BEN

A MEMOIR,
FROM
STREET KID
TO GOVERNOR

BEN

A MEMOIR, FROM STREET KID TO GOVERNOR

BY BENJAMIN J. CAYETANO

WATERMARK
PUBLISHING

ISBN 978-0-9790647-0-8 (softcover)
ISBN 978-0-9821698-0-3 (casebound)

Library of Congress Control Number: 2008943582 (softcover)
Library of Congress Control Number: 2008943494 (casebound)

Design
Gonzalez Design Company

Production
Marisa Oshiro
Wendy Wakabayashi

All photography from the *Honolulu Advertiser* library except on the
following pages:

Front cover portrait	Daniel E. Green
121, 125 bottom, 127 bottom	Benjamin J. Cayetano
125 top	Justice Frank Padgett
259 top	Hawai'i State Art Museum
259 bottom	University of Hawai'i

A portion of the proceeds from the sale of this book support the
Cayetano Foundation Scholarship Fund administered by the Hawai'i
Community Foundation.

Watermark Publishing
1088 Bishop St., Suite 310
Honolulu, Hawai'i 96813
Telephone 1-808-587-7766
Toll-free 1-866-900-BOOK
sales@bookshawaii.net
www.bookshawaii.net

Printed in the United States

Contents

For Eleanor and Ansing,
with love

Foreword

Every man has his fault, and honesty is his.

—*William Shakespeare,* Timon of Athens

Candor is a notoriously rare commodity in political memoirs. That's what makes *Ben: A Memoir, from Street Kid to Governor* as bracing as it is revealing. Ben Cayetano delivers not only an account of his political career but an unflinching look at the human being at the center of the action. This book is not a bland lesson in civics, but a revealing exposure of legislation as it is actually made in the political sausage grinder of compromise and betrayal, loyalty and courage, fear and rage.

In it, the core attributes of the man shine through: honest, tough and smart. Those were the qualities I saw in him in 1974 when we were first elected to the Hawai'i State Legislature. Those were the virtues I cited in support of his race for governor in 1994. They were the essential requirements needed for that time.

Hawai'i's immediate post-statehood era was over. It was a time of retrenchment, reevaluation and readjustment. The generation returning from World War II had transformed Hawai'i from an ethnically stratified plantation territory to a state that honored the values of racial equality and progressivism. The forces that had driven and shaped the transformation were far from spent, but their basic goals had been achieved, and the state's future direction seemed uncertain. What was needed above all was resolute leadership; a strength of character, hard-earned and well-honed.

Ben Cayetano's background included elements of both the old and new Hawai'i. He was born a Filipino American in a U.S. territory in which ethnicity, by and large, determined a child's prospects. By the time he returned home in the early 1970s, after working his way through UCLA and Loyola Law School, opportunities had broadened greatly for non-Caucasians. Ben's talents blossomed. His ambition and willingness to risk failure led him to run for office against the conventional wisdom that a Filipino could not win.

When Ben and I entered the Legislature as freshmen in 1974, I was drawn to his sense of confidence, intellect and readiness to question received wisdom. I enjoyed his sardonic wit and ready, self-deprecating sense of humor, not always apparent to the public. It was the beginning of a 30-year friendship, both personal and political.

The voters found Ben's truth-telling refreshing enough to reward him with multiple terms in the Legislature and twice with the state's highest office. There were those for whom his unvarnished style sometimes seemed too brutal or unpolished. They found him impatient, truculent and irascible. While many recognized a keen ability to comprehend and articulate the big picture, others felt wounded by a perceived dismissal of people who did not share his manifest intellect. But for those in either camp, everyone knew there was no daylight between Ben the politician and Ben the human being. That directness is evident throughout this book.

The rewards of *Ben: A Memoir, from Street Kid to Governor* go beyond accounts of politicking and governing. They include a deeply felt but unsentimental rendering of a childhood and early adulthood that may discomfit many middle-class readers. Its hardships and disorder offer insight into Cayetano's personality. To have scaled the heights of public life from an impoverished childhood in Kalihi testifies to his native intelligence and the origin of the hard-edged nature of his moral and ethical demands on himself and everyone around him. It goes far to explain the disdain for politesse which still informs his words and actions. In terms of his political values, it illuminates his instinct to side with those to whom life has dealt a poor hand.

Ben Cayetano's life vividly illustrates the truth that politics is the great paradox of modern life. We live in an age when meaningful personal interaction between individuals from different social and economic strata is increasingly uncommon. In the political arena, however, people of diverse backgrounds still must routinely talk with one another and work together. Technology provides a cascade of information, yet we seem less able than ever to communicate. Ben Cayetano always got his message across, if not in words, then with a look as pointed and final as any summary judgment.

Mediocre politicians fail to grow beyond the limited perspectives they bring with them into office. The successful ones find the strength and vision to subsume their own interests and bridge the social and political differences that separate them from their colleagues. It is upon the latter that society depends for the resolution of conflicts and solutions to its challenges. It is in that context that Cayetano excelled.

He could and did work with, overcome or outflank representatives of every interest. He ran at every issue and never retreated from any conflict. His virtue was his vice. Whether by sheer force of stubborn will, or as a willing partner to those who recognized that an even-handed deal was the only way to get him to the table, Ben played the game straight.

The readers of this book will find that same man reflected in these pages: a complex and compelling human being and a politician—honest, tough and smart.

Neil Abercrombie
U.S. House of Representatives

Introduction

This I believe is the great Western truth: that each of us is a completely unique creature and that, if we are ever to give any gift to the world, it will have to come out of our own experience and fulfillment of our own potentialities, not someone else's.

—Educator Joseph Campbell, The Power of Myth

In writing this story, I've tried to stay true to Campbell's belief. I share my opinions about the political, social and economic history of the times. However, the reader should keep in mind that I am not a historian or social scientist, nor am I an economist. The opinions, the interpretations I give here are based on my experiences in politics, my education and the life I've lived thus far. If there are errors, they are not intentional.

We are all creatures of our experiences. Our upbringing, parents, ethnicity and culture all shape us in some way, as do events that are not always under our control or foresight, and people—friends, relatives and even strangers who pop up sometimes unexpectedly to lend a hand or give advice and, because we admire and respect them, influence our lives. And good fortune—fate—plays a huge role in what we become and achieve. At least in my life it has.

I write about these various factors, often in anecdotes that may seem small in view of the big things I've experienced during my 28 years in public office, but are meaningful personally, because of their significance in my life.

There is an inherent reticence, a "pressure of self-censorship" as Virginia Woolf once described it, in writing a memoir. It is natural for the writer to want to win the reader's approbation and to avoid disapproval; therefore, there is often a reluctance to reveal the unflattering and sometimes darker side of the writer's life. From autobiographies and memoirs I've read, politicians seem most susceptible to this pressure.

I don't reveal everything about my life, but I reveal a lot more than most, some of which has to do with a series of regrettable and youthful transgressions against the law (most of which happened during my junior and senior years in high school). I reveal more than enough, I believe, to help the reader better understand

1

why I hold certain values and why I made certain decisions on public issues during my time in public office.

My mother was one of the strongest people I knew. But under the veneer of that strength she suffered demons linked, at least in part, to her upbringing and her failures in marriages and with men in general. Her father—my grandfather—was a hard, too-often-cruel man who seemed incapable of loving anyone—including, I might add, his grandchildren. And Mom, being the oldest, was almost always the victim of his anger, his frustrations, his abuse. But Mom developed toughness, a grittiness that kept the demons under control and commanded respect from most who knew her. Until, that is, her will, her mind—that toughness—were finally conquered and destroyed by her addiction to drugs—not illegal street drugs, but legal drugs prescribed by her doctors.

Drug addiction has been the bane of modern American society. And it will continue to be so unless politicians summon up the courage to deal with it honestly and eschew the political agendas that have been the biggest obstacle to finding solutions to the problem. Indeed, there are times when I imagine that the only way drug addiction can be conquered, if that is possible, is for every person to experience it first-hand—either personally or as a witness to its destructive effects on a loved one or dear friend. Then, perhaps, real progress in preventing or curing it can be made.

With his consent—I would not have done it otherwise—I write about my younger brother's homosexuality. When we were growing up, the only gays we saw or knew about were the female impersonators, drag queens and publicity seekers whose outrageous public behavior created the perverse caricature that continues to subject gays to discrimination, ridicule, derision and, worse, acts of violence. But there was, and continues to exist, a "silent majority," to coin a worn political phrase, of gay people who remained in the closet and who did their best to lead ordinary lives.

My brother Ken was one of them; he lived a quiet life for more than four decades. He served his country in the Vietnam War, held a steady job, is law abiding, votes and found a loving partner. They saved enough money to buy a modest home (now paid off) and, unlike the more than 50 percent of heterosexuals whose marriages now end in divorce (I am one), he and his partner are still together and remain reasonably happy after more than 35 years.

I write about my father—my stepfather, really—who I consider the only father I ever had, and how he took care of Ken and me and how, without really thinking about it, we tried to repay him by supporting him and, after dementia set in, caring for him until his death. Dad never knew that I knew he was not my real father—but there was no need for me to tell him. We loved each other.

These experiences profoundly affected my political positions on gay rights, drug addiction, latchkey children and long-term care. They strengthened my belief that for too many of our citizens, their government is the last hope for improving the quality of their lives.

I write with the hope the reader will learn from my personal struggles—marked too many times by ignorance, contradiction and missteps—in dealing with my family's crises.

Twenty-eight years in public office taught me that politics is a microcosm of the larger society. Today, at least, it is not quite the noble, idealized undertaking for which we all hope. For while high school civics teachers teach our young people—as they should, in order to continue to instill hope and trust in their governments—that "we are a nation of laws, not men," my experience adds a caveat to that notion. It is, after all, men (and women) who give true meaning to and execute the laws.

One can only wonder, for example, whether Hawai'i would have become the first state to provide women with the right to an abortion if its governor at the time, John A. Burns, a devout Catholic who was known to attend Mass every day, had not honored the doctrine of the Separation of Church and State. Rather than vetoing the bill, he allowed it to become law without his signature. Contrast Burns to George W. Bush, who is also devoutly religious and admits, openly and proudly, that his decisions are heavily influenced by his religious beliefs—and by a "higher father," as he once put it.

There is much about ethnicity and race in this book. There is no getting around it. The remarkable evolution of Hawai'i is all about ethnicity and race. Any discussion about these topics in Hawai'i, of course, is always a complex and sensitive subject, far more so than I write about here, and perhaps, in the long run, it's best left to the expert sociologists and political scientists to analyze and explain in greater detail. But what I offer here is what I saw and lived with.

I grew up at a time in Hawai'i's history—the '50s and '60s, mainly—when race and ethnicity were still huge factors in Hawaiian society, as they were throughout the nation, affecting how jobs were dispensed, how privileges were granted and political and social status was determined. It was also a time when "local people," who, in today's politically correct world, would be called "people of color," grew up in an environment that taught them to be wary of haoles (Caucasians) and to perceive them as social and political antagonists. It was a time when the haole culture imbued many haoles with a sense that they were superior to locals. Some locals succumbed to it: Gov. Burns described their mindset as a "plantation sense of inferiority."

Hawai'i was different from other places, though. Two major factors made the distinction.

The first is Hawai'i's limited land area, which, unlike on the Mainland, virtually forced people of different ethnicities to live, work and play together. The second, and most important, is the widespread acceptance of the unique Native Hawaiian culture that promoted tolerance and caring—the "aloha spirit." While the concept of aloha is often overused by the tourism industry to promote its special interests, it is of such importance to the local culture that the State Legislature, perhaps fearful that Hawai'i was losing its aloha spirit, and naively believing that law can preserve culture, passed a law defining it.

Today, Hawai'i's society boasts the highest rate of interracial and interethnic marriages in the world. Indeed, some experts predict that the extraordinarily high rate of such mixed marriages may one day reduce ethnic distinctions in Hawai'i to the point that they become insignificant.

Changes in politics usually reflect changes in the larger society. For example, as of this writing, in the nearly 50 years since Hawai'i became a state in 1959, three of Hawai'i's six governors were minority Americans—a Japanese, a Hawaiian and a Filipino (me)—who could trace their roots to Asia or the Pacific. By comparison, since the birth of our nation more than two centuries ago, only five other minority Americans—black Americans Edward Brooke and Deval Patrick (Massachusetts) and Douglas Wilder (Virginia), Chinese American Gary Locke (Washington) and Indian American Bobby Jindal (Louisiana)—have been elected governor.

Since statehood, Hawai'i has been America's poster child for racial tolerance—a model for the world to follow, as many have called it. It is uncertain, however, whether in the years ahead Hawai'i can maintain its lofty position, for there are some profound changes occurring. Among them: the influx of Mainland haoles and immigrants from Asia bringing new values that often conflict with the old; a young local population that has little awareness of the historic struggles of their grandparents and is less likely to care about preserving the old values that made Hawai'i what it is today; and finally, a Hawaiian sovereignty movement that, if achieved, may impose some form of segregation between Hawaiians and non-Hawaiians, potentially eroding the chemistry—the culture of aloha—that has made Hawai'i the most tolerant multicultural society in the world.

Having written this, however, I add another caveat: There is a common tendency among local people to view racial and ethnic discrimination as a story of the haole versus everyone else. Indeed, the Civil Rights Movement of the '60s was seen as one pitting whites against blacks, but the truth is that the movement would not have succeeded had it not had strong white support.

The reality, of course, is that there has long existed a pecking order among Hawai'i's racial and ethnic groups. Haoles, after all, do not have a monopoly on racism. Locals understood that the Portuguese, who were never accepted as equals by the haoles, were wary of the Japanese and Chinese, who were in turn wary of the Filipinos, Hawaiians and everyone else. As history reveals, however, the use of power is fundamental to the haole culture. And during the times I write about, the haoles often did use power to keep other ethnic groups in line.

But the 1954 Democratic Revolution eroded their political power, and many haoles began to find themselves in the minority and see themselves as victims of racism, a role foreign to their experience in Hawai'i. The inevitable resentment this change caused among them manifested itself in Hawai'i's 1998 and 2002 elections, the story of which remains virtually untold today and on which I hope to shed some light, at least in the political context, later in this book.

In writing about my personal experience as a legislator, I tried to give the reader a look at the realities of the legislative process, at the fact that what happens in the caucus rooms and the House and Senate chambers is influenced by the ideology, special interests and self-interest of their occupants.

And while Hawaiian activists continue to pursue Hawaiian sovereignty, it is worth noting that in 1986, politicians of Hawaiian blood controlled the State government: John Waihee was governor, Richard (Dickie) Wong was the Senate president and Henry Peters was Speaker of the House. The actions of these three powerful leaders had a profound impact on Hawaiian issues and the Hawaiian people's revered Bishop Estate.

I never had any long-range plans to become governor; rather, I was guided to the office by unforeseen events and circumstances. Nor did any person, any political insiders, any political machine or party leaders anoint me to run for governor. It pretty much just happened.

During my governorship, I was confronted with and dealt with the big issues that frustrated and at times divided our people: same-sex marriage, the *Rice v. Cayetano* case, the state's dispute with the Office of Hawaiian Affairs over ceded lands, and the worst and most prolonged economic crisis in Hawai'i's history.

And in wrestling with these complicated and politically charged issues I often found myself at odds with the organizations (labor unions) and people who had played a large part in making possible my 28-year journey from the State House to the governor's mansion. At some point in every politician's career, this will probably happen. And in almost every instance, the politician must decide whether to risk incurring the wrath of his past supporters in order to do the right thing

I also mention some of the politicians I worked with—perhaps best described by the Clint Eastwood movie title *The Good, the Bad and the Ugly*—which may give the reader a keener insight about the current state of politics in Hawai'i and verify my contention that politics reflects society and that the final responsibility for the state of political affairs falls on the voters themselves.

As governor, I felt honored and privileged to lead our state into the new millennium. There was so much to be optimistic about. Hawai'i's economic recovery had begun in late 1998, and it seemed that the worst was over. But no one could have foreseen September 11, 2001. The terrorist attacks profoundly changed our lives forever.

The reader may find satisfaction in learning how the State Legislature set partisanship aside to find ways to deal with the problems caused by September 11, but will surely be disappointed in learning how short a hiatus it was. Moreover, they may be as shocked as I was at the time at how unprepared the State, federal and County governments were in responding to such suicidal acts of fanaticism. On the other hand, they may be pleasantly surprised to know that although September 11 inflicted great economic damage to all 50 states, Hawai'i and Wyoming were the only states whose economies bounced back within a year.

Ironically, Hawai'i's tourism industry stands to benefit from the fear caused by the September 11 attacks and worldwide terrorism. Security and serenity are higher priorities than ever before for tourists everywhere. Hawai'i, the world's most isolated inhabited landmass, has long been famed as an ideal place for relaxation and serenity; September 11 has made Hawai'i one of the world's safest tourist destinations.

There are two great books that influenced my thinking about Hawai'i. The first, James Michener's best-selling historical novel *Hawaii*, gave a worldwide audience of readers an insight into the incredible story of our beautiful island state. The second, Lawrence H. Fuchs' *Hawaii Pono* ("Hawai'i the Righteous") is considered a classic—an objective, scholarly and provocative interpretation of Hawai'i's sociological and political history.

But both books tell Hawai'i's story only from its birth to 1959 (*Hawaii*) or 1961 (*Hawaii Pono*). Subsequent works usually stop at the end of the era of John Burns (1974). This is not surprising. The Islands' post-World War II socio-political history is a great, inspirational story—the kind that historians and novelists love to write about and from which movies are made. A lot, however, happened in the 30-plus years that followed.

Today, Michener would be pleased to learn that the unwritten prohibition against Asians, which angered him and kept him and his Japanese-American wife from buying a home in upscale, haole Kāhala, is a relic of the past. He might also be surprised to learn that many of the "Golden Men" he wrote about in his novel—his fictionalizations of the real people who shaped modern Hawai'i—have either faded into the past or fallen on hard times. One example is Walter Dillingham, the powerful, arrogant, racist leader of the old haole oligarchy. Dillingham's influence was considerable, reaching the halls of Congress and the likes of General George Patton and even into the Oval Offices of Franklin D. Roosevelt and Dwight D. Eisenhower.

The "Old Patriarch," as Dillingham was described by *TIME* magazine when it featured him on its cover, died a year after his son, Ben, was crushed by local war hero Daniel K. Inouye in the 1962 election for U.S. Senate.

In 1970, Ben, who was born and raised in Hawai'i, moved to Australia, ostensibly to manage the Dillingham Corporation's interests there. Faced with increasing Mainland competition, especially from Henry Kaiser, and having lost its political power, the Dillingham family, led by Ben's brother Lowell, began selling off the Dillingham Corporation's Hawai'i assets to invest in Mainland and international businesses. The sale of Dillingham Corporation's flagship asset,

Hawaiian Dredging & Construction Company, marked the end of the family's once-pervasive and powerful influence in Hawai'i.

Then there is the sad ending to the storied life of Hiram Fong, the Chinese-American Kalihi boy who bootstrapped his way through Harvard Law School, succeeded marvelously in business and became the first Asian American to sit in the U.S. Senate. However, in the last remaining years of his incredible life, he found himself entangled in lawsuits with a son and other relatives over money. Meanwhile, creditors were vying in the bankruptcy courts for a piece of Fong's once-considerable fortune. This should not detract from Fong's respected place in Hawai'i's political history—but to this romantic's eye, his life deserved a better ending.

Professor Fuchs, who recently retired from Brandeis University, should find great satisfaction in the prescience of his work in *Hawaii Pono*. His socio-political interpretation of the rise of Hawai'i's different ethnic groups proved uncannily accurate. Among his many predictions, Fuchs' conclusion that Hawai'i's Filipinos, while lagging behind the Chinese and Japanese, would eventually "make it" has occurred, at least in politics and the State Judiciary. And his observation that many Hawaiians, given that their native culture does not prepare them to compete for success in American culture, may seek reparations and a restoration of the past, has certainly manifested itself in the present-day sovereignty movement and the fight to persuade Congress to pass the Akaka Bill.

Finally, I write about growing up in Kalihi. Someone once described Brooklyn, New York, as the "cradle of tough guys and Nobel laureates … and proof of the power of marginality." The same chemistry which made Kalihi as different from other places in Hawai'i as Brooklyn is from the rest of New York produced four of Hawai'i's six governors, our nation's first Samoan-American mayor, the first Asian American to sit in the U.S. Senate, two Rhodes Scholars, State Supreme Court justices, two State House Speakers, two of Hawai'i's three world champion professional boxers, some of Hawai'i's greatest entertainers—and, of course, more than its share of Hawai'i's most notorious criminals. Kalihi is Hawai'i's Brooklyn.

Kalihi is where this story begins.

CHAPTER ONE

Life in Kalihi

The Cayetanos of Kalihi

Roughly translated, the Hawaiian word "Kalihi" means "place of transition." I was born there on November 14, 1939. I grew up and lived there until I left for Los Angeles in 1963.

Today, much of Kalihi is light industry, but back then it was a predominantly blue-collar residential neighborhood. I drive through it occasionally, mostly out of nostalgia; everyone I knew has moved out, so there is usually no other reason for me to go there.

A few years ago, the *Honolulu Advertiser* did a story on me and a former Kalihi youth gang leader who in his early 20s had reformed his ways. They set up a photo shoot at the duplex where I once lived.

Not surprisingly, the duplex looked rundown; after all, many years had passed. But time was only part of the reason for its demise. There was considerable rubbish strewn throughout the yard, and the empty beer cans stood out prominently. Window screens were torn and left unrepaired. Inside the duplex, I was stunned to find that the same gas stove from my youth was still being used—the thick black soot, which had accumulated over decades of use and poor maintenance, had become a permanent part of the stove itself. And the same small bathtub, the porcelain inside yellow with age, was still being used as well.

Mr. Leonida, our landlord back then, would never have tolerated such neglect. I suppose the fact that he and his family also lived there made a big difference. The current tenants had an absentee landlord who apparently was not inclined to pay attention to his or her Kalihi investment. Neither were the tenants. It was a sign of people not giving a damn. Kalihi had changed—but not for the better.

It wasn't always that way. Kalihi was not even always blue collar or light industry. In the early 1900s, it was a residential district for middle- and upper-middle-class Chinese, Hawaiian and Portuguese residents. By the late 1930s, however, Kalihi had evolved into a predominantly blue-collar community. Working families were attracted to the area mostly because rents and homes were affordable. Among these families were many Japanese and a lesser number of Filipinos who had left the plantation to work in the city. Kalihi became a kaleidoscope of ethnicities: Japanese, Filipinos, Hawaiians, Chinese, Koreans, Puerto Ricans and

Portuguese. There were a few haoles: mostly military families who lived at nearby Fort Shafter.

Asato, Ching, Hayashida, Koda, Mau, Okuda, Pratt, Tawata and Steinhoff—these were the last names of my close childhood pals. The guys I played with as kids and hung out with as teenagers. We had different ethnic surnames, different skin tones, different facial features—and if asked about our ethnicity, we would answer, "Chinese, Filipino, Japanese, Hawaiian-Chinese," whichever the case may have been, but we were different from our Mainland counterparts. Indeed, it would have been more accurate to describe us all as "local," rather than by our ethnicity, for we were born and raised in Hawai'i, spoke pidgin, loved local food and had a greater affinity for the Hawaiian culture—the culture of Hawai'i's native people—than for the ethnic culture of our grandparents' homelands, about which most of us knew little or nothing.

The homes in the area were modest, usually small and inexpensive; the well-kept yards were a sign of pride of ownership. The residents in my part of Kalihi were mostly Japanese, with an ample sprinkling of Filipinos, Hawaiians and Chinese. Most of the Puerto Ricans and Portuguese lived in upper Kalihi and Kalihi Valley, which are located mauka (mountain-side) of King Street. This is a major street running parallel to Nimitz Highway, the highway that leads to Honolulu International Airport and Hickam Air Force Base on the western side of O'ahu and to downtown Honolulu and Waikīkī on the eastern side. We lived in a rented, second-story duplex on Silva Street in lower Kalihi on the makai (ocean) side of Nimitz Highway.

Kalihi was destined to become blue collar. It was close to the harbors and airport and, at the time, it was the western edge of the city's unofficial borders. The politicians saw Kalihi as a convenient and politically correct place for public work projects. Even today, Kalihi still has the largest concentration of low-income public housing in Hawai'i—at one time there was more there than in all of the rest of the state combined.

In 1914, the Territorial government built Oahu Prison—"OP"—Hawai'i's largest prison at the time, at the corner of Pu'uhale Road and Dillingham Boulevard—a stone's throw from my school, Pu'uhale Elementary School, about a mile from where I lived. Children walking to or from school on Pu'uhale Road would often see the prisoners playing sports or working in the prison yard. Sometimes the children would wave hello when they saw family friends or relatives among the inmates. I never knew anyone in the prison, but I would always wave to the prisoners—and to the guards armed with rifles in the two towers facing the road.

Two or three miles away, next to the Kapālama Canal—which was once clean enough for crabbing and fishing but today is polluted—dark gray or black smoke spewed from the smokestack of the city's 100-foot-high incinerator, as the daily collection of garbage and rubbish was burned. Decades later, the city shut it down, which actually improved air quality in the area.

Kalihi was an ideal place for light industry. Amid trucking companies, auto repair shops, junkyards and other small companies and businesses were Hawai'i's three largest pineapple canning companies—Hawaiian Pineapple (later Dole), Libby's and Del Monte. For two summers, during my sophomore and junior years in high school, I worked as a tray boy at Hawaiian Pineapple.

On Kalihi Street, a few blocks away from our duplex, was the Kalihi Poi Factory, owned and run by Japanese Americans. A few blocks away, on Homerule Street, was a crematorium—the "make (dead) man place," as we called it. On Mokauea Street, a hundred yards or so from our duplex, was the McCabe Stevedore Company, where stevedores would gather every morning before being transported to work on the docks.

At the end of Silva Street there is the Associated Steel yard, where steel workers cut rods and assembled frames for construction projects. Next to it was a wood shop where beautiful wood Hawaiian carvings were made, until the shop was closed because it could not compete with the flood of mass-produced foreign "Hawaiian" artifacts which tourist vendors found cheaper and more profitable.

Kalihi was a good place to grow up. Its residents were friendly and helpful. Most did not lock their doors at night. Most were hard working. There was respect among them.

Writers often romanticize Kalihi, describing it as "rough," "tough," "impoverished" and "poor." By most standards Kalihi was a "poor" and "impoverished" place—but frankly, I did not know it. I might not have had the healthiest and most balanced meals to eat or expensive clothes to wear, but my father made sure there was always something to eat and that I always had clean clothes and shoes.

Most poor kids, I believe, don't realize they are poor. They don't miss what they never had or knew anything about—unless, of course, they can make comparisons or are told they are poor and try to figure out why.

I believe they do know, however, if they are happy or sad. I probably went through all of the emotions and developed the insecurities of kids whose parents are divorced—divorce carried a stigma back then—but I made adjustments in my social life to deal with it. Overall, I was happy growing up in Kalihi.

My father, Bonifacio Marcos Cayetano (everyone called him *Ansing*), raised my brother and me. Like us, our next-door neighbors, the Estiamba brothers, were raised by their dad, as were the Steinhoff boys who lived on the corner of Mokauea and Silva Streets a few houses away.

I was about six or seven when my parents divorced. I don't remember anyone ever explaining to me why Mom was not living with us—in fact, I don't remember how or when the word "divorce" crept into my child's vocabulary. I learned quickly, however, how to take care of myself and make sure my brother, Kenneth, who is two years younger, brushed his teeth, took a bath, had breakfast and dinner, dressed and got ready for school. Ken learned fast and soon was often more conscientious than me, doing it all by himself.

One thing that caused me some anxious moments was having to relight the pilot light on our gas stove when it went out, which happened often. Not knowing anything about gas stoves, except that they could be dangerous, I saw relighting the pilot light as an early test of my manhood. First, I'd tell Ken to step outside. Then I got a box of matches and virtually shut my eyes while nervously trying to relight it, expecting at any moment I might be blown up. As I got older, I found out that it wasn't as dangerous as I thought. I'm not sure why I remember this story, but I chuckle every time I think of it.

Dad worked as a waiter for the Outrigger Canoe Club, a private social club whose membership was limited to haoles and affluent Hawaiians. He worked there six days a week. Monday was his day off. He would leave home at 7 a.m. to catch the Kalihi bus. After two bus transfers, he'd get to the Outrigger about 8:30 and work the breakfast shift. When we were very young, he would come home by bus between shifts to cook dinner for us. It was a big strain on him, so often he would cook before he left for work. It didn't make sense for him to come home between shifts, so he would stay there, work lunch and dinner, and get off work at 9 p.m., sometimes 10. If he was lucky, he caught a ride home with a fellow worker. Otherwise, it would take him at least an hour by bus to get back home. By then, Ken and I would be fast asleep.

I knew Dad felt bad about his long work hours. Sometimes on a Saturday or Sunday, he'd take us with him to work, and we would go swimming or play on the beach while he worked. At lunchtime, the chef would prepare lunch for us and we'd eat in the employees' locker room. And on most Mondays, his day off, Dad would take Ken and me to the movies. We looked forward to it. Most of the time, we went to the old King Theater downtown to see cowboy movies. Those starring Hopalong Cassidy, the Durango Kid, Red Rider and Little Beaver, the Lone Ranger and Tonto, and Roy Rogers and his horse, Trigger, were among our favorites. (As we got older, John Wayne and Randolph Scott would replace them as my heroes.) Movies were simple in those days. The good guys always won. Most of the time, Dad would fall asleep about two thirds of the way through the movie while Ken and I would be stuffing ourselves with popcorn and hot dogs, washed down with soft drinks.

Often, we'd go to the Palama Theater, which resembles a smaller version of the famous Grauman's Chinese Theater in Hollywood. The theater closed decades ago but still stands today, unusable and falling apart. It was legally designated a historical building and therefore cannot be torn down—stark testimony to how a well-intentioned law can have unintended consequences.

Dad liked the Palama Theater because it was easy to get to by bus, and after the movie, he would take us to eat saimin noodles and barbecue beef at a little

Japanese saimin restaurant on Robello Lane right next to the theater. The place was always packed because they served the best saimin in Honolulu. I heard it closed sometime in the late 1960s because the owners' children had all gone to college and did not want to carry on the family business.

As we got older, Dad gave us a daily allowance for lunch and dinner. Health-wise, this was not a good idea. Too often, Hershey bars, Babe Ruths, ice cream and Cokes were happily substituted for healthy meals. Usually, however, my brother and I would eat dinner at Dot's Hut, a local restaurant owned and run by the Hamamura family. Dot's Hut was housed in a Quonset hut on Kalihi Street, a 10-minute walk from our duplex. The food was great. But I never felt comfortable having dinner there with Ken or by myself while my friends were having dinner at home with their families.

The Hamamuras were very kind to us. When Ken was about 10 years old, he began working for them, washing dishes and even helping to serve customers. He could keep his tips and got free meals. They couldn't hire him, because he was too young. But they knew our family situation, took a liking to Ken and found a way to help us. They were hardworking, honest and humble people—the sort one never forgets.

Like the Hamamuras, the Estiambas were good people. They lived in the other half of our duplex apartment. Ken and I felt safe with them as neighbors. Mr. Estiamba was a shipyard worker, a technician of some kind. In those days, it was a big achievement for an immigrant Filipino to have that kind of job. He enrolled his two sons, Albert and Carlos, at St. Louis High School, a private Catholic school. We knew when he got home from work because after dinner, around 6 or 6:30 p.m., he would sit on the back porch, light up a cigar, play his guitar and sing Filipino songs.

I looked up to the Estiamba boys, especially Albert, who was eight years older than me. Back then, for young Filipino boys like me, getting into St. Louis was like getting into Notre Dame. It was a big deal. Albert was a starting halfback for the 1949 St. Louis Crusaders football team. High school football was big in those days. Sell-out crowds at the old Honolulu Stadium were common. One year, either 1949 or 1950, Mom took Ken and me to the championship game against McKinley. St. Louis won, 13 to 6, with Albert scoring the two winning touch-downs. For a long time, I told everyone who would listen that Albert Estiamba, star halfback for the St. Louis Crusaders, was my next-door neighbor.

Once, Albert got into a fistfight with a neighbor that spoke volumes about life in Kalihi. Albert wasn't a troublemaker; he was actually quiet and soft spo-ken. I never saw him get angry or heard him raise his voice. The neighbor was a guy named Henry (not his real name), who seemed like he was always moody or angry at something. Most of the kids avoided him. Henry got into an argument with Albert's younger brother, Carlos, which ended up with Henry slapping Carlos around. Henry was in his 30s. Carlos was only 15 or 16, still a kid. Whatever the reason, it didn't seem right to me. I was angry and frightened.

As soon as I heard Albert walking up the steps, I went to the front door. Carlos told him what happened. Albert went straight to Henry's apartment downstairs. I could hear them talking below. Pretty soon, Henry's voice sounded louder and angrier. Finally, he shouted repeatedly, "What? You young punk, I'll break your ass!" I saw Henry give Albert a hard shove, then another. Albert motioned calmly with his open hand, pointing to the street, and said, "Let's go." There, right in front of our duplex, in the middle of Silva Street, they squared off and started fighting.

My heart raced as I watched them from the porch. Henry, a stevedore, was a little bigger than Albert, and he already had the muscular build of a grown man. Almost as soon as the fight began, a dozen or more stevedores came running over from the McCabe Hamilton Stevedores building on Mokauea Street, about 100 yards away. When I saw them, I got really scared. I was frightened when the fight began, but now I was so scared I began trembling. I was worried that one or more of the stevedores would jump Albert.

But no one did. Instead, they stood in a circle around the two fighters. The circle got bigger as some male neighbors joined the crowd. A couple of drivers parked their cars to watch. No one said or did anything. The only sounds I heard were the thumps of punches and the grunts of two men wrestling and hitting each other.

The fight couldn't have lasted more than three to five minutes, but it seemed like it went on longer than that. Coming off the football season, Albert was in great physical shape. He had fast hands and knew how to use them. Soon youth and determination made the difference. Albert knocked Henry down two or three times. Each time Henry got up. His face was a bruised, bloody mess, and he looked exhausted. Once, after he went down, Henry called out desperately, "Times ... times ..." (pidgin for "time out"). It sounded so funny that as scared as I was, I wanted to laugh. But none of the adults laughed. Finally, after Albert knocked Henry down again, a huge Hawaiian stevedore stepped in between the two, helped Henry up and said, "Okay, fight over. He had enough. Everybody go home." No one argued. The fight was over.

Fifteen minutes later, the cops finally arrived. By then, the crowd was gone, the street deserted. When the cops questioned Albert and Henry, they both dismissed it as a "misunderstanding." Back then, that's the way things were done in Kalihi.

Later in the evening, I saw Henry, his face still red and swollen, walking slowly down the street, apparently looking for something. The next day, a grinning Carlos told me that Albert had hit Henry so hard, so many times, that he'd knocked Henry's gold fillings out of his mouth. That, along with the fact that Henry had called for a "time out" in a fight he had started, made him a subject of ridicule. The story of the fight was repeated in the neighborhood for a long time.

Jerry and Ansing

One day I heard the bell ringing from the ice cream man's car (I think it was a Jeep with a built-in freezer on it) as it was coming up Silva Street. I began rummaging through my father's dresser looking for some loose change, and then I found his life insurance policy. I must have been only 10 or 11 at the time, but I knew what life insurance was for. Later, as I went through it, I noticed that there was only one name listed as a beneficiary: Ken's. *Where is my name? Is it just a mistake? Why have I been left out?* These kind of thoughts ran through my mind. I was fearful I had done something wrong, although I had no clue what it could be.

I recalled once my brother Ken and I got into an argument that ended with me punching him out. Reduced to tears, he shouted angrily at me in pidgin, "You not my bruddah!" At the time, Ken's words went right over my head. Brothers, after all, argue all the time and say all kinds of nasty things to each other. But the insurance policy made me wonder. Physically, Ken and I do not look like brothers. I resemble my mother. Ken is a dead ringer for Dad. I had often wondered why Ken and I looked so different. Now I wondered whether we were real brothers—and whether Dad (Ansing) was my real father. I was afraid to bring it up with him or Mom—how does a 10- or 11-year-old ask his parents about something like that? I was worried how they would answer, and yet at the same time I had no idea what they would say. I decided that at the right time, I would ask Auntie Violet, Mom's youngest sister.

I was close to Aunt Violet. I often stayed over weekends at her home in Damon Tract. She was married to a haole from West Virginia—Ken and I called him Uncle Jack. She met Jack through her job at the Pearl Harbor Naval Base during World War II—he was a former Marine. I heard that he was wounded somewhere in the Pacific, sent to Tripler Army Hospital for treatment and later became an MP at Pearl Harbor. But I never heard him talk about his war experience.

Uncle Jack came from a very poor family. His full name was Jack Ayers; he was German American. Once I heard my Aunt Violet kidding him about his life as a hillbilly: how they were more backward than we were in Hawai'i because they were still using outhouses in West Virginia. Whenever Uncle Jack criticized some of our local ways, Aunt Violet would bring up his hillbilly roots. Most of the time, it was good natured.

You couldn't miss Uncle Jack. He was handsome, brown-blond-haired, and stood at least six inches taller and weighed 50 pounds more than any of the Filipino men in our family. He liked fishing and struck up a friendship with a couple of older Filipino fishermen and regularly went fishing with them. It was nice to see this big haole exchanging fish stories with his shorter, brown-skinned friends. It took awhile for him to understand pidgin laced with a Filipino accent, but he eventually got the hang of it and learned how to speak pidgin with them. He was the only haole living on "N" Road in Damon Tract. He was always nice to me, and I liked him a lot.

They had three sons: Patrick, Jack Jr. and William. Each was taller and bigger than me. You could not tell they were part Filipino. My cousin Jack Jr., especially, with his blond hair, looked pure haole. The only way you could tell he was local was when he spoke pidgin. Billy also had mostly haole features, and I often joked with him that he was the biggest Filipino I ever knew (years later, he played center on the University of Hawai'i football team). I was the oldest among all of my cousins, and they all kind of looked up to me. We were all close; I was especially close to Pat, who was two years younger than me.

Damon Tract was located next to the old John Rodgers Airport, which is now part of Honolulu International Airport. It was in the flight path of the Hickam Air Force Base. In fact, during the Japanese attack on Pearl Harbor, the enemy planes that bombed and strafed Hickam Field flew right over Damon Tract. A couple of houses were strafed, and even though the owners patched up the bullet holes, you could still see the impressions under the newer paint.

Like Kalihi, Damon Tract was a blue-collar neighborhood. At the time, it was not the big industrial area it is today. Back then, there were mostly old homes, a pig farm run by the Oshiro family, the Asagi Chicken Farm, a grocery store, an elementary school and a Catholic church.

The roads in Damon Tract were named with the letters of the alphabet. Each road ran perpendicular from the edge of the airport up to Nimitz Highway, the main highway leading to Hickam. Every road was a dead end, ending at the fence that separated the airport from Damon Tract. It was a great place for cockfights because the cops would have to drive in from Nimitz Highway and could be easily seen from the dead-end side of the road where the cockfights were held.

To Filipinos, a cockfight was a sporting event—in their eyes it was just like a rodeo, except the dead cock became someone's dinner whereas the used-up rodeo horse might end up in a glue factory or as dog food. Typically, dozens, sometimes hundreds, of people attended. The yard would be teeming with activity; the few women there were usually selling snacks (most often Filipino pastries) and drinks. Owners proudly displayed their fighting cocks for the bettors to see. Gaffers could be seen expertly tying the razor-sharp gaffs onto the fighting cocks' spurs. Bets were made verbally, on the honor system (anyone who welched on a bet put his life in danger). There was even a weigh-in. A designated person would weigh the fighting cocks by holding one in each hand, his arms serving as a scale, and then he would announce whether one cock was heavier or lighter than the other. It wasn't very scientific, but everyone seemed to trust the system.

The cockfights I saw were swift and deadly, usually ending within a minute or two. But there were rules. Before a cock could be declared a winner, it had to peck the loser's comb within a certain time limit—otherwise the cockfight would be declared a draw.

Most of the cockfights in Damon Tract were held in a big yard next to my Aunt Violet's home. Whenever the cops managed to pull a surprise raid, it resulted in chaos—people would be scattering everywhere, climbing over fences, running through yards, hiding in closets—it was hilarious.

I looked forward to staying at Damon Tract. Usually, Mom would pick me up and drop me off there—except the one time I walked. I had lost all of my dinner money playing the pinball machine at Dot's Hut. I was hungry and went home to see if there was anything to eat, but the only thing in our refrigerator was a quarter-piece of raw onion. I ate all of it with soy sauce, but of course, I was still very hungry. It was a Friday, so there was no school the next day. I decided to visit Aunt Violet. It was a five- or six-mile walk, mostly along busy Nimitz Highway. I told Ken to let Dad know.

Along the way, I stopped briefly to look for crabs along a bridge by Keʻehi Lagoon. There were two bridges, which still stand today. We called them "First Bridge" and "Second Bridge." Cars were whizzing by, but I wasn't worried about them—I was more worried about the pack of wild dogs that frequented the area. So I picked up a baseball bat-sized piece of wood to protect myself. Fortunately, the dogs weren't there.

When I finally got to the street where my aunt lived, it was already getting dark. Aunt Violet happened to be standing outside her yard when she recognized me walking down the road. "Boy … [that was my nickname]. Boy, did you walk from Kalihi?" she asked in astonishment.

"Oh, it wasn't hard, Auntie," I replied, trying to sound nonchalant.

"No, but it is so dangerous with all those cars driving on Nimitz, don't you ever do it again, okay?" she scolded. Finally, she smiled and asked, "I bet you didn't eat dinner. Are you hungry?"

So one day, I finally worked up the nerve to ask Aunt Violet about my father.

"Auntie, is Ansing my real father?"

She hesitated for a moment and then confirmed what everyone else in my family but me seemed to know. Ansing was not my biological father, she said. He was my legal father—his name was on my birth certificate—but my biological father was a guy named Jerry. Jerry left Mom while she was still pregnant with me.

"Boy, I think you are old enough to know. He comes here all the time for the cockfights," she replied, "Next time he comes, I'll show you who he is."

Months later, when I was staying over, she called me to her second-floor bedroom window. "Boy, there he is, that man is your real father," she said, pointing to a man among dozens of Filipino men who were milling around awaiting the cockfights. He was short, of medium build and fair skinned. I don't remember his facial features except that I sensed that he truly was my biological father.

From then on, every time I stayed over, whenever there was a cockfight, I looked for him among the crowd. I saw him a couple of times, but he did not notice me. Then one day, I felt someone tap my shoulder. It was him. He asked, "You know me?" I was stunned by the tone of his voice. He sounded like he was doing me a favor by just talking to me—not a hint of warmth or friendliness, not even a smile. Who did he think he was? I glared at him and shot back sarcastically, "Yeah, I know you"—then turned my back and walked away.

That was it. He knew who I was and saw me often, but he never acknowledged me, not even a smile or hello. I was unimportant in his life. I don't recall feeling hurt, but any inner feelings I might have had for him would remain submerged forever. We never spoke to each other again. Sometimes I wonder whether things would have been different if he had shown some warmth, expressed some genuine interest in me.

When Mom was alive there were times I hoped she would tell me the real story about Jerry. Years later, I asked her why my middle name was "Jerome," and she said it was the first name of a famous lawyer she admired. She never knew that I knew the truth. I figured it was a part of her life she did not want me to know about. I never asked. It was okay. In the end, it didn't matter; I was glad she married Ansing. (In 1973, Jerry's name would come up again in an extraordinary case in which I was the lawyer defending a man accused of murder.)

Love for another, a psychologist friend once told me, grows largely from personal interaction rather than blood ties. When I first met Jerry my reaction was one of curiosity, not filial emotion. Ansing—Dad—was, after all, the only father I knew. He treated me as if I was his natural son. He was the only father I grew to love. My brief encounter with Jerry only strengthened my feelings for Dad.

The life insurance thing hurt, but I accepted it. *Maybe one day he'll add my name,* I thought. Besides, I was the big brother. I could handle myself. Ken was younger; he was smaller, timid and quiet. He would need help if Dad died. Looking back, that's how I rationalized it. I wasn't Dad's real son but he treated me as if I was. Even to this day, whenever I hear people say "blood is thicker than water," I am amused. It's more folklore than reality.

Dad was born and raised in a small village on the outskirts of the city of Urdaneta, Pangasinan Province, Philippines. He told me he came to Hawai'i in 1928, imported along with thousands of other Filipino immigrants by the plantation owners who were searching the world for workers to plant and harvest Hawaiian sugar cane. His older brother, Pablo, became a steward on a merchant ship, leaving behind a wife to whom he would faithfully send money but whom he would never see again.

Dad was Ilocano. Ilocanos were considered better workers than the fair-skinned Visayans, who were more heavily influenced by the Spanish culture and had a reputation for preferring frivolity and shunning hard work. Once, Dad told me that the difference between Ilocanos and the Visayans was that "Ilocanos work hard…. Visayans, they think they better than us but they lazy," a point of view disputed by Mom, who was part Visayan.

The haole plantation owners preferred Ilocano workers to Hawaiians, who often left the plantation fields, mainly because they could not adjust to plantation life and found it demeaning to work under the hot sun side by side with Asian immigrants. They also preferred them to the Chinese and Japanese, who were inclined to marry, start families and move to the city to find jobs or start small businesses, while most Filipinos saw working on the plantation as a temporary sacrifice. One day, they believed, they would return home with a nest egg to better the lives of their families.

Once, when I was in high school, I read a newspaper story about an old Filipino man who, after working on the plantation for nearly four decades, was finally returning to the Philippines to retire. Somehow, he had saved enough money to buy a small tractor, which he intended to take back with him. The story included a nice photo of him sitting on it. With his new tractor and his pension (a pittance in Hawai'i, but good money in the Philippines) the old man would make a heroic return to his village. The story was good public relations for the plantation owners—but the reality was that the old man was the exception rather than the rule.

By the late 1940s, two thirds of the plantation workers were Filipinos. For these men the biggest problem was the lack of women. One historian estimated that in 1930 Filipino men outnumbered Filipino women by more than 10 to one. All of the male Asian immigrants faced the same problem, of course, but they dealt with it in different ways. The pragmatic Chinese married Hawaiian women, thus accounting for the many Chinese Hawaiians in Hawai'i today. The ethnocentric Japanese shunned interracial marriage, opting instead for Japanese "picture brides." Most Filipinos, however, still clung to their dream of returning to their homeland one day. Tragically, too many Filipino men, unable to afford a ticket back to the Philippines or unwilling to return, lived out their senior years in loneliness, often in near- or abject poverty.

Bachelorhood brought social problems. Some Filipino men turned to prostitutes and gambling to make up for their loneliness. Some doted on their godchildren, showering them with gifts and money. Worse, competition for the few women available too often bred jealousy, manipulation and sometimes violence.

One day, an example of that kind of violence struck close to home. I must have been about 11 or 12 at the time when I saw my next-door neighbor, Carlos, crying, and later his older brother, Albert, teary-eyed. I had never seen Albert cry before, and I knew something was very wrong. I saw Dad talking to our landlord,

Mr. Leonida, and some of our neighbors. When they were done, I asked, "Daddy, what happened?"

"Oh, son, a crazy man kill their mother," he replied sadly.

"Why?" I asked Dad.

"Because he is so jealous of her," he said, shaking his head.

Murder was big news in those days—and it seemed even bigger if Filipinos were involved. The story was plastered in large headlines on the front pages of the two major daily newspapers. My heart sank when I read them. The sight of Albert and Carlos weeping made me weep too. I thought about Mom. It was a terrible day for the Estiamba family. It would be a long time before we heard Mr. Estiamba play his guitar and sing his songs again.

Such tragedies bolstered the widespread stereotype that Filipinos were a people given to vice and violence. And Filipinos such as my father paid a steep price for it—suffering discrimination in the job market, being looked down upon socially and treated unfairly by the government. Years later, I was shocked to learn that until capital punishment was abolished in Hawai'i in 1957, nearly one-half of those executed were Filipinos. Things are much better today, but back then Filipinos ranked near, if not at, the bottom of Hawai'i's socioeconomic hierarchy.

Education has long been the key for minorities to attain parity in society. But for the haole plantation owners, the less educated the worker, the better. Illiteracy encouraged docility. Docility discouraged ambition, kept the workers on the plantation. Ironically, life was so bad in the Philippines that some well-educated immigrants would lie about their education to increase their chances of being chosen to work on Hawai'i's plantations. I recall that on a few occasions my father would run into a friend and say to me, "Son, you see Maximo? He was a schoolteacher in Urdaneta." Or at a Filipino function the leader of a Filipino club would be introduced as "engineer" because he had been one in the Philippines, even though he was a hotel worker in Hawai'i.

Like the majority of the Filipino immigrants he came with, though, Dad did not have much schooling. His third-grade education in a rural school in Urdaneta had taught him beautiful penmanship but only the basic elements of reading, writing and arithmetic.

But that did not stop him from leaving the plantation. The plantation was not what he wanted. The sun was hot, the work, backbreaking—and he did not want to get involved in the rising labor unrest, which eventually led to strikes and sometimes violence. Eventually, he found a job in the hotel industry, first as a busboy and then as a waiter at the old Palm Tree Inn in Waikīkī, and finally as a waiter at the Outrigger Canoe Club, where he worked for more than 20 years. Dad was a hard worker, and his warm personality and neat appearance made him well suited for the service industry.

I never learned how my father and mother met or why they married. I never asked and no one ever told me. We just never talked about it. I was born on November 14, 1939. They divorced when I was about six years old. So they must have been married for at least six years.

But their divorce was inevitable. They were so different. Mom was aggressive and independent; Dad was easygoing and laid back. Intellectually, Dad was not curious—he took each day as it came. Mom, on the other hand, was always trying to learn. She was smart. Had she been born 50 years later, she could have been a lawyer or a teacher. The divorce was amicable, and they agreed that Dad would get custody of me and Ken.

Mom would drop by every other weekend to pick us up. Most of the time, she took us to places she wanted to go, places for adults. One day, she took us to lunch at Ciro's, a popular upscale restaurant in the old Alexander Young Hotel building in downtown Honolulu. "Boy, when you eat always use your fork to push the food away from you," she said. When I used my butter knife to cut a roll, she took the knife from my hand and instructed, "Boy, never cut a roll, always use your hands to break it," demonstrating how. I was getting a lesson in table manners. People at nearby tables would look and smile. I was embarrassed, but I wanted to please Mom. But I was still a kid, and I wanted to go to the beach, to the zoo, to be with other kids—with my cousins, my friends—and not have to worry about how I combed my hair, how I dressed or what my table manners were at Ciro's or other fancy places Mom took us.

As much as I wanted to see Mom, I dreaded going with her. She had a fetish about neatness. Wherever she lived, her home was super neat, everything in place, clean as a whistle. And whenever she visited our apartment, she would inspect the place and either clean something up or tell us to do it later. If we knew she was coming, Ken and I would scurry about trying to straighten up the house.

Every time we went out with her we had to wear clean, stiffly starched pants and shirts. She insisted we comb our hair in what she thought was a proper fashion. I had to use a big glob of greasy Three Flowers Brilliantine pomade to make it the way Mom wanted: left side parted, slicked straight down. I looked like a real Mommy's boy.

Mom was a great dresser, but conservative, preferring dark blues, browns, grays and muted greens. She never wore jeans. Once she saw me wearing a bright red shirt. She laughed and told me, "Boy, people with brown-skinned complexion [like me] should stay away from colors like red, orange and purple." Except for my old favorite light red, gingham-design shirt, which I wore a lot in high school, and a few ties, to this day I have never bought clothing that is red, orange or purple.

As I reached my teens, I'd often hide whenever Mom came to pick us up. I'd tell (threaten, actually) Ken not to tell her where I was. Sometimes I could hear her calling my name repeatedly, and I'd hide in the backyard until she left with Ken. She knew I was hiding, and it probably hurt her feelings.

Small-Kid Time Memories

Kalihi was like a big playground for me. Often, I'd walk a mile or so to play basketball or just hang out at nearby Puʻuhale Park, or a couple more miles to the Kalākaua Gym or the Kalihi YMCA. On weekends, if I wasn't staying over at my aunt's home, I would go with my friends to Sand Island.

Today Sand Island is crowded with warehouses, trucking companies and light industry. Back then, there were few businesses located there. A major part of Sand Island belonged to the U.S. Army, including the many abandoned buildings that became part of our playground. On weekends, the place was deserted, and, except for a lone MP at the gate by the entrance to Fort Ruger, we had it all to ourselves.

At the small harbor where sampans (wooden boats 10 to 15 feet long) were moored parallel to each other, I taught myself how to swim by kicking off one sampan and stroking my arms like crazy until I hit the next one. I learned how to "pump hole" for crabs in the adjoining mud flats by pumping one foot into one end of the crab's tunnel while someone was at the other end with a scoop net to catch the crab as it was pushed out by the force of the water.

As I got older, I became more adventurous. My friends and I would build canoes (we called them "tin boats") out of a sheet of corrugated roof iron, tar and pieces of wood to paddle out to Mokauea Island, about 300 to 400 yards offshore.

Usually the tin boat would start leaking as soon as the tar gave way; then it would sink and we would have to swim back to shore. But we would build another and try again. The closest we ever got was the halfway point. There are probably a half-dozen tin boats buried in the mud between Sand Island and Mokauea Island.

Thirty years later, I found myself chairing a hearing of the State House Committee on Transportation and listening with amused skepticism to a well-known environmental activist testify about the "sacred history" of Mokauea Island. Before the haoles discovered Hawaiʻi, the ancient Hawaiians had no written language. Their knowledge, customs and traditions were passed on to younger generations through chants, prayer, dances and art. As far as I can remember, the only people living on Mokauea Island were two or three elderly Filipino men, living in small shacks built on stilts above the water, eking out an impoverished existence. There was nothing "sacred" about the island back then.

My mother—to get back to her—was the oldest of three sisters, christened "Eleanor Infante." Mom and her sisters, Rachel and Violet, were the prettiest trio of sisters in all of Kalihi. Mom was about 5 foot 8, tall for a Filipina. She was fair skinned—a mestiza. Her parents were Visayans from Cebu. She had only an eighth-grade education, but she was very bright. She was "street smart"—but she could have been book smart, too, if she'd had the chance. She taught herself how to speak the Visayan, Ilocano and Tagalog dialects. Dad could only speak Ilocano.

Mom had a reputation for being tough. She was like the character played by the fine actress Gena Rowlands in the 1980 movie *Gloria*. In the movie, Gloria is a beautiful, tough but soft-hearted former mob moll who saves a young boy from being murdered by the mob. When I first saw the movie when it came out, Gloria reminded me of Mom. Mom was no mob moll, but she was beautiful, compassionate and tough.

One evening, Aunt Violet got into an argument with a male neighbor that ended with her being punched on the nose. Rather than call Uncle Jack, the first thing she did was to telephone Mom and tearfully tell her what happened. I was there and I could hear Mom's raised voice on the other end of the line. "What!" she said; "that bastard! I'll be right there!"

About 15 minutes later, I saw the headlights of a car turning from Nimitz Highway onto the street where my aunt lived. There were no streetlights in Damon Tract, so it was pitch black. As the car came closer, I saw the "TAXI" sign on the roof. Mom had arrived. She stepped out of the taxi, dressed in an expensive dress and high heels—also like Gena Rowlands in *Gloria*—took one look at my aunt (who made sure there was still some blood showing on her nose) and stormed over to the neighbor's house. We—my cousins and I—followed her like ducklings following their mother. Meanwhile, the neighbor had locked himself in his bedroom. I watched as Mom started kicking the door and shouting, "Come out here and pick on someone your own size, you coward! Come out, you punk, step outside!" The guy never came out. Mom was just awesome that night.

I was about 12 when Dad bought me my first bicycle. I could hardly contain my excitement. It was a blue Schwinn, complete with horn, headlight, chrome fenders and whitewalls with spoked rims. I remember the price: $56. Ordinarily, Dad would not have been able to afford it, but he won some money gambling and decided to spend some of it on us. So he bought new bikes for Ken and me. Dad didn't make a lot of money, but when he had it, he was very generous.

With my new bike I became a home delivery boy for the *Honolulu Advertiser*. A 12-year-old businessman! Every morning I'd wake up at 3:30 a.m. and ride my bike about two miles to Dee-Lite Bakery at the corner of Dillingham Boulevard and Mokauea Street. Along with a couple of other delivery boys, I would wait there for the *Advertiser* dealer to drop off the morning newspapers. As soon as we got them, we would roll up each newspaper, bind it with a rubber band, put the bundles into the newspaper bag specially made to fit on bicycle handlebars and take off on our different routes to make deliveries.

My route was scary. Most streets in the neighborhood did not have streetlights, so it was usually very dark. Sand Island was our playground during daytime, but at 4:30 a.m. it was deserted and so dark I could hardly see the road. None of the handful of companies there were open at that hour. I was always worried about running into the pack of dogs that roamed the area. I was also very worried about running into Wilson.

Wilson, who looked like he was pure Hawaiian, might have been Hawai'i's first homeless person. None of us knew anything about his background or his family. We just knew that he was a hopelessly incurable alcoholic who lived in a huge, abandoned concrete pipe at Sand Island. Whenever we saw Wilson during the day, he would be drunk, wandering Sand Island, sometimes the neighborhood, holding a bottle in a brown paper bag, talking incoherently to some imagined person.

We thought Wilson was pupule (crazy), but no one ever teased him. We felt sorry for him. Sometimes we'd take up a collection of loose change and give it to him. Wilson was a good-sized man. Whenever I ran into him during the daytime I was wary but not afraid of him. The thought of running into him in the dark at 4:30 in the morning, however, was different. I got scared just thinking about it.

Whenever I was making deliveries, every time I heard a sound or saw a movement in the dark, my 12-year-old imagination ran wild. The worst was having to ride by the crematorium on Homerule Street. The crematorium was a mysterious place to kids in the neighborhood. If we saw smoke coming out of the high smokestack, we figured they were cremating a body. One morning, a movement in the dark scared me—prompting me to ride my bike past the crematorium as fast as I could. At the same time, I threw a newspaper on the run so hard that it broke the glass window on the customer's front porch. Later, I returned and apologized to the customer. Fortunately, he told me he would fix it himself, but just to be more careful the next time.

Almost every morning, I would go through some hair-raising experience. After six months, my father asked me to quit delivering newspapers. When I told him that I was doing it because I wanted to pay him back for the Schwinn, he laughed and said, "No need, son, you look so tired every morning and I worry you get hurt."

Having greater mobility opened new adventures for me. With our bikes, my friends and I were able to go to places we had never been before. We would bike to Waikīkī to bodysurf at "the wall" (which still stands today) or to Ala Moana Park to swim or to the reservoir (we called it "Tin Roof" because the water tower had a tin roof) way up in Kalihi Valley to catch crayfish and catfish.

But not all of our adventures were good ones. Once, four of us rode our bikes all the way from Kalihi to go spear fishing at the beach off Kāhala. We packed our Hawaiian sling spear guns, a floater, net and lunch. Bicycling the 10 miles from Kalihi to Kāhala was duck soup for us. We were young and fit. We parked our bikes at one of the public rights-of-way and began spear fishing along the reef, parallel to the shoreline. We were in the water a couple of hundred yards from the right-of-way when we heard someone shouting at us, "Hey, you kids get out of here!" A big, barrel-chested haole man was standing at the water's edge, yelling at us at the top of his voice. He was definitely annoyed by our presence in front of what I assumed was his home.

We were about 50 yards from shore, so we moved back further, into deeper water, hoping to placate him. But he continued to yell. Red-faced, arms waving, he shouted, "I said get out of here, goddammit!"

One of my friends said, "Benny, we better go, the haole man is really mad."

"Why?" I asked. "He doesn't own the ocean!"

"No, let's go, the man is really mad," my friend repeated.

"Goddammit! I said get out of here!" the man shouted again.

By then we were angry ourselves—and a safe distance away from the haole man. I looked back at him and shouted, "Ah, fuck you!"

"Yeah, up yours!" someone else yelled, giving him the finger, as we all swam back to the right-of-way. We weren't in the water long enough to spear anything. We had nothing to show for our long bike ride.

Before leaving, we decided to eat lunch there. The four of us sat with our backs against the chain-link fence, eating our rice balls, Spam and Vienna sausage. The fence separated public from private property. As we ate, each of us did an impersonation of the angry haole man, each performance eliciting hilarious and loud laughter.

After about 15 minutes, we saw a policeman park his car and begin walking toward us.

"Hey, you kids have to leave, you're making too much noise," the cop ordered.

"Oh, sorry about the noise, we'll keep our voices down," I said.

"No, you guys have to leave now," the cop said, this time almost apologetically.

"Why? This is not private property," one of my friends said.

"Because the lady," the cop said, motioning to the fence, "wants you kids to leave, that's why."

"Can we finish our lunch?" I asked.

"Come on, don't give me a hard time, go now," he said in a way that left me feeling he had done this before.

Standing about five feet from the other side of the fence with her arms crossed was an elderly, white-haired haole woman. She did not say a word, but her stern look, her pursed lips, said everything she wanted to say. As I was packing up to leave, I kept looking back at her. I wasn't angry—I was perplexed. This had never happened to me before. First, the big haole man, now this distinguished-looking white-haired lady—I wondered, *What did we do to make them so angry? Do they hate us, or what?*

It was a different Hawai'i then. Later, as an adult, I would learn more about Hawai'i's history and how a small group of haoles—an oligarchy—ran Hawai'i like a South American banana republic. As a kid, the only haole I knew personally was Uncle Jack. I guess he was different because he came from a poorer background than I did. Other than him, I just assumed whenever I saw a haole not in a military uniform that he was the boss. If I saw a haole working at a service station, a bakery, a hotel or any business, I assumed, subconsciously at least, that the guy was in charge.

Years later, I shared the story of being chased out of the water with former Chief Justice William Richardson. He chuckled and told me how as a kid he had had to stand at the water's edge at Waikīkī to watch people dancing in the hotels. Back then the hotel management treated the beach as if it was the hotel's private property. In 1973, as chief justice of the Hawai'i Supreme Court, he ended this practice by ruling in *County of Hawaii v. Sotomura* that the State owned the beaches all the way up to the vegetation mark, which effectively abolished all private beaches in Hawai'i.

A Primer in Politics

My introduction to politics came when I was elected treasurer of the eighth-grade class at Kalākaua Intermediate School. I swamped my opponent, getting about 80 percent of the vote. The president was Linda Au Hoy, a Chinese-Hawaiian girl. Larry Miike, who came from Damon Tract, and Nancy Oshiro, both Japanese Americans, were elected vice president and secretary.

We were good students (I never got a "C" in my report card until my junior year in high school). However, I must confess, I don't remember much about being in student government except trying to master Robert's Rules of Order, which I never succeeded in doing even as a State legislator. The following year both Linda and Larry transferred to private schools. Linda transferred to Kamehameha School (a private school for Hawaiians only, which, with its $10 billion trust, is probably the richest prep school in the nation), and Larry went to 'Iolani School, a private school well known for its academic excellence, where he became a star baseball player. (Years later, after I became governor, Larry, armed with medical and law degrees, would join my administration as director of the Department of Health.)

There were good reasons for their transferring to private schools. Kalākaua, named after King David Kalākaua, was a school with serious problems. Its nearly 2,000 students came from seven or eight feeder elementary schools. Half of the student body was teenage boys from Kalihi, for whom proving their toughness and courage became a rite of passage—a sure formula for trouble. Hardly a school day went by without a fight or incidents of hijacking and bullying. The school was simply too big for teachers and administrators to control. Not surprisingly, parents who could afford it did their best to send their children to private schools.

There were many good teachers at Kalākaua. Mrs. Burmeister was one of them. A local haole, she was known for her feisty, no-nonsense approach to teaching. She was best known, however, for her uncanny accuracy with erasers, usually thrown a fair distance from the blackboard at the disruptive student, always a boy, at the back of the room. The class would then carry on, with the guilty student sporting a white chalk mark on his head for the remainder of the class period. Today, she would be charged with criminal assault and the school would be sued. Back then, parents welcomed this kind of corporal discipline, and a student beaned by a Burmeister eraser would probably suffer a worse fate at home if his parents found out.

My favorite teacher was Harold Higa, the band teacher. The boys in the band—there were no girls in it back then—respected him. Great teachers have that something extra that separates them from the ordinary. Mr. Higa had it. We could tell he was completely devoted to his work. And he had the ability to inspire his students to do their very best. Most important, we all knew he respected and cared about us. Slightly built, stoop-shouldered, always looking over his eyeglasses, he appeared very ordinary—but he left an indelible mark on me and many of his students.

One day, Mr. Higa announced that he was being transferred from band to teach orchestra. This was a shock. To the boys in the band, the orchestra was for girls and sissies. Moreover, the orchestra at Kalākaua was pretty bad, often eliciting giggles and stifled laughter whenever we heard the violins screeching during practice. "Sorry, fellows," he said, "the decision has been made. I'm going to miss teaching you guys, but I'll still be here at Kalākaua. If you need help, come see me." Without exception, the boys were unhappy, but there was nothing we could do.

He then introduced his replacement, a Mr. Oga (not his real name). Mr. Oga was stepping into big shoes, but the boys were open to him. As soon as he started talking, though, I got the feeling he wasn't going to make it with us. He was tall and slim, and whenever he smiled it seemed more of a leer than anything else. The man was no Harold Higa.

Mr. Oga came across as very cold and stern. He didn't seem happy to be at Kalākaua. I got the impression he was just biding his time until he could be transferred to a school more to his liking. His attitude and teaching showed it. Unlike Mr. Higa, he would make sarcastic remarks whenever someone made a mistake. He always seemed to be annoyed.

Then came the foot-tapping incident. Nothing upset him more than musicians who tapped their feet when performing. One day, in the middle of a score, he stopped the band and announced that this was his pet peeve. He considered it unprofessional. "What's the matter with this Japanee?" someone said later. "It never bothered Mr. Higa."

In those days, the Kalākaua Band had some of the toughest boys in the school. Antonio Pascua, a clarinet player, was an amateur boxing champion, and later as a high school student at Farrington he would win the light-heavyweight crown at the Seattle Diamond Belt Tournament in Washington. And there were others, like Gerado Paet, a saxophone player built like a fire hydrant, who was about as nice a guy as one could meet but not someone to mess around with.

One day, Mr. Oga stopped the band and began lecturing us. I saw some of the guys signal each other. When the band resumed playing, they began to tap their feet again, louder than ever. Soon more joined in, until finally everyone was stomping their feet on the floor as hard as they could. The sound of 60 teenage boys pounding their feet on the old wood floor could be heard well beyond the band room. We'd had enough—and we wanted Mr. Oga to know it. Ignoring his orders for us to stop, we kept stomping until he stormed out of the room in disgust and anger. As soon as he left, the room erupted with loud "yahoo!"s and raucous laughter.

Word about the foot-stomping spread quickly—and it got to some of the thugs in the school. The next day, a couple of them confronted Mr. Oga, roughed him up and told him to get out of Kalākaua. We never saw him again.

Like most of the boys in the band, I felt badly for Mr. Oga. What happened to him was wrong—but I was glad he was gone. A few of the guys were not so charitable.

The next day, Mr. Higa was back. He was very somber, and the entire band was quiet. He lectured us about the wrongness of what happened. Coming from him, however, it did not sound like a lecture. Whenever he said something, everyone just listened.

The boys were so happy he was back that someone came up with the idea of buying Mr. Higa a present. Each band member chipped in a dollar for a total of about $60. It was rumored that the watch cost only $40 and that the guys who thought up the idea kept $20 for themselves. But a $40 watch in 1953 was still a pretty good watch. It was a fitting gift for a great and highly revered teacher. Mr. Higa choked up a bit when the watch was presented to him. He was surprised and at a loss for words. He thanked us, looked at the watch and said softly, "Gosh, nothing cheap about you guys." We gave him a standing ovation.

(Years later, I learned that Mr. Higa had served as an interpreter for the U.S. Marines during the battle for Iwo Jima in World War II. To make sure that he wasn't mistaken for the enemy, he would sing or whistle American jazz tunes. He was so unassuming, quiet and humble it was difficult to envision him serving his country under such dangerous circumstances.)

As a teenager, I was always looking for ways to earn spending money. One day, as a bunch of us were walking to Sand Island, we noticed a lot of brass and copper wires, pipes and fixtures lying around in vacant lots and in old abandoned warehouses. To us, it was junk no one wanted. Someone got the idea of collecting the brass and copper and selling it to the scrap metal company at Sand Island. We were too young to sell it ourselves, so we paid an adult to do it for us. Our first sale exceeded our expectations. So we decided to do it again.

The second time, the boss of the company handled the sale. He looked at the brass and copper items, frowned a bit and asked, "Where did you kids get this stuff?" It was the first time it occurred to any of us that the stuff might not have been discarded waste after all. But he approved the sale anyway and paid us about 20 percent less than the going prices. We weren't happy about it, but we shrugged it off. In the next sale, however, the boss paid us only half the regular price. When someone pointed to a posted sign listing the prices per pound, he smirked and said, "If that's how you feel, go somewhere else." Well, there was no place else.

The next Sunday, we were walking to Sand Island to go swimming. As we passed the scrap metal company, someone noticed that there was nothing but loose coral at the bottom of the company's chain-link fence. One of the guys dug a hole in the coral, and the smallest among us squirmed under the fence. From there, he began throwing brass and copper items over the fence. We picked the stuff up, mixed it with the other brass and copper we had collected and, the next weekend, when the boss was out to lunch, we had someone sell the items back to the company. The guy had cheated us, but we more than evened the score by selling him back his own stuff. We never went back.

During my eighth-grade year, Ken was living with Mom and our new stepfather, Rudy, in Whitmore Village. I lived in Kalihi with Dad. I was alone a lot, especially at night. But sometimes I would hang out someplace and come home late at night, even after Dad returned from work. After Mom found out that I got into a nasty fight with a kid at school, she decided I had too much time alone and that I was heading for more trouble. She convinced Dad that I should move to Whitmore Village and live with her and Rudy. Dad agreed. Ken and I switched places. He moved back to Kalihi and I moved to Whitmore Village.

Whitmore Village was the kind of rural community where everyone knew each other. I recall staying over with Mom one weekend in 1951 or 1952. I was visiting Ken, who was still living there at the time. The Korean War was being fought, and a neighbor's son (I think his name was Eddie) was killed in action. He was a handsome, local Filipino in his 20s. Mom kept his photograph in the living room. In those days, it was legal to have a wake held in the home. In the Filipino culture, a panaje, or prayer ceremony, is held for nine days, with the deceased lying in state in the home. It seemed everyone in Whitmore attended Eddie's panaje. During each panaje, I could hear the voice of the priest carrying throughout the still night as he led the mourners in prayer. The people of Whitmore, mostly Filipino and Japanese plantation workers, were good Americans—as good as one could find anywhere in the country.

Mom owned and managed a dance hall in Wahiawā called the Rainbow Dance Hall. She took me with her to work a couple of times for an hour or two. A six-piece band provided the music. A couple of bouncers kept order. The customers were mostly single Filipino men and soldiers from nearby Schofield Barracks. The dance hostesses were tough ladies. They had to be. Most of their customers were lonely, horny men who were continually hitting on them.

The dance hall would usually close at around 2 a.m. A few times, I got up from bed and watched Mom count the night's cash receipts at the kitchen table. The bills were stacked in neat piles by denomination alongside the small, pearl-handled .25-caliber automatic that Mom took with her whenever she went to the dance hall.

Later, I found out that the dance hall was going broke and Mom was becoming harder to live with as she worried herself sick trying to figure out ways to save it. Dance halls were very popular during World War II and the immediate postwar period. But by 1954, the business had begun to fade.

A year later, Mom closed the hall. Because of their financial situation, she took a job on the plantation as a field worker—something she'd sworn she would never do. Mom respected people who worked hard, but she saw working in the pineapple fields as a personal failure. Picking pineapples under the hot sun was a tough job for a man—but it was far tougher on a woman. It was tough on a woman's skin and complexion, and it hardened her hands. Regardless of the precautions they took, such as wearing heavy clothing that covered their faces, large hats and goggles, making them look like beekeepers, prolonged work in the fields was bound to affect women's physical appearance. Women who worked in the fields aged faster. There was no getting around it. Mom worked in the fields for only a year because she developed severe back problems, which would later require surgery and lead to a serious crisis for the entire family.

In 1955, I moved back to Kalihi to live with Dad and Ken again and enrolled at Farrington as a sophomore. I enjoyed living in Whitmore City and had made many good friends there. But I was a city boy, and I longed to return to Kalihi. I was glad to be home again.

Farrington High School was one of the largest high schools in the western United States. Named after a former governor, Wallace Rider Farrington, the school was reputed to be the toughest in Hawai'i.

Contrary to popular perception, school discipline at Farrington was good. If there was trouble, it usually took place off campus. Things never got out of hand for a couple reasons: First, none of the teachers at Farrington were ever intimidated by students; second, the male teachers, coaches and ROTC instructors all worked together to help enforce school rules and discipline. They did not always follow the book. When necessary, one of them would take troublemakers into the boy's restroom or to the back of the ROTC building for a "talk."

Once during an ROTC parade, our company was ordered to "march time" (march in place) when a guy named George started fooling around, jumping up and down on two feet as if he were on a pogo stick. One of our ROTC instructors, Sergeant Jelf, walked up behind him and, as George began his ascent, gave him a swift kick in the rear, leaving a streak of dark brown shoe polish on the seat of George's pants. A sharp look from Sergeant Jelf stopped our giggling. George became the talk of the school for a long time.

Years later, in 1995, I met another one of my ROTC sergeants, Sergeant Arnold, at the 50th reunion of Farrington's Class of 1945. Sergeant Arnold, who bore a striking resemblance to the actor Ernest Borgnine, was living in a retirement community in Arizona but came home for the reunion. "Cayetano," he asked, "do you remember what I made you guys do when I caught someone chewing gum?" Remember? How could I forget? Sergeant Arnold took gum-chewing in his class as a personal insult. Whenever he caught someone chewing gum, he'd order the entire class to do push-ups. But that did not stop the gum-chewing—until the next (and final) infraction when he ordered everyone in the class to chew the same piece of gum and the guy who started it all to swallow it!

"Sergeant, if you did that today you would be in big trouble," I said with a chuckle. He smiled and retorted, "That's the trouble with the schools today. No discipline. No respect for teachers. Teachers are afraid of the students. But look at you guys—you all turned out okay, right?"

Encounter with the Law

The year 1958 was a turning point in my life. I was totally focused on cars and my girlfriend, Lorraine. I was working part time, pumping gas at a service station. Repeated counseling by my teachers, who kept assuring me I was college material and urging me to keep my grades up, fell on deaf ears. During my junior year, C's began appearing on my report cards. In my senior year, the roof fell in. I was on the verge of flunking out.

I had no desire to go to college. Instead, the few times I thought about life after graduation, joining the U.S. Air Force seemed like a reasonable option for me. But in June 1958, I graduated from Farrington. That year turned out to be unforgettable.

One August evening, I was sitting in my car with three friends at Scotty's Drive-In, back then a popular hangout for high school students. As usual, the place was packed with cars. Suddenly, we noticed two guys arguing with one of the security guards. They were the Kaeo brothers, Walter and Kalani. The brothers were very close and were always playing pranks on each other. The security guard, a guy nicknamed Dandy, had a reputation as a real hardnosed guy. Apparently, Walter had been using the restroom and Kalani had deliberately left the door open, exposing Walter to the people sitting in their cars or passing by.

Dandy, acting as if he was a cop, ordered Walter to leave the premises. Kalani tried to explain it was his fault, not his brother's. But Dandy was not interested in explanations and grabbed Walter by the shirt collar to physically throw him off the premises. Kalani punched him. The two other security guards quickly ran over to help. Simultaneously, the other boys from Pālama jumped out of their cars and joined in the fray. Outnumbered three to one, in a minute or two all three security guards were knocked to the ground.

While the guards lay dazed, the boys began dousing them with malts and Cokes and pelting them with half-eaten hamburgers and French fries. Four male workers burst out of the building to help the security guards. One guy, a huge haole, was dressed in a chef's uniform and waving a big pot in his hand. The Pālama boys got in their cars and quickly drove away.

Shige, one of the guys in my car, said, "Benny, we better get out of here, too." We had nothing to do with the fight, but we were parked right next to the Pālama boys, and leaving seemed like a good idea. It turned out to be a big mistake.

As I drove out of the drive-in and turned left on Keʻeaumoku Street, I looked in my rear-view mirror and saw a couple of cars moving fast toward us. I turned right on Kapiolani Boulevard and looked in the rearview mirror again and saw one of the cars coming up fast. It was the Metro Squad—the police vice squad unit feared for its roughhouse tactics.

One of the cops motioned for me to pull over and I did. "Move over," he said as he got in the driver's seat and drove my car back to Scotty's. I told him we had nothing to do with the fight. "Just shut your mouth," he retorted. Back at the drive-in, they ordered us to stay in the car. One of our guys, Clarence Pratt, managed to sneak away. He had just enlisted in the Army, so no one minded his getting away.

I watched the Metro cops talking to the chef, who was still holding the big pot. He pointed at us and said, "Yeah, those are the guys who jumped Dandy and the others." That was all it took. Before any of us could say anything, a couple of the younger Metro cops—these guys were all in great physical shape—came over, flung open the car doors, grabbed each of us by the shirt and threw us against the drive-in wall. "Don't move, punk, or I'll kick your ass," one said to me.

The place was packed with a couple hundred customers and onlookers who watched the cops manhandle us. When Shige protested the rough treatment, one of the cops grabbed him by the hair and pounded his head into my 1951 Ford coupe's right front fender, leaving a small indentation. I got angry and complained to one of the cops about what had been done to Shige. He looked at me sternly, and said, "Sonny, I tell you what, we call it even. I won't say anything about all those empty beer cans we found on your car floor and you forget what happen to your friend, okay?"

Unhurt but shaken, Shige was taken to and detained at the Juvenile Detention Center a few streets away from Scotty's Drive-In. At 18 years old, both Reynold and I were adults, and we were detained in the holding cell on the third floor of the old police station on the corner of Merchant and Bethel Streets.

When we were taken to the holding cell, I saw Harvey Pratt, Clarence's older brother. Back then, the police used inmates to do work at the jails. They were called "trustees." Harvey was wearing a blue denim trustee uniform. "Benny, what you kids doing here?" he asked, grinning. I told him the story and he just laughed. "So, my fat brother Clario made it, eh?" he smiled. "Well, you kids just take it easy; I'll be here all night."

Harvey was Portuguese Hawaiian, and like all of the Pratt brothers, he had that handsome part-Hawaiian look. He stood about 5 feet 10 inches and was solidly built. He was a nice guy, a tough guy, a motorcycle rider who was quick to use his fists. Once, he made the news when he punched out Richard Tregaskis, the famous writer of *Guadalcanal Diary* and other books, after a traffic accident in which Tregaskis' car damaged his motorcycle. To Harvey, it didn't matter who the other guy was or whose fault it was; he loved his Harley, and anyone who damaged it was in for trouble.

On another occasion, Harvey got drunk and was raising hell in the old Kalihi Bowling Alley. The management could not get him to leave and called the cops to arrest him. When the cops arrived, they found that Harvey had stationed himself between two racks of bowling balls with his back to the wall. When they approached him, he started rolling bowling balls at their feet to keep them at bay. Bowlers looked on incredulously, some laughing at the sight of the cops jumping up, down and sideways to dodge the heavy balls. Finally, they got to him, handcuffed him, took him outside and worked him over a bit before taking him to the police station.

Reynold and I weren't the only ones in the holding cell. There was an older guy who looked like he was in his 30s. He appeared to be Portuguese. He was big, about 5 feet 10 inches and at least 250 pounds. He was lying on a cot and appeared to be sleeping. I whispered to Reynold that the guy's nose was bleeding. He wasn't sleeping. "What? You punks talking stink about me?" he asked angrily. Despite our denials, he got up and started toward us. Soon he was chasing Reynold and me around a long, iron table. Soaking wet, I weighed about 125 pounds, and Reynold was only slighter bigger than me. The guy looked like he wanted to kill us. "Take it easy, bruddah, we neva talk stink about you," I said several times in pidgin as we ran around the table as if we were playing musical chairs.

Hearing the commotion, Harvey came into the room and asked, "Benny, what's the matter? This Portagee bothering you guys?"

"Yeah, he thinks we were talking stink about him," I stammered.

Harvey looked at the guy and ordered, "Eh, Portagee, come heah!" He reached through the bars, grabbed him by the shirt collar and started banging the guy's head against the cell bars. Each time his head hit the bars it made a loud sound. "Leave the kids alone (bong!), otherwise I'm coming in there (bong!) and I'll break your fucking ass! (Bong!) You understand, fucker?" (Bong! Bong!) The big guy slumped to the floor, holding his head, and just sat there, obviously dazed. We had no more trouble after that.

(Several years later, Harvey's free-spirited lifestyle caught up with him when he was killed in a motorcycle accident.)

The next morning, Mom came in a taxi to pick me up. A police captain questioned me for the last time: "Okay, Benjamin, you say you were not involved in the fight and I believe you [he didn't], but I know you know the guys who were involved. Now standing before your mother, if you love her, tell me the names of the guys who caused the fight." There was no way I could squeal on the guys. After a long pause, I said meekly, "I don't know." Mom had a pained look on her face.

It was the first time I had ever been arrested and jailed. Luckily, no charges were filed against me, Reynold or Shige. The fear that ran through me as we were chased in the holding cell made me vow I would never do anything to land in jail again.

(Years later, Walter Kaeo came to my law office for some legal advice. He had just gotten out of Oahu Prison, having served 10 years for armed robbery. We talked and joked a bit about the Scotty's incident. He was no longer the kid I remembered from years ago. He was all muscles, his body chiseled like a body-builder's. "Walter, you're a little bigger than I remember," I joked.

"Benny," he laughed, "we had nothing to do at OP except lift weights and smoke joints. Besides," he continued, "I had to hold my own against the bulls in OP ... know what I mean?" A year after we talked he was dead—shot by his wife. She said he was beating her and she shot him in self-defense. She was never charged.)

A few weeks after our night in the holding cell, I was shooting pool with my friends at our usual hangout, the Waiakamilo Pool Hall on Dillingham Boulevard and Waiakamilo Street. Around 9 p.m., a car stopped in front of the pool hall. A guy named Alex stepped out. Alex was from Pālama and we all knew him. We did not know the other guys. "Eh, howzit guys," Alex said. "We going to Pālolo Housing to settle some business there. Can you guys come to back us up?" Without giving it much thought, three of us—me, Gary and Warren—got into our friend Kabo (Herbert Koda)'s car (he was driving his mother's 1954 Mercury) and fol-lowed them to Pālolo Housing.

"What is this all about?" I asked Kabo.

"I don't know, but Alex said if there is a beef, it will be between two guys and we just have to make sure it is up-and-up," he replied. Beef?

We arrived at Pālolo Housing at around 10. "Eh, you guys can wait in the car, but if anything happen come give us a hand," Alex said. "Shit, we don't even know these guys," I complained again. Three of us got out of the car and stood by silently. Kabo stayed in the car in case we had to get out of there quickly. We watched as five of the other six guys approached two guys sitting outside one of the apartments. For a minute or so, we heard them talking. Suddenly, someone threw a punch, and then blows were being exchanged. It was five against two, so we just stood watching, expecting the fight to end quickly. Unknown to any of us, there was a bunch of older men, probably construction workers, drinking at another apartment on the other side of the building. Quickly, they came running to see what was going on. And then they got into it. Other men were pouring out of the apartments. It seemed all of

Pālolo Housing was jumping into the melee. Quickly it turned into a rout. The driver of the other car had locked himself in his car as his attackers were smashing his windshield, one of them wielding a two-pound sledgehammer. The other five guys were either beaten unconscious or had run away. Then someone shouted, pointing to us, "There's more of them over there!"

"Kabo, get your car out of the parking lot," I said, trying to remain calm. One of the first men who reached us shouted, "You punks came looking for trouble, eh? Now we going give you the same thing we gave your friends!" Another guy joined him, and they tried to grab us and take one of us down. We began backing up, fighting back when we were attacked. We could see more men running quickly toward us. It was time to get out.

The three of us started running down the street with the men in pursuit. We were younger and faster. Soon we outdistanced them. While we were running, we could hear the cries of the guy who was trapped in his car: "Enough, brah, I had enough." His cries echoed through the quiet night in Pālolo Valley. We just kept running as fast as we could. My heart was racing like crazy. Finally, we reached Wai'alae Avenue. It was near midnight and the streets were deserted. Then we heard the police sirens and saw the police cars driving up to Pālolo Housing. We ducked behind a building and watched.

In our panic, we had run across a field. I had stepped on some kiawe thorns that pierced one of my slippers. Apparently, my adrenalin level was so high, I did not feel a thing while running. But the cuts began to hurt and I was trying to nurse my foot. We were out of breath and sweating heavily.

Warren said, "Eh, we gotta go back, we left Kabo behind. If we don't go back everyone will think we yellow." Gary and I looked at each other in disbelief and shook our heads.

"Kabo drove out of the parking lot," I said. "I think he is okay."

"Yeah, but the other guys going think we yellow," Warren replied.

"Fuck them, we don't even know those guys—why the hell did we come in the first place?" I asked, angry and humiliated.

The next day, September 4, 1958, the story of the fight (the newspaper called it a "riot") was on the front page of both daily newspapers, along with a photograph of the car with its windshield and windows smashed. "They came looking for trouble and they found it," a police detective was quoted as saying.

Later, we met Kabo. He was unhurt. While we ran away from Pālolo Housing, he was trapped and was forced to run farther into the housing and hide for an hour. After the cops left the scene, he began to make his way back to his mother's car in the parking lot. Luckily for him, one of our friends visiting her relatives there saw him and asked the Pālolo guys to leave him alone. Kabo drove off in his mother's car, the two headlights and windshield smashed by the guy wielding the sledgehammer.

The story did not end there. The day after the fight, nearly 100 cars filled with high school boys and men from Kalihi drove through Pālolo Housing looking for revenge. And for months afterward, any Pālolo guy who ventured into Kalihi put himself at risk of a beating.

Alex, who was arrested, never informed the police about us. Alex was a tough kid. If he'd squealed on us he would never have been able to live it down. It was a close call, but we lucked out. We were just in the wrong place at the wrong time.

Family Man

Several weeks later came the biggest turning point in my life. On September 20, 1958, Lorraine and I got married. Kabo was my best man. I was 18 years old.

Lorraine was only 17. My cousin Billy once told me when he first saw her he thought she was the "prettiest Filipino girl" he had ever seen. Because she was a minor, her father had to sign the marriage application on her behalf. He wasn't happy. He told Lorraine he didn't think I would amount to anything. He didn't show up at the wedding. It angered me because I knew he had hurt Lorraine's feelings. "He'll soften up when the baby comes," Mom told me. At that point, I didn't really care if he did or not. I'd had my fill of fathers who didn't support their kids.

Our first-born, Brandon, came two months later. I was totally unprepared for fatherhood—but happy to become a father. A year and a half later, our daughter, Janeen, was born. My first priority was to find a better job. I quit my summer job as a laborer at Oʻahu Metal Supply, a company owned by the Fujino family. Rick Fujino was one of the nicest bosses one could hope to have. But I needed a better-paying job.

I got a good break when I was accepted in the IBEW (International Brotherhood of Electrical Workers) apprenticeship program. I was excited. At $1.64 per hour, I would be earning much more money. After four years of apprenticeship, I could become a journeyman electrician.

I worked for a company called Halfhill Electric. The haole owner, Stanley Halfhill, seemed like a good man. His workers, who were mostly AJAs, were very loyal to him. It was a good company to work for.

One day we were working on a project at Fort DeRussy in Waikīkī, and our foreman came over to me carrying a shovel and a five-gallon can. "Cayetano," he said, pointing, "I want you and Roger [another apprentice] to clean out the mud in that manhole. You'll need a ladder and rope for the five-gallon can." *Ladder? Rope?* I thought. *What for?*

Roger and I walked over to the manhole and lifted the cover. The manhole was filled with mud right to the top. So we took turns: One would shovel the mud into the can and the other would carry the can and dump the mud. More than a week later, I found out why we needed a ladder and rope. The manhole was about the size of a small bedroom, but a couple of feet deeper. We needed the ladder to get in and out.

I complained to one of the journeymen: "Why are Roger and I doing this kind of work? We're apprentices; this is work that should be done by laborers."

Clearly annoyed, he asked, "Cayetano, how much do you make an hour?"

"A dollar sixty-four," I replied, beginning to realize that I had asked the wrong question.

"Well, a laborer makes $1.90 an hour and you make $1.64—now do you understand why you and Roger are doing it and not some laborer?" I stared at him blankly.

I enjoyed being an apprentice. For a while, I thought seriously about becoming a journeyman electrician. But the construction industry suffered a downturn in 1959, and I was laid off. Like many others, I waited for a call from the union to go back to work. Meanwhile, I collected unemployment compensation.

Back then, there was a bit of a stigma to collecting unemployment. It was as if one was collecting welfare but really did not deserve it. Each time I went to collect my unemployment check, I wore dark glasses and a cap.

I began worrying about how we were going to make ends meet once the unemployment benefits ended. After two months of waiting for the union to call me and collecting unemployment, I decided to look for another job, any job. I found one, driving a truck for a company called Hawaiian Wholesale Food Plan, which paid $1.35 an hour for delivering frozen meats and vegetables to people's homes. Freezers were not in common use with local people, and most of the customers were upper-middle-class or wealthy haoles. For the first time, I would get a better insight into how they lived.

And although I would often deal with maids or housekeepers, on the few occasions that I dealt with the homeowner directly, usually the wife, some of my experiences were pleasant, while a few were unforgettable.

Once, I was walking alongside a swimming pool, carrying a 50-pound box of frozen beef cuts on my shoulder, when a huge dog came out of nowhere and blindsided me into the pool. Fortunately, I fell into the shallow end and did not drop the box into the water. The lady of the house, a haole woman in her 60s, came running out the house, grabbed the dog, whose tail was wagging, and asked, "My goodness, are you all right?" Except for standing in four feet of water with the box still on my shoulder, I was fine—just soaking wet. She asked her maid, a Japanese woman, to bring some towels while I sat dripping on a chair by the pool. "Oh, I'm so sorry about our dog. You can stay here until you dry off," she said.

"Thank you, ma'am, but I have other deliveries to make," I replied. Putting her hand to her mouth, she stifled a laugh. I wanted to laugh, too. The whole episode was pretty funny. Without doubt, I would be the topic of conversation at her home for a long time.

On another delivery in the Kāhala area, I saw a woman painting by the pool. She was tall and very pretty. "Good morning," I said as I entered the yard, "I'm here to deliver your order from Hawaiian Food Plan."

"The service entrance is on the other side of the garage!" she said sternly, cutting me off with an angry look. I apologized and headed for the service entrance, recalling what one of the old-time drivers told me: Remember, the customer is always right—especially the rich ones.

One day in August 1959, I was making deliveries when it was announced that Hawai'i had just become a state. Everyone celebrated the news throughout the Islands. On O'ahu, church bells rang everywhere, motorists beeped their horns, emergency sirens blew and it seemed celebrations were being held everywhere.

As I was packing frozen foods into a customer's freezer, I could hear the national anthem being played at a nearby school. I paused for a moment. The customer, the wife of a naval officer, smiled and said, in a well-intentioned but ludicrous attempt at pidgin, "You be state now."

"Yes, we be state now," I replied, smiling, mimicking her and trying to sound like an Indian chief at a powwow.

The majority of Hawai'i's people supported statehood. Around 1954, I recall statehood supporters holding a pro-statehood petition-signing drive in downtown Honolulu. The response was terrific. The newspapers gave the event front-page coverage. Nearly 120,000 people signed it—remarkable for a population of only about 500,000 at the time. The petition, a 250-pound roll of paper, made quite an impression on Congress.

Of course, not everyone supported statehood. Opposition came mostly from the haole elite and the upper-class Hawaiians who feared that statehood would result in their losing political power to the "Asian menace"—the ever-growing Japanese-American population, which had become the biggest ethnic group in Hawai'i. But the anti-statehood people were in the minority. In the 1959 general election, the overwhelming majority—estimated at 96 percent—of Hawai'i's voters supported statehood.

The 1959 election produced some historical milestones: Republican Hiram Fong was elected to the U.S. Senate, Democrat Dan Inouye to the U.S. House of Representatives. They were the first Asian Americans elected to Congress.

The big surprise, however, was the Republican Bill Quinn's victory over Democrat John A. Burns. No one did more than John A. Burns to get the statehood bill passed. But instead of returning home to campaign, Burns stayed in Washington, D.C., tending to his duties as Hawai'i's delegate to Congress. It was a big mistake.

Quinn had the advantage of serving as Territorial governor—in terms of patronage and duties, it was a post more powerful than many State governorships. Moreover, he was handsome, articulate, a graduate of Harvard Law School and the first governor to have his own television program. In fact, he was seen as something of a boy wonder. And he was quite a singer, an important asset for the festive Hawai'i style of politics of those times. (Singing, by the way, did not save Inouye's Republican opponent, Ben Dillingham, who was known for singing "Three Blind Mice" in Hawaiian. Inouye won by a huge margin.)

I knew little about Burns until he was he was pitted against Quinn in the 1959 special election to elect Hawai'i's first State governor. I knew Burns was Hawai'i's delegate to Congress and that he was considered the architect of the "Alaska First" strategy that subsequently opened the way for Hawai'i's statehood. The strategy was simple: Once Alaska became a state, its two new United States senators would support statehood for Hawai'i. Moreover, because Alaska, like Hawai'i, was not contiguous to the mainland United States, one of the most effective arguments against Hawaiian statehood—that Hawai'i was too far from the Mainland—would be eliminated. Some congressmen, I suspected, used this argument as a convenient smokescreen for the real reason they were against Hawaiian statehood: racism against Hawai'i's non-white population.

Burns did not get many accolades for his role in achieving statehood for Hawai'i from Hawai'i's two pro-Republican daily newspapers—but many among those who favored statehood acknowledged his work. The talk on the street was that Burns was favored to win the election hands down.

I was a skinny 19-year-old too preoccupied with learning about parenthood and supporting Lorraine and our year-old son to take a strong interest in local politics. But I admired Bill Quinn. It was hard not to. Handsome, charismatic, articulate, able—the Harvard lawyer was a popular Territorial governor. His sunny disposition and optimism won over a lot of local people. Back then political rallies were colorful events, and Quinn often used his sonorous Irish tenor voice to belt out songs like "Blue Hawaii" and "When Irish Eyes Are Smiling," to the delight of the crowd. And when *TIME* magazine put his photograph on the cover of its 1959 statehood issue (a post-election gift from Clare Booth Luce, *TIME*'s powerful and politically shrewd owner and a part-time Hawai'i resident) Quinn's political stature got a great boost.

In the last two weeks of the 1959 campaign, Quinn's announced his "Second Mahele"—a land-distribution scheme by which Quinn, if elected, would release a couple hundred thousand acres of State land for sale to ordinary citizens. The idea caught everyone by surprise. It sounded bold and visionary, and the pro-Republican news media, particularly the *Honolulu Star-Bulletin*, played it up.

Quinn's promise of making it possible for the common person to be able to buy land in fee for $50 an acre, in a state where most homeowners were forced to lease, struck home with many local voters. Land reform had been a winning political issue for the Democrats. For Republicans, who usually fought the Democrats on land reform, Quinn's Second Mahele was their answer.

Caught flat-footed, the Democrats attacked the proposed Second Mahele—among them, I would find out years later, the first Hawai'i lawyer I worked for, Frank Padgett. It was a measure of Padgett's character that he set aside his friendship with Quinn to expose what he thought was a virtual hoax on the people. But it was too late. As political consultants will attest, more elections are won by emotion than by merit. And the Second Mahele generated a lot of emotion.

In many ways, Quinn was like Ronald Reagan. His warm and charismatic personality made it seem improbable that the man was capable of engaging in political hi-jinks. On its face, the Second Mahele seemed like a great idea—and I was one among thousands of people who believed Quinn's bold proposal could make it possible for us to own our own homes. I had grown up in rented housing, and Quinn gave me hope. I was only 20 years old, a year short of being eligible to vote, but had I been old enough, I would have voted for Quinn. On Election Day, Quinn upset Burns by 4,000 votes.

As it turned out, Quinn and the Republicans won the battle, but they would lose the proverbial war. Quinn's days were numbered. Democratic legislators, who dominated the new State Legislature and were angered by Burns' loss, blocked him at every turn, dumping some of his appointees to key boards and commissions.

As Quinn himself would admit later, his choice of the title "Second Mahele" was a big mistake. Apparently, Quinn and his advisors were not well versed in Hawaiian history (I wasn't either back then). If they had been, they would have known that most Hawaiians considered the "Great Mahele"—a land-distribution scheme proclaimed by Kamehameha III that among other things allowed haoles to buy and own land—the foot in the door which allowed the haoles to "steal the land" from their ancestors. Not surprisingly, the Democrats, led by well-known Hawaiians like Bill Richardson, attacked Quinn's Second Mahele as an "insult to Hawaiians." The Second Mahele was hung like an albatross around Quinn's neck.

Adding to Quinn's problems was his rift with Lieutenant Governor Jimmy Kealoha. Kealoha, apparently angered that Quinn did not live up to his alleged promises to share political appointments with him, vented his anger by running against Quinn in the 1962 Republican primary.

To me, Kealoha came across as a rank opportunist. It seemed a bit much that the part-Hawaiian Kealoha, an accomplice to Quinn's Second Mahele in 1959, was now asking local people like me for our vote. Kealoha, a former mayor of the Big Island and seasoned politician, was in a real bind. His complaints about Quinn breaking his promise to share power with him would hardly move voters who saw such behavior as common among politicians. So Kealoha played the "local boy" card.

"If you want to see your local boy, your son of the land, be governor, this is your chance," Kealoha said at one rally. Kealoha's plea fell on deaf ears among haole Republicans, and few Democrats crossed over to vote for him in the Republican primary. Quinn beat him handily—sending Kealoha into retirement from politics.

Anger is a powerful motivation for people to act. By 1962, angry was how many local voters felt about Bill Quinn. Like many who had supported Quinn in 1959 I felt betrayed. The Second Mahele was just another in history's real or imagined long list of shenanigans by the haole elite to take advantage of locals.

Scores of State workers, ignoring the State law prohibiting their getting involved in political activity, joined in helping the Burns campaign. I was one of them. Like the others, I felt as if I had been had. "We were like the sand ʻōpū [a scavenger fish]; he threw us the bait and we swallowed it hook, line and sinker," a fellow State worker complained ruefully.

Hawaii Pono

The fallout from Quinn's Second Mahele hurt him badly in the 1962 election. But adding fuel to the fire was the book *Hawaii Pono*, authored by visiting professor Lawrence H. Fuchs and released in 1961.

Hawaii Pono is shunned today by Hawaiian activists but is still considered by many to be the classic study of Hawaiʻi's social and political history (it was cited by the U.S. Supreme Court in *Rice v. Cayetano*). It chronicled the impact of the haole entrepreneurs and missionaries on the Hawaiian Kingdom, the growth of the Asian immigrant groups and the events leading to the Democratic Political Revolution of 1954.

Fuchs, a distinguished and respected scholar who would later become dean of the American Studies Department at Brandeis University, wrote as a detached observer. The reaction, however, was anything but detached. *Hawaii Pono* generated great controversy. Republicans took issue with many of the Fuchs' findings and accused him of being unfair and distorting the facts. Democrats, Japanese and Filipinos in particular, found verification that the haoles had unfairly wielded their economic and political power to treat them like second-class citizens.

For me, *Hawaii Pono* was a political clarion call. I had heard all the stories, but it was the first time anyone had laid out in plain terms the social and political history of our state. Fuchs was no political pamphleteer for Democrats—indeed, unlike some of the revisionist Hawaiian historians today, he did not lay the blame for the plight of Hawaiians solely on the haoles; he noted the good the missionaries had done and how the Hawaiian monarchs themselves had helped the haoles to acquire economic and political power, albeit eventually at the expense of their own people and culture.

Those nuances of history escaped my attention at the time. I was young, and what caught my eye was how the haole elite had treated Asian immigrants like my father as if they were second class.

Fuchs' depiction of the powerful, arrogant and racist Walter Dillingham hit me hard. Testifying before the U.S. Senate in the 1920s, the virulently anti-Japanese Dillingham was asked why Hawai'i's plantation owners did not import white workers. Dillingham's unforgettable response was the kind of racist talk that would assume a life of its own and stigmatize the Republican Party as the "haole" party for decades:

"When you are asked to go out in the sun and go into the cane brake, away from the tropical breeze, you are subjecting the white men to something the good Lord did not create him to do. If He had, the people of the world, I think would have had a white pigment of the skin, and not variegated colors."

Dillingham was the stereotype of how many locals viewed haoles during those times. Stereotyping any ethnic or racial group is hardly fair, but to a political neophyte like me, Dillingham was no different from the big haole man who had chased me and my friends out of the ocean in front of his home when we were kids.

Unrepentant in his views about Asians, fearful of the growing Japanese-American political power, Dillingham used his considerable influence with members of Congress to oppose statehood for Hawai'i. His son, Ben, described by *TIME* magazine as a "turn-of-the-century conservative," was the chairman of Hawai'i's Republican Party. There were, of course, moderate haole Republicans who disagreed with Dillingham's racist views and saw the need for social reform, but Dillingham overshadowed them all. There was no room for people like me in the Republican Party. I became a Democrat—and never looked back.

About the only thing Burns and Quinn had in common was that they were both tall haoles. Unlike Quinn, Burns was unsmiling, seemingly dour at times, and he was not a good speaker. A former Honolulu police captain, Burns did not have a college degree. Quinn was a Harvard lawyer. When Burns and Quinn debated on television, Burns stuttered at times and struggled for the right words. It was painful to watch. Art Woolaway, who was the chair of the Republican Party, quipped, "The debate showed why John Burns should not be elected governor."

For those who saw verbal agility as a sign of leadership, Woolaway's words hit home. Quinn performed like an animated John F. Kennedy. Unfortunately for him, the Second Mahele debacle colored everything he said. On the other hand, Burns' sincerity and conviction seemed utterly genuine. He wasn't as polished as Quinn, nor was he a good speaker—but those traits, which so many haoles saw as shortcomings, were seen as superficial by local people who had come to identify with Burns as one of their own. For them, character more than anything else was what they sought in their governor.

Early election returns showed clearly that Burns was on his way to a decisive victory, the only question being the size of the margin. I drove to the Burns head-quarters on Merchant Street to watch the celebration. Standing outside and look-ing through a window, I saw Burns in person for the first time; he was laden with leis, among which a red carnation rope stood out conspicuously, and he stood on a chair to speak to the overflowing and boisterously happy crowd. I couldn't hear what he said. It didn't matter; all I knew was that Hawai'i was in for big changes—changes for the better for local people like me. I was happy—and hopeful.

In a complete reversal of his narrow defeat in 1959, Burns defeated Quinn by 30,000 votes—a huge landslide back then. Quinn, the once-popular governor, whose name had been bandied about as a potential vice presidential running mate to Nelson Rockefeller, seemed finished politically. But in 1976, GOP leaders coaxed him out of retirement to run for a U.S. Senate seat against Democrat Sparky Mat-sunaga. He was badly beaten. Timing is everything in politics—and Quinn's time had long passed. He never ran for public office again. A promising political career came to a sad end.

When John F. Kennedy met Quinn when he visited Hawai'i in 1960, he reportedly said, "I like that Quinn fellow better than Burns"—a story that, according to University of Hawai'i history professor Dan Boylan, Quinn himself loved to tell.

Indeed, likeability was Bill Quinn's biggest asset. I never stopped liking Quinn. He had many of the attributes I wanted in a political leader. Many agreed he had been a good Territorial governor. His Second Mahele—which some believe was the creation of the popular disc jockey J. Akuhead Pupule—seemed out of character for him. There is, however, little sentiment in politics, and there are few second chances. Quinn's lapse of judgment, his moment of weakness in succumb-ing to winning at any cost, cost him dearly and, sadly, tarnished his reputation. No political office was worth such a high price. It was a lesson I would take with me into my own political career.

During my first term as governor, I appointed Quinn to the prestigious East-West Center Board of Governors. Unknown to many, Bill Quinn had a role in start-ing the East-West Center, for which he never got much credit. By the mid-1990s, U.S. House Speaker Newt Gingrich and his band of conservative Republicans who dominated Congress saw the East-West Center as just another Democratic pork-barrel project and made huge cuts to the Center's operating budget.

Had it not been for the efforts of U.S. Senator Dan Inouye, who used his con-siderable influence with his Republican colleagues to get funding, the State either would have been forced to step in and take over the East-West Center or abandon it. Besides the huge cost involved, I believed that turning the Center into a State institution would diminish its status as an independent and international body. Bill Quinn, I thought, could help lobby the Republicans to restore the funding.

Deep down, as I began to become more experienced in politics, I was saddened that Quinn's political career had ended the way it did. To be sure, his 1962 defeat was largely self-inflicted, but as the years passed and I learned more about him, I felt badly that his one misstep had denied him the privilege of public service. As governor, I believed it was fitting that he be given the opportunity to serve again.

He eagerly accepted my appointment to the East-West Center Board. Out of the hundreds of appointments I made as governor, few pleased me more than this one. I was glad he accepted. Unfortunately, three months later, Quinn resigned for personal health reasons. He was nearly 80; the passage of time had taken its toll.

The Interview

Shortly after the 1959 election, I accepted a position as a rodman with the State Highway Department. A year later, I took an exam and was promoted to civil draftsman. I worked indoors and got a nice pay raise. I enjoyed drafting, something I had been good at in high school.

In 1962, an unforeseen event had a profound impact on the course of my life. The State announced several openings for higher-paying draftsman positions. I was very interested in competing for a position in a section that did structural work. I spent long hours preparing for the test. Finally, along with 100 or more applicants, I took the test. My score exceeded my expectations. A 99.1 percent! Almost perfect. I was ranked first on the list. But the written test only accounted for 70 percent of the application process. The remaining 30 percent would turn on the personal interview.

I felt well prepared for the interview. However, a few minutes after it began, I knew I wasn't going to get the job. The guy who interviewed me was just going through the motions. At the end, he handed me back the samples of my work and said, "You do good work, but I'm looking for someone who has completed his military obligation. With your high score, I'm sure you'll be picked up by another section."

I was very disappointed. But I've always felt guilty about never serving in the military. In 1962, there were still many veterans of the Korean War who were competing for jobs. I recalled reading that on a per capita basis, Hawai'i's casualties were the highest in the nation. Most came in the early years of the war when poorly trained and equipped U.S. Army units stationed in Hawai'i were rushed to Korea to fend off the North Koreans. The Hawai'i boys had served with great courage against overwhelming odds. No, I had no complaints if a veteran who had served his country got the job instead of me. They deserved higher priority.

I ended up in the Advanced Planning Section. It was an important section. One of its big projects was planning the route for the proposed H-3 freeway through Moanalua Valley. I liked the people I worked with, but the work was not at the level I expected. Soon I was bored.

Quintin Alfafara was a close friend and former classmate at Farrington. Quint had been raised by his divorced father. Like me, he married his high school sweetheart, Sally, right after graduation. Sally is Japanese, and Filipino-Japanese marriages were uncommon back then.

One day, Quint called and told me, "Benny, Sally and I are moving to Los Angeles. I think there are better opportunities for work and school up there. Besides, Filipinos don't have much of a chance here. If you are not haole, Japanese or Chinese, you can't get ahead. They just don't think we're good enough. I'll keep in touch and let you know how we're doing." Quint had no relatives in Los Angeles; he and Sally were going up cold. That took guts—something Quint never lacked. I respected him and felt sad he was moving away. But I realized I had never fully appreciated the depth of his feelings about racial matters in Hawai'i.

One day, nearly a year after the interview, while I was making copies at the copy machine pool, I struck up a conversation with a young local guy who was using another machine. "Where do you work?" he asked me.

"Advanced Planning," I replied. "What about you?"

"Structural," he said.

After a few minutes, it became apparent that this young man was the person who had gotten the job I wanted. I found out he was only 20, had never been in the military and had a draft status of 1-A (mine was III-A), which meant that if war broke out he would be among the first to be called.

I had been lied to. I had studied hard for the test. I had gotten a nearly perfect score. I was ranked first—and the guy lied to me. I was devastated. Disillusioned. And angry. By the time, I got home from work, I was furious. *This is what Quint was talking about. This was the kind of shit that angered him so much he moved to L.A.*, I said to myself. It wasn't the first time something like this happened to me. But this one really hit home; it hit me hard. It was unfair not only to me but to Lorraine and the kids.

It gnawed at me. It affected my work. I became more sensitive to slights, real or imagined. One day, an engineer named Roy suggested, "Ben, why don't you go to the Mainland? You can work during the day and get a college degree at night." Over the next couple of months, Roy and several other engineers, all of them AJAs in their 30s, told me about their experiences on the Mainland, urging me to go and take advantage of the opportunities for school there.

Go to college? At Farrington, going to college had seemed beyond my reach, a distant dream all but forgotten. When I was in the eighth grade, I did a book report on Clarence Darrow, the famous lawyer. It inspired me, at least at the time, to think about becoming a lawyer. Reality—poor grades, no money, no ambition, no college graduates in my family—brought me back to earth.

Thereafter, my dream of becoming a lawyer was left to my imagination, Walter Mitty stuff. I thought seriously about joining the police force, but I was too short to meet the 5-foot 8-inch height requirement—a requirement that is now illegal but which, historically, was a big reason the Honolulu Police Department was dominated by the taller haoles, Hawaiians and Portuguese. And so I turned to thoughts of the military. I decided to join the U.S. Air Force, which seemed like a good idea at the time. Beyond that, I had nothing planned.

But marriage and children had changed everything. Getting a good job was my highest priority, but time after time, I felt doors were closed to me because of my lack of education or connections, or my ethnicity—or a combination of all these things. I was learning fast about the realities of adult life.

Life in Hawai'i in the 1950s and early 1960s was a paradox when it came to ethnicity and race. Socially, most people got along very well. But those were times of dramatic social and political change, and each ethnic group took care of its own. When it came to employment, ethnic or racial preference was often listed as a requirement in many of the newspaper classified ads.

Today, one may find it surprising that job ads back in the 1950s and early 1960s calling for "Caucasians only" or "Japanese only" or "Chinese only" were not only legal but commonplace. But that's the way things were then. The practice of overt discrimination began to fade in the mid-1960s when the Civil Rights Movement began to peak. To their credit, Hawai'i's two major newspapers, the *Honolulu Advertiser* and the *Star-Bulletin*, both announced they would no longer run classified ads which promoted racial or ethnic discrimination. The 1964 Civil Rights Act outlawed racial discrimination in the job market—but old and long-accepted attitudes and practices did not die easily.

In those days, Filipino Americans had little political and economic power—and even less community respect. In the hierarchy of Hawai'i's ethnic groups, Filipinos ranked down at the bottom, a place shared with Samoans and other Pacific Islanders. In my eyes, the only way to break down those barriers and change minds—win respect—was through education. A high school diploma was not enough—getting a college degree was the key.

"Let's move to Los Angeles. Quint and Sally will help us get settled," I said to Lorraine. She agreed, and we began planning for it. Mom did not like the idea. Brandon and Janeen had added a joy to her life that she had never experienced before. The thought of her grandchildren being so far away in a place she knew little about was hard to accept. She took some comfort, however, in knowing that we didn't have the money to move, that it would take time for us to save what we needed. In the interim, she would spend a lot of time trying to change our minds.

Mom was right about the money. We began scrimping and saving and I accumulated as much vacation time as State regulations allowed—all with an eye to moving to L.A. Then fate lent us a helping hand. I was no stranger to gambling; I'd learned how to shoot craps in high school, and for a couple years I had been buying football and baseball pool tickets from Uncle Jack, who was selling them for a guy who worked in the shipyard. Back then, the shipyard was always a good source for them. I had never won anything.

Then came the day of a Los Angeles Rams-San Francisco 49ers game. For the first time in years, I had a shot at winning. It came down to the point after the touchdown. If the kicker missed the conversion, I would have the winning ticket. At the time, Lorraine and I were sitting in our 1954 Ford, waiting for the traffic light to change on Ward Avenue, listening to the game on the radio. Pro kickers rarely miss a conversion, so I was resigned to being disappointed. Not this time, however. When I heard that the kicker missed the kick, I went wild with joy. "A thousand bucks!" I shouted. Drivers in the cars beside mine must have thought I was nuts. Unbelievably, a month later, I hit another one! Another $1,000 within a month! I couldn't believe our good luck.

I called Quint and told him we were ready to move to Los Angeles. He and Sally were going to buy a new home in Whittier. If we could wait a couple months, he said, we could take over renting his apartment in Los Angeles. A new home? Quint and Sally had been in L.A. for only three years! We waited three or four months before leaving Hawaiʻi.

"Boy, why do you want to go to Los Angeles?" Mom asked. "You already have a good steady job here, you don't even know what to expect on the Mainland. It's so dangerous there … people are different."

"Mom," I replied softly, "there's not much for us here. We can't make it here … and I don't want to live in Hawaiʻi anymore. I have to go. On the Mainland I can work during the day and go to college at night. I want to become a lawyer."

"Boy … think of the kids, they'll be so far away from our family … it's good to be ambitious, but don't reach for the moon," she said, tears welling up in her eyes. She was thinking, of course, about Brandon and Janeen. Her two grandchildren had become such a big part of her life.

In March 1963, we left for Los Angeles. Dad was at Queen's Hospital, still recovering from stomach surgery for ulcers. Lorraine and I and the kids visited him before leaving for the airport. "Dad, after you get well and we get settled in Los Angeles, come up and live with us," I told him.

"Son, you take care the kids," he replied, hugging them. Like many Asian men of his generation, Dad hardly used the word "love." He showed it through his actions, not words. As expected, Mom was very emotional, hugging Brandon and Janeen as if she would never see them again.

That night, we headed for Los Angeles. "Unless things change, I don't want to ever come back," I said to Lorraine. Despite my harsh words, leaving Hawaiʻi was tearing me up inside. But it was time for us to go—time for us to reach for the moon. ❖

CHAPTER TWO

Los Angeles

Culture Shock

Our flight on Pan American Airways to Los Angeles was the first time any of us had been on an airplane or off O'ahu. Our departure was a difficult one, especially for Mom. Since their births, she'd doted on Brandon and Janeen. The kids gave her a second chance at raising children, something she never really had with me and Ken.

Between bouts of air sickness during the flight, I felt uneasy about leaving Dad, still recovering from his surgery, and Mom, who had gone through a series of major operations herself, including a complicated back surgery which still caused her pain and for which she was increasingly relying on medication for relief. Finally, I fell into a deep sleep.

It was early morning when we landed. Los Angeles looked like someone had sprayed the sky gray. I didn't see any mountains, although we would a week later after a big rain hit the area and washed away the smog. Quint and Sally met us at the airport. Soon we were on a long drive to their new home in Whittier. We stayed there for a week while the apartment was being cleaned.

During the first week, we played tourists; our kids were thrilled to be visiting Disneyland, Universal Studios, Hollywood and other attractions. As we drove by new housing subdivisions, the affordable prices advertised on the billboards caught our eyes. No one in our families had ever owned a home. Here, in L.A., it seemed possible.

At the week's end, Quint took us to the apartment on Albany Street. It was a two-bedroom, clean but small. The area was blue collar and predominantly "Chicano," as Mexican Americans preferred to be called then. Located a few miles away was the University of Southern California—an oasis of beautiful buildings occupied by mostly well-to-do white students, surrounded by a crime-ridden black ghetto where poverty was the norm and danger lurked. Tragically, a few years later, for no apparent reason, the son of a prominent Hawai'i corporate executive would be murdered by thugs in front of his fraternity house.

Earlier, Quint had remarked that the neighborhood was a "little rough." As usual, he tended to understate things. In fact, there was a spate of shootings and killings between rival Chicano gangs the first month we were there. The repeated warnings and crime horror stories I had heard before coming to L.A. made me wary.

After we moved into the apartment, whenever we needed groceries, I would walk Lorraine to the nearest grocery store. I could easily pass as a Chicano, Lorraine as a mestiza. To convince the neighborhood tough guys who hung out by the grocery store that I was just a harmless, peace-loving Hawaiian, I wore the loudest aloha shirt I owned. In Kalihi, a mere look could cause problems; so when I ran into the Chicanos, I avoided eye contact when I could, nodded courteously when I could not and tried to appear about as humble as possible without showing fear. These neighborhood safaris prompted me to buy a car, which I did a month later (a beautiful 1956 Chevy hardtop coupe, which after six months proved to be a lemon), so I could drive to malls and shop in areas I considered safer.

Our first few months in Los Angeles were somewhat of a cultural shock. I had never seen so many black people congregated in one area before (I would have the same experience with Chicanos on my first visit to East L.A.) The only black person I had met in Hawai'i was a military dependent named Burl Malone who became a popular track star at Farrington. Besides Malone, who, by the way, was lighter skinned than most locals, I remember only one other black student at Farrington (we jokingly referred to them as "Royal Hawaiians") out of a student body of nearly 3,000.

The first Chicano I met was a co-worker at the California State Highway Department. And then there was a guy named Birdsong—the American Indian who lived in the apartment above ours. Back home Native Americans were as rare as the Hawaiian nēnē, a native goose found only on Maui and the Big Island.

One morning I saw a refuse-collection truck being driven on Albany Street. It looked just like the trucks the city used back home, but there was a big difference— the crew was all white. Never in my wildest dreams could I have imagined a haole working as a refuse worker or "rubbish man," as we called them in Hawai'i. I was like the proverbial country jack who goes to a big city and is awed by its skyscrapers. I felt like laughing out loud. As the truck passed by me, one of the men saw me smiling. He smiled back and waved. "Good morning," I said as I waved back.

Like Hawai'i, L.A. was a mix of ethnic groups. And yet people behaved differently than in Hawai'i. Japanese Americans in Hawai'i jokingly referred to their Mainland counterparts as "Katonks"—the name emulates the sound one gets by pounding on a coconut. Hawai'i Japanese Americans considered most Katonks "coconuts"—hardheaded, and brown on the outside, white on the inside. Indeed, the Mainland Japanese were different. They were more insular and actually *more* "Japanese" than Hawai'i Japanese, who were more outgoing and open.

The difference between the ethnic groups in L.A. and Hawai'i, I concluded, was due mainly to two factors: geography and the Hawaiian culture. Los Angeles was "Balkanized," with almost definite geographic boundaries separating the habitats of each ethnic group. The Chinese lived in Chinatown, the Japanese in Little Tokyo or Gardena, the Chicanos in East L.A., the blacks in Compton and so forth. About the only place these people would meet was at work. Interaction was limited.

Hawai'i, too, had its Chinatown, Little Tokyo and Filipino camps, but as the population grew, the limited land area eventually forced these ethnic groups to live, play and work together. Hawai'i's geography forced people to get along. It's much easier to disrespect, dislike or hate other people if one doesn't know much about them. But when people live next to each other, invite each other to birthdays, weddings and other functions, when their kids go to the same schools and play together, then acceptance and tolerance and respect, rather than disrespect and intolerance, are more likely to develop.

Moreover, the different ethnic groups in Hawai'i had a tremendous advantage: Most were imbued with the culture of Hawai'i's native people, an infectious valuing of tolerance and acceptance—the "aloha spirit" that is often touted as Hawai'i's gift to the world.

A few weeks after we arrived, I began work as a draftsman for the California Highway Department, which was near the L.A. Civic Center. Quint, who had been working there for a couple of years, set up an interview for me. It went well. I was hired and earned significantly more than I earned in Hawai'i. L.A. was beginning to live up to its star billing.

About three months later, we moved to a two-bedroom duplex in Lawndale, which was closer to the L.A. International Airport where Lorraine would work. Lawndale was a working-class white neighborhood. As far as I knew, we were the only non-white family living on our street. Our next-door neighbors were cordial, very nice people, but many in the neighborhood were aerospace workers who were new to California themselves. Everyone pretty much kept to themselves.

By the year's end, I left the State highway department to take a job as a draftsman for North American Aviation, located next to L.A. International Airport. This section of the company was building the Saberliner, a medium-sized commercial airplane for private corporate use. The pay was much higher than with the State highway department, and the company was conveniently located a few miles from where we lived.

Meanwhile, Lorraine had already gotten a job as a waitress at the famous Theme Restaurant at the L.A. International Airport. She worked there until I graduated from law school. In 1965, we moved to a duplex on Aviation Boulevard on the outskirts of Inglewood, only a mile or so from the airport. It was a nice, working-class predominantly white neighborhood with a good elementary school a block away that Brandon and Janeen attended.

By late 1964, we decided I should attend school full time. I was already 24. It would take too long to finish college and then law school through night classes. I found a part-time job as a draftsman for the Waltco Trucking Company in Gardena. My boss was a guy named Don Jordan.

"I like Hawaiians because they work hard," he said before he hired me. Don was the stereotypical Middle American—the kind one would expect to find as a member of the Lions or Rotarians. He was a good man and a good boss—easy to get along with, respected and well liked by his workers. And helpful. He gave me as much flexibility as I needed to accommodate my class schedule and exams. If all bosses were like Don, there would be no need for unions.

"I see you were a little distracted in high school," the counselor at Harbor Junior College joked, perusing my high school transcript. My free-spirited junior and senior years at Farrington had left me on the verge of flunking out.

As she spoke, I mused about my years at Farrington. "Benjamin, your test scores are very good; you are definitely college material," Susan Chun, one of my teachers at Farrington had counseled me. "You know," she continued, "there are very few Filipinos from Kalihi who go to college. You can do it if you study."

Back then, her words went in one ear and out the other. Now, to calm the anxiety I was feeling about going back to school at age 24, I sought refuge, verification, in them. *I'm good enough to make it through college*, I assured myself. *Mrs. Chun said so.*

In the fall of 1965, I enrolled full time at Harbor Junior College in San Pedro, a 15-minute drive on the freeway from Lawndale. Harbor JC was a great little college. Black students from the Compton and Watts area, Asians from Gardena and Torrance, Chicanos from San Pedro and middle- and upper-middle-class white students from Rolling Hills made for a diverse student body.

At that time, California guaranteed the top 12.5 percent of its high school graduates admission as freshmen to the University of California system by law. This meant the other 87.5 percent would have to attend junior colleges or the California State University system. This system worked well, I believe, for the junior colleges and State universities, in that it provided them with many bright students.

At Harbor JC, I was usually the oldest student in my class. For most of my first year, all I did was listen to some of the bright, verbally adept young students engage our professors and each other in class. My writing skills were still good enough to be competitive with my Mainland classmates, but coming from Hawai'i I wasn't accustomed to the level of verbal dialogue I heard in class. Mainlanders could talk up a storm. It didn't take me long to adjust, though. By my second year, I was actively engaged in class discussions.

I felt reborn as a student. Most of the professors I had were great—many were young, idealistic Ph.D.s who seemed to really love teaching. Soon I was eagerly deep into my studies. Surprisingly to me, English literature became my favorite course. It helped that our professor was a dynamo of energy with movie-actress good looks. She knew her stuff, and her manner of teaching inspired me to want to learn more about the great writers with names like Keats, Shelley, Tennyson, Joyce,

Homer and others whom I had never heard about before. At age 24, I found myself actually looking forward to going to class each day.

Lorraine and I developed a routine for school days: I'd go to my classes in the morning until about noon and then rush off to my part-time job; I'd finish work at about 5 p.m., rush home, pick her up and drive her to work; then the kids and I would have dinner and I would hit the books. Around midnight, Lorraine would call me and I'd drive to the airport to pick her up. We followed this routine like clockwork for more than seven years.

Ronald Reagan and Me

In 1966, I got my first taste of California politics. Democrat Gov. Pat Brown was facing Republican Ronald Reagan. The campaign was bitterly fought. But Brown—considered by many historians today to be one of California's great governors—was an old-school politician. He was awkward at best and often inept in his public appearances as he struggled to make the transition from backroom politics to the television age. The Republicans successfully portrayed Brown as bumbling, inept and indecisive. Symptomatic of the Republicans' hard-hitting campaign was a bumper sticker that read: "If It's Brown, Flush It!"

Brown was no match for the telegenic Reagan. Reagan might have been a mediocre movie actor, but his speaking skills and charismatic personality were too formidable for Brown to overcome. It was "show time." Television was in; old-school campaigning was out. Reagan beat Brown in a landslide—by more than a million votes. Spin, image—form—counted more than substance.

Reagan promised he would restore fiscal integrity to California's State government. He tried to do just that—by making drastic budget cuts to social programs for the poor and to Pat Brown's greatest achievement—the world-class University of California system.

By the time I transferred from Harbor JC to UCLA in 1968, most of the UC administrators, faculty and students were up in arms over Reagan's huge budget cuts. Rightly or not, many among the faculty, who were overwhelmingly liberal and Democratic, saw the budget cuts as Reagan's retaliation for their strong endorsement of Pat Brown.

This was a time when student demonstrations for civil rights or against the Vietnam War were sweeping the nation. Emotions were high. In California, students and faculty demonstrations targeted the despised Reagan. It did not take long before Reagan himself developed a real animus towards student demonstrators.

In 1970, an angry Reagan lashed out at student demonstrators: "If it takes a blood bath, let's get it over with. No more appeasement." Four days later, Ohio National Guardsmen opened fire on students at Kent State, killing four and wounding a score of others. It was mind-boggling. When President Johnson sent the 101st Airborne troops to escort black students to school in the South, the troops were ordered not to carry loaded weapons. Why in the world were National Guardsmen using loaded weapons at Kent State?

When confronted by the media about his provocative words, Reagan shrugged it off as just a "figure of speech"—and, to my amazement, he got away with it. He seemed impervious to blame.

The man was an enigma. He came from a poor and humble background, yet he espoused policies that devastated poor people and divided everyone. Carl Albert, former Speaker of the U.S. House, once said that the difference between FDR and Ronald Reagan was that FDR was a man born rich who understood what it was like to be poor, whereas Reagan was "a poor man who became rich and forgot what it was like to be poor."

I got the feeling that Reagan was acting out a role, as he had done many times in his movies, and finally morphed into the character he was playing.

Nothing about Reagan rankled more than his attacks on the poor. I grew up with people living on welfare, and the ones I knew weren't on the dole by choice. If anything, most of them felt ashamed about it. Reagan's speeches—always masterfully delivered in his "aw shucks" style—usually included a reference to "welfare queens driving Cadillacs"—racist code words for black welfare cheats. He never said a word, of course, about corporate welfare—the subsidies paid to white farmers not to grow crops, the tax breaks given to the giant oil companies.

The 1964 Civil Rights Act was a major step toward achieving equal rights for minorities. Most of the white people I met seemed to support the law in principle. In a short time, however, the growing unrest, the violence spinning out of the demonstrations, the implementation and enforcement of new civil rights laws and court decisions to compel the racial integration of schools caused a backlash of growing resentment among white people.

Like Barry Goldwater and Richard Nixon before him, Reagan was not above playing the race card to win white votes. The Republican Party's Southern Strategy, which capitalized on the growing resentment of white people about the Civil Rights Movement and the dismantling of racial segregation, was at the core of Reagan's campaign for president.

For me, Reagan erased any doubts when he chose Philadelphia, Mississippi, to deliver a symbolic message. This was the county where the infamous murders of three civil rights workers, Andrew Goodman, Michael Schwerner and James Chaney, had taken place 16 years earlier. There, Reagan kicked off his general election campaign at the Neshoba County Fair, an annual event that became famous for racist diatribes by segregationist politicians. The central message of Reagan's speech: "I believe in states' rights."

Because Reagan was governor of California, his signature was affixed to my

UCLA diploma. I covered the signature with a piece of tape, and it stayed that way for nearly 25 years—a personal protest, a trivia conversation piece for anyone who noticed it on my diploma on the wall of my law office.

Nearly 20 years after my graduation, when I was lieutenant governor, I met President Reagan at the White House. I was predisposed not to like him. After only a few minutes, however, I was struck by his persona. A handsome man, Reagan exuded warmth and charisma like no other political leader I had ever met. In person, he was a real charmer—an authentically charismatic figure. *How in the world, I thought, could such a seemingly nice man have such nasty social policies and say such mean-spirited things about poor people who could not defend themselves?* He seemed oblivious to people's suffering. I could not help feeling that Reagan just didn't know any better.

In 1996 or 1997, I met Reagan again, this time at the Los Angeles Country Club. He was sitting in a golf cart with a Secret Service agent. Not surprisingly, he did not remember me. Dressed in golf garb, he still looked great but seemed distracted. I found out later that he was already in the early stages of Alzheimer's disease. I disagreed with many of Reagan's policies, and there was a time when I literally hated his guts—but the passage of years cooled my animosity.

I was glad to have had a glimpse of the more personal side of him. Predictably, when Reagan died in 2004, his stature grew larger in death than it had been in life. The embellishment of his accomplishments fueled by fervent supporters and widespread public sympathy for a president stricken with Alzheimer's disease swelled Reagan's popularity to such levels that there was serious talk among conservatives about giving him a place on Mount Rushmore and replacing Franklin Roosevelt's portrait with Reagan's on the dime.

Greatness, like beauty, is in the eyes of the beholder. For me, if one looks carefully, no amount of political spin or revisionist history can hide the tragic human consequences of his domestic policies, nor the fact that Reagan did more than any modern American president to polarize the American people along racial lines.

Life in Law School

In 1968, I received my bachelor's degree from UCLA. It was a special day for my family. I was the first to graduate from college. Dad came over from Las Vegas for the ceremony. Ken was still in the Air Force and was unable to come. He called to congratulate me. Mom did not attend. I knew she was sick, but we had lost touch with each other. The few letters I sent her went unanswered. Still, graduation day was a special day for us.

In September, I began my first year at Loyola. I harbored some doubt as to whether I was good enough to get through law school. I heard repeatedly that the first year is the most difficult. Reluctantly, I gave up my part-time job with Waltco so I could concentrate full time on law school. Don Jordan, my thoughtful boss, invited me to come back if I needed a part-time job. I never forgot his kindness.

Unlike Loyola's beautiful main campus on the bluffs overlooking Marina Del Rey, the law school consisted of a handful of buildings located a few miles from the center of downtown Los Angeles. The campus was small, no more than two or three acres at most, enclosed by a high concrete wall. There were only two entrances to the school—the main entrance to the admissions office and the entrance to the rear parking lot. The school had a fine law library, but there was no cafeteria, only vending machines that too often offered stale sandwiches, snacks and soft drinks. But the smallness of the campus provided an intimacy that made it easier for students to get to know each other; close friendships were forged.

In 1968, the nation's law students were overwhelmingly white and male. Loyola was no exception. Out of the approximately 210 students in my first year class, less than a dozen were women (today, at least half of the students in most law schools are female). I was one of two or three Asian Americans in the daytime class. Considering their numbers in the general population, blacks and Chicanos were woefully underrepresented—not only at Loyola but also at universities across the nation.

To address the imbalance, law schools worked with private foundations to develop affirmative action programs for minority students. What it boiled down to was giving preference to selected minority students over better-qualified white students. The program at Loyola was limited to blacks and Chicanos. It provided free tuition and books—and an annual living stipend of about $2,400.

Along with most of the white students, I supported affirmative action. However, Loyola's program experienced some growing pains. The biggest was with the selection process. With good intentions, program administrators thought it a good idea to include black and Chicano political activists on the Admissions Committee. Not surprisingly, students who were active in the politics of race had an edge in being selected.

One Chicano student in the program, Bob, and I became good friends. Bob was one of the leaders of the Chicano group. He was a rugged-looking, easy-going guy, but he could get riled up quickly when it came to issues involving racial discrimination.

I was among the handful of law students he invited to his wedding reception when he married a pretty white girl in Venice. In the '60s, Venice was considered L.A.'s counterpart to San Francisco's famous Haight-Ashbury district, the famed home of America's hippies.

The reception in Venice was for the couple's friends and an exchange of their wedding vows—activist style. The collection of guests was an interesting, if not colorful, array of contrasts. The Chicano males were all dressed in traditional Mexican long-sleeved, white, embroidered cotton shirts similar to the barong shirts worn in the Philippines. Some of the hippies lived up to the stereotype of being non-practitioners of basic hygiene. A pretty hippie woman standing next to me, perhaps in her mid-20s, was barefoot; a glance at her bare feet revealed rings of dirt like the growth rings of a redwood tree. As for the dozen or so law students who were present, the non-Chicano males, including me, were all dressed in suits and ties—standing out clearly like Secret Service agents at a presidential rally. The highlight of the wedding reception came when the bride and groom exchanged their wedding vows. One of the Chicano law students was a reverend (at least that's what we were told) and performed the wedding service, which included a long recitation of all the alleged wrongs committed by the United States against Mexico and Mexican Americans since California became an American possession. The reverend's main point was that because California was illegally taken from Mexico, Anglo (American) law did not apply to Chicanos. Therefore, Bob and his wife could not be legally married under the law of the Anglos but had to legitimize their union under the ritual that was being held before us.

One could easily have been amused by the ceremony, but as I stood listening to the reverend (I think his name was Leon), I sensed that the Chicanos were dead serious. Rituals and ceremonies are ways people remind themselves of values they hold dear and help instill a resolve to preserve and protect those values. That's what Bob's wedding ceremony was all about. Unknown to most of the guests, however, the couple had been legally married under California State law a week or so earlier. Just in case.

As I mentioned, politics played a big role in the selection of Chicano students into the affirmative action program. Political activism, however, does not ensure one is ready for law school. By the first year's end, many of the Chicano students were on the verge of flunking out. Soon their frustrations were directed toward the Loyola administration. The Chicano group decided to hold a demonstration to air its complaints about the "relevance" of the curriculum, and other issues, at the quarterly administration and faculty meeting that was going to be held in the school's auditorium.

The demonstration became unruly. Shocked Loyola administrators and faculty at the meeting were forced to call the LAPD, which forcibly removed the demonstrators. The sight of some of my classmates, cuffed at their hands and ankles and being carried away like hogs to the slaughter, caused me mixed emotions. It was demeaning to see the police treat people that way—but I felt the demonstration was unjustified. Loyola had done nothing to deserve this kind of negative publicity.

The next morning, the student demonstrators and their supporters called for a strike. As I drove into the school's parking lot, I saw a line of about two dozen student demonstrators, arms locked, standing two deep across the steps of the entrance at the school. They were blocking the only entrance to the law school from the parking lot. I sat in my car a few minutes, thinking about whether I should cross the picket line. I was a first-year student and was struggling in a few subjects. Attending the class lectures was important to me. More important, I didn't think the strike was justified. Loyola was an eager and willing participant in the affirmative action program, but it never deviated from holding its students to its traditionally high academic standards.

I knew nearly every one of the student demonstrators. A few were good friends. Standing in the middle of the picket line was a tall white student named Michael. I learned later he had helped organize the strike. Under ordinary circumstances, Michael was a nice guy, but just from listening to him in class I had pegged him as an ideologue who supported every purported liberal cause regardless of merit—sometimes just for the hell of it. Michael was probably the best-dressed student at Loyola. Compared to the rest of us, he dressed as if he were a model for *GQ* magazine. Even when he wore jeans, they were always a designer brand.

"Cayetano, you more than any one else [referring to the white students crossing the picket line] should know better," he said. He usually called me "Ben," so when he called me "Cayetano" I knew he was upset with me. And I was getting pissed at him. The last thing I needed was a lecture about civil rights from an affluent, self-righteous white guy.

"Listen, man, get the fuck out of my way! I'm going to class," I said angrily, looking him in the eye, as I brushed by him. Bob, who was standing next to Michael, said nothing and just stared ahead.

Later that day, Professor Laurence Simpson, who was considered one of the national authorities on the law of agency, started his class with a short lecture about the strike and the demonstration. Professor Simpson was in his late 70s, a big heavyset man, a terrific teacher with a great sense of humor who was respected by his students. A hush fell over the class as he began to speak.

"If you fellows really want to help the poor; if you want to help uplift the lives of our minority communities," he said in his booming voice, "then you had better master the laws of real property, contracts, criminal law, torts and the State and federal constitutions! Do you know why? Because you can bet that the lawyers for the other side will know the law, they will know the court rules and procedures—and if you don't, they will make short work of you in court! All this talk about the curriculum being 'irrelevant' is nonsense!" I respected Simpson because he never let politics get in the way of what he thought was right.

By the end of the first year, many of the affirmative action students left Loyola. Although a few excelled, the Chicanos and blacks had a much higher dropout rate than the whites. The Chicano students suffered more because of their focus on politics. Most of the black students made it—presumably because they were admitted more on their academic potential than their political activism.

Bob was one of the Chicanos who left, halfway through the second year. He was smart and idealistic, but he did not have the patience to spend three years in law school; the country was in the midst of the Civil Rights Movement, and there was so much going on in the Chicano community. I never had a chance to talk to him before he left, and we lost touch with each other.

A decade later, after I was elected to the State Senate in 1978, I got a telephone call from him. He was in Hawai'i for a visit. We met and talked about our days at Loyola. He had put his bachelor's degree in social work to good use and become a social worker.

Social workers are the unsung heroes of government. They serve the poor, the handicapped, people and families that have been devastated by drug and alcohol addiction, sexual abuse, incest and child abuse. Their clients have little or no political power, which is a big reason why social workers suffer a paucity of funding for their programs and end up carry impossibly huge caseloads. Every day they struggle to help people get their lives together or just to get by. And the only time people pay attention to what they are doing is when they screw up. Not surprisingly, they burn out quickly compared to those in other professions. The ones who survive are usually driven more by compassion and dedication than anything else. Bob was one of them; he was in his element.

I was happy to get his call. We never talked about the strike when we were at Loyola. He never held my crossing the picket line against me. We remained friends.

If the goal of Loyola's affirmative action was to increase the numbers of minority lawyers, the chances of success were obviously greater if the students selected for the programs were the best prepared academically rather than the most politically active. Throwing ill-prepared minority students into law school without tutoring or extra assistance was a formula for failure—and a disservice to the students and their communities. Moreover, a bigger problem was that the number of black and Chicano students in the undergraduate schools was disproportionately small—there simply were not enough of them to choose from. Failures were inevitable. Despite its flaws, though, I continued to support affirmative action. On balance, I thought it was a step in the right direction.

Most white Americans supported the civil rights law—the big challenge was in its implementation. People react differently when they are affected in some negative way. The qualified white student who was denied admission to law school because a less-qualified minority student was given preference could hardly be expected to be supportive of the affirmative action program. Every time a black or Chicano student failed it would erode support for the program and provide more fuel for its critics. This was why it was important for affirmative action students to succeed.

Personally, I was glad Asians were not included in Loyola's program. Like it or not, the terms "minority" or "affirmative action" student carried a stigma that suggested that such students were intellectually inferior to "regular" students. As the years have passed and the program has been refined, that stereotype has been pretty much disproved, mostly because the minority students selected for the programs were those who were better prepared academically rather than those most politically active. At Loyola, I didn't want to wrestle with that problem. I knew law school would be tough, but it was important to me that I make it on my own.

In fact, most Asian students were making it on their own. Most came from stable families with parents who would sacrifice almost anything to give their kids a good education. In my final year at Loyola, Asians were finally admitted to the affirmative action program. The students were Japanese, Korean and Chinese. There were no Filipinos. I found this amusing—an example of how little even the best-intentioned white people knew about Asian Americans. On a per capita basis, the Chinese, Japanese and Koreans ethnic groups matched, if not exceeded, the white population in terms of college graduates. Filipinos lagged behind, but they would get there in good time.

Today, after more than 40 years, my views on affirmative action have changed somewhat. Studies show that the increased numbers of blacks and Chicanos in law schools have not kept pace with those of their white counterparts. White women, however, have fared well and today make up nearly one-half of the nation's law students. The success of white women reveals what some educators have known for a long time: Those who succeed in college have a better chance if they come from stable families and learn the fundamentals of education in grade school. Thus, real, effective affirmative action for blacks and Chicanos and other minorities begins with providing them better education in grade schools, where teachers have the best opportunity to shape the children's young minds, and with programs that help strengthen their family lives.

Affirmative action is a form of reverse discrimination. But one has to be blind not to acknowledge the impact of our nation's shameful history of racial discrimination against blacks, Chicanos, Native Americans and Asians. In 1968, I considered affirmative action a modest means of reparation for blacks and Chicanos. Blacks, in particular, suffered more than any other minority. Something had to be done to help them catch up with the rest of the nation. After four decades, however, I believe it is time to reassess the affirmative action programs with an eye to making poverty rather than race the determining factor for college and professional school admissions.

As a general rule, most law firms did not hire first-year students. I decided to try anyway. I must have called at least 50 law firms but was rejected each time. Finally, I lucked out. I called the law firm of Harris & Hollingsworth, which was located next to the Los Angeles International Airport. Somehow I convinced the office manager to let me speak directly to the senior partner, Richard Harris. Our brief conversation led to a personal interview, which resulted in a part-time job I would hold until I graduated from law school. Harris was a highly regarded lawyer, soft spoken, a gentleman. It didn't take me long to see that his staff was devoted to him. In a short time, I felt the same way; we grew to like and trust each other. He was kind and thoughtful. To help me with my law studies, he gave me a key to the office so I could use its law library on weekends and evenings. The law firm's main office was located within walking distance from our new duplex in Westchester. Things were going well.

Besides doing legal research, part of my job was to serve or file legal documents, such as subpoenas, restraining orders, summonses and complaints. This was the best part because, in addition to my hourly wage of $3.50 per hour, I was paid $3.00 for every document that I served and also got a mileage allowance. Little did I realize that the job would lead to some unforgettable experiences.

Once, Mr. Harris asked if I would serve a subpoena on a witness who lived in Northridge; the trial was scheduled to begin the next day. The witness was in Las Vegas and was not expected to return to his home until between 11 p.m. and midnight.

"Ben, don't feel like you have to do it; we can get a professional process server to do it," he said. "The person is a friendly witness [a witness favorable to our client's case], but I want to make sure he shows up for the trial."

Of course I was going to do it. My respect for Mr. Harris was such that it never crossed my mind to refuse any assignment he asked me to do. The witness was important to our client's case. Mr. Harris knew he could rely on me to get the job done.

I figured it would take me about three hours to drive there from my home, serve the witness with the subpoena and return. Lorraine usually got off work about midnight and could catch a ride home. I had to take the kids with me, so I dressed them in warm clothing, bundled them up with a blanket and pillow in the backseat of our VW Beetle and drove to Northridge.

The witness' beautiful, two-story home was in a cul-de-sac. I got there at about 10:30 p.m., a little early. I parked next to his garage, made sure the kids were warm and comfortable, and waited.

As I sat there, it soon occurred to me that someone might notice my car and call the cops. Northridge was an all-white, well-to-do neighborhood. The cops would have a lot of questions for someone like me if they found me there. Fortunately, no one noticed my car.

Around 1 a.m., I saw the headlights of a car enter the cul-de-sac. Sure enough, the witness was driving the Cadillac described by Mr. Harris. I got out of my car. The witness saw me and stopped his car with his headlights shining at me. He was a big, middle-aged white man.

"Hi, good morning," I said. "I'm from Richard Harris' office. I have a subpoena for you to appear at the trial today." The man had already agreed to testify, but the subpoena was to assure he did not change his mind.

"Oh, yes," he said, smiling, as he accepted the subpoena. "How long have you been waiting here?"

"About two hours," I replied.

"Tough way to make a living," he said, glancing at the kids asleep on the backseat.

"I only do this part time; I'm a student at Loyola Law School," I replied.

He took a long look at me, as if he had been pleasantly surprised, and smiled. "Oh, a law student … I see. Well, good luck … and take care of those kids of yours," he said, nodding at Brandon and Janeen asleep on the backseat.

Not everyone was as good natured. Serving people with subpoenas, restraining orders or complaints is not a job likely to win friends. And too often, the person directs his resentment or anger toward the messenger.

I had heard enough stories about process servers being beaten up, stabbed and even shot to convince me to take extra precautions whenever I went into tough neighborhoods. I dreaded having to serve papers in the tough black and Chicano areas—especially the Chicano ones. Black toughs could never mistake me for a member of a rival gang; Chicanos could. With my brown skin, I could easily pass for one.

Ironically, though, the only time I had a problem was when I served divorce papers on a white guy in Long Beach. Our law firm represented his wife, a pretty, petite, eight-months-pregnant blond who had tearfully recounted to us how her husband had beaten her. The sight of her bruised face disgusted me. *What a punk,* I thought to myself.

Ben Aranda, the firm's first Chicano lawyer, was handling the case. "Ben, she talked to her husband and he agreed to settle everything," he instructed me. "He knows you're going to serve him with the papers, so there shouldn't be any problems. She told him she would telephone him at home about noon, so if you get there about then, you can serve him with the papers. The house is the only one with a white picket fence in the front yard." *This one will be easy,* I thought.

I got there at noon, parked my Beetle in front of the fence, walked through the gate and knocked on the door. A short, heavyset woman opened the door. It was the guy's mother.

"Good afternoon, I have some papers for Mr. King [not his real name]," I told her. "Yes, he is expecting you," she said. Looking past her, I could see him talking on the telephone at the end of a long, narrow hallway. He was shirtless, wearing jeans and stood about 6 feet 2 inches tall, and weighed about 190 pounds.

"Come in," he said cordially, beckoning me in with one hand. I walked in and placed the papers in his outstretched hand as he continued talking on the phone while reading the papers at the same time. *That was easy,* I thought. "Thank you, Mr. King," I said, already thinking about my next assignment, and turned to leave.

"Hey, wait a minute. Is this a complaint for divorce?" he asked, looking at the papers.

"Yes, it is," I replied, sensing something had gone wrong.

Turning to the telephone in his hand, his face twisted with anger and he began screaming at his wife, who was still on the other end of the line, "You lying bitch, you fucking whore, this is not a restraining order, it's a fucking complaint for divorce!" A slew of epithets followed; then he slammed the telephone down on the receiver. He was becoming angrier by the second. No longer able to yell at his wife, he turned on me.

"Get the hell out of my house and take these fucking papers with you!" he shouted, throwing the papers at my face. Taken by complete surprise, I felt as if he had spat on my face. Annoyed, I reached down, grabbed the papers off the floor and put them on a nearby table.

"Sorry, mister, you are served," I said curtly. In hindsight, it was one of the most asinine remarks of my life. I had waved the proverbial red flag before the bull. As I walked quickly down the long, narrow hallway to the door, I kept on looking back, watching him. He picked up the papers, crushed them into a ball and started for me. Fortunately, his mother stepped in front of him, attempting to calm him down. Instead, he began screaming at me, his contorted face an angry mask. Now red-faced, the guy was nearly incoherent. My worst fear was happening. The guy was pissed! At me!

"Sir!" his mother shouted desperately as she struggled to stay between me and him, "Sir, leave! Get out of here!" It was the first time a white person had called me "Sir."

I got out of the house and closed the door behind me. I knew she couldn't hold him off for long. I had to make a decision. *Do I leave the way I entered, through the gate and walkway? Or do I jump over the fence to get to my parked car?* His mother's screaming now reached a couple of octaves higher. "No! Leave him alone! Sir! Go! Sir! Go!" she shouted.

The fear in her voice made my decision easy. The shortest distance between two objects is a straight line—which was about the only thing I remembered from my geometry class. Adrenalin raging, I started running toward the three-foot-high white picket fence and somehow managed an Olympian-like leap over it!

Just as I got to my car, the house door flew open. And there he was, framed in the doorway, his eyes big and wild—like a couple of sunny-side-up fried eggs. He was dragging his mother, who had fallen to the floor but was heroically hanging onto the backside of his jeans and belt. "No! Leave him alone!" she yelled, as he dragged her along, like a Clydesdale horse pulling a beer wagon. Dr. Jekyll had turned into Mr. Hyde. Growing up in Kalihi, I had been beaten up before. But never by a crazy man! To put it mildly, I got a little excited.

I had prepared for something like this—but I'd always imagined the attacker would be black or Chicano. I managed to get into my car, start the engine and lock all the doors. I reached down under my seat, pulled out the baton-sized iron pipe that I kept for self-protection and placed it on the passenger seat.

Within seconds, my red-faced, wide-eyed antagonist was at my car door. He threw the summons and complaint—now torn into confetti—on my car's windshield. I had the car in gear, ready to drive off. But first, I wanted to give him a piece of my mind. I rolled down the window about six inches. *Okay, you bastard, put your arm through this window, and I'll give it a worse beating than you gave your wife—and I'll take you for a ride down the street for a block or two!* I yelled at him in my mind. I had been humiliated and I was hopping mad.

I started yelling at him: "Listen, pal, why in hell you pissed with me for? I'm just a working man trying to do my job! What the hell's the matter with you? You punched out your wife [I found out later he also did a number on his best friend], you just put your mother through hell—you should be ashamed of yourself, you damned coward!"

Having vented, I was ready to drive away. But my verbal assault had had an impact on him. Suddenly, he was silent, looking down at his feet. Shaking his head side to side, his eyes welled up with tears. He started sobbing uncontrollably.

"She told me she was going to get a restraining order because I hit her—but she never said anything about getting a divorce," he sobbed. "Yeah, I hit her. I'm really sorry about it. But I came home early from work one day and caught her screwing my best friend. In our house! My best friend! She was seven months pregnant, for God's sake! We were going to have our first baby! What would you do if you came home to something like that?" he wailed.

I'd probably try to kill the guy. I was shocked. I sensed he was telling me the truth. My feelings of support for our pretty, petite, pregnant client began to wane. She had not been candid with us (experience would later teach me that most clients tell their lawyers what they want to remember), and I'd nearly gotten beaten up because of it.

"I'm sorry I took it out on you," he continued. "I just lost it when I found out the papers were for a divorce and not a restraining order. She told me she was not going to divorce me. She lied to me again," he said softly. I was dumbfounded.

"I don't want a divorce," he sobbed. "No matter what she did, I still love her; she's my life … Mister, can you help me?"

Help him? I was just a law clerk, not a lawyer. But the guy was now a broken man. His Jekyll/Hyde transformation had scared the living daylights out of me. But now, he was mush—emotionally beaten, a human wreck.

"Sir," his mother intervened, "he loves her so much; if you can help him, we'd be so grateful." So she too—this nice lady who kept on calling me "Sir" throughout this ordeal—was ready to forgive her daughter-in-law.

I wondered how I would have reacted under the same circumstances. I couldn't bring myself to just leave without trying to help. I felt sorry for him.

Besides, his mother had protected me—I owed her. And I was afraid he would explode in anger again and hurt someone—or worse, maybe blow his brains out.

I had to trust my gut feelings about this guy—something I've done many times throughout my life. I wanted to help, give him some hope. Warily, I stepped out of my car, put my hand on his shoulder and said, "Mr. King, let me call my boss. He'll talk to your wife, and maybe we can arrange for you two to meet and get some counseling."

"Thank you, thank you," he muttered, barely able to get the words out.

We went back into the house, his mother with her arm around his waist. I got on the telephone and called Ben Aranda.

"Hello, Ben, I'm here at Mr. King's home. Listen, the guy blew up and came after me … but he's calmed down now. Emotionally, he's really messed up.…"

There was silence on the other end of the line. Finally, Aranda asked, "Ben, did he attack you? Are you all right?"

"Well, he got a little angry, but everything's okay now," I said, understating what had actually happened. "He doesn't want a divorce … I told him perhaps we could arrange a meeting between him and his wife or they could go to counseling."

"Is he near you?" Aranda asked anxiously.

"No, he's in the living room with his mother," I replied.

"Listen, this guy has a terrible temper. Don't take any chances, just leave him the papers—and come back to the office."

"Well, can we arrange for them to meet, get counseling?" I persisted naively.

"Ben," Aranda said firmly, "we represent the wife. She is our client. Not him. She is adamant about getting a divorce. Remember that. Tell him we'll discuss this with his wife later. But I want you to leave now."

I hung up and walked over to Mr. King and his mother. "I spoke to my boss about you and your wife meeting and perhaps getting some counseling."

"What did he say?" his mother asked.

"He has to discuss it with your son's wife. We'll get back to you."

His mother walked me back to my car. The last I saw of her son, he was sitting, his face buried in his hands. His mother kept on apologizing for his conduct.

As I drove back to the office, I wondered whether I was out of line. *Perhaps,* I thought, *I should have just driven away and not gotten involved; perhaps I gave the husband false hope.* If what he said was the truth, there was little chance the marriage would survive. Moreover, Aranda was right. We represented the wife, not the husband. She'd hired our law firm to get her a divorce. Lawyers are supposed to be advocates—not social workers. Years later, however, as a lawyer with my own practice, I would eventually handle hundreds of divorces and family-type cases. I discovered there were some clients who were best served when I acted more like a social worker than a lawyer. It cost me some fees, but I learned a lot about human nature—and I felt pretty good about it.

Racial Turmoil

The assassination of John F. Kennedy in 1963, followed by those of Robert Kennedy and Martin Luther King, Jr., as well as the antiwar movement, the civil rights demonstrations and the race riots, were all signs of a troubled nation. How different, I thought, it must be for the people in Hawai'i whose knowledge of these events came mainly from the television news, than it was for us living in Los Angeles and witnessing firsthand the daily occurrences underlying the city's antiwar demonstrations and racial flare-ups.

The spectacle of redneck cops and sheriffs angrily wielding billy clubs and using tear gas and dogs against black and white civil rights demonstrators protesting Jim Crow laws in the South was something foreign to this local boy from Hawai'i. It angered me and only aggravated the already poor relationship between police and minorities throughout the nation, especially in the black ghettos of the nation's large urban centers in the Midwest and Northeast.

Los Angeles was no exception. While most of the nation's attention was focused on the black community, there were serious problems brewing between the black and Chicano communities and the Los Angeles Police. Nothing troubled me more than how local law enforcement dealt with minorities. The propensity of white cops to shoot to kill shocked me.

One evening, I watched a television news report about a police shooting that was especially disturbing. A young Chicano in his teens standing in line at a fast-food restaurant attempted to steal an extra taco when the clerk's back was turned. Another worker saw him and told him to put it back. Just then, an LAPD patrol car happened to be passing by, and the workers summoned the cops. The young Chicano started running across a ball field. The cops gave chase and ordered him to halt; when he didn't, one of the cops shot him in the back of the head, killing him.

I couldn't believe it. The next morning I checked the newspaper. The report was correct. Mexican-American leaders protested and demanded that the cop be prosecuted.

At work, a white guy, Dean, and Bobby, a Chicano, had a running chess game. Every lunch hour, they would play each other, picking up where they left off the day before. A chess player myself, I would often watch them, enjoying their banter and jokes. They were obviously good friends.

The day after the shooting, however, was different. As they played chess, Bobby began talking about the shooting. He was obviously upset and grew more agitated the more he talked about it.

Dean listened for a while and then, clearly exasperated, said, "Bobby, the kid should have listened to the cop. When a cop with a gun says 'stop,' you stop."

Bobby looked up incredulously, rose from his chair and shot back angrily,

"Hey, man, since when is it right to shoot a kid for taking a taco? The fucking prick shot him in the back! You think the cop would have shot the kid if he was white? Where the hell is your head at, man?" Bobby got up and walked away.

Dean looked at me sadly, shaking his head. "I should have kept my mouth shut," he said. They would resume their marathon chess game a week later, but on that day these two good friends saw things so differently it was as if they came from different planets. The blow-up was indicative of the difference in how whites and minorities viewed the police.

More police shootings followed. The pattern of the city government's response would almost always be the same: White cop would shoot and kill unarmed black or Chicano civilian; minority community leaders would protest; the mayor would call for coroner's inquest, which invariably absolved the cop.

Another shooting was especially egregious. The LAPD raided an apartment they believed was occupied by armed robbers. Instead, it was a group of illegal Mexican immigrants, "wetbacks," as they were derisively called then, playing cards. As the cops broke down the door, three of the immigrants tried to flee by jumping out of windows. Staked out outside were LAPD cops who shot and killed each immigrant who came through the windows. None were armed. A tragic mistake, perhaps—but it was just another incident that strengthened the perception in the Chicano community that racism was at the root of how the predominantly white LAPD cops dealt with Chicanos.

Once the cops shot and killed a white guy: the young son of a former mayor of Pasadena who had the misfortune of getting drunk in a bar, falling asleep in the restroom and setting off the burglar alarm as he stumbled around trying to get out of the place after it had closed. The cops arrived and ordered the guy to come out. When there was no response, one of the cops shot a tear gas canister through the front door, killing the unfortunate and still-drunk young man who was on the other side trying to open the locked door. The shooting was a one-day news item. Back then, life was cheap in L.A.

Coming from Hawai'i, where the cops rarely drew their guns, though they would not hesitate to slap people around or rough them up to make their point, I was shocked by the seeming ease with which police shootings of unarmed people occurred in Los Angeles.

Police shootings had become a problem to minorities nationwide, so much so that the famed CBS program 60 Minutes did a story on it, mentioning in the process that the Honolulu Police Department had the strictest regulations on use of firearms by its members and had the lowest incidence of shootings in the nation.

In the black community, the frustration and fury of young black men at the shootings—and the failure of the government to do anything about it—led to the formation of radical groups, such as the Black Panther Party. The group rejected Dr. Martin Luther King, Jr.'s "turn the other cheek" philosophy of peaceful civil disobedience. Parroting Chief William Parker and the LAPD, the Panthers preached using "any means necessary" to protect themselves against violence by the police. Black Panther leader Rap Brown summed up their feelings when he said, "Violence is as American as apple pie."

In August 1965, less than two years after the JFK assassination, things came to a head when a riot erupted in Watts, a predominantly black community in South Central Los Angeles. The riot grew out of an argument between a Los Angeles police officer and a black motorist that escalated out of control. Police reinforcements were called and, wielding batons, they made arrests and restored order.

Hours later, however, hundreds of blacks rallied to protest the police action. Soon more people joined the protests—and six days of rioting followed. Thirty-four people were killed, 29 of them blacks—all shot by police or National Guardsmen. More than 1,000 people were injured, and hundreds of buildings were destroyed by fire.

Los Angeles was in a virtual state of siege. Everyone seemed to be arming themselves, and I was no exception. For the first time in my adult life, I went to a sporting goods store to buy a firearm. I had plenty of company. I found myself in a line together with several hundred blacks, Chicanos, Asians and whites. The line stretched completely around the block. The people were buying up all of the guns and ammunition. It was bizarre.

When I finally got to the counter, there were two handguns left. I opted for the biggest one: a four-inch, .357-caliber Colt revolver, which was so big and heavy it felt like I was carrying a 10-pound dumbbell. The people in line behind me had to settle for pellet guns, knives, hatchets, bows and arrows and spear guns. The sporting goods store was sold out of guns. It was absurd, bizarre—but it was the reality of the moment.

Waltco Truck Co., where I was still working at the time, was located in Gardena, and Watts was only three or four miles away. Flames and smoke from torched buildings were clearly visible. We could hear the sirens of the police cars and fire engines—and occasionally what sounded like shots. The governor sent in the National Guard. Waltco closed for a couple days. When it reopened, I went back to work and found that most of my fellow workers—blacks, whites and Chicanos—were carrying firearms in their cars.

For six days, a great human tragedy unfolded before a national audience. One unforgettable television news clip showed a grim-faced cop sitting in a passing police car, displaying three fingers to the camera as if he had been on a hunting expedition. The message was clear: Three fingers meant he had shot three people, black people. Repeatedly shown on national television, the news clip manifested what Chief Parker meant when he ordered the police to "use all necessary force" to put down the riot.

Parker, who was considered a "cop's cop," was arrogant and foolish with his public statements. When asked about the cause of the riot, he was quoted as saying, "Someone threw a rock, and like monkeys in a zoo, others started throwing rocks." Not surprisingly, Parker's ill-chosen words made sensational news, causing newspaper headlines that fueled a furor among even the most moderate and well-educated black Americans.

It was difficult to understand the results of the rioters' anger. Not only did they burn down more than 1,000 dwellings and buildings, they also destroyed hundreds, perhaps thousands, of jobs held by blacks and wiped out hundreds of businesses, including many that were owned by blacks. I could not imagine the same thing happening in Kalihi. We loved Kalihi—it was pretty obvious that many blacks who lived in Watts hated the place.

Watts became the catalyst for a half-dozen major race riots in cities across the nation. The 1967 Detroit Riot, for example, resulted in 47 dead, hundreds injured and more than 1,000 buildings destroyed. At the heart of these riots were charges of police brutality.

Most of the white people I knew saw the police as the difference between order and chaos: Rioters were considered criminals who should be arrested or shot. Most blacks and Chicanos, on the other hand, saw the predominantly white LAPD as racists, heavy-handed protectors of the white community.

In 1967, President Lyndon Johnson appointed Gov. Otto Kerner of Illinois to head a blue-ribbon commission to investigate the causes of race riots. In 1968 the Kerner Commission, as it was called, concluded that police misconduct led to the outbreak of violence in half of the riots.

This decade in American history had a great impact on my perspective on American justice. As a citizen, I became skeptical of my government. As a young lawyer, I would opt to remain in private practice and defend the accused rather than prosecute them. Watts had confirmed what I learned from history: In times of crisis the majority will choose order over individual liberty.

Vietnam

In 1962, James Gabriel became the first Hawai'i-born soldier killed in Vietnam. A Kalihi boy and a 1956 Farrington graduate, Gabriel was a member of the elite Green Beret Special Forces, sent in increasing numbers by President Kennedy to assist the South Vietnamese government in its fight with the Viet Cong. Gabriel was badly wounded while leading the defense of a South Vietnamese hamlet under Viet Cong attack. Captured, he was carried away by the Viet Cong and later found executed.

I knew little about what was happening in South Vietnam. For a while, I remained ambivalent about the war—school, work and our kids took up most of my time. But by 1965, I began reading everything I could about Vietnam, about the role of the French, about our policy and why our leaders said we had to be there. The more I read, the more I watched the news, the more I began to sense that Sen. William Fullbright was right: The United States was acting "like Boy Scouts dragging reluctant old ladies across the streets they do not want to cross." All the deaths, the wounds, the suffering of our troops and their families, the ingratitude and incompetence of the South Vietnamese military, were tearing our country apart.

That year, Ken was sent to South Vietnam. He was in the Air Force and spent a year stationed at Cam Ranh Bay. Then I got word that Bobby Natarte, a good friend of mine, was killed. For me, the high cost of the war struck home. My interest in it became very personal.

Bobby Natarte and I were close. A former Marine, he had worked himself up to sergeant before being discharged in 1959. When I first met him, we were both members of the same martial arts club. Bobby was born to be a Marine; he loved it, but he got out because the pay for enlisted men at the time was shamefully low and made it tough on his family. Like James Gabriel, Bobby was a Filipino American, born and raised in Hawai'i. We talked often about our families and our futures. I told him I wanted to go to college and become a lawyer. Like an older brother, he was very supportive and enthusiastic. "Benny," he said, "college is not for me. I'm not good with books and studying. But you can do it, I know you can. Go for it."

After leaving for Los Angeles in 1963, I lost touch with Bobby for a while. The last I heard he was still working as a refrigeration mechanic. In November of 1965, I sent Bobby a Christmas card, telling him that I was in school full time, that Lorraine and I were both working and we were all fine. In January 1966, Bobby wrote back. He was happy to hear from me. He was back in the Marine Corps.

"I joined up again to save my marriage," he wrote, without explaining why, "but don't worry about me because I'm with a Marine air mobile unit that supplies our troops. Compared to the guys on the ground, I have it easy. Study hard, I know you'll make it. Proud of you, brah," he concluded in pidgin.

In March 1966, a month after I got his letter, Bobby was killed. Later, I was told his helicopter crashed into a river. It was an accident. Trapped in the wreckage, Bobby drowned. I was sick thinking about it. I knew Bobby well. He was a gung ho Marine. If he had to die, he'd want to be killed in action. But not like this. *I hope he was unconscious when it happened,* I said to myself; *I hope he didn't know....*

I thought about Bobby a lot thereafter. I still do today, usually on Veterans Day. Years after the war ended, on my business trips to Washington, D.C., I'd visit the Vietnam War Memorial Wall, find Bobby's name etched in the black granite and recall our moments of friendship.

Another name I looked for was that of Abraham Ahuna, another good friend and classmate at Farrington. Abe, who was a Native Hawaiian, lived across from my grandmother's home in Damon Tract. There were many poor families living in

Damon Tract, but none poorer than Abe's.

I knew Abe well. Among the guys we hung out with at school, he was often the object of jokes; he was the kind of guy who would be asked to hold the bag on a snipe hunt. After his junior year ended in 1957, he dropped out of Farrington and joined the Army. There was good-natured wisecracking among Abe's friends that the Army was "scraping the bottom of the barrel" when it took Abe. *How did he get into the Army with that crooked pinkie?* I wondered. Abe had injured his left pinkie playing barefoot football, and it was permanently bent at a 90-degree angle. He never went to the doctor to get it fixed, probably because he couldn't afford to.

The Army was good for Abe; he earned his GED (general education degree) and eventually was promoted to sergeant. Abe had found his niche in life—at least for what little of it he had left. Later, I found out that Abe had been badly wounded by a mine or booby trap; he hung on for months, fighting for his life, before he finally died.

Bobby and Abe are just two among the nearly 58,000 Americans who were killed in Vietnam.

In a short time, I concluded our government was lying to us. They knew the war could not be won and was not worth the cost—but they continued to feed the flower of our youth into the meat grinder. Tens of thousands of Americans soldiers paid with their lives—and thousands more were wounded—for nothing.

By 1968, President Johnson's political standing had plummeted. He would not seek reelection. I found myself drawn to Eugene McCarthy, the antiwar U.S. senator. McCarthy, liberal and intellectual, read poetry and could quote from the classics. He was very popular among college students, but there was a much bigger, older electorate out there that he could not reach. Robert Kennedy beat him in Oregon in the Democratic primaries, but was shot soon afterward. McCarthy's campaign petered out. It taught me that idealism alone rarely wins elections.

The 1968 Democratic National Convention in Chicago was a disaster. After a peace plank offered by antiwar delegates was rejected, a riot broke out outside the convention center where thousands of antiwar demonstrators had gathered. Mayor Richard Daley's cops responded with police dogs, tear gas and batons to such an extreme that a congressional committee would later describe their actions as a "police riot."

Vice President Hubert Humphrey won the Democratic nomination. I admired him and believed he would make a good president. But the "Happy Warrior," as the news media called him, found himself nearly 17 points behind the Republican nominee, Richard Nixon. Humphrey would make a terrific comeback—only to fall short and lose narrowly. America had elected a devious politician who would make "Watergate" a household word and become the first American president to resign from office in disgrace.

By the late 1960s the antiwar movement had gained tremendous momentum. I joined an antiwar draft-counseling group made up of Loyola law students working with a Santa Monica law firm that specialized in selective service law. We advised clients on the legal requirements for qualifying for conscientious objector and other deferment status.

Shortly, it became apparent that our free draft-counseling service worked best for the guys from middle-class or wealthy families. Avoiding the draft could be costly. It spawned a profitable business for the lawyers, orthodontists, psychologists, psychiatrist and even some clergy who offered their services for a fee. Psychologists, psychiatrists and clergy were usually used to support the potential draftee's application for conscientious objector exemptions or to establish that the draftee was a homosexual. Orthodontists also did well, fitting clients with heavy braces (even if they were not needed), which was a surefire way to get a deferment. At $1,500 to $3,000 a head—big money in those days—most guys could not afford it.

Money and privilege made a difference. Those who had them could afford the professional help. Those who had the political connections used them to get into the National Guard—where only 1 percent of the Guardsmen were deployed to Vietnam. It was that simple.

In the end, it didn't matter much; our clients were mostly college types, middle class or wealthy. Our outreach efforts revealed a pattern of behavior: If working-class whites, blacks, Asians or Chicanos got a draft notice, most would report for duty regardless of their feelings about the war. Many of the students we counseled were genuinely opposed to the war. But for some, the draft was simply an unwarranted intrusion into their lifestyle, and they would do whatever they had to do to avoid it.

The old adage that wars are started by the rich and powerful but fought by the poor and working-class was as true for Vietnam as it was for past wars. After a few months, I quit the draft-counseling group.

Vietnam was a time of contradictions. When the 1967 Israeli-Arab Six Day War broke out, hundreds of young Jewish-American men and women flocked to a recruiting station set up in Los Angeles to join the Israeli military to defend Israel. And yet Jewish Americans were usually in the forefront of the antiwar movement—a fact not overlooked by supporters of the Vietnam War. Young Americans who were labeled as cowards because they opposed the Vietnam War nevertheless were willing to risk their lives defending Israel or joining the struggle for racial equality in the hostile Deep South.

In 1971, President Nixon ended the draft. Not surprisingly, the student antiwar movement, purportedly based on high moral and philosophical grounds, ended virtually overnight, even though young Americans continued to serve and die in Vietnam for nearly two years afterward.

News reports of antiwar demonstrators spitting on returning troops or yelling obscene remarks at them angered me; the infamous photo showing Jane

Fonda seated on a North Vietnamese anti-aircraft gun just about blew my mind, to put it mildly. While my brother Ken and close friends like Bobby and Abe served in Vietnam, self-indulgent, privileged hypocrites like Fonda put our troops at greater risk.

The Vietnam War had been waged dishonestly for a flawed policy—and American presidents kept feeding our young into the slaughter because of politics. Eleven years and far too many dead and wounded later, America lost the war. It was a sad chapter in our country's history.

In 2002, my last year as governor, I visited Vietnam. Our guide, a young Vietnamese man in his 30s, briefed us: After North Vietnam won the war, the government's attempt at establishing a Russian-model economy utterly failed—and a great famine swept the country. Malnutrition had stunted the physical growth of an entire generation of Vietnamese children. These were 40- and 50-year-olds who had the physiques of children. The only things that betrayed their age were their worn faces.

Our tour guide had experienced much sadness himself. His family was South Vietnamese. His two older brothers had served in ARVN, the South Vietnamese Army. One was killed. The other, a former lieutenant, was badly wounded, permanently crippled and spent several years in a North Vietnamese "reeducation camp." He eked out a living by running a small bicycle repair shop.

"What is the unemployment rate of Vietnam?" I asked Greg Wong, a Foreign Service officer from the American Embassy, who had been assigned to brief us. A hapa (Chinese-haole), Greg had parents who were from Hawai'i.

"There is no unemployment in Vietnam, only underemployment," he said. "Everyone works; there just aren't enough full-time jobs to go around."

Greg predicted we would be surprised to find a lack of bitterness toward Americans. I was skeptical. After all, the war had claimed the lives of more than a million Vietnamese. Compared to our 58,000 killed, the Vietnamese paid a horrific price for the right to govern themselves.

But surprised we were. Experiencing the Vietnamese postwar attitude toward Americans proved to be touching and rewarding. Of course, they won the war. And winners could afford to be gracious. It was a sobering experience to visit a Vietnamese war museum and see America depicted as a defeated enemy. Even more sobering was the realization that Vietnam is run by the same Communist Party that was once our enemy, which the U.S. government now considers a trade partner and a source of cheap labor for U.S. business.

The week before we hired him, our tour guide had been hired by a group of Marine veterans who held a reunion in Hue to honor their war dead. "They were very sad; it was a very emotional gathering," he said. I thought about Bobby and Abe and wondered sadly how those Marine veterans felt about the war now.

"Do the people still harbor ill feelings against Americans?" I asked, seeking verification of Greg's briefing.

"No, we like Americans the best."

"Why?" I asked.

"Because the other foreigners who visit Vietnam come only to find ways to make money; when Americans come, many give money to orphanages and schools. We like Americans best because they have big hearts," he smiled.

The day we left Vietnam, we met Brad Wong and two women at the airport. Wong is a surgeon from Queen's Medical Center, Hawai'i's biggest and most modern hospital. One of the women was also a doctor, the other a nurse. Without fanfare or government funding, they had gone to Vietnam to train Vietnamese doctors and nurses. I was proud of them. *Yes*, I thought, *Americans have big hearts.*

Family Matters

In 1966 or '67, Mom called to say she was coming to L.A. to visit us. Over a five-year period, she had undergone a series of major surgeries, none of which seemed to have been fully successful. Her back surgery, in particular, left her with what seemed to be permanent residual pain. Prior to the surgery, she expressed a great deal of confidence in her doctor, Ralph Cloward, who gained a degree of fame for his development of a new surgical technique that allowed the doctor to perform back surgery from the patient's front side rather than from the back. Whatever the advantages of this technique, it did not help Mom's recovery. Increasingly, she relied on drugs to deal with the residual pain.

I sensed she was having problems the year we left Hawai'i, but I believed it was because of recurring pain. That she had become addicted to drugs never occurred to me. I thought of her pain as a physical problem that would heal in due time, when there would be no need for her to take drugs. I was dead wrong.

The day I picked her up at the airport, I was shocked at her appearance. She had lost a great deal of weight, as if she suffered from anorexia, and she wore heavy makeup to mask her ashen complexion. Still, I was glad to see her again.

As she unpacked, pulling out gifts for the kids, I noticed a large vial that appeared to contain hundreds of pills, Seconals or "reds," as they were called on the streets because of their dark red color.

"Mom, why so many pills?" I asked, pointing to the vial.

"I have a three months' supply … you know, Boy, I needed FBI clearance to travel with this many pills," she said. I looked on silently, thinking it was an indication of how long she intended to stay on the Mainland.

"Can you take me to see a doctor tomorrow?" she asked later.

"What for?" I asked.

"Oh, I want to have something checked," she said, flipping through the telephone directory.

The next day I took her to a doctor in nearby Inglewood. As she got back to the car after her visit with him, I asked, "Everything all right, Mom?"

"Oh, yes, I'm fine. Boy, can you take me to this pharmacy?" she asked, showing me an address she had written on a piece of paper.

"Okay, it's not far from here," I replied as I drove out of the parking lot. At the pharmacy, I waited in my car in the parking lot. Shortly, Mom emerged from the pharmacy and I drove her home. At home, she took out a vial of pills from the package. They were more Seconals. I began to worry.

"Mom, why do you need so many of those pills?"

"Oh, I'm going to visit your father in Las Vegas and stay there a while."

The next day, she asked me to take her to the doctor again. This time, however, she had a list with the names and addresses of three different doctors. By then I had figured out this was her way of getting more pills. I got very worried.

"Mom, you've got so many pills already, why don't you wait until you really need more before going to the doctor again?" I asked.

"No, I may not be able to get them when I go to Las Vegas to visit your father," she replied guardedly.

"Well, I can't miss class and take off from work anymore; besides, you have enough pills to last you at least three months. Why don't you wait a few days?" I replied, trying to find an excuse to keep her from getting more.

"All right, I'll wait until the weekend."

Later that day, I dropped Lorraine off at the restaurant and then went shopping for groceries. I got back home about an hour later. I was surprised to see the living room in disarray, sofa cushions on the floor, desk drawers open; I thought the place had been burglarized. Where were Mom and the kids?

Slowly, a head rose up from behind the sofa. It was Mom's.

"What happened here?" I asked.

"Oh, I thought I lost these," she sighed, a look of relief on her face; her speech was slurred, and she was unsteady on her feet as she held up the vial of reds with one trembling hand and tried to steady herself on the sofa with the other.

I had seen what the drugs—those little red pills—did to her physically. But this was the first time I saw how they affected her emotionally. It confirmed what I had been subconsciously denying for too long—Mom was a drug addict, hooked on a legally prescribed drug.

The next morning, as I was getting ready to leave for school, I saw Mom looking through the phonebook.

"Mom, what are you looking for?"

"I need a taxi."

"A taxi?"

"Yes, Boy, don't worry about me," she said impatiently. "You go to school. I'm going to see a doctor."

My heart sank. She was obsessed with getting more pills. There was no sense trying to talk her out of it. She had made up her mind and there was nothing I could do. I would have to miss class again, but it would have been irresponsible of me to let Mom, in her drugged state, take a taxi to the different doctors and pharmacies. She was "doctor shopping," a colloquial term for drug addicts who tried to get overlapping drug prescriptions by deceiving unwary doctors.

"Mom, forget the taxi, I'll drive you to the doctors," I replied, increasingly frustrated.

This was the '60s, when most people knew little about drugs. I was like everyone else. I knew nothing about how to help someone who had become addicted. I saw the drug scene as the world of hippies, wild college students who smoked marijuana and musicians who shot up heroin. This was the stereotype created by the media.

These were the days when the State and federal governments' answer to drug use was reactive and punitive. Drug users were tried and thrown in jail. In some cases, young people could get up to 20 years in jail just for getting caught smoking pot. But while the government struggled to deal with illegal drug use and public awareness about it grew, addiction to legal drugs, prescribed for patients by their doctors, was a hidden but growing crisis.

As I drove her from doctor to doctor, she disclosed something that had been bothering her.

"Boy, do you know that your brother is a homosexual?" she asked. I looked at her quizzically but said nothing. "I found out he was writing letters to a guy who lives in California. They met when your brother was stationed in Vietnam," she continued.

"You read his letters? Mom, that's private. You spied on your own son, for crying out loud! You had no right to do that," I blurted out, scolding her.

"I always wondered about your brother; I just had to find out," she said, sounding like a detective who had just broken open a case. I said nothing and continued driving. I wasn't surprised. I had never given Ken's sexual orientation much thought, but now Mom's words brought out what I had sensed deep in me about my kid brother for many years. As she continued talking about it, she got a little emotional and teary eyed.

Back then the social consequences, the potential ridicule and pain to self and family were too great and painful a burden for most gay people to come out. Families reacted to their children's gayness in different ways, mostly bad. It was not unusual to hear of a gay son or daughter being "disowned" by their family.

Among Asians in Hawai'i, the topic of homosexuality was an absolute taboo. Before coming to Los Angeles, I had never met or heard of a gay person who was Chinese, Japanese or Korean. Not that they did not exist, of course; they just weren't visible. They remained closeted. The times mandated it.

America, after all, was the home of the rugged individualists. John Wayne country. Homosexuals were seen by many as something less than normal people; they were to be pitied, ridiculed, disowned or ostracized. That kind of thinking was the norm in the '60s.

Once, when I was 13 years old, a group of my friends and I walked past a nightclub after we had seen a movie at the Hawaii Theater. A well-known female impersonator, whose stage name was Prince Kalima (not his real name), was setting up a marquee in the club's showcase window. His back was to us, so he did not see us standing there. Some of the guys started giggling; then someone tapped on the window and, as Prince Kalima turned around, he was surprised to see five 13-year-old boys, giggling and waving their limp wrists at him.

"Yoo-hoo ... hi, sweetie," someone teased.

"You fucking bastards," he shrieked as he rushed for the door. He was a big man, about 250 pounds. Still screaming obscenities at us, he charged out of the nightclub and chased us down the street. Laughing, we quickly outran him. And after putting a safe distance between us and him, we started teasing him again, leaving him standing in the middle of the street, screaming in a high-pitched voice at us. Looking back, it was not a proud moment in my life.

The irony of the times was that in the midst of the great Civil Rights Movement, an era that had the most significant impact on America's social and cultural fabric since the Great Depression, the overwhelming majority of the American people, of all races, of all social and economic classes, were bigots—when it came to homosexuals.

Few gays dared to come out publicly. In college, I recall that famous writers such as James Baldwin and Gore Vidal made no bones about their gayness. But their courage in doing so was exceptional. Most were like Liberace, the famous entertainer who history has revealed was gay but who threatened to sue any writer or columnist who suggested it.

Over the years, whenever I thought about Ken, I felt remorse and guilt thinking about all the times I teased him, calling him a sissy whenever we argued or fought about something. What a struggle it must have been for him as a kid growing up in a place like Kalihi. He always tried hard but never quite fit in when we played the kinds of roughhouse games boys play. The fact that I was just a kid then didn't assuage my feelings of guilt and remorse as I recalled the incident as an adult.

How will Dad take this? I wondered. Dad was a quiet, easygoing man but one of the things he prided himself on was his manhood, that he could handle himself. This was important to Filipino men. Dad would never brag and was reluctant to talk about himself.

Once, however, Mom told me about the time Dad and four of his Filipino friends got into a street fight with a group of local boys on Maunakea Street. It was a one-sided affair, and when the cops finally got there to break it up, Dad was the only one of the Filipino immigrants still standing. The first time I asked Dad to tell me the story, his eyes lit up.

"Dad, tell me about the time you and your friends got into a fight with the local boys on Maunakea Street," I asked.

"Oh, it was nothing, son," he replied.

"Come on, Daddy, Mom told me you were the only one left standing up," I teased him.

"Oh," he smiled, his one gold front tooth gleaming (he almost always began a story with "Oh"), "the local boys don't like Filipinos, so they like cause trouble; they call us bad names, so my friend Romeo, he answer them back. Then they want to fight and start punching us so we try to fight back," he told me.

"And what happened?" I asked.

"Oh, there was more of them and they bigger than us. Pretty soon, all my friends on the ground—they all knock out!" He laughed as if it was a big joke.

"What about you?" I asked, playing the straight man.

"Oh, I back up against the corner of the wall like this [demonstrating] so they have to get me one at a time; every time one come I punch and kick him," he said, showing a left-handed boxing stance.

"So the first one, I knock him down," he laughed again.

"No kidding? Was he a big guy?" I asked, still playing the straight man.

"Oh, yeah … he's a big Portagee guy, over 200 poun'." (Dad weighed about 135, soaking wet). "He try grab my shirt collar so I hit him with a straight left. He went down."

"Where did you hit him?"

"On the chin. You know, son, I can hit [hard, he meant] because I turn my hand—like this—I follow through," he said, demonstrating a straight left hand and turning motion, like the famous "anchor punch" Muhammad Ali used to knock out Sonny Liston.

"But I'm so lucky the policemen come and break up the fight and they take everybody to jail," he said with a big laugh.

I loved this story because Dad loved telling it. Throughout the years, especially in his final years when he was slipping into dementia, I would ask him to tell the story over and over again. And he always told it as if it was the first time. No one ever tired of hearing it because it made him happy. My father never bragged about anything, but when we asked, he was proud to share this memorable moment of manliness.

Dad, Ken and I never discussed Ken's gayness. We didn't know how. It was like the inane "Don't Ask, Don't Tell" policy the U.S. military follows today in dealing with gays among its ranks. And from 1967, when Mom found out, for as long as he lived—Dad died on January 1, 1994, the year I was elected governor—he never let anyone know that he knew. If Dad was disappointed or angry about Ken, he never showed it, never treated Ken any different. Dad loved Ken deeply—and that made the difference.

We were not a family that knew how to discuss problems. I never confided about any of my personal problems with either my father or mother. Neither did Ken. More than 35 years passed before Ken and I finally talked openly about his homosexuality. We were both in our 60s by then—both old enough to collect Social Security.

Not airing it out stifled our understanding of the issue. Not surprisingly, Ken suffered through bouts of depression and self-doubt over the years. He lived a quiet life, his social life limited mostly to our family and his gay friends who, like him, remained in the closet. After I got into political office in 1974, he began avoiding me as much as he could. I felt we were estranged, but I couldn't put my finger on the reason why. Later, he told me that he stayed away because he thought I was ashamed of him and he was afraid he might embarrass and hurt me politically if he was found out. His words broke my heart. Precious years—wasted in silence.

After a week with us, Mom left by Greyhound bus for Las Vegas. That day I got a telephone call from Ken, who was stationed at McGuire Air Force base in New Jersey. He told me Mom and Rudy had divorced. I was stunned. She had not said a word about it to me. Moreover, Ken said she did not have a place to stay in Hawai'i and was running low on money because she was unable to work; she was going to see Dad in Las Vegas to ask him for support.

"How was she when she left for Vegas?" he asked.

"Ken, she's been high on her medication—stoned—drugged—most of the time she's been here."

"I'm on my way to Hawai'i, and I'll be stationed there for my final two years. I'll stop in L.A. and take her with me," Ken replied.

A few days later, Uncle Paul, Dad's older brother with whom he was living in Las Vegas, telephoned me. "Ben-ha-min, your mama is very sick," he explained in thick pidgin. "She cannot stand up so good. And she wants to go to the doctor all the time. I'm scared something will happen to her," he said. "When she come to your house, you betta send her back Hawai'i quick."

The next day, Mom got back from Las Vegas looking worse than ever. She was only 46, but she looked a very old 60. She was so unsteady on her feet that the bus driver had to help her off the bus. Later, Dad described her behavior in Las Vegas as "like a crazy woman." The same day, Ken arrived in Los Angeles. He and Mom stayed over a few more days with us and then returned to Hawai'i.

When I took her and Ken to the airport, I felt relieved she was going back. *Everything will be better once she gets home*, I said to myself unconvincingly. I was the oldest son, and I felt guilty about not being able to do more. But I also felt angry that this was happening. I told Ken I would send money to help out.

"Ben, take care of Lorraine and the kids; I'll take Mom back home and see if we can get some help." My kid brother—mild mannered, soft spoken—was a better man than I. After all that Mom put him through, he was there for her when she needed help—even though she had not been there for him when she found out he was gay.

Mom was the toughest person I knew, but her addiction had reduced her to a sad shell of her former self. As the years passed, it became pretty clear that her addiction had consumed her—she could not control herself even if she wanted to. The only way she could have beaten her addiction was to have gone to jail or gotten professional help in a detoxification center. Of course she was not going to jail; her addiction was caused by legally prescribed drugs, and there were no detoxification centers in Hawai'i back then.

My three years of law school passed like a blur. Compared to my turmoil-filled first year at Loyola, my second year was mild—and I welcomed the mildness. That year, I studied hard and made the Dean's list. There was light at the end of the tunnel. For my final year, my main objective was to survive—to do whatever it took graduate. I coasted and began thinking seriously about whether I really wanted to return to Hawai'i. Mr. Harris had offered me a position as an associate attorney with the law firm. I could become a partner in three years. I could never thank him enough. But after thinking about it, I made up my mind. It was time for us to go home. (Years later, Mr. Harris was appointed as a Superior Court Judge; a fitting way to cap off a career for an excellent lawyer, a great boss and dear friend.)

I had received a good job offer from Frank Padgett, one of Hawai'i's top trial lawyers at the time. Padgett not only offered a substantially higher starting salary than the two other Hawai'i firms that offered me jobs; he also agreed to pay for all of our airfare and moving expenses, including the shipping of our German Shepherd, Blitz. With our savings down to a few hundred dollars, the offer was a gift, one I found hard to refuse.

I graduated from Loyola on a hot, sunny Saturday in June 1971. The graduation ceremony was long, and everyone was sweltering in the terrific heat. The law school graduates were scheduled to receive their diplomas last. Someone estimated it would be at least another hour before they got to us. Then the president of our class went from row to row and asked if we wanted to sit through the ceremony or get our real diplomas at a previously designated room. Almost en masse, the majority of my class stood up and left the ceremony to get our diplomas. Meanwhile, the dean of the law school was still sitting on stage thinking about the speech he was scheduled to give.

We behaved terribly—I cringe every time I think about today—but it was symptomatic of my generation of college students. For many, public service was high on our list of priorities, but we were also an anti-authoritarian bunch not impressed in the least with rituals and ceremony.

I longed to return to Hawai'i. But Lorraine, who had worked full time for eight years and borne the brunt of attending to our kids' needs at home and in school, had misgivings about going home. Materially, she had pointed out, there was so much more we could do for ourselves and our two kids if we stayed in Los Angeles. Moreover, as a lawyer with Richard Harris I would eventually earn enough for us to buy a home in a good neighborhood where the kids would attend good schools. These were all good reasons for us, as so many local people from Hawai'i had done, to make the Mainland our home. But she knew how badly I wanted to go home and deferred to me.

Eight and a half years on the Mainland made me realize how unique a place Hawai'i is. We had been treated well by our neighbors and friends, and I never experienced any kind of racial discrimination in Los Angeles. But I saw it happen to others daily. I was like an unnoticed locker room attendant. I heard white people talk about blacks and Chicanos—and blacks and Chicanos talk about white people or each other. I was disturbed by what I heard. Watts and the race riots, which followed in the urban cities, the bombings of black churches, the murder of white and black civil rights workers, the police shootings, were all symptoms of the deep chasm that divided the races—as the Kerner Report concluded—into two Americas, one white, one black.

Moreover, the Vietnam War had divided the country, inflicting deep wounds that would take a long time to heal. America was going through a period of turmoil, an introspective search for its national conscience. *Things will get worse before they get better*, I thought. Granted, Los Angeles provided better opportunities for material growth, but Hawai'i was the best place for Brandon and Janeen to grow up into caring and tolerant adults. Moreover, there were greater opportunities for me as a lawyer to serve the community I cared most about. Although Lorraine had deferred to me, I knew how much she had invested over the past eight years. My getting a law degree would not have been possible without her. She had mixed feelings about going home. As if to reassure her that life would be better in Hawai'i, I told her, "When we get home, I never want you to work again."

Living in Los Angeles for nearly nine years had changed me. I was returning with a law degree, of course, but more significantly, I had seen and experienced events which dramatically shaped my views on race, politics, government and religion.

After the graduation ceremony, we stayed overnight at a nearby hotel. The next day we boarded a flight for Hawai'i. Compared to the Boeing 707 we had taken in 1963, our United Airlines 747 (brand new, we were told) was a remarkable development in aircraft technology. In about five hours we would be back in Hawai'i. This time for good. ❖

CHAPTER THREE

Home Again

Changes

From my window on the 747, Oʻahu still appeared strikingly beautiful; the rugged Waiʻanae and verdant Koʻolau mountain ranges stood majestically amid the lush patchwork of Island colors surrounded by ocean blue. Nearly nine years had passed since we had left Oʻahu, and the island seemingly had not changed.

But as we descended, some changes became apparent: Oʻahu traffic congestion appeared worse than ever—like a mini-version of Los Angeles. A new highway, H-2, leading to Schofield Barracks, Wahiawā and the North Shore, had been completed.

I looked for signs of whether construction of H-3, Oʻahu's third freeway, on which I had worked as a draftsman for the State Highway Advanced Planning Department, had been started. It had not; lawsuits brought by well-funded environmentalists had forced the State to abandon the Moanalua Valley route and plan for an alternative through Halāwa Valley a few miles away.

For nearly a decade, Hawaiʻi's economy, fueled mainly by heavy Japanese investment, had grown at nearly double-digit rates at times while the rest of the nation lagged behind. By the '70s, more than half of the Japanese investment in the United States had found its way to Hawaiʻi's real estate developments, such as hotels, luxury condominiums, high-end homes and golf courses.

The growing economy created more jobs and wealth, but it also attracted immigrants and Mainland haoles seeking work or business opportunities. In nearly nine years, Hawaiʻi's population increased from about 633,000 in 1959 to 770,000 in 1970—an increase of 22 percent. New condominiums and housing subdivisions were popping up like nut grass. Housing costs were higher than ever. Joe Pao, one of Hawaiʻi's big local housing developers back then, predicted that one day there would be no sugar or pineapple grown on Oʻahu and that the vacant fields would be used for new housing subdivisions and real estate developments. Time would prove him prescient.

Indeed, tourism permanently displaced sugar and pineapple as the driver of Hawaiʻi's economy. Hawaiʻi's sugar plantations, which were the most productive in the world, still could not compete with subsidized foreign sugar. Over the next two decades these plantations shut down one by one, falling as if they were dominoes, throwing thousands of workers out of jobs throughout the state. The plantations transitioned some of their lands mostly into real estate developments where the profits were not only greater but virtually assured. Pineapple would follow in sugar's footsteps.

As the sugar plantations closed, the beauty of the huge expanses of green sugar cane fields would disappear as well, replaced by urban development or barren dirt. New hotels, the symbol of the new economy, emboldened the Waikīkī skyline, in some places blocking the once-clear vistas of world-famous Diamond Head and the ocean.

Politically, the Democratic Party was in full control, having won the Territorial House of Representatives in 1954 and, in 1962, the governorship, both houses of the State Legislature, and Hawai'i's three congressional seats. (Hawai'i's Democratic Party would earn the distinction of being the longest-lasting political machine in the nation.)

The idealism that drove the 1954 political revolution produced some of the most progressive social legislation in the nation, including the 1967 Hawai'i Land Reform Act, a controversial, landmark law intended to expand fee simple homeownership by breaking the grip of the handful of private estates on residential land, which in 1987 would be upheld by the United States Supreme Court. In 1970, Hawai'i became the first state to give women the right to have abortions. A year after I returned, in 1972, Hawai'i was the first state to ratify the proposed Equal Rights Amendment. And, in 1974, the passage of the Prepaid Health Care Act gave Hawai'i the distinction of being the only state to require employers to provide health insurance for their full-time employees.

The University of Hawai'i system, never a high priority with the Republicans, who usually sent their children to Mainland institutions, was seen by Democrats as the only hope for local children who could not afford to attend Mainland universities. The Democrats provided generous funding for UH, and it had grown significantly, achieving world-class status in subjects such as astronomy, ocean marine sciences, tropical agriculture and Asian studies. A two-year medical school had been established in 1965, and the old Honolulu Vocational School, where I took classes as an electrician apprentice in 1959, was replaced by Honolulu Community College, one of six new community colleges built throughout the state after 1963.

June 1971 was also marked by a number of significant events. Hawai'i's then-largest hotel, the $62 million, 1,900-room Sheraton Waikiki, opened on June 1. By 1974, Japanese multimillionaire Kenji Osano would own all of the Sheraton hotels, including its flagship, the legendary Royal Hawaiian Hotel. Osano became Hawai'i's largest individual hotel owner, with 20 percent of the rooms. Local people were ambivalent about Japanese investors like Osano. While some welcomed the creation of jobs and business profits, many others resented the fact that foreigners had become dominant players in Hawai'i's tourism industry.

On June 18, the Hawai'i Supreme Court set off a firestorm of protest when it appointed Matsuo Takabuki as a trustee to the Bishop Estate, a trust established by the beloved Princess Bernice Pauahi Bishop mainly for the benefit of Hawaiian children. Many Hawaiians, who already felt strongly that more Hawaiians should be appointed as trustees, were furious that a Japanese American had been appointed. Kawaiaha'o Church's Rev. Abraham Akaka protested emotionally, "We felt like strangers in our own homeland."

A week before I got home on June 20, Gov. John Burns had appointed Lt. Gov. George Ariyoshi to head the Kohala Task Force to help the hundreds of people thrown out of work when the 108-year-old sugar plantation was closed by its Big Five owner, Castle & Cooke, Inc. The Task Force was the first of many futile attempts by the State to revitalize the dying sugar industry and save the jobs of thousands of plantation workers.

These three events forebode major controversial political trends that would later confront me after I entered public office, but in June 1971 they were just casual curiosities, news and headlines. I was much too focused on my new job with Frank Padgett and preparing for the dreaded bar examination. Politics was just about the last thing on my mind.

Becoming a Lawyer

It is hard to overstate the anxiety that the mandatory bar exam provokes in law school graduates. In 1971, Hawai'i's bar exam was a five-day affair. The stakes were huge. One cannot practice law without passing the bar exam. Anecdotes of employers retracting job offers for failures abound. Worse was the social stigma attached to failure. Flunking it once usually evoked a "there but for the grace of God go I" empathy from colleagues; flunking it twice or more imposed a life sentence of gossip about the level of one's intelligence ("He was an affirmative action student ... how did he ever get into law school?").

One person, a man named Earl, earned unsolicited notoriety among lawyers. When I took the bar exam in 1971, he had already failed it more than a dozen times. A graduate of a well-respected law school, a former aide to a U.S. senator and a nice, soft-spoken man, outwardly he seemed unaffected by his failures. Yet he was a Nisei and a World War II veteran, and I could not help feeling that his failures must have eaten him up inside. He stood out among the other examinees, many of whom were 20 or more years younger. Sadly, he failed again in 1971. Finally, in 1980, he passed, I was told by a mutual friend who tutored him, on his 26th attempt. It was an incredible story of perseverance. Unfortunately, his many failures were like a scarlet letter branded on his forehead. Not surprisingly, no one hired him.

Small wonder then that every lawyer has stories in his or her trove of bar exam vignettes—some humorous, most not—ranging from some guy pissing or shitting in his pants during the exam or puking afterward, to stories of anxiety attacks, depression, nervous breakdowns, heavy drinking and drug use.

Padgett gave me two weeks off to study for the bar. Two weeks? I was horrified. Most law firms gave their new associates at least a full month to study for the exam. Some of the guys in my study group had taken off two months. Moreover, I was working long hours at the firm, often leaving work after 6 p.m., and like everyone else I worked at least a half-day on Saturday and would attend the bar review course at night. Two weeks? Was the man serious?

"Well, if you don't have it down after three years in law school, a three-month review won't help you. Two weeks should be plenty," he said, without a hint of empathy.

The five-day exam started at 8:30 each morning. Examinees were given five hours to write essay answers to five or six questions on designated subjects. Allocation of time for each question was left to the discretion of the examinee.

The first two days were uneventful. On the third day, however, everyone was talking about the guy who got up in the middle of the exam, announced, "I can't take this shit," and walked out. Just freaked out. Later, someone said that the guy was from Harvard. Harvard? *The* Harvard, arguably the best law school in the nation? Jesus.

"Yeah, the kid didn't study, he came here to surf and took the bar exam on the fly," someone said. "Probably one of those trust fund kids who doesn't have to work for a living," another speculated. As with most of the people taking the bar exam, failing the bar was absolutely not an option for me. I had to pass. Period. My anxiety ramped up a couple of notches. Foolishly, I tried to deal with it by studying harder, reviewing my notes into the wee hours of the morning.

On the fourth day I had had only about two hours sleep but my adrenalin was soaring. I felt confident. The test was on torts—one of my strongest subjects. I waded confidently into the questions. Finally, it was over. I felt good about my answers. But I could feel my energy draining; I needed sleep. Then, during the usual post-test discussion, I heard some of the guys in my study group discussing the question about the defective lawnmower. The central issue was what the law describes as "product liability."

Lawnmower? What defective lawnmower? Product liability? I couldn't remember. Then it hit me: Departing from my routine of taking each question in order, I had skipped that question, intending to return to it later. Unfortunately, I had spent so much time writing what I thought were brilliant answers to the other questions I had forgotten about it. No wonder I had so much time left. Arrogance, overconfidence—screwed by my hubris.

Shocked, I wallowed in self-recrimination and self-pity. Frantic, I started doing the math in my head. I needed a minimum of 84 on each of the five questions I had answered just to average 70, which was the minimum passing grade. *Possible*, I thought. But later, as I discussed the test with the guys in my study group, my heart sank. I had missed a couple of big issues on two questions. An 84 average? Unlikely.

The fifth day covered subjects such as real property, negotiable instruments and secured transactions, things that I found boring and had treated as such in law school. After all, I had no intention of becoming a corporate lawyer—wouldn't dream of it. I was going to be a trial lawyer like the lawyers on television—*The Defenders* or *The Storefront Lawyers*—fighting for the poor and the working class.

I told Lorraine about the missed question. She had been the family's bread-winner while I was in law school, and after I graduated I told her I never wanted her to work again. I had to pass the bar exam to make good on my promise. She deserved to know. Besides, I needed a shoulder to lean on.

"Just do your best tomorrow; I know you'll pass," she said with a slight smile, reassuring me, supportive as she always was. My mind was a blank. There would be no review of notes for me that night. Nothing. I was exhausted. I went straight to bed and fell into a deep sleep.

On the fifth day, I cringed at the thought that there would be questions on subjects such as "the rule against perpetuities" and "negotiable instruments," which I hated, never really understood and had barely passed at Loyola. The chances of my scoring well on such questions were about the same as my mastering the puzzle of the Rubik's Cube. At the end of the day, however, I felt I had done about as well as I could, but nowhere close to what I had hoped for.

Over the next six weeks, I could tell everyone in the firm knew how I had messed up. The word had gotten around. People were sympathetic. I didn't hear the usual office jokes and small talk. Most of the time I sat in self-imposed exile in my office with my door closed and buried myself in work. I cranked out legal documents, memoranda and whatever I was assigned to do. I wondered if Padgett would fire me if I flunked. I was just as worried at the thought of being the first from Loyola to flunk the Hawai'i Bar. That would be a first I could never live down. I even thought about calling my former boss, Richard Harris, and asking him whether his job offer was still open. But then he would know I had failed. *Suck it up, Cayetano, and face the music*, I scolded myself. It was a tough six weeks.

Finally, one afternoon I got a telephone call from Lorraine. The mailman had just delivered a letter from the Hawai'i Bar Association. Cringing, I asked her to open it and tell me the result.

"I already did," she said, pausing; then, her voice teasing, "didn't I tell you that I knew you would pass? I'm so proud of you." I let out a loud "Whoopee!" I felt like dancing a jig. It was like winning the football pool all over again. My secretary heard my shouts of joy through the office wall and chimed in her congratulations over the intercom. The long journey had ended. Finally, I was a lawyer.

The word soon got around. One by one the partners and associates dropped by my office to congratulate me. Padgett was the last. Popping his head into my office, he said, "Congratulations, Ben, I heard you did it the hard way." He was smiling.

Padgett and Wally

I can't imagine anyone who worked with Frank Padgett not being affected by the experience in some way. He was just about the most complicated person I have ever met. I didn't learn much about being a trial lawyer from him. Padgett did not teach; it seemed he expected his associates to learn how to become good trial lawyers by osmosis. But there was much to learn from and respect about his character.

Padgett was born in a small town in Indiana. He was a sophomore on scholarship at Harvard when Japan attacked Pearl Harbor on December 7, 1941. Like many of his classmates, he decided not to wait to be drafted. He left Harvard and joined the U.S. Air Force. He was 20 years old.

At 22, he was piloting a B-25 bomber on combat missions against the Japanese in the Pacific. On his final mission his bomber was hit by enemy anti-aircraft fire, forcing Padgett and his crew to bail out over Indochina (now Vietnam). All would survive the war, but Padgett and three of his crew were captured.

Tall and gangly, Padgett stood out among the prisoners. He was the captain of his bomber. Thus, he became a regular target for interrogation and the cruel torture that went with it. One day he was turned over to the Kempetai, the feared Japanese equivalent of the Gestapo. Padgett did not know it, but his luck had just changed for the better. He and the Japanese Kempetai officer who was assigned to interrogate him had something in common: They were both Ivy Leaguers. The Kempetai officer was a graduate of Columbia University and apparently looked back fondly upon his years in America. He also realized that Japan would lose the war.

"If they beat you, don't say anything, don't fight back. The war will soon be over and you will be back in your country within a year," he advised Padgett. "Once or twice a week I will call you in for questioning. I will invite a few of my friends and we can discuss other more interesting and important things besides this war." To help Padgett fight beriberi, a debilitating condition that afflicted many prisoners, the man sometimes gave him limes and peanuts.

Under the circumstances, they were hardly equals, but a bond of humanity had developed between the two former Ivy Leaguers. And while thousands of prisoners died of cruelty and disease in Japanese prison camps, the man's decency probably saved Padgett's life.

Six months before the war ended, however, Padgett was transferred to another prison camp. There he fell seriously ill with malaria. At the war's end, his

6-foot, 3-inch body weighed less than 100 pounds. He was so ill that he was rushed back to the States for hospitalization. Fate intervened again—one of the nurses treating Padgett was an attractive blonde named Sybil who later became his wife.

Using the GI Bill, Padgett returned to Harvard after the war. Harvard waived the requirement for a bachelor's degree and admitted him to its prestigious law school. Three years later, he graduated near the top of his class. Job offers came quickly, but he accepted one from Garner Anthony, who was a senior partner at a top Hawai'i law firm, and a former Territorial attorney general during World War II.

Typical of the times, the Anthony law firm was all haole and nearly all Republican. Padgett was the exception. Most Mainland haoles who came to Hawai'i to work and live were expected to become Republicans. The choice seemed simple: Hawai'i's Republicans controlled business, Territorial and County government, the Territorial Legislature and the governorship. Indeed, until Hawai'i became a state, haole Republican leaders like Walter Dillingham had more influence on Democratic presidents than local Democratic leaders. Becoming a Republican would open doors to opportunities in government and business that were not open to Democrats.

On the other hand, the Democratic Party was the party of locals, led mostly by Japanese Americans and labor unions. The unions were locked in a continuing power struggle with big business. It made good sense for Padgett to turn Republican. But he was cut from different cloth. For nearly a century his Indiana family had brooked no Republicans—they were diehard Democrats. For Padgett, Democratic values ran deep, too deep to change.

Seventeen years later, Padgett set up his own law firm. The former POW invited two Japanese-American lawyers, Asa Akinaka, a Stanford graduate, and Wendell Marumoto, the son of former Supreme Court Justice Masaji Marumoto, to join him. The two AJAs were graduates of Punahou, which meant they were very bright—in those days few Asians were admitted to the exclusive private school founded for the children of the haole elite. Padgett's two other partners were Hod Greely and Keith Steiner, both from longtime Hawai'i families. Padgett Greely Marumoto & Akinaka was Hawai'i's first haole-AJA law firm.

Prior to graduation, I had received job offers from two Hawai'i law firms. I had heard the stories—and was warned about how difficult it was to work for Padgett. But he impressed me during my interview. Besides the financial considerations he offered, Padgett was reputed to be one of Hawai'i's top trial lawyers. I wanted to work with and learn from the best.

Padgett was a tough taskmaster. He was often moody, quick to anger and given to moments of sulking, which sometimes caused me and others to wonder how much of it was due to his experience as a prisoner of war, but he was honest and fair. Socially, however, he could be a different person, friendly, warm, even fun to be around.

Even his adversaries acknowledged his brilliance as a trial lawyer, but his biggest weakness was his impatience—which bordered on contempt—for those who differed with him on legal matters. Rarely would he admit he was wrong on a legal point. Once he dismissed an error he made with a laugh, "Well, I can't fire myself, can I?"

His style was hardball all the way. If a case could not be settled, he gave no quarter to his foes and expected none from them. His take-no-prisoners style, however, created diehard enemies among some of the best defense lawyers in Hawai'i. His intransigence had its price.

Once, in a trial with Marty Anderson, himself a top lawyer and senior partner of one of Hawai'i's largest law firms, Anderson all but called Padgett a liar in front of the jury. Padgett, the story goes, erupted in anger, took off his coat and virtually leaped over a table to get at Anderson. Anderson, a Stanford graduate who had developed an intense dislike for Padgett, took off his coat and urged him on.

There were no blows exchanged, as by the time both had their coats off, they were restrained by their associates. It must have been great theater for the jury to see these two skilled and distinguished-looking lawyers go after each other like schoolboys. Their antics were clearly unprofessional, but the incident undoubtedly raised the esteem of both in the eyes of their young associates. While most laypeople may frown on this kind of behavior, trial lawyers thrive on it.

My first major assignment was a case in which Padgett was being sued personally. The lawsuit was instigated by an attorney named Ralph Corey, who was a stockholder tenant in The Kalia, one of the few cooperative housing projects in Hawai'i. Unlike condominium owners, who own their apartments in fee, cooperative buyers own shares of stock and are entitled to an apartment for each share.

The lawsuit alleged that Padgett, and the developers who controlled the initial board of directors, had committed fraud and breached their fiduciary duty as directors, unfairly allocating the common areas and diminishing the value of stockholder shares by financing the project through an intricate bond scheme designed by Padgett to reduce the taxes paid by the developers.

Padgett was livid. After all, he reasoned, one could argue whether the allocation of the common areas was fair, but the bond scheme had been approved by the Internal Revenue Service. So how could it be fraudulent? To make matters worse, the principal attorney representing Corey and the stockholders was Harold Wright, one of the senior partners in the Honolulu law firm Cades Schutte Fleming & Wright. Like Marty Anderson, Wright was an avowed enemy of Padgett. The feeling, of course, was mutual. What's more, Padgett suspected that Wright's enmity toward him was why Cades Schutte had taken the case in the first place, which angered him even more. His response was to call on his good friend Wallace Fujiyama to represent him.

Fujiyama, or Wally, as everyone called him, was already established as one of Hawai'i's great trial lawyers. He and Padgett admired one another. Once, when Padgett was told that someone had described him as the "haole Wally Fujiyama," he chuckled and retorted that Wally was the "Japanese Frank Padgett." A big ego can be a prerequisite to becoming a great trial lawyer.

Wally first heard of Padgett when one of Honolulu's newspapers ran a human interest story about how Padgett, the former POW, was representing a Japanese temple in a civil lawsuit. Coming at a time when the polarization between the haole and local communities was worse than ever, the story made a favorable impression on locals like Wally.

"You know, Ben, Frank suffered a lot in the war," he once told me. "If he was a lesser man, he would be like those other haoles and have nothing to do with local guys like us."

To Wally, Padgett was a "good haole," a mantle he bestowed as a high compliment for his haole friends, though haoles who did not know Wally would likely have found it patronizing. In Wally's mind, "good haoles" were those who "accepted and respected local people."

One good haole who understood Wally was his longtime law partner, James Duffy, an Irish American from Minnesota. Duffy, who came to Hawai'i to work for a haole law firm, was so new he did not even know how many islands made up the state. But he worked so well with locals that word got back to Wally that Duffy was a "good haole." One day Wally called Duffy for lunch, a friendship developed, and Duffy joined Wally's firm as its junior partner. Duffy, who now sits on the Hawai'i Supreme Court, expressed his feelings at Wally's funeral in 1994 in a heart-rending eulogy in which he described Wally as "My hero, my partner, my friend."

Like most Japanese Americans who were adults during the World War II years, Wally was deeply affected by the racial discrimination against AJAs. He was too young to join Nisei like Dan Inouye and Sparky Matsunaga in the famed 442nd Regiment and 100th Battalion, but he joined the Army as soon as he came of age and was stationed at Schofield. After an honorable discharge, he joined the Honolulu Police Department, where his fellow police officers began taking notice of his exploits.

Once, when Wally was a rookie cop, he stopped an Army officer who was driving erratically. When he asked the officer to step out of the car, the intoxicated man called him "a fucking Jap." Wally's reaction was a punch that broke the officer's jaw. No disciplinary action was taken against him. "The guy actually apologized after he sobered up," Wally explained, as if the apology excused his misbehavior.

In another incident that assured his celebrity status among his fellow police officers, Wally, then on the plainclothes Metro Squad, and his partner, Neil "Corky" Donahue, were called to break up a fight between two haole sailors at the Brown Derby Club in Chinatown. As Wally and Donahue tried to break up the fight, the two servicemen—spewing racial epithets against Wally (Donahue was a local haole)—turned on the two cops. Immediately, a dozen other sailors, all apparently more or less drunk, jumped into the fray. Using their fists, blackjacks, chairs, and anything else they could get their hands on, Wally and Donahue, according to prevailing folklore, knocked out all of the sailors. Unfortunately, they also managed to nearly destroy the inside of the club, and the irate owner filed a claim for the damages against the city.

At the prompting of his friend, Bill Richardson, who later became chief justice of the Hawai'i Supreme Court, Wally left the police force for law school. He never forgot his fellow cops and often would represent individual police officers for free on personal matters.

By the time he returned home after law school, Wally had built an impressive resume: He was an editor of the University of Cincinnati Law School Law Review; graduated first in his class and compiled a grade point average which, according to a speech given by the law school's dean in 1993, was never surpassed. He was also admitted to the esteemed Order of the Coif, a prestigious national honor society limited to the nation's top law students.

Today, this remarkable academic record would have brought generous offers from the nation's best law firms. Back then, however, things were different. When Wally returned home and applied for a job with a big all-haole law firm, he wasn't even granted an interview. Instead, the law firm hired someone from the Mainland. The haole elite was an insular bunch; they married each other, sent their children to the same schools, belonged to the same racially exclusive social clubs, controlled business and government, and dominated the Republican Party.

Nevertheless, a young, idealistic Wally joined the Republican Party, thinking he could "make a difference" in opening doors of opportunity to local people. On a personal level, Wally probably hoped that it would open doors for him. He wanted badly to become a tax lawyer and, of course, the big haole law firms had a monopoly on corporate tax work in Hawai'i. Wally made an impression and was selected as a delegate to the 1956 National Republican Convention. Later, he confided to me that he felt like "window dressing." Moderate Republicans were in the minority, and conservatives like the racist Walter Dillingham still ran the GOP. Wally's stint as a Republican was short. Republican conservatism conflicted with his social liberalism, most of his close friends were Democrats and, as he once joked, "most of the time I was one of the few who had black hair at those [Republican] meetings."

His rejection by the big haole law firm was the best thing that ever happened to him. The experience was one of those quirks of fate that changed his life. It lit a fire within him that sent him to the courtroom with a vengeance. Always superbly prepared, Wally took special delight in taking on Hawai'i's mostly haole establishment. He vindicated himself by either gaining their respect or inculcating fear in them.

Wally was actually fairly tall for a Japanese man, standing nearly 5 feet 10 inches, but he was overweight and flabby, and walked with a slight stoop, all of which made him look shorter. He wore expensive suits and ties to court but never wore them well, usually appearing somewhat disheveled. He always wore long-sleeved silk shirts, probably because his arms seemed disproportionately skinny compared to his torso. He had a craggy, slightly pockmarked facial complexion, but nevertheless he exuded a rugged charisma that made his presence felt in the courtroom. Women found him attractive. In trial, his biggest assets were his razor-sharp and innovative mind and his extraordinary ability to read people and to connect with a jury. Like most great trial lawyers, Wally was a superb storyteller. He could speak the King's English with the best of them or lapse into pidgin when it served his purpose.

"Ben, most haoles equate intelligence with how you speak. That's their culture," he once told me. "So many times they take local guys like us for cheap. In trial, there is nothing better than the other side underestimating you, especially before a local jury. That's an advantage for us; remember that." I never forgot it.

Probably the most repeated story about Wally among lawyers was the "stepladder case." In the 1960s, Sears, then known as Sears, Roebuck and Co., carried a stepladder that turned out to be defectively designed. People were injured wherever the ladders were sold. Today, Sears would probably issue a notice of recall of the stepladders. Back then, however, recalls were unknown (they were instituted years later when the growing number of huge jury verdicts for injuries or deaths caused by defective products and the adverse publicity made recalls economically feasible). Then, though, it was cheaper for big corporations like Sears to fight such lawsuits in court. In the stepladder case, there were so many suits that Sears hired top-notch law firms that traveled from state to state to defend the company in court. Wally's lawsuit against Sears would be the first defective stepladder case against Sears in Hawai'i.

Sears sent a defense attorney from San Jose, California, to defend the case. Settlement negotiations failed and the case was tried. The highlight came at the close of the trial. As Wally was making his final argument to the jury, the Mainland lawyer, apparently concerned with how the trial was going, rose and objected, stating that he was having "difficulty understanding what Mr. Fujiyama is saying." It was a mistake.

Ever quick on his feet, Wally "humbly" apologized to the jury for "not being able to speak as well as our good friend from the Mainland." To which a juror quipped in pidgin, "Dat's awright, bruddah! We understan' yu!" The jury returned one of the highest verdicts of its kind for Wally's client. His Mainland adversary, an outstanding defense attorney named Bob Propelka, had watched with growing admiration how Wally "home-towned" him before the local jury. Thereafter, he gave Wally the ultimate accolade a trial lawyer could give an adversary—they became lifelong friends.

The Cades law firm was one of the oldest and biggest in Hawai'i. Harold Wright assigned attorneys Singleton Cagle and Tom Huber to handle the Kalia case. Cagle, originally from Kentucky, was nicknamed the "Kentucky Colonel" by the younger associates in his firm. He was a good choice to replace Wright against Wally. Well-respected, genteel, likeable, Cagle was a highly skilled trial lawyer, as was his soft-spoken associate, Huber. The jury would find it hard not to like these two. They would be tough adversaries.

I was one of three associates working on the case; the other two were from Wally's law firm. I was the only one who had no trial experience. My task was to do research and conduct discovery. Basically, the discovery process is intended to allow each side to "discover"—by oral depositions (sworn testimony) and written interrogatories—the facts that are relevant to the other's case. Wally instructed me to take the depositions of the plaintiffs. I assumed he meant just Ralph Corey and the Board of Directors. No, he corrected me; he meant deposing every one of the more than 300 Kalia stockholders. As a matter of standard practice, the oral deposition of a plaintiff is not taken until the plaintiff has answered the written interrogatories. This meant I had to draft and serve written interrogatories on each one of the 300-plus plaintiffs! I thought deposing all of the stockholders was a waste of time and money. But, as I quickly learned, much of the case was more about Padgett's pride than anything else.

Once, I wrote a memorandum on the case citing a string of New York Supreme Court rulings on "co-op" cases, which favored the plaintiff stockholders. The "cooperative" concept was fairly new, and the New York courts were far ahead of their counterparts in other states in ruling on the issue. Padgett and I were on Maui at the time. He read my memorandum, blew up in anger, sulked and did not say a word to me the rest of the day.

The next morning, Asa Akinaka dropped by my office. "I heard the old man got angry with you," he said, smiling.

"Yeah, he was something else," I replied.

"Yes, he came back to the office and said he was worried about your 'defeatist attitude,'" Akinaka said, still smiling.

"Defeatist attitude? What's the matter with the guy? If he thought my memo was full of shit, it would have been nice if he told me why. But for him to go off sulking is beyond me," I replied defensively, irritated by the accusation.

"Well, Mr. Ca-ye-tano," Akinaka said, slowly measuring the pronunciation of my surname, "you have to understand this man you are working for. He may have white skin, but inside this haole is a samurai. In another life he was probably Japanese. And he is taking this lawsuit very personally. You have to understand that."

I nodded in agreement as Akinaka got up to leave.

"Besides, his bark is worse than his bite," he continued, still smiling. "If he didn't like you or didn't think that you had the potential to become a good lawyer we wouldn't be having this discussion, you know what I mean?"

So we would wage the kind of legal war that the big law firms always used to defend insurance companies, corporations and well-heeled clients against ordinary people who had the temerity to sue them: besiege the opponents with interrogatories and depositions, subpoena records, file motions. The idea was to wear them down, make the lawsuits very expensive, encourage settlements and discourage potential lawsuits.

About a month before the trial, we began holding settlement conferences with Cagle and Huber. Wally had one rule for the upcoming settlement conferences: "I'll do all the talking. You guys just listen and watch how they react. After each conference I'll tell you what happened," he said.

The conferences were very cordial. Singleton Cagle was impressive, always impeccably dressed. When he wore a bow tie, he seemed like a character out of a movie or novel about the South.

While everyone addressed Cagle as "Sing," I always called him "Mr. Cagle." Out of respect. I liked the guy. He reminded me of Richard Harris, whom I had worked for as a law clerk in Los Angeles. Wally liked and respected Cagle, too. At the settlement conferences, there were no raised voices. The discussion seemed so civil one could easily have been bored. Not me, of course—I was eating up every word they were saying.

After one important conference, as we were walking back to his office, Wally asked me and the other associates, "You guys notice anything unusual about Cagle today?"

Silence. It was as if the three of us were on a quiz show. We exchanged glances. No one knew the answer.

"What happened when I filled his cup with coffee?" Wally asked, eyebrows raised, an exasperated look on his face.

"Uh ... his hand was trembling a little," I said, pleased with myself for picking up Wally's cue.

"That's right," Wally replied, with an annoyed look at my two fellow chastened associates, "and I think he is very worried about taking this case to trial."

To Wally, details, no matter how seemingly small, could make the difference in court. If Wally represented a client who was injured in an automobile accident at 3 in the morning, his associates knew that one day they would have to go with Wally to visit the scene at the exact hour the accident happened.

Wally often invited me into his private office to "talk story." I enjoyed it and looked forward to it. Occasionally, Jimmy Duffy would join us, but more often than not it was just Wally and me. The first thing he would do was kick off his shoes and walk around in his socks. Then he'd open the overhead cabinet behind his desk where he stored dozens of vials of prescribed drugs for his many ailments and take a couple of pills. Then he would start telling his stories. Sometimes he would talk about his past cases, describing the actions of witnesses, the judges, opposing lawyers and his trial strategy. He had a great sense of humor and would often regale me with funny and sometimes bawdy stories from the courtroom or the political arena. It was his way of teaching; I learned a lot by just listening. On a personal level, I knew we had hit it off.

"Ben, we're going to settle this case. We can win it, but it's costing everyone so much money," he said later.

"What about Frank?" I asked, mindful about Padgett's strong feelings on the case.

"Frank can be one stubborn haole," Wally replied, lapsing into pidgin. "But with Frank, his clients always come first. Those four developers, especially Kep Aluli [he was a full-blooded Hawaiian with roots in ancient Hawaiian royalty] and Ogami, are not only his clients, they're his good friends. And Frank is loyal to his friends. So if I can negotiate a settlement that is good for them, Frank will go along."

"And you know the other reason I want to settle this case?" he asked.

I just looked at him as I tried to think of some legal point I had missed.

"Ben, after all of the depositions you took, how would you describe the people who live at The Kalia?" he asked.

"Retirees: white-collar workers, teachers, former federal and State workers," I replied.

"That's right. They're not rich people. And many are local. Their apartments are life investments. The longer this case goes on, the more it's gonna cost every stockholder. No sense penalize everyone because their board of directors made the big mistake of listening to Ralph Corey. Right? Ben ... fight hard to win for your clients, but if you win, never kick the other side when they are down. That's not our style."

The Kalia case was settled on the day the trial was to begin—literally on the courthouse steps. The settlement was favorable for Padgett and the four developers. According to Tom Huber, Harold Wright was very angry when he learned about it.

As the years passed, Wally's influence in law, business and politics grew immensely; a local magazine designated him as one of Hawai'i's "powerbrokers." Our friendship grew as well. Wally was a strong supporter in all of my political campaigns. He died in 1994 before I became governor. I was given the privilege of speaking at his funeral services.

By mid-1973, I decided it was time for me to move on. I wanted to be on my own and not have to answer to anyone. I left with high regard for Padgett. The tough, moody, hardnosed trial lawyer had a soft, compassionate side to him that only a few saw. A few years later, Akinaka left, and around 1976, the law firm broke up and Padgett started a small practice with his son-in-law, Rick Rost.

In 1980, Gov. George Ariyoshi appointed Padgett to the Intermediate Court of Appeals and in 1982 to the State Supreme Court. Unknown to Padgett, his loyal former partner, Asa Akinaka, who sat on the Bar Association's Board of Directors, had lobbied hard for Padgett's appointment. I was a member of the State Senate by then, and I urged my fellow senators to confirm his appointment.

Loyalty was an integral part of Padgett's character. When I ran for governor in 1994, Padgett, who left the Supreme Court in 1992, appeared in one of my campaign television spots—a role totally out of character for him. Joe Napolitan, my political consultant, was elated over Padgett's endorsement. "Ben, our poll shows you are getting your ass kicked among white voters. Do you have any more white supporters like Padgett?" he said, only half joking. (At the time, I was running a poor third, more than 30 points behind the leader, GOP Congresswoman Pat Saiki; Mayor Frank Fasi was in second place.)

The Guardian

On Oct. 26, 1973, Samantha, our youngest child, was born. Brandon and Janeen were still in high school; I had only a handful of clients and no secretary, and I was sharing office space with two other struggling young attorneys, Simeon Acoba and Dennis Potts.

I had saved enough money to carry my law office for about six months. Beyond that I would have to borrow money or close the office if I did not generate enough income. I was worried about how my law practice would fare, but I felt a deep satisfaction that I would not have to answer to anyone else, that the success or failure of my law practice was solely in my hands.

Eventually, the cases began dribbling in. Small stuff: divorces, adoptions, wills and traffic cases. I also asked for and got court appointments to serve as guardian ad litem for troubled children—incest victims, abused children, runaways and children in foster homes. Later, I got court appointments to defend people charged with crimes.

These were the kinds of cases that the big firms almost never took. They could not afford to. For a young sole practitioner like me, however, the small fees the cases brought would help pay the rent for my small law office. More importantly, I would discover, they taught me invaluable lessons about people who were in need and in trouble. Many of the cases revealed the dark side of society; a side not normally visible, or spoken about, even in Kalihi. The most troubling were those that exposed the terrible crimes inflicted by adults on those least able to protect themselves—our children.

In 1976, I was appointed as guardian ad litem for a pretty 10-year-old hapa (Japanese-haole) girl. Ramona (not her real name) was born out of wedlock, the offspring of a haole father and a Japanese mother. Abandoned by her father, Ramona was raised by her mother, a rail-thin barmaid in her 40s who used heavy makeup to mask her plain looks. Father gone, mother estranged from her family, which saw her illegitimate child and lifestyle as a disgrace, Ramona and her mother were on their own.

When Ramona was about 10, her mother began leaving her home alone with her new boyfriend while she worked at night, often not returning home until after the bar closed at 2 a.m. It wasn't long before the boyfriend started sexually molesting Ramona—an ordeal that continued for more than a year. It was only after the boyfriend left Hawai'i to work on a construction project on Johnston Island that Ramona mustered the nerve to tell one of her teachers that she had been abused. The school authorities quickly notified the State social services agency and the police. The Family Court assumed jurisdiction over Ramona and appointed me to represent her in the formal legal proceedings that would determine her future.

I first met Ramona when a State social worker brought her to my law office. As the social worker narrated the sordid and tragic story to me, Ramona sat quietly in the reception room, her hands folded on her lap, staring at the floor.

"I've been doing this for more than 20 years," the social worker, a local Chinese woman in her late 40s, said softly, "but I never get used to it. The kinds of terrible things these kids go through just break my heart. And what's really tragic is that the kids often feel guilty and blame themselves," she continued sadly.

Later, I explained to Ramona who I was, what a lawyer did, and that I was appointed to represent her as the court tried to figure out how to help her. Ramona sat passively, still staring at the floor, hands folded on her lap. Her two-year ordeal had hardened her; she had heard a lot from many people who had told her they were trying to help her.

Finally, I said softly, "Ramona, my job is to protect you. I promise that man will never hurt you again. And I will ask the police to arrest him and put him in jail." Her upper lip tightened and quivered as she struggled not to cry. Finally, her eyes welled up—first, just enough to allow a solitary tear to flow down the side of her face, and then the dam broke and the tears came as she sobbed silently, her shoulders shaking.

As she gently ran her hand through Ramona's hair, the misty-eyed social worker looked up at me and said, "See what I mean? You never get used to it."

Anger swept through me as I imagined what I would do to the boyfriend if Ramona were my daughter.

"I want to press criminal charges against the mother's boyfriend," I said to the social worker. "He has to pay for what he did to her."

"We don't think pressing criminal charges is in Ramona's best interests, "she replied.

"Why not?" I asked incredulously.

"Our psychiatrist examined her and he thinks Ramona is right on the edge emotionally. A public trial may cause her greater emotional damage than she already has suffered. And we are very concerned about Ramona's mother. She feels enormous guilt and is extremely depressed."

"Don't you think if the guy who did this to Ramona is not punished she will have a tougher time healing?" I asked.

"Our experience is that in cases like this, the kids never heal. They cope. We work with them to help them cope, to learn how to live with it, to move on. The scars will always be there," she said somberly.

"When Ramona was born out of wedlock, the mother's family disowned her mother and avoided contact with Ramona. The mother's family is very Japanese. They feel great shame that Ramona is an illegitimate child. And the fact that the father is not Japanese made it worse," she continued.

"Does the family know what happened?" I asked.

"We try to keep these cases very confidential. No one in the family knows anything. But if the man is prosecuted, it will become public," she said. "You know, Ramona and her mother only have each other—no one else. And both are right on the edge. You're her guardian, but I think you really should discuss this with the psychiatrist before you go further," she concluded.

Like most lawyers I had developed an inbred skepticism about psychiatrists. Psychiatry is more art than science. And I had been a lawyer long enough to know that if one looked hard enough, lawyers could almost always find and hire a psychiatrist to testify favorably for their case.

But Ramona's psychiatrist struck me as highly credible and knowledgeable. After a long and exhaustive discussion with him, I was convinced he was right: Ramona could suffer greater emotional damage if she had to go through a public trial. In my gut I felt anguish and frustration. I had promised Ramona that the boyfriend would be punished, but I had spoken too soon, too impulsively. As a lawyer, I knew it would not take much to prosecute the mother's boyfriend for at least statutory rape, a Class C felony that carried a mandatory sentence at the time. But my duty was to do what was in the best interests of my client. I decided against seeking prosecution. The mother's boyfriend had committed a terrible crime with impunity.

The best I could do was to write him a letter: "If you ever set foot in Hawai'i again … I will have you prosecuted for raping a minor. Govern yourself accordingly," I wrote. I got no satisfaction from my threat. It was like the dozens of demand letters I wrote to people who owed my clients money. In those cases, at least I could follow up by suing them. In Ramona's case, there was little I could do if the boyfriend disregarded my threat.

Later, when Ramona asked me whether "the man is going to court," I told her the police could not get him because he was never coming back to Hawai'i. It was a white lie, albeit one which was justified under the circumstances.

By 1980, Ramona's case was closed and I lost touch with her. In 1986, I was elected lieutenant governor and was required by law to give up my law practice. A few years later, I was jogging at Ala Moana Park, when I heard someone call out my name. "Mr. Cayetano, Mr. Cayetano! It's me, Ramona! Remember me?" she said, smiling and waving her arms.

I hadn't seen her in more than five years. I was a bit taken aback by her appearance. She had grown up, of course, but she looked worn out, appearing much older than she really was. Her hair was cut short—a "butch" was how it would be described in street talk. She was dressed in blue jeans, a denim jacket and boots. She looked like the moll of a motorcycle gang leader. Her male companion, who eyed me warily, seemed much older. As she extended her hand to shake mine, I noticed the tattoo of a cross between the forefinger and thumb of her hand. The years had hardened her, but she greeted me with a warm smile and a hug. Inside there was still some of that pretty 10-year-old girl I had met many years ago.

I smiled, trying to mask my first impression. We exchanged greetings and engaged in small talk for a few minutes. I found out she had quit high school; she was single, unemployed and "just hanging out." I saw my jogging companions waiting for me up ahead. "Ramona, I no longer practice law, but if I can help you, call me. Take care of yourself, okay?" I said as I started to jog away.

Years later, during my first term as governor, Ramona called my office. I returned her call. She had married, then divorced, and now was struggling to support her two children. She was back living with her mother, who was still working but no longer as a barmaid. They had gotten closer. The kids were their common bond.

"My kids are the most important thing in my life. I just want them to have a better life than I did," she said.

"Do you get help from their father?" I asked.

"Yeah, he doesn't make a lot of money, but he usually pays the child support on time. He's good about that. The problem is that it takes the CSEA so long to pay me. It's been really hard on all of us. When I call them they give me all kinds of excuses. Can you help us?" she asked.

The CSEA (Child Support Enforcement Agency) is a federal-State agency established by Congress to collect child support from absent parents. The intent was to assure parental financial support for children and to reduce the number of children receiving State or federal assistance. The ideal, however, did not match up with reality. CSEAs were not efficient operations, a consequence of the complexity of the task, inadequate funding and State government bureaucracy. Hawai'i's CSEA, plagued by especially bad funding deficits and inadequate staffing, was one of the worst in the nation. I did not want to get her hopes too high, and so I explained how we were trying to fix the problems with the CSEA. I would see what we could do to help her. We spoke for a more few minutes and then she concluded by warmly thanking me "for everything." It was the last time I heard from her.

There was no happy ending to Ramona's case. The failure of her marriage left me speculating whether she had developed a distrust for men, as her psychiatrist advised she would years ago. I wondered whether she would ever marry again or have a meaningful relationship with any male.

The future did not look bright. She was already in her 30s, and her job skills were minimal. She was having a tough time finding a job that paid enough to provide the basic needs for her two kids. However, she was getting financial support from her mother and the State. She was struggling, and I urged her to take advantage of the State program for mothers with dependent children that would allow her to go back to school. But she had been through so much that I worried that she would be overwhelmed and just give up one day.

But there was a sliver of hope. There was no hint of self-pity in Ramona. When she called me, she politely asked for help rather than demanding it. And the focus of her concern was always her kids. "Thanks for everything," she had said in parting. It was difficult to feel deserving of any thanks in a case like this. But her words suggested there remained a generosity of spirit found only in persons who still have hope. Life would be a struggle, but it seemed she had learned to cope, to move on and that was the best one could hope for under the circumstances.

Not all of the cases turned out badly. Once I was appointed as guardian of three haole children whose mother, hopelessly addicted to drugs, was deemed unfit to have custody of the children. Their father was dutifully sending monthly child support, but he refused to take custody of them. The court had no choice but to place the kids in a foster home.

The foster parents were Filipino immigrants in their mid-60s; their home was in Waipahu where the population was overwhelmingly Filipino. I didn't think this was a good placement. I put in a telephone call to the social worker.

"Placing three blond, blue-eyed haole kids with immigrant Filipino foster parents in Waipahu is like placing me with black foster parents in Harlem," I said to her. "Can't we do better?"

"Well, there weren't many choices. Most of the people who are willing to become foster parents come from poor or working-class families. Many of them do it to supplement their incomes. Filipinos, Hawaiians, part-Hawaiians; we have very few haoles or Japanese or Chinese foster parents," she replied.

"Why won't the father take custody of his kids?" I asked.

"I've talked to him many times. I suggest you call him and find out for yourself," she replied.

The father was an employee of an overseas airline. He refused to meet with me so I spoke to him by telephone. It was not a pleasant conversation.

"Sir, it's not in the best interest of your three children that they live with foster parents in Waipahu. They'll be better off living with you," I said politely.

"I'm sorry, it's not possible," he replied.

"Not possible? Why not?" I asked.

"It's just not."

"But these are your children, your own flesh and blood."

"It won't be easy, but I can increase the child support I pay monthly," he said, trying to evade my question.

"Sir, your kids need you more than they need more child support money," I replied, trying to prick his conscience.

"I'm sorry, it's just impossible."

"Listen, your boys will be the only haoles in their schools. They'll be getting their asses kicked daily. Do you understand what I'm saying?" I scolded, beginning to lose my cool.

"I'm sorry, it's just impossible," he repeated.

"Tell me, my friend, why in hell do you have kids if you don't want to take care of them?" I asked angrily.

The oldest child was Lawrence, a scrawny, nerdy-looking 15-year-old. He would have a key role in how his 11-year-old brother, Timmy, and 10-year-old sister, Judy, fared in this foster home. I met with Lawrence privately in my office.

"Lawrence, do you know why your father doesn't want to take custody of you and your brother and sister?"

"He can't take pressure. He's kind of weak," he said.

"How do you feel about it?" I asked.

"I was real hurt at first but I've kind of gotten over it."

"What about your brother and sister?" I asked.

"Timmy and Judy are taking it harder. They don't understand why he doesn't want us. Anyway, he was never real close to us like Mom was. He was gone a lot because of his job."

"Lawrence, you're the only one left. There is no else in your family who can help Timmy and Judy. So you have to help them. Teach them how to keep their rooms clean and brush their teeth, and help them with their homework. They look up to you, so you got to be there for them, okay?" I asked.

"Yes, sir, I know that."

"How do you feel about living with Mr. and Mrs. Garcia in Waipahu?" I asked, fishing for how he felt about living in Waipahu.

"It's okay, they are nice people. They've treated us pretty good."

"Have you had any trouble in school or in the neighborhood?"

"No, sir, not yet. I try to be friendly to everyone; otherwise I just mind my own business."

"How about Timmy and Judy?" I asked.

"Judy's a little shy so she pretty much sticks to herself. Timmy's made a few friends."

"Okay, now listen good. Don't give the tough guys in school any reason to try you out, you understand? Once they think you are some kind of uppity haole, they will make life miserable for you. You know what I'm getting at?"

"Yes, sir."

"Now, if anyone tries to make trouble, you just walk away. If that doesn't work, go to the principal or your teacher and you call me. But no matter what happens, don't show anyone that you are afraid, okay?"

"We'll be okay, sir," he said softly.

I was impressed with the kid. He was very smart and possessed a maturity beyond his years. Maybe he could fill the void his father had left.

Later I met with the Garcias at their home in Waipahu. They had migrated to Hawai'i from the Philippines nearly 30 years before. Their three sons were all adults; two were in the military, and the youngest was attending a college on the Mainland. The home was small but neat. Lawrence and Timmy shared one room; Judy had her own.

"How are the kids doing?" I asked Mr. Garcia.

"Oh, Ah-torney Cayetano, dey are doing good," he replied, addressing me by my title as a matter of courtesy, like most Filipino immigrants.

"Do you prepare Filipino food for them?" I asked, smiling at Mrs. Garcia.

"Oh, no, Ah-torney, dey not used to Pilipino pood. So I make American pood—like de hamburger an de hot dog an sometime we go buy de pizza an de spaghetti," she said, her broken English laced with a strong Filipino accent.

"Ah-torney, we do our best to make dem happy because we peel so much peeti for dem. De mother sick, de father he run away," Mr. Garcia cut in, shaking his head sadly.

"But sumtime, I see Judy—she cry by herself in her room; she is so quiet, she seem sad all de time, so I try compert her, I take her shopping, I teach her how to wash clothes. I tell her when her mother gets well, they will all see her again," Mrs. Garcia added.

As he spoke, I thought: These three blond, blue-eyed kids, who looked like poster children for a Wisconsin cheese company, would be raised, at least for part of their lives, by a poorly educated, immigrant Filipino couple of modest means, who spoke pidgin and had little else to offer—except something money could not buy—a lot of compassion and caring. Perhaps things would work out better than I feared.

Once the court proceedings were over, my role as guardian was eventually terminated. The social worker, however, kept me posted on the kids' progress. One day, a few years later, she called me at my law office. She sounded elated.

"I have good news. I just want you to know that Lawrence will be graduating from Waipahu High. His teachers tell me that he is popular with his classmates and he is in the top 10 percent of his class," she said.

"Great! What about Timmy and Judy?" I asked.

"After Lawrence graduates, Timmy and Judy may be going back to Wisconsin to live with their grandparents. And their mother is getting better, so they may be able to visit her and perhaps live with her again. It took a long time for us to get all of this done, but now things are looking up for them," she replied.

"And Lawrence?"

"He's going to join the Air Force, which has a program that will pay for his college education."

A few years later, I got a telephone call from Lawrence. He was in the Air Force; he told me he was doing well and training to be a journalist. He spoke warmly about the Garcias, stressing that he kept in touch with them. Timmy and Judy were doing fine. He thanked me warmly. I told him I was very proud of him.

I called the Garcias to congratulate them. "Oh, Ah-torney Cayetano, we so happy for dem! We so proud of Lawrence, he help Timmy and Judy so much. We lob dem. We will miss dem so much," Mrs. Garcia said, her voice cracking with emotion.

A happy ending; but it was an unusual case. But for the fact that the kids and the foster parents were of different races, it was a good match-up. And it made a big difference that despite all the heartache the kids went through with their parents, they were emotionally stable.

Most cases, however, are far more complicated and frustrating. Many foster children suffer from severe emotional troubles that cause them to become runaways or discipline problems. Foster parents tend to be laypeople who, notwithstanding the State's attempts to train them, are often not well qualified to deal with these problem children. Consequently, many foster parents quit the program within a year—as many as 70 percent, according to one national survey. There is a critical and growing shortage of qualified foster parents, not only in Hawai'i but throughout the nation, which may one day cripple this highly important program.

Incest and sexual molestation cases afflict children from every social class. But the ones that surface tend to involve the children of working-class people. As one psychologist explained to me, "The rich and upper-middle class have the capability to pay hush money [for out-of-court settlements] or to hire professionals like me to help the victims. The poor and working class have no real choice but to get help from the State."

Government exists for many purposes, but one of the most important is to help those who are least able to help themselves. Unfortunately, it is easy for politicians to be distracted, especially the young ones who have little life experience and who are too often wooed by powerful special interests hoping to influence them. There are some things that cannot be taught fully in the classroom without some measure of personal experience; understanding what it's like to be poor or a foster child or a victim of sexual abuse are among them.

101

The lessons learned from personal experience tend to stick. For a few years at least, I was part of the life struggles of Ramona, Lawrence and others like them. What I learned would stay with me forever.

The Criminal Justice System

Criminal defense law came naturally to me. Growing up in Kalihi, I knew that the kids who grew up there were far more likely to get in trouble with the law than kids from better neighborhoods. I could no more prosecute kids like them than I could squeal to the cops on my friends when I was a kid.

After only a few years in Los Angeles, I had become convinced that there was more than a grain of truth to accusations by blacks and Chicanos that the Los Angeles Police Department (LAPD) used a double standard when it came to the treatment of minorities. Coming from Hawai'i where the worst one could expect from local cops would be a beating, I was shocked and outraged that hardly a month went by without the LAPD cops shooting and killing an unarmed black or Chicano over a trivial incident. The coroner's inquests that followed the shootings seemed pro forma—without fail absolving the incident as "justifiable homicide." LAPD Chief Bill Parker's inflammatory description of blacks during the 1965 Watts Riot as "monkeys in a zoo" summed up the prevailing attitude in the LAPD.

Any doubts I had about fair law enforcement in Los Angeles were erased by the news coverage of the Civil Rights Movement. The incredible television news coverage exposed how widespread it was that local officials, at the State and County level, used the authority of the law to mistreat blacks and their supporters.

Coming from Hawai'i where the black and Chicano populations were infinitesimal, I knew little about their history. College changed that. It unveiled for me the shameful history of the oppression of black Americans: slavery, Jim Crow laws, the lynching of thousands of black men—at times in carnival-like atmospheres—and the misconduct and, often, complicity of local police in crimes against blacks.

American history textbooks uniformly provide examples of great American presidents who, succumbing to the widespread fears of the majority or their own personal biases, made decisions that violated the rights of Americans because of their skin color, religion or political beliefs. Among them were such distinguished presidents as Abraham Lincoln and Franklin D. Roosevelt.

Once, after writing a paper on Andrew Jackson at UCLA, I was struck not by the achievements for which historians rated him a great president, but by his defiance of Chief Justice John Marshall and the U.S. Supreme Court in his relentless pursuit of his Indian relocation policy, which led eventually to the deaths of thousands of Cherokee Indians on the infamous Trail of Tears. The "common man's president," the former slave owner, had turned imperious when it suited his purpose. It was not his finest hour.

"We are a nation of laws, not men." Those high-sounding words, repeated by my teachers from elementary to high school, took on a new meaning for me: Our laws are only as good as the men (and women) who are given the responsibility of carrying them out. There was no way I could become a prosecutor. Others could have that responsibility. I wanted to be on the side that checked our government, the side that would fight to assure that the rights guaranteed under the U.S. Constitution meant more than eloquent words on paper.

A few months after I started my own law practice, I received my first court appointment in a criminal case. It would be my first jury trial, but not quite the kind of high-minded, inspirational case for which I had hoped.

My client was a Hawaiian in his 20s. His nickname was "Whitey," a local takeoff on his dark skin. He and Masa, his buddy, were charged with burglarizing a jewelry store on Campbell Avenue in Kapahulu. These two guys were not model citizens. Both had criminal records. They were streetwise, tough—and fun loving. Always cracking jokes about each other, they acted on impulse rather than planning. I hardly ever heard them call each other by their names or nicknames. Most of the time they addressed each other with obscenities. Interestingly, they always called me "Mr. Cayetano."

The case seemed like a defense lawyer's worse nightmare. A slam dunk for the prosecution. The facts were horrible—and comical.

One night, at about 10:30, Whitey and Masa were just "cruising around" in Masa's girlfriend's car. Suddenly, Whitey asked Masa to stop the car and back up to a jewelry store on Campbell Avenue. Whitey stuck his head out of the car and could see that someone had carelessly left some jewelry and watches on display.

After parking the car a block away, they walked up to the store where Whitey picked up a big rock, threw it through the display window and scooped out the jewelry and watches. As the burglary alarm rang, they ran to the car, threw the jewelry and watches (mixed with bits of broken glass) on the back seat and drove straight down the road to an apartment building less than a mile away.

Alerted by the sound of the burglar alarm, two startled people saw them running from the jewelry store to the car. One was a 70-year-old woman who lived across the street from the store, the other an off-duty cop who was sitting on the back porch of his two-story home. Masa had happened to park the car on the street in front of his front porch.

As the two men ran by the cop's house, he caught a glimpse of them, jumped up and rushed to his front porch, from where he said he saw the two men get into the car. Being the good cop that he thought he was, he watched, eyes on the car's taillights, as it was driven straight down the street to the apartment building less than a mile away. He then called police dispatch and described the building.

Meanwhile Masa parked the car in front of the apartment building, leaving the jewelry and bits of broken window glass on the back seat, and he and Whitey ran up to an apartment on the fourth floor. Incredibly, they were spotted by another off-duty cop who happened to be smoking on the front porch of his house, next to the apartment building. This cop did not realize what was going on until he saw a half-dozen police cars, red lights flashing, converging into the parking lot. Looking up at the fourth floor, he saw Masa hiding behind a column, peering at the cops below. "He's up there!" he shouted, pointing to Masa, who rushed back inside the apartment.

When Whitey and Masa entered the apartment there were three other men inside who would play a key part in the case. Hearing that the cops had arrived, Whitey locked himself in the bathroom, where he tried to wash off the blood from the small cuts he had sustained when he reached through the broken store window. Masa, meanwhile, realizing that the cops had seen him and were coming up the stairs, took off for the sixth floor, leading half of the cops on a wild chase all the way to the rooftop. Before he ran off he inexplicably placed an ironing board against the bathroom door—a fact which, during the trial, would cause jurors to smile and shake their heads in amusement.

When the cops burst into the fourth-floor apartment, one of the three other men who were there pointed to the ironing board, which was now like a beacon to Whitey's hideout. Tossing the ironing board aside, one of the cops pounded loudly on the bathroom door, identified himself and ordered Whitey to come out. Although Whitey had managed to wash the blood off his arm, he was puzzled to discover that the numerous small cuts on his arm stood out against his dark skin. So he placed the towel he had used to wipe off the blood over his cut arm and emerged like a waiter from the bathroom to find himself facing a half-dozen angry and winded cops with guns drawn. They pushed him against the wall and handcuffed him.

When the evidence against your client is strong, negotiating a plea bargain with the prosecutor to avoid or minimize jail time is usually the client's best bet. In this case, I told Whitey he would be foolish to go to trial because the evidence was overwhelming. Moreover, if he insisted on going to trial in a slam-dunk case like this, the judge would probably get angry and impose a harsher sentence.

Cliff Nakea, who was the deputy prosecutor handling the case, and I had studied for the bar exam together. We were good friends. Nakea, I explained to Whitey, was a reasonable and fair-minded person. I was confident I could work out a good plea bargain with him. Unfortunately, Whitey had a long criminal record, had spent a year in prison and feared being imprisoned again. No way would he plead guilty.

"Eh, Mr. Cayetano, in Hālawa if you no can beef, no can handle yourself, no mo boys [gang] then you in trouble ... and if you māhū [gay], you in big trouble. I gotta fight this all the way, I no like go back to Hālawa," he pleaded.

As Nakea made his opening statement, reciting the facts of the case, he portrayed my client and his partner as if they were characters out of Jimmy Breslin's *The Gang That Couldn't Shoot Straight*. He was having a good time. He was good. Most of the jurors were smiling; a few stifled laughter, shaking their heads when Nakea mentioned the ironing board. I pretended I was enjoying myself and smiled.

Unless they have a good shot at winning, most prosecutors, especially elected prosecutors, are reluctant to try criminal cases in court. Consequently, most people they charge with crimes are probably guilty of something, but not necessarily the multiple counts of crimes with which they are charged. Theoretically, prosecutors should win every case they take to court. They don't, of course, because criminal trials are often fraught with events and forces beyond their control.

I decided to keep my opening statement short. I urged the jurors to keep an open mind on the evidence, reminding them that Whitey had the right not to testify and that the State had the burden of proving him guilty "beyond a reasonable doubt." The concept of "beyond a reasonable doubt" is a powerful tool for the defense—and it would be the heart of Whitey's defense.

Preparation is the key to winning. Even the smallest detail may make the difference. One evening, at approximately 10:30, the same time the burglary was committed, Whitey and I visited the crime scene and he led me step by step through what had happened that night. A couple of hours later, I had pretty much mapped out the sequence of events and, most important, I had observed the vantage points from which the two witnesses said they had seen Whitey and Masa. I was about as prepared as I could be. I felt a little better about our chances. If we lost, it would not be for lack of putting up a vigorous defense.

Experienced trial lawyers know that eyewitness testimony is one of the most unreliable forms of evidence. I experienced this firsthand when the prosecution's case began unraveling with its first eyewitness. Under cross-examination, the 70-year-old woman conceded that from a distance of nearly 100 yards away she did not see the faces of the two men she saw running down the street that night. She identified the two defendants in a police lineup, she admitted, because "they looked like the two men," but now she wasn't sure.

The second eyewitness, the off-duty cop who lived on the corner where the car was parked, also admitted he did not see the men's faces as they ran by his back porch, but insisted that he saw them as they got into the car.

Catching a witness in an outright lie or mistake is rare. But in a case like this, the objective was twofold: find a few facts that could cast doubt on the witnesses' testimony and give the jury an opportunity to observe the witnesses' demeanor. The cop was not a good witness. He acted as if he was cocksure about what he had seen. I sensed the jury did not like him. My main objective was to show that it was unlikely the witness had actually seen the two men's faces. The fact that it was late at night and dark raised some doubt as to what the witnesses had actually seen.

Too often, luck is an important element in how cases turn out. Here, the police bungling of the evidence was like a chapter from *The Keystone Cops*. First, they lost the bloody towel that my client had had over his arm when he was arrested. They also lost the big rock that had been used to break the window. They did not find any gloves, which they should have if they had looked hard enough, as Masa had stuffed them in a garbage can on the sixth floor. They allowed the three other men in the apartment, including the one who had pointed to the ironing board, to leave without identifying themselves. Furthermore, the car keys could not be found, leaving open the suggestion that the other men might have been the robbers.

We presented no evidence. After final arguments, the case went to the jury for deliberation. Four hours later, the jury came back with its verdict: not guilty. Nakea was stunned.

In discussing the case with the jurors later, it was clear they thought the police had bungled the case so badly that they concluded that the State had not proved guilt beyond a reasonable doubt. The first vote taken was eight to four for "guilty." The four minority jurors then set off an intense and long discussion about the meaning of "presumption of innocence" and "proof beyond a reasonable doubt." By the third vote, the jurors agreed unanimously on a "not guilty" verdict. It wasn't easy, but this conscientious jury had done its civic duty.

This was my first trial. My obvious nervousness faded quickly once the trial began, but my inexperience showed. I was sure the jurors noticed. But I must have done a few things right. A few years later, the jury foreman, a man named Rob Perez who worked for the *Honolulu Star-Bulletin*, and another juror retained me to do some civil work.

Soon I was getting referrals for criminal defense work from lawyers and former clients. A string of court victories followed. Each case taught me some lessons not only about the law but also about human nature.

Pedro was a Filipino immigrant in his 20s who had emigrated from the Philippines and had lived in Hawai'i for about 10 years. A drywall worker for a construction company, Pedro had a wiry build, standing about 5 feet 6 inches tall and weighing about 130 pounds. Friday was payday, and every Friday after getting paid, Pedro went to a home near where he lived in Kalihi to play cards.

One Friday evening in 1974, as Pedro and five others sat around a table playing cards on the front porch of a house, four vice squad cops burst upon them. The cops were dressed in plain clothes and, according to Pedro and other witnesses, did not announce they were cops. Instead, one of the vice cops, a burly guy named Roger, dove head first onto the table yelling loudly.

"He wen dibe on de table on de money and de cards," Pedro told me.

"Did he say anything?" I asked.

"No, he jus wen yell and dibe."

"Okay, show me how he yelled."

"He wen like 'aaaarrgghh!' and he wen grab my arm," Pedro replied.

"He yelled like Tarzan in the movies?"

"Sound same ting."

"And what did you do?"

"I get away and run in de kitchen."

"Why did you run?"

"I don' know who he is … I'm scared."

"And what happened?"

"He chase me and tackle me in de kitchen and he punching me."

"How many times did he punch you?"

"I don' know … I knock out."

"Did you fight back?"

"No, Ah-torney … I just try and run away."

"How long were you knocked out?"

"I don' know … I wake up in de ambulance."

"Now, Pedro, the cop said you pulled a knife on him, is that true?"

"No, Ah-torney, I no pull nipe on him."

"But the cops said you had a knife on you, is that right?"

"Yes, Ah-torney, but it one small steak nipe that I use por my job."

"Why were you still carrying the knife?"

"Because I no go home, I go play card straight prom work."

"How were you carrying the knife?"

"I make scabbard from cardboard and tape … I wear it on my belt."

"Was it hidden under your shirt?"

"No … anybody can see."

"Did you know the guy was a policeman?"

"No, Ah-torney … If I know he is a policeman, I no run, I gib up."

"You ever been arrested before?"

"One time, dey catch me por gambling."

"And what happened?"

"Da judge he pine us. I jus pay de pine."

Pedro's version of the raid was confirmed by other witnesses. However, what happened in the kitchen was problematic. The only witness was the vice cop named Roger, a Chinese Hawaiian. The leader of the vice squad was a local Filipino American named Peter. The third was a Portuguese Hawaiian named Thomas. The fourth was another Chinese Hawaiian named Ralph.

Roger, who stood about 5 feet 10 inches tall and weighed 200 pounds, had beaten Pedro unconscious. By the time Pedro retained me months later, his face had pretty much healed, but when I saw the police photographs I was outraged. He was beaten so badly I could not recognize him. His face was badly bruised, both eyes were swollen nearly shut, and, as I found out later, he had suffered a ruptured eardrum and a fractured eye socket.

Trying to piece together what happened in the kitchen, I came up with several scenarios: Pedro might have pulled the knife to defend himself; or Roger, seeing the knife, might have been angered—I did not think anything could scare the guy—and reacted by giving Pedro a brutal beating.

The key to the case was whether Pedro knew Roger was a cop. Two cops, Peter and Thomas, testified that Roger identified himself. Ralph was bringing up the rear and did not hear anything. The five men who were playing cards with Pedro all testified that Roger did not identify himself, and that he dove on the table, yelling like Tarzan.

The consequences to Pedro could be severe. Assaulting a police officer with a deadly weapon was a crime that carried a mandatory penalty of five years in prison. If he were found guilty, the judge had no recourse but to sentence Pedro to prison. I explained the law to him and suggested a plea bargain. He asked if he would have to go to jail. I told him I could not guarantee he would not but it would not be for five years. Near tears, angry, Pedro replied, "Ah-torney, I no do it … I no do 'em … I'm innocent. Why dey do this to me?" The prosecution had a strong case. They would not plea-bargain without Pedro serving some jail time. We had to go to trial.

As weird as his story sounded, I believed Pedro. The cops, I figured, had wanted to have some fun when they raided the place. I could understand Pedro and the others trying to get away, but there was no reason for Pedro to pull a knife unless he did not know they were cops.

Back then, gamblers were usually just fined by the court. Few got more than a few days in jail. My father was arrested for gambling several times. He'd plead guilty and pay the fine. It didn't stop him from gambling. Gambling was in his blood, part of the Filipino culture. So why would a small man like Pedro pull a knife on a cop who outweighed him by 70 pounds? Why would Pedro and the others make up such a wild story? *No respect*, I thought. No way would Roger pull such a stunt if the gamblers were local boys or haoles. His horseplay set off a sequence of events that he could not have foreseen.

The trial boiled down to who the jury would believe: the three cops or Pedro and his five friends. I was worried about our witnesses. All were single, in their 30s and inarticulate in English. They spoke with heavy Filipino accents and all had prior convictions for gambling. Juries tend to give police witnesses the benefit of the doubt. Pedro needed jurors like Rob Perez. I had doubts about this jury.

The prosecutor was Michael Weight. Weight was a friend and a fine trial lawyer who I knew would be a tough adversary. He knew only the evidence as it was presented by the cops to the grand jury. His job was to convince the jury that the evidence was sufficient to prove guilt. He was good at his job.

Allan Hawkins was the judge. Hawkins, who had a striking resemblance to Franklin D. Roosevelt, was considered by most lawyers an independent thinker and a fine judge.

I felt the trial went better than I expected. The cops were caught contradicting themselves on certain aspects of their testimony. The downside was that Weight gave our witnesses a scathing cross-examination, which raised inconsistencies as well. Their inarticulate answers made it worse. Regardless, at the close of the evidence, I thought we had a chance for acquittal. The final argument would be crucial.

Just before the prosecutor began his final argument, the four cops entered the courtroom and sat in the front row nearest to the jury. Cops do this routinely to influence jurors, especially in criminal cases, which may lead to civil lawsuits against them. If the cops were worried, their worries ended when, after only three hours, the jury came in with a verdict. The jury foreman was the juror I worried about most: a retired Marine sergeant who had served with the military police. I braced myself. "Your honor, we find the defendant guilty," he announced, standing ramrod straight as if he had never left the Marines.

Pedro's head dropped. Staring at the floor, he whimpered softly. "I no do 'em ... I no pull nipe on him ... I no do 'em ... I'm innocent." As the jury filed out of the jury box, none looked at me or Pedro. Weight was somber. He was a good trial lawyer, and fair. He took no joy in the verdict. He did his job. (Years later, Weight told me he thought the cops' evidence was "flimsy.") I kept patting Pedro on the back, trying to comfort him. There was little I could say.

After the jury left, I made a motion for the court to set aside the verdict. Such motions are rarely granted, and defense attorneys make them almost pro forma. During the trial, however, I felt Judge Hawkins was leaning toward my client.

"Mr. Cayetano, you know the rule. The determination of the truth of the evidence is best left to the trier of fact, the jury. In this case, the jury had reasonable grounds to believe the police or your client. They chose to believe the police. This court has to respect their findings," he said in denying my motion. The first hint I got that Hawkins did not like the verdict was when he ruled that Pedro could remain free pending sentencing. Weight did not object.

At the sentencing, Hawkins removed any doubts I had that he believed Pedro. "The court suspends the imposition of sentence for a period of five years, during which should the defendant suffer no arrests or convictions, the charge shall be dismissed," he ruled.

Hawkins had taken a bold step. He used his discretion as a judge to grant Pedro a sentence similar to what is known today as a "deferred acceptance of guilty plea." I was stunned. The law was clear. It called for a mandatory five-year prison sentence. Surprised, I turned to Weight with a *Can the judge do that?* look. He grinned and said, "Ben, I'm not going to argue about it."

Later, at my law office, I explained to Pedro his options. He could accept the sentence, or we could appeal the jury's verdict. I urged him to accept, pointing out that if he won on appeal, he would be retried and, if convicted under a different judge, he could be given the mandatory five-year sentence. Pedro was angry and bitter—beyond hearing what I said.

"I no like do this anymore … I not guilty … I no do 'em, why dey do dis to me?" he said, shaking his head. I could see that this time he was also angry at me for losing the case, for not saving him from injustice. There was no appeal. After a few more meetings, I never saw Pedro again. I wondered whether his conviction would result in his being deported back to the Philippines.

For years, the case haunted me, left me second-guessing myself, wondering whether I could have done more, done better.

Then one year, I think it was in 1976, as I was walking and knocking on doors in Pacific Palisades, seeking votes for my reelection to the State House of Representatives, I met a local Portuguese-Hawaiian woman in her 40s. Her eyes brightened when she opened the door and saw me.

"Mr. Cayetano, do you remember me?"

"Uh, you look familiar," I lied.

"I was on your jury. You know, the case with the police and the Filipino guy."

"… the Filipino guy … oh, yes," I replied.

"Yes, poor thing, he was really beaten up, wasn't he?"

"That would be an understatement," I replied.

"Did he go to jail?"

"He should have, but he was lucky we had a good judge."

"Oh, I'm so glad," she said earnestly.

"Why did you and the other jurors find him guilty?" I asked.

"Actually, the jury was split. Six for guilty, four for innocent and two undecided. I voted not guilty. I did not believe the police."

"Why did you change your vote?" I asked, trying to hide my frustration.

"Well, the foreman kept arguing that we had to support the police. He said he was in the military police and he told us what dangerous work it was. There were only four of us who thought he was innocent, so we went along …"

As she spoke, a number of questions ran through my mind: *If you believed he was innocent why didn't you stick to your opinion? Support the police? What about reasonable doubt? Presumption of innocence? Where in the Constitution does it say the jury has to support the police?*

But I said nothing. The case was over. She seemed happy to have met me. She greeted me warmly as if I had won rather than lost the case. She might not have been the ideal, strong-minded juror Pedro needed, but she deserved thanks for being a good citizen.

"I know it was a tough decision for you," I said.

"Yes, I'm just a housewife," she replied, self-deprecatingly, by now apparently sensing my disappointment. "I don't really understand these kinds of things, but I did my best," she replied.

"I know you did and no one could expect anything more, thank you," I said, handing her a brochure as I turned to leave.

Years later, when I recounted this case to a young lawyer, he remarked that Pedro was lucky that Michael Weight was a fair prosecutor, and that Judge Allan Hawkins was a good judge. Yes—but Pedro was also unlucky: unlucky he encountered a bad cop, unlucky he was at the wrong place at the wrong time and unlucky he was a Filipino immigrant who didn't speak English well—and was still carrying the small steak knife he used at work.

"Our Father Would Have Been Proud"

In 1977, Rolando was charged with the murder of his brother-in-law. I was appointed by the court to defend him. Rolando was a short, dark-complexioned man. His pockmarked face betrayed little emotion. He never smiled and I got the feeling he had a lot of anger bottled up within. Rolando said little, leaving the talking mainly to his older brother, Jun. Like most Filipino immigrants, Jun was always courteous and deferential in our conversations. He spoke with an accent, but he was very articulate, smart and very concerned whether his brother could get a fair trial.

The basic facts were clear: The brother-in-law was leaving Rolando's sister for another woman. At the time of the shooting, he was loading a set of stereo speakers into the back seat of his car. His 10-year-old son was with him. Rolando had used the brother-in-law's own revolver in the shooting. An argument ensued and ended when Rolando shot the brother-in-law five times: once in the left shoulder, once in the right thigh and three times in a neat, four-inch-diameter group through the heart. Rolando had a deep, one-inch cut on his right thumb, which suggested there was a struggle for the gun. And although the victim's son was the only eyewitness, a neighbor told the police that she heard the men arguing loudly in a foreign language and a sequence of shots fired.

Rolando's story was that he did not intend to shoot his brother-in-law, but that during the argument, the brother-in-law threw the two stereo speakers at him and lunged for the gun. He remembered only the struggle and the first two shots; he didn't remember firing the final three. When I asked Rolando why he took the gun with him when he confronted his brother-in-law, he replied that the gun belonged to his brother-in-law and he wanted nothing that reminded him of him left behind.

The prosecutor was a guy named George Yamamoto. He was a big man, aggressive and, in this case at least, cocksure of himself. Unlike Mike Weight, Yamamoto had a reputation for being hardnosed. Plea bargains did not come easy from him. He had a sardonic sense of humor, but we got along fine.

"Ben, I'll bet you a steak dinner that I get at least second-degree murder in this case," he smiled, baiting me.

"Shoot, I got you covered," I replied.

Jury selection was important. Yamamoto was no racist, but he was practical and used his two preemptory challenges to bump two Filipinos off the jury. Meanwhile, I used my two challenges to bump off a haole and an AJA, both white-collar, upper-middle-class men who looked like the law-and-order types. Back then, jury selection was not the science it has become today (for those who can afford it). Lawyers relied mainly on their life experiences and intuition about people and human nature.

There was one juror, however, who Yamamoto asked me not to bump. "Ben, don't be stupid and bump juror number 11 now," he joked, referring to a slender, pretty woman in her 20s whose ethnicity neither of us could figure out. *He wants to put on a show for her*, I thought.

The prosecution's case was simple: Rolando, angry at his brother-in-law for leaving his sister for another woman, took the brother-in-law's revolver from his room and walked over to the garage where the brother-in-law was loading a stereo set into his car, shooting him five times as he emerged from the back seat. The only witness was the victim's 10-year-old son.

The first break in the case came with the prosecution's ballistic expert, who testified that the trajectory of the three bullets over the heart came from a lower elevation. The prosecutor dutifully pointed out that the victim stood about 5 feet 9 inches tall while Rolando was about 5 feet 1 inch. The prosecutor then asked if the trajectories were consistent with shots fired by a shorter man in a crouching stance and a taller man who had just stood upright after putting something in the car. The expert agreed. But I noticed the three bullet slugs that were recovered were smashed as if they had hit something hard. The only thing hard behind the victim when he was shot was the car, which measured about 5 feet 7 inches from the ground to the roof. The photograph of the car, which was admitted into evidence, showed that all of the windows were rolled up; there were no bullet holes in the car. This was inconsistent with the prosecutor's theory. I was puzzled at how he could have missed the inconsistency.

Not wanting to bring attention to these two seemingly inconsistent facts, I decided not to cross-examine the expert.

The son's testimony was critical. However, instead of letting the boy testify freely, Yamamoto asked a series of leading questions designed to elicit testimony that he wanted to hear. I objected.

"Objection, your honor; if the prosecutor wants to testify, he should take the stand. He is leading the witness."

"Overruled, Mr. Cayetano. Given the boy's young age I will allow some flexibility," the judge said.

After an hour of direct examination, it was apparent that the son was struggling to answer the questions. He began to come across as scripted.

Under cross-examination, it became even more apparent that the son was unsure of his answers and, at times, whenever he got stuck, he looked at the prosecutor as if to ask for help.

As it turned out, the boy had not seen what happened during the actual shooting. When his father and uncle started arguing, he got scared and ran to a telephone pole about 10 yards away. His back was turned as he ran, so he didn't see what happened. He heard the first shot and hid behind the telephone pole as the other shots were fired. In other words, he did not know whether his uncle shot first or if his father threw the stereo speakers first. A few jurors frowned as they listened to the son's testimony.

The next morning as I walked to the courtroom, an incredible thing happened—the kind that can create so much uncertainty and drama in a trial. The victim's son, a cute and polite boy, was sitting on a bench with his mother outside the courtroom. He always said "hi" to me, and I'd smile and reply "good morning" or "howzit." This time, however, he wanted to speak to me.

"Mr. Cayetano, I remember now ... last night I had a dream and I remember now."

Taken aback, I asked, "You remember what?"

"I remember what happened."

Because the son was a minor, I wasn't sure whether it was appropriate for me to question the State's witness without the presence of the prosecutor, but I had heard enough and I abruptly stopped the conversation.

Later, a few minutes after the trial resumed, I asked the judge for permission to reopen my cross-examination of the son on the basis of our conversation that morning.

The prosecutor objected on the grounds that I would be going over old grounds. "Did you initiate the conversation with the boy, Mr. Cayetano?" the judge asked with a stern look on his face.

"No, I did not, your Honor; he surprised me. What he said is new, and I should be allowed to ask him a few questions."

The judge consented, overruling the prosecutor's objection. My cross-examination of the son was brief.

"When you approached me this morning, you did it on your own, isn't that correct?"

"Yes."

"And what did you say to me?"

"I said, 'I remember now ... because I had a dream last night.'"

"Now, I did not ask you what you dreamed about, did I? I told you we can talk about your dream only inside the courtroom, isn't that right?"

"No, you never asked me about my dream," he replied.

"But if I, or Mr. Yamamoto or the judge—were to ask you questions now, in this courtroom, about what you saw when your father was shot your answers would be based on your dream?"

"Yes ... mostly," he replied.

"Thank you. No further questions."

The son's testimony, which had been a little shaky the other day, was now fully compromised. In my final argument, I would mention the dream repeatedly to stress to the jury that the son's testimony was unreliable. The prosecutor rested his case on a Friday. On Monday, we would present our defense.

In preparing to present our case, I discovered that the prosecutor had not called the neighbor, who heard the loud voices and shots, as a State witness. She was the wife of an Air Force pilot stationed at Hickam Field. At the time of the shooting, they were renting a home right across the scene of the shooting. The home was built on stilts on the side of a hill, giving her a view of the street below. Her statements to the police seemed important to our defense. According to the police report, she and her husband were watching TV in their living room when they heard "loud voices arguing in a foreign language," then a shot followed by more loud voices arguing, another shot followed by more argument and finally three rapid shots.

I could see why the prosecutor did not call her as a witness. Her statement supported Rolando's story that there had been a struggle for the gun as shots were fired. The prosecutor had presented the evidence in a manner that suggested that all five shots had been fired rapidly as the victim was emerging from the back seat of the car.

I telephoned the witness and asked if I could meet with her to discuss the case. She agreed to meet on Saturday. Since the shooting, they had moved from their temporary residence to officer's quarters at Hickam. On Saturday morning, I drove to Hickam.

She was a tall, strikingly beautiful woman from Alabama in her early 30s. Except for her black hair, she looked like the movie actress Virginia Mayo. I had never seen anyone with gray-blue eyes before. She spoke with a Southern accent, her manner so courteous and refined that I wondered whether she came from one of those aristocratic Southern families I saw in the movie *Gone with the Wind*.

As we sat in her living room, I introduced myself and explained that I was Rolando's lawyer. Before I could ask her a question, however, she interrupted me.

"Sir, will I get in trouble if what I say in court is different from what I told the police?" she asked politely.

"No, you weren't under oath when you spoke to the police, but in court you will be sworn to tell the truth. Can you tell me what happened?" I asked with growing apprehension.

Her eyes began filling with tears and she broke into a soft sob.

"It was horrible. My husband and I were watching TV in our living room when we heard these loud voices ... we couldn't understand what they were saying ... and then we heard a shot ... and the loud voices arguing again ... and, then another shot...."

Tears were flowing down her cheeks, smearing her mascara. I handed her my handkerchief.

"After the second shot, I rushed to the window and I saw him ... he was standing over the other man who was lying flat on his back on the ground. He shot him three more times," she said, her voice breaking in anguish, as if it had just occurred.

I was stunned.

"You know, sir, he's not a big man, but when he's drunk the children are all afraid of him," she continued.

"Why didn't you tell the police this?" I asked.

"My husband said we're strangers here and we shouldn't get involved any more than we had to."

"So that's why you didn't tell the police that you actually saw the shooting?"

"Yes."

"Where's your husband now; may I speak with him?"

"No, he's away. He flew to Guam. He won't be back for a week."

"Are you going to call me to appear in court?" she asked.

"No, I won't, but perhaps the prosecutor will. If he does, you have nothing to worry about if you tell the truth."

"Should I call him?"

"I'm afraid that's your decision, not mine."

I thanked her, and as I drove to the office I thought about the horrific impact her testimony would have on our defense. Hawai'i law permits a person to use deadly force to protect oneself—but only to the extent necessary. Once the person knows or has reason to know that his attacker is no longer a threat, he may not continue to use deadly force. If the jury believed her testimony, Rolando could not claim self-defense in shooting the victim as he lay on his back on the ground.

Her testimony would explain why the bullets were so badly smashed, and it was consistent with the police expert's testimony on the trajectory of the bullets: When he fired the last three shots Rolando was not crouching, shooting up; instead, he was shooting down, a scenario totally missed by the prosecutor.

Self-defense is an affirmative defense. In other words, the defendant must testify to prove his defense, effectively waiving his constitutional right to remain silent. I believed the woman's story but I wanted to hear from Rolando before deciding what to do. By the time I got to the office, however, I was angry with Rolando.

Unfortunately, I betrayed my feelings when I telephoned him and demanded that he meet with me at my office.

His appointment was for 1 p.m. He didn't show up. For a couple hours, I tried unsuccessfully to reach him and Jun. Finally, at about 5 p.m., I reached Jun. He had dropped off Rolando right in front of my office building and did not know where he was. I told him it was important for him to find Rolando and bring him to my law office. Finally, at about 8 p.m., Jun telephoned to tell me he had found Rolando and would bring him over. Fifteen minutes later, Jun and Rolando were at the door. Jun left to park his car. Rolando and I were alone.

I scolded him for not keeping his appointment and angrily told him what the witness had said. How could I defend him if he did not tell me the truth, I asked. He never answered my questions and just kept looking at the floor. After a few minutes I noticed the smell of alcohol. He was drunk. I kept questioning him. Then I heard a strange sound. Rolando was grinding his teeth. Slowly, he looked up at me, his eyes bloodshot, his face purple with anger. Startled, I lowered my voice, but he kept on staring at me, kept on grinding his teeth. I remembered the witness's words about how the children were afraid of him when he was drunk. And now, for the first time in my law career, I was afraid of a client. Rolando was short, but he was well-built, with big hands. He worked as a construction laborer. He looked strong.

I looked for something that I could use to defend myself. Within my reach was a statue of a Chinese lion someone had given me. It weighed about eight to 10 pounds, heavy enough for me to bash his head in. We stared silently at each other for a few seconds, and then there was a knock at the front door. It was Jun. He had had a hard time finding a parking space, he said. He had arrived just in time.

I explained to Jun what the witness had said. "Take Rolando home. Sober him up. We meet tomorrow morning here at 9 a.m. Jun, I want you here with me and Rolando," I instructed him.

The next morning we went over Rolando's story. Everything happened so fast, he said; there was a struggle over the gun, but he didn't remember firing the last three shots. That was his story, and he stuck to it. And that's the story we would present to the jury.

Experienced trial lawyers know that a trial can be like the famous Japanese movie *Rashomon*, where each party to the incident has a different perspective as to what happened and why. Frankly, I believed the woman from Alabama, and I gave deep thought to the ethics of the situation. The prosecutor had not called her because what she had told the police was not helpful to his case. Her testimony would hurt our case, but my sworn duty was to defend Rolando—it was the prosecutor's duty to present the evidence of guilt to the jury.

On Monday, we presented our case. Rolando was our only witness. He told his story to the jury just as he had told it to me repeatedly. Once, during my direct examination of Rolando, I picked up the gun to make a point to the judge and the jury. Suddenly, the prosecutor rose up from his seat, grabbed the gun from my hand, flipped out the revolver's six-shot cylinder, looked through it as if he was checking to see if it was loaded, and then handed it back to me. It was a cheap theatrical stunt for which I normally would have objected and asked for a mistrial, but I could see that most of the jurors were not impressed. Besides, I did not want to retry the case.

Throughout the weekend, I worried whether the woman from Alabama would be called as a witness. I worried more about whether she had called the prosecutor to tell him the truth about what she actually witnessed. At the close of our case, I told myself not to show any emotion to the jury if the prosecution called her as a rebuttal witness to Rolando's testimony. She did not appear.

During my final argument I argued that the jury could not rely on the testimony of the victim's 10-year-old son, "as it would be an injustice to deprive a person of his liberty [I never used the word 'convict'] on testimony based on a child's 'dream.'"

But the fatal blow to the prosecution's murder case came from their inept analysis of the forensic evidence. Holding up the photo of the car with all of its windows rolled up, I asked the jury why—if, as the prosecutor had argued, the victim was shot in an upward direction as he emerged from the back seat of the car—were there no bullet holes in the car? The answer, of course, was self evident: that was not the way the shooting happened.

Preparation is the key to winning in trial. I learned that from some of the great lawyers with whom I practiced. Caught up in hubris, Yamamoto was ill prepared.

After a four- or six-hour deliberation, the jury foreman announced a verdict of not guilty on the first- and second-degree murder charges. But the jury found Rolando guilty of manslaughter. It was a compromise verdict. Rolando was a very lucky man.

As the jurors filed out, I stood at the entrance of the jury box to thank each for their verdict. Finally, juror number 11, the pretty young woman, stood next in line before me. During the trial, while the other jurors were watching the witness being questioned, as jurors normally do, I caught her watching me instead several times. Each time she gave me a slight smile. I wondered whether we had met before.

As I extended my hand to shake hers, and before I could say anything, she said, "Our father would have been proud." I was speechless. "My father is Jerry," she said smiling. "I'm Barbara, your half sister."

Later, over a cup of coffee, I learned that Barbara's mother was Japanese and that she had worked as a flight stewardess for Hawaiian Airlines for a number of years. She had an older brother who worked for United Airlines. My mother, she told me, had kept Jerry informed about my progress through UCLA and later Loyola Law School. "Your mother would call him every time something important happened to you," she said. Mom never knew I knew about Jerry, but she apparently never got over him, even after he left her pregnant with me for Barbara's mother.

"Barbara, you know that you should have disqualified yourself during jury selection when the judge asked if any of the jurors was related to the lawyers or parties involved, don't you?" I asked her. "You could have gotten into a lot of trouble for not disclosing we were related."

"Well, we've never met before, and besides I wanted to see what kind of lawyer my older brother was," she smiled. "You know we [the jury] could not buy self defense, but the prosecutor did not prove his case. So we compromised and agreed on manslaughter.

"I think our father would have been proud to see you in court. Why don't you give him a call?" she asked.

"Maybe I will one day," I replied.

After that day, I saw Barbara once when she dropped in my law office for some legal advice on a small matter. Since then, the last I heard was that she married a guy from the Mainland. He became a minister, and that they moved to Nevada. I never got the chance to make that call to Jerry, my real father. I felt ambivalent about it and kept putting it off until one day, several years later I read his obituary in the newspaper.

I've long believed that the practice of law is among the noblest of professions. Many who grew up poor yet somehow managed to summon the determination to overcome what might have seemed like insurmountable odds would just as soon, once in the rarefied world of law, forget their past. But some of the cases I handled not only profoundly shaped my perspective of our judicial system's institutional strengths and flaws; they made it impossible to forget where I came from. The lessons I learned from these cases and the people I represented made it difficult for me to just walk away. They, and others like them, needed someone to go to bat for them. And I wanted to be among those who did. ❖

CHAPTER FOUR

A Freshman Legislator

Commissioner from Kalihi

Shortly after I opened my own law practice, David Paco, an executive assistant to Gov. John A. Burns, paid me a visit. The governor, he said, wanted to appoint me to the Hawaii Housing Authority Commission. I had never heard of the HHA Commission before.

"Why me?" I asked. "I've never met the governor."

"Well, he'd like to see more Filipinos in State government."

"And you threw in my name?"

"Yeah, I told him all about you. He knows your story ... that you came home with a law degree and a little chip on your shoulder ... he frowned a little when I described your long hair and a mustache and how you sometimes wore a white suit with red pinstripes and platform shoes to court," Paco said with a little laugh.

"But the clincher was when I told him you were from Kalihi. You know, he has a real soft spot for Kalihi boys."

Indeed, nothing seemed to endear local people to Burns more than the fact that this tall haole, born in Montana, had grown up among locals in Kalihi. What made it special was that Burns fit in; he became one of the boys. One story that assumed legendary proportions was about Burns and Hiram Fong, Sr., another Kalihi boy, who would become the first Asian-American U.S. senator, shooting craps together.

The HHA, I soon learned, was the State agency that developed and managed public housing for low-income people, about half of which is located in Kalihi. Some of my classmates had lived in public housing—including my wife, Lorraine, who grew up in Mayor Wright Housing in Pālama.

"It's an important commission ... and some of the governor's diehard supporters may not like the fact that the he wants to appoint one of us and not one of them," Paco said.

At the time, I was struggling to build my law practice. I had few clients, and attracting more was a high priority. Family and law took up much of my time. Nevertheless, I felt drawn to public service. Out of more than 900 graduates from my high school class of 1958, I was the only one among the small number of college graduates to become a lawyer. Good luck had had much to do with it. I felt an obligation; I had made it but knew of so many others who were smarter than I who had not. I owed, and I wanted to give back. Public service was one way to do it. And a governor I had never met opened the door to that world for me: It was a turning point in my life.

The Governor's Ceremonial Room is a magnificent room. Its 16-foot koa ceilings and walls are strikingly beautiful. The ceremonial desk, where the governor sits and signs official documents, is also made of beautiful koa. Centered behind the desk is a huge replica of the state seal etched with the state motto: "Ua mau ke ea o ka 'āina i ka pono (The life of the land is perpetuated in righteousness)." Adorning the walls that day were the larger-than-life-size portraits of the last five governors. Burns' would be the sixth. With the exception of Gov. Samuel King, who was part-Hawaiian and gave part of his inaugural address in Hawaiian, every one of Hawai'i's governors had been haole. After the swearing in, Gov. Burns came over to congratulate the new commissioners. I was carrying our 6-month-old daughter, Samantha; Lorraine stood next to me with Brandon and Janeen. As I waited for him to get to me, I was anxiously searching for the words I would say to him.

Finally, we shook hands. I thanked him for the appointment and then asked, "Governor, why did you appoint me? We've never met before, and I was on the Mainland for the past eight years while you were running for office."

Burns stood a little over 6 feet tall but seemed several inches taller because of his ramrod posture. His usually unsmiling, serious demeanor had earned him the nickname "Old Stone Face." He looked me in the eye, smiled slightly and said, "Well, Ben, there aren't many young Filipinos from Kalihi who go on to become lawyers. I think you can make a contribution to the state." That was the only conversation I ever had with him.

Burns, of course, understood the importance of symbolism in politics. A few months before I left for Los Angeles in March of 1963, he publicly rejected the customary honorary membership the exclusive, haole-only, Pacific Club had offered to every governor. No doubt his action angered some haoles, but it likely gave sway to the more progressive haole members who managed to bring about the repeal of the racially discriminatory policy a few years afterward.

Burns' words had a profound effect on me. I wasn't connected, politically or in any other way, and the fact that he had reached out to bring an outsider like me into public service touched me deeply. The admiration and respect I developed for him had come gradually, at times grudgingly, but they also became enduring.

Twenty years later, as governor, I would appoint a young Jewish-American woman from New York named Margery Bronster as Hawai'i's first woman State attorney general. As was the case with Burns and me, I did not know Margery Bronster beforehand, nor did she seek the appointment. But a lawyer friend recommended her, and, after learning more about her background and interviewing her, I offered her the job. A few of my close supporters voiced some concerns about

Top: Ben (back right), Ken (with glasses), Grandma Blasa and cousins. Bottom left: Ben's father, Bonifacio Marcos Cayetano, was known to his friends as Ansing. Bottom right: Ben's mother, Eleanor, greets Ken upon his return from Vietnam.

Top: Wally Fujiyama. Bottom (left to right): Former Republican
gubernatorial candidates Fred Hemmings, Frank Fasi and Andy Anderson.

Governor John A. Burns

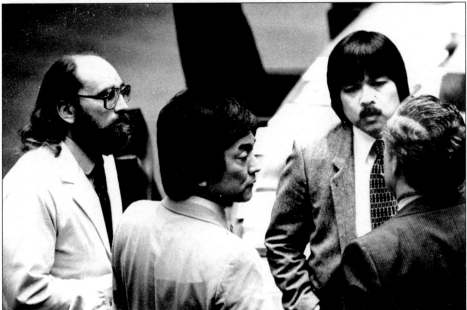

Top: In 1983 Senator Ben listens to the floor debate prior to State Sen. Dickie Wong's purge of Ben and his fellow Senate dissidents. Bottom: Dissident Democrats Neil Abercrombie, Charles Toguchi and Ben Cayetano confer with Republican Buddy Soares during the purge.

Top: As a young lawyer, Ben learned much from Justice Frank Padgett. Bottom: Ben and family during his 1986 campaign for lieutenant governor (left to right): Brandon, Samantha, Ben, Lorraine, Janeen, son-in-law Michael, grandson Micah and Bonifacio

Top left: Former Honolulu Mayor Eileen Anderson, Ben's opponent in the 1986 Democratic lieutenant governor primary. Top right: Tom "Fat Boy" Okuda. Bottom: U.S. Senator Dan Inouye (left) and former Congressman Cecil Heftel, who still maintains that he was smeared in the 1986 gubernatorial election

Top: Lieutenant Governor Ben presents Philippines President Corazon Aquino with a koa bowl on behalf of the State of Hawai'i. Bottom: At age 6 Vicky Cayetano, then Vicky Tiu, played opposite Elvis Presley in the movie *It Happened at the World's Fair*.

On May 5, 1997, Governor Ben and First Lady Vicky
are married at Washington Place.

my appointing a Jewish-American woman from New York to such a coveted post.

"Eh, Ben, she's been here only five years—and those New York Jewish wahines don't know how to stop talking," a lawyer friend said, only half jokingly. But I had a good feeling about her, and, as I will explain later in this book, she would serve the people with distinction and courage—she would make history.

My role as a commissioner gave me a keen insight into the workings of State government. I attended as many legislative hearings as I could to watch HHA Chair Bill Cook testify and to learn more about the HHA and the Legislature. Although I was interested in politics, I had never considered a political career, mainly because I did not think I was qualified. I wanted to practice law, to make a mark as a trial lawyer. But the more I watched the legislators in action, the greater my interest became. *I can do this*, I thought.

The Run for the House

Shortly after I was sworn in as an HHA commissioner, I got a phone call from Richard Dumancus, president of the Sheet Metal Workers' Union. Revocato Medina, another labor union officer, had told him about my appointment. He congratulated me and invited me to have lunch. "I want to meet you and talk story," he said.

Filipinos were a big part of the labor movement. It was the one segment of Hawaiian society in which they had achieved great success. Dumancus stood out, however, because, unlike the other Filipino labor leaders, whose union memberships were heavily Filipino, his union was mostly comprised of Japanese, Chinese and Portuguese workers. There were few Filipinos in the sheet metal industry. I looked forward to meeting him.

Dumancus was tall for a Filipino, standing a little over 6 feet. He had big-boned hands that seemed disproportionate to the rest of his slim, wiry body. He smoked heavily for years, and when we first met he was already in the early stages of emphysema, from which he would eventually die. Dumancus had a reputation for being tough when it counted, but always fair.

"Ben, the Old Man [that's what people called Burns] thinks you have potential. You ever think about getting into politics—running for office?" he asked.

"Well, I told Rev I would think about it," I replied. "But he told me that I wouldn't have a chance running from Pearl City because 60 percent of the voters are Japanese who will not vote for a Filipino. He said that I should move to either Kalihi or Waipahu, where there are large numbers of Filipino voters."

Dumancus paused for a few seconds, looked down at me through those thick glasses he wore, and sighed, "That's the problem with Filipinos. We can't get ahead because we stick to ourselves. If you think small like that, Ben, you'll never get anywhere.

"It may be easier for you to win in Kalihi or Waipahu, but if you want to run for higher office you will need to win the votes from every group, not just Filipinos—there are not enough of us.

"Most of my men [members] are Japanese, Chinese or Portuguese. There are few Filipinos. And not one of the companies they work for is owned by a Filipino.

"You know why I've been the only president this union has since it started in 1955? Because I know the sheet metal business better than anyone," he said, answering his own question. "The men know my word is good; they trust me to do what's right for them. The day I let them down, that's the day I deserve to be kicked out."

"I found out that every Filipino who ran in the Pearl City district lost—and pretty badly," I said, interrupting him.

"Well, you can be the first to win. If you want to live in Pearl City, that's fine. Remember, family first, take care of your family. But don't be afraid to run from there just because most of the voters are Japanese. Look at it this way: If you can win there, you can win anywhere. If you lose, it's not the end of the world. I heard you're a good lawyer—if you lose, go practice law. Politics is not everything," he said.

A week later, I called Dumancus.

"Richard, I decided to run from Pearl City," I said.

"Good, I'll ask two of my top guys, Mel Murakami and Howard Tasaka, to help you. I'll see if I can raise some money from the companies that are not Republicans. And I'll call Roy [Yamashiroya] at Service Printers to help out with your brochures and bumper stickers. Roy and I are close—if I ask for help, I can always count on him; he'll give you a good deal," he said.

The Reapportionment Commission had recently created the new 19th Representative District, which included all of Pearl City. There were two State representative seats. One seat was filled by an incumbent, Tats Kishinami, a six-year veteran legislator. My goal was to win the vacant seat.

One day, while visiting the State Capitol, I was introduced to State Sen. Anson Chong. Chong, who was in his mid-30s, was a favorite of the news media. A veteran of the Peace Corps, a liberal, handsome, he was portrayed by the media as youthful, idealistic, pro-environment, independent—the kind of politician to whom young people could relate. Roddy Rodrigues, who worked as a researcher for the Legislature, introduced me to Chong at the State Capitol.

"Senator, I want you to meet Ben Cayetano. He's going to run for the State House," Rodrigues said.

"Hey, great, man. We could use some new blood in the State House," he said, flashing a big smile as we shook hands.

"What district are you going to run from?" he asked.

"I'm going to take a shot at the open seat in the new 19th District," I answered.

His jaw dropped. "The new 19th? Oh, man, you picked the wrong district. Have you ever heard of Norman Mizuguchi?" he asked with an amused look.

"No," I replied.

"Why don't you move to Kalihi or Waipahu? Your chances are better there," he said.

Yeah, and maybe you should move to Chinatown, you pake, I thought to myself. Move to Kalihi or Waipahu? I had been given that advice so many times I was getting tired of hearing it—and I was disappointed that even liberals like Chong had stereotyped notions of Filipinos. *Quint was right—even the guys who are supposed to be on our side don't think we're good enough*, I thought.

It didn't take me long to find out who Norman Mizuguchi was. A former all-star basketball player at Hilo High School, he held a Ph.D. in education from the University of Utah; his wife, Harriet, had been appointed by Gov. Burns to the University of Hawai'i Board of Regents. Together, they made an attractive couple. Mizuguchi had strong ties to the labor unions, especially the powerful Hawai'i Government Employees Association (HGEA) and its fiery leader, David Trask. Moreover, he had shrewdly garnered the support of many community groups, particularly the Little League baseball team parents, whom he wooed with donations of soft drinks and cash for their teams. Willy Cadavona, my campaign manager, referred jokingly to Mizuguchi as "pretty." A less jaundiced view came from Lorraine and some of our female campaign workers, who found him "good looking."

No wonder Chong felt sorry for me. It was clear to me that my chances of beating Mizuguchi in Pearl City were slim. At times, I started second-guessing my decision to run there. Perhaps Chong and the others were right—maybe I should have moved to Kalihi or Waipahu. Later, however, after reflecting on my talk with Dumancus, I decided that living in Pearl City was best for our family and that we would stay there. Fortunately, the 19th had two State-representative seats, and both were up for election. If I couldn't beat Mizuguchi, maybe I could beat Kishinami. I went to Dumancus for advice.

"I know Norman—he lives right down the street from me in Pearlridge. He's Najo's boy. [He was referring to retired State Sen. Nadao Yoshinaga, whose political instincts, if one believed his admirers, rivaled Machiavelli's.] Najo is grooming Norman to become governor or U.S. senator one day. If he runs against you, it will be a tough race," he said.

"What about Kishinami?" I asked.

"Well, I hear a lot of complaints about the guy," Dumancus replied. "My Pearl City friends tell me once the guy was elected he became big-headed—arrogant. I think you have a better chance of beating him than Norman.

"You know, Ben, I've watched Hawai'i politics for a long time. And to me, the Japanese voter is probably the fairest of all of the ethnic groups," he said.

"Really? Why do you think so?" I asked.

"Since 1954, they have been very successful in opening things up for them-selves; in politics, in business, in State government. And I think some of them feel a little guilty that their success has not been shared by other ethnic groups. Do you remember when Oren Long and Wilfred Tsukiyama ran against each other for the U.S. Senate in 1959?" he asked.

"Not really; the only thing I know about Tsukiyama is that he was a former chief justice of the Supreme Court," I replied.

"Right, but in 1959, the Republicans put up Tsukiyama against Oren Long. So it was a haole-versus-Japanese election. Tsukiyama was a well-known law-yer and legislator, and he was well respected in the AJA community. He was the Republicans' token Japanese," Dumancus said.

"You see, the haoles who ran the Republican Party thought that Tsukiyama would get a lot of Japanese votes because he was highly regarded by the Japanese community. They figured that combined with the votes of haole Republicans he could beat Long. Well, when the votes were counted, it wasn't even close," he said, smiling. "Long beat Tsukiyama badly."

"Why?" I asked.

"What happened was that many Japanese voters who lived in Democratic districts voted for Long—while the haoles who lived in strong Republican districts like Kāhala also voted for Long. So the Japanese voters, who are usually Demo-crats, voted for Long because he was a Democrat, while the haole Republicans also voted for Long—because he was a haole," Dumancus chuckled.

"There must have been a lot of red faces among the Republican Party lead-ers—Dillingham, Woolaway and that crowd. What a slap in the face for Tsukiyama. That's why Bill Quinn appointed Tsukiyama as chief justice. They had to make it up to him," Dumancus said.

"Why did Tsukiyama become a Republican?" I asked.

"Hell if I know. Most people can't figure it out. Idealistic, I guess. Blind to history. Frankly, I can't understand why any Japanese or Filipino would become a Republican," he said, shaking his head.

"Why are so many Hawaiians Republicans?" I asked.

"Because they hate the Japanese more than the haoles. It's crazy, it was the haoles who screwed them, but Hawaiians are like crabs in a bucket; they can't stand others getting ahead of them," he replied.

"Now the reason I tell you about Long and Tsukiyama is because it shows that the Japanese will vote for a non-Japanese over one of their own kind."

"Under the right circumstances, I guess," I said. "But Long was a former governor [Territorial]—I'm just a young lawyer with no political experience."

"Well, I think that's good enough for a House race. Remember, Jack Burns appointed you to that commission because he was impressed with your back-ground—you need to tell that story to the voters in your district: Voters respect people who work hard and struggle. People like underdogs. Now—there are two seats, right?"

I nodded in agreement.

"Well, if Ariyoshi beats Gill and Fasi [George Ariyoshi, Tom Gill and Frank Fasi were the front runners in the Democratic primary election for governor], I think you will get a lot of votes from the haoles, Hawaiians and everyone else who thinks there are too many Japanese in the legislature. These people will have a hard time voting for two Japanese. So if you can get enough Japanese voters to give you one of their two votes, you might surprise all these guys who said you don't have a chance in Pearl City. So just work hard, give it your best, don't bad-mouth anyone. And don't forget to show people you have a nice family—Lorraine and your three kids will be very helpful.... I have a feeling you'll do fine," he said confidently.

Dumancus was a mentor and an inspiration to me. I had great respect for him. And he was respected by his members—he was the union's only president and business manager from when it was formed in 1955 to his death in 1987. Dumancus built a respected union that to this day has never been tainted by scandal or wrongdoing. He helped me get started in politics but never asked for a favor for himself or his union; the only promise he asked of me was to "never do anything that will bring shame to your family and the Filipino community."

My 1974 campaign for the State House was a classic case of on-the-job training. At the outset, nearly every one of my campaign workers lived outside of the district. Most were former classmates at Farrington. No one had any political experience. But we followed Dumancus' advice almost to the letter—except I did not cut my hair.

Lorraine and I walked door-to-door, meeting people throughout the district. Most people were friendly—but few wanted to discuss issues. I was fast beginning to realize how important the personal side of a campaign at the House level had become. Dumancus was right; it was more important than issues, probably because there were few differences on issues between the candidates, and the voters saw personal background as a better barometer of character. The second time we walked the district, I noticed people were much friendlier and more open. It was a good sign.

A big part of our strategy was to follow Mizuguchi wherever he appeared. We were both young (34) and college educated, and we both had good-looking families that were heavily involved in our campaigns. Our hope was that some of Mizuguchi's strong supporters would give us their second vote.

Kishinami, on the other hand, started his campaign late. Apparently, he had conceded Mizuguchi would win handily and therefore he would have to be satisfied with coming in second. We got the impression he was supremely confident that he would win the second seat.

"Yeah, Kishinami is relying on getting a strong Japanese vote—he is really playing it up … even his bumper sticker is red and white just like the Japanese flag," Cadavona said jokingly.

A month or so before the primary election, I was at the Pearl City Library awaiting my turn to be interviewed by the Hawaii State Teachers Association (HSTA) Political Action Committee. None of the other unions had endorsed me. Even the ILWU, dominated by Filipino workers, remained neutral. The HSTA was my last shot at getting a union endorsement. As I waited, Roddy Rodrigues arrived. "Ben, don't take too long. It's a waste of time. I was just told HSTA is going to go with Mizuguchi and Kishinami," he said.

I wasn't surprised. Kishinami was a six-year incumbent and Mizuguchi was well connected with labor and held a Ph.D. in education. Having worked many years as a researcher for the Democratic legislative majority, Rodrigues had become a political insider. I had no reason to doubt him.

"Why does HSTA even hold these endorsement interviews when they've already made up their mind? I feel like just going in and giving them a piece of my mind," I said, a little irked.

"No, don't do that, keep cool," Rodrigues replied. "There will be another time."

"But only if I win … the last time something like this happened, I ended up going to law school," I chuckled.

By the time of the interview, I was relaxed, resigned to the fact that nothing I could say would make a difference. We were allotted a half-hour for the interview. I gave a 10- to 15-minute opening statement in which I poured out my experiences, feelings and views about public education. I could tell from their reaction that I had gotten their interest. Then came the question-and-answer period, which went on for over an hour. Finally, it was over. The interview had lasted nearly 90 minutes.

"Roddy, are you sure they've already made up their minds?" I asked. "I was in there for more than an hour."

"That's the word I got from a member of the HSTA board," he replied.

I felt good about the interview: It was the same kind of good feeling I had when I connected with the jury in a trial. The interview had tired me, so I headed straight for home, took a shower and went to bed at about 10 o'clock. At about midnight, the phone rang. It was Sally Waite, the chairperson of the HSTA PAC.

"Hello, Mr. Cayetano? This is Sally from the HSTA PAC. I'm happy to tell you that the PAC decided to endorse you for the primary election. Congratulations," she said.

I was stunned. "Really? I'm at a loss for words. All I can say is thank you very much," I stammered.

"Yes, we liked the way you answered our questions. And we really liked the fact that you didn't duck any and that if you did not know the answer, you owned up to it," she said. "That went over very well with our committee members."

"May I ask whether your committee endorsed anyone else?" I asked.

"Yes, we endorsed you and Tats Kishinami," she replied.

I was dumbfounded. I'd thought it was a foregone conclusion they would endorse Mizuguchi. A few minutes later, Rodrigues called to congratulate me. I asked him why the PAC hadn't endorsed Mizuguchi.

"Well, I was told they thought he was too cautious and too political in the way he answered their questions," Rodrigues replied. "By the way, my source apologizes for his screw-up; he thought Norman had it in the bag."

The HSTA endorsement gave a real boost to our campaign. A group of teachers augmented our small campaign organization. A few were Filipinos; most were either Chinese or Japanese. Many became fast friends, and they would support me in every election I had during my 28 years of public service.

Political campaigns run the gamut of emotions, filled with peaks and valleys of excitement, depression and elation. A few months before the primary election, I was discouraged to learn that a union poll showed me a distant third behind Kishinami. Mizuguchi was first. But in the remaining two weeks before the election, I sensed things were changing fast and that we had a shot at winning.

On Election Day, we campaigned right up to the time the polls closed. As we awaited the returns that evening, I wasn't as nervous as I'd thought I would be. Our small band of campaigners had given me more than I had expected. We had done all we could. There was nothing else to do but wait for the returns.

At about 9 p.m., Alex Cadang, one of our campaign chairmen, called me aside. "Partna [Alex's nickname for me] ... we're going to win," he whispered. "I just heard on the radio we're leading Kishinami by 250 votes." The final return showed I had won by a little over 500 votes.

Nineteen seventy-four was the beginning of the post-Watergate Period. In August, Richard Nixon, the most powerful leader in the world, was driven to resign as president to avoid impeachment; a number of his assistants followed him, several ending up in jail for perjury and various charges. The year before, Vice President Spiro Agnew had resigned, and he too was charged, indicted and imprisoned on unrelated charges of corruption.

Hawai'i's voters wanted "new blood" and expressed their strong desire for change at the polls. I was one of 22 freshmen legislators elected to the 51-member State House of Representatives—a 43-percent turnover.

Lt. Gov. George Ariyoshi beat reform-minded Democrats Mayor Frank Fasi and former U.S. Congressman Tom Gill to become the first Asian American to be elected governor in the United States.

A week or so after the general election, the Democratic Party held a reception at the Ilikai Hotel for all Democratic legislators. Carl Takamura, another newly elected State representative, and I were heading for the elevator when we ran into Sen. Chong, who was also going to the reception.

Takamura, who knew Chong personally, stopped to introduce me to Chong.

"Senator, have you met Ben Cayetano?" Takamura asked.

Chong, sounding as if he was offering his condolences at a funeral, replied, "Oh, yes, we've met before … gee, Ben, I'm really very sorry that you lost."

"Lost? Senator, what have you been smoking?" I retorted, smiling, as I stepped into the elevator. We left Chong standing there, with a puzzled look on his face, his eyes blinking rapidly. As the elevator door closed, Carl shook his head and chuckled, "That's typical Anson … man, he can say the weirdest things."

Chong wasn't the only politician who was shocked. Over the next two weeks, word got back to me that some veteran legislators had expressed their surprise in different ways—one dismissed my election as a "fluke." I could sense a hint of resentment from some of those who were loyal to Kishinami. A natural reaction, I supposed. But most of the veterans, Democrats and Republicans, welcomed us and offered to help. And I was eager to learn.

Organizing the House

"No one will be allowed to leave this room until we organize the House," intoned Minoru Hirabara, the affable chairman of the Hawai'i Democratic Party. His words elicited some bemused grins. "Mino" was well liked and a good chairman, but I felt, as did most, that the organization of the House was none of his or the Party's business.

Once elected, a legislator owed a single fiduciary duty—to the public, not to the Party or any other special interest. Not that Mino's involvement made much difference to the freshmen. Except for Mizuguchi, who had worked as a Senate staff member, and Gerald Machida from Maui, who worked for the HGEA, the rest of us knew little about the players vying for leadership roles or the internal politics among veteran Democrats.

James Wakatsuki, a longtime veteran of the House and the city Council, was elected Speaker. Wakatsuki was called the "'opihi," after a species of limpet found only in Hawai'i and known for its ability to cling tenaciously to rocks despite pounding surf. His calm, close-to-the-vest approach on political issues created the perception that he was a stereotypical politician who did his real business in smoke-filled rooms.

In fact, he belonged to a generation of local politicians that harbored an inbred distrust of the press. This was hardly surprising. The haole-dominated Republican Party had controlled Hawai'i's newspapers and used them desperately, unfairly, and, at times, viciously to stem the looming tsunami of Democrats and labor unions that would finally overwhelm them in 1954.

I don't recall Wakatsuki holding a single press conference during the four years I served with him in the House. More often then not, if he had something to say to the news media, it was done through a written press release. If he spoke to a reporter, it was an indication that he trusted him to be fair and accurate, and he would usually do it one-on-one in the quiet of his office.

A lawyer in his early 50s, Wakatsuki was smart, tough and politically savvy. He was careful not to use his office for personal gain. As Speaker, for example, he was in a much stronger position than most legislators to raise campaign funds. Most politicians see fundraising as a necessary evil. But I don't recall Wakatsuki ever holding a fundraiser. I asked him how he financed his campaigns, and he told me that he relied on a close circle of friends. "Besides," he asked, "how much money do you need for a House race?"

Wakatsuki stood head and shoulders above House Speakers who followed him. The 1975 legislative session, however, his first as Speaker, would be his most difficult. He would need all of his political skills to deal with the new reform-minded Democrats and some highly controversial bills. One bill provoked such public outrage that the majority Democrats in both the House and Senate would petition the Governor to veto the bill, which they had passed just a few days before.

"All politics is local," former U.S. House Speaker Tip O'Neill wrote in his memoir. Indeed, House veterans knew this only too well. Rather than seek a committee chairmanship, many vied to sit on the Finance Committee, where it was easier to insert their pet projects into the State Budget Bill and get something done for their constituents.

The Finance and Judiciary committees were reserved for veterans. These two important committees were the hub of the bill-review process. Every bill introduced during the session was referred for disposition to one or the other committee and often to both. The committees performed an important screening process. Thus it was important for the Speaker to appoint representatives to these committees whom he could trust and rely on.

There was a tacit understanding about the Finance Committee: If the Speaker was from O'ahu, then the Finance Committee chairperson would have to be from the Neighbor Islands, or vice versa. In 1975, the Finance Committee was chaired by Jack Suwa, an old-time Democrat from the Big Island.

Moreover, the Neighbor Island Democrats had their own caucus, ostensibly to assure that the Neighbor Islands would be treated fairly by O'ahu legislators. This was hardly necessary, as O'ahu representatives seemed incapable of uniting over any issue which would adversely affect the Neighbor Islands. Nevertheless, a dozen Neighbor Island representatives voting as a bloc could not be ignored. Any O'ahu issue of significance, such as H-3 or rail transit, required trade-offs to get Neighbor Island support.

A surprising number of important chairmanships were left open to freshmen. The Culture and the Arts, Environmental Protection, Housing, Health, Public Assistance, Tourism, Energy and Transportation, and Youth and Elderly committees would be chaired by new, inexperienced legislators. Most of our 1974 freshman class saw ourselves as reform politicians; we tended to be an idealistic group, more interested in focusing on influencing legislative policy than on pork-barrel politics, of which we knew little. Most were eager to assume committee chairmanships. There were, of course, some risks.

As one veteran explained, "You want the glory? Fine—but you have to be willing to take the grief, the crap that goes with it. If everything goes well, the chairman may get some credit. If not, he takes the heat for his committee members." *Fair enough*, I thought.

Working with the Republicans was another challenge. As the minority party, they had the role of challenging and checking the positions taken by the majority. Inevitably, for some, politics often shaped their tactics and positions on bills. Not that one could fault them. In those days few, if any, Republican bills were passed.

Republicans were left with two choices: play the loyal opposition to the extreme, drawing media attention but getting little or nothing constructive done, or give up pride of authorship and ask a Democrat to introduce the bill for them and work cooperatively to get it passed.

Republicans who put pragmatism above politics got a surprising number of things done by working with Democrats. The House had a number of talented and experienced Republicans. Most were moderates. Some were liberals in the mold of a Jacob Javits or Nelson Rockefeller. None were conservatives—at least not of the Newt Gingrich breed. Those would come later, after the Religious Right finally took over Hawai'i's Republican Party in 1988.

Many of the Republicans were experienced businesspeople. House Republican leaders, such as Minority Leader Andy Poepoe and Minority Floor Leader Buddy Soares, were business executives who were respected and well liked by their Democratic counterparts. These two leaders did much to downplay politics and encourage a cooperative, bipartisan working relationship.

I was given the chairmanship of the House Energy and Transportation Committee (not because I had asked for it—actually, I knew little about the subject matter—but because no one else seemed to want it).

Once the House was organized, we were invited to a number of receptions hosted by special-interest groups, mostly business organizations, labor unions, professional associations and lobbyists.

At one reception, David Trask, the fiery and controversial leader of HGEA, came and sat next to me. He reached over and slipped an envelope into my shirt pocket.

"Ben, here's a little something from the HGEA to help with your campaign expenses. Work with Norman [Mizuguchi]. You two guys will make a good team,"

Trask said softly. The envelope contained a check from the HGEA PAC for $250, the largest contribution I had ever received at the time. The election had left me in debt, and I welcomed the HGEA's post-election support.

I had never met Trask before. I had heard of him, of course, but mostly through the news media. I knew of his brothers, Arthur and Bernard, who were both well-known lawyers. From what I knew about them and what I heard about David Trask, it seemed as if the Trask family was born into controversy.

Trask was not a big man physically, but he had the dour demeanor of a pit bull. As one House veteran said, "It's hard to tell if David's pissed off, because he looks like that all the time." Trask understood the trappings of power very well. Whenever he visited the State Capitol, he always had two or three men with him who, as they say in Kalihi, looked as if they could "handle" themselves.

During the few times we spoke, Trask hardly looked me in the eye. Instead, he had a furtive look, an air of feigned detachment, looking askance as he spoke. I felt as if he was about to "sucker punch" me at any minute.

Some found Trask an obnoxious bully. Indeed, Wakatsuki enjoyed telling the story of how once, when they were both members of the Territorial House, Trask got gotten him so angry he had challenged him to step outside and settle things man to man. Considering that Wakatsuki was known for his ability to keep cool, it was quite a feat on Trask's part.

Intimidation might have been part of Trask's style, but most politicians put up with him because the reality was that the HGEA had become one of the most influential labor unions in Hawai'i. By 1974 its membership swelled with the tremendous growth of State and County governments. It rivaled in political power the International Longshore and Warehouse Union (ILWU), which had been the heart of the Democratic Revolution of 1954.

Trask was often heavy handed in using his power against those who disagreed with him. (He once denounced me at the State Capitol before a rally of 4,000 to 5,000 State workers). Consequently, people tended either to love or to hate him. I knew that some HGEA members were ambivalent. They disliked his bullying style, and were quick to say so privately, but they were usually pleased with the generous pay raises and fringe benefits he got for them.

Perhaps the best example of Trask's power was his success in organizing Hawai'i's public school principals. Most thoughtful labor union leaders and pro-labor legislators understood that collective bargaining worked best and most fairly when there was a fair balance of power between labor and management. Unionizing public school principals created an obvious imbalance of power in the management of Hawai'i's public schools. To this day, many believe this has been a major obstacle to reforming public education in Hawai'i.

But Trask was all about getting more power, leaving others to deal with any collateral consequences. I didn't like Trask's style, but I had to give him his due.

The man was doing his job for his union—and I had to admit that he was effective. If anyone were to blame for Trask's excesses, his overreaching, it was the politicians who allowed themselves to be intimidated, or stooped to groveling to get his political support.

Trask's suggestion that I meet with Mizuguchi was something I had intended to do anyway. As a former Senate staff member to the once-powerful State Sen. Nadao Yoshinaga, Mizuguchi had seen firsthand the inside world of legislative politics. He knew the key players and had influence with them. He had valuable experience and knowledge about issues that I hoped he would share with me.

I must have given him the impression I had come with my hat in hand. Our meeting was cordial but short. "I'll have my staff develop a sexy highway beautification program for you," he said, somewhat dismissively. Mizuguchi had a lot going for him; political powerbrokers like Trask and Nadao Yoshinaga had high hopes for his political future, but, over the years, his penchant for erring on the side of caution would prove to be a liability rather than an asset.

I was no expert on transportation issues, but I found highway beautification neither "sexy" nor a priority. Indeed, the state faced major transportation issues that would prove controversial and difficult to resolve. Among them were an increase in the fuel tax to stabilize the highway fund, the construction of the new H-3 defense freeway, the search for a second general aviation airport, a proposed state ferry system and a proposed limit to the percentage of live-aboards at the Ala Wai and Keʻehi small-boat harbors. The importance of highway beautification paled in comparison.

Fortunately, I managed to hire competent and experienced staff. With help from Roddy Rodrigues, a researcher for the majority research section, and, later, Earl Anzai, an analyst with the Legislative Auditor's Office and formerly with the federal GAO (Government Accountability Office), I slowly became more knowledgeable about these issues.

Eventually, I discovered the main reasons there wasn't much competition for the chairmanship of the committee. One, the position carried with it the responsibility for proposing an increase in the fuel tax to keep the highway fund from going into deficit, and any politician proposing a tax increase risks incurring the wrath of the public. Two, it meant facing outraged environmentalists and angry Hawaiian activists who were dead set against the construction of the H-3 freeway.

Living in Los Angeles for nearly nine years, I had grown accustomed to the give-and-take, rough-and-tumble style of Mainland politics. Notwithstanding its excesses, this style kept politicians on their toes and raised the public's awareness of what their politicos were up to.

Midway into the 1975 legislative session, however, it became clear that, with a few exceptions, most of the veteran House Democrats shared Wakatsuki's views of the news media and airing their views publicly. The overwhelming majority of the legislators were AJAs. There was a cultural gap between haoles and AJAs: Haoles favored blunt emotion and free expression, while most AJAs preferred to withhold their feelings and temper their words, a view shared by most non-AJA local legislators.

"If you no can say nothing good about anyone—no say nothing," one House veteran, quoting in pidgin an old, overused local bromide, reminded us. Like most local boys, I had grown up with the "no talk stink" credo. Fair or not, many local people saw verbosity as a character flaw to which haoles seemed most susceptible.

John Burns embodied this attitude when he declared, "Any fool can take a stand"—an oblique backhand to the articulate, outspoken and acerbic Tom Gill, Burns' former lieutenant governor, who would challenge Burns in the 1970 Democratic primary.

In his successful 1974 gubernatorial campaign, George Ariyoshi used the slogan "Quiet but Effective," created by his political consultants, Jack Seigle and Joe Napolitan. The two believed that the slogan accomplished two objectives: It honestly depicted Ariyoshi's inner strength and character, and it sent a subtle message to local people, Japanese Americans in particular, that Ariyoshi was more likely to share their values than would his three opponents in the Democratic primary, Honolulu Mayor Frank Fasi, Gill, and State Senate President David McClung.

In his opening-day address as Speaker, Wakatsuki proudly pointed out that House rules required open decision-making. The reality of legislative politics is that ever since legislatures have existed, bills and other sensitive matters have usually been debated and votes counted behind closed doors. Closed caucuses encouraged open discussion. Legislators who were uncomfortable speaking publicly opened up. Sensitive, personal matters occasionally were aired. To be sure, at times, discussions could get heated. On several occasions, heated arguments degenerated into near-fistfights.

The reluctance of legislators to reprise in public what went on behind closed doors was understandable. For one thing, the practice rarely changed votes and served mainly to put things on the public record. Less debate meant the bills would move along with greater efficiency. One veteran quoted Winston Churchill that "the best argument against democracy is a five-minute conversation with the average voter." In other words, public debate was considered a waste of time.

All of this, of course, came at the expense of the public's right to know. Experience is a great teacher, but, for some House veterans, it jaded the youthful idealism that had drawn them to enter politics in the first place.

The 1975 legislative session, however, marked the beginning of incremental changes in the political culture of the House. It was inevitable. Twenty-two freshmen—43 percent of the House—had promised to reform the existing political system. Most believed deeply in bringing more transparency to the legislative process. In the final days of the session, the fallout from a controversial bill involving the pensions of legislators would help move the Legislature slowly but irreversibly in that direction.

On March 13, 1975, a contentious and, at times, acrimonious debate over a bill took place in the closed majority caucus. The bill, HB 1840, was introduced to stop the banks from getting into the industrial loan business. Feelings over the bill ran high among some House veterans. An informal count among the veterans indicated the official vote would be close. Some of the freshmen votes were up for grabs. For the first time in the session, the veterans engaged in a full public debate on a bill.

I was delighted at the prospect of watching the veterans argue the bill publicly on the House floor. This did not happen often. For most of the session, they moved as one, pestered with occasional questions mostly from a small group of freshmen that included me, Neil Abercrombie, Russell Blair, Richard Ho and Carl Takamura. "Well, well," Takamura chuckled, "the old boys finally have a little fight among themselves."

I knew little about the industrial loan dispute. Having less than a month before the start of the session to get up to speed on energy and transportation issues and prepare for public hearings, which required reading each of the dozens of bills referred to my committee, I focused almost exclusively on my committee work. Except for a quick briefing by my staff the day of our majority caucus, the dispute between the banks and the industrial loan companies was new to me. Most freshmen were in the same boat. None of the freshmen rose to speak during the debate. Instead, we were like spectators at a tennis match, watching silently as the opposing sides exchanged volleys.

During the 1970s, Hawai'i's real estate market was still booming, fueled mostly by Japanese investment, which accounted for more than half of the total Japanese investment in the United States. Investors, speculators and developers were always on the lookout for easy access to capital. But it was difficult for them to get financing for high-risk projects from the conservative, federally regulated banks.

The industrial loan companies filled the void nicely. The companies were creatures of the State. As such, they were governed exclusively by State regulations, which were far more liberal than the stringent federal regulations governing the banks. To attract the savings deposits that provided the cash for loans, industrial loan companies offered interest rates of 18 to 20 percent, nearly double the rates paid by banks. Another big difference was that personal savings accounts at banks were insured up to $10,000 by the Federal Deposit Insurance Corp. (FDIC), whereas industrial loan company accounts were not.

On the Mainland, banks were allowed to get into the industrial loan business through holding companies. Hawai'i law was silent on this approach. In 1974, First Hawaiian Bank, then Hawai'i's second-largest bank, formed a holding company that applied for an industrial loan license. The application was denied by the Department of Regulatory Agencies. Shortly thereafter, the bank's holding company filed a second application, which was still pending when the 1975 legislative session opened in January.

Industrial loan company lobbyists and their supporters were not about to leave the fate of First Hawaiian's application to chance. They persuaded the chairmen of the Consumer Protection Committee and the Judiciary Committee that First Hawaiian Bank was trying to circumvent the law and something had to be done to stop it. Thus, HB 1840 was introduced to close what some thought was a loophole the bank was exploiting. True to his role as speaker, Wakatsuki lent his support to the two chairmen. Most of the House leadership followed suit.

Tony Kunimura or "Uncle Tony," as he was called by some, led the opposition. The ex-butcher from Kaua'i (he had two missing fingertips to prove it), was not a college graduate. He was self educated, much like Eric Hoffer, the former longshoreman turned author and social commentator. Kunimura was no intellectual, but he was a crafty tactician and an excellent speaker fully capable of moving an audience to anger or tears. (I sat next to him for two years.) There was a flair about him; he could be flamboyant at times, mostly in his attire—he once wore a red suit, complete with red suspenders and a red bow tie, to the session.

Kunimura often delighted in baiting his younger, better-educated colleagues. At one public hearing, his needling got freshman Neil Abercrombie, a former University of Hawai'i professor, so angry that the infuriated Buffalo, New York, native challenged Kunimura to a fistfight.

The Democratic Neighbor Island caucus had shucked its usual "all for one, one for all" attitude and was hopelessly divided over HB 1840. The four Big Island Democrats were split: Stanley Roehrig and Minoru Inaba supported the bill, while their colleagues, Herbert Segawa and Yoshito Takamine, opposed it.

Kunimura, the senior representative from Kaua'i, was pitted against his two younger Kaua'i colleagues, Dennis Yamada and Richard Kawakami. The three Maui Democrats supported HB 1840.

Roehrig and Yamada argued like the lawyers they were. In his long floor speech, Roehrig recounted the history of the haole Big Five corporations, how they had stifled competition and controlled Hawai'i's economy through "interlocking directorates"—an often-repeated bit of history that usually raised the ire of old-time Democrats. "Every member of this House who is for the small guy ought to vote for this bill," he concluded, leaving me wondering what "small guy" he was talking about. Industrial loan companies such as GECC Financial, Servco and Finance Factors were financially solid companies, rivaling some of the smaller banks and savings and loans in assets.

Yamada followed and, using words like "vertical integration," argued that allowing banks to engage in fields other than banking encouraged the development of "monopolistic practices." By prohibiting banks from getting into the industrial loan business through holding companies, he argued, HB 1840 would foster, not reduce, competition. This was another "small guy vs. big guy" argument.

Dan Kihano, a Democrat from Waipahu, opposed the bill, pointing out that Mainland banks were allowed to use holding companies to get into the industrial loan business and that it would be unfair to prohibit Hawai'i banks from doing the same thing. HB 1840, he argued, would stifle, not promote, competition.

Kunimura, apparently sensing that arguments about "monopolistic practice" and "competition" had run their course, rose to make the most sensible argument of the debate. Noting that the Department of Regulatory Agencies, which was created by the Legislature to regulate financial institutions, had already denied First Hawaiian's holding company its first application, Kunimura argued:

"What are we trying to do here tonight, Mr. Speaker? Are we trying to be inconsistent and say that the [Department of] Regulatory Agencies does not have the qualifications and the proper people to make the right decisions? Then we should do away with it and put the money someplace else? Are we trying to say that we are afraid they may approve this? Mr. Speaker, I think we are trying to put the cart before the horse."

Just before the vote was called, Republican Hiram Fong, Jr., and Democrats Minoru Inaba and Charles Ushijima each rose, declared conflicts of interest and requested a ruling from Wakatsuki on whether they could vote on the bill.

Fong, who was the Republican minority floor leader and the son of former United States Sen. Hiram Fong, held substantial shares in Finance Realty and Finance Factors, two industrial loan companies his family had helped start. Inaba was a director on the board of an industrial loan company. Ushijima was the Democratic majority leader and an executive at First Hawaiian Bank.

Wakatsuki ruled that none were in conflict and all who were present on the House floor were required to vote. If all three were allowed to vote, the supporters of the bill would net one more vote, as Fong and Inaba supported the bill, while Ushijima did not.

Republican Ralph Ajifu, who opposed the bill and a few years later would work for First Hawaiian, moved to appeal the Speaker's ruling. Kunimura seconded his motion. An apparently perplexed Kunimura rose to speak:

"Mr. Speaker ... what is the conflict of interest?"

Wakatsuki replied, "I have ruled that there is no conflict on the basis that each member makes a disclosure. We have a disclosure law that each member of the House file his financial statements with the Ethics Commission.... I believe that each one of us was elected by his constituents, presumably knowing each member's interest and his employment, and that the members here vote according to their conscience and what's good for the state."

In an oblique reference to Hiram Fong, Jr., Kunimura pressed the issue: "Then, Mr. Speaker, are 1,000 shares of Finance Realty and 450 shares of Finance Factors to you immaterial?"

"On the question of voting on a question, the chair rules there is no conflict," Wakatsuki said.

"Then, Mr. Speaker, am I to understand that, in your honest opinion, the ethics law and the requirement to file our interests is a hoax?"

"That is your opinion, not the Chair's," Wakatsuki answered.

Kunimura, who had a turn for the dramatic (one of his close friends was the famed Japanese actor, Toshiro Mifune) rose on a point of personal privilege and showed why he was a better politician than he was a butcher:

"I am aggrieved, Mr. Speaker.... We have gone to our constituents ... and declared that we shall do everything in our power to represent, not private interest, but public interest. It grieves me, Mr. Speaker, I have known you for many years and many times we have been shot by the same firing squad because of our closeness, and tonight, maybe temporarily, we part company. But, Mr. Speaker, I'd rather stand alone in this House, trying to do a job that is required of me by law and conscience, than to make convenient decisions ... and sit here quietly accepting all these conveniences.... Mr. Speaker, count me as an independent from tonight."

Smiling slightly, Wakatsuki replied, "Representative Kunimura, the issue before the House is whether the chair's ruling is sustained. After tonight, we will still be friends."

Under the House rules, any member could request a roll call vote. Unlike a voice vote, in which the individual's vote is expressed as one among many, a roll call vote required each representative to publicly announce his vote as his name was called.

"Mr. Speaker, I request a roll call vote," Ajifu said.

"A roll call vote has been requested. Mr. Clerk, call the roll," Wakatsuki ordered.

In alphabetical order, the clerk called out the names of all 51 members of the House. As the roll call droned on, the House chamber grew so quiet that the voices of the clerk and each individual representative echoed throughout. I busied myself checking off the "aye" and "nay" votes on the House roster as they were being declared. Kunimura looked at me with a grin and shook his head slightly, as if to say, "Don't bother. The vote on HB 1840 was decided hours ago in the closed caucus."

At 10:30 p.m., the clerk announced that HB 1840 had passed by a 28-22 margin (one member was absent). I was one of 13 Democrats and eight Republicans who joined Kunimura in voting against the bill. Twenty-one Democrats and seven Republicans voted for it.

A recess was called immediately after the vote. The ebullient Roehrig acted as if he had just won a major trial, strutting around the floor, literally high-fiving members who had voted with him. Roehrig's antics were too much for Kunimura to take. Losing his temper, Kunimura accosted Roehrig as he walked by, grabbing him by his necktie and spewing epithets into the Hilo Democrat's startled face.

I was sitting next to Kunimura and jumped up from my seat to restrain him. My timing was perfect. If somehow things had gotten out of hand—I knew they wouldn't—Roehrig, who was about as physically fit as a Marine just out of boot camp, could have done some real damage. To his credit, the younger Roehrig walked away, his feelings hurt, surprised that his much-older, portly and out-of-shape friend from Kaua'i had taken the defeat so personally.

The floor action on HB 1840 was a learning experience. Whatever Kunimura did on the House floor, he did fully aware that the public and media were watching. He was in top form that night. I enjoyed all of it. *This is how it should be,* I thought. *Everything out in the open. Playing by the rules. Clean. On the record for the public to know. Every legislator held accountable for his or her vote.*

HB 1840 did not raise any monumental issues. This was a battle between two special interests, one trying to use the law to shut out the other to protect its economic interest. It was the kind of struggle that I would see repeatedly, albeit with different special interests, during my 12 years in the Legislature.

On principle, there was little to choose from on either side. Each had presented a reasonable argument. The bill was not about the poor or the disadvantaged—it was about financial institutions fighting to make money. Banks and industrial loan companies are not sympathetic figures. Whether HB 1840 passed or failed, the loser would survive.

Under these circumstances, intangibles such as friendship, intuition, trust, resentment, distrust or any of the wide spectrum of other human feelings could play a bigger role than usual in influencing how one voted. Indeed, Kunimura never struck me as a water-carrier for the bank. His opposition to the bill arose more out of his close friendship with Ushijima than anything else. Ushijima was one of the most popular members of the House. When Kunimura stepped forward to support Ushijima, he brought with him others who were his allies and close friends, such as Dan Kihano, Henry Peters and others.

For me the issue was marginal. At this point in my legislative career, I felt little empathy for the banks and the industrial loan companies. I could have flipped a coin to decide which side I would support. I voted with Kunimura mainly because I admired him for taking on the House leadership and for standing by Ushijima, who I also liked and respected. My high school civics teacher would have been disappointed at the reasons for my vote.

The Manoa Finance Crisis

The industrial loan story did not end with the vote on HB 1840. As the real estate market began to cool, industrial loan companies whose portfolios were heavily weighted with real estate began to run short of the cash they needed to pay the high interest rates promised to their depositors.

In 1976, an industrial loan company, THC Financial, closed. Fortunately, a plan was developed by which it managed to repay its depositors in full over a five-year period.

The THC Financial failure caused enough concern among legislators that, in 1977, they established the Thrift Guaranty Corp. of Hawai'i to insure industrial loan savings accounts, as the FDIC did with bank savings accounts. The FDIC was an independent corporation established by Congress to insure bank deposits and was funded by assessments on member banks. Similarly, Thrift Guaranty was set up as a private Hawai'i nonprofit corporation funded by assessments on member industrial loan companies totaling $2 million per year. To get Thrift Guaranty started, the State loaned it $29 million, of which $20 million was used to start the fund.

In February 1983, the State bank examiner ordered the closure of industrial loan companies Manoa Finance and Great Hawaiian Financial, for their failure to meet statutory financial requirements.

State officials looked to Thrift Guaranty Corp. to provide relief. The Thrift funds, however, had been partially depleted by the earlier failure of other industrial loan companies, such as Imperial Finance. Thrift Guaranty paid only about one-third of the deposits and was $32 million short of finishing the job.

Some legislators wanted the State to contribute the $32 million and be done with the problem. Others felt, as I did, that the State had already made substantial loans that would probably never be repaid, and that the industrial loan companies should be assessed and a repayment plan worked out.

In an ironic twist, the State bank examiner approached First Hawaiian Bank's Walter Dods to develop a plan to bail out the depositors. Dods, then First Hawaiian's vice president of marketing, had good reason not to get involved. First Hawaiian had been so badly out-lobbied by the industrial loan companies on HB 1840 that Dods once joked to me that he "felt as if [he] had been run over by a truck."

By the time of the crisis, however, First Hawaiian had managed to get into the industrial loan business by buying Hawaii Thrift and Loan, a failing industrial loan company, so the bank had an interest in how things turned out.

Still, Dods' first response to the State bank examiner's request was negative: "My initial reaction was, 'Hey, these elderly Japanese were getting higher interest rates. They took the risks. Tough luck' … but when I actually saw the people, it became a cause for me. It wasn't greed. They trusted [Manoa Finance CEO] Yamamoto."

Human faces had been put on the depositors. The thousands of elderly, mostly AJA depositors, many of whom had their life savings in Manoa Finance, hardly fit the stereotype of greedy investors. Perhaps in some other place, people could say "too bad" and forget about it. But Dods, the son of a police officer and a coffee shop waitress, wasn't brought up that way; moreover, First Hawaiian Bank itself had gotten into the business by purchasing a failing industrial loan company. For three hectic months he immersed himself in developing a plan to make the depositors whole again.

Dods agreed to work with the court-appointed trustee of Manoa Finance, Charles Klenske, Thrift Guaranty and the remaining industrial loan companies to develop a solution. In April 1985, Dods' modified plan was approved by the State Legislature. The plan called for the remaining industrial loan companies to loan $21.2 million to Thrift Guaranty and for the State to loan the balance of $9.5 million. Both loans were secured by the real property that Thrift Guaranty had taken over from Manoa Finance and Great Hawaiian for the benefit of the depositors.

Among the senators, Abercrombie and I were Dods' two biggest supporters. Immediately after the plan was approved, Dods, misty-eyed and emotional, came over to thank us for standing by him.

Dods' fervent leadership had worked a near-miracle. In a little over two years after Manoa Finance was closed, its depositors were repaid. It would take another three years to liquidate the real property assets to repay the loans made by the State and the industrial loan companies.

In 1989, Dods became president and CEO of First Hawaiian Bank, and in 1996 he became the first Hawai'i banker to be selected as president of the prestigious American Banking Association.

In 1982, Kunimura left the Legislature and was elected mayor of Kaua'i. He was reelected twice thereafter. But by 1988, Kunimura had reached a point in his political career which I think all politicians reach if they are in office too long, at which he couldn't have cared less what anyone thought about him. That attitude showed when he was caught on television, bare-chested, cooking chicken hekka for the boys at then-U.S. Rep. Dan Akaka's apartment in Washington, D.C. A reporter asked him about a controversial Kaua'i housing project, about which he quipped: "If God wanted everyone to have a house, he would have made all of us turtles."

In 1988, he was badly beaten in his bid for reelection by Joanne Yukimura, a young liberal-environmentalist Democrat he had beaten in 1982. That defeat marked Kunimura's retirement from politics.

The Firestorm

On April 7, the 56th day of the 1975 legislative session, the House was formally notified that Gov. John A. Burns had lost his long battle with cancer. In his 1974 farewell message to the joint session of the State Legislature, Burns spoke with eloquence:

"With no regrets, with an unclouded conscience, and with the knowledge that we have done our best within our limited abilities, I shall leave this office in due time; I shall leave enriched with the countless and cherished friendships, with nothing but warm memories of the years of mutual toil toward noble ends, and with a deep and abiding love for the people in whose cause we have sought a life of public service."

On April 8, the 57th day of the session, the House paid tribute to the fallen leader. The outpouring of heartfelt sentiments from both Democrats and Republicans was inspiring and moving.

Speaker Wakatsuki eulogized Burns as one of the "finest public servants ever to serve Hawai'i's people." Republican minority leader Andy Poepoe described Burns as "a man who will be cited by our state's history books as a truly great leader of Hawai'i. Every word, every honor, every tribute is rightfully his."

Big Island Democrat Yoshito Takamine, a former ILWU official, spoke of how much Burns had done to improve the lives of working people. Kaua'i Democrat Kunimura lauded Burns as "our Great White Father" and the "Messiah" of the Democratic Party.

As the tributes from both sides continued, I reflected on how Burns had brought me into public service and, finding myself caught up in the emotion that filled the House chamber, I vowed that I would do everything I could to live up to the trust he had placed in me.

The 1975 legislative session had been a highly productive one; we had done some good work for the people of Hawai'i. It would have been ideal to have adjourned sine die as we paid tribute to John A. Burns on the 57th day.

It was not to be. On the 60th and final day of the session, a monumental lapse in good judgment by the House leadership over two bills would tarnish the session.

Kenneth Lee was the chairman of the Labor and Public Employment Committee. At the time, I did not know much about him, except that he was one of two representatives from the 17th District in Kalihi. Lee gained notoriety when he punched out *Honolulu Star-Bulletin* reporter Gregg Kakesako over a story Kakesako had written that criticized Lee. Kakesako suffered minor bruises but decided not to press charges. Although the veterans I spoke to thought Lee's actions were stupid and inexcusable, a few could hardly hide their delight that for once it was the reporter who had taken it on the chops.

Lee's biggest responsibility that year was to manage the bill that provided funding for the recently negotiated collective bargaining agreement for State workers.

The bill in question was Senate Bill 1645. Under existing conference rules, if the House and Senate disagree on a bill, they can send the bill to conference. House and Senate conferees, appointed by the Speaker and Senate president, then meet in conference to work out the differences. If the conferees agree on a final version of the bill, it is then referred to the full body of the House and Senate for a vote. Neither side can propose amendments at that point, and a majority of each house must approve the bill. If the bill fails to get approval in either house, it dies.

When SB 1645 was sent to conference, it only covered pay raises for State workers. The conferees amended the bill to include pay raises for the judiciary, the governor, the lieutenant governor and the governor's Cabinet. When done without a public hearing, this questionable practice is referred to as "piggybacking."

To critics who argued that the pay raises for the judiciary and the governor had not had a public hearing, Lee's response was that separate bills relating to pay raises for the judiciary and the executive branch had received public hearings; therefore, he argued, the subject matter had undergone public hearing, albeit in separate bills. The conference committee's decision to lump these pay raises with those for State workers, of course, was just a ploy. Voted on separately, the chances of a pay-raise bill for judges and the governor were problematic. Tying them to negotiated pay raises for State workers made a big difference. Politically, it was difficult to vote against a bill for 45,000 State workers just because it also included pay raises for the Judiciary and the governor.

Thus, the legislators were given a Hobson's choice: A vote against the bill would anger the unions and thousands of State workers whose pay raises had been legitimately negotiated, whereas a vote to give pay raises to the newly elected governor, lieutenant governor and Cabinet would likely anger the public.

I didn't like the piggybacking. Yes, the Republicans could play politics if the pay raises for the governor, his cabinet and the judges were in a separate bill, but I believed there were sound reasons to justify the raises. Lee's game-playing was underhanded; it would place a cloud over the heads of every House member who voted for SB 1645 and add to the public's already negative perception of politicians.

I was annoyed. The piggybacking seemed unnecessary and foolish. One would have to be blind to not foresee the negative public reaction. But I sensed that Lee's many years in politics had jaded his idealism. By most accounts, Lee had worked hard to better the lives of his constituents in Kalihi. But at some point, he had become a "game-player"—a malady that often strikes those who have held political power for too long.

I voted for the bill because I supported giving the judiciary and the governor pay raises. Back then, the salaries for high-level State executives, such as the president of the University of Hawai'i and superintendent of education, were set by law at 95 percent of the governor's salary. Thus, the governor's salary (about $47,500) acted as a ceiling for high-level State executive jobs. Compared to salaries in the private sector, the State salaries were too low, making it difficult to recruit highly qualified people.

As expected, the Republicans had a field day attacking the piggybacking approach. On a roll call vote, the bill passed 37-14. But the passage of SB No. 1645 was just a prelude to the firestorm to come.

SB 1645 wasn't the only surprise Lee pulled out of the conference: Mindful that his efforts had delivered pay raises not only to 45,000 State workers but to the judges, governor, lieutenant governor and the governor's Cabinet, he must have thought it only fair that legislators share in the State's largesse as well.

This time, Lee outdid himself. He convinced the House and Senate conferees that it was time to increase legislative pensions. To this end, he gutted a bill relating to interest rates on the State employees' retirement system and inserted a provision that would increase legislative pensions by 150 percent. The idea came out of the blue and began to take on a life of its own.

The discussion in the closed majority caucus was intense. But aside from Lee defending his actions, few of the House veterans said anything. Nevertheless, some troubling issues emerged: The attorney general acknowledged that the bill in its amended form might have been unconstitutional; there had been no public hearing on legislative pensions, and there was an inherent conflict of interest in legislators voting on a bill that would enhance their own pensions. His words were of no avail. Yoshito Takamine, Lee's vice chairman, ended the debate. "Okay, there's been enough discussion, let's go out and vote," he said.

As we headed out of the caucus room, Vice Speaker Richard Garcia looked at me and shook his head. "Ben, this is a bad bill, but I gotta support the Speaker and the chairman." Majority Floor Leader Bob Kimura and Majority Assistant Floor Leader Steve Cobb felt no such compunction, and both decided to vote against the bill. Kimura told the Speaker he was going to vote against the bill, but that he would not speak against it. "Ben, make sure you guys speak out against it on the floor. The Republicans are going to kill us on this," he said.

During the floor debate, I attempted to question Lee.

"Mr. Speaker, will the chairman yield to a question?" I asked.

"No," Lee replied.

"Mr. Speaker, will you yield to a question?"

"Not today," he replied.

It was pretty clear that the majority wanted to get the vote over with as soon as possible. I finished my floor speech, once again raising the same issues that other freshmen legislators and I had raised in the closed caucus, virtually pleading with the members to vote against the bill.

Carl Takamura rose and quoted from a *Star-Bulletin* editorial praising the Legislature: "'Most major questions up for decision have been fully and freely discussed, not ramrodded past an unsuspecting public.'"

The chamber was so quiet one could hear the proverbial pin drop. Fed up, Takamura made a final and futile plea: "Personally, I refuse to be sandbagged again. Now I know how this thing works, and I know that the votes have been counted and we're probably speaking to ourselves … but, maybe not, and maybe to some of the people here, and I doubt if these words will change anybody's mind …

but if there is somebody who's still on the fence, I hope you will consider carefully what's happening here tonight and vote with your conscience."

As Bob Kimura had predicted, the Republicans had a field day: "Our collective pledge ... that we would support open government ... is now a mockery.... We have so amended the original HB 1779 that it would not be recognized by its own parents," Kinau Kamalii said.

Jack Larsen mocked the Democratic majority by reading from Webster's Dictionary the definition of words such as "avarice" and "greed."

Buddy Soares warned, "I think it's remiss that we allow ourselves to come down to the wire ... and cloud our whole session by passing this bill."

Andy Poepoe sat silent, waiting for the train wreck that was about to happen.

Lee, unwilling to answer questions on the floor, stopped speaking in defense of his bill, resorting instead to having the clerk insert his prepared written statements into the record.

The day before, the news media had gotten wind of HB 1779, and their early reports had spurred many people to personally confront their legislators at the State Capitol. It was about 10 p.m., but the House gallery was packed with hundreds of people. HB 1779 had taken on a life of its own.

A roll call vote was requested. As the clerk called for Blair's vote, he responded, "Kanalua." (In Hawaiian, this means "I doubt," but as used in the Legislature, it means "not ready.") Under House rules, a legislator could respond with "kanalua" two times, after which he was required to declare his vote.

Like most of the freshmen, Blair was under tremendous pressure. Just 24 years old and fresh out of law school, he was the youngest person ever to be elected to the State House—an impressive accomplishment that made him a favorite of the news media. He was in a tough spot for someone with so little life experience, and he had only a few seconds to make up his mind.

Among the standing-room-only crowd in the House gallery were members of Blair's young staff. When Blair declared "kanalua" the first time, his staff could be heard urging him to "Go down! Go down!" When the clerk called on Blair for the second time, Blair voted "aye," and a collective groan of disappointment could be heard not only from his staff but also from others in the gallery who had taken a liking to the young legislator as well.

HB 1779 passed final reading by a vote of 30 ayes to 21 nos. Only seven Democrats—Clarence Akizaki, Abercrombie, Cobb, Kimura, Takamura and I—had voted no. At 11:56 p.m., April 11, 1975, the House adjourned sine die.

The next day, the *Star-Bulletin*, which had praised the Legislature for its open decision-making, headlined its afternoon issue "150 PERCENT PENSION INCREASE!!" in letters so big they took up nearly half of the front page. The *Honolulu Advertiser* weighed in with a stinging editorial that repeated what we all knew: The fiasco over the legislative pension bill had ruined an otherwise productive legislative session. HB 1779 was the news media's top story. Radio stations repeatedly played excerpts from our floor speeches. An outraged public vented its fury at the Democrats by bombarding them with telephone calls and letters. This was not a media event that would pass in a few days.

Three or four days after adjournment, Wakatsuki called for a closed-door meeting of the majority caucus. The six House Democrats who had voted against HB 1779 were not invited. A similar meeting was held by the Senate majority caucus. An hour or so later, we were told that the caucuses had decided to jointly petition the governor to veto HB 1779.

On April 18, 1975, Gov. Ariyoshi vetoed the bill, noting in his veto message that he had done so at the request of the legislative petitioners.

I knew of no one among the six Democrats and 15 Republicans who had voted against HB 1779 who took pleasure in the debacle. For 59 days, the 75th Legislature had done excellent work. But after the 60th day, few among the public would remember, or care.

Overall, I believed Wakatsuki was a fine Speaker, but it would take a few years before his good works erased the stigma of his lapse of leadership on the legislative pension bill. Before I left the House for the State Senate in 1978, I met with him to thank him and wish him well. I asked him, of course, why he had not tried to stop the bill. He smiled and replied, "That was a big mistake … but you know, Ben, a Speaker doesn't have the luxury of being a dissident. There are a lot of bills I don't personally support, but I have to respect the work put into them by the chairmen and their committee members."

"Like what?"

"Like when you held the fuel tax bill in your committee to force the Finance Committee to report out your engine displacement tax bill, some of the guys thought you were being unreasonable, because we all knew how important it was to increase the fuel tax. And some of the guys in leadership were so pissed off because you made the issue so public that they wanted to throw you out as chairman, but I stopped them."

"Why did you?" I asked.

"Frankly, I didn't think an engine displacement tax would stop anyone from buying a big car. But I understood what you were trying to do—I was once young and idealistic like you…. I knew how much work you and your committee members did on your bill. And I respected that."

I said nothing.

"But hey … maybe that was another big mistake on my part … maybe I should've let them throw you out," he said, chuckling. "One day, Ben, you will find out that being a leader is not so easy."

Gov. Ariyoshi appointed Wakatsuki to the State Circuit Court in 1980 and to the Hawai'i Supreme Court in 1983. I was a member of the Senate Judiciary Committee, which would recommend confirmation or rejection to the Senate body. He was publicly criticized by the Republicans, who argued he should have resigned as Speaker when he accepted the nomination. *Better for a Democrat to raise the issue than to leave it to the Republicans*, I thought. And so I grilled him about it at the hearing. As expected, he fielded my questions with ease. Along with the rest of committee, I voted to confirm him.

The day after the Senate confirmed his appointment, he sent me a handwritten note: "Ben, you would make a good prosecutor. Aloha, Jimmy." A few years later, Ariyoshi appointed him to the State Supreme Court, where he served honorably until his premature death in 1992.

The 60th day of the 1975 legislative session was a defining moment for me. I was one of only three of the 12 freshmen Democrats who fought against the legislative pension bill. Many of the House veterans voted for the bill out of loyalty to Wakatsuki. Wakatsuki's misstep was a consequence of his strong belief in consensus. "The House Chairman wants it … and the Senate leadership want it too," he explained to the caucus.

The word "consensus" is so overused in politics that every time I hear it I think of Abba Eban, Israel's former ambassador to the United Nations, who once described "consensus" as "what many people say in chorus but do not believe as individuals." Every political leader seeks consensus. In a democracy, the word itself sounds like a worthy goal. Indeed, Burns and Ariyoshi were "consensus" leaders; independents like Tom Gill and Nelson Doi were not.

But seeking consensus for its own sake can cause problems; it may lead to undesirable compromises inimical to the public interest, as it did on HB 1779. Finding the point of departure is the difficult challenge. HB 1779, however, taught me what should have been obvious: My conscience would be my guide, and if I had to err, I should do so on the side of the public's interest.

I understood how difficult it was for many of the freshmen to oppose the House veterans on the bill, but my experience as a criminal defense lawyer made it easier for me to deal with the pressure. As a lawyer, I had devoted myself to assuring that my defendant clients would be treated fairly and accorded every constitutional right, regardless of what anyone thought of me. I found honor in that. As an elected public servant my only client was the public, and I had sworn to uphold its trust, regardless of the political consequences. It meant much to me that I did so on HB 1779.

The experience drew Neil Abercrombie, Carl Takamura and me closer. Abercrombie was a former probation officer who became a university professor and had been a leader at UH in protests against the Vietnam War. Takemura had been deeply involved in community service. The three of us had been in college during the mid-1960s and emerged from those years as political and social liberals possessed of a healthy skepticism of government. Thereafter, on most controversial issues, we tended to vote together.

The Freeway and the Train

As the 1976 election got closer, I heard that the former incumbent, Tats Kishinami, was preparing to run again. I had been criticized by some community leaders in the district about my opposition to the University of Hawai'i's proposed new West O'ahu College (years later, I would change my position after O'ahu Sugar Company closed its plantation in West O'ahu). There were others who did not like my outspoken style.

I had beaten Kishinami narrowly in 1974. He had been overconfident and taken me lightly, a mistake I knew he would not repeat in 1976. The thought that my political career might end after only two years was disconcerting. But I knew if I held back as a legislator, if I didn't speak out publicly and do what I thought was right in the time I had left, I'd never forgive myself if I was defeated. *Go for it, go for broke—you may never have a second chance*, I thought. And that would be my political creed for the 28 years I served in public office.

There were some good signs. I received a handwritten note along with a $50 check from Tom Kiyosaki, Farrington High School's legendary football coach. "Ben, don't forget where you came from. Keep up the good work," he wrote. Kiyosaki had joined Farrington after I graduated in 1958. I had never met him, but his reputation as a great coach had reached me even while I was living in Los Angeles. Kiyosaki was as revered at Farrington as Paul Bear Bryant was at Alabama or John Wooden at UCLA. One of the great anecdotes about him was about the night when people who attended a night event at the school returned to the parking lot to discover that vandals had systematically ripped off every car in the parking lot—except Kiyosaki's. He was a World War II veteran and, like his brother Ralph, who became superintendent of public education and later ran for lieutenant governor as a Republican, had devoted his life to public service.

I also got a note with a $50 check from Keiji Kawakami, founder of 'Iolani Sportswear. His handwritten note said the same thing: "Ben, don't forget where you came from …" Like Kiyosaki, Kawakami was a combat veteran, having served with the famed 442nd Regiment in World War II. Later, I found out that Keiji and his wife, Edith, were dedicated and generous patrons of local art and music, particularly Hawaiian art and music. Keiji's note was the beginning of a cherished friendship.

To beat Kishinami I had to get a decent share of the AJA vote in Pearl City. The unsolicited notes from Kiyosaki and Kawakami lifted my spirits and gave me confidence that I would win.

A few hours after the polls closed in the primary, I learned that I had handily won. Mizuguchi and I were easily reelected in the general election. A post-election poll revealed that 63 percent of the AJAs in my district had supported me—only 2 percent less than had voted for Mizuguchi, who had received 65 percent of the vote. This time, however, I led the ticket in overall votes, polling more than 1,000 over Mizuguchi and garnering the highest vote total for a House race in the state.

My victory taught me another truism of Hawai'i politics: Though the voters may disagree with a politician on issues, they are likely to support him if they believe he is honest and fighting for their best interests.

A few years later, a UH study on voting patterns in Hawai'i concluded that when it came to voting, AJAs were the most liberal of all ethnic groups in Hawai'i. I was living proof of that conclusion. In every election I ran in thereafter, Pearl City would be my strongest district.

From 1976 to 1978, much of my time was spent dealing with controversial transportation issues, such as the proposed H-3 freeway and Fasi's proposed mass transit program, the Honolulu Area Rapid Transit (HART) system, which would be publicly reviewed by my committee.

H-3 was one of many freeways built across the nation under President Eisenhower's greatest legacy—the Interstate Defense Highway Program, a massive capital-improvement program designed to move military equipment and personnel more efficiently intrastate as well as interstate. The short- and long-term economic impacts of the program were enormous. For the states, the big carrot was the federal government's promise to pay for 90 percent of the construction costs.

Ostensibly, H-3 was planned to provide a quicker, more efficient transportation link of Pearl Harbor Naval Base, Schofield Barracks and the Kāne'ohe Marine base. But at the Legislature, the importance of H-3 for military purposes held little significance and was rarely brought up. Rather, the debate focused on whether H-3 would relieve the daily traffic congestion caused by commuters heading to work in downtown Honolulu by allowing other commuters an alternate route to West O'ahu's huge employment centers, such as Pearl Harbor Shipyard, Hickam Air Force Base and Schofield Barracks. Labor unions and businesses argued that the huge construction project would give the economy a big and needed boost by creating hundreds of new jobs and an increased demand for goods and supplies.

But the thought of a 16-mile, six-lane concrete freeway running from the beautiful 3,700-acre Moanalua Valley through the pristine Ko'olau Mountains infuriated the environmentalists. The Moanalua Valley Foundation, an organization financed by the wealthy kama'āina Damon family, which owned much of the valley, joined in the fight. The two groups sued the State in federal court and managed to delay the H-3 project for more than a decade, forcing the State to change H-3's route from the Damon family's Moanalua Valley to Hālawa Valley. When H-3 was finally completed in 1997, the delays had driven its cost from an estimated $70 million in 1977 to an outrageous $1.2 billion. Fortunately for Hawai'i taxpayers, the federal government paid for 90 percent of the construction costs.

Angry Hawaiian activists, asserting that H-3 threatened historic sites and desecrated the land, weighed in as well. Archaeologists found heiau (religious sites), which would be destroyed by the construction. The State was forced to adopt measures to preserve them. On the other hand, some of the activists impaired their credibility with exaggerated claims—piles of rock were suddenly transformed into historical and sacred heiau. Emotions ran high, so much so that one activist leader, Lilikala Kameʻeleihiwa, a University of Hawaiʻi professor, prayed publicly for the deaths of anyone who worked on H-3. Her crass, arrogant remarks proved prophetic, as several workers were killed and dozens injured during the construction of H-3.

My committee's public hearings were held before packed crowds; the hearings often became contentious as tempers flared and accusatory statements were exchanged. Committee members and I were heavily lobbied by groups on both sides.

I supported H-3. The City General Plan had designated West Oʻahu as the site for Oʻahu's second city, today called Kapolei. West Oʻahu was already the fastest-growing area in the entire state, traffic congestion had grown worse, and the bulk of the state's private and public housing was being built there. As a resident of Pearl City, I experienced the negative impact of the growth firsthand; traffic congestion had reached intolerable levels, affecting air quality and mobility, and there seemed to be little relief in sight. Under the circumstances, I thought it was unfair to expect West Oʻahu residents to absorb the full impact of urban growth over the next two decades. H-3 would divert some of that growth to Windward Oʻahu.

The majority of my committee members agreed that the H-3 appropriation should be included in the State's Capital Improvement Bill, which was being developed by the Finance Committee. The debate over H-3 ranged from issues relating to the environment and historical Hawaiian sites to transportation, traffic congestion, jobs and the economy. But no matter which side of the debate one was on, at its core was an overriding public concern about urban growth and its impact on the quality of life.

Ever since Stanford Professor Paul Erlich's bestselling doomsday book *The Population Bomb* had been released in 1968, predictions about population growth had become a staple of discussion among politicians and academics. In 1974, First Hawaiian Bank economist Thomas Hitch calculated that, if Hawaiʻi's population growth rate were to continue, the state would have a population of 14 million people by 2074. No reasonable person could rely on the accuracy of such a prediction, but it seemed to me that the well-respected Hitch's sole purpose was to make a satirical point about the adverse consequences of growth to the current crop of politicians who, in his eyes, seemed indifferent to it.

In 1977, Fasi got into the business of forecasting population growth, predicting that Oʻahu's population would grow to 3 million in two decades. (How he reached that conclusion remained a mystery.) Thus, he argued, Honolulu needed a rail transit system that would relieve traffic congestion and move people around efficiently. Fasi's hyperbole on population growth notwithstanding, his proposed rail transit system, the Honolulu Area Rapid Transit (HART) was bold and innovative. To fund the system, the City wanted the authority to levy a

1-percent general excise tax. My initial reaction to the proposal was favorable.

Shortly after the legislative session ended, I decided to take three of my committee members on a tour of several Mainland rail transit systems. San Francisco's BART (Bay Area Rapid Transit) was the first. The presentation made by BART officials was impressive and professional. The BART train was very impressive; it was clean and spacious, and the ride was surprisingly quiet and comfortable.

Our next stop was an appointment with Professor Melvin Webber, the director of the Institute of Urban and Regional Development at the University of California at Berkeley. Webber was renowned nationally for his work on urban and regional planning. He had been a consultant on the BART project and had later formed misgivings about such heavy rail transit systems.

A 15-minute courtesy call turned into an hour. Professor Webber, who had studied HART, invited us to his home for dinner, where more discussion about HART and the poor performance of rail transit in other cities followed. We had to leave just before midnight, or we'd miss the last BART scheduled for San Francisco. We had spent about five hours engaged in a fascinating discussion with a highly interesting man.

"Rail transit is not for every city," Webber said. Rail transit made sense for cities like Chicago and New York, he argued, but for Honolulu, it could be a costly mistake. The HART ridership projections were unrealistically high, he pointed out, comparing them to actual ridership for other rail systems. Moreover, HART would have to rely heavily on a feeder bus system, because there was little available land for park-and-ride lots to which commuters could drive and leave their cars. BART, he noted, had huge park-and-ride lots, as well as a feeder bus system to get passengers to the stations, but its actual ridership still fell far below original projections. Moreover, he concluded, Honolulu's projected population of between 1.2 to 1.5 million people (in 2008—33 years later—Oʻahu's population is a little more than 900,000) over 20 years was too small to generate the volume of ridership necessary to keep tickets at reasonable prices. The population projections were critical because fewer people meant lower ridership, which in turn meant either an increase in fares or reduction in services. If ticket prices were not affordable, ridership would fall, requiring a higher operating subsidy from the City real property taxes to keep the system going.

We had never before heard anyone critique the HART proposal in such detail. At least not anyone from the State Department of Transportation (DOT), which avoided publicly criticizing HART. Politics was in play.

The State wanted federal funding for H-3. If Fasi opposed H-3, it would likely jeopardize the State's chances for federal approval and funding. On the other hand, if the State opposed HART, the project was dead. When Fasi once made some critical comments about the feasibility of H-3, the DOT got the message.

It therefore remained for the Legislature to analyze HART. Webber had given me and my committee members a lot to think about, and I assigned my staff to research some of the issues he had raised.

Fasi had hired a rail transit consultant named George Villegas to manage the HART project and head the city's team in trying to sell the project to the Legislature. Villegas was an experienced rail transit proponent, but each time he testified before my committee, his credibility suffered. He tended to engage in hyperbole, making dubious claims about how HART would benefit the community. Incredibly, he once testified that, among other benefits, HART would result in savings of millions of dollars (he even gave a specific dollar amount) in automobile insurance premiums for people who would forego buying a second car. As one bemused committee member told me later, "This guy must think we're stupid." Villegas' usefulness to Fasi was compromised each time he testified. About a year later, Villegas was gone. Ostensibly, he had resigned to work as a consultant on a rail transit project in South America.

As a precondition to qualifying for federal funding, the federal Urban Mass Transit Authority (UMTA) required the City to do a thorough alternative analysis to ensure that the City had considered all reasonable alternatives to rail transit.

Astrid and Donald Monson, two well-known experts in city planning who had moved to Hawai'i to retire in 1973, had taken it upon themselves as citizens to review the City's "alternative analysis" statement. They concluded that it had been done pro forma and was biased on the side of the rail transit alternative. My staff concurred with the Monsons, and we began focusing on the City's statement.

Fasi had little patience for any person who questioned the City's work on HART. Once, after I suggested at a public hearing that the City take a closer look at the feasibility of converting Hotel Street into a dedicated busway, as had been done in Portland, Oregon, Fasi immediately announced the City would hold a demonstration to show that a busway was not feasible. The next day, Fasi ordered between 50 and 100 city buses to drive down Hotel Street. The buses were driven in one lane, horns honking, bumper to bumper—so close they looked like circus elephants walking single file, each animal's trunk gripping the tail of the one before it. It was so outlandish, so bizarre, that when I heard the horns honking and saw the buses I smiled and said to Roddy Rodrigues, who was my committee clerk at the time, "Whatever people may think about this guy ... the man has balls." When a reporter asked me what I thought about Fasi's demonstration, I said that I thought it was "funny." To many House veterans, however, it was just another Fasi antic that reflected poorly on his character.

In 1977, Wakatsuki approved my recommendation for holding a conference on the proposed HART system. He was concerned about the cost, but agreed that it was the best way for the public and legislators to get more information about HART. The format was simple: The City would invite its experts to present the case for HART; I would invite Mainland experts to present the other side.

I invited Webber and asked him to invite other experts who had analyzed HART. Webber brought professors from Princeton, Harvard and a few other universities.

The City brought in experts who were experienced in running rail transit systems in Mainland cities such as Chicago and New York, and a professor of engineering from the University of Pennsylvania.

The conference was packed, with legislators, councilmen, labor leaders and community leaders among the audience. The news media gave the conference excellent coverage. The experts on both sides were excellent, very professional in giving their opinions. But most important, the conference enhanced public awareness of the pros and cons of HART.

HART was Fasi's creation, but at the Legislature, he turned out to be its worst enemy. His attitude and antics offended legislators who were undecided and eager to learn more about it. Many Neighbor Island legislators had become increasingly skeptical about supporting a costly rail transit system which would benefit only Oʻahu. Rather than meeting with them personally to allay their concerns, Fasi seemed inclined to play politics through the news media. Each time he opened his mouth he drove another stake into HART.

I had nothing against Fasi. In fact, I thought he had done some good things as mayor. But I was one of only a handful of House Democrats who felt that way. After Fasi's stunt with the buses, a veteran House Democrat put his hand on my shoulder and chuckled: "Now you know, Ben, why we don't trust the guy: He thinks he's better than anyone else; you can't believe anything he says."

By 1978, HART was dead. In 1986, the City renewed its rail rapid transit proposal—but this time opted for a "light rail" system. The State Legislature passed a law that authorized the City Council to levy a half-percent increase in the general excise tax. Led by its chairman, Arnold Morgado, the Council rejected the tax increase by a single vote. Rail transit was dead again—only to be revived in 2005 by newly elected Mayor Mufi Hannemann. ❖

CHAPTER FIVE

OHA and the Affairs of State

Growth and the Economy

The hotly contested 1978 Democratic primary race between incumbent Gov. George R. Ariyoshi and Honolulu Mayor Frank F. Fasi dominated the news coverage. Ariyoshi's narrow come-from-behind victory pretty much decided his reelection; he overwhelmed Republican John Leopold in the general election.

The most significant political event of the year, however, was the 1978 Constitutional Convention. A number of constitutional amendments were proposed, the most significant of which established the Office of Hawaiian Affairs (OHA). The Hawaiian cultural and historical renaissance had expanded into the political arena. Self-determination would from then on become the dominant Hawaiian issue confronting future political leaders.

But in 1978, the impact of economic growth on Hawai'i's quality of life remained a big issue. Surveys revealed that although the people welcomed the new wealth that was being created, they were highly concerned about its impact on the quality of life.

Ariyoshi responded by revealing his "preferred future" policy in a State of the State address. Some shrugged it off as political rhetoric. His policies seemed contradictory at times: He supported H-3, which would encourage growth on the Windward side of O'ahu; on the other hand, he resorted mainly to land banking to help keep the area rural for future generations.

To discourage the immigration of Mainland hippie types who, according to widespread anecdotes, headed straight for the State welfare office from the airport, Ariyoshi established residency requirements for welfare benefits and State jobs. Many believed his policy, in light of recent federal court rulings, to be unconstitutional.

The real catalyst for Hawai'i's surge in population and its attendant problems was the growth of tourism and real estate development, not Mainland hippies. After Burns was elected governor in 1962, Hawai'i's appeal as one of the world's premier tourist destinations brought in billions of dollars from outside investors, many of them Japanese, such as Kenji Osano.

Between 1962 and the passage of the State Plan in 1978, nine new hotels had been built, among them the Sheraton Maui at Ka'anapali; the Kahala Hilton on O'ahu and the Mauna Kea Beach Hotel on the Big Island. A 1969 First Hawaiian Bank report predicted that Waikīkī would reach a peak of 31,000 hotel rooms (as of 2007, there were 34,000), second only to New York.

For more than a decade, Hawai'i had one of the hottest real estate markets in the nation. Construction boomed, bringing in thousands of out-of-work Mainland construction workers ("snow birds," as they were called by locals), many of whom later decided to make Hawai'i their home.

In a free capitalist economy, there was only so much the State and County governments could do to control growth. Among the most effective tools for managing growth on O'ahu were the policies set by the State Land Use Commission, the State Land Board and the City's Zoning and Planning commissions.

One of the goals of the 1954 Democrats was to break up the Republican stranglehold on economic opportunity. By the early 1970s tremendous gains had been made. The state economy was booming. Hawai'i's real estate market showed no signs of waning. New business investors tended to hire lawyers and consultants who had access to those who held political power. Thus, Mainland corporations such as Boise Cascade hired Big Island Senator John Ushijima; Daiei, the big Japanese corporation, retained Wally Fujiyama. Many legislators and politically connected members of boards and commissions got involved in real estate. There was nothing illegal about public officials getting into business unless it influenced their work at the Legislature or on boards and commissions.

State and County politicians found themselves struggling with the dilemma of freeing up land for housing and economic development for Hawai'i's fast-growing population. On O'ahu, the City Council tended to be a developer-friendly bunch, and Fasi, in touting HART, accepted that rapid population growth on O'ahu was a given. Instead, he chose to exact a heavy price from developers by imposing "impact fees" as a precondition to approval of a development. The problem with this approach was that while it made development more costly, it didn't control it.

The general populace seemed ambivalent about economic growth, tourism in particular. One poll showed that although a majority of residents supported the growth of tourism they opposed the building of new hotels on their particular island. Politicians who responded to this sentiment often had to deal with intense opposition from groups that favored more development. Once, in December, 1976, when a proposed construction moratorium on high-rise buildings was being considered by the City Council, the council members were picketed by between 4,000 and 5,000 construction workers, while a caravan of big construction trucks continuously circled City Hall, horns blaring, creating a horrendous traffic jam. I could hear the tumultuous din from my office at the State Capitol. The moratorium was not passed.

At the State level, Ariyoshi attempted to bring coherence to his policy on growth by introducing the Hawai'i State Plan in 1977. The plan was two tiered. The upper level framed its broad objectives and "priority directions." The second level outlined the implementation phase, requiring State departments and agencies to develop 13 "functional plans" covering specific areas, such as agriculture, housing and tourism.

Creating the Hawai'i State Plan was a big step for Ariyoshi. Like many legislators, I was impressed by its breadth and boldness. The broad concepts stated in the upper tier were criticized by some as too much "motherhood and apple pie," but the plan had value in the way it pulled those concepts together.

In one of my final floor speeches as a member of the House, I praised the plan as a significant step forward in managing the resources that affect the quality of life in our state. Ariyoshi deserved credit for trying to do what no other governor had done—develop a coherent, all-encompassing plan designed to help State and County governments establish policies to preserve and maintain the high quality of life unique to Hawai'i. On the 60th day of the 1978 legislative session, Democrat and Republican legislators paid tribute to his efforts by overwhelmingly approving the Hawai'i State Plan.

In 1978, I decided to run for one of the four Senate seats in my district. My political stock was up. For every one of the four years I had spent in the House, the *Star-Bulletin* had rated me as one of the 10 best legislators. Similarly, the *Hawaii Observer* rated me as one of the four best. I had done my best; I had followed my political creed faithfully, saying what I thought had to be said publicly and doing what I thought was right regardless of the political cost.

I was one of the first to use television in a State Senate race. Compared to the more sophisticated television ads I would use in my later campaigns for lieutenant governor and governor, my 1978 television ad (I could afford to produce only one) was crude and technically inferior. But the ad proved highly effective—probably because none of the other candidates were using television.

I won and led the ticket in both the primary and general elections. Patsy Young, Joe Kuroda and Norman Mizuguchi won also. I was pleased that I won but felt badly that incumbent Donald Ching did not. I admired and respected Ching. He was smart, honorable and one of the leaders of the Senate. Occasionally, I'd ask him for advice, which he gave freely. Unfortunately, the good guys don't always win in politics.

Then my focus turned, for a time, to more personal things.

Mom

"She's gone, Ben. Mom's gone...." Ken said, his voice trailing off. He was calling from our mother's tiny apartment on Vineyard Street. She had died in her sleep. I was in my new office at the State Senate at the time. Mom's apartment was less than a five-minute drive from the State Capitol. I hurried to the parking lot and drove to the apartment.

When I arrived, Mom was still in bed. Ken was sitting next to her. She felt cold and hard to my touch, her eyelids slightly open. "At least she won't suffer anymore," Ken said, tears welling in his eyes. Pop, Mom's elderly husband, was sitting on the sofa in the living room, staring out the door. Pop was already in his mid-70s—an age when most people come to grips with the inevitability of death. Having lived with Mom as she went through the torment of her drug addiction, Pop had gone through some hard times himself. But he had been patient and taken care of her. He looked sad but not surprised.

On the nightstand next to the bed I found a big vial of pills—the same Seconal she had been addicted to for years. There were only three capsules left. I picked up the vial and looked at the date of the prescription: December 9, 1978. This was the morning of December 11. In less than two days, she had taken 47 capsules. Ken and I looked at each other; without saying a word, I knew we were both thinking the same thing. My doctor told me later that people who suffer from drug addiction often become confused and forget how many capsules they've taken. Mom's official cause of death was listed as "cardiac arrest."

Mom had lived a star-crossed life. She was beautiful and smart, but she suffered at the hands of her cruel father. Once, my Aunt Rachel told me, my grandfather hung my mother suspended by her wrists from the ceiling. Mom was about 12 at the time. Only after Aunt Rachel, who was about 10, started screaming and pulling on his arm did he let Mom down. "And then he told your mother to pack her things and get out of the house," Aunt Rachel said. "I looked through the window and saw my sister crying, walking up the road and carrying her clothes in this small suitcase—I cried and cried."

"Boy, don't be too hard on your mother, she had a very hard life," my Aunt Rachel told me another time when she found out I used to hide when Mom came to pick us up. "Your grandfather was very mean to her. She was the oldest. So if anything went wrong he would take it out on her. If he did not beat her he would do mean things to her. Once, he sprinkled uncooked rice on the floor and forced her to kneel on it with her arms stretched out, holding something in each hand. If she moved, he would beat her."

I was stunned. Mom had never mentioned those things to me. She hardly talked about my grandfather. However, once she told me he was the kind of guy who, on a one-car driveway, would not back his car up for an oncoming car even if the other car had entered first and was almost at the end. The other driver would have to back up, or there would be trouble. She also recalled how during Prohibition my grandfather made and sold bootleg liquor. As little as she was at the time, Mom had to help out, capping bottles and running errands for him.

I never really got to know my grandfather. He divorced my grandmother, married a Japanese woman and fathered six or seven children, including one who was my high school classmate. Then he divorced her, married a young woman from the Philippines and, in his late 60s and 70s, fathered three more children. He never visited us and literally stepped out of our lives.

But Mom never said anything bad about Grandpa. On more than one occasion, I heard her telephone him to ask how he was doing. Or she'd go over to his home and drop off some fruit or his favorite Filipino food. Ken and I didn't learn about how Grandpa had abused her until we were both in our 40s.

Mom had bad luck with men. She was married five times. Her first husband, Frank, died shortly after they married. Her second husband, Jerry, who was my biological father, divorced her for another woman while Mom was still pregnant with me. Before I was born, Mom married her third husband, Bonifacio Cayetano. I doubt if she really loved him; I think she married him to avoid the social stigma of being an unmarried woman giving birth to a child. My surname is Cayetano because Bonifacio Cayetano is listed on my birth certificate as my father. They divorced when I was about six and Ken four. Her fourth husband, Rudy, divorced Mom when her drug addiction got so bad that he couldn't take it anymore.

When Ken brought her home from Los Angeles in 1967, Mom had been devastated emotionally and physically by her addiction. She was not the same person. She had no place to live, so Aunt Rachel took her in. For nearly a year she lived with Aunt Rachel and Uncle Billy and my six cousins in a small three-bedroom house on Kahai Street in Kalihi.

"You know, Boy, your mother was so skinny, so weak and sickly, I was afraid she might die," Aunt Rachel told me. "Every day I'd cook for her, help her take a bath. I'd massage her feet and talk to her, tell her everything would get better."

Things did get better, and Mom moved to Damon Tract to live with my grandmother, Blasa, whom my grandfather had divorced to marry another woman. One day, Mom telephoned Aunt Rachel. "Mediong [Aunt Rachel's Filipino nickname], I'm going to get married, but mostly for companionship," Mom told her almost apologetically. Grandma Blasa had encouraged the marriage.

Maximo Dacanay was Mom's fifth husband. We called him "Pop" because he was about 25 years older than Mom, who was then in her mid-40s. He was a good man, soft-spoken and humble. Pop was intelligent and had been an engineer in the Philippines. He held a good job as an electronics technician at the Pearl Harbor Shipyard There weren't many Filipino men who had those kinds of jobs back then. Until the early 1950s, approximately 70 percent of Hawai'i's Filipino population was single men. Max was part of that generation. It wasn't that difficult for Grandma to find a husband for Mom.

For a while, it seemed Mom was doing well. She gained weight and seemed to have her drug problem under control. She looked good again. She doted on her grandchildren—Brandon was her favorite. There were times that I got the feeling she was trying to make up for not raising Ken and me.

But after a few years, things started getting steadily worse. Mom started to complain about suffering intense back pains again. She resumed "doctor-shopping" to get more Seconal—and we would see her high more often. Physically, she lost a lot of weight and looked sickly in her complexion and in her eyes.

There was little anyone could do. There was no legal recourse; Mom was still considered a competent adult. I was frustrated by the ease with which she got doctors to prescribe Seconal—even though she showed all of the physical signs of addiction. Once, I telephoned her doctor and voiced my concerns about Mom's drug abuse. Yes, the doctor replied, he was aware there was a problem and had substituted a placebo for the Seconal, hoping to wean her off the drug. It didn't take long for her to figure it out and change doctors.

Back then the only non-invasive procedure doctors could use to diagnose back problems was the X-ray. Her doctor told me her X-rays showed no abnormality. So I concluded there was nothing wrong with her back; she had just become addicted to Seconal the way others were addicted to heroin or cocaine. She was such a tough person, I often wondered why she couldn't fight the addiction—why couldn't she beat this thing? It wasn't a conscious decision, but soon I found myself avoiding doing things with Mom and instead immersing myself in my law practice and my duties as a newly elected State senator.

Ken took Mom's death especially hard. When Mom found out he was a homosexual, after he returned from serving in Vietnam, she put him through hell. Once, when she was living with him when he was stationed at Hickam, Ken was awakened at about 2 a.m. by Mom pounding on his bedroom door. "What kind of creature did I bring into the world?" she screamed. For a long time, Ken suffered from depression and guilt, in part because of things she said about him. But he never held it against her. He told me this story just a few years ago—after keeping it bottled up within himself for more than 30 years. "She only said things like that when she was high; she didn't mean it," he said. My kid brother was a bigger man than I could ever hope to be.

Though it wasn't readily obvious, Dad also took it hard when she died. He never remarried. He never stopped loving Mom. Sometimes he would joke about her "coming back." But it was no joke—it was a hope he harbored for a long time. The first time I saw Dad cry was at Mom's burial service. I was standing next to him, and as each of us got ready to throw the traditional handful of dirt into the grave, a solitary tear streamed down from the corner of his right eye.

I shed no tears that day; I couldn't. I was long past feeling grief. The only emotion I felt was relief—relief that Mom's suffering had ended and relief that it was over, that this long, sad episode was behind us.

My experience with Mom's drug addiction influenced my views on drugs, religion and God. *What kind of God*, I wondered, *would allow a person supposedly created in His image to be degraded and to suffer as Mom did?* When the Catholic priest recited the Mass at Mom's funeral services, I tuned him out.

In public office I opposed draconian laws that imposed mandatory sentences and harsh penalties for drug use. I felt strongly that just throwing drug addicts in jail was not the answer. Most legislators disagreed and took a hard line. There were times when it was only a few of us—sometimes only Neil Abercrombie, a former probation officer, and me—who argued for treatment rather than incarceration of first-time nonviolent drug offenders. Nothing annoyed me more than the law-and-order types who argued that the best way to fight the drug problem was to throw every addict in jail.

Years later, as governor, I submitted a bill to require treatment rather than incarceration for first-time drug offenders. This was not a new idea. Arizona, hardly a bastion of liberalism, was the first state to enact the idea into law. Despite the objections of law enforcement officials and judges, an overwhelming majority of Arizona voters approved it at the ballot box—not once (it was declared unconstitutional the first time) but twice. Shortly thereafter, California followed Arizona's lead. In Hawai'i our bill was strongly opposed by law enforcement officials. In 2001, however, the Legislature approved it, and I felt great satisfaction and pride when I signed it into law.

A few years ago I shared Mom's story with my doctor. "You know, Ben," he told me, "X-rays only show clouded images of bone. They couldn't have helped your mother's doctor find out whether she was suffering from damage to her nerves and therefore experiencing real pain. Today, an MRI would clear that up for him. Your mother's reaction to the placebo suggests she was probably suffering extreme pain. Seconal isn't like cocaine or heroine; those drugs are so highly addictive because they give the user a big high. Seconal numbs its users to pain; they get addicted to it because it's the only way for them to get rid of the pain. Seconal is so addictive, powerful and destructive that today it is rarely prescribed."

I wish I had known this when Mom was struggling with her addiction. I think it would have helped me understand better what she was going through; perhaps it would have helped me to be a more understanding son.

The New Senate

Immediately after the 1978 September primary election, Richard S. Wong, or "Dickie," as we all called him, made it clear to all senators that he was seeking the Senate presidency, which was held by Big Island Senator John Ushijima. Wong had been chairman of the powerful Senate Ways and Means Committee, which ranked second only to the presidency. But Wong professed a vision for a "New Senate"—one which was more independent and open.

Over the course of a month or so, Wong demonstrated why he was such an adept political organizer. Unlike Ushijima, who never asked the freshmen senators for support, Wong took care to meet with each of the six new Democratic senators, engaging each of us in an exchange of ideas and explaining his hopes for the Senate.

Wong was a former labor leader. While serving in the House, he developed a reputation as an independent, reform-oriented legislator. So when he pledged that he would work with us to make the Senate more open, I was impressed.

John Ushijima had a notable legislative record himself. Like many of the World War II veterans (he served with U.S. Senator Dan Inouye in the famed 442nd Regiment) who were part of the 1954 Democratic Revolution, Ushijima's idealism manifested itself in his work. He was, for example, a key legislator in the passage of Hawai'i's landmark Prepaid Health Insurance law and other important legislation.

By 1978, however, the Democrats had pretty much won the fight for social justice and equal opportunity, idealism waned—and the focus had long been turned to the state's rapid economic growth. Many of the '54 Democrats sought to take advantage of the opportunities they had opened in business. Ushijima was one of them.

He was a lawyer, and his status as a former Judiciary chairman and Senate president attracted clients. He stirred up some controversy when he introduced a bill which seemed to benefit one of his clients, the real estate development company Boise Cascade. Nevertheless, he was considered a key legislator and was selected by the *Honolulu Star-Bulletin* as one of the 10 outstanding legislators from 1975 to 1978.

But Ushijima's inexplicable indifference to the new senators had its effect: Freshmen senators Neil Abercrombie, Dante Carpenter, Steve Cobb and I pledged our support to Wong. A week later, Charles Campbell, the only African American in the Legislature, became the fifth freshman senator to join us. The sixth, Norman Mizuguchi, stayed neutral. He had little choice. Like Ushijima, he was born and raised in Hilo, and they knew each other well.

Thirteen votes were needed to organize the Senate. But Wong had only 12 Democratic votes. Republican Ralph Ajifu, Wong's close personal friend, was his ace in the hole. If no other Democrat joined Wong, Ajifu would step forward and vote for him. Ajifu's personal loyalty to Wong was well known and at times irritated the other Senate Republicans.

For obvious political reasons, Wong preferred to organize with 13 Democratic votes. Hawai'i Kai Democrat Dennis O'Connor, who was off vacationing on the Mainland with his family, offered to support Wong if he got the chairmanship of Ways and Means. O'Connor would be the 13th vote needed. But Wong, who considered O'Connor a fence-sitter and felt he could not rely on him in tough situations, was not about to turn over the Senate's most powerful committee to him.

I had already been slated to chair the Judiciary Committee. I was the only attorney supporting Wong, and I was delighted at the prospect of chairing the committee. But Wong asked if I would give it up to O'Connor, who was also an attorney, and serve as chair of Ways and Means instead. I was stunned by his offer.

"Ben, you'll learn more about politics and the State government on Ways and Means than you will on the Judiciary Committee. You'll see the different kinds of special interests and which senators are helping them. I've been in politics for a long time [since 1966], but it wasn't until I became Ways and Means chairman that I learned about these things."

"You know that I have no experience in this area. I'm a freshman senator, and I have trouble balancing my own checking account," I said jokingly.

"Ben, if we get Dennis we can organize the Senate—get good staff, they'll help you learn fast."

Even if I had wanted to, I could hardly refuse. As it turned out, my years as Ways and Means chairman were the most valuable in my legislative career.

During my first year in the House, Tony Kunimura once scolded me for being too deferential to the governor's transportation budget requests. "Ben, remember this: We [the State Legislature] are an equal branch of government. The governor proposes, and we dispose. That's what we're here for."

Indeed, Ways and Means was the Senate's clearinghouse for all of the governor's proposed programs with financial implications, and it was responsible for the development of the Senate's version of the State budget.

My inexperience made me uneasy. I needed good and trustworthy staff. I found it in two young men, Earl Anzai and Colbert Matsumoto.

Anzai, a former State legislative federal auditor, became my committee clerk and managed our budget analysts and office staff. He had spent a couple of years auditing U.S. military bases in Asia and the Pacific Islands.

As a federal auditor Anzai was, as I learned from one of his former fellow auditors, considered the proverbial "pain in the ass." Unlike some federal auditors, Anzai refused to rely solely on written reports from the people who worked for the federal entity he was supposed to audit. Once, for example, while auditing fuel consumption at a military base in Thailand, he climbed on top of a huge fuel tank and used the measuring stick to determine actual usage, comparing it to the written reports.

Anzai grew up in rural Ka'a'awa where his parents owned a grocery store. Education-wise, we had something in common: We were both late bloomers. He flunked out twice from UH before he buckled down, attended Emory University in Georgia in the mid-1960s (he claims he was the only AJA student), and went back to UH where he got his BA and MA. (Later, at my urging, he enrolled at the UH law school and got his law degree).

I left it to Anzai to hire 13 budget analysts. Time was of the essence, but he insisted on giving each applicant a test which he had to pass before Anzai would even consider him, a first for the historically patronage-oriented Legislature. (One of the applicants who flunked the test was Rod Tam, who later became a legislator and gained national notoriety for introducing a bill that would give every State employee the right to take a 15-minute nap.)

Matsumoto, a Lāna'i boy whose parents were plantation workers, became my staff attorney. I first met him when he and fellow attorney Allan Murakami popped into my campaign headquarters one day, introduced themselves and offered to help on my 1978 Senate campaign. Matsumoto had just completed a three-month spiritual retreat at a renowned dojo (Buddhist temple) in Kalihi Valley. His head was shaved completely bald, and he looked like a monk from David Carradine's popular television series *Kung Fu*.

Anzai and Matsumoto were not only very bright; they were highly ethical and idealistic men. I knew I could trust them, and I relied heavily on their advice. I would need it. Ahead of us were some hot issues: the Hawai'i State Plan, collective bargaining, OHA and the State budget.

Prior to the 1979 legislative session, my committee reviewed every one of the proposed 12 or 13 State functional plans. Eventually, the functional plans proved to be the Achilles heel of the State Plan. The broad goals of the plan were to be lauded—but, as has often been said, "The devil is in the details."

Ariyoshi had delegated the implementation phase of the Hawai'i State Plan, the functional plans, to his department heads. It soon became clear that the plans reflected the personalities of the directors. Some functional plans were innovative, but too many fell far short of the bold concepts set forth in the first phase of the plan. Often the functional plans showed little to differentiate them from ordinary departmental budget proposals for operational funding. And where a legislative committee disagreed with the specifics of a functional plan, the plan was amended to the committee's satisfaction.

Moreover, the Hawai'i State Plan served as a planning guide, but with no sanctions for non-compliance. For future governors and legislatures the plan had no effective philosophical or political authority. Few would disagree with its broad concepts, but Ariyoshi's attempt to bring order to the planning process through the more detailed functional plans was a different story. In a floor speech, O'Connor stated that, while the broad concepts laid out in the Hawai'i State Plan were useful guidelines, the functional plans were not needed—an opinion shared by many.

Many of the senators were frustrated by Ariyoshi's tightfisted economic policies. A fiscal conservative, Ariyoshi often restricted legislative pork-barrel appropriations. The State constitution entrusts the governor with the duty of managing State government and maintaining its fiscal integrity. In this connection, the governor's power to restrict legislatively approved appropriations is mainly intended to provide the flexibility needed to adjust spending due to revenue shortfalls and other unforeseen events.

Theoretically, if a governor is opposed to a program, his appropriate response should be a veto or a line-item veto, which the Legislature has the power to override, not a restriction. When a governor restricts an appropriation, there is not much legislators can do except complain or lobby the governor to release it. The power to restrict gives the governor a great deal of leverage.

Few were surprised when an independent like Wong criticized Ariyoshi's restrictions of legislatively approved appropriations as "a dangerous usurpation of legislative power." But when House Finance Chairman Jack Suwa, an Ariyoshi loyalist, denounced the governor's repeated rewriting of budgets passed by the Legislature, it revealed the intensity of the hard feelings felt by many legislators. The respected and well-liked Suwa, ordinarily a man of few words, spared none in expressing his frustrations over Ariyoshi's actions:

"If a Constitutional Convention is called by the people, I will urge the delegates to review how to stop the governor's assumption of complete authority over the appropriations and the erosion of the Legislature's traditional power of the purse."

But Suwa's words were mild compared to the harsh criticism by T.C. Yim, chairman of the Senate Economic Development Committee. The hot-tempered Yim was furious that Ariyoshi had restricted the funding for some of his pet energy programs, and he vented his ire by threatening to reject the confirmation of Hideto Kono, the governor's choice for director of the DPED.

Unlike Wong's and Suwa's, Yim's criticism was extreme. Kono took the brunt of it. Senators would blanch as Yim angrily dressed down Kono at committee hearings. I could see people in the audience shaking their heads, shocked at the way Kono was being treated.

Kono was one of the governor's best directors. A World War II veteran who had served in the U.S. Military Intelligence Corps, he had spent nearly 30 years as CEO of a Japanese corporation before returning home to Hawai'i to retire. Urbane, intelligent and articulate, Kono never raised his voice in anger. I watched with growing respect as he calmly responded to Yim's harsh questions. In the end, Wong intervened, calming down the mercurial Yim, and Kono was confirmed by the Senate.

Kono was confirmed by a 24-1 vote. The only senator to vote against his confirmation was Neil Abercrombie. A few days after the vote, Kono paid him a visit. "He had good reason to be angry at me," Abercrombie told me. "But he shook my hand, told me he respected me and offered to work with me. He sounded very sincere. I was surprised." By the time Kono retired in 1986, Abercrombie was a strong supporter of his.

For a governor to release every appropriation approved by the Legislature would be irresponsible. The development of the State budget is a political process that, too often, includes appropriations that are not well thought through but rather are intended primarily to satisfy constituents' demands.

A Parent-Teacher Association, for example, may ask its legislator for State funding to build a new gym for its school. Although the legislator knows that the chances of a new gym being built are slim, because it is not a high-priority project on the Board of Education's list, he puts in funds for planning as part of his "pork-barrel" request. His constituents are satisfied. The governor, after being advised that the gym is not a high priority, restricts the planning money, which, if not used, lapses after three years. The legislator tells his constituents that it is up to the governor to release the funds. The constituents petition the governor, who, after the money lapses, ends up being blamed for the gym not being built.

Aside from pork-barrel capital improvements, which are pretty much left to the discretion of individual legislators, the Ways and Means Committee is supposed to weed out projects that cannot be justified financially.

In Yim's case, Ariyoshi restricted State funds pending receipt of matching federal funds, which seemed reasonable to me. Yim, however, somehow got Ways and Means to include a proviso that required the governor to release the State funds regardless of whether federal funds were provided. I thought the proviso was clearly illegal. By law, the governor has the authority to restrict funding if he deems it necessary to balance the budget or to keep the State solvent. That discretionary authority cannot be undone by a proviso, which is basically a statement of legislative intent. But Wong, who was Ways and Means chair at the time, was not inclined to consider such legal technicalities. As with Ajifu, Wong and Yim were very close friends.

"Earl," I said, "I don't want to ever see a proviso like that in any budget coming out of this committee … I don't care who wants it. It's nuts. You can't force the governor to spend money."

Whenever legislators complained to Ariyoshi about his restrictions of appropriations, he would say something like, "Okay, you guys tell me what I should restrict to keep the State solvent." Few legislators, of course, even knew where to begin. Legislators have a much narrower fiscal perspective than the governor—usually limited to the needs of their constituents and special interests. Ariyoshi asked a good question. I had an idea that I thought would provide an answer.

I proposed what we called the "A-B" budget format. It was simple in structure, and it would inform the governor where, if he had to restrict appropriations, the Legislature thought he should start.

Part A included what the respective Senate committees considered high-priority appropriations. Part B was made up of appropriations of secondary priority. If revenues were short, and the governor decided restrictions were needed, he was required to restrict appropriations from Part B. This format, I thought, would pressure the governor to use his line-item veto of appropriations for projects he thought unworthy of funding. In such a case, the Legislature would at least have the option of overriding the veto.

House Finance Committee Chairman Suwa liked the concept, and, for the first time in Hawai'i's history, the Legislature approved a State budget that clearly indicated its priorities to the governor. The idea was simple but unique, and it attracted national interest from legislatures and government associations across the nation. The A-B budget concept, however, would be followed for only six years before the Legislature reverted back to the old budget format in 1985.

Collective bargaining was another hot issue. A controversy erupted when the Firefighters Union was awarded a contract with a provision for a cost-of-living allowance (COLA). The potential financial ramifications were ominous. The State was still negotiating contracts with 13 other bargaining units. If they demanded and got COLA, the financial cost to the State would be enormous.

A newspaper reporter buttonholed me after a public hearing and asked whether I supported the COLA award. "No, the State can't afford it," I replied. The next day the newspaper's front-page headline read: "Key Lawmaker Opposes COLA." David Trask and other labor leaders were furious at me. The following day, the public worker unions mounted one of the biggest demonstrations ever seen at the State Capitol. The crowd, made up of thousands of State and County workers (teachers, UH faculty, custodians and office workers), gathered in the Capitol rotunda after work.

As I sat in my Senate office on the second floor, I could hear Trask excoriating me for being against working people. When it came to giving fire-and-brimstone union speeches, Trask had no peer. "He forgot where he came from," Trask fumed. John Radcliffe, of the teachers' union, followed, blasting me for "betraying working people."

I could hear the crowd chanting my name. I decided to show myself. As I stepped out of my front office, I could see a huge crowd, estimated by some at about 4,000, most wearing white T-shirts emblazoned with their union name.

"Stay back ... don't let them see you," warned Anzai, who was standing at the railing on the second floor. *Better for them to see me than think I'm cowering in my office*, I thought.

As I stepped to the railing, the crowd stopped chanting my name and started booing. Among them, I saw some of my strongest campaign supporters standing around looking up at me, while the boos from their fellow workers reached a crescendo so loud I could hardly hear myself speak. Later, a senator asked how I felt when I heard the cascade of boos. "It's quite a high. You should be so lucky as to experience it one day," I joked halfheartedly, bemused by the question.

The next morning, Wong asked me to meet with him, Speaker Wakatsuki and House Finance Chair Jack Suwa in his office. As we shook hands, Wakatsuki smiled and said, "Mr. Cayetano ... there's no law that says you have to answer a reporter's question, you know."

"Oh, I thought I'd liven things up a bit. It's been a little boring around here,"

I joshed.

Suwa sat silently, smiling at the banter.

"Okay, look, Ben," Wong said. "Jimmy and I spoke with Ariyoshi today and we all agreed that the State can't afford COLA. So we are going to send him a letter signed by the four of us stating that we oppose the COLA award and will not agree to fund any contract that has COLA. Ariyoshi will then renegotiate the firefighters' contract."

"Just the four of us will sign this letter?" I asked as I read it.

"Yeah. We got to take our members off the hook. Next year, the entire House and half of the Senate are up for reelection ... they don't need the unions pissed off at them," Wakatsuki replied.

The letter was sent to the governor and made public. There was no press conference. The import of the letter was clear. The Legislature was not obligated to fund any collective bargaining contract, and the four of us would oppose funding any contract that included a COLA. The firefighters backed off, a new contract was negotiated and, along with those for the other collective-bargaining units, the contract was approved for funding by the Legislature.

Political Lessons

As the Ways and Means chairman, I had the responsibility of leading the Senate conferees in the budget negotiations. Each legislative session, hundreds of bills are passed. The appropriation for every bill that requires State or federal funding is included in the State Budget Bill. The purpose of the budget conference was for the House and Senate to iron out their differences and come up with a balanced State budget.

Suwa and I had a good working relationship. We had worked together in the House; there was mutual respect between us. Suwa had served as House Finance chair for nearly eight years, and he knew everything a finance chair needed to know about State government. He was a veteran chairman; I was a rookie. But I felt comfortable because I knew he would play straight, as he had with all those he dealt with in the past.

Wakatsuki and Wong agreed to leave the budget negotiations exclusively to Suwa and me. The committee members all agreed: The negotiations would be closed to the public.

The members of both committees were provided with folders that set forth the House and Senate positions on each budget item, and they were put on call. Some remained in their offices; others went home; and a few went to their favorite bars. "Ben, we'll be at Crystal Palace until about 2 a.m. Call me there if you need us," a Neighbor Island senator told me.

The format was simple. The conference was held in the Senate Majority caucus room; the only people there were me; Suwa; our committee clerks, Anzai and Jeff Agader; and a few selected staff. Our budget analysts stood by in case we needed more information about a budget item. Anzai and Agader had already flagged the items over which the House and Senate differed.

We began the conference at about 8 p.m. Suwa and I took turns explaining our positions on each budget item. The atmosphere of civility between us encouraged compromise. At times, Suwa or I would call in a committee chairman to further explain the importance of a budget item to the subject matter (e.g., transportation, education, etc.).

I tended to negotiate like a lawyer, setting forth the arguments pro or con on the item before us. It was a reflection of my inexperience. In the next few hours, I would learn some lessons about the role of parochial politics from my House counterpart.

Once, a House appropriation for a major overhaul of Hilo Airport came up. The appropriation was for about $50 million (I've forgotten the exact amount). The Senate opposed it. Our analysis showed it could not be justified. Anzai and my staff had done a great job analyzing the project. They found that Hilo's population was diminishing and that increasingly tourists were choosing to visit Kona, where the weather was sunny and the beaches were beautiful, instead of Hilo, where it rained often and there were no good beaches. Moreover, with the demise of sugar, business travel to Hilo, with its already depressed economy, was going to decline.

Suwa listened closely as I rebutted each of the reasons the House listed to support the appropriation. Finally, I said, "Jack, I'm sorry, but the Senate cannot agree with the House position. Our analysis shows that your numbers don't add up. The projections don't justify spending millions to overhaul an airport that fewer people are going to use."

"You know, Senator," he said slowly (Suwa never called me Ben), "I congratulate you and Earl, your staff—the analysis was outstanding. But I tell you the real reason I want this money for the Hilo Airport—equal opportunity, to give the people there some hope. O'ahu is doing fine, and I'm happy for you folks, but Hilo's economy is depressed. It needs new jobs, something to boost its economy."

I glanced at Anzai. He was smiling. So was Agader. The state airport system was funded by a special fund supported mainly with landing fees paid by the airlines. I turned to Anzai. "There is a huge surplus in the airport special fund," he said anticipating my question.

We all knew that the $50 million or so to renovate the Hilo Airport would hardly make a dent in the airport special fund, which was flush with nearly half a billion dollars. Moreover, the fund could only be used for airport purposes; it would have no impact on funding for public education and other services, which were paid for by the general fund. Nevertheless, on paper at least, it did not make good fiscal sense to spend that kind of money for Hilo. But Hilo's economy was lagging behind that of most of the state. Something had to be done.

There was nothing more for me to say. Government is not a business. A government run by accountants has no soul. Giving people hope when things are tough is what government is supposed to do. Moreover, interpersonal relationships sometimes play a big role in politics. Suwa and I had a good relationship—one of mutual trust and respect.

"Okay, Jack, I agree to the House position ... equal opportunity ... hope for Hilo. One day, I'm going to ask you to do the same for other people who I think need the same kind of kōkua [help]."

"You know me, Senator; if I'm here, I always kōkua you Oʻahu boys," he replied.

By about 8 a.m. the next day, Suwa and I had finished our negotiations. It had taken just 12 hours. Our staffs reviewed the budget agreement, then we met with our respective committee members to review the final proposal. Everyone was satisfied with the final budget. It was a good compromise.

I felt pretty good about what we had accomplished. Suwa, who had been through this many times, seemed happy, too. At about 10 a.m., we let in the waiting news media for a short photo-op.

Our staffs worked together to fine-tune the State Budget Bill for submission to the full Legislature, which gave its overwhelming approval. The 1979 legislative session would prove to be the most productive and enjoyable of my 12 years as a legislator.

Most legislators held full-time jobs: many with businesses, some with labor unions, others with nonprofit and charitable organizations; a handful were self-employed. As with any part-time legislature, potential conflicts of interest abounded.

It is impractical to disqualify every legislator who has a conflict of interest from voting on bills which may affect him or his employer; moreover, determining that one conflict of interest is greater than another is subjective—dependent on the opinion and sometimes whim of the current Speaker or Senate president.

Back then, the House and Senate rules provided that at the committee level a committee member must declare his conflict and could ask the chairman for permission to be excused from voting. In voting before the full House or Senate, however, the legislator was required not only to disclose his conflict of interest; he was also required to vote if present when the vote was taken.

Theoretically, full and public disclosure of the conflict of interest made the legislator's constituents the final arbiter of the appropriateness of his vote. If a legislator's conflict was seen as egregious by enough of his constituents, they could vote him out of office.

Once, when I was chairman of Ways and Means, Buddy Soares found out that Big Island Democrat Stanley Hara had proposed a $6 million appropriation for the draft of the State Budget Bill. The appropriation was for the State to buy a parcel of Big Island land called Kapoho Tidelands. The problem was that Hara, who was into real estate speculation on the Big Island, did not disclose that he had a big financial interest in the land. Kapoho Tidelands was a speculative venture that had soured, and Hara wanted to palm it off on the State. Soares had done some research and gave me a copy of the title search, which revealed Hara's interest.

It wasn't the first time Hara had tried something like this. Once Anzai found out that Hara had proposed a $70,000 appropriation for a jojoba bean project, which somehow found its way into the Higher Education Committee's proposed UH budget. The appropriation was a legislative initiative; it was not requested by UH. Hara was not a member of the committee, so we assumed the appropriation had been approved by Higher Education chairwoman Pat Saiki.

"Hara kept on checking on the appropriation; he did it so often I figured he had an interest in it, and I found out that he did," Anzai said. "Take it out of the draft," I instructed him. Hara did not say a word about it, nor did I say anything to him.

Kapoho Tidelands, however, was the last straw. I was embarrassed that we had missed it. After Soares gave me the copy of the title search, I found Hara in the Ways and Means conference room. He was standing in front of the blackboard on which Kapoho Tidelands was listed along with other parcels of land recommended for our land-banking program.

"Beautiful, beautiful," Hara said to himself. I brushed by him, went to the blackboard and with one brisk stroke, erased Kapoho Tidelands from the list. I turned and angrily confronted him. "Stanley, if you ever pull this shit again, I'll report you to the Ethics Commission," I said. My harsh words were like water running off a duck's back; Hara looked at me as if nothing had happened.

A few months later, I got a phone call from Mack Kamikawa. Kamikawa was an investor in a hui of which Hara was a trustee. He suspected Hara had sold one of the hui's parcels of land as if he owned it and without disclosing the sale to the members of the trust. I had never met Kamikawa before, but I was told he was quiet and honest. Like Hara, Kamikawa was a war veteran, part of that Nisei generation that produced Dan Inouye and Sparky Matsunaga.

I told Kamikawa I would analyze the case but he would have to find another lawyer to take Hara to court if it came to that. I concluded that Hara had breached his duties as a trustee and Kamikawa should sue him. Hara's son, Glen, now a State Circuit Court judge in Hilo, called me to propose a settlement. Terms were negotiated and I discussed them with Kamikawa.

"Sue him, Mack, you've got a strong case," I advised him.

"No need, I just wanted to make a point; go ahead and settle the case."

"You sure? You've got a strong case," I replied.

"This was never about money, Ben. Settle the case and send me your bill."

A few years ago, Vicky and I attended a fundraising dinner for the Democratic Party. It was a big affair, packed with at least 1,000 people. The young Democrats who had planned the event decided to honor two old-timers for their outstanding contributions to the Party. It was a nice touch but also a clear indication that they knew little about the legislative histories of those they were about to honor.

One of the honorees was Stanley Hara; the other was former Kaua'i Sen. Billy Fernandes, a controversial figure who had just left the Senate when I was first elected to the House in 1974. One memorable news story about Fernandes involved a State road on Kaua'i. Somehow, State highway engineers had been persuaded to ignore the basic geometric theorem that the shortest distance between two points is a straight line and had diverted the road to run by land owned by Fernandes, enhancing the land's value. *These two old-timers are like peas in a pod,* I thought.

As Hara walked by my table on his way to the stage to receive his award from the smiling but unsuspecting and uninformed young Democrats, our eyes met. "Congratulations, Stanley," I said with a smile. Appearing unflappable as ever, he nodded furtively and scurried away to get his award.

The Political Gets Physical

Suwa retired early in 1980 and Ted Morioka, his vice chairman, replaced him. Morioka was a nice, amiable man. As far as I could tell, he was fully capable of handling the negotiations for the House. As a result of changes in the House and Senate rules, the conference would be open to the public for the very first time.

Wakatsuki apparently did not have much confidence in Morioka. He assigned Peters, the House majority leader, to negotiate the State budget for the House. Morioka showed no outward emotion, but the 60-something AJA must have been embarrassed and hurting inside.

Peters had gained the confidence of Wakatsuki, who became a mentor of sorts to him. Some believed that Wakatsuki, who would leave the House to become a Circuit Court judge in 1981, was grooming Peters to succeed him as Speaker. In Wakatsuki's eyes, Peters was a good choice: He was a natural leader, intelligent and charismatic. He was well liked by nearly everyone, even House dissident leaders such as Mits Uechi, who had been a perennial thorn in Wakatsuki's side. Moreover, Peters had been loyal not only to Wakatsuki but to Ariyoshi as well.

From my talks with him, I got the impression that Wakatsuki felt, all things being equal, that it would be good for the House and the Democratic Party to have a non-AJA Speaker. AJAs had led the 1954 Democratic Revolution and dominated the Legislature thereafter.

When I was elected in 1974, AJAs made up more than half of the Legislature. Prior to 1954, many Hawaiian legislators had been Republicans who, along with their fellow haole Republicans, had controlled the Territorial Legislature. The

1954 revolution had wiped them out. A Native Hawaiian like Peters—the only one among 36 House Democrats—would be a perfect choice for Speaker.

But there was a side to Peters that Wakatsuki had not seen. He had a terrible temper. Legislators who had quick tempers were hardly unique—none, however, stood over 6 feet tall, weighed 230-plus pounds and were as young and physically strong as Peters.

I first got a glimpse of that side of him in 1975, during our first year in the House. Back then, it was not unusual for public hearings to go on late into the night. Unlike today, there was great public interest in the Legislature, and the hearings were usually well attended.

At about 10 or 11 one night, Peters was standing at the rail on the fourth floor. A few of the House members and I were standing there with him. Peters started singing. The outdoor acoustics at the State Capitol are such that at that hour a normal conversation on the rotunda could be heard by someone standing at the fifth-floor rail. Peters had a great voice, and he loved to sing, but there was a public hearing going on and someone complained.

Richard Garcia, the majority floor leader, came out and asked Peters if he could keep it down. Garcia, who was slightly taller than Peters, had a big smile on his face when he said it.

Peters turned to Garcia, and, pointing to the rotunda four floors below, said matter-of-factly, "You know how high it is from here to there?" I couldn't see Peters' expression, but I saw Garcia's—his smile vanished instantly as he backed away and said, "Okay, okay, I'm just telling you what the chairman asked me to."

I didn't think much of it then, but as the years passed, I heard of other similar incidents. The general feeling among House members was that Peters could be intimidating.

Once, during the 1979 budget conference, Peters came to see me about a budget procedure. I don't remember what it was about specifically, but Peters seemed upset it was in the proposed State budget. "It's required by law," Anzai said, interrupting him. Peters turned to Anzai and warned, "You better be right." (He was right, as Peters found out when he checked with Suwa's staff.)

Anzai was taken back by Peters' demeanor and the inflection of his voice. So was I. "Henry," I said, "if you've got a problem with what we've done, don't take it out on my staff." Anzai, who looked like he would rather be elsewhere, said nothing.

Later, after Peters and Suwa left, I tried to make a joke of the incident. "Earl," I said, "did you remember your aikido training when Henry came on like that?" Anzai chuckled and replied, "You know that he's pissed off at you, not me, don't you?" *Yeah, and it won't be the last time,* I thought.

One night at about 10 o'clock during the 1979 legislative session, I was walking through the State Capitol basement when I saw Ollie Lunasco, the Waialua Democrat, walking toward me, slightly bent over and holding his stomach.

"Ollie, what's the matter? Are you hurt?" I asked.

"That fucking Henry's crazy," he said, grimacing.

"What happened?" I asked.

"He false-cracked [pidgin for 'sucker punched'] me!"

"What?"

"I saw Henry and Danny (Kihano) coming out of Mits' office, walking up the hall toward me, and I said, 'Bruddah Henry, howzit,' and the crazy bastard punched me in the stomach," Lunasco said.

"Why?" I asked.

"I don't know—he just walked up to me and punched me in the stomach; I didn't expect it. I went down," Lunasco replied.

"Did he say anything to you?" I asked.

"I don't know, I was in so much pain, rolling around on the floor … trying to catch my breath."

Lunasco was part of a group of dissident Democrats who demanded certain changes to the House rules and organizational structure. The leader was Mits Uechi. Others included Charles Toguchi and Clifford Uwaine. Relations between Uechi's group and the majority Democrats had deteriorated so badly that, on more than one occasion, the majority had locked them out of the caucus room.

Uechi was no shrinking violet when it came to political infighting. He was an expert on parliamentary procedure and knew the House rules by heart. He was smart but had a knack for getting under people's skin. Once, he got Kaua'i's Richard Kawakami so angry that the normally cool-headed Kawakami told Uechi, "Mits, I notice one of your eyes is smaller than the other; keep fucking with me and I'll fix it so they both match." The 5-foot, 5-inch, 150-pound Uechi took those kind of comments in stride.

As majority leader, Peter had the responsibility of dealing with them. In fact, Peters and dissidents like Uechi and Lunasco had once been good friends.

For weeks, Uechi and the dissidents had frustrated Peters with their parliamentary mischief. Whatever had happened earlier that day must have been the final straw for Peters. Temper raging out of control, he had barged into Uechi's office where Uechi was meeting with Toguchi. "I don't think he even turned the doorknob," Toguchi would recall later.

With one motion of his big arm, Peters swept everything off Uechi's desk. Shouting angrily that he was "sick of you guys," Peters began furiously upending furniture and knocking things off shelves as he continued his tirade, which was mostly directed against his once-good friend Uechi, who was now, in Peters' words, a "fucking Japanee."

Toguchi, meanwhile, stepped out of the office, got on the telephone and called Wakatsuki's office. Told by his secretary that Wakatsuki was in conference, Toguchi shouted angrily over the phone, "You tell him to get his ass over here,

Henry Peters has gone crazy!"

Peters was like the proverbial bull in a china shop—except this bull was raging mad. Having already swept Uechi's desk clear and torn up the office, Peters reached over the desk, grabbed Uechi by the jaw with one hand—squeezing and contorting his pudgy cheeks, lips and slanted eyes into a weird mask—lifted him off his chair and cocked his arm to punch him. At the last minute, he punched Uechi's desk instead, breaking its glass top and the two knuckles on his big right hand.

By then, Wakatsuki and Dan Kihano were there. Wakatsuki calmed Peters down while Kihano was reduced to tears and helplessness when he saw the dazed Uechi sitting on the floor in the mess that had been his neat office.

After Peters flattened him, Lunasco picked himself off the floor and went to Uechi's office to find out what was going on.

"Henry tore up Mits' office," Lunasco later told me, "chairs, books thrown all over the place … even Mits' desk was turned on its side—the fucking Hawaiian went crazy. And then Chip [Clifford Uwaine] came by … I couldn't believe the expression on his face—he was white with fear; he was scared shitless. Chip said Henry found him at the Higher Ed hearing and told him he was 'going to get all of us.'"

A few days later, Uechi lost control of his car while driving to the State Capitol; it careened over a traffic island and knocked down a sign. The news media reported it as a minor accident, but those who knew what had happened that night in Uechi's office speculated that he had suffered a nervous breakdown.

The news media never got the full story. Instead, the incident was reported as an "organizational dispute"—a topic unlikely to generate public interest. Obviously, the media had gotten Peters' version, but not that of Uechi, Lunasco or Toguchi. I wondered what the public's reaction would have been if they had known the full facts.

The media's failure to get the real story was a blessing in disguise for the Democrats. The 1980 elections were less than six months away, and all 51 members of the House were up for reelection. Lunasco had a tough campaign ahead of him. If the full story had come out, it could have hurt him and other House Democrats.

Lunasco asked Wakatsuki, who, for the same reasons, did not want the news media to get the full story, what he was going to do about Peters. Wakatsuki's answer gave him little comfort: "Stay away from him … don't get caught with him alone," Wakatsuki warned.

"I couldn't believe what Jimmy said," Lunasco told me later.

Henry Peters was never criminally charged or sued for damages. Nor did he ever apologize to Uechi or Lunasco or anyone else for his rampage. According to Lunasco, Uechi was "never the same again."

"I'm worried about the budget conference," Anzai said afterward. "I don't know how Henry is going to get up to speed on the budget. It's crazy to think he can jump into it in mid-session and know what's going on."

"Well, he was on the Finance Committee for four years.... Henry's a smart guy. He's experienced," I said.

"Yeah, but Jack [Suwa] did everything. The committee worked with him for years, and as long as he took care of Henry's pet projects, he left everything to Jack. That kind of experience is worthless to someone who is going to chair the committee."

A few days after Peters replaced Morioka, he invited me to lunch to discuss the ground rules for the upcoming budget conference. Our discussion about the rules was brief, and soon we were trading war stories about our growing-up days—his in Wai'anae, mine in Kalihi.

I left the luncheon remembering two anecdotes about Peters: For two years, he had studied at Jackson College in Mānoa to become a priest before transferring to Brigham Young University, where he was a star volleyball player. It was there that Peters punched out a BYU football player whom he felt had offended his wife, Carolyn.

"I caught the guy flush, and he went down and out!" Peters said. "And his friend ... you ever heard of Merlin Olsen?"

"You mean the all-pro defensive end for the Los Angeles Rams?" I asked.

"Yeah, that's the guy.... Well, he stood there looking at me. So I told him, 'Eh, haole, you want some, too?' And he said, 'No, friend, this is not my fight.'"

I didn't have a story to match this one. The thought of Peters spiking his huge right hand—it looked like the size of a ham hock—into the poor guy's jaw as he would a volleyball made me wince.

Later, Anzai asked me, "How did your lunch with Henry go?"

"Henry was born 200 years too late; he thinks he's King Kamehameha."

"What happened?" Anzai asked.

I told him the story.

"Oh, shit," he replied.

"Brush up on your aikido, Earl; I'm afraid it's going to be a tough conference," I replied, "real tough."

"I'll be nowhere to be found," he chuckled.

We both laughed.

The Trouble with Twenty Percent

The 1978 Hawai'i State Constitutional Convention proposed 34 constitutional amendments, all of which were subsequently ratified by the voters. The convention was dominated by special-interest groups with different agendas.

Public labor union delegates, for example, blocked efforts to pass amendments to establish initiative and referendum; establishment Democrats pushed through a "resign to run" amendment aimed at blocking Mayor Fasi from running for governor again.

Hawaiian activists managed to get five amendments relating to Hawaiian culture, history and governance passed, marking the transition of the Hawaiian Renaissance from issues of culture and history to self-governance and politics. The most important of the five amendments established the Office of Hawaiian Affairs (OHA).

Constitutional amendments are rarely self-executing, and it remained for the Legislature and the governor to approve the "enabling" legislation that would give the amendments their effect. The most troublesome was shaping enabling legislation for the funding of OHA.

The amendment provided that a pro rata share of the revenues from the 1.4 million-acre ceded-lands trust mandated by Section 5 (f) of the Statehood Admissions Act be used to fund OHA. Section 5 (f), however, does not specify a fixed percentage for any one of the five purposes. It leaves it to the State to manage and dispose of the income "for one or more of the foregoing purposes." In other words, setting the pro rata share was solely up to the State Legislature.

My personal view, shared by the majority of my committee and Judiciary chairman O'Connor, was that setting the pro rata share at 20 percent was like giving OHA a blank check. There would be little accountability. OHA, after all, was still a State agency. Section 5 (f) specifically described one of the five purposes as "the betterment of Native Hawaiians." OHA, however, was set up to benefit all Hawaiians—Native Hawaiians (those with 50 percent or more Hawaiian blood) and part-Hawaiians (those with less than 50 percent Hawaiian blood). The part-Hawaiian population at the time was estimated at nearly 150,000, compared to 60,000 Native Hawaiians. How would OHA be held accountable for its use of the ceded-lands income? Did the word "income" mean gross or net income?

Until these and other questions were answered, it made more sense to set the pro rata share at a low percentage and require OHA to submit an annual budget request for general funds, which it would have to justify like all other State departments.

At the end of the 1997 session, the Legislature approved Act 196, which set the pro rata share at 4 percent in addition to providing general operating costs, funds which OHA was required to justify like all other State agencies. Peters supported the new law.

By 1980, however, Hawaiian activists began demanding that the pro rata share be set at 20 percent; Section 5 (f), they argued, listed the "betterment of Native Hawaiians" as one of the five purposes for which the ceded-lands trust income could be used. One of five equal parts is 20 percent.

This was logic of convenience. Section 5 (f) did not specify a percentage, but instead left it to the State to decide. Theoretically, the State could set the pro rata share at anywhere from 1 percent to 100 percent for one or more of the five purposes. In fact, historically the State had spent most of the Section 5 (f) money on public education.

Nevertheless, the 20-percent pro rata share argument took on a life of its own among many Hawaiians. By the 1980 legislative session, Peters was converted to its cause and became its champion. A House bill (Act 273) was introduced to amend Act 196 and increase the pro rata share to 20 percent. It would be the most difficult issue I had to address in the weeks ahead.

Although we followed the same conference format as we had in 1979, from the outset the budget conference did not go well. Anzai was right; there was little chance that Peters would be as well prepared as he should have been to negotiate the budget and related bills.

For the first time, the conference negotiations were open to the public, and Peters' inadequate preparation began to show. After a few conferences, I could sense he was getting frustrated and annoyed at having to turn to his staff for answers when my committee members or I asked questions about the House position on a bill. I was getting frustrated and annoyed at Wakatsuki for having put us in this situation.

The details of a bill did not seem to mean much to Peters. He had the analysis done by his staff before him and would use it to explain the House position or rebut a Senate position, more to impress the audience than convince us of the merit of his argument. I sensed that Peters knew what he wanted, and he would do whatever it took to get it.

About a week before the 60th and last day of the regular legislative session, he changed his negotiating strategy. He made it clear that he would hold certain bills unless the Senate agreed to the 20-percent pro rata share in the OHA bill. Among the bills Peters held hostage were the Supplemental Capital Improvement Bill, the Pensioners' Bonus Bill and a bill for a work-training program for unemployed people called SCET.

To be sure, holding bills hostage was not a tactic invented by Peters. It was the nature of the bills he held hostage that indicated how far he would go to get what he wanted. It didn't take long for groups of retired State workers to meet with me and express their concerns about the fate of the Pensioners' Bonus Bill. Most of them had retired in the 1960s when State salaries were low. When I started as an entry-level rodman for the State highway department in 1960, my salary was $289 a month, so I understood how much the bonus meant to most of them.

"Don't worry, I'll do everything I can to make sure the bill passes," I vowed, "but you should also go talk to Representative Peters."

If the Pensioners' Bonus Bill died, 11,500 retirees and their families would be affected. "Man," Anzai said, shaking his head, "how can Henry do this?"

"It's easy," I said, "if you don't give a shit that people might get hurt."

Most of the Hawaiians who lobbied me for the OHA bill were reasonable and polite. The activists, however, never bothered to meet with me. "They think you're a lost cause," Anzai chuckled.

Emotions were running high, and things soon got ugly. The pre-conference public hearings I held on the OHA bill were packed with standing-room-only crowds. Pro-OHA Hawaiians who gave reasonable, well-thought-out testimonies were overshadowed in the news media by outspoken activists who demanded that the 20-percent pro rata share become law.

In one public hearing, Frenchy DeSoto, who had been a delegate to the 1978 Constitutional Convention and one of the architects of the OHA bill, gave an angry recitation of the historic injustices she believed had been suffered by Hawaiians. She was playing, of course, to the news media and the crowd at the hearing. When it came to pure political demagoguery, DeSoto had few peers. As she went on and on, her testimony morphed into a tongue-lashing that elicited applause from her supporters whenever she emphasized a point. It was quite a performance.

My committee members didn't deserve this kind of treatment. When she was done, I pointed to the people sitting at the conference table and said, "Frenchy, take a look at the faces of the members of this committee. None of our ancestors had anything to do with the historic injustices you just talked about."

In fact, with the exception of Abercrombie, a Scottish American from a working-class family in Buffalo, New York, the committee members were all local: Chinese, Filipino, Japanese, part-Hawaiian and Portuguese. DeSoto, who was reveling in the audience's approbation, glared at me but said nothing.

Then came the threats and intimidation. In floor speeches, Anson Chong noted he had received a telephone threat and Abercrombie, who met with Hawaiian activists, decried their behavior and vowed that he would never be influenced by intimidation.

In politics, threats relating to controversial issues are a fact of life. The higher one's profile on such issues, the more likely it is there will be threats. Most of the threats I received were from guys who wanted to punch me out. But I never got any death threats until the OHA bill came up for hearing. One in particular warranted taking precautions.

"Yeah, we got another one today," Anzai said. "This guy telephoned; he claims he's a hunter and can drop you at 300 yards. He said he'll nail you on the freeway when you drive home. We should look into this one a little more." Having no desire to become an addition to this alleged hunter's list of trophies, I agreed to take precautions.

Wong heard about it and arranged for the Honolulu Police Department to investigate and provide security for me. During the last month of the legislative session, I'd often leave the State Capitol between 2 and 3 a.m., even sleeping over at times. For three mornings, an HPD officer followed me home, the blue light on his car roof revolving and shining; once we reached my home, he asked me to remain in my car while he walked around my house with a flashlight to check the premises.

This is ridiculous, I thought. My neighbors might think there was a domestic squabble between Lorraine and me. On the third morning, I thanked the officer and told him I did not want an escort anymore. But the threats kept coming. An HPD lieutenant phoned me and offered to tap my telephones. "If the calls don't stop in two days, with your permission we'll install the tap," he said. Strangely, the next day the threatening telephone calls stopped, adding to our suspicions that the calls were made by persons who worked in the State Capitol.

"Ben, I don't want you to meet with Henry alone, okay?" Wong told me one day.

"Is he upset with me?" I asked, even though I knew the answer.

"A little ... just stay out of his way and don't meet with him alone," Wong replied.

"Dickie ... my name is not Mits Uechi. You tell Henry if he lays a hand on me I'll have him prosecuted and I'll sue his ass," I said, trying not to sound like the proverbial boy whistling in the dark.

"Stay cool ... nothing's going to happen," Wong assured me.

A few nights later, I was sitting in Wong's office awaiting a call from Peters to reconvene the negotiations. At about 2 a.m., Wong got the call. "They're ready to reconvene," he said.

As I got up to leave, Wong said, "Ben, don't go alone. Take Duke [the vice president of the Senate] with you."

Duke's real name was Edward Kawasaki. During the 1950s and '60s, Kawasaki was a professional musician and a bandleader with his own 16-piece band. He was a big Duke Ellington fan, and began calling himself "Duke" because he thought it sounded more appropriate for a bandleader than "Edward." He loved big-band music, and he named his only son "Guy" after another famous bandleader he admired, Guy Lombardo (Guy is today a nationally renowned high-tech marketing guru).

Kawasaki was a political iconoclast. He was contemptuous of legislators who, as he put it, "can't stand on their own two feet." That was why, he said, he liked then-Mayor Frank Fasi. Kawasaki was an articulate speaker and enjoyed robust debate. He hated those who tried to get their way through intimidation rather than persuasion. He thought David Trask was a bully and told him so. When Abercrombie blasted Trask, calling him a "gangster" for physically threatening one of his staff members, Kawasaki roared with laughter and beamed his approval.

As we walked to the House Finance conference room, Kawasaki looked at me and, with a big smile, said, "Ah, don't worry, Ben, if Peters tries anything, there'll be either a dead kanaka or a dead Japanee."

I looked at the 60-year-old former amateur sumo wrestler and burst out laughing. *They don't make them like Duke anymore,* I thought.

On the last day of the session, we were still stalemated over the OHA bill, and Ariyoshi granted a one-day extension. Five more one-day extensions would follow.

Wakatsuki disliked extensions, not so much for the public criticism they provoked but because he believed that deadlines were set to be met. Too many extensions would defeat the purpose of the 60-day session, which was to pressure the Legislature to finish its work. He felt extensions should only be granted as last resorts.

My own view was that the Legislature should take as much time as it needed to get the job done. If the Legislature's final product was in the public's best interest, the people would respond favorably; if not, there could be political consequences. Wong did not like extensions either, but he was much more flexible. "Just get it done," he said to me.

During a conference I was having with Peters and others, Wakatsuki called O'Connor, who was a conferee, out of the meeting. Later, O'Connor told me that Wakatsuki had implored him, "Stop it. Stop it. Give them [the Hawaiians] the 20 percent, otherwise they'll just come back again and again." Wakatsuki made the same plea to other key senators. He must have figured me for a lost cause; he never made the same plea to me.

By the 63rd day, I could sense from the comments of several senators that Wakatsuki's message was beginning to have an effect. Soon, O'Connor started to have second thoughts. The labor unions ran ads on the Pensioners' Bonus Bill, targeting certain senators. OHA supporters ramped up their efforts. House and Senate members started worrying about their pork-barrel projects. I could tell that some of the senators were beginning to feel the pressure.

By the 64th day, I knew I had to make a decision. Half of the Senate and the entire House would be running for reelection in less than six months. If the Pensioners' Bonus Bill failed, 11,500 retired county and State workers would have to wait at least a full year before it could be passed. If the supplemental capital improvement budget failed, legislators would not be able to tout their "pork" to their constituents as accomplishments.

"This shouldn't be a personal contest between you and Henry on who can hold out the longest," Anzai reminded me. "What if the Pensioners' Bonus Bill falls through the cracks? A lot of those retirees will be hurt."

"Yeah, but there's so much we don't know about the OHA bill. There is no inventory of the ceded lands; we don't know how much income is generated every year, and we can't agree on the definition of 'income.' Is it gross or net? Now if it's gross income, it'll virtually bankrupt the State. And there is nothing in the House bill which will require OHA to spend the 20-percent pro rata share only for Native Hawaiians and not all Hawaiians. It's irresponsible to pass a bill with so many unanswered questions and loose ends, and it pisses me off just to think about it," I replied.

"Well, you know that old saying, 'There's nothing more powerful than an idea whose time has come'?" Earl said, paraphrasing Victor Hugo's famous quote.

"Yeah, even if it's a bad idea," I replied.

Most of the Republican senators understood the importance of a well-reasoned OHA bill and refrained from playing politics. Except for one. Andy Anderson saw an opportunity to gain support from Hawaiian voters for his bid for the governorship in 1982 and jumped on the OHA bandwagon. His floor speech reeked of pure politics.

"If you vote against this bill, you are against OHA ... I think the Hawaiians are entitled to win a few skirmishes, if not the war, at this time.... If the chairman of Ways and Means ... wants to review this budget, he needs but put a bill in changing the 20 percent to 12, to 19, to 8, to 5 ..."

Anderson praised Peters' methods, saying, "I happen to believe ... that if it were not for the packaging concept that the House was adamant [about], this bill would not be here on our desks today."

Abercrombie voted for the bill, but with strong reservations: "I regret very much that the bill is before us in this manner. I fear that those who are interested in seeing this office move forward have won a pyrrhic victory, that this is merely a skirmish in a very large battle," he said.

Abercrombie's remarks would prove prophetic. The adoption of Act 273 was a major victory for Peters and OHA. But Peters' disinterest in detail caused him to overlook the unusual "severability" clause of the OHA bill we had inserted. Basically, the clause provided that Act 273 would be nullified in its entirety if any part of it conflicted with federal law. In the jargon of politics, such clauses are called "poison pills."

(In September 2001, the Hawai'i Supreme Court ruled that Act 304—Act 273 revised—was null and void because it violated federal law.)

There was one other matter on which Peters refused to budge: the appropriation for the Hawai'i Natural Energy Institute. There was no disagreement between the House and Senate over the appropriation itself. But there was strong disagreement over whether the State Department of Planning and Economic Development (DPED) or the University of Hawai'i should be designated as the expending agency.

T.C. Yim demanded that UH be the designated agency. It did not matter to me which State department was designated, as there were good arguments on both sides of the issue. There was little doubt that a big reason Yim opposed designating DPED was because Hideto Kono was still its director. There was also little doubt that Peters' intransigence was based in part on Yim's shameful treatment of Kono in 1979.

After negotiating with Peters for more than a week on this issue and consulting with Yim every day, neither Yim nor Peters would budge. I warned Yim that the negotiations were stalemated and that the appropriation could be lost. He still refused to budge.

I had served for four years as the chairman of the House Energy and Transportation Committee and had worked with Yim before. In my first year, I developed a package of alternative energy bills, which the House approved and sent over to the Senate. Yim held the bills in his committee, and in the following session introduced most of the bills as his own, while killing mine. I had been taught a small lesson in political maneuvering. But it didn't matter, because I felt what counted was that the ideas became law. Moreover, I was preoccupied with some big, controversial transportation issues at the time.

Because Yim was close to Wong, I had bent over backward for two consecutive legislative sessions to accommodate him. But by the 64th day of the 1980 session, I was fed up with Yim's unyielding, uncompromising style.

I was not about to cause a further extension of the session because of his pique. As chairman, it was my call. Once we agreed to the 20-percent OHA bill, I wasn't going to prolong the session any longer just to accommodate Yim. The Pensioners' Bonus Bill was one thing—elderly retirees would get hurt if it didn't pass—but I would not give in on this bill to Peters. The state's energy programs would survive another year. I broke off negotiations and the appropriation was lost.

Yim was furious, and in an angry floor speech he caustically attributed the loss of the appropriation to "small, petty politics"—ignoring the fact that Peters and others loyal to the governor had thought the same about his treatment of Kono in 1979.

Yim was angry at me as well. At the end of the 66th day, I ran into him in Wong's office. He told me he would no longer support me as Ways and Means chairman. "You're out!" he said angrily. My immediate reaction was to tell the 5-foot, 1-inch martinet to go and have sex with himself, but I was so exhausted that I just looked at him and smiled.

I liked Yim, but when it came to his energy projects he was impossible to deal with. Unfortunately for him, the 1980 legislative session would be his last. Yim was defeated in the 1980 Democratic primary by State Rep. Milton Holt—a young, Harvard-educated Kamehameha Schools alumnus who many political observers touted as a sure bet to become governor or U.S. senator one day. Asked to comment on his apparent loss on election night, Yim deplored the voters' short-sightedness: "Well, I guess the people don't care about energy," he said.

Peters emerged from the 1980 session smelling like the proverbial rose. He got the 20 percent OHA bill passed, and he got even with Yim for his mistreatment of the well-liked and respected Kono.

In 1981, Peters succeeded Wakatsuki as Speaker of the House, after the latter was appointed by Ariyoshi to a Circuit Court judgeship. Most of the dissidents who were the targets of Peters' angry rampage were gone: In the 1980 election, Lunasco was defeated and Uwaine was elected to the Senate. Uechi retired from politics. And in 1982, Toguchi was elected to the Senate.

In March 1984, the Hawai'i Supreme Court appointed Peters as a trustee of the multibillion-dollar Bishop Estate. Despite calls for his resignation, Peters continued to serve as Speaker while collecting a salary of about $900,000 annually from Bishop Estate. Finally, in 1987, Peters was pressured to step down as Speaker by a group of reform-minded House Democrats led by Richard Kawakami of Kaua'i and future Lt. Gov. Mazie Hirono.

Although he lost the Speakership, Peters was undaunted and continued to serve in the House, reinforcing his relationships with certain House Democrats by parceling out Bishop Estate contracts and jobs to them.

As a trustee, Peters had as his highest priority at the Legislature the protection of the Bishop Estate. It was during this period that he began to assert his "Hawaiianness."

In 1994, Peters retired, culminating 20 years of service as a State legislator. Shortly thereafter, he became the dominant trustee for Bishop Estate. By 1999, however, Peters' leadership style would prompt an investigation by the Internal Revenue Service that jeopardized the estate's tax-exempt status, and a lawsuit by the State attorney general that would cost him and four other trustees their jobs and bring about major reforms to the estate. ❖

CHAPTER SIX

Coalition Politics

Solidarity and Diversity

I n post-election November 1980, the two Democratic factions in the State Senate were hopelessly divided. With the 1981 legislative session less than two months away, Wong found himself three Democratic votes short of the 13 he needed to organize the Senate. His strongest supporter, Yim, had been beaten in the 1980 Democratic primary, and former supporters O'Connor and Campbell had defected to the Ushijima faction.

Except for O'Connor, who was too independent to get close to anyone, and Campbell, who remained an enigma to most, the Ushijima faction was seen as close to the old-line Democratic establishment. Ushijima and fellow Big Islander Stanley Hara were heavily involved in real estate development. Kauaʻi's George Toyofuku was in the insurance business, Gerald Machida worked for the HGEA; Milton Holt and Norman Mizuguchi were HGEA favorites.

Wong's faction—the "New Senate"—was viewed as more independent, with no close ties to the governor or Democratic Party leadership. In terms of style, the Ushijima faction was less likely to question or publicly criticize the governor's policies; some tended to view such criticism as a sign of disloyalty. In contrast, robust and at times heated debate, even against each other, was commonly practiced, even encouraged, by the Wong faction.

With the Democrats hopelessly stalemated 10-7, both sides were hoping to organize a coalition with the Republicans. If successful, the coalition would be the first in Hawaiʻi's political history. Most mainstream Democrat leaders strongly opposed a coalition with Republicans.

Republican floor leader Andy Anderson, who was contemplating a run for governor in 1982, was quick to milk the situation politically. In a floor speech, Anderson said: "We would like to be informed, Mr. President, if somebody can inform us in this body, just what the hell is going on. Is somebody talking to somebody; are the Democrats meeting?"

Anderson, who had boasted in another floor speech that he could command the attention of the news media as well as any senator, demonstrated exactly what he meant. In truth, however, he knew full well what was going on because he was heavily involved in the negotiations with both the Ushijima and Wong factions.

Among the Republicans, Anderson, Wadsworth Yee and Pat Saiki favored a coalition with the Ushijima group, preferring to continue their time-tested relationship with them rather than having to deal with Wong's more independent, outspoken and unpredictable senators. Soares, Ajifu, George, Henderson and newcomer Ann Kobayashi were open.

O'Connor, the negotiator for the Ushijima group, made it easy for the Republicans to decide. His group, O'Connor said, was willing to give the Republicans vice chairmanships, bigger staff allotments, trips and other perks, but not committee chairmanships. In other words, they wanted the Republicans to help them gain political power over the Senate, but were unwilling to share it.

"Are you saying we [Republicans] are not qualified to be committee chairmen?" Soares asked incredulously.

Soares' rhetorical question all but killed O'Connor's offer. There was a lot of talent and experience among the Republican senators. Andy Anderson, Scotty Henderson and Wadsworth Yee, for example, were all successful, self-made businessmen. Buddy Soares, Ralph Ajifu, Mary George and Pat Saiki were respected and popular community leaders. How could the Republicans *not* be offended by O'Connor's offer?

Wong would not make the same mistake. Democrats, Wong told the Republicans, would reserve the presidency and chairmanships of the Ways and Means and Judiciary committees—all other committee chairmanships were up for grabs. It was an offer they could not refuse.

On January 30, 1981, the eighth day of the session, Wong formally announced the Democratic-Republican Coalition. It was a milestone in Hawai'i politics.

The seven Ushijima Democrats could hardly hide their chagrin. Ushijima, who was not inclined to say much publicly, spoke like a man betrayed. With thinly veiled sarcasm aimed at Anderson, he said, "I would like to offer my congratulations to the former members of the minority, especially to Senator Anderson ... I think this is one of the greatest things that has happened to the minority—one of the great robberies ... again, Andy, congratulations. You did a great job ... please treat your 'hostages' [the Wong faction] well."

Minoru Hirabara, chairman of the Democratic Party, broke his usual reluctance to make comments to the news media by speaking out in what amounted to a lecture on party loyalty. New Speaker Henry Peters, we were told, had vowed privately to a few House members that the House would not pass any Coalition bills.

It remained for Milton Holt, the freshman senator, to reveal why the Ushijima faction had tied Dennis O'Connor's hands in his negotiation with the Republicans. "A coalition vote to organize is one thing, so long as the majority retains leadership and chairmanships of all committees. Responsibility remains with one party. But a true coalition such as this ... obscures party lines and party responsibility. Where, oh, where, is the 'loyal opposition'?" Holt asked.

I was unmoved by the criticism. There were enough examples to show that, when it suited their purpose, the Democratic establishment was willing to cross party lines to help Republicans defeat Democrats.

It did in 1964 when Republican Hiram Fong, Sr., beat Democratic Congressman Tom Gill in the U.S. Senate election. It did in the 1972 election for mayor when Gov. Burns himself covertly supported Republican Andy Anderson in his unsuccessful race against incumbent Democrat Frank Fasi. (The only high-ranking Democrat who never crossed party lines was Dan Inouye. In the 1972 election, Inouye openly endorsed Fasi.)

So when Holt asked rhetorically: "Where, oh, where is the 'loyal opposition'?" *Where indeed?* I thought. Six years in the Legislature had taught me that the Republicans hardly measured up to the loyal opposition one learns about in a high school civics class. And there were practical reasons for it.

Anderson, a bedfellow to establishment Democrats when it suited their mutual purposes, was a successful businessman; Wadsworth Yee was the major principal of Grand Pacific Life Insurance; Pat Saiki sat on Hawaiian Airlines' board of directors; Scotty Henderson had extensive business investments on the Big Island.

With those kinds of personal economic interests, it made sense for them to have cordial relationships with the Democratic appointees to various State departments and agencies, boards and commissions that could affect their economic interests. Pragmatism, more than idealism, governed the Republicans.

The real loyal opposition during my six years in the Legislature was the independent Democrats—the senators and representatives who not only believed that the Legislature was a separate and equal branch of government but practiced that belief. The independents were populists—a natural development, I believed, in persons who neither have nor covet material wealth.

Unlike the Ushijima faction, the senators of the Wong faction owned no more real estate than their own homes. In fact, a few, like Abercrombie and Wong, owned no real estate at all. In terms of employment, a number were full-time legislators: Abercrombie and Wong; Patsy Young, a widowed housewife; Mamoru Yamasaki, a retired ILWU officer; Joe Kuroda, a retired school principal; and Clifford Uwaine.

When I was first elected to the House in 1974, I wasn't experienced in politics, but based on what I read and heard in the news media, I was under the impression that some Democrats were becoming a bigger problem to the public interest than Republicans.

Indeed, one reason I supported Tom Gill was that I shared his belief that too many Democratic legislators and supporters were moving away from the ideals that fueled the 1954 Democratic Revolution. To Gill, John A. Burns wasn't the problem—it was some of his "alarming friends."

One of the objectives of the 1954 Democrats was to unlock the Republican oligarchy's stranglehold on economic opportunities, and they succeeded mightily. But the Democratic tide did not raise all boats equally. Too many used the government to make it easier to achieve their self-interested goals.

With Gill's defeat and retirement from public service after the 1974 gubernatorial primary, and Fasi's quitting the Democratic Party after his loss to Ariyoshi in 1982, the Democratic Party's two major independent leaders were gone.

I was deeply concerned, and in a floor speech I warned that if the leaders of the Democratic Party valued conformity over diversity, the Party was headed for trouble. There was no better example, I noted, than the homogenized, one-shoe-fits-all Republican Party, which was swept out of power in 1954.

When a reporter asked me what I thought about the rumors that Democratic Party officials would seek disciplinary action against us, I told him to ask the Party chairman whether all 17 Democrats who had sought a coalition with the Republicans would be disciplined—or only the 10 who were successful?

It would have been foolish for the Party leaders to attempt to discipline 10 of the Party's own senators, several of whom were its top vote getters in the state. Nevertheless, at the 1982 Democratic State Convention, anti-Coalition Democrats—led by Milton Holt—managed to ram through new Party rules, which set forth the grounds for disciplining future Democrats who crossed party lines or supported non-democratic candidates.

In 1994, Holt revealed his hypocrisy by endorsing Frank Fasi when he was Best Party candidate against me for governor. It was no surprise to me that the rule that Holt sanctimoniously and successfully argued for in the 1982 Democratic Convention was never enforced against him—or any other Democrat who crossed party lines.

Organizing the Coalition

As the only attorney in the Coalition, I was slated to be chairman of the Judiciary Committee. Wong asked me to help organize the Coalition. There were two problems: Abercrombie and Saiki both wanted to chair the Higher Education Committee; similarly, both Carpenter and Henderson wanted to chair the Committee on Economic Development.

Abercrombie and I had been close friends since our days in the House. Abercrombie, as a former UH professor, knew the University system well. He was clearly better qualified. The UH administration, however, made it known that it preferred Saiki over the outspoken Abercrombie. Wong, leaving no stone unturned to avoid squabbles among Coalition members, decided to accommodate them.

Moreover, we were already three or four days into the legislative session and still not organized; a sense of urgency prevailed over all of us.

"Ben, if anyone can convince Neil, it's you. This thing between him and Pat is holding up the organization. Talk to him, he'll listen to you," Wong said.

Abercrombie, of course, marched to his own drummer, but Wong was right: He would at least listen if I talked to him.

"Ben, Saiki doesn't know a damn thing about the University," Abercrombie argued.

"Yeah, but this dispute between you and her is holding up the organization," I replied.

"Saiki's a former teacher, she should take the Education Committee," he pointed out.

"Yeah, but she's a Republican—every one of her kids went to private schools, she's not really interested in the Education Committee," I said. "Neil, that's the difference. You give a shit. I know you do. You're the one who opened my eyes to the importance of early childhood education."

He was silent.

"How many times have we discussed how poorly prepared some of your former public school students at UH were? Well, you can do something about it with the Education Committee," I told him.

He began to smile.

Finally, I argued politics. "Neil, how many faculty members are there at UH?" I asked.

"Three thousand or so," he replied.

"Well, most of them are going to support you anyway. But there are more than 11,000 teachers and between 2,000 and 3,000 principals and vice principals. Their unions have supported you in every one of your elections—do a good job with the Education Committee, and their rank and file will bust their asses for you," I said.

"Okay, okay," he chuckled, "but Chip [Uwaine] wants Education too, so you got to work it out with him."

There were two committees open—Human Resources and Labor and Health. Chip was as anxious as everyone else to get organized and agreed to take Human Resources. That left Carpenter and Henderson.

In the 1978 election, newcomer Carpenter had beaten out incumbent Henderson for one of the three Big Island Senate seats. Once, while relaxing in Henderson's office, I asked him how it felt when he lost to Carpenter. Henderson, a successful Big Island businessman, had a great sense of humor. "I cried," he joked. Carpenter had beaten Henderson by only 178 votes. I sensed there was a bit of an estrangement between the two men.

Carpenter, the former Big Island councilman who Abercrombie called the Senate's "Victor Mature" because of his resemblance to the famous actor, had chaired the Health Committee for two years; he wanted no more of it. Neither he nor Henderson would budge on the Economic Development Committee.

As a last resort, I offered Carpenter my Judiciary Committee, hoping that he would not take it because he was not a lawyer, that he would come to his senses and return as chairman of the Health Committee. I should have known better. Carpenter was always up to accepting challenges, and he was delighted to become the first non-lawyer chairman of the Judiciary Committee. "Yeah, like the man said, 'Damn the torpedoes! Full speed ahead!'" Carpenter said, quoting Adm. David Farragut's famous words.

That meant I would have to take the Health Committee.

That night, as the Coalition members were gathered in Wong's office watching the 10 o'clock news report on the Coalition's organizational structure, I stood in the back, next to the door. As the list of committee chairmen was being scrolled down on the television screen, I finally realized how much of a fall it was from chairing the powerful Ways and Means Committee to the Health Committee. I felt as if I had been banished to Siberia. I motioned to Wong that I was leaving, walked to the parking lot and took the long drive home.

I doubt if there is any other profession that is as full of continuous highs and lows as politics. As I drove home, I was definitely feeling low; I had been full of ideas for developing an agenda for the Judiciary Committee, and now the opportunity was gone. Self-recrimination and self-pity began to set in. *I should have kept my mouth shut*, I scolded myself.

Ten minutes after I got home, I got a telephone call from Wong.

"Ben, you okay?" he asked.

"Yeah, I'm fine," I lied.

"We couldn't have organized if you didn't talk Neil and Dante into moving off their first choices," he said.

No shit, I thought.

"I want you to be the majority policy leader," he said.

There was no such position, so I knew he had just thought it up. "Look, Dickie, don't feel sorry for me. The Senate is not kindergarten. I'm a big boy. I don't need some useless, save-face title," I replied.

"No, no, Ben, this is important. You'll be the majority policy leader for our Democrats, and Buddy Soares will be the minority policy leader for the Republicans. A lot of people are expecting our Coalition to fall on its face, so we got to prove it will work. You and Buddy will review all of the bills and try to work out the differences between us and the Republicans. If you two can't work out the differences, then you guys recommend to the caucus whether we should hold the bill, kill it on the floor or put it out for a vote," Wong explained.

I had learned long before how to live with the hand dealt to me. The idea sounded sensible, so I agreed to give it a try.

Soares and I met the next day. We developed a plan of action, instructed our staffs to do some preparatory work and began reviewing bills the following day. We spent long hours together reviewing and discussing the bills and negotiating differences between our respective caucuses. Before taking a bill to the Senate floor, the Coalition would always meet with us to discuss our recommendations. We did this for two consecutive years, and it succeeded beyond my expectations. The only bills we did not cover were those reported out of the conference committees to the full Senate.

Interpersonal relationships are important to getting anything done in politics. Soares was in charge of marketing for Aloha Airlines; he was smart, especially in reading how certain senators would react and pointing out their special interests; he was gregarious and had a good sense of humor. And he was a good family man. Whenever one of his handsome sons came over to visit him, Soares would always hug and kiss him before he left. "Ben, I always hug and kiss my boys, no matter how old they are," he told me. I wondered whether all Portuguese fathers were like Soares, or if they were like Asian fathers, who rarely hugged or said, "I love you" to their kids, taking it for granted that somehow their children knew how they felt.

Working with Soares was like working with Suwa. No games were played. Everything was up on the table. There was mutual trust and respect. For two years, we worked well together. Not one of our recommendations was rejected by the caucus, nor did we ever lose a floor vote on a bill. We got to know each other well, and a strong friendship grew out of the many hours we spent working together, one that remains today.

The Seven Dissidents

The seven dissident Democrats, still chafing over being left at the altar by Anderson and Yee, unleashed a barrage of sniping each day of the legislative session on everything from staff allocation to parliamentary procedure. Led by O'Connor and Holt, they directed their ire mostly at Wong and Anderson. On one of Anderson's bills, the normally reticent Ushijima weighed in with questions:

"What does the amendment do? Will the senator explain?" Ushijima asked, trying to look serious.

"The amendment would make the playing of video or electronic game machines by minors a penalty, as it is with pinball machines," Anderson replied.

"What is a video machine?" Ushijima deadpanned.

"A video machine is a television electronic game played by electronics," Anderson, a little annoyed, replied.

"Is it bad for minors?" Ushijima asked, trying to keep a straight face.

"Yes, I think it's bad for minors, Senator, as is a pinball machine … I think school lunch money is spent on the machines … I personally feel very strongly about this," Anderson replied, his irritation beginning to show.

"I had the impression that it was very educational," Ushijima concluded with a smile.

"That could be your judgment," Anderson replied.

O'Connor got into the act: "Mr. President, this is a bad year for children. We've taken away their dogs; we've taken away their cats; and now we are going to take away their Star Wars games. The momentous things before this body are astounding."

Steve Cobb, trying to help the irritated Anderson, explained, "The effect of this amendment is … [to] eliminate any distinction [between] the playing of ball and marble machines and the playing of video games."

O'Connor got the last word: "I guess poor old Kane Fernandez [a well-known carnival promoter] loses all his games, too, because the kids have a terrible time with their lunch money at Kane Fernandez's games at all the school carnivals."

As a Republican minority member, Anderson had had the luxury of sitting back and skewering the Democratic majority on whatever came to his mind. As a member of the Coalition, however, he found himself with the shoe on the other foot. O'Connor and Ushijima had given Anderson a taste of the medicine he had been dishing out for years.

In 1980, two events caused the State to cut back on spending. The first was the new constitutional expenditure ceiling on general fund spending; the second was the election of Ronald Reagan as president.

Reagan had promised to cut federal spending. Shortly after he took office, he announced his "New Federalism" program, which was designed to devolve dozens of federally funded social programs to the State governments.

David Stockman, Reagan's ultraconservative director of the Office of Management and Budget, embarked on what he called a "starve the beast" policy to reduce federal spending. Funding for the devolved programs was not only drastically reduced but, in many cases, was given in so-called "block grants," purportedly to give the states greater flexibility in allocating the funds.

"Politics," as the disillusioned Stockman would write after serving only one term with Reagan, "triumphed the Reagan Revolution." In fact, Reagan left the nation with the biggest deficit in history up to that point and actually increased the size of the federal government. The only "starvation" that occurred was at the state level, where social programs for our most vulnerable citizens suffered dramatic cuts.

Many of Lyndon Johnson's "Great Society" programs had been continued by Richard Nixon and Jimmy Carter. Most were partially federally financed, with the states making up the balance. The percentage of funds provided for a program varied. Thus, if the federal government covered 70 percent of the program cost, the state would provide the balance of 30 percent.

When Reagan reduced or eliminated federal funds, State politicians had to decide whether to make up for the cuts with State funds, reduce the scope of the program in question or eliminate it.

Reagan often sprinkled his "New Federalism" speeches with bromides about "home rule" for the states; similarly, his speeches attacking waste in social programs almost always included pointed and misleading remarks about "welfare queens" and "fraud."

To be sure, among the plethora of private social programs that emerged out of Johnson's Great Society, some were wasteful, ineffective or even fraudulent. As chairman of Ways and Means in 1979, I had set up new standards to scrutinize the programs that applied for State funding. This had never been done before, and a surprising number of these private vendors were forced to scramble to provide proper accounting documents to justify their programs.

The jury was still out on the effectiveness of many programs. This was true especially of drug addiction treatment programs. The Legislature was anxious for answers on drug addiction, so private vendors that provided treatment were given the benefit of the doubt when it came to State funding. (By the mid-1990s most programs were found to be ineffective, and many closed).

Ariyoshi followed a "warm-body" policy, which meant no layoffs. Under Peters, the House was like an arm of the executive branch and strongly supported the governor's policies. Warm-body policies work only for the short term, though; in any long-term fiscal downturn, a warm-body policy is inefficient and wasteful. (When I became governor in 1994, for example, our audits found civil engineers doing the work of lower-paid draftsmen in the Department of Transportation.)

In my Health Committee, we merged some department programs and reduced funding and the scope of services for others. The biggest casualties were the private vendors, who suffered bigger cuts in State funding and whose services, in a few cases, were terminated. Clearly, additional State funds were needed just to maintain the current level of services for these programs.

The Legislature, however, was constrained by the new expenditure ceiling law on general fund expenditures. I was the author of the new law, and I knew that in order to exceed the ceiling, a "declaration" approved by a two-thirds vote was required. In the urgent circumstances of the time, however, pragmatism was the order of the day. Special funds, which were not counted against the expenditure ceiling, and other budgetary techniques, were used to avoid exceeding the ceiling. Most Coalition senators had a "no harm, no foul" attitude toward the use of such methods.

What made the situation appear incongruous was that, while budget cuts were made to programs to comply with the expenditure ceiling law, Ariyoshi's frugal policies had accumulated a $241 million surplus over two consecutive budget years, triggering a tax rebate mandated by the State constitution.

Article VII, Section 6 of the State constitution addresses the disposition of excess revenues: "Whereas the State general fund balance at the close of each of two successive fiscal years exceeds 5 percent of general fund revenues for each of the two fiscal years, the Legislature in the next regular session shall provide for a tax refund or tax credit to the taxpayers of the state, as provided by law." If the Legislature wanted to avoid a tax rebate, it had to develop and approve a State budget that had a surplus that did not exceed the percentage set by the State Constitution. In other words, it had to spend down the surplus.

To Ariyoshi—a liberal on social issues but a fiscal conservative—the mandated tax rebate was verification of his frugality. In 1981, the Legislature approved a one-time $100 tax rebate for every resident; for a family of four, this meant a total of $400.

Most legislators saw the tax rebate as a boost for the economy as well as good politics. I wasn't so sure. A letter to the editor of one of our daily newspapers argued that the tax rebate was proof that Hawai'i taxes were too high. And an elderly man once stopped me in a supermarket and asked: "Why you folks give tax rebate when da school buildings all fall down? No make sense."

The Coalition was working well internally, but its relationship with the seven dissident senators was so polarized that winning a floor vote on contested bills seemed to be the only thing that counted. The upside for the public—if there was one—was that both sides were usually very well prepared to debate the bills on the floor.

Under less-polarized circumstances, the arguments might have swayed some votes on either side. Indeed, there were times when I found myself agreeing with some of the points made by the dissidents in their arguments. I had no doubt that some of the dissidents felt the same way about arguments made by Coalition members.

Unfortunately, the polarization was so intense that no matter what was said, regardless of the merits of an argument, the vote was routinely divided along factional lines. "Mr. President, 18 ayes, 7 nos, the measure passes final reading," the Senate clerk intoned so many times that he was beginning to sound like a recording.

With Peters as Speaker, the House had firmly aligned itself with the governor. Many House bills merely restated the governor's position on various issues. The Coalition remained the only real check on the executive branch.

One of the bills pushed strongly by the House for the governor was one that would have given several thousand non-unionized State executives and managers an 18-percent pay raise. Senate conferees, led by Ways and Means Chairman Mamoru Yamasaki, told House conferees the Senate would not agree to 18 percent but, instead of ending the negotiations, unwisely agreed to the House's request to put the bill before the full Senate for a vote.

The House's request was typical of the tenacious negotiating style of Peters. In trying to accommodate the House, however, the Senate conferees gave proponents another opportunity to pressure Coalition senators into changing their votes on the bill. In fact, two Coalition senators did switch their votes. The rest, however, held firm, and the bill was rejected by a 16-9 vote.

Conference bills are take-it-or-leave-it propositions, with no amendments allowed. Four House bills agreed to by Senate conferees, which retroactively approved appropriations for the past State budget biennium, did not have the declarations required by law to exceed the expenditure ceiling. As the author of the expenditure ceiling law, I could not overlook that the bills were legally flawed, and, along with several others, I voted against them.

The Coalition had emerged intact from the 1981 legislative session. However, some big challenges lay ahead; the biggest was the 1982 election. ❖

CHAPTER SEVEN

Duty to the Public

Fasi and the Election

Seven of the 10 Coalition Democrats, including Dickie Wong and me, would be running for reelection. How resentment of the Coalition would manifest itself at the polls in the Democratic primary, only eight months away, was anyone's guess.

A *Honolulu Advertiser* poll, however, suggested that the public felt differently than the old-line Democrats. The 1981 Legislature was given high favorable ratings, the highest in years.

"The best kind of politics is getting the job done," House veteran Tony Kunimura once told me, recalling an often-quoted but seldom-practiced political adage. The Coalition had done just that in the Senate, and although the House had killed most of the Senate bills, particularly those opposed by the governor, nevertheless there seemed to be widespread public approval of the fact that Democrats and Republicans had set aside partisanship and were working cooperatively.

The most important race, of course, was for governor. It was pretty clear that Ariyoshi's two main opponents would be Frank Fasi and Andy Anderson. Ariyoshi had narrowly beaten Fasi in the 1978 Democratic primary, overcoming a 10-point deficit in the last two weeks. This time, however, Fasi, having quit the Democratic Party, would run as an independent, which meant that in the general election there would be more voters who would be inclined to support Fasi than Ariyoshi.

Fasi had been estranged from the Democratic establishment ever since he jumped into the 1954 Democratic Primary to challenge incumbent Mayor John Wilson. Fasi, who claimed he decided to take on Wilson after he experienced a religious epiphany urging him to do so, committed one of the biggest political sins of all when he openly urged Republicans to cross over to vote for him in the primary. Given an opportunity to defeat the highly regarded Wilson, they crossed over in droves to give Fasi an upset victory. Fasi found out, however, that crossover voting can work both ways, when many angry Democrats voted for Blaisdell to defeat Fasi in the general election.

That election showcased Fasi's politics. In subsequent elections spanning nearly a half century, he touted himself as the "little guy's champion" and deliberately played to the disenchantment felt by Mainland haoles, Hawaiians and other ethnic groups who, for their own reasons, felt left out of political power after the AJA-led 1954 Democratic Revolution. This strategy helped elect Fasi to Honolulu's mayorship in 1968—but never to any higher office beyond that. John Burns, who publicly supported the part-Hawaiian Wilson for appointment as Territorial governor, never forgave Fasi for Wilson's defeat.

Thereafter, establishment Democrats—most who saw Fasi as dishonest, unethical and a rank opportunist—resorted to a series of attempts to either defeat Fasi or hurt him politically.

When he ran for reelection in 1972, Burns and other Democrats covertly supported Republican Anderson in a failed attempt to beat him.

In 1975, Fasi was indicted on bribery charges brought by special prosecutor Grant Cooper, a well-known Los Angeles trial lawyer hired by State Attorney General Ronald Amemiya. Cooper had represented Sirhan Sirhan, the assassin who had gunned down Bobby Kennedy in 1968. The mere fact that a lawyer of Cooper's stature had taken the case suggested there was substance to the state's charge. However, Cooper was forced to dismiss the charges when Hal Hansen, the key prosecution witness, recanted his story and refused to testify against Fasi. "A great injustice has been done," Cooper said before he returned to the Mainland. Legally, Fasi was innocent of the charges against him. Politically, however, his reputation was damaged.

In 1976, the Hawaii Community Development Authority was established by the Legislature to control and develop the 676-acre Kaka'ako district located in the heart of urban Honolulu. This State takeover of land from the City's jurisdiction was motivated in large part by anti-Fasi politics.

It was a classic case of common sense trumped by politics, for although the State could build infrastructure such as sewers and streets in Kaka'ako without City permits, it would have to connect with the surrounding City sewers and streets. During Fasi's terms as mayor, the City did little to facilitate development of the area. As a result, the redevelopment of Kaka'ako was delayed for more than 20 years. To compound the problem, as the State began spending hundreds of millions of dollars to improve Kaka'ako infrastructure, in 1978 the voters approved a constitutional amendment that gave the counties exclusive rights to the real-property taxes. Thus, as the State paid for infrastructure improvements in Kaka'ako with State general funds, the City collected the real property tax on the enhanced land values.

In 1978, anti-Fasi delegates to the 1978 Constitutional Convention engineered the so-called "resign to run" constitutional amendment, seen by many as a "stop Fasi" measure designed to force him to resign his mayorship if he decided to run for governor or any other higher office again. (In a similar vein, after World War II, Republicans introduced the 22nd Amendment limiting presidents to two terms in office. They wanted to avoid having to deal with a parade of liberal presidents like Franklin D. Roosevelt, who was elected to four terms.)

In the 1980 mayoral election, anti-Fasi Democrats had rallied behind former Ariyoshi Cabinet member Eileen Anderson and finally booted an overconfident and arrogant Fasi out of the mayor's office. Embittered by the loss, he resigned from the Democratic Party.

One could hardly blame Fasi for discarding his Democratic credentials, but much of the enmity the former Marine captain from Connecticut seemed so easily to provoke was his own doing. He was dismissive of Democrats who disagreed with him, had a blatant proclivity for political opportunism and, when it came to politics, seemed to possess little loyalty to anyone or anything.

My personal experience with Fasi only reinforced that image. In 1980, I proposed merging two underutilized elementary schools a little more than a mile apart and using the site of the smaller one for the new UH law school. The land had been transferred by the City to the State when the State took over the County school system in 1968 on the condition that it be used for public schools. A month or so before the idea was made public, I called Fasi and explained it to him. "Sounds like a good idea," he said. "No problem." A few days later I sent him a letter confirming his consent.

School mergers are almost always controversial, and this one was no exception. Within a week, the principal of the smaller school, along with the faculty and the students' parents, organized a protest. Petitions were circulated and politicians were lobbied. Still, the university's Board of Regents and five of the nine members of the Board of Education supported the idea.

It did not take long for the protesters to meet with Fasi to ask for his support. The next day, Fasi, who was up for reelection, announced that the City would not agree to the land being used for the new law school. I was shocked. The proposal was dead. Later that evening, a few minutes after I watched the 10 o'clock news, Fasi called me at home.

"Ben, much ado about nothing, eh?" he said.

"I just finished watching you on the news. You looked good with all those parents and cute little kids around you," I replied, with a hint of sarcasm. "Listen, Frank, I wouldn't have made the proposal without your okay. I even sent you a letter confirming it."

"Well, Ben, I didn't think all hell would break loose, but this morning I met with a group of angry parents," he said.

"Hey, Frank, when I explained it to you, didn't you say it was a good idea?" I retorted.

"Ben, let me tell you something, I've been in this business longer than I can remember, and you know as well as I do that it's the people who are mad at you who remember when it's time to vote. The ones who agree with you never remember anything good you've done."

"Oh, fuck it; I don't know why we're even having this discussion."

"Oh, come on, Ben, it's nothing personal," he said.

"Right. Good night, Frank."

The next time I saw Fasi he acted as if nothing had ever happened. It was hard to stay angry at the man. I always liked him (even when we ran against each other in 1994 and he accused me of taking a bribe from one of his weird supporters and discussed my separation from Lorraine over his radio show), but I never forgot. In the 1980 election I worked hard to help Eileen Anderson beat him in the Democratic primary.

I did vote for Fasi in his 1972 and 1976 mayoral elections. I thought he was a good mayor, perhaps the best since statehood. He had done good things for the city. The centerpiece of his achievements was Honolulu's bus system, which was rated one of the best municipal bus systems in the nation. There was some truth to his campaign slogan "Fasi gets it done." Moreover, he had surrounded himself with talented Cabinet members, most of whom had good relationships with mainstream Democratic leaders and State legislators. Often they would successfully accomplish what Fasi himself could not—lobby legislators to support city-related issues.

In every poll that I saw, though, Fasi received low marks for honesty and ethics. If he wasn't aware that there were questions about his character, his political polls must have surely revealed it to him. When he sought to regain the mayor's office in 1984, a seemingly chastened Fasi ran a television ad in which he and his wife, Joyce, assured viewers that he was a changed man. It must have helped, as he defeated Eileen Anderson, whose unimaginative, bureaucratic style of leadership had produced little over her four-year term.

For me, Fasi's startling mea culpa only verified the past complaints about him and revealed the extremes to which he would go to win an election. Frankly, I was embarrassed for him.

Despite Andy Anderson's evasiveness, it was an open secret that he was also gearing up to run for governor against Ariyoshi in the 1982 election. As a candidate, Anderson had a lot going for him. He was part-Hawaiian and a successful small-businessman; he had movie-star good looks; and he was experienced, intelligent and a good speaker.

Politically, Anderson and Fasi were like peas in a pod: They were ardent practitioners of doing whatever worked for them at the moment, a tactic that could bring short-term benefits but also long-term liabilities. (In 1984, for example, newly elected Mayor Fasi hired Anderson as City managing director—one result of this marriage of convenience came in 1987 when a jury found both men had committed fraud in managing a City housing project, though the verdict was reversed later by the State Supreme Court).

This "politics of convenience" helped Fasi become mayor—but it was a big reason why he was never elected governor or to Congress. And it never worked for Anderson, who lost every election for higher office that he entered.

Ariyoshi had won a close victory over Fasi in the 1978 Democratic Primary, overcoming a 10-point deficit in the last two weeks, before going on to trounce Republican John Leopold six weeks later in the general election. In 1982, however, Ariyoshi and Fasi would face off in the general election, in which haole and Hawaiian Republicans and independents would be voting. These voters were more likely to vote for Fasi than Ariyoshi.

Under the circumstances, conventional political wisdom suggested that Coalition Democrats should minimize or avoid controversial disputes with Ariyoshi. In fact, during my eight years in the Senate, the 1982 legislative session would be the most contentious with the governor.

On many issues, we worked hard to accommodate Ariyoshi. We knew, for example, how badly he wanted the Legislature to complete the second phase of his State Plan—i.e., the 12 functional plans. Ariyoshi had called the State Plan a "gift to our children." By the end of the legislative session, we had finished and approved all 12 plans, which, inexplicably, were rejected by the House (an indication that Ariyoshi himself did not like the Senate's versions). The plans would be taken up again in the 1983 legislative session.

Separation of Powers

When appropriate I was an adversary to the governor, but I never saw him as an enemy. My differences with him were on issues. I respected him, but, unlike too many legislators with whom I served, I never deferred to him. I believed strongly that the Legislature was an equal and separate branch of government and should conduct itself accordingly. Throughout each legislative session, we did what was expected of us under the State constitution's system of checks and balances. When we had to, we "checked" the governor. In 1982, two major disputes emerged.

The first involved the Senate's unique constitutional power of advice and consent, a power that traces its roots to the United States Senate. Except for Nebraska, which has a unicameral legislature, the power of advice and consent is invested in every State Senate in the nation.

Alexander Hamilton, in Federalist Paper No. 6, explained the purpose of advice and consent: It is "an excellent check upon the spirit of favoritism in the President, and would tend greatly to prevent the appointment of unfit characters from State prejudice, from family connection, from personal attachment, or from a view to popularity."

The power has its limits. The Senate is restricted to either confirming or rejecting a governor's nominee—it cannot replace him or nominate another. Thus, if the Senate rejects a nominee, the governor must submit another, and still another if that nominee is rejected, until one is finally confirmed.

During a four-year term, a governor nominates hundreds of people to various State boards and commissions. The overwhelming majority are usually easily confirmed by the Senate, as were the majority of Ariyoshi's nominees. During the 1981 legislative session, however, five of his nominees—one to the Boxing Commission, another to the University of Hawai'i Board of Regents and three to the Hawaii Housing Authority Commission—faced strong opposition in the Senate. The reasons varied, but it did not help when most of the nominees failed to appear at the public hearings on their nominations. As a matter of courtesy, Senate President Wong met privately with Ariyoshi and urged him to withdraw the nominations, which he did.

After the close of the 1981 legislative session, however, Ariyoshi gave the five nominees interim appointments to the very positions from which he had earlier withdrawn their nominations. And in the 1982 legislative session, he inexplicably resubmitted the nominations for Senate confirmation.

His decision was like a shot across the Senate's bow. Why Ariyoshi did not bother to inquire whether the senators had changed their minds since 1981 remains a mystery. Regardless, the issue was no longer whether the nominees were qualified. Instead, it had become a matter of principle and political power. This was not a fight sought by the Coalition. But to confirm the nominees would set the bad precedent of allowing not only Ariyoshi but also future governors to circumvent the advice and consent process. The dispute was about the fundamental principle of separation of powers.

Under the State constitution, once a governor submits the names of the nominees to the Senate, they are exclusively under the Senate's jurisdiction, and he can withdraw them only if the Senate agrees. As he had done in 1981, Wong tried in 1982 to privately persuade Ariyoshi to withdraw the nominations; Ariyoshi's response was that he would do so only if the nominees asked him.

The die was cast. A visibly grim Wong took the unusual step of relinquishing the Senate president's podium to Vice President Kawasaki so he could speak from the floor against the nominations.

Wong weighed into Ariyoshi's actions, arguing that by appointing the nominees to existing vacancies after the Senate agreed to let him withdraw the nominations, Ariyoshi had denied the Senate its right to vote to either confirm or reject the nominees and was trying to "end run" the State constitution. Under the circumstances, Wong argued further, to confirm the five nominees would make a mockery of the Senate's power of advice and consent and reduce it to a rubber-stamp for the governor.

Wong noted that as a delegate to the 1968 Constitutional Convention, Ariyoshi had spoken in opposition to a proposed constitutional amendment to rid the Senate of its power of advice and consent. Moreover, as a former State senator himself, Wong argued, Ariyoshi understood the importance of the Senate's power of advice and consent to the principle of separation of powers. To drive that point home, Wong stressed, the Senate must reject all five nominations.

Whatever his motives, Ariyoshi must have known that the Senate would reject the nominations. The seven dissident Democrats spoke for confirmation, arguing that the nominees were "good people" who deserved the Senate's approval. They were good people and, in fact, some were personal friends of a few Coalition senators. Nevertheless, friendship had nothing to do with the issue at hand. The five nominees were caught in the middle of a struggle between the governor and the Senate. By majority vote, all five were rejected.

Unlike Anderson and Fasi, Ariyoshi could be loyal to a fault when it came to his supporters. In 1984, he appointed then-deputy attorney general Michael Lilly as attorney general. In reviewing Lilly's background, Senate researchers discovered things that senators found troublesome; among the most troubling was the fact that Lilly had made telephone calls from his State office on behalf of a former client who was being sentenced for crimes committed in Canada. The client, who Lilly had represented while in private practice, was the head of a family of gypsy shysters who had committed fraud against mostly elderly people in Hawai'i before moving their scams to Canada. There was nothing wrong with Lilly's representing him while he was in private practice, but to call from his State office under color of his deputy attorney general status was inappropriate.

Although his chances of being confirmed were slim, Lilly, who denied all of the allegations, refused to withdraw, and Ariyoshi stood by him. Lilly's nomination was rejected by the Senate.

The Heptachlor Crisis

March 18, 1982, marked the worst public-health crisis since statehood. The State Department of Health announced that State and federal laboratory tests had detected traces of the pesticide heptachlor in milk and ordered the recall of homogenized milk, 2-percent milk, acidophilus milk and half-and-half from all civilian grocery stores. For the next six months, two terms, previously unknown to most people, would dominate news reports and everyday conversation: "heptachlor" and "green chop."

Heptachlor is a pesticide that was used by Hawai'i pineapple plantations during the 1970s to control ants in the pineapple fields. In 1978, the federal Environmental Protection Agency (EPA) banned its use, but in a negotiated agreement with Hawai'i pineapple companies granted the plantations an exemption to use up their existing stocks.

"Green chop"—shredded pineapple leaves—was considered good cattle feed and was sold by the pineapple companies to Hawai'i dairy farmers. The EPA approved the practice, but required that the green chop be held for a year before it was sold to allow the heptachlor on the leaves to dissipate. This precaution was not taken. Inevitably, the dairy cows that were fed the contaminated green chop produced milk with traces of heptachlor.

After the March 18 recall, it seemed hardly a week went by without the Health Department recalling other Hawai'i dairy products such as yogurt, cottage cheese and ice cream.

In a little over a month, all milk and dairy products had disappeared from O'ahu's grocery stores and supermarkets. Moreover, because of a State law designed to protect Hawai'i milk producers from unfair Mainland competition, the stores could not buy Mainland milk as a substitute. Mainland milk could only be bought on O'ahu's military bases, which used it exclusively.

O'ahu's 19 dairy farmers, most of whom had been struggling to stay financially solvent even before the recalls, were forced to dump 3.2 million pounds of milk, worth an estimated $600,000—big losses for the already marginal businesses. The recalls eventually cost O'ahu's two largest milk producers, Meadow Gold Dairy and Foremost Dairy, millions of dollars in lost sales.

The initial public reaction to the first recall was one of concerned curiosity. Few knew anything about heptachlor. My office received a couple of dozen phone calls, mostly from mothers of children and infants who wanted to know more about the pesticide. But when the news media disclosed that the State laboratory technicians who had detected the heptachlor in January of 1982 had not informed their superiors until March 11, the public's concern turned into outrage.

The overwhelming majority of the calls I received were from irate mothers who were terribly worried that their children's health might be at risk. Public confidence in the milk industry was sinking fast.

On March 24, 1982, barely a week after the first recall, the *Honolulu Advertiser* ran an editorial that stated cryptically, "The State Department of Health is no place for poor leadership. The record suggests more than contaminated milk should be recalled."

On March 30, just four hours after the department ordered a fourth recall, George Yuen, the department's director, announced his retirement. Yuen, who by most accounts was considered a fine administrator, had been done in by the negligence of some of his department's timid and overcautious employees.

More State recalls followed and, on April 19, 1982, the U.S. Food and Drug Administration announced it had banned the use of Meadow Gold milk and dairy products on all airline flights and ships traveling from Hawai'i to the Mainland because of the unacceptable levels of heptachlor. Subsequently, the FDA banned the sale of beef from cattle that had been fed contaminated green chop.

On April 20, the new State health director, Charles Clark, issued an order barring Meadow Gold Dairy, Hawai'i's biggest milk distributor, from processing any raw milk produced on O'ahu. Meadow Gold attorneys sued for a court order to enjoin the Health Department from enforcing Clark's order. By then, public confidence had hit rock bottom.

In response, the Senate established the Special Senate Investigative Committee on Heptachlor. Unlike the regular legislative committees, the Investigative Committee was empowered to subpoena records and witnesses and take testimony sworn under oath. It was the first committee of its kind in state history. I would serve as its chairman.

Committee resources were limited. We would have to do the job with a secretary, two researchers and a used Wang word processor (back then, computers, email and the Internet were not available), which I bought from a UH astronomy professor for $13,000 using my campaign funds (legally permissible at the time). Fortunately, I was authorized to hire my former committee clerk, Earl Anzai, who had just graduated from the UH law school.

After a week of intense preparation, the Special Investigative Committee held its first hearing on May 14. To persuade the witnesses to speak freely, I closed the first session to the news media and public while the committee interviewed five State milk investigators about their inspection practices and standards.

If there were standards, none of the inspectors seemed to know anything about them. Over time, a friendly, casual relationship had developed between most of the inspectors and certain employees of the two milk-processing companies. When one inspector was asked to explain how he chose the milk samples for inspection, he admitted sheepishly that the samples were selected by a company employee. There were other revelations to come.

In subsequent public hearings, a sorry tale of misplaced priorities and mismanagement by the State began to unfold. The State employees seemed more concerned about the milk companies than the public.

The investigative committee's highest priority was to determine whether heptachlor was, in fact, a health hazard if consumed in milk or other dairy products. Experts were called in to provide answers.

Lawrence Piette, executive director of the Cancer Center of Hawai'i, testified, "The evidence is sufficient to strongly implicate heptachlor as a carcinogen in man as well as in laboratory animals."

But Dr. John Hylin, an agricultural biochemist, testified there was no evidence to prove that heptachlor was a health hazard, provoking murmurs from members of the packed crowd, some of whom shook their heads in disbelief. After the hearing, a visibly annoyed woman buttonholed me and asked, "If heptachlor is not a health hazard, why did the EPA ban it?"

In fact, the evidence was mixed. There was not enough evidence to show that heptachlor directly caused cancer in humans. But tests on laboratory animals provided ample evidence that heptachlor was highly toxic to humans and had the potential to cause a number of illnesses, including severe liver damage. The risk of a human being suffering health problems from the ingestion of heptachlor would depend on the amount ingested and the period of time over which it took place.

The evidence was not conclusive, but the EPA decided to ban heptachlor because of its highly toxic properties and its potential to cause harm to humans.

Unfortunately, the January test results were sent to a federal laboratory on the Mainland for confirmation and were not reported to Department of Health superiors until March 11. Meanwhile, Oʻahu dairy farmers were allowed to continue using green chop as cattle feed.

Then there was testimony that implied the March 18 recall was announced hurriedly to preempt a news reporter who, having been tipped off by a concerned State employee, was about to break the story.

The recalls continued into late April. Since the dairy farmers and the state's two milk producers began dumping the contaminated milk after the March 18 recall, it was asked why so many more recalls were ordered. And why only of Meadow Gold products?

One answer was provided by a Meadow Gold employee who met surreptitiously with Anzai and me. "The company," he said, "is still using skim milk, because they think skim milk is safe."

Heptachlor is known to lodge in fatty tissues. In milk, it would be in the cream. If what the employee said was true, then his bosses had assumed that it was safe to process skim milk, because the cream (and thus, presumably, the heptachlor) had been skimmed off.

Unlike Foremost Dairy, which wisely chose to dump all its contaminated milk and suffered few recalls, Meadow Gold played hardball; its attorneys were uncooperative, and the committee was forced to subpoena its records. When the State Department of Health ordered the company to stop processing all raw milk because tests kept detecting heptachlor in its products, Meadow Gold lawyers sought a court injunction to stop the State from enforcing its order.

Proving that Meadow Gold had deliberately used contaminated milk was a big challenge. Here, Anzai's experience as a federal auditor proved invaluable. Under the State milk law, Meadow Gold's monthly records showing raw milk quantities and the production records of every milk and dairy product were available to the State milk commissioner.

Anzai developed a methodology that would allow for comparisons of the volume of raw milk purchased by Meadow Gold, the volume of raw milk dumped and the volume of milk used to make skim milk and other dairy products. Working weekends and late nights, he and the staff calculated the volume of milk used to make milk products by breaking down its ingredients and adding up the amount of milk used to make everything from skim milk to ice cream. The Wang word processor was used to the point of overheating. The results were not precise, but they were accurate enough to make the comparisons.

"I think our whistleblower is telling the truth," Anzai said. "Our comparisons show the company did not dump as much raw milk as it reported."

The investigation was not without its lighter moments. One night, the whistle-blower told Anzai that the company was going to transfer the skim milk to a warehouse in 'Aiea. Armed with doughnuts and coffee, Anzai and I staked out the plant from about 9 p.m. to 2 a.m., waiting in my car for the milk to be delivered. The only person to appear was a police officer, who confronted us and asked why we were parked next to the warehouse.

By the end of May, Beatrice Foods, Meadow Gold's parent company, had had enough. The Chicago-based corporation, a major food-processing company that back then specialized in milk and dairy products, sent one of its vice presidents to Hawai'i to resolve the situation.

"Senator, we [Beatrice Foods] are embarrassed by what has happened in Hawai'i. We take great pride in our reputation for producing high-quality dairy products, and I can assure you we will resolve things very quickly," he said.

They did. The vice president told me that, besides production procedural changes, Meadow Gold's CEO would be transferred to a Beatrice Foods subsidiary on the Mainland and the manager of its milk production had decided to retire.

Two months after the March 18 recall, O'ahu groceries and supermarkets were once again stocked with fresh Hawai'i milk and dairy products. The committee concluded its investigation with a comprehensive report in June. Long-term studies would be conducted to determine whether any person had been adversely affected by the heptachlor. The crisis was over.

The heptachlor milk crisis was an example of how easily government can lose its way. It demonstrated what happens in the increasingly risk-averse culture that permeates government. State laboratory technicians revealed their lack of confidence in their own skills by sending the milk samples to a federal laboratory for confirmation before reporting them to their superiors. As a result, dairy farmers continued to use the contaminated green chop for cattle feed for another two months. Clearly, if the department, relying on erroneous test results, had ordered the dairy farmers to stop using green chop and the milk processors to stop processing raw milk, there would have been enormous economic damages and the potential for lawsuits against the State. But the State had a duty to protect the public health. It might have been a tough choice—but if there is a risk of error, the government should always err on the side of the public. This fundamental principle of government was not followed.

The negligence of his employees cost George Yuen his job. But Yuen was the only casualty—no other State employee was reprimanded, suspended or fired for failing to protect the public health.

A Look at Gambling

In his opening day speech at the 1982 Legislature, Dickie Wong, anticipating the need to replace federal funds lost under Reagan's New Federalism policy, proposed two new revenue sources. One was a State lottery.

Gambling is one of those issues that many politicians denounce as sin but do little about. Church bingo games continue; Hawai'i's "social gambling" law allows people to gamble in the privacy of their homes as long as each gambler keeps his winnings and no profit is made by a third party (the so-called "house").

The proposed State lottery had little chance of passing. Religious groups opposed the lottery for moralistic reasons; law enforcement warned against an influx of Mainland organized crime to Hawai'i; civic groups and Hawai'i's two daily newspapers cited social ills such as gambling addiction.

It was difficult getting worked up for a bill doomed to rejection, but few ideas become law in the first session. Often, educating one's peers and, more important, the general public on the merits of a bill was the first step in the legislative process of turning ideas into law. Groundbreaking laws—civil rights and workers' compensation, for example—took years of debate and public hearings before sufficient public and political support were mustered for them to pass.

Lotteries have roots in our history. Some of the first lotteries were held during the American Revolution to finance Gen. George Washington's Continental Army. Under the Hawaiian Monarchy and into the early 1900s, horse racing—the "Sport of Kings"—was legal in Hawai'i. I saw nothing immoral about gambling.

Anti-gambling groups tend to view all types of gambling as the same. Allow one form, they argue, and the floodgates to others will be opened. I disagreed. Las Vegas-style 24-hour fast-moving casino gambling was pernicious, and I opposed it. But a State lottery was different, more comparable to the bingo games played to raise money for churches than to shooting craps, roulette or any of the other casino games in which one could lose thousands of dollars in just a few minutes.

Law enforcement officials opposed all gambling and warned that a State lottery would attract Mainland criminal elements to Hawai'i. After living in Los Angeles for more than eight years, I returned with a healthy skepticism about the claims of law-enforcement and other government agencies. There was a lot of information on casino gambling but little on State-run lotteries. I asked whether the officials were opposed to horse racing for the same reasons. Horse racing, they answered, was even more likely than a lottery to bring in Mainland organized crime. If that were the case, I asked, why was it that FBI director J. Edgar Hoover, who was America's most famous crime fighter at the time, was such an ardent horse-racing fan that he attended the races regularly and was often seen sitting in his reserved seat at the racetracks? The question answered itself.

The strongest argument against gambling was its social costs. Gambling addiction was the most serious. But there were no reliable statistics on the incidence of gambling addiction related to lotteries. Most of the studies were done in places like Las Vegas where there was widespread casino gambling.

Politics is an art, not a science. Weighing the different interests is always a challenge. If, for example, the State proposed to build a new highway along a certain route, it might come at the expense of longtime residents of the area, whose homes might be condemned to make way for it. For the proposed State lottery, the question was whether the revenues raised to fund social programs were worth the cost in social ills.

There are risks inherent to living in any free society. If the legality of every activity was predicated on the fiscal and human costs of the social problems it imposed on society, then activities such as alcohol consumption and tobacco smoking would be made illegal. They remain legal because the majority of Americans believe that the freedom to decide those issues for themselves is more important than the social cost to society. The history of the failure of Prohibition, and the repeal of the 18th Amendment, which turned many ordinary Americans into lawbreakers, taught us that lesson.

There was no better proof of the penchant for gambling among Hawai'i residents than the fact that, on a per capita basis, they frequent Las Vegas' casinos more than residents of any other state except Nevada itself. Indeed, some hotels, such as Boyd Gaming Corp.'s California Hotel and Casino, cater specifically to Hawaiians, going to the extent of serving favorite local foods and selling local products. Each year, thousands of Hawai'i residents spend hundreds of millions of dollars in Las Vegas casinos.

Polls indicated that nearly 70 percent of the public supported a State lottery, a remarkable statistic, given the strong opposition by the newspapers, churches and law enforcement.

In his 1982 State of the State address, Ariyoshi had warned that the New Federalism could cause as much as a 25-percent reduction in federal funds for State social programs for the needy and poor. New sources of revenue were needed to make up for the anticipated loss of federal funds. While the Senate offered a lottery and a hotel room tax as potential new sources of revenue, critics offered nothing but criticism.

Through his New Federalism and his attempt to reduce the size of the federal government by "starving the beast," Reagan did more than any other president to move the states to legalize gambling. During his two terms as president, 18 states adopted State lotteries. As of this writing, Hawai'i and Utah are the only states that do not have legalized gambling. ❖

CHAPTER EIGHT

End of the New Senate

The Coalition Disbands

On April 26, 1982, the 60th day of the regular legislative session, Andy Anderson and Pat Saiki announced their resignations from the Coalition and their candidacies for governor and lieutenant governor, respectively.

The Coalition had worked well in 1981, passing bills for initiatives, referendums, a State lottery and a hotel room tax (both were killed in the House). In 1982, however, the Coalition struggled somewhat, mostly on issues such as workers' compensation reform, over which there had been a historical divide between Democrats and Republicans, partly because Coalition Democrats were wary of doing anything that would enhance Anderson's anticipated run for governor.

Complicating matters would be the Coalition's dispute with the governor on the issue of advice and consent and the Senate's investigation of the heptachlor milk crisis, which exposed mismanagement by the State Department of Health and caused the resignation of its director and well-respected member of Ariyoshi's Cabinet, George Yuen.

Still, public opinion of the Coalition seemed to remain high—mostly, I thought, because the people sensed we had kept partisanship to a minimum in trying to do our work. In 1982, all seven Coalition Democrats were reelected by comfortable margins. I got a free ride, running unopposed in both the primary and general elections. In the governor's race, Anderson and Fasi split the anti-Ariyoshi vote, and Ariyoshi beat both by a wide margin.

The 1982 election marked the end of the Democratic-Republican Coalition. But there were other changes as well. The constitutionally mandated, bipartisan Reapportionment Commission, struggling to maintain the current multimember legislative districts, developed a reapportionment plan based on registered voters. The Republican Party joined in a lawsuit by GOP House member John Carroll seeking a ruling that the plan should have been based on census population, not registered voters, and therefore was unconstitutional. Carroll, a lawyer, was unhappy with how the commission had reapportioned his House district.

On January 25, 1982, a few days after the opening of the session, U.S. District Court Judge Martin Pence issued a ruling that dramatically changed the legislative districts. In ruling for the Republicans, Pence appointed a citizens' panel to develop a new reapportionment plan based on census population. The Republican Party's celebration on Pence's ruling was short-lived. The Party and the unhappy Carroll had won a pyrrhic victory.

On May 4, Pence approved the citizens' panel's new reapportionment plan— single-member districts. All multimember legislative districts were eliminated. This meant no legislative district could have more than one legislator—something no sensible Republican could have wished for.

Single-member districts are the bane of minority political parties. In a state like Hawai'i, which is heavily Democrat and independent, Democratic candidates are more likely to win single-member districts than Republicans. A Republican had a better chance of winning a seat in the old multimember districts even if the district was heavily Democratic. The same was true for ethnic minorities. I doubt seriously I would have been elected in 1974 in the old 19th Representative District, where more than 60 percent of the voters were AJAs and I was the only non-AJA running in the Democratic primary. Fortunately, the 19th was a two-member district, and the voters had choices.

Moreover, single-member districts give well-financed incumbents a tremendous advantage over newcomers. There is probably no better example than the U.S. House of Representatives, where an average of 98 percent of the incumbents are routinely reelected.

The Reapportionment Commission, comprised of an equal number of Democrats and Republicans, resorted to using registered voters as a base for its plan to avoid the so-called "canoe districts," which include parts of two or more islands. Unfortunately, the "one-man, one-vote" rule does not include exceptions for an island state like Hawai'i.

For the minority Republican Party, the impact of single-member districts was devastating. In 1980, there were eight Republican senators, but in 1992 through 1998 there would be only two in the 25-member senate. In 1982, one of the casualties was Republican minority leader Wadsworth Yee, who found himself having to take on Democrat Neil Abercrombie in a heavily Democratic district. Yee was soundly defeated. (Predictably, demographic shifts in a district were usually reflected in the election. By 2004, the number of Republican senators increased to five.)

There were a number of significant changes in the 1982 Senate. Following the departure of Anderson and Saiki to run for higher office and the defeat of Yee, Democratic dissidents Ushijima, O'Connor and Toyofuku, facing another four years with Wong as president, all chose not to run for reelection. (Stanley Hara retired in 1980 and Charles Campbell, another victim of the new reapportionment, was defeated in 1982.)

Notwithstanding some of our floor fights, which at times must have provided great theater for the news media, these veterans often contributed valuable input in committee work. With their departure went a great deal of expertise and political savvy, not to mention the life experience that many of today's young legislators lack. The exodus of these veteran legislators signified a generational transition in the Senate. By the close of 1982, the only Democrat left in the Senate who had been part of the 1954 Democratic Revolution was Mamoru Yamasaki.

The Democrat-Republican Coalition lasted two years; by 1982, Anderson's anticipated bid for governor had eroded its viability. To no one's surprise, Anderson took every political advantage he could of the Coalition. Meanwhile, the seven dissident Democrats attacked Coalition Democrats almost daily for allegedly aiding Anderson's anticipated campaign.

Wong, who was the main target of these attacks, repeatedly reaffirmed his support for the Democratic candidate in the coming election and pledged to reorganize the Senate with Democrats in 1983. Wong's most vehement antagonist was Milton Holt. There was little love lost between them. Holt, who had defeated Wong's close ally and friend, T.C. Yim, in 1980, must have taken great pleasure in goading Wong into what amounted to a weekly loyalty oath to reaffirm his Democratic credentials.

Prior Concurrence

In March of the 1983 legislative session, Wong's "New Senate"—which from 1979 through 1982 had touted openness and encouraged debate and independence from the executive branch—began to fall apart.

At the heart of the demise was the Senate's "prior concurrence" rule. This rule, for which I beg the reader's patience as I try to explain it here, plays an important role in assuring that the Senate's committee system operates with transparency and fairness. Among other things, prior concurrence, a milestone procedural reform that was years in the making, provides a check against any abuse of power by the Ways and Means Committee and, by extension, the Senate president.

At its core, the rule was intended to give all appropriate parties notice of changes. It required the chairman of Ways and Means (or any committee chairman) to inform the subject committee chairman of any changes in subject matter content proposed in the subject-matter committee's bills.

The legislative process lends itself to political game-playing. If, for example, the president were against a bill, he could refer it to three or four subject-matter committees and virtually ensure it would be killed by one of them.

The potential for game-playing was greatest in the Ways and Means Committee. This was the committee of last resort where legislators, the governor and the Cabinet or lobbyists for special interests whose bills had failed to get approval in subject-matter committees could get another crack at their passage by lobbying to resurrect them in some form. This was true for appropriations rejected by

217

subject-matter committees as well. Little wonder, then, that some senators referred jokingly to Ways and Means as the "Lazarus committee."

At times, questions as to which committee had jurisdiction over an issue led to inevitable conflicts over who had the final authority over content and policy. These conflicts were often at their worst when the subject-matter committee was not notified of the changes made by Ways and Means.

The prior concurrence rule was designed to obviate such conflicts. Thus, once the subject-matter chairman was notified of a change, he would meet with the chairman of the committee that had proposed the change to seek an agreement. If they could agree, the subject-matter committee chairman would consult with his committee members for their consent. If they could not agree, the Senate leadership would intervene to help resolve their differences.

From 1979 through 1982, prior concurrence was not an issue in the Senate because, while subject-matter chairmen in the House could not sit on the Finance Committee, Senate chairmen were allowed to be members of Ways and Means. This was made necessary by the deep schism between the Wong and Ushijima factions, which left Wong with only 10 Democrats to run the Senate. Thus, as members of Ways and Means, subject-matter committee chairmen participated in any changes made to their committees' proposals, which constituted more than adequate notice.

After 1982, the number of Democratic senators increased from 17 to 21. With the proliferation of Democratic senators, the old practice of not allowing subject-matter chairmen to sit on Ways and Means was reinstituted. Thus, prior concurrence took on renewed importance.

In anticipation of a severe revenue shortfall caused by Reagan's New Federalism policy, subject-matter committees were asked to trim current operating costs for all State departments and agencies. The concern was so great that Ways and Means approved a Senate bill that provided for a temporary 1-percent increase in the 4-percent general excise tax to make up for the shortfall. A memorandum from Ways and Means chairman Yamasaki instructed all subject-matter committee chairmen to cut their budgets.

I was assigned to chair the Senate Committee on Economic Development. I welcomed the assignment and quickly immersed myself in developing an agenda for the committee. As it turned out, my chairmanship, along with those of five others, would be short-lived.

Midway through the 1983 session, a number of subject-matter committee chairmen started to complain that it was difficult to get information about the State Budget Bill. In the past, they had been allowed to read (but not make copies of) worksheets of the bill. The worksheets were an important source of detailed information, revealing any changes made by Ways and Means to the committees' bills or proposed department budgets.

Instead of access to the worksheets, we got the runaround, leaving us totally in the dark as to what Ways and Means had done to our respective committee programs. Even Wong seemed to be avoiding our inquiries. Finally, on March 31, 1983, a few of us decided to ask for information during the floor session, making our requests public and part of the Senate Journal.

Still, we never got the worksheets. The rule of prior concurrence—for which Wong fought hard during his days as a dissident and reformer—had been ignored by Yamasaki and Wong himself. Some subject-matter committee chairmen went with the flow and took the changes in stride. I was one of six Democratic senators who did not.

Two major committees, Hawaiian Homes, chaired by freshman Lehua Sallings from Kaua'i, and Higher Education, chaired by Abercrombie, suffered major changes to their programs.

Abercrombie was a fierce advocate for the University of Hawai'i's faculty and students. He believed the UH administration was top heavy and inefficient, and he proposed eliminating some administrative positions and services and shifting the funds to services for faculty and students. In fact, the UH administration, adhering to the governor's warm-body policy, was carrying positions that had long since outlived their usefulness.

A student housing bonds coordinator position, for example, was filled with a warm body, but no one could recall or determine the last time, past or present, that any student housing bonds had been issued. UH administrative salaries also seemed excessive. In 1983, the salary for the UH vice president of fiscal affairs was about $100,000 a year, compared to approximately $55,000 for the State director of Budget and Finance, who managed the fiscal affairs of the entire State government, including oversight of the UH budget.

Not surprisingly, Abercrombie's proposed changes were opposed by the State UH administration. Although the majority of his committee approved the proposals, a few members were opposed. Rather than express their opposition in committee, however, one skeptical member summed up their attitudes when he muttered to no one in particular, "Ways and Means will take care of it."

My committee oversaw the State Department of Planning and Economic Development (DPED). Only about $13 million of DPED's annual budget of more than $250 million was for its staff and operations; the balance was for a number of separate agencies and commissions that were attached to DPED for budgetary accounting purposes.

One such agency was the Commission on Population and the Hawaiian Future. My committee and staff analyzed the commission and concluded that it should be "sunsetted," or abolished; the vice chairman of the commission agreed, saying the commission had completed its work and, if more was needed, it could be handled by the current DPED. My recommendation to abolish the commission and terminate its four staff positions (one vacant) was unanimously approved by my committee members. What happened later in Ways and Means was an example of how difficult it was to make reforms.

Ways and Means, I later learned, had adopted a House bill that extended the life of the commission and transferred the four positions to DPED. I was not informed that my committee's recommendation had been rejected. What was worse, no one was willing to give a justification for the change. The commission's operating budget was minuscule—"manini," as the Hawaiians say, compared to DPED's huge $250 million budget. But the seemingly inconsequential issue, I sensed, was an ominous portent of things to come.

"It looks like the Senate is dancing the old one step, two step—one step forward, two steps backward," Carpenter observed wryly.

"I want to get straight answers to two questions: Why weren't we given notice, and what is the justification for the changes?" I said. "The Population Commission is manini, but if they're going to play games with this kind of small stuff, what else is going on?"

That afternoon, prior to going into the evening floor session, I spoke with Bert Kobayashi, the vice chairman of Ways and Means. Kobayashi was one of three senators who held a Ph.D. He had taught at a Mainland university before coming back to Hawai'i. As the former executive director of the Population Commission, he was familiar with its work. He was not, however, one to rock the boat.

"Bert, what's going on with the Population Commission?" I asked.

"Well, we've got some warm bodies involved here, and it seemed rather drastic to eliminate the commission," he replied.

"I know the governor has a warm-body policy, but since when did the Senate adopt one? Dickie and Yama [Yamasaki] warned us about the revenue shortfall, we even passed a bill to raise the general excise tax by 1 percent and you guys [Ways and Means] instructed us to cut spending, and that's what we did."

"Well, it's a little more involved than that," he replied. "Chip's wife works for the commission."

"Chip's wife? Is this what all of this is all about?" I asked. "So why didn't Chip let me know?"

"You have to ask him that question."

"Look, our position is not carved in stone; if the governor or Ways and Means wants to keep those warm bodies in DPED, then he can use some of the 20 or so civil service positions we put in the budget for him to use at his discretion. The Population Commission's biggest expense is its staff. If we don't cut staff, what do we save on—the electricity bill? How can we cut spending if we follow a warm-body policy?"

"I'm not the chairman," he replied.

That evening, March 31, 1983, the 45th day of the session, I made a motion to amend the State Budget Bill to restore my committee's proposal to abolish the commission and its five staff positions. Toguchi seconded my motion.

I was under no illusion that our amendments would pass. Even if the four Republicans supported us, which they did, we would have only 10 votes. We needed 13. But there was little chance of anyone taking on Wong and Yamasaki to vote with us. Our goal was to get them to justify their actions on the record—in the Senate Journal and before the public and news media. At 8 p.m., I made my motion, kicking off a four-hour debate. This is an excerpt from the Senate Journal:

> *Senator Cayetano then rose and stated as follows:*
> Mr. President, the Committee on Economic Development held a hearing on this matter ... and we determined that the work of the commission staff could be dealt with in other ways; that there was no need for an office of population in DPED and that the four positions should not be transferred from the Commission on Population and the Hawaiian Future (to DPED).... This was the recommendation to Ways and Means and it was a recommendation which was approved unanimously by every member of the Committee on Economic Development. We have to remember that this was not an easy decision for the committee. We were operating under the instructions from Ways and Means....
>
> Mr. President, I would like to know from the chairman, the vice chairman ... or from the members (specifically, Uwaine) who have friends on this population commission, what is the reason for overriding the subject-matter committee's recommendations and placing back into the budget those four particular positions.
>
> What is the reason, when we are faced with fiscal constraints and were told to make devastating cuts, when we had to make agonizing decisions after long and hard hearings where evidence was presented to us, what is the reason?
>
> *Senator Yamasaki then responded:*
> Mr. President, to clear this matter up, I would like to just state that we have a letter from the Department of Planning and Economic Development (DPED) requesting that the functions of the Commission on Population and the Hawaiian Future be transferred to the DPED and, also, that the three warm bodies ... be also transferred to the Department of Planning and Economic Development.

The amendment was defeated by a vote of 11 ayes and 14 nos.

Lehua Sallings then introduced the first of four amendments to restore her committee's proposals in the State Budget Bill. Again, we wanted Ways and Means to state the justification for rejecting the subject-matter committee's recommendations. The Senate Journal continues:

> *Senator Yamasaki responded:*
> ... as I said in my committee, over the 25 years that I have been serving in the Legislature, this is the first time that a subject committee chairman has ignored the request of the department and completely changed the projects and the programs of the department.
> And after conferring with the department, an individual by the name of Mr. Fletcher of the Department of Hawaiian Home Lands, confirmed that these projects are essential and that we should support the request of the department....
> *Senator Abercrombie then continued:*
> I have not served as long as the good Senator ... but surely these halls and perhaps the halls over in 'Iolani Palace never heard a remark that a Mr. Fletcher from the Hawaiian Home Lands came in and said that he wanted the money and that, therefore, the recommendation of the (subject) committee authorized by yourself and this body, to conduct investigations, hearings and find conclusions about it, be ignored....
> And perhaps we ought to bring the people from the various departments in and accept their recommendations at face value ... and send them to the executive, somewhat like the activities that take place in the Soviet Union, for example, when the presidium meets.
> *Senator Yamasaki replied:*
> Mr. President, all I can say, is that this project is priority Number 2 of the Department of Hawaiian Home Lands.

Yamasaki's replies left nothing to be said. He had deferred to the State administration and changed our committee budgets recommendations without informing us. He had ignored the rule of prior concurrence.

"I put in a lot of hard work for four years to make this so-called 'New Senate' work," Abercrombie said. "I'm not about to sit silent while Dickie and these guys take the Senate back to the past."

After only three years, Dickie Wong's "New Senate" was becoming "old." I felt betrayed.

The Hawaii Crime Commission

After the legislative session had ended, several of us sat in Duke Kawasaki's office discussing the events that had just transpired. There was unanimous dissatisfaction among the six of us with the way Yamasaki had handled the development of the State Budget Bill. In anticipation of the coming revenue shortfalls, every subject-matter committee chairman had followed Yamasaki's instructions to come up with savings by cutting the budgets of the various State departments, only to have him arbitrarily reject our proposals without notice and in violation of the "prior concurrence" rule. To make matters worse, in most cases Yamasaki had simply capitulated to the State administration's requests and in a few instances promised to "take care" of the personal interests of some senators. *So much for the so-called "New Senate,"* I thought.

Duke Kawasaki was particularly peeved with Yamasaki's treatment of the Hawaii Crime Commission. Kawasaki—a strong supporter of the commission—noted that while on the one hand Yamasaki had used the governor's warm-body policy to justify saving the staff of the Commission on Population—even though the chairman of the commission himself had proposed abolishing the commission—he had not applied the same policy to the Hawaii Crime Commission and had inserted such a paltry appropriation in the State Budget Bill that the commission's end was all but assured.

The Hawaii Crime Commission, which had been modeled after the famous Chicago Crime Commission, was created by Lt. Gov. Nelson Doi. Doi, who had served as a State senator from the Big Island for 14 years, was a close political ally of Kawasaki and Tom Gill. In 1974, Doi and Gill ran for lieutenant governor and governor respectively. Although Doi won, Gill was defeated by Ariyoshi in the Democratic primary. In the general election, Ariyoshi and Doi defeated their Republican opponents.

Almost since its inception, the Hawaii Crime Commission had begun to investigate corruption in government. This evoked different levels of resistance from some local law enforcement officials, who seemed to resent the idea of a commission of civilians intruding on their jurisdiction, and hostile opposition from legislators like Milton Holt, who made it a high priority first as a State representative and later as a State senator to abolish the commission.

A longtime veteran of the State Senate, Doi had developed a reputation as an independent, fearless and honest legislator. As long as Doi headed the Commission, it was safe from political attacks. In August 1978, the Commission issued a report finding that organized crime had infiltrated political and social circles. The fact that no individuals were named provoked angry criticism from some legislators.

In 1979, when I chaired the Ways and Means Committee, I agreed to meet with Hikaru Kerns, a hapa-haole in his mid-30s who had been designated by Doi to serve as the commission's director. Born in Japan and raised in Tacoma, Washington, Kerns was the son of an American army captain and a Japanese mother. He had been a 1969 Rhodes Scholar. He was very bright, articulate and idealistic about the commission's work.

With the Crime Commission under attack and facing probable abolishment, a desperate Kerns contacted my office and asked if he could meet with me. I agreed, and we met.

"Sen. Cayetano, the Crime Commission is in a terrible position," he said. "Our critics attack us for being ineffectual and not doing anything. The problem is the commission's rules of confidentiality make it a crime for me or any other staff member to tell legislators what we are doing.

"I'm probably breaking the law with the information I want to show you, so if you don't want to see it, I understand perfectly," he continued.

"Why are you coming to me?" I asked.

"There are only two senators I feel comfortable with in discussing the commission's work, and you're one of them," he said.

"Who is the other?" I asked.

"Dennis O'Connor, but he's not in a position to help. In your position, you can help."

"What about Sen. Kawasaki? He is the Commission's strongest supporter in the entire Legislature," I asked.

"Yes, but I think Lt. Gov. Doi was privately briefing him all along. He knows what the commission is doing. He's been very helpful."

"Are you going to speak with anyone in the House?" I asked.

"Well, I have to be careful because Rep. Holt is leading the charge to abolish the commission. But I am thinking about speaking to Rep. Dennis Yamada [the Judiciary chairman from Kaua'i]; he's a lawyer, and I believe he is open minded and honest."

"Yeah, Dennis is a straight shooter. Okay, let's see what you got for me," I said.

"We call this project 'Operation Cassius,'" he said somberly. "This is an example of our work. It's an investigation of the Honolulu City Council."

As Kerns unveiled a chart, I began to feel uneasy. I was personally acquainted with all of the Honolulu City councilmen, either through Democratic Party activities or because of working with them on City projects for which they sought State funding.

"We received information that two councilmen might be taking bribes," he said. "We think one councilman took a bribe disguised as a real estate transaction; in the case of the other, we think one of his staff is hitting on people who are seeking permits and variances for home construction or real estate development. We are investigating whether the councilman himself was directly involved.

"This chart shows two real estate sales between Mr. Horibe [not his real name], who as you know is a big real estate developer, and Councilman Kealoha [not his real name]," he explained, pointing to the chart.

"Here you see the councilman buying a new home from the developer. The developer took the councilman's old home as a down payment. At first glance, there is nothing wrong with the transactions, until you compare the sales price paid by the developer for the councilman's old home to comparable prices for homes in the area. We did a comparison of the sales prices for similar houses and lots in the area. And, as you can see, the sales price for the councilman's old home was $50,000 higher than the highest price for a similar home in the area. And our research revealed that the developer later sold the councilman's old home at market price, taking a loss of more than $50,000.

"A year later, they went through the same kind of transaction. This time the councilman bought a home in one of the developer's high-end subdivisions. Here [pointing to the chart] you can see that the developer paid approximately $100,000 more for the councilman's home than comparable sales prices for similar homes in the area. Again, the developer sold the councilman's old home for market price, taking a big loss on the sale.

"So over a period of a little more than two years, the councilman bought two new homes from the developer, and each time the developer credited the councilman inflated prices for his old homes."

"So what's the quid pro quo?" I asked. "Without proof of a quid pro quo there is no case to be made for a charge of bribery. Arguably, the inflated prices for the old homes paid by the developer are discounts that may raise ethical questions, but they are not illegal."

"Yes, you're right, Senator," Kerns replied. "But as you know, this developer needs a lot from the City—things like permits, variances, etc. And through his companies, he's raised a lot of campaign money for not only this councilman but others as well. So the stakes for the developer are very high. We suspect there is strong motivation for the developer to buy votes and influence for his projects. And so we have an ongoing investigation to determine whether there is any evidence of quid pro quo. We can't do it if the Legislature cuts our staff or, of course, if the commission is abolished."

"Did the councilman report these transactions in his financial disclosure forms?" I asked.

"Yes, but unless someone who knows what he is doing connects the dots, it will be very difficult for anyone to figure out what really happened just from the financial disclosure forms," Kerns replied.

The commission had its detractors. Some law enforcement officials resented the commission's intrusion into matters under their jurisdiction. And Doi might have stepped on some politically powerful toes when in a public speech he seemed to confirm that the commission had uncovered proof of the existence of a "Godfather" and the presence of organized crime in political circles in Hawai'i.

Technically, Kerns might have violated the law in disclosing the information to me, but pragmatically he had little choice if the commission was to survive. I had good feelings about Kerns. I believed he was truthful, a dedicated public servant. Gov. Ariyoshi, Kerns told me, was not supportive of more funding for the commission. As chairman of the Ways and Means Committee, I was in a good position to get funding for the commission to continue its work. Moreover, Senate Vice President Duke Kawasaki, a close friend and ally of Doi's, was a strong supporter of the commission.

In 1980, however, Doi decided to retire from politics to take a federal judgeship in the Marianas. Kerns, seeing the handwriting on the wall, stayed awhile to help the transition but left the commission later that year. In 1981, I was no longer chairman of Ways and Means, and by 1983 Kawasaki and I were out of favor with Wong. We were dissidents and had been stripped of our committee chairmanships.

Meanwhile, the commission found itself immersed in controversy. Gov. Ariyoshi had appointed Neil Okabayashi—one of his strong political supporters—as its chairman. The commission members saw Okayabashi's appointment as a potential conflict in that its task was to investigate possible corruption in State government. In a public hearing well covered by the news media, the commission unanimously voted to remove Okabayashi as chairman. Obviously, the commission's action did not please Ariyoshi, who had not been a supporter of the commission but had put up with it for as long as Doi was there. But with Doi gone and me and Kawasaki stripped of our political power, Holt finally succeeded in abolishing the commission. In 1984, the Crime Commission was formally abolished. "Operation Cassius" was never consummated.

(After Wong left the Senate to become a Bishop Estate trustee in 1993, Holt emerged as one of the most powerful members of the State Senate. By 1998, however, he had developed a well-publicized history of drug abuse problems and spouse abuse. That year, Holt was indicted by the federal government for six counts of mail fraud relating to his illegal use of campaign contributions for his personal use. In a plea bargain, Holt agreed to plead guilty to one count and was sentenced to serve a year in federal prison. His once-promising political career was over.)

"They Don't Shoot Losers"

In late March 1983, the six of us (Abercrombie, Carpenter, Toguchi, Sallings, Kawasaki and I) met and concluded that Yamasaki should be replaced as chairman of Ways and Means. The floor debates had revealed that the Maui senator was more an ally of the governor and the establishment than the reformers in the Senate. With the four Republicans, we had only 10 votes. We needed 13. Once we had them, we decided, we would confront Wong and demand that Yamasaki be replaced or that strong measures be taken to assure that the prior concurrence rule was honored.

I was skeptical because I knew Yamasaki would not do anything without Wong's approval. But I also knew that Kawasaki would not join a move to oust Wong. They had been close and longtime friends, and Kawasaki truly believed that Wong would come to his senses and "work things out."

It was nearly midnight when we decided to offer the chairmanship of Ways and Means to Norman Mizuguchi, who was the most experienced and best qualified among the other Democrats. If he accepted, we knew he would bring Holt and Gerald Machida with him. We were well aware, of course, that if Mizuguchi declined, it would be the end of our efforts to replace Yamasaki. As it transpired, Mizuguchi not only declined, but, as we learned later, he immediately telephoned Wong to give him the news. Mizuguchi, Holt and Machida, who before our phone call were on the "outs" with Wong, were now "in."

At this point, it didn't matter, because none of us would put up with the way business was now being conducted in the Senate any longer. "I didn't run for the Senate to be taken care of," Abercrombie said.

Yamasaki was a good man and a dedicated public servant; he was unselfish and would never do anything for personal gain. But he was also a good soldier, loyal to a fault. What happened to our subject-matter committee programs in Ways and Means would not have been done without Wong's approval. Wong ran Ways and Means, not Yamasaki.

I knew Wong would react strongly, just as he had when he led the Senate Coalition in rejecting five of Ariyoshi's nominees to various boards and commissions in 1982, ostensibly to uphold the Senate's power of advice and consent.

It wouldn't matter that Abercrombie, Carpenter, Kawasaki and I were his strongest supporters; Wong would have to punish us, if for no other reason than to save face and set an example for anyone else who wanted to challenge his style of leadership.

We learned about our fate the next day on the evening television news: The Senate would be reorganized; we would be stripped of our committee chairmanships and Kawasaki of his vice presidency.

"Hmmm, I think the man overreacted," Carpenter joked.

"Dickie wouldn't be president without us," Abercrombie said, a point we would hear repeatedly. "While I was working 20 hours a day trying to do my committee work, all the time Dickie was reorganizing the Senate around us."

"Yeah, I wonder what he would have done if Ushijima, O'Connor and those guys were still around," I said cryptically.

Kawasaki, who had thought Wong would try to work things out, was only partly right.

Wong wanted to make examples of Abercrombie, Sallings and me. Sallings and I had moved to amend the State Budget Bill—a "no-no" move that would usually have been made only by Republicans. Abercrombie had led the floor debate on all five amendments, revealing that neither Yamasaki nor any member of Ways and Means could offer any justification for rejecting the subject-matter committee proposals.

Carpenter and Toguchi had not participated in the debate. Kawasaki had, but, because of their long and close friendship, Wong overlooked it. Wong met with Kawasaki and Carpenter individually. He offered to leave them alone if they did not support Abercrombie, Sallings and me.

The big problem for Wong was that Carpenter, Kawasaki and Toguchi believed we were right and that the fault lay with Yamasaki and the Ways and Means Committee—and Wong himself. Carpenter and Kawasaki declined Wong's offer and told him they would stand firmly with us, and if that meant they would lose their current positions, so be it.

Wong sent Yen Lew, his committee clerk, with a message for Toguchi: If Toguchi continued to support us, he could forget about the trip to China Wong had promised him, and he would be stripped of his chairmanship of the Senate Agricultural Committee. Toguchi, whose committee proposals had not been revised by Yamasaki, was incensed that Wong thought he could be bought off by the China trip.

"You tell Dickie that Ben, Neil and Lehua are right—and he can take the Ag Committee and that trip to China and shove it up his ass!" he said angrily to Yen Lew.

Toguchi had the most to lose. He had just been elected to the Senate in 1982, and the Agricultural Committee was important for his district. Moreover, he had no problems with the State Budget Bill. But he had been a dissident in the House, struggling against the leadership for the reforms that had been adopted by the New Senate. He knew if the rule of prior concurrence could be ignored for three committee chairmen with impunity it could happen to his committee or others as well.

April 6, 1983, was a Wednesday, the 48th day of the 1983 legislative session. The Senate gallery was packed with staff members, news media and other people. Nearly every member of the House came over to watch Wong take us down.

"The nice thing about American democracy is that the winners are not allowed to shoot the losers," I joked, as we waited, along with the four Republicans, for Wong and his band of 14 Democrats to come out of the Senate caucus room.

Once the session began, all six of us spoke, pledging our cooperation to the senators who were designated to take over our committees and explaining for the record—Wong had already heard it many times—our reasons for our actions. I was touched by the three senators, Kawasaki, Toguchi and Carpenter, who stood with us on principle. As the Senate Record recounted:

Senator Kawasaki then rose on a point of personal privilege and stated:
Mr. President, upon learning that three of our more diligent,

capable, intelligent committee chairman, generally known to do their homework, known to burn the midnight oil here, and known to come out with intelligent solutions of their recognition of the State's problems ... when I learned that these three people were to be removed from their positions, as a result of their disagreement with the budget process and belief that the Senate rules are to be honored, Senators Carpenter, Toguchi and I declared our support of the three committee chairmen....

I wish to express to you, Mr. President, personally, my appreciation of your support ..., urging me to remain in my position....

However, I must say that I cannot in good conscience assume any other posture than to fully, unequivocally support the posture taken by Senator Abercrombie, Senator Cayetano and Senator Fernandes Salling....

The decision I've made to support these people ... is my own. One that I've made because this is the only right thing to do, and if I have to vacate my position as vice president of this Senate, so be it.

Dante Carpenter laid out the specifics of our complaints:

Senator Carpenter then rose on a point of personal privilege and stated:

Let's look at the chronology of events. Every subject-matter committee, Mr. President, worked diligently to get their budgets within the Senate's initial guidelines that was the current year's budget plus seven percent. This is presumably based on anticipated revenues that the State could reasonably collect.

It wasn't easy, but priorities were indeed established and funding assigned within those limits. The results were basically no program expansion and, in short, no innovation ... holding the line at current spending and even cutting, where necessary.

Then we received an expanded budget, the budget bill from the House requiring unaffordable expenditures; and then we barely [passed] a tax bill to the House to show that the Legislature would have to pass a tax increase to fund it; and now we've positioned the "Senate version" of that House bill with everything in it on the condition that the tax increase is passed.

Mr. President, the vote yesterday to get the bill out to the House is not really the Senate position, it's the Dickie Wong position for whatever reason. We've not been informed of that whatever reason.

In short, Mr. President, both the Senate and House have essentially overloaded the budget and we're both acting somewhat less than responsible unless we take one of two tasks. One, either we stand by the original cuts which are indeed within the State's means or we strongly support the tax increase to pay for everything, but not both.

We either take a responsible position … or we abrogate our responsibilities and leave the decision to the executive, once again.

Charlie Toguchi took the floor and took Chip Uwaine to task, noting that Uwaine was Wong's strongest supporter for ousting us, and reminding Uwaine that as dissidents in the House both he and Uwaine had challenged the House leadership on the very same principles. Abercrombie, Toguchi and I had helped Uwaine get elected to the Senate. We raised money and worked hard for him because we thought he was independent and for legislative reform. For Uwaine to disagree with us was one thing, but he was the one who was most vociferous in urging Wong to oust us. Toguchi made clear he stood with us on principle:

I had no "beef" about the budget. I think we did a decent job with the agriculture budget … [but] I think, Mr. President, you know very well what I'm talking about, and yesterday, you also indicated to me, "Charlie, I understand where you are coming from."

Mr. President … I will continue to do my best here to serve … the people of this state. At this point, I don't really care what happens later. You can take the chairmanship, you can take the titles, you can take everything, and I will not feel sad or depressed. But, Mr. President, if the Senate continues to operate the way it has operated for the past three months that I have been here, and according to others, the past five years, then to me, it will be a sad day for all of us, everybody who is looking to us for leadership.

Wong responded:

I respect the rights of others and I really and truly appreciate the comments made today; however, I must respond to a real situation. The anticipated action to be taken later is in response to an attempted takeover of the Ways and Means Committee by six very disgruntled Senators. I take these actions with some regret because I've counted the six among my strongest and most ardent supporters in the Senate. The six also included longtime personal friends of mine and I'm sorry to see us on opposing sides.

Even though we are now adversaries, I tell my longtime friends that I hope we can remain friends.

I was elected Senate president on the basis of an organization that was worked out and agreed by 20 Democrats. I have an obligation to protect the integrity of that plan which we designed, to distribute power and responsibility broadly among all Senators. I cannot and I will not tolerate any attempt by any Senator or group of senators to grab power for themselves, or to dump other senators from their positions. This is contrary to my whole legislative philosophy of how things can be done around this place.

I want to make it very clear that these actions are strictly in response to the takeover attempt by six Democrats. It has nothing to do with their disagreement on the budget or their attempts to filibuster last week. I have no problems with debate and disagreement on the issues. That is, to me, a very legitimate component of the legislative process.

Throughout my legislative career, I have always advocated fair, open, and full discussion and participation by senators and legislators.

The basic issue, really, in this whole controversy has been the organizational integrity of the Senate. That's it, pure and simple.

Wong's words about debate and "distributing power and responsibility broadly" did not match his actions. He was willing to cut deals with Carpenter, Kawasaki and Toguchi if they would not support Abercrombie, Sallings and me—despite the fact that the three had been participants in the move to oust Yamasaki. And the rule of prior concurrence, which had been the linchpin of Wong's campaign against Ushijima for a "New Senate," was not worth the paper it was written on. Our subsequent requests for the budget worksheets were never granted. Kawasaki, who was the most optimistic in our group that Wong would "work things out," once waited for hours before he was finally told by Ways and Means staff that the worksheets would not be available.

The importance of the worksheets is that they provide much more detailed information as to why certain appropriations were made part of the State Budget. There is no better source for exposing political game playing via the budget. I learned this all too well when I was chairman of Ways and Means.

We had made such a fuss over the worksheets that if Wong had just provided them to us, there would have been little left for us to argue about. By refusing, however, he only heightened our suspicions that there were things in them that he did not want us to know about. (As I will describe later, Wong's intransigent attitude about sharing information with others would ultimately cost him his job as a Bishop Estate trustee.)

In the political arena, a dissident's most effective tool is public disclosure. Thus, we filed a lawsuit seeking a court order to force the release of the worksheets.

We knew we would lose, because historically our Judiciary has avoided ruling on disputes on internal political matters. But our purpose was to focus public attention on the dispute. On every one of the remaining 15 days of the legislative session, we took to the Senate floor to question publicly why certain bills were being passed. Unlike the Ushijima dissidents, we made sure we did our homework on each bill. Too often, chairmen who were accustomed to having their bills passed without questions were caught unprepared. The news media had a field day.

Finally, on the 60th day, Wong, who had said he had "no problems with debate and disagreement on the issues," resorted to a parliamentary maneuver to limit debate on the State Budget Bill. The maneuver had never been used in the history of the State Senate.

Toguchi had the floor when the Senate recessed during the day session. At the opening of the evening session, Steve Cobb made a motion for a special order to limit debate on the budget bill. Uwaine seconded the motion. Cobb's motion set off an intense floor fight, as described in the Senate Journal:

> Senator Abercrombie then objected: "Mr. President, I...."
>
> The President then interjected: "This vote requires a two-third majority. Mr. Clerk, call the roll...."
>
> ... Senator Cayetano then rose and queried: "Mr. President, are you going to recognize the Senators?"
>
> The President replied: "No, I will not...."
>
> Senator Abercrombie then interjected: "Yes, then are you prepared to hear discussion...?"
>
> Senator Cobb then asserted: "Mr. President, the motion is not debatable. It is a privileged motion requiring a two-thirds vote."

The motion was passed 19-6.

> At this time, Senator Carpenter rose and stated: "... under the representations that you made to us as our leader for the past five sessions, you've always invoked a very open kind of atmosphere, allowing full and free discussion?"
>
> The President replied in the affirmative and Senator then queried: "May I ask at this time, then, why you have taken this route?"
>
> The President replied in the affirmative and stated: "... I have come to the conclusion, from the media accounts, it is not one of the ways to conduct the people's business by filing suit against the Senate for the purpose of retrieving worksheets, which some people feel are valuable in their determination of the budget....
>
> "But, more importantly ... I have been hearing direct accounts

attributed to certain Senators in the dissident group, of their plans for a filibuster. And that, I will not condone...."

Senator Carpenter then replied: "I appreciate your response, Mr. President. I think that one of the reasons the court action ensued, certainly, was the fact that the coordination and communication which you so eloquently expounded from the podium essentially dried up. Mr. President, during the last 48 hours, you may recall a direct plea to you, as the president of this body, for the information [worksheets] that would make it more appropriate for us, as fellow senators, to make a fully informed decision as regards the outcome of the bills before this honorable body.

"Mr. President, you gave us no choice, you certainly gave me no choice, but to leave these chambers at this time, in disrespect for the chair."

Toguchi, who had the floor at the close of the day session, refused to give it up.

Senator Toguchi asserted: "Mr. President, I am speaking on a point of personal privilege!"

The President instructed the Clerk to call the Roll, and Senator Toguchi maintained: "Mr. President, I have the floor!"

Senator Toguchi then began to continue his remarks on the budget and the President interjected: "Will the Sergeant-at-Arms please remove Senator Toguchi."

Senator Abercrombie then queried: "What's the vote on, Mr. President?"

The President replied: "We are voting on the budget. Mr. Sergeant-at-Arms, would you please remove Senator Toguchi?"

Senator Abercrombie then remarked: "You would be awfully good in El Salvador. No, remove me too. It would be an honor...."

The President maintained: "I will not allow six individuals to dictate whether or not the Senate will adjourn this evening on time."

Sen. Abercrombie then asserted: "But you'll allow yourself to dictate to us, when you make up your secret budget and your secret agendas and you come in with all this cockamamie routine about [us] taking over and all the rest of it! So, don't go preaching about that stuff, Dickie. You want to remove us, you remove us! You got the guts, go ahead and do it!"

There was nothing left to be said. The six of us walked out. The State Budget

Bill and dozens of other bills were passed in our absence.

The 1983 legislative session was over.

There was no peace between us and the Wong faction during all of 1984. We continued to press for reforms and scrutinize bills and subject the various chairmen to rigorous questioning on the Senate floor. If there was one good thing about it, the chairmen who anticipated our questions began paying more attention to their work.

The 1984 Legislative Session was Dante Carpenter's last. He left the Senate to run for mayor of the Big Island. All five of us—Abercrombie, Kawasaki, Toguchi, Sallings and I—helped in Carpenter's successful campaign.

The 1984 election also marked the end of Uwaine's political career. In February of 1983, he and 22 others were indicted for voter fraud. We all believed that he had masterminded the scheme, but we never made it a public issue. As disappointed as we were in him, we respected his right to a fair hearing of the criminal charges against him. Besides, I felt, as the saying goes, "When a train wreck is about to happen, just get out of the way."

It didn't take long for Uwaine to be convicted in the forum of public opinion; in 1984, the voters showed their displeasure with him by voting him out of office. He was convicted in 1986 after one of his fellow conspirators testified against him. Sadly, Uwaine's wife was convicted in 1985. I saw her as a quiet, sweet woman who did whatever he told her. She was the stereotypical AJA wife.

As a former criminal defense lawyer, I knew Uwaine could have struck a deal with the prosecutors to save his wife. Instead, he stood by silently, hoping, it seemed, that there was a chance he could escape the charges—while she was convicted and spent three months in jail.

As for Cobb, his political career would end in 1989 when he was caught and prosecuted for soliciting an undercover cop posing as a prostitute. The crime ended not only his political career but also, sadly, his marriage. Last I heard Cobb, a former U.S. Army officer, was teaching at a university in Russia.

By the end of the 1984 legislative session, I had decided to leave the Senate. Despite our blow-up in 1983, I was still fond of Dickie Wong. I felt, however, that he had lost some of the idealism that had made him a respected dissident leader in the House. I was disappointed for him. The years had taken their toll on him, and I got the feeling that finding financial security had taken a greater importance in his life. One evening I was sitting in Wong's office watching the television news when he looked up from a set of papers he was signing and lamented reflectively, "You know, Ben, I've been in this business now for 20 years and I don't have an economic pot to piss in." I understood fully—there weren't many job offers or economic opportunities for retired dissidents or independents who rocked the boat.

In 1985, we resolved our differences with Wong. Wong reinstated his old friend, Duke Kawasaki, to Senate vice president. I became chairman of the Senate

Transportation Committee, Abercrombie of the Human Services Committee and Toguchi of the Committee on Education. Sallings did not get a committee chairmanship, but she was assigned to sit as a member of the Ways and Means Committee.

I was told that in 1983 when Kawasaki refused Wong's offer to keep him on as vice president if he would not support us, Wong got emotional and wept. And while Kawasaki lost his title, Wong let him keep the vice president's big office (the rest of us were moved into smaller offices). I think that if nothing else many of the senators felt good that he was vice president again.

A Long-Overdue Tax

Nothing demonstrated more clearly the economic and political power of Hawai'i's tourist industry than the long struggle over the hotel room tax. Since statehood, tourism had replaced agriculture—sugar and pineapple—as the major driver of Hawai'i's economy. Between 1963, when I left Hawai'i for Los Angeles, and the 1982 legislative session, 10 new hotels opened in Hawai'i while Dole's Moloka'i pineapple plantation and the Big Island's North Kohala sugar plantation were closed.

Tourism had blossomed into the proverbial Golden Goose. The new hotels provided thousands of jobs; inspired new tourist-related businesses; enhanced high-end real estate values, which drove up the tax-assessed values of every home in the state; and fueled the construction industry. In 1982, tourism accounted for nearly 20 percent of the state's gross product.

In my first year in the House, I asked Speaker Jimmy Wakatsuki why he did not propose a hotel room tax. "The time is not right," he replied. What Wakatsuki, who personally supported the tax, meant was that the governor was opposed to and would more than likely veto it. Indeed, in several of his State addresses, Ariyoshi had proudly touted not raising taxes as one of his accomplishments.

During the 1974 governor's election, Tom Gill made a persuasive case for a hotel room tax. Gill had done his homework: Hawai'i hotel prices, he noted, were 15 percent below the national average, and the industry was raking in the highest profits in the nation—an average of 21 percent on each dollar. A hotel room tax could bring in revenues of up to $60 million a year. I was convinced more than ever that the tax was justified.

There was a downside to the growth of tourism. It created a lot of jobs, but most were low paying. And there was an ethnic divide in terms of who got the better jobs. The more numerous lower-paying jobs usually went to local residents, whereas top executive and middle management positions were almost exclusively taken by Mainland haoles or Japanese from Japan.

Moreover, the millions of tourists who visited Hawai'i during the early '80s

(6 million by 1989) took a toll on the state's infrastructure (highways, parks, water and sewage systems), its natural resources and its environment. The beaches fronting or adjacent to hotels were usually the finest in the state, but the sheer numbers of tourists enjoying them often caused residents to stay away, resulting in de facto segregation between the two groups.

Once during the late '70s I took Lorraine and our three kids for a one-day stay at the Royal Hawaiian Hotel. We had never stayed at the Royal before and decided to take advantage of a one-day discounted room rate offered to kamaʻāina.

The next morning, as we sat on the beach watching our kids frolic in the sand and warm water, I noticed the place was packed with tourists from Japan and the Mainland, as far as I could see. Besides the beach boys, we seemed to be the only local residents there.

These visitors, I thought, *will use and enjoy the world-famous Waikīkī Beach more in a week than I will in my adult lifetime.* Yet they paid only the general excise tax on purchases while they were here, whereas local residents paid general excise as well as income and real-property taxes year round.

In my eyes, a premium—a hotel room tax levied on visitors—was appropriate and would help ease the residents' tax burden by exporting a substantial percentage (25 to 30 percent) of the burden to non-residents.

Listening to industry leaders tout the benefits of tourism, I sensed a bit of paternalism in their attitudes. "Look at all of the jobs and wealth tourism has created for Hawaiʻi; why all the fuss over a hotel room tax?" they seemed to be saying. Sadly, there were some politicians who agreed and gave virtually unconditional support to the industry. I found this frustrating—a reflection, from my point of view, of the so-called plantation mentality, the sense of inferiority which, as John Burns once stated, afflicted too many local people.

I appreciated tourism but never felt grateful for it. The difference may be slight, but there is a difference. The corporations that owned the hotels invested in Hawaiʻi for one reason only: It was profitable.

And the State had been a good partner, not a mere beneficiary. Compared to other tourist destinations, the State had taken good care of Hawaiʻi's superb natural resources; our environment remained beautiful and clean; our air was unpolluted; our drinking water rivaled the purest in the world. The State's infrastructure—its highways, airports and harbors—was in as good or better condition than that of its competition. The State provided millions of dollars to the Hawaiʻi Visitors Bureau every year to promote tourism, a subsidy that was not provided to any other business except the sugar industry. Hawaiʻi consistently ranked in the top 10 most-desired tourist destinations in the world, and the aloha spirit of our people persuaded nearly half of the visitors to return.

During this period of high profits, the tourism industry fought the hotel room tax tooth and nail. Tourism, it repeatedly argued, provided thousands of jobs, enhanced real estate values and made up approximately 20 percent of the State gross product; a hotel room tax would hurt Hawai'i's ability to compete with other tourist destinations.

At every public hearing, tourism industry representatives repeated their longstanding arguments that a hotel room tax would make Hawai'i less competitive, reducing the number of visitors and resulting in a loss of hotel jobs.

Legislators were presented with petitions signed by hundreds of hotel workers from nonunion hotels opposing the proposed tax. Dozens of hotel workers were given time off to testify against the tax. The hotels' drumbeat public relations spin had taken its toll. Many hotel workers genuinely believed their jobs were at stake.

Industry leaders were well-traveled, experienced businesspeople who knew more about world tourism than the average layperson. They were well aware that Hawai'i was the only state in the nation (perhaps the only tourist destination in the world) that did not have a tourist tax of some kind. They could not produce any evidence or studies to prove that a tourist tax was a deterrent of any kind, anywhere, and yet, that's what they led their less-knowledgeable, less-experienced workers to believe.

My views on the hotel room tax took a few years to develop fully. Before the advent of the Internet, Hawai'i's location as the most isolated inhabited place in the world made it more difficult and time consuming to research issues.

Often, researchers looked to the University of Hawai'i, the Department of Planning and Economic Development (DPED) and/or the HVB for information. When it came to matters of tourism, politicians who were not well traveled were at a disadvantage, having to rely on information provided in large part by the industry itself.

I had serious doubts about the industry's warnings of the negative impact of a hotel room tax, and I openly advocated for its passage; nevertheless, I harbored a scintilla of uncertainty about my position. I wanted firsthand information, some final assurance that the tax would not endanger the jobs of hotel workers.

In 1980, any doubts I had about the justification for a tourist tax were resolved when I was invited to participate in Pan American Airways' Tourism Mission. Pan American's purpose was to give Hawai'i politicians a firsthand look at major tourist destinations in France, Italy, Monaco, Spain and London over a 22-day period. For this not-so-well-traveled State senator, it was the dream trip of a lifetime.

Fifteen public officials (five senators—Ralph Ajifu, Dante Carpenter, Dennis O'Connor, Mary George and me; five State representatives; one County Council member from each of the four counties; and State DPED Director Hideto Kono), along with *Honolulu Advertiser* senior editor George Chaplin and five business executives, made the trip. Our first stop was Rome.

"Why all the soldiers with the submachine guns?" I asked our guide.

"To guard against the Red Brigade," he replied.

"The Red Brigade?"

"Yes, it's a Marxist terrorist group which wants to overthrow the Italian government by violence. They've already killed several politicians and bombed some government buildings. You'll see signs of them everywhere in the city."

It was hard not to notice them. As we drove to our hotel, the widespread Red Brigade graffiti and the pollution surprised me. This was not the Rome I saw in travel pictures. The graffiti was everywhere. Sadly, few of the famous centuries-old Roman statues and busts that adorned the great city were spared.

To be sure, any 2,000-year-old city is bound to show signs of age, but this was Rome, one of the greatest cities in the history of the world, and the pollution detracted from its incredible architecture and glorious history.

A visit to the famous Spanish Steps the next day revealed one source of the problem. The site was packed with tourists. *Too many tourists and inadequate maintenance*, I thought. The Fontana di Trevi at the bottom of the Steps, which I had first heard about in the movie *Three Coins in a Fountain*, was filled with coins, including three of mine, but it also overflowed with discarded Coke cans, bottles and other debris. There were simply too many tourists. The great city was a victim of its own success.

We were later told by an American Embassy staff person that the Italian government was poor and was struggling to find the resources to properly maintain the city and deal with other problems such as the rapid growth of tourism and the terrorism of the Red Brigade.

At our hotel, I asked the doorman how long they had had a hotel room tax.

"Oh, ever since we have been in tourism—perhaps 2,000 years," he chuckled, apparently amused by my question.

A week later, in Nice, France, I noticed that there was no room tax shown on my hotel bill.

"You don't have a tourist tax?" I asked the hotel manager.

"Oh, yes, of course, we do," he replied.

"But I don't see it on my hotel bill," I said.

"Why should we tell you?" he said, smiling mischievously. "Our guests are concerned only with the overall cost of the room; no one ever asks about the tax. Does the tax make a difference to you?"

"No, it doesn't," I replied, trying to hide my surprise at discovering that the practice of listing the tax on a hotel bill was apparently uniquely American.

There were other lessons to be learned. Overdevelopment and pollution, for example, were major problems with which the governments of every tourist destination we visited were struggling.

On the island of Capri, real estate development had run wild, finally prompting the government to impose a moratorium on building. Capri's mayor told us that living costs on the island had risen so high that many workers were forced to live in Naples and take the 40-minute ferry to go to work on Capri. The government's reaction (it did not appear to have a plan), he told us, was to impose a moratorium so strict one could not even get a permit to build a swimming pool.

In Spain, the expansion of commercial jet travel in the 1960s led to a tourist boom in places like Malaga and Majorca. One consequence in the places we visited was there was a plethora of discotheques and bars bearing American names and a sprinkling of shops selling pornographic products. Once a group of us were walking through the city when we passed a porn store, and I noticed that the clerk was one of the picadors we had seen at a bullfight the day before. *A bit of a culture clash in Catholic Spain,* I thought; *one day the guy is sticking bulls, the next he is selling dildos.*

In Cannes, I noticed many women, including beautiful, rich jet-setters, sunbathing topless on the beach (mostly on huge, smooth black boulders; there was little sand), but no one was in the ocean.

"Why isn't anyone swimming?" I asked our host.

"Because the water is polluted," he answered, matter-of-factly.

"But it looks clear, almost like our beach at Waikīkī."

"Yes, but it became polluted years ago and so no one swims anymore."

In Sorrento, Italy, I found out what the word "Hawai'i" meant to people. Browsing through a shop one day, I saw some tropical plants (anthuriums, I was told) for sale. The clerk, noticing our interest, said, "The good ones are on the other side [of the display counter]." The "good ones" were advertised as being from Hawai'i. Whether they were or not, I had no way of knowing; what was significant was that, wherever we went, we discovered to our delight that the word "Hawai'i" had a special meaning to people.

The tourism industry mounted a campaign that killed the hotel room tax in 1982, as it had done for nearly two decades. I was disappointed but not surprised. Wakatsuki was right: Given Ariyoshi's opposition to the tax, the time was not right. The governor, we were told in caucus, would support the tax only if the industry was ready for it; that comment created quite a stir—provoking some guffaws—as no one in the caucus believed that the industry would ever be ready. Meanwhile, industry lobbyists continued their efforts to get more State funding for the Hawai'i Visitors Bureau, the tourism industry's marketing agency.

Under Gov. Burns, the HVB received 50 percent of its funding from the State, with HVB members contributing the other 50 percent. By 1982, however, the State's subsidy had increased to about 70 percent of HVB's funding.

Industry leaders, however, were never satisfied. In 1985, they proposed a bill to increase the general excise tax, with the proceeds going to tourism promotion. It was a classic case of overreaching. More "corporate welfare." I wasn't the only legislator who felt this way. The proposal was rejected.

In 1986, the industry leaders, after failing repeatedly for years to persuade the Legislature to appropriate State funds to build a convention center, proposed a 2-percent hotel room tax, with the proceeds to be earmarked for marketing and for financing a new convention center. The House and Senate disagreed over the 2-percent bill, and it was sent to the conference committee. By proposing the tax, the industry had demonstrated it was "ready" for it, if the proceeds were used for its benefit. The time for a hotel room tax had come.

The bill that emerged from the conference committee was not what the industry wanted. Instead of a 2-percent room tax, the bill was amended to establish a 5-percent transient accommodations tax (TAT), which covered all accommodations, not just hotel rooms. To the industry's chagrin, the TAT was not earmarked for a new convention center, as there was no agreement that one should even be built. Instead, the TAT proceeds would go into the general fund.

Industry pleas that anything higher than 2 percent would hurt their competitiveness rang hollow, as it was pointed out that the airlines had just increased their fares by 5 percent, an indication that they were reacting to make greater profits because of the increased demand for travel to Hawai'i. Moreover, as Duke Kawasaki pointed out, the industry was unable to explain satisfactorily why a 5-percent TAT would hurt its competitiveness when it raised room rates as much as 30 percent during the peak season.

The conference bill passed by a 21-4 vote, but not before some senators expressed the frustrations they had harbored during the many years they had waited for the long-overdue tax. No senator knew more about how much the delay cost Hawai'i taxpayers than Mamoru Yamasaki, the chairman of the Ways and Means Committee. Recalling the defeat of the hotel room tax in 1973, the normally passive and soft-spoken Yamasaki stood on the Senate floor and scolded the industry:

"There were dozens and dozens of telegrams that came from the Mainland to defeat the room tax.... And at the time, I told the gentleman who represented the hotel industry, Mr. Don Bremner, and also another gentleman who is now working for the tourist industry in Japan, that sooner or later the hotel industry must face a room tax of some kind.

"I believe it is a fair bill, a compromise ... to let the people of the state of Hawai'i know that the visitors ... will also share the burden of improving Hawai'i to make Hawai'i a better Hawai'i that we all can enjoy ... the residents as well as the visitors that come to the state of Hawai'i."

I remained silent. Yamasaki had said everything that needed to be said. Wong stood at the president's podium with a slight grin and a *better-late-than-never* look on his face.

It remained for Abercrombie to break the tension with a light but revealing touch to the evening:

"I recall my first year [1975] in the House when the tax was defeated ... and I said to Mr. Bremner that ... the night it [the tax] passes you folks will be in the gallery and the very next day ... after all the hue and cry about its passage, you will be prepared with a list of projects for funding out of that hotel room tax. I remember clearly the words Mr. Bremner said to me at that time; he said, 'Oh, you've got it all right except one thing.' I asked, 'What's that?' He said, 'We'll have the projects ready the same night.'"

Abercrombie happily concluded his floor speech with a much-deserved accolade to Wong, who for more than a decade had doggedly championed the hotel tax: "I can just see, Mr. President, you can't wait for that vote; you've waited so long and we're all so happy for you."

But the fight was not quite over. If Ariyoshi vetoed the bill, we knew the House would not join the Senate in overriding the veto. Like most of us, Speaker Henry Peters supported the tax, but he would not allow the House to support an override.

On June 13, 1986, Ariyoshi, in his final year as governor, signed the Transient Accommodations Tax into law. It had taken nearly 22 years after I was first elected in 1974 for the Legislature to pass a tax that had long been taken for granted in virtually every other tourist destination in the world.

The difficulty in passing the tax demonstrated the political power of Hawai'i's tourist industry. One could only speculate how much in untold hundreds of millions of dollars had been lost to the State over the years, dollars that could have been used to fund social programs for the poor and needy, for public education and other worthwhile services.

Farewell to the Senate

On the last day of the 1986 legislative session, there was a farewell ceremony of sorts for Abercrombie and me. Duke, Toguchi and several senators made humorous speeches bidding us farewell.

"Windmills '0'-Abercrombie '10'" was Buddy Soares' opening line in the floor speech he gave about Abercrombie and me on our last day in the Senate. I laughed aloud when I heard it, but it was an apt description of the long-haired, bearded University professor who seemed to fight every battle, big or small, that offended his sense of justice or fairness.

Wong spoke last. His speech about Neil and me was sprinkled with humor and evoked laughter from the senators. At one point he tossed us two huge cardboard boxes labeled "Tylenol Tablets"—souvenirs of our many encounters during the past eight years.

I enjoyed the humor. Later I reflected on my years in the Legislature. The high points and the lows, the accomplishments measured against the defeats—and the friendships and alliances.

The two years I spent as a Senate dissident fighting Wong left me emotionally drained. Although a settlement was reached, I knew nothing had really changed. The New Senate we had established in 1980 was once again the Old Senate. Dickie Wong had the votes to do whatever he wanted.

Concentrate on your law practice, make some money, spend more time with your family, I thought. But shortly after the legislative session ended, as the 1986 elections drew closer, I began having second thoughts. There were too many important things happening in State government, too many unresolved problems for me to walk away from politics completely. Like many politicians, I had a love-hate relationship with politics. I loved having the privilege and power to help make things better, but I hated the intransigence of the system—its resistance to change, the self-dealing and the powerful and pervasive influence of special-interest groups.

There were few alternatives that appealed to me. Congress, I thought, was better suited for others. National and world affairs always interested me, but the thought of serving as one of 435 members of the U.S. House did not. Moreover, Washington, D.C., was not the kind of city in which I wanted my kids to grow up.

Nor was I interested in City politics. I wanted to serve at the State level; public education, social services and economic development interested me more than parks, sewers and bus service.

In terms of its statutory powers, Hawai'i's lieutenant governor is among the weakest in the nation, responsible mainly for the management of the elections (this responsibility was repealed in 1996), whereas its governor, because of the high concentration of statutory powers in the office, is considered one of the strongest. Those who hold the lieutenant governorship often struggle to find ways to give the office more importance and credibility.

Critics call it a "do-nothing" job, and silly jokes about it abound. With a few exceptions, the position of lieutenant governor has long suffered from the widespread perception that it is a post that, to paraphrase comedian Rodney Dangerfield, "gets no respect."

In fact, not one of the seven lieutenant governors before me served more than a single term. Three—Republican Kealoha and Democrats Gill and King—ran unsuccessful races against the incumbent governors; two (Richardson and Doi) left to accept court appointments, one (Ariyoshi) served only three years before succeeding the terminally ill John Burns; and the last, John Waihee, ran for the open seat left by the retiring Ariyoshi.

The importance of the post, however, becomes apparent when a succession actually occurs. Then, theoretically, at least, the cause of democratic government is better served because the successor—the lieutenant governor—is elected statewide.

I had 12 years of valuable legislative experience that could be useful in public service. But there was more to it than that. I believed then, as I do today, that there is something noble about being chosen out of a population of more than a million of one's fellow citizens to serve the public's trust. It's a privilege, an experience that cannot be bought, although many a rich person has tried.

I had learned that the political system was not as I had been taught in high school. Decisions on too many important bills, for example, were increasingly made privately, long before the bills were debated at public hearings which in those instances had become pro forma affairs. The influence of special-interest lobbyists had grown immensely. The common citizen had been increasingly relegated to the role of bystander. I felt obligated to stay in politics.

Once, in an unscripted television political advertisement we used during my 1994 gubernatorial campaign, my former boss, Frank Padgett, described me as an idealist. I took it as a compliment. Not all politicians do. Most begin their careers with a sense of high idealism, hoping to influence events that affect people's lives, but, at some point, their idealism fades and at times it even becomes the object of scorn as they pride themselves in becoming "realists" and maneuver or connive to acquire power to achieve certain ends.

The danger is in the way power, once acquired, is used. The famous British historian Lord Acton's warning that "power corrupts, and absolute power corrupts absolutely" is likely to become a self-fulfilling prophecy unless checked by the politician's idealism—his continued belief that he was elected to serve the people's best interests first and above all else. Or to paraphrase Lincoln, nearly all men can stand adversity; if you really want to test a man, give him power.

I was not a pure idealist. Like many, I looked for pragmatic, realistic ways to deal with our state's problems, but I never subordinated my idealism to realism. There is, I believe, a touch of Don Quixote in all politicians and criminal defense lawyers—I was both, so perhaps I had a little more of it than most.

On the last day of the 1986 legislative session, my good friend Neil Abercrombie urged me not to retire. "We can't let those guys take over," he said. Ultimately, that's what it boiled down to for me. ❖

CHAPTER NINE

Behind the Scenes

Eileen Anderson

The 1986 Gubernatorial election would usher in a new governor for the first time since 1974. Three major contenders entered the Democratic primary: former Honolulu Mayor Eileen Anderson, U.S. Congressman Cec Heftel and Lt. Gov. John Waihee. A poll taken in early May 1986 showed Anderson with a slight lead over Heftel and a larger one over Waihee, notwithstanding her defeat by former Democrat Frank Fasi in the 1984 general election for mayor.

Anderson, who was had once been seen as the Democratic establishment's choice to succeed Ariyoshi, had fallen out of favor with the governor. Her upset win over Fasi in 1980 was mainly due to the strong support she received from Ariyoshi. Many believed Anderson was encouraged to run against Fasi to weaken him in his anticipated bid for governor against Ariyoshi in 1982. Indeed, Anderson's 1980 victory denied Fasi the political power of the mayorship, and Ariyoshi beat him handily in the 1982 general election.

Ariyoshi felt slighted, it was said, when Anderson later seemed to want to distance herself from him. "Not even a simple 'thank you' to the governor," one of his supporters told me. Whether or not it was true, the perception was widespread that she was indifferent not only to Ariyoshi but to others who had helped her in 1980.

I had been a strong Anderson supporter in 1980. She had testified many times before my Ways and Means Committee. She was articulate, highly professional and straightforward; like many legislators, I thought she was one of Ariyoshi's best Cabinet members.

When Anderson beat Fasi in 1980, I was thrilled. Ariyoshi had been governor for nearly two terms and was expected to serve an unprecedented third. I was among those who looked to Anderson to succeed Ariyoshi and provide new, fresh leadership.

When Anderson ran for reelection in 1984, I expected to be called upon to help her again. The call never came—at least not until it was too late. There were others who had helped her in 1980 and weren't called in 1984. Anderson and her people were caught up in the hubris that grew out of her earlier victory. They felt they didn't need anyone else.

When my good friend Carl Takamura, who was helping in the Anderson campaign, called to ask me to help less than two weeks before the election, I asked him why I had not been called sooner (a question, no doubt, asked by others who were contacted at the last minute).

"Well, months ago, when I suggested we call you to help out with the Filipino community," Takamura sighed, "Bob Awana said, 'No, why should we owe chits to anyone when we're in the driver's seat?'" (Awana, who was a key leader in the Anderson campaign, would later turn Republican and chair Linda Lingle's unsuccessful 1998 campaign for governor.)

"You know, Carl, I never asked Eileen for anything after the 1980 election; I just wanted her to win. But ever since she won, I've been hearing talk all over the place that Eileen has changed, that being mayor has gone to her head. In fact, I've hardly seen her over the past four years," I replied.

"Well, she's left the running of the campaign to Awana," he replied.

"So now that she's in trouble they want help? For crying out loud, there's less than two weeks left," I replied tersely.

"What can I say? I agree with you. But now I want to know if you're willing to help," Takamura replied.

"Tell Eileen that it's too late for me to do anything—and that I think she's going to win anyway."

That was a white lie. In fact, I was convinced she was going to lose, but I didn't want to hurt her feelings.

Anderson had underestimated Fasi, who was a skilled, innovative campaigner. He hit Anderson where she was vulnerable—with a powerful television ad that asked, "Name one thing that Eileen Anderson has done in the past four years?" while a huge clock ticked loudly in the background. It was one of the most effective political ads I had ever seen on television.

To make matters worse, Anderson could not respond effectively—because, in fact, she had done little except spend money for planning, a result of her methodical, bureaucratic approach to solving problems. Fasi ran the TV ad repeatedly, which not only had people talking about how good it was but also had them asking themselves just what, in fact, Anderson had done in her four years as mayor.

A month or so before the election, Anderson's once-comfortable lead began to shrink, and her campaign was in an irreversible downward spiral. She needed a miracle to turn it around, and I didn't think there was one to be found.

She lost badly. I could see the hurt in her eyes as she conceded the election to Fasi on television on election night. It was a sad thing to watch, but her pain was self-inflicted; there was little else to be said.

But when Anderson jumped into the governor's race two years later, I was glad for her. She sounded like her old self again. My old positive feelings about her becoming governor returned, and I made it known to my key supporters that

I favored her over Heftel and Waihee.

At the time, I was pondering whether to run for lieutenant governor. Anderson was ahead in the polls then, and like many of the pro-Anderson people working on my campaign, I thought we would make a great team: A haole woman-Filipino combination that could attract strong AJA support would be hard to beat in the general election. I was optimistic about my chances.

In discussing the matter with my campaign committee, one of the many "what if" questions that arose was the possibility of Anderson dropping out of the governor's race to run for lieutenant governor instead. "I heard some talk that some of the 'old boys' are trying to convince Eileen to drop out and run for LG instead, to clear the way for Waihee to take on Heftel," said Lloyd Nekoba, my campaign manager.

"Why should she do that? I heard she's leading right now," I replied.

"Without them, she can't raise money for the governor's race. I heard they are drying up her fundraising sources to pressure her to drop out and run for LG," Nekoba said. "And if it's between you and Eileen, they'd rather have her because a lot of those guys don't like you because of the shit you gave Ariyoshi in the past—and the coalition you guys formed with the Republicans. You should clear the air with Eileen before jumping into the LG race," he concluded.

He was right. Besides, I really did not feel that strongly about running for lieutenant governor; as a senator, in fact, I had introduced a bill to abolish the office. If Eileen was thinking about running for lieutenant governor, I would not run. I'd retire from politics.

I called her later that day. "Eileen, I'm thinking about running for lieutenant governor," I said.

"Oh, that's great, Ben; I think you'll do well," she replied.

"Thanks," I said, "but I won't run if you are thinking of dropping out of the governor's race to run for lieutenant governor. I'll support you instead."

"Oh, no, Ben, I'm going to run for governor. I'm already 59; the lieutenant governor's job is for a younger person [I was 46] like you," she replied.

With that assurance, we continued planning our campaign, and a few weeks later I announced that I would run for lieutenant governor and that my campaign headquarters would open on May 9.

A few days before the opening, Nekoba answered a phone call and said, "Ben, it's Eileen."

"Hi, Eileen," I said.

"Ben, I won't be able to make it to your opening."

"Oh, too bad, we'll miss you," I replied.

"Ben, I'm calling to give you the courtesy of knowing that I'm thinking of running for lieutenant governor," she said.

I was stunned. The rumors were true.

"Eileen, I asked you just a few weeks ago whether you were going to run for lieutenant governor and you told me, 'No, that it's a job for a younger person,' like me," I reminded her.

"Well, things change, Ben, but I'm only thinking about it at the moment," she said.

"Eileen, I told you I would not run for lieutenant governor if you were going to run for …"

"Oh, Ben, don't make it any harder," she interrupted. Her tone sounded as though she were lecturing a little kid.

"Okay, Eileen, I'm very disappointed. And let me tell you this: I'm going to end your damned political career!" I snapped and hung up.

"She's going to run," I said angrily to Nekoba. "She's already made up her mind. She didn't even have the courtesy to tell me the damned truth. Thinking about it? Bullshit! She caved in to those pricks who think they own this state!"

Nekoba, who had been watching me during my conversation, looked at me calmly and asked, "How're we going to do it?"

"Do what?" I asked.

"End her political career."

"I don't know," I said, and we both burst out laughing.

Later, Nekoba reminded me that the official filing deadline for my candidacy was in July (it was then May), so there was still time for me to drop out.

"Not like this, not after I announced I'd run," I said. "We have so many people committed throughout the state; no, I can't drop out now. We'll take her on."

On May 9, the day we opened my headquarters, there was a tsunami warning. This was no drill; the governor ordered the schools closed, State and City workers were dismissed and advised to take their kids home, and businesses closed as well. Soon, a traffic jam of monumental proportions, probably the worst in Oʻahu's history, made it virtually impossible to get anywhere by car. Scores of my supporters were stranded in traffic, many trying to get to their families. Only a handful made it to our opening. I wondered if this was an omen of things to come.

Anderson's announcement caused great concern among my supporters, many of whom had supported her in the 1980 campaign and would have supported her for governor, too. I was worried, as well, but I had to be careful not to show it.

It wasn't difficult to figure out why the Democratic establishment wanted Anderson out of the governor's primary. Many felt that Heftel was a Democrat by convenience and, unlike Eileen Anderson, just another Mainland haole who did not respect local people. Moreover, he was politically independent—he had no ties, no allegiance owed to the Democratic establishment or anyone else.

If Anderson stayed in, she and Waihee would split the AJA vote to the advantage of Heftel, whose base in the primary was mainly independent AJAs, Filipinos and haoles. Moreover, Heftel was a multimillionaire and didn't have to rely on the traditional Democratic donors to raise the big dollars he would spend on his campaign. He made a big point of this as an example of his independence.

Ariyoshi favored Waihee. As lieutenant governor, Waihee had been very helpful in bringing about a settlement in the United Airlines strike. And, unlike his predecessor, Jean King, Waihee had been loyal to Ariyoshi, whereas as mayor, Anderson had been indifferent. Moreover, the ambitious, risk-taking Waihee, who ran for lieutenant governor after serving only four years in the State House, was not about to serve another term as lieutenant governor, waiting another four, or more likely eight, years for another crack at the governorship.

From a purely political perspective, it made sense for the Democratic establishment to get Anderson to drop out. In this scenario everyone else—including me—was expendable.

"Lloyd, these are the same kind of guys who told me I couldn't win in Pearl City in 1974. These bastards think they know everything about politics," I said. "Screw them; tell our people what happened between Eileen and me, that'll fire them up."

A union poll taken a few weeks after Anderson's announcement showed she was leading me 55 percent to 30 percent among those likely to vote in the Democratic primary. I needed a few breaks to turn things around. Over the final two months before the primary elections, the breaks came.

Ten days before the September 20 primary, Vicky Bunye, one of four Republican candidates for lieutenant governor and Mayor Frank Fasi's director of the Office of Human Resources, charged that administrators of Japanese ancestry in the Department of Education (DOE) had made a "conscious effort" to discriminate against Filipinos and Caucasians in hiring.

Her words hit like a bombshell. It was the first time a candidate made race and ethnicity so openly an issue in the campaign. Bunye was no fool; she was well educated, having earned a bachelor's degree from the University of the Philippines and a master's degree from Georgetown University before joining the Peace Corps. She came to Hawai'i in the late '60s to teach Peace Corps trainees who were going to be deployed to the Philippines, later became a U.S. citizen and joined the Fasi administration.

She wasn't the first Filipino immigrant to make allegations of racism against the DOE. Moreover, Professor Michael Haas of the University of Hawai'i had written a book in which he used statistical analysis to argue that "institutional racism" existed in the DOE.

I was at a function when the news media confronted me for a comment about Bunye's charges. I was caught cold—it was the first time I heard about the issue. I was shocked. Racial discrimination by individuals in State government there surely was—I had experienced it myself—but it was a bit of a stretch to argue there was "institutional" racism in the DOE against any ethnic group.

I could understand Bunye's frustration. It is difficult, for example, to explain to a teacher who was educated at Ateneo University, which is considered the Harvard of the Philippines, and who speaks fluent English, why he or she is not qualified to teach in Hawai'i's public schools. I've had many complaints, not just from teachers from the Philippines but from those from Canada and even the Mainland about the DOE's seemingly restrictive hiring policies (a topic worthy of extended discussion in another book).

I knew Vicky Bunye personally. I liked and respected her, but she had crossed the line on this one. I was upset she had injected race into the election. If voters voted strictly along ethnic lines, I wouldn't have a chance of winning. Since 1974, my political campaigns had been structured to appeal to people of all races, a strategy that was not only consistent with my core political beliefs but was smart politics as well. My response to the reporters was short and terse:

"Fasi should fire her," I said, without further comment. I had just given the media their headlines for the evening news.

Later in the day, my political consultant, Jack Seigle, who had been anxiously trying to get in touch with me with a statement he had prepared, finally got hold of me.

"That was great, Ben. You got terrific coverage on radio today; for sure it will be the lead story on TV tonight and in the newspapers tomorrow. It'll go over well with the AJAs," he said happily.

"It was my gut instinct, Jack; I just said what I thought was right," I replied.

"Well, Ben, it was perfect—short, sweet, right on point. We couldn't have written anything better," Seigle replied.

Meanwhile, a political donnybrook ensued after the press managed to question Fasi. According to the *Honolulu Advertiser,* prior to Bunye's remarks, Fasi had met with his Filipino appointees, and told them to support Andy Anderson and Bunye or "look for work elsewhere." "You're patronage, you're not exempt," he said to them. When questioned by the press about it, Fasi replied that the U.S. president "and the governors of all 50 states" did the same, provoking a heated rebuttal from retiring Gov. George Ariyoshi, who argued that while he told his Cabinet of his "personal preferences," he never instructed them whom to support.

Anderson waited nearly three days before she said anything about Bunye. Her comments went virtually unnoticed—it was a case of saying too little, too late.

Prior to the Bunye incident, our poll showed Anderson leading me 55 percent to 27 percent among AJA voters and 55-35 overall. Seigle commissioned a quick poll to weigh the impact of my reaction to Bunye. In an incredible turnabout, the new poll showed me leading Anderson 50 percent to 35 percent among AJA voters. It was a pivotal turning point in our campaign.

"Ben," Seigle said, "we've squeezed about as many votes as we could from our soft TV spots about your life and from Bunye; there're still a lot of independent votes out there for grabs, and we need to go after them."

"What do you have in mind?" I asked.

"Phil [Wood] came up with some negative ads which I think are powerful and will work," Seigle said.

"The ads were designed to get the attention—and votes—of the people who don't care if you were born in a manger or raised in an orphanage or found on the doorsteps of a church," Wood said impishly.

Jack Seigle and Phil Wood were the best in town; they had never lost a state-wide election. Seigle had handled the gubernatorial campaigns of Jack Burns and George Ariyoshi, winning every one of them.

"Jack, don't you think running negatives against a woman is risky?" I asked.

"Yeah, negative campaigning is risky. It can backfire. That's why we have to make sure that our material is accurate and truthful. It may lose you some votes, but we think it will gain you more. We'll be attacking her record; as long as we tell the truth, it's fair game. That's how Fasi beat her in '84."

My gut instinct was to go for it.

Wood put up a storyboard on an easel and explained the ad to us.

"It's a comparison ad," he said, "comparing Anderson's record as mayor to Ben's as a senator. The text reads like this: 'In four years as mayor, Eileen Anderson did 59 studies, including one which cost the taxpayers $65,000 to study the impact of painting the curb red at the Honolulu Zoo.... Ben Cayetano, on the other hand, fought to save the life savings of the depositors at Manoa Finance and created the Hula Mae program to provide low-interest loans for affordable housing.'

"Because Eileen is haole," Wood explained, again smiling, "we're using a haole woman with a smooth, soothing haole voice to do the voice-over. The ad ends with a photo of Ben smiling telescoping to fill nearly all of the screen."

"Is the information about her record accurate?" I asked.

"Yeah, your people did a heck of a job researching it," Wood said. "Some of the studies Eileen did are downright ridiculous. We have another ad which focuses on a study on the impact of moving a house."

"We'll run the ads during three of the last five weeks before the election; we'll take them off the air about 10 days before the election, and while she responds with her ads, we'll close with our soft ad about you and your family," Seigle interjected.

The response to the ads gave us reason to worry. Dozens of our supporters from all over the state called or wrote, pleading with us to stop running them. "Take the high road, don't attack her," was the common complaint. Nekoba and I quickly met with Seigle and Wood.

"Jack," I said, "the response from our own people has been horrible. The phones are ringing off the hook in all of our headquarters. They think the ads are hurting us. Should we pull them off the air?"

"Ben," Seigle said calmly, "your people are going to vote for you no matter what they think of the ads; remember, the ads are targeting the voters we haven't been able to reach with our other stuff. I read that Eileen is complaining that the ads are 'mudslinging,' which means they are worried. Phil and I think the ads are working—but it's your election to win or lose."

I remained silent for a minute; then Seigle interjected, "Ben, you've got good gut instincts. Your instinct on Bunye was right on. We couldn't have written a better script for you. So trust your gut on these ads."

I was worried our ads had backfired, but I trusted Seigle's judgment. "Okay, Jack, let's keep running them and see what happens," I replied.

"Ben, take a deep breath and smile … you're going to win," Seigle said with a grin.

By the third week of running the ads, I knew we would win; the comparison ads had exposed Anderson's weak record as mayor far more specifically than Fasi's clock ad. I could feel an upsurge in our campaign everywhere I went.

Seigle was right; on Election Day, I beat Eileen Anderson by nearly 43,000 votes. We had overcome a 20-point deficit to score an incredible victory. She never ran for public office again.

The Smear

About 10 days before the primary, I got a call from Cec Heftel.

"Ben, it's going to be you and me against the Republicans in the general election. I'd like for us to meet at my condo at 1320 Ala Moana so I can brief you on my campaign platform for the general," Heftel said.

"Cec, there are 10 days left till the election; don't you think we should meet after the primary?" I asked.

"Well, he [Waihee] cut into my lead a little, but my polls say I'm still leading by 12 points. I don't think he can make it up in 10 days," he replied.

I wasn't so sure.

Heftel exuded a cool confidence when we met. The centerpiece of his campaign platform for the general election was a plan to establish Hawai'i as the premier healthcare center of the Pacific. He would use his strong connections to the world-renowned Mount Sinai Medical Center to help make his vision a reality. He had done his homework, citing facts and figures to support the proposal. I was impressed (so much so that I adopted his proposal during my 1994 campaign for governor). *No small wonder*, I thought, *that this guy is a multimillionaire.* "He's very bright," I told Nekoba later.

During the primary election, I'd often appear at campaign events with either Heftel or Waihee, or both. There was a big difference in their styles and personalities.

Heftel might have been impressive in the corporate boardroom, but he was a novice when it came to political campaigning. His speeches were flat and boring, without the spark that could lift a crowd. He showed little passion for his ideas and, more important, little warmth when he went around shaking hands as politicians are expected to do.

A friend who dined with Heftel on several occasions told me he was taken aback by his table manners. "He treats food like fuel, as if eating is something he has to do just to keep his body going. I don't think he enjoys it." I got the impression Heftel felt the same way about campaigning.

One afternoon, I attended a rally for Heftel at McKinley High School. There was a big crowd of between 1,500 and 2,000 people there. As I wandered through the crowd, shaking hands and talking to people, I asked an elderly Chinese woman whether she was there to support Heftel. "No, I came for this," she replied with an impish smile, pointing to a partially eaten roasted half-chicken in a box.

"A half a roasted chicken!" Nekoba exclaimed. "For 2,000 people? Man, Cec is spending big bucks."

Waihee's rallies were different. His crowds were boisterous, enthusiastic and emotional. Waihee's speeches were pure populism, delivered with great passion and often ending with Waihee dripping in perspiration. Heftel was not a good campaigner; while shaking hands with people it seemed as if he was gliding through the crowd with a Cheshire cat grin fixed on his face. His support was like the Nile River—a mile wide and only a few feet deep.

Heftel must have known Waihee was chipping away at his big lead, but with a huge television buy to flood the airwaves with his television commercials for the final two weeks, he remained confident, he told me, that he could hold off Waihee.

Lurking in the undercurrent of the campaign, however, were two documents that were being circulated to defeat Heftel.

One was a political screed written by Roland Kotani, a Democratic State representative. A gifted writer, Kotani had essentially penned a long narrative about the contributions of the Democratic Party to Hawai'i and the importance of maintaining local values, indicting Heftel as just another Mainland haole who did not understand or care about local values or local people. In essence, Kotani merely regurgitated what many locals who did not support Heftel were already thinking. I did not think it was an effective indictment of Heftel himself.

The other document, however, was potentially far more damaging. It bore the imprimatur of the U.S. attorney general. Several weeks before the primary election, copies of a five-page confidential summary of an investigation by the U.S. attorney general of allegations of sexual misconduct by, among other people, U.S. Congressman Cecil Heftel were circulated to about 20 people, including some news reporters.

The summary included a confidential report of an informant's 1983 hearsay statement to a federal drug-enforcement agent accusing Heftel of involvement in drugs and sexual relations with "young males and females," suggesting that Heftel was a bisexual pedophile.

To their credit, the news reporters did not cover the document. No one knew for sure whether only 20 people received copies, so it was difficult to determine the impact of the document on voters. All through the primary, traveling throughout the state, not once did I hear anything about the document.

In the election, Waihee defeated Heftel with 44.8 percent of the vote, with 35.6 percent going to Heftel.

The day after his defeat, an angry Heftel blamed the Democratic establishment for circulating the smear against him. Leaking federal documents is a crime. The governor ordered the State attorney general to conduct an investigation to find the source of the leak. A Mainland expert was brought in to conduct the investigation. Working on the proven theory that no two copy machines produce like copies and that each copy machine has its own "fingerprint," the expert traced the document to a copy machine in the office of City prosecutor Charles Marsland, a Republican. Many suspected that Rick Reed, Marsland's deputy and confidant, was behind the leak. Reed was a born-again Christian. A former hippie pothead and member of a local religious sect headed by a guy named Chris Butler, Reed had made attacking Democrats a personal crusade, leveling all kinds of wild charges. His choirboy looks belied a dark side. As far as I was concerned, he was the reincarnation of Sen. Joseph McCarthy.

During the primary election campaign, Neil Abercrombie, Duke Kawasaki and I met with Frank Fasi, who, having been elected mayor in 1984, was sitting out the 1986 governor's race. Abercrombie and Kawasaki had a good relationship with Fasi (Kawasaki would later become Fasi's deputy director). I went along for the ride.

Fasi told us that Heftel "would never win the election."

"The Republicans have a 'red book' on Heftel," he said. "They've got copies of airline tickets, hotel bookings of Cec and this black guy who is supposedly his personal physical therapist [Heftel had been badly injured in an automobile accident] traveling together—he'll never make it." (Fasi would later deny he ever said this).

In post-election coverage of the smear, the news media stories focused on Heftel's angry allegations that the Democrats were responsible. What the news media missed, however, was the probability that the Republicans preferred to face Waihee rather than Heftel in the general election.

To be sure, there were many establishment Democrats who preferred Waihee, but the early polls showed that Heftel led Waihee in the Democratic primary, indicating that he had strong support among the Democratic rank and file.

Republicans preferred to run against Waihee, because Heftel could draw the votes of the haoles and businessmen who made up the overwhelming majority of the Republican Party—Waihee could not. It was not in the best interest of

Republican gubernatorial candidate Andy Anderson to run against a Democrat like Heftel who could take votes from Anderson's Republican base.

None of this thinking mattered to Heftel, who continued to blame the Democrats for the so-called smear throughout the general election. As late as 1998, he repeated his charges that the Democrats had smeared him in 1986, warning my Republican gubernatorial opponent Linda Lingle to "watch out."

No one really knows if the "smear" was a reason for Heftel's defeat. During the campaign, I met and talked to hundreds of people. Except for the conversation with Frank Fasi, not once did I hear anyone suggest that such a document existed or that Heftel was a homosexual; I heard nothing derogatory about his personal life. And when I met with Heftel at his condominium to plan our campaign for the general, he never uttered a word to me that such a document existed or that the Democrats were trying to smear him. I only found out about the document after the primary, when Heftel charged that he had been smeared.

One of Waihee's bumper stickers had the words "Heart and Soul" emblazoned on it. And that's what the 1986 primary election amounted to; I believe that Heftel lost not only because he ran a poor campaign and was a passionless campaigner—he lost because too many voters concluded that he did not have the heart to be governor of Hawai'i.

John Waihee and I would go on to defeat Andy Anderson and Pat Saiki in the 1986 general election. For the next eight years, I served as lieutenant governor. It would be the most frustrating period of my nearly three decades in Hawai'i politics. ❖

CHAPTER TEN

Hawai'i's Lieutenant Governor

"The Hawaiians' Turn"

first met John Waihee in 1978. At the time I was chairman of the Senate Ways and Means Committee and a member of the Legal Aid board of directors. Waihee was one of two finalists being interviewed for the vacant Legal Aid executive director's position; the other was a guy named Mel Masuda, a graduate of Yale Law School who was active in the Democratic Party.

During the 1978 interview, I questioned—"grilled" would be more accurate—Waihee about his experience and found that while attending college on the Mainland he was involved in organizing community groups, trying to get poor people and urban minorities more involved in political action.

But I also learned that Waihee had been practicing law for less than two years. Moreover, his practice was limited mostly to workmen's compensation (today it's called "worker's compensation"). Masuda, on the other hand, had been practicing for 10 years and had a track record of doing pro bono legal work for the poor and Native Hawaiian causes. (He once represented pro bono the famed Hawaiian activist George Helm and the Protect Kaho'olawe 'Ohana).

"Give the guy credit, he has balls applying for this job even though he has little experience," I said to one of the directors. But Masuda's impressive background was the big difference, and we selected him for the job. What struck me, however, was that, despite Waihee's obvious inexperience, there were still a few directors who argued strongly on his behalf. After listening to their arguments, it became apparent that they were acting solely out of loyalty to him. I was impressed. *Not many people inspire that kind of loyalty*, I thought.

Eight years later, in November 1986, I was waiting for Waihee to arrive at my office (he had insisted earlier that we meet in mine instead of his, a nice personal touch on his part). I wondered whether my role in blocking his bid for the Legal Aid position had colored his thinking about me.

"I guess I did you a big favor in 1978," I said, somewhat jokingly. "Just imagine if we had selected you to head Legal Aid; we might not be having this conversation today."

"Yeah, you know, I really wanted that job, I had all kinds of ideas about reorganizing Legal Aid," Waihee replied, smiling. "It would've been exciting and fun. If I got it, I don't think I'd have run for the House."

Amazing, I thought, *how a little detour, a missed opportunity, a rejected job application, led Waihee on the road to the governorship.* The man was born under a lucky star.

"Ben, I was lieutenant governor for four long years. I know how frustrating it can be. I want to work with you. If you have projects in mind that you'd like to work on, let's get together and talk about them. I'll come up with a few that I want you to head," he said.

"Thanks," I replied. "You know I'll support you whenever I can, but on big issues, like rail transit, which I opposed while I was a legislator, I have to give my honest opinion."

"No problem. But on other issues I hope we can discuss them before you take a public position," he replied.

"Fair enough," I said, pleased with our meeting.

Waihee's storybook climb to the governorship was truly amazing. In 1980, just four years after he received his law degree, he was elected to the State House. Two years later, he became Hawai'i's seventh lieutenant governor, and in 1986 he was elected governor. He was the first governor with Hawaiian blood since statehood. At 40, he was also the youngest governor in state history.

His success was in large part due to his keen political instincts and his willingness to take risks. Under the circumstances it made sense for a young Hawaiian with Waihee's ambition to run for lieutenant governor. He ruled out running for the Senate seat in his district because it was held by Milton Holt. Had Henry Peters not become Speaker in 1982, Waihee might have remained in the House with an eye on the Speakership. But Peters was the first Speaker of Hawaiian blood since statehood, and Waihee would face much criticism from the Hawaiian community if he tried to oust him.

Ariyoshi was term limited, which meant the governorship would be up for grabs in 1986. As lieutenant governor, Waihee would have statewide recognition, whereas he was a virtual unknown in the House. But first he had to beat veteran State Sen. Dennis O'Connor in the Democratic primary. He did, scoring a close and surprising come-from-behind win.

Waihee's timing was near perfect. By 1986, the time for a governor with Hawaiian blood had come. Before Waihee appeared on the political scene, Peters and Holt were the two men most political observers thought had the inside track to becoming the first Hawaiian governor. In 1984, however, Peters took himself out of contention when he accepted a lucrative appointment as a Bishop Estate trustee. Holt looked good on paper, but he lacked what Peters and Waihee had plenty of—charismatic leadership quality. The all-state high school quarterback from Kamehameha Schools and Harvard graduate, who had been biding his time waiting for the right moment, was left standing at the altar.

Top: The Hawai'i Convention Center combines state-of-the-art, high-tech facilities with generous displays of Hawaiian art and culture, while its architectural design reflects the Islands' beauty, environment and natural resources. Approved during the Waihee Administration, the Center (here under construction) was completed on time and on budget by the Cayetano Administration in 1997. Bottom: Running for office in Hawai'i sometimes means taking the campaign to the beach.

Top: In December 1998 Hawai'i Intermediate Court of Appeals Justice Simeon Acoba, Jr., administers the oath of office to Governor Ben for a second term, as First Lady Vicky looks on. Bottom: Completed in 2002 adjacent to historic Washington Place, this plantation-style residence for future governors was completely financed with $2.2 million in private funds raised by First Lady Vicky Cayetano and the Washington Place Foundation.

Top: The Hawai'i State Art Museum building was purchased in 2001 for $22.5 million from a bankrupt Japanese corporation that had invested $80 million to buy and renovate the one-time Armed Services YMCA. Bottom: The $150-million John A. Burns School of Medicine in Kaka'ako was designed as the centerpiece of Governor Ben's vision to establish Hawai'i as the premier health care center of the Pacific. Construction started in October 2002, and the school's first phase was completed in 2004.

Top: Governor Ben greets President Jiang Zemin of China upon Jiang's arrival in Honolulu. Later, at a reception at Washington Place, the president played his steel guitar while First Lady Vicky sang "Aloha Oe." Bottom: On a post-9-11 visit to Japan, Ben gets a taste of Japanese Prime Minister Junichiro Koizumi's sense of humor, when the prime minister shows him a photo of a movie poster—for Gary Cooper's *High Noon*—that he presented to President Bush at the White House.

Top: President Hu Jintao of China visits Hawai'i. Bottom: With First Lady Vicky looking on, Philippines President Gloria Arroyo presents Ben with the 2002 Philippines Legion of Merit Medal.

The much-revered and highly respected Gladys Brandt (right) greets
Office of Hawaiian Affairs trustee Frenchy DeSoto.

The ancient Romans had a term for a certain political process: *cursus honorum*, the honors race. It was the process by which Roman politicians moved up the ladder. They were evaluated along the way until, finally, some made it to the top. In American politics, the process is known as "paying your dues." My journey to the governorship took 20 years; Waihee's took six.

Since 1954, Hawai'i's Japanese had enjoyed success in virtually every aspect of Hawaiian society, particularly politics and business. They dominated the Legislature, the executive branch and the Judiciary; many were heavily involved with investors from Japan in hotel acquisitions, new hotel construction and real estate development.

Among Hawaiians and other ethnic groups that did not share in the wealth created by the new economy, there was an undercurrent of resentment against the Japanese. The reality, however, was that among all of Hawai'i's non-haole ethnic groups the Japanese were best positioned to take advantage of the new economic opportunities. Hawaiians, like the Filipinos, were simply not prepared for it.

In 1971, for example, I was one of only a dozen or so Filipino attorneys practicing law among more than 1,500 Hawai'i attorneys; the Hawaiians had only a few more. By contrast, there were hundreds of Japanese, haole and Chinese attorneys. The same held true for accountants, bankers, engineers and other professionals. Moreover, the big foreign investors were Japanese, and they felt more comfortable with and tended to employ or partner with Japanese Americans.

To those envious of the AJA successes, none of these facts seemed to matter and, as is usually the case between the haves and have-nots, emotion ruled over reason. The result, as Fuchs pointed out in *Hawaii Pono*, was one of the great anomalies of Hawai'i politics—Hawai'i's Japanese had displaced the haoles as the objects of Hawaiian enmity. These feelings played themselves out in the post-statehood Hawai'i elections.

When I ran for the State Senate in 1978, I led the ticket in a field of four Senate seats, racking up the highest vote total for a Senate race that year. In analyzing the election results, I concluded that I had received a significantly higher number of non-Japanese votes than the other three senators, who were Japanese Americans. During the campaign, there were times when people would sidle up to me and tell me they were voting for me because they felt there were too many Japanese in State government.

Once, an Ariyoshi supporter lamented that no matter what the governor did for the Hawaiians, it never manifested itself in votes. In predominantly Hawaiian communities such as the Nānākuli-Wai'anae area, Ariyoshi's vote total in his three gubernatorial elections remained basically unchanged, regardless of how much he did for the people who lived there. Nevertheless, Ariyoshi never wavered in his efforts to help the Hawaiians.

If Hawaiians resented the Japanese for their successes, some Japanese felt obliged to help young Hawaiian politicians move ahead. Waihee would not have won without the support of Ariyoshi and the majority of the Japanese community, Peters would not have become the state's first Hawaiian Speaker without the support of Jimmy Wakatsuki, and Milton Holt would not have been elected a senator in a district where Hawaiians were a minority. (Similarly, I would not have been elected in Pearl City.)

Contrary to widespread perception, back then (and currently), as I mentioned before, the Japanese were and are probably Hawai'i's most liberal ethnic group when it comes to voting.

Waihee's election as lieutenant governor gave him the opportunity to nurture his relationship with Ariyoshi. Interpersonal relationships—trust, friendship, loyalty, respect—are probably more important in politics than in any other profession. Waihee's people skills and his warm, outgoing personality were among his biggest assets. In a short time the two men grew closer but, as Ariyoshi himself has said, ultimately it was Waihee's skillful work in helping to settle the United Airlines strike that sealed his support for Waihee in the 1986 election.

At a rally during the 1986 general election, a middle-aged, slightly balding local Japanese man wearing a *Waihee for Governor* T-shirt approached me and said, "Ben, we AJAs had our chance for governor with Ariyoshi, now it's the Hawaiians' turn with Waihee—you be patient ... the Filipinos will have their turn next time."

It would not be the last time I would hear such words.

Later, I found out the man was Mike Tokunaga, one of two of Burns' chief political lieutenants. At the time, I had heard of Tokunaga but we had never met. Often, supporters caught up in the excitement of a political campaign tend to say things they feel at the moment only to forget them later. I wasn't sure what to make of what he said at the time. But, true to his words, when I ran for governor in 1994, Tokunaga showed up at my campaign headquarters one day, offering to help. He later even appeared in one of my television advertisements. It didn't matter to him that as a legislator I had been a strong critic of the Ariyoshi administration: Tokunaga, a 100th Battalion combat veteran of World War II, was a true believer in the precepts of '54. Time had not diminished his belief in the ideal of equal opportunity for all. His idealism humbled and inspired me.

Leasehold Conversion

In 1984, Hawaiians despaired as the U.S. Supreme Court upheld Hawai'i's 1967 Land Reform Act (more commonly known as the "leasehold conversion law"), a landmark law passed by the Legislature to break up the big estates' stranglehold on private land in Hawai'i. Many Hawaiians (except, perhaps, those who like tens of thousands of non-Hawaiians longed to own the land on which they resided) saw the 1967 Act as a threat to the Bishop Estate and its prestigious Kamehameha Schools.

When the Hawai'i Supreme Court appointed Peters to the Bishop Estate board of trustees, he became the first trustee who was also a member of the State Legislature. When asked, he refused to step down as Speaker; his trusteeship, he argued, was a "part-time job," similar to jobs held by other legislators. The big difference, however, was that, as a trustee, Peters owed a fiduciary duty to the Bishop Estate, a higher duty than other legislators owed to their employers. Moreover, Bishop Estate was no ordinary employer; it was the biggest private landowner in the state, and its influence extended far beyond its primary responsibility to Kamehameha Schools and its beneficiaries. Most important, Peters' compensation as a trustee was directly linked to the estate's income.

Five years later, this potential conflict of interest would emerge in the bitter struggle over whether leasehold conversion should be made legal for condominiums, cooperatives and townhouses.

The U.S. Supreme Court's 1984 ruling upholding the 1967 Land Reform Act had encouraged owners of condominiums, cooperatives and townhouses to seek the same right of leasehold conversion given to owners of single-family homes. The sheer number of the lessees, of whom there were thousands statewide, created a demand for a political solution that could not be ignored.

In response, Waihee submitted a bill for a new leasehold conversion law for lessee owner-occupants of condominiums, cooperatives and townhouses. He asked me whether I would take the lead for the administration and lobby for the bill at the Legislature. I would not have agreed if Peters had still been Speaker, as there was no chance he would have allowed the House to pass the bill.

But in 1987, Democrats Richard Kawakami and Mazie Hirono led a majority of House members who, keenly aware of the looming leasehold conversion issue and the political embarrassment that a Bishop Estate trustee was the Speaker of the House, forced Peters to step down. Kawakami was elected Speaker. The Kaua'i Democrat was no political novice and had his own special-interest favorites, but he was respected by House members as being open and fair. Unfortunately, in March 1987, midway through the legislative session, Kawakami died of a heart attack. He was Speaker for less than three months.

Peters tried to regain the Speakership, but Hirono and others blocked him. Vice Speaker Daniel Kihano became Speaker. Kihano was quiet, soft-spoken and considered one of the real "good guys" of the House. Always eager to please and to get along, he was everyone's friend (which was probably the main reason he was selected to be Speaker).

The mild-mannered Kihano, however, was no match for the strong-willed Peters. Peters had lost the Speakership, but he still maintained a coterie of loyal followers for whom he had used his considerable powers as both Speaker and Bishop Estate trustee to liberally dispense favors in the form of jobs and personal services contracts.

It would be an oversimplification to say that Peters had bought their loyalty ("rewarded" might be more appropriate). He had won them over by the sheer force of his personality. Peters was a likeable, tough, fearless, street-smart and charismatic leader. One senator and former House member, Marshall Ige, went so far as to publicly and fawningly describe Peters as his "role model and mentor." (In 2001 and 2002, Ige would fall into disgrace when he was convicted and sent to prison for extortion, tax fraud and other charges. "I just want to say that my family is being sacrificed to reelect Governor Ben," Ige protested shamelessly after he was indicted by the attorney general. Ige was echoing the same charge Peters would make against me when I ordered the attorney general to investigate the Bishop Estate in 1998.)

From 1989 to 1990, Waihee's proposed condominium leasehold conversion law was one of the hottest issues before the Legislature. Public hearings on the bill were packed with lessees and landowners, testimony was often emotional and contentious, and there were so many witnesses who wanted to testify that the hearings often lasted until the early hours of the following morning. Legislators dreaded those hearings.

For nearly three decades, Hawai'i's real estate market had been one of the hottest in the nation. As lease rent reopening deadlines loomed, landowners sought to maximize profits from lease rents they believed had long been undervalued. Lessees, on the other hand, most of whom acknowledged that their lease rents were low, worried desperately that the rents would be increased beyond what they could afford. Moreover, some argued, the low, long-term fixed lease rents about which the landowners complained had been set by the landowners themselves during times when lessees had little or no negotiating leverage.

As a trustee, Peters owed a fiduciary duty to Bishop Estate. As a representative, he owed a fiduciary duty to the people of Hawai'i. Peters was reported to have attended every public hearing on the proposed bill, and in a short time there was little doubt that he was there to protect the interests of the Bishop Estate.

I never doubted that Peters believed in what he was doing. He was a proud Hawaiian. The 'āina (land) had special meaning for him, as it did for most Hawaiians. Peters believed it was wrong for the government to force Bishop Estate to sell its land. One of the reasons Peters was appointed was to defend the Bishop Estate interests at the Legislature, and he made no bones about it. He had little sympathy for the lessees. But I also felt that Peters was deeply hurt by his rejection as Speaker and that fueled, at least in part, his tenacious defense of the estate.

At the hearings I attended, Peters was a man on a mission as he led the opposition against the bill. His line of reasoning was clear: Leasehold conversion was unfair to landowners such as the Bishop Estate; ergo, it was unfair to its beneficiaries, the Hawaiian people. Besides, didn't the lessees read the leases they signed? Didn't they enjoy long-term low lease rents? These were powerful arguments that gave many legislators pause for thought.

Armed with research done by his Bishop Estate staff, Peters repeatedly cited examples of former lessees who made huge profits from the sales of their homes and condominiums while enjoying low lease rents. He quoted reports by experts hired by Bishop Estate to show that for decades Bishop Estate lease rents were undervalued and, although the proposed increases were high, they were fair given the skyrocketing prices in Hawai'i's booming real estate market.

The 1967 act was designed to apply to single-family dwellings, which effectively limited its impact on subdivisions on tracts owned by the big landowners. But Waihee's proposed new law would extend the right of leasehold conversion to condominiums, cooperatives and townhouses. It doesn't take much land—perhaps two to three acres—to build a condominium or a cooperative.

Thus, the self-described "small people" with land holdings of five acres or less on which condominiums or cooperatives had been built joined the opposition to the proposed law. A few were part-Hawaiian families for whom the land—often passed from generation to generation—was their biggest asset. Many legislators, particularly those from the Neighbor Islands, where leasehold conversion was not much of an issue, empathized with them.

However, there were lessees who were empathetic figures as well. One was a Mr. Gouveia, a local Portuguese man who owned a condominium in the Sandalwood, a medium-priced condominium building located near downtown Honolulu. Mr. Gouveia, a retired City employee in his 70s who had to use a cane to walk, testified that his lessor was going to raise his lease rents by more than 1,000 percent. "I knew our lease rent was low, so I expected an increase—but they want 10 times more rent now and I cannot afford to pay it," he said.

There were sound arguments on both sides, but Peters' and the Bishop Estate's take-no-prisoners, uncompromising stance did not address the hard fact that there were thousands of lessees who, like Mr. Gouveia, faced unaffordable increases in lease rents or the prospect of having to sell or lose their homes. Peters never proposed a reasonable solution—he wanted unconditional surrender.

The most vocal supporters of the proposed bill who showed up at the hearings were lessees from East Honolulu, many from Hawai'i Kai—an area that was seen by legislators as predominantly Republican. Many were retirees, living on fixed incomes and worried about the proposed rent increases, but they were usually not in the leadership and not visible. Most of the leaders of the lessees were haoles who felt strongly about leasehold conversion.

Ideally, race should not have mattered, but the political reality was that pitting Hawaiians against any non-Hawaiian ethnic group over land issues was a sure formula for trouble, more so for haoles, who tended to be more outspoken and aggressive than local people and, as an ethnic group, were burdened with the baggage of the land-grabbing history of those who came before them.

It didn't take long for the debates over the bill to degenerate into a "local-versus-haole" battle. Indeed, after one public hearing, a legislator taking note of the overwhelmingly haole audience referred sarcastically to the Hale ("house") Coalition (an ad hoc organization of lessee owners) as the "Haole Coalition." That Peters had gotten caught up in this feeling revealed itself in an incident at the State Capitol.

Mazie Hirono, the chairperson of the House Consumer Protection Committee, recalled how, after one particularly contentious hearing, Peters stopped abruptly as he was walking out of the hearing room and confronted an elderly haole woman who was standing by the door. Towering over her, he said, "Haole, you're not going to steal any more of our land." A horrified Hirono saw what happened, admonished Peters and apologized to the startled woman, trying to calm her.

There were some sound arguments against the proposed bill, but they were obfuscated as the hearings became more confrontational and accusatory.

Despite Peters' opposition, the bill was approved by the House and passed over to the Senate, where President Wong referred it to a committee chaired by Mike Crozier, a part-Hawaiian and another former House member who was closely allied with Peters.

When Wong referred the bill to Crozier's committee, I knew it was finished. Nevertheless, I called Crozier to ask that he give the bill a public hearing and at least let the lessees have their say. He quickly disabused me of any hope for a public hearing.

"Eh, let me tell you something, your bill is dead," Crozier said, obviously irritated I had called.

"Mike, it's not my bill, it's the governor's. I'm just the messenger. All I'm asking is for you to put the bill up for public hearing," I replied.

"Eh, look, it's dead, it's dead, okay? Got it?" he repeated impatiently.

"Yeah … I got it," I replied, swearing under my breath.

Later, I met with my chief of staff, Nekoba.

"You don't look too happy. What did Crozier say?" Nekoba asked.

"Oh, nothing much. He just told me to go fuck myself," I deadpanned.

"No shit?" Nekoba replied, chuckling.

"That's about what it amounted to…. Lloyd, I'm not going to waste any more time pushing for the damn bill. As long as Henry is in the House and there are guys like Crozier in the Senate, there's no chance it'll pass."

"Why don't you ask Waihee to talk to Crozier?" Nekoba asked.

"Yeah, but Waihee knows what Crozier's answer will be," I replied.

Stalemated at the Legislature, the lessees shifted their efforts to the Honolulu City Council. The Council went through the same painful public hearing process, and in December 1991 it approved a City law that incorporated the provisions of Waihee's bill. Leasehold conversion was always a bigger issue on O'ahu than on the Neighbor Islands. Thus, when the City Council passed its leasehold conversion law for O'ahu, for all intents and purposes the issue was dead at the Legislature.

Peters' opposition to leasehold conversion did not stop with the enactment of the new City law. If anything, as an incident in Hawai'i Kai would reveal, things got uglier.

The City law required lessees who wanted to buy their fee to hold a public hearing to show that they had met the legal conditions for leasehold conversion. Jane Sugimura, a leader of a lessees' group, recalled one such public hearing in Hawai'i Kai to which Peters brought in two busloads of Hawaiians, most of whom she believed were Kamehameha Schools alumni, wearing T-shirts with the words *Thou Shall Not Steal* printed on the front.

"A lot of them were very big, tough-looking men," Sugimura recalled. "They didn't threaten anyone … they just stood around watching us … but some of the lessees felt really intimidated."

Not every big landowner took Peters' hard-nosed approach to leasehold conversion. The Campbell Estate, for example, had set up a voluntary leasehold-conversion process whereby its representatives negotiated buyout prices for the lessees. One of the lessees who bought his fee was Crozier, a fact that did not go unnoticed by the lessees.

"Crozier paid a reasonable price for the fee to his townhouse, which was another reason we were really upset with him," Sugimura recalled. "We thought he'd understand how the lessees felt, but I guess, because we weren't from his district, he didn't even care. At least Campbell was reasonable; they were open to negotiation. But with Bishop Estate the prices were set extremely high and their attitude was 'take it or leave it.'"

As with the Bishop Estate, all the beneficiaries of the Campbell Estate were of Hawaiian blood. But unlike Bishop, Campbell was a for-profit entity whose beneficiaries traced their lineage to Hawaiian royalty. Under Peters, Bishop Estate took a hard line on leasehold conversion. Campbell trustees, who were all haole except for Fred Trotter, a part-Hawaiian, took a more objective, less emotional view of the politics of leasehold conversion.

As Trotter explained to me years later, "We thought long and hard about taking a hard line like Bishop, but we figured out that it was in the long-term best interests of the Campbell Estate to work things out with the lessees. We owned about 2,000 leasehold lots on O'ahu, most in the Leeward area. Many of the lessees were people who worked for our companies. Unlike Bishop, because of tax considerations, we couldn't negotiate individually with the lessees, so we had to set prices across the board per square foot for all of our leasehold lots. We knew if we set the prices too high, many would not be able to buy the fees. Unlike in Hawai'i Kai and those areas, our lessees were mostly local, blue-collar working people. Ed Burns, Gov. Burns' brother, convinced us to take the long-term view. We had other big projects planned for the area and Burns said, 'Do you want thousands of enemies or thousands of friends who will support your projects?' We agreed with him. The people's goodwill was important for the estate's long-term interests.

"Ed Burns did appraisal work and we worked with him and came up with a fee schedule. We offered the leases for an average of $1.25 to $1.50 a square foot, which, given current values, was really on the low side. We sold something like 97 percent of the leasehold lots to the lessees. The sales generated about $15 million in cash, which was good money back then. We leveraged that cash in investments which were very profitable for the estate. It turned out to be the most profitable deal in the Campbell Estate's history. Our beneficiaries were satisfied; our lessees were happy. I can't count the number of lessees who thanked us for giving them the chance to own their own homes."

(Trotter, one of the heirs to the Campbell Estate, was once the manager of the Kahūkū Sugar Plantation. A Republican, he was well liked and highly respected by the plantation's workers. Once, when word got around that the plantation had fired Trotter, 500 Filipino workers protested by going out on strike. Trotter was reinstated. He is generally credited with helping many of his workers buy the fees of the land they were leasing from Campbell Estate.)

One day in June 1989, Nekoba brought news about Crozier. "I just got word that the ILWU is putting up a guy named Brian Kanno to run against Crozier," he said.

"Who is this guy?" I asked.

"He was an aide to Congresswoman Patsy Mink. Sounds like he's pretty smart ... graduated from Yale. He's Herb Takahashi's nephew," Nekoba replied. (Takahashi was a highly regarded labor lawyer whose main client was the ILWU.)

"Why are they doing it?" I asked.

"Crozier's vulnerable. I mean, after the way he treated you, just imagine how he treated the average guy. He's pissed off a lot of people in and out of his district," Nekoba replied. "I checked with our people in his district, and I can't find anyone who is going to support him."

"Lloyd, see if they are willing to get actively involved in Kanno's campaign," I said.

I liked Crozier personally, but when it came to the leasehold conversion issue he was close-minded and arrogant. He used his power as chairman of the committee to arbitrarily kill the bill. There was no debate, no hearing; he simply pronounced it dead. And he had also misused Senate funds for personal trips and was required by the ethics commission to repay the Senate. Dozens of lessees from outside Crozier's senatorial district volunteered to help in Kanno's campaign. They did sign-waving, stuffed envelopes and raised money for him. "We didn't know who Kanno was ... never heard of him before, but we wanted Crozier out because of the way he treated us," lessee leader and attorney Sugimura recalled.

Voter dissatisfaction with Crozier was so widespread in his district that the virtually unknown, untested Kanno beat him in the 1992 Democratic primary by a whopping 62 percent to 30 percent.

"Man, he got his ass kicked!" Nekoba said, astonished at the election returns.

"Lloyd, politics is a contact sport. If someone hits you, you hit him back; that's the way it is. Crozier played hardball and he paid for it," I replied. Crozier never ran for public office again. A year or so after his loss, Waihee gave him a job as a consultant with the Department of Hawaiian Home Lands. When I was elected governor in 1994, I kept him on at the department. He left voluntarily several years later.

Shortly after the close of the 1992 legislative session, Peters announced his retirement. He had served for 18 years in the House and probably would have been a shoo-in for reelection. His tenacious and sometimes ruthless defense of Bishop Estate angered many non-Hawaiians, but, as one prominent Hawaiian leader observed, "To the Hawaiians in his district he remained their champion." In 1998, Peters would fight another battle—this time to save his position as a Bishop Estate trustee.

Danny Kihano, who was Hawai'i's first Speaker of Filipino ancestry, served as Speaker until 1992, when he retired under the impression, he would tell people, that Waihee had promised him a job. But there was no job forthcoming. Sadly, the trappings and duties of being Speaker had consumed his attention, and his insurance business eventually failed. Desperate and financially strapped, Kihano used his campaign funds for his personal use. Embittered by Waihee's failure to give him a job, in 1993 he accepted a job offer from Fasi, apparently to get his "high three" and boost his legislative pension. In 1994, Kihano served as co-chairman of Fasi's gubernatorial campaign. I was running, of course, but during the campaign, he never said a harsh word about me. There were no hard feelings, no disappointment; I understood why he had taken the job with Fasi. In 1996, Kihano retired to spend more time with his wife and their grandchildren. Sadly, his past misuse of his campaign funds soon caught up with him.

When the U.S. attorney's office investigated him in 1996, Kihano made things worse by urging his campaign treasurer to cover up for him, which she rightly refused to do. When I heard about the attempted cover-up, my heart sank. I felt like weeping. As a former criminal defense attorney I knew all too well that the federal government's response to people who lie is to throw the book at them. In 1997, the U.S. attorney did just that, convicting Kihano on federal charges of wire and mail fraud, money laundering, conspiracy to obstruct justice and witness tampering.

In May 1998, U.S. District Judge Allan Kay granted Kihano a "compassionate release" from prison after he suffered a near-fatal heart attack while serving the first year of a two-year sentence in Lompoc, California. According to his lawyer, Kihano's doctors gave him about a year to live. In 2000, Kihano died of heart failure. It was an ignominious end for an otherwise decent man who entered politics with the best of intentions, only to succumb to its destructive temptations. For too many, politics can be a seductive mistress. ❖

CHAPTER ELEVEN

The Republicans

The Race Question

The 1988 Democratic National Convention in Atlanta was my first. It was hot and humid, but the excitement of attending the convention and the friendliness of the people more than made up for my personal discomfort in the heat.

Atlanta was touted as the most cosmopolitan city in the South. I was told it had the highest percentage of African-American millionaires of any city in the nation. One morning, I read a big story in the *Atlanta Constitution* (now the *Atlanta Journal Constitution*), the South's equivalent of the *New York Times*, about a debutante ball held the night before. Debutante balls, I recalled from some old *Gone with the Wind*-type movies I had seen as a kid, served as a rite of passage celebrating the transition for teenage girls into the world of high-society womanhood. I was always under the impression they were for white girls only. But this story was about a debutante ball for the daughters of middle- and upper-class black Americans.

Atlanta had a strong and thriving black middle class that produced outstanding political leaders such as its then-mayor, Andrew Young, who would later become U.S. ambassador to the United Nations, and Maynard Jackson, who had served one term as mayor before Young and two terms thereafter.

Along with several other Hawai'i delegates, I had the opportunity to chat briefly with Jackson. He was a big man, standing 6 feet 3 inches and weighing nearly 300 pounds, light skinned, with eyes that suggested he was part white. He was charismatic, not in the evangelical way of a Jesse Jackson, but more like Bill Clinton. He seemed highly personable, articulate and down to earth in casual conversation (he told me that he had relatives who lived in Kāne'ohe). He had been, I was told, an outstanding mayor. (Jackson died in 2003.)

I had been to Atlanta before, but only passing through. During the five days I spent there for the 1988 convention, what I learned about the city broke my stereotypical impression about blacks in the South. I had never imagined a Southern city in which black Americans played such a prominent role in politics, economy and social hierarchy.

Atlanta was like an oasis in a desert. I left with the lasting impression that this city could teach its counterparts in the North a thing or two about how black Americans can prosper and win the respect that comes with the acquisition of economic, political and social power. Compared to the rest of the nation, they seemed to have done well there.

The convention presented some historic firsts: The Reverend Jesse Jackson and Massachusetts Gov. Michel Dukakis were the first African American and Greek American, respectively, to run for the Party's nomination for president.

The Democratic Party was used to firsts; in 1960, the Party had nominated John F. Kennedy, the first Catholic nominee, and in 1984, it nominated U.S. Congresswoman Geraldine Ferraro, the first woman to run for vice president.

The faces of the convention delegates mirrored the diversity of the American people, which was an integral part of the Party's creed. It was then and remains today the big difference between the Democratic and Republican parties. It's a big reason I'm a Democrat.

Conventions are choreographed affairs, designed to inspire and entertain and to celebrate the Party's history as the delegates select the Party's candidate for president of the United States. The highlight of the convention, of course, is the appearances of the Party's political superstars and the candidates themselves.

There were many fine speeches given at this convention, but those by Jesse Jackson and the keynote speaker, Gov. Ann Richards of Texas, were outstanding. I had my doubts about Jackson. At first he struck me as overly opportunistic as he vied to fill the leadership vacuum created by the assassination of Dr. Martin Luther King, Jr. But the night he spoke at the convention, Jackson was in top form, moving many delegates to tears with his rousing "Keep Hope Alive" speech. On the other hand, the silver-haired, distinguished-looking Richards had the delegates rollicking with laughter as she displayed her Texas wit at the expense of patrician, Connecticut-born George H.W. Bush ("George was born with a silver foot in his mouth," she quipped) and voiced an eloquent clarion call for victory in November.

Most of the speeches given that night prompted cheers, standing ovations or at least appreciative applause, except for one—Bill Clinton's. Clinton, who had been given the unenviable task of serving as the convention's wrap-up speaker, gave a long, tedious speech that seemed to repeat every point made by each of the major speakers.

The crowd grew restless as Clinton struggled to get through the speech, with which he was obviously not comfortable. When he finally uttered the words, "In conclusion…," a loud cheer and applause erupted from the thousands of weary delegates, who by then must have been looking forward to the post-convention receptions and the posh, by-invitation-only parties, most of which were given by special-interest groups or wealthy Democrats. It was an embarrassing moment for the future president.

(I first met Clinton in 1987 when he, Hillary and their daughter, Chelsea, visited Hawaiʻi. Clinton was still the governor of Arkansas, and he and Waihee had become good friends. On the evening the Clintons arrived in Honolulu, the Waihees hosted a dinner for them at Washington Place. As the Clintons drove up in their rental car, Waihee and I stood outside the front door waiting to greet them. Waihee turned to me and said, "This guy will be either a U.S. senator or president one day.")

Later, as we waited for other Hawaiʻi delegates to join us in the convention center parking lot, Clinton and Hillary happened to walk by. Waihee greeted his good friend with a hug. I shook his hand. Before we could say much, a crestfallen Clinton complained, "The Dukakis people wrote that speech; they put in all that stuff I didn't want in it; I knew it would be too long, but they insisted.... I'll never give a speech I don't like again."

"Actually, I thought it was a pretty good speech, there was a lot of substance to it," Waihee said, trying to offer some solace to Clinton. Every politician experiences moments of embarrassment they would rather forget—I've had more than my share of them—but few are unlucky enough to do so before a national audience.

I had taken a liking to Clinton when we met in Hawaiʻi and compounded Waihee's white lie with my own by trying to assure him that I also thought it was a good speech. Hillary Clinton stood there with a slight but knowing smile, aware, I was sure, that Waihee and I were trying to boost her husband's spirits.

Within a week after the convention, however, Clinton showed his remarkable ability to turn things around. He silenced his political opponents by appearing on several popular late-night shows where he joked self-deprecatingly about his convention speech and topped it off by playing some passable jazz on his saxophone. The audience loved it. Not many politicians could bounce back like that. I was amazed. The little-known governor from Arkansas had become a national figure. Waihee was right: This guy was something special.

I walked out of the convention feeling inspired and optimistic about Dukakis' chances of winning. Dukakis had given a fine speech that included a few lines in Spanish, a nice touch which evoked cheers, particularly from Hispanic delegates. A week later, the post-convention polls showed him with a 17-point lead over Bush. Even taking into account the so-called "post-convention glow," I thought 17 points was a good lead. But in the ensuing months I watched in awe as the Republicans waged an aggressive, no-holds-barred, hardball campaign against Dukakis. It was dirty and racist, but it certainly was something to behold.

Dukakis was the first Democratic presidential nominee to fall victim to the Republican's "Southern Strategy." Developed in the 1960s by Richard Nixon, the strategy called for Republicans to court white voters by exploiting their fears about racial issues.

Ronald Reagan sanctioned the Southern Strategy in 1980 when he kicked off his bid for president by giving a speech touting "states' rights" in Philadelphia, Mississippi, the site of the infamous murders of civil rights workers James Chaney, Andrew Goodman and Michael Schwerner. It was not one of Reagan's shining moments.

Dukakis was a seasoned politician, but I doubt if he expected the brutal, racist campaign Bush ran against him. It was run by two hardnosed political consultants: Lee Atwater, who was chairman of Bush's campaign committee, and Roger Aisles, who currently runs the conservative Fox News. Atwater once described Aisles' campaign strategy as "attack and destroy." To these two, everything about Dukakis, including rumors about his wife, Kitty, was fair game.

During the Democratic primary, then-U.S. Sen. Al Gore had criticized Dukakis for Massachusetts' liberal prison furlough program. Subsequently, Aisles and Atwater discovered that one of the prisoners who had been furloughed had gone on a crime spree, robbing and raping a white woman. The inmate was a black man named Willie Horton. Atwater vowed to make Horton Dukakis' "running mate," which he did in his infamous "revolving door" television ad. The ad showed photos of Dukakis and Horton—who looked like everyone's worst nightmare—side by side. The ploy was a blatant appeal to racism—and it was highly effective.

Rumors about Dukakis' wife were spread through "push polls"—a technique by which the pollster insinuates damaging, false or sensitive information about a candidate to targeted groups under the guise of taking a poll. The pollster might ask, "Would it make a difference in how you vote if you knew that candidate X's wife is an alcoholic?" Whether or not the information is true, the thought is planted in the person's mind.

Atwater and Aisles were masters at this stuff. Their 1988 racist, anything-goes attack became part of the Republican campaign playbook and sadly is today a norm in American politics.

Dukakis added to his demise by taking the so-called "high road," which made it appear he was not fighting back. If there is anything the American voter hates more than bullies, it is people who don't fight back. (Joe Napolitan, the political consultant for my two gubernatorial campaigns, had a "24-hour rule," which called for a quick response to negative attacks. If they were not answered promptly, Napolitan once explained to me, then the public was likely to take my silence as an admission that the allegations were true.)

Dukakis also committed a couple of memorable political faux pas.

To blunt criticism that he was uninformed about military matters, Dukakis held a photo op which showed him wearing a helmet while driving a tank around a field, waving to the crowd. It was an incredible blunder. One news story described Dukakis's appearance as "Snoopy-like," and the Republicans used the television footage in ads that mocked Dukakis to no end. This kind of blunder usually happens when a candidate defers unconditionally to the suggestions of his public relations people.

The second big mistake came during his second televised debate. According to news reports, most viewers thought Dukakis had won the first debate, but Bush's subsequent "Willy Horton" campaign had erased Dukakis's early lead. He was behind and needed to do well in the second debate to win.

Whatever points Dukakis scored in that debate were wiped out when Bernard Shaw, one of the panelists, asked Dukakis whether he would support the death penalty if his wife were raped and murdered.

What a cheap shot, I thought. Shaw, an African-American newsman, had asked a question that brought back thoughts of the "Willy Horton" ad and played to Bush's campaign theme that Dukakis was soft on crime.

Dukakis, who was against the death penalty, had to hit this question out of the park. "Show anger, emotion, say you'd like to kill him—and then explain why you're against the death penalty," I muttered to myself. Instead, Dukakis answered as if he was speaking at a seminar, rattling off statistics to show the ineffectiveness of capital punishment. There was a collective groan from the small group I was with. Dukakis had struck out, confirming the Republicans' portrayal of him as a cold person. (He wasn't, as I would learn a year later when I met him while he was a visiting professor at the University of Hawai'i.) I knew the election had been lost; Dukakis had no chance of catching up to Bush. In November 1988, he suffered a crushing, career-ending defeat.

In 1990, Atwater was diagnosed with an inoperable brain tumor. Apparently, he experienced a religious epiphany and, in an act of contrition, he publicly denounced the campaign tactics that he and Aisles had made part of the Republican playbook and apologized to the man he cast as Willy Horton's running mate, Michael Dukakis. Political campaigns are prone to be rough-and-tumble affairs, but the campaign against Dukakis was extraordinarily dirty, and Atwater's mea culpa confirmed it.

Fifteen years later, on July 14, 2005, Republican National Committee Chairman Ken Mehlman apologized to the National Association for the Advancement of Colored People for the GOP's Southern Strategy. Admitting that the GOP exploited the racial fears of white voters to blame pro-civil rights Democrats for the nation's racial unrest, Mehlman said, "It's not healthy for the country for our political parties to be so racially polarized. I am here today as the Republican chairman to tell you we were wrong.")

But before that apology, by 1994 the Republican strategy had produced a string of victories that gave them the majority of the nation's governorships and Congress. It also left black Americans and other minorities little choice but to vote for Democrats. Indeed, a joke that had regularly made the rounds among Democrats during every GOP Convention since 1988 was that "there were more black people on the stage entertaining than there were among the delegates."

One exception was the 1994 election of former star Oklahoma quarterback

J.C. Watts to Congress; Watts became the first black Republican congressman since Oscar De Priest (R-Ill.) in 1928.

When Watts' father was asked what he thought about his son becoming a Republican, the father joked, "I don't know about my boy ... but for a black man to vote for a Republican is like a chicken voting for Colonel Sanders." Watts was an aberration. He retired in 2002 and, since then, there have been no black Republicans in Congress.

The GOP Turns Right

Race was just one part of the Republicans' strategy. Religion was the other. In the mid-1970s and '80s, Gallup poll surveys showed that one-quarter to one-third of the U.S. population identified themselves as "born-again" evangelicals.

Evangelical leaders blamed liberal Democrats and judges for racial turmoil, the sexual revolution, feminism, pro-abortion sentiments and gay rights. They vowed to cure these sins by mobilizing their followers to help elect politicians who were supportive of their beliefs. The Democratic Party was seen as the antithesis of their Christian values and way of life.

"The mission of the Christian Coalition is simple," said the Coalition's leader, Pat Robertson. "It is to mobilize Christians—one precinct at a time, one community at a time—until once again we are the head and not the tail, and at the top rather than the bottom of our political system."

Another prominent evangelical leader, Jerry Falwell, once proclaimed, "I have a divine mandate to go into the halls of Congress and fight for laws that will save America." Falwell, an ardent segregationist in his early years, succeeded the disgraced Jim Bakker as head of Bakker's popular Praise the Lord (PTL) television ministry and established The Moral Majority, an organization that called for fundamentalists and evangelicals to set aside their differences, to unite and form a voting bloc within the Republican Party. Once, in an amazing and memorable moment of candor, Falwell said, "Good Christians, like slaves and soldiers, ask no questions.

During the early 1980s, while the Religious Right was making its presence felt on the Mainland, it was still pretty much ignored by both Democrats and moderate Republicans in Hawai'i. Like many other politicians, I found it difficult to believe that the Religious Right could make much headway in Hawai'i.

Compared to the highly respected evangelist Billy Graham, who eschewed getting involved in politics, Falwell and Robertson seemed like snake oil salesmen. Moreover, the public sex and corruption scandal of Jim Bakker in 1987 was followed by the fall of one of Bakker's chief rivals and critics, evangelist Jimmy Swaggart, who in 1988 was exposed for (and tearfully confessed to) having patronized prostitutes. These incidents created the impression that the Religious Right had suffered a serious political setback. *Surely, they would fail in Hawai'i,*

I thought. In the years ahead, I would learn I was dead wrong.

To be sure, there were signs of the growing influence of the Religious Right in Hawai'i politics. On bills relating to issues such as abortion, pornography and sex crimes, the testimony given by an increasing number of people took a more strident, moralistic tone.

One person who stood out among them was Stan Koki, a self-confessed former drug user who had become a born-again Christian. Koki, a successful businessman, became a familiar face at public hearings regarding pornography and drugs. In 1998, he would emerge as the Republican Party's candidate for lieutenant governor.

But like many Hawai'i politicians, I was preoccupied with other important issues such as economic growth, public education and the environment. The thought that the Religious Right could rise to power in Hawai'i was the farthest thing from my mind.

In late January 1988, however, Hawai'i Republican Party officials were taken by surprise when a surge of new applicants began registering to vote in the Party caucuses and its unofficial presidential primary. There were so many new applicants that Republican Party officials moved the date of their presidential primary from January to early February.

On February 4, liberal and moderate Republicans were shocked when the new Republicans elected Christian evangelist Pat Robertson in the Republican Party's presidential primary, dominated the caucuses and adopted an anti-abortion Party platform. In protest to the religious right "pro-life" agenda, four veteran Republican women legislators—State Sens. Donna Ikeda and Ann Kobayashi, as well as State Reps. Virginia Isbell and Kinau Kamalii—resigned from the Republican Party and became Democrats.

Pat Saiki and Andy Anderson, the GOP's most viable candidates, chose not to run. Saiki was serving only her fourth year in Congress while Anderson, having lost an expensive campaign in 1986, had a 1987 jury verdict for committing fraud on a City housing project hanging over his head (the verdicts against both Anderson and Fasi were reversed by the Hawai'i Supreme Court in 1989). The Republicans were hard pressed to find a viable candidate for the 1990 gubernatorial election.

In 1990, Fred Hemmings, a three-term Republican State representative facing only token opposition, won the Republican gubernatorial primary election. Hemmings, a local-born haole, graduate of Punahou School and former world-champion surfer, had been elected to the State House in 1984 and reelected in 1986 and 1988.

His public statements suggested a brand of conservatism essentially similar to that practiced by U.S. Congressman Newt Gingrich, the former college history professor who authored the conservative screed "Contract with America" and led the Republican takeover of the U.S. House in 1994.

There was a difference, however. Gingrich was a highly knowledgeable, articulate and formidable advocate of the conservative philosophy. Hemmings was facile in speaking the conservative rhetoric, but his words never materialized into specific programs or ideas. It was enough, however, to win him the 1990 Republican gubernatorial primary.

The twice-divorced Hemmings was hardly a poster boy for the Religious Right's position on marriage, but they appreciated his consistent and strong opposition to proposed laws intended to assure gays and lesbians equal rights in areas such as housing and employment. He was their champion, at least in 1990.

Hemmings' rise to statewide recognition began shortly after his election to the House in 1984, when he joined the "law and order" campaign launched by prosecutor Charles Marsland.

Marsland, a former corporate lawyer for the City and trust lawyer for First Hawaiian Bank, joined the City prosecutor's office in 1975, shortly after his 19-year-old son, Charles Marsland III, who was working as a doorman at a popular Waikīkī discotheque, was found murdered gangland style on a lonely road in rural Waimānalo.

My first encounter with Marsland was in court. Then a deputy prosecutor, he was prosecuting a client I represented on a drunk-driving charge. As most experienced prosecutors and defense attorneys know, a properly prosecuted drunk-driving charge is very difficult to defend against. Nevertheless, my client was acquitted. Marsland lost the case in large part because he was unable to control his emotions. His antics helped create rather than erase the reasonable doubt which would lead to the acquittal of my client.

He reacted angrily to the verdict, storming out of the courtroom, swearing as he brushed by me. "It's not the first time; he takes it very personal, that's how he is," one of the court clerks said to me. (It wouldn't be the last time. Once, after he was elected prosecutor, Marsland blew up and got into a scuffle with defense attorney Patrick Tuohy.)

In 1980, Marsland ran as a Republican in the City's first election for prosecutor since the 1930s. Television was starting to play an important role in elections, and the telegenic Marsland, riding a wave of public empathy generated by the murder of his son, crushed his Democratic opponent, former Deputy Prosecutor Lee Spencer.

"The hardest job in the world is to be a 'good cop,'" a famed New York police commissioner once said in a panel discussion on police brutality. A good cop, he explained, was one who understood that the Bill of Rights was intended to protect the individual citizen from the excesses of the government and understood the limitations of his authority in carrying out his duty. Given the kinds of people and the dangers cops encountered daily, it was a miracle that most remained good cops.

The same tough standards, I believed, should apply to any public official who has the power to affect the life and liberty of an individual citizen. I wondered whether Marsland had what it took to be a "good" prosecutor.

As events unfolded, Marsland proved to be more politician than prosecutor. He made headlines with his complaints and personal attacks against judges who issued rulings not to his liking, the governor, legislators and defense attorneys.

It soon became obvious that Rick Reed, his chief of staff, was the architect of Marsland's public relations war. Reed was the former owner-publisher of a small Maui newspaper called the *Valley Isle*, which had run a story alleging that Big Island rancher and influential Democrat Larry Mehau was the "Godfather" of organized crime in Hawai'i and was connected in some way to the deaths of George Helm and James Kimo Mitchell, two Hawaiian activists who were actually lost at sea when they attempted to paddle by surfboard from Moloka'i to Kaho'olawe.

Mehau, a former Honolulu Police Department vice squad officer who had long been the subject of such rumors, sued Reed for libel. Reed claimed that, since Mehau was already a public figure, his statements were protected by the First Amendment. A jury verdict in Reed's favor was reversed by the court. Reed's newspaper had already failed, and he had no assets. Rather than go through the expense of a new trial, Mehau agreed to settle if Reed issued a public apology. Reed apologized but did not retract his accusation.

Reed's allegations about Mehau did not end with the settlement. After Reed joined the prosecutor's office, Marsland picked up where Reed left off. Although Marsland never openly accused Mehau of being a crime boss, he seemed to be suggesting as much. Using the term "the Ariyoshi-Mehau machine" frequently in his public speeches, Marsland tried to bait Ariyoshi into the controversy. As was his style, Ariyoshi took the so-called high road, virtually ignoring Marsland's charges except to state once that he and Mehau were longtime friends and, as far as he knew, Mehau was not involved in any criminal activities. If he was, he said, Marsland should prosecute him.

Mehau's lawyer, David Schutter, was one of the state's top trial lawyers. Schutter, whose law firm I joined in 1983, had publicly denounced Reed as part of a "cabal of comic strip" characters. Schutter was often inclined to hyperbole in his public statements, but privately he told me that Reed was no comic book character, that he had been part of a religious sect in Kailua and was truly "evil" and "ruthlessly ambitious" and had a strong influence on Marsland. Schutter was easily the most flamboyant criminal defense lawyer in the state; he had represented some of Hawai'i's most notorious criminals, but I had never heard him describe any of them as he did Reed.

As an individual, Reed had the right to express his opinion about Mehau, but it was clearly unprofessional, unethical and irresponsible for Marsland, as City prosecutor, to parrot Reed's suspicions and try to taint Ariyoshi by association.

The rumors about Mehau led to intensive investigations by the federal government. Nothing ever came of them. To their credit, the federal law enforcement agencies were highly professional and made no public statements about Mehau or anyone associated with him. The difference between federal law enforcement officials and Marsland was like night and day.

Mehau was no fan of mine. After I joined Schutter in 1983, he told me that Mehau had called him to express his disappointment that Schutter had invited me to become part of the law firm. Mehau's displeasure with me was in large part due to my criticisms of Ariyoshi and some of his Cabinet members. Moreover, Mehau was close to Andy Anderson and Dickie Wong, with whom I had gotten into political battles. In 1986, Mehau supported Anderson for governor against John Waihee and me. In 1994, he supported Pat Saiki against Fasi and me. In 1998, mainly due to the efforts of Jimmy Takushi, one of my Cabinet members, Mehau supported me. Prior to 1998, I knew Mehau did not like me. The feeling was mutual. And when Takushi told me that he had persuaded Mehau to support me in the 1998 election, it was Mehau's choice; I never asked for his support. But although his political influence had waned considerably, I knew I would be a big underdog in the 1998 election and wasn't about to turn down anyone who wanted to support me.

Mehau was an imposing figure. Standing slightly over 6 feet and weighing nearly 300 pounds, he exuded a powerful presence. A martial arts expert, he had become somewhat of a legend as head of the Honolulu Police Department's feared Metro Squad. Jay Toguchi, Charlie Toguchi's older brother, who was a former member of the Metro Squad, described Mehau as an old-school cop who didn't hesitate to use his fists to deal with the bad guys. The rumors about Mehau came about in part because he knew many of the state's top criminals. But as a former cop, it was his business to get to know as much as possible about them. Moreover, he had also grown up with some of them—like some of the tough Irish- and Italian-American cops who grew up with boyhood pals turned criminals in the tough neighborhoods of big cities like Chicago or New York. Growing up in Kalihi, I understood this.

Despite the rumors about him, political leaders like John Burns and George Ariyoshi—two governors whose integrities were beyond reproach—considered Mehau a trusted and loyal friend. To this day, after nearly four decades of rumors and investigations, Mehau has never been charged with any criminal wrongdoing.

Marsland's attacks on the judges were one sided. The judicial code of professional conduct prohibits judges from engaging in public debates over their rulings. Thus Marsland's attacks were met with silence, creating an environment that could only undermine public confidence in the court system. His office once orchestrated a public demonstration of several hundred people to protest a judge's ruling.

His disdain and disrespect for judges who ruled against the prosecution trickled down to a few of his deputies. In one case, a deputy prosecutor named Kenneth Nam protested an adverse ruling by Circuit Court Judge Simeon Acoba by turning his back as the judge verbally issued his ruling. Nam, knowing full well that reporters were present, stated that he was turning his back in "disrespect of the court." Acoba held Nam in contempt of court and sentenced him to a week in jail. Marsland reacted publicly with a barrage of tirades at the judge.

Marsland's public attacks against judges were unprecedented in Hawai'i, but the tactic had become increasingly common on the Mainland, where conservative Republicans and evangelicals routinely attacked the courts for "judicial activism." The big difference was that Marsland's attacks had a sharp, bitter, personal edge to them.

One day, I was told by a personal friend who was a deputy prosecutor that Marsland had given a speech in which he had mockingly spelled out Judge Acoba's first name as "S-i-m-i-a-n" ("apelike") rather than "Simeon."

Among friends, jokes and joshing about each other's ethnicity are widely accepted in Hawai'i. But Marsland and Acoba were hardly friends. I had known Acoba for many years and considered him not only a fine attorney but also a highly ethical and conscientious person. Years later, I appointed him to the Hawai'i Supreme Court. In my opinion, Marsland had gone too far. No one was holding him accountable for his disrespect of the judges.

A few days later, Marsland appeared at a Senate public hearing. I was a member of the committee and grilled him with questions about his proposed bills and then asked whether he had made the racist remark about Acoba. He denied it. I expected as much, but several people who had heard him confirmed he had said it. I thought it was important to put it on the public record. It didn't take long for things to get out of hand between us. After the hearing, we got into an angry swearing match outside the conference room.

"Don't let him take you down to his level," a good friend, who had read about the encounter, advised me later. "Take the high road."

Frankly, I was sick and tired of being advised to take the high road.

"Take the high road? This guy is running around town like a madman, attacking everyone, no one holds him accountable, the CJ [chief justice] is nowhere to be found, others are running for cover—and you're telling me to take the high road?" I replied defensively.

"Let him hang himself; the people will figure him out," my friend said.

"Yeah, but if no one takes this guy on, if no one responds to his wild charges, how is the guy on the street going to understand what's happening?" I replied.

"I know you're pissed, many other people are too. But no need getting into one of these fuck-you exchanges with him. Hey, Ben, you're my State senator, I voted for you, you represent me—so don't lose your cool."

He was right. It wasn't the last time I would get angry at another politician, but it was the last time I would use that kind of language in public. Frankly, though, I felt no regret over my exchange with Marsland. It was something that had to be said at least once.

During the legislative sessions, Marsland submitted bills designed to make it easier for his office to prosecute and convict people. I saw most of the bills as weakening the long-standing protections set forth in the Bill of Rights of the individual citizen against the excesses of their government. I made up my mind to do everything I could to kill the bills or to amend them to assure fairness and due process.

No legislator wants to be labeled as "soft on crime." The label has cost some legislators their elections. Indeed, in recent years, I've seen too many of the current crop of legislators cowed into voting for bills they privately oppose to avoid such accusations. Fortunately, during the 1970s and 1980s, the majority of legislators I served with saw through Marsland's ploy and had the political will to either reject or amend the bills.

Tom "Fat Boy" Okuda

Hemmings had targeted Tom Okuda, the deputy administrator of the courts, as an example of political corruption. Okuda had already established himself as the unofficial lobbyist for the Judiciary when I was elected to the Legislature in 1974. There were many outstanding and highly respected lobbyists then (the image of lobbyists has since changed), and Okuda was among the best.

Well liked and respected by legislators on both sides of the aisle, the slightly disheveled, unassuming, pleasant 50-something Okuda could easily have been mistaken for someone who was not the brightest of lights. He was, of course, very bright, but he had an uncanny ability to make the other guy think otherwise.

Okuda—I never called him Fat Boy—stood about 5 feet 5 inches and, as his moniker suggested, was overweight. Except for formal occasions, his usual daily attire consisted of khaki pants, casual loafers, an outdoor-type vest over his aloha shirt and his signature soft, weathered porkpie hat (I don't recall ever seeing him without it). When he sat at his desk, he would nearly always loosen his belt, which gave me the impression his pants waist size was too small. And when he spoke, he often would close his eyes, which gave his round face the appearance of a "happy face" icon.

But for the fact that Okuda was Japanese American he could have been one of those characters from Brooklyn or the wards of Chicago who are immortalized in the writings of authors like Jimmy Breslin and Mike Royko.

He was a master teacher, but not the Ph.D. type. He taught from his life experience, often driving lessons home through parables. As with many local boys, his manner of speaking was often sprinkled with pidgin idioms. Once he was invited by a group of State librarians to share some tips on lobbying the Legislature. Abercrombie and I happened to be present. "If you want the Legislature to give you one dollar but they can give you only 50 cents, no grumble, take the

50 cents—but if times are bad, tell them you will take 25 cents instead of 50, and always say thank you very much. And the next time, they will give you one dollar because you showed them respect and understanding. Be patient, be humble and be understanding. And you will be successful in the long run."

It was a virtuoso performance, and the librarians gave Okuda a standing ovation.

Okuda had a legion of loyal friends and supporters. One of his closest friends was his boss, Les Cingcade. Cingcade, a tall (at least 6 feet 2 inches), slender Mainland haole with a Ph.D., and Okuda, a short Japanese American with an advanced degree in street smarts, were like Mutt and Jeff at legislative hearings. As popular as he was, Okuda never undermined Cingcade, who was relatively new to Hawai'i. "Les is the boss," he told me; "he is a good man and deserves respect. If you respect good people, they will become your good friends."

The late Bob Rees, who was probably Hawai'i's best investigative journalist during the 1990s, once did a story on Okuda and told me he could find no evidence that suggested he had done anything to enrich himself personally. That was the consensus of those who knew Okuda. He was totally devoted to the Judiciary, and his sole objective was to persuade legislators to support the Judiciary's budget requests. In this regard, he was no different from other State administrators and State employees who lobby to persuade legislators to support their bills or budget requests.

Unlike the lobbyists for private interests, Okuda never raised money for campaign donations. Instead, he developed strong personal relationships with legislators from both parties. I never ceased to be amazed at his ability to marshal a small army of Judiciary employees to take time off from work to prepare platters of sushi, noodles, fried chicken and other local dishes for dinners or lunches to which legislators, staff, news media and other lobbyists were invited. These feasts were usually held in a conference room (a common and legal practice available to lobbyists back then). They were like after-work beer busts—no political speeches, no programs, just lots of food and soft drinks and talk.

Okuda started in the Judiciary as a court reporter in the 1960s and then worked himself up to head the Traffic Violations Bureau (TVB). The TVB was established in the early 1960s after a scandal that exposed police officers who would withdraw tickets for favors or bribes. Under the new system, once a police officer issued a ticket it was taken out of his hands and became the responsibility of the TVB. For a variety of reasons, there were always some traffic tickets which had to be dismissed. Only the judges could authorize a dismissal, but they were too busy to research whether there was justification for it. Therefore, administrative judge Millard White set up a procedure through which Okuda researched the reasons for dismissing the tickets and then made his recommendations to the administrative judge. If the judge agreed he would dismiss the case, and the initials "ABC"

(Action by the Court) would be stamped on the file. This procedure was followed by every administrative judge thereafter.

To simplify the process, Okuda followed the expedient of contacting the police officer who issued the ticket and asking whether he or she really wanted to pursue the matter in court or was willing to withdraw the ticket. If the officer was willing to withdraw, Okuda would recommend to the judge that the ticket be dismissed.

Police officers have a lot of discretion in giving traffic tickets. It's not unusual for a cop to give a driver a break and let him off with a warning. Eventually, Okuda acted as if he was a cop issuing traffic tickets. Routinely, he'd listen to a person's story and then decide whether he would recommend that the ticket be dismissed.

As for legislators, Okuda once explained to me that there was an existing law that gave them immunity from being issued violations or petty misdemeanors during the legislative session. He was also known to fix tickets for news reporters, particularly the television news crews, who would often double-park and rush off to cover a hearing or legislative session.

It was no secret that Okuda could fix tickets. And his largesse in accommodating such requests, along with his success in lobbying, caused concern among citizen watchdog groups such as Common Cause. The system was clearly fraught with the potential for abuse. Marsland focused on this and had his investigators screen more than 14,000 traffic tickets to find ones that might have been improperly dismissed.

Among them were tickets that had been issued to politicians (Pat Saiki was one), news media and judges, including several from the Supreme Court. Marsland's costly and time-consuming investigation uncovered 32 questionable tickets.

To create the appearance of objectivity, Marsland hired an attorney named Darwin Ching as a special prosecutor. To those who knew Ching's background it was a cynical ruse. Not only was Ching one of his former deputy prosecutors and a close friend, he was another one of Marsland's pack of true believers.

In a politically charged and highly public trial, Okuda was prosecuted for committing 32 petty misdemeanors. Because the charges were the lowest level of all criminal charges (punishable by a maximum of 30 days in jail), Okuda was not entitled to a jury trial. Many of the judges on Oʻahu had to recuse themselves because they knew him personally. Judge Thomas Kaulukukui, Jr., the newest judge in the Judiciary, was assigned to hear the case. Hilo-born attorney Michael Weight, himself a former prosecutor, was retained to defend Okuda. After a trial that lasted a little more than a month, Judge Kaulukukui found Tom guilty on 13 of the petty misdemeanors and dismissed the other charges.

On these 13 traffic tickets, the police officers who issued the tickets testified that they were never contacted or asked by Tom or anyone else whether they wanted to pursue or withdraw the traffic violations.

Under State law, a State employee convicted of a crime in the course of his employment stood to lose his State pension. To save his pension, an appeal was filed to give Okuda the opportunity to retire. In 1989, after serving the Judiciary for 41 years, he left it. Later that year, the Supreme Court affirmed eight of the 13 petty misdemeanors and dismissed the other five. Tom tried to hide his feelings, but many of his friends knew that he was a broken man.

Shortly after the verdict I visited Okuda to offer my support. It was a visit I never forgot. "Governor (I was lieutenant governor), I want to show you something," he said as he opened his office safe and pulled out some documents.

"What are those?" I asked.

"Oh, the court clerk gave me copies of a DUI ticket and two court dockets," he replied, handing me the ticket.

I was startled by the surname of the person I saw on the ticket. Without saying a word, I looked up at Okuda and he replied, "It's his son, not him."

Okuda then handed me the copies of the two court dockets. One had the date of the appearance for arraignment and plea; the second and later one noted that the DUI charge had been dismissed.

"Why was the DUI dismissed?" I asked Okuda.

"I think the police officer [Okuda never said 'cop' and always addressed politicians by their titles] did not show up. So the judge dismissed the case."

"Did the prosecutor ask for a continuance [to try the case later]?"

"According to the court clerk, there was no request for a continuance," Okuda replied.

"Tom, you know as well as I do that DUIs almost never get dismissed; there are games being played here," I said.

"I know," he replied.

Strange things can happen when a person with connections to the prosecutor's office is cited for a drunk-driving offense: A police officer issues a ticket; the prosecutor recognizes the name or is contacted by someone who has influence with the office; the arresting officer is told not to show up at the trial; when the judge dismisses the case because the police officer has not shown up, the prosecutor does not ask for a continuance (which in such cases is routinely granted) to try the case at a later time; and the judge has no choice but to dismiss the case.

I was certain that is what had happened in this case. Okuda had copies of the documents, had verified the identity of the person arrested for the DUI and also knew who his attorney had been. That was all I needed. I had more than a few questions I wanted to ask Marsland, the boy's politician father and their lawyer.

"Well, let me have copies of the documents. I'll publicly confront Marsland and ask for an explanation of why the case was dismissed, or maybe I'll ask the attorney general to investigate," I said, my anger growing.

"No, please, the boy is still young," Okuda pleaded. "You know, you and

Marsland, you guys chose to run for political office, to make it your career, but your children did not have a choice. They stuck because you are their father."

(A few years earlier, while I was still a senator, Okuda had hired my son Brandon as a summer hire—a minimum-wage, temporary job. I didn't ask him to do it, but Okuda and I had become close friends, and he knew from our talks that Brandon was going through some difficult personal issues. "I go hire him and keep an eye on him for you ... I try help him, he's a good boy," he said to me. Marsland and Hemmings had made a big political issue out of it—and the news coverage mentioned Brandon's name.)

"Yeah, but those bastards wouldn't hesitate a minute to use this kind of stuff against me, you or anyone they did not like," I replied.

"I know, but if you have to hurt the son to show that the father did something wrong—that's no good. If you do that, you become just like them," Okuda replied.

"But the public is entitled to know the truth. Tom, this is for a DUI, not a parking ticket," I protested.

"I know, but do you think it is worth hurting the son because he made a mistake? We all make mistakes when we young—when you were growing up you got in trouble too."

"But what that kid will really learn is that if you have the right connections you can get away with that kind of crap," I replied.

Okuda did not reply. He had already made his point.

"Tom, who knows about this?" I asked.

"The judge, the bailiff, the court reporter, the police officer, some of my staff ... the court clerk is the one who told me about it."

"Well, Tom, it'll get out eventually," I said.

"But only if the police officer says something, and I don't think he will—the others will not say anything; they leave it up to me."

"Damned hypocrites, I'm so pissed...." I replied.

"Governor," Okuda replied with a slight smile, "because the father pull strings for his son it will affect their relationship."

"What do you mean?" I asked.

"Well, now the son knows that his father does not practice what he preach. And when the father tries to teach the son to be honest, to follow the law—the son will not believe him. So you see, Governor, even though the father save his son from being punished by the law, he has hurt his son more than the law ever could. The son will always remember this, and if he grows up to be a good person, he will feel guilty and think less of his father."

I was at a loss for words. Finally, I replied, "Okay, Tom, I won't say anything, unless you say so."

"Maybe one day I will write a book about this kine stuff.... I know plenty good stories," Okuda chuckled.

Years later, Michael Weight, Okuda's fine defense attorney, told me how frustrated he was with Okuda during the trial. Weight, a part-Hawaiian born and raised in Hilo, lamented, "Tom was a samurai. He refused to turn me loose. He refused to let me subpoena witnesses and pursue certain lines of defense that I was confident would have gotten him acquitted. He just didn't want anyone else to be hurt."

That was Tom Okuda. He never hurt people; he helped them. He was loyal to the Judiciary but was left out to dry after he was indicted. One day during the trial, Weight was flabbergasted when a court clerk handed Tom a handwritten note from Chief Justice Herman Lum: "Tom, we're having problems with our budget at the Legislature."

"I couldn't believe it," Weight told me. "Tom was loyal to the CJ and did whatever the CJ asked him to do, but the CJ never offered an encouraging word to him. And here we are in the middle of the trial and the guy has the nerve to send that note asking Tom for help."

Marsland, Reed and Hemmings had politicized the trial. Many were intimidated by Marsland and ran for cover. I was one of the few politicians who stood up for Okuda. He was entitled to due process and a fair trial, and I wanted to do everything I could to make sure he was treated fairly.

I had no doubt that the three of them were trying to squeeze every political advantage they could out of the situation. But as they would soon discover in the years ahead, their ploy would backfire.

Tom Okuda never wrote that book—but Les Cingcade, who had left the Judiciary to become president of Mid-Pacific School and was one of the few to openly support him, was appalled by what had happened and began writing a book of his own.

When Okuda died of heart failure in 2001, Cingcade, who a few years earlier had left Mid-Pacific for another job on the Mainland, returned to give the eulogy at his funeral. He was still working on the book. Unfortunately, he died a few years after Okuda. The book was never finished.

Charles Marsland is a good example of why prosecutors (and judges) should never be elected. For personal political purposes, he used the full power of his office, spending hundreds of thousands of dollars in a trial which lasted a month, to convict Okuda of committing eight petty misdemeanors. Politics should never govern the administration of justice. The two simply don't mix.

In 2006, a young reporter for *Hawaii Business* magazine interviewed me for a story she was writing on the evolution of lobbying in Hawai'i. She mentioned Okuda in her story and seemed to suggest that he was "corrupt."

I sighed and bristled when I read the story. Okuda had never been out for personal gain. He had been given power and discretion in an obsolete system that invited sloppiness and abuse, lacked accountability and had not caught up with the changing ethics of the times. He made the mistake of fixing eight out of more than 14,000 tickets over a period of more than 20 years. Guilty? Yes. Corrupt? No. I'll always believe Okuda was a good man.

"Don't Forget"

It took the voters of O'ahu eight years to figure out Marsland. While he was still basking in Okuda's conviction, the overconfident Marsland was soundly beaten by Keith Kaneshiro in the 1988 election for City prosecutor. The voters had had their fill of his brand of law and order and threw him out.

He did not take his loss well. As a matter of common courtesy, an outgoing office-holder usually worked with his successor to ease the transition between them. Obviously, it was in the public's interest that the transition be smooth. Kaneshiro, however, was not allowed to set foot in the prosecutor's office from the day he beat Marsland in September until the day after he was sworn in in January 1989.

There were earlier times when Marsland's name had been bandied about as a candidate for governor. But by 1988, caught up in his hubris, he had squandered the huge political capital that gave him runaway victories in 1980 and 1984. And by the time he figured out Rick Reed, it was too late. Marsland never ran for public office again.

In 1990, Hemmings met the same fate (at least temporarily) when he was beaten by a 2-to-1 margin by Waihee (and me) in the gubernatorial election. Hemmings' conservative message did not resonate well with the majority of voters. Moreover, his crusade to root out alleged corruption, cronyism, nepotism and other "isms" was seen by many as political rhetoric rather than a sincere effort to make government better. His association with Marsland had backfired.

When, in 1987, the attorney general's investigation of the so-called "Heftel smear" in the 1986 gubernatorial election traced the copies of the federal documents used in the smear to a copy machine in Marsland's office, Marsland and Reed for once remained silent and made no response. Prior to the report, the relationship between Marsland and Reed had soured. Reed and his wife, Cutter, were estranged. Both worked for Marsland. According to news reports, Reed had physically attacked his wife while both were at work. Marsland sided with Reed's wife, and Reed, who had earlier announced he would run for lieutenant governor, moved back to Maui.

Subsequently, I learned that the schism between Reed and his wife led her to inform the attorney general's office that Reed had copied the smear documents and passed them on to a Fasi aide. As I would discover from personal experience during the 1994 gubernatorial campaign, Fasi knew of more unsubstantiated allegations about the personal lives of his political opponents than any other politician—and he did not hesitate to use them to his advantage.

In 1988, after Marsland was voted out of office, Reed was elected as one of Maui's State senators. Like a cat, he had once more landed on his feet. In 1992, he ran for the U.S. Senate against Democratic icon Dan Inouye. Reed produced a tape-recording in which a woman claimed that Inouye had sexually molested her 17 years before. The surreptitious recording was made by a young woman believed to be a member of a religious sect in Kailua. Reed used the tape-recording in a slick television ad to attack Inouye. When the woman, who was unaware she was being taped, refused to confirm the allegations, Reed's scheme began to crumble. Maggie Inouye, Inouye's highly respected and dignified wife, also appeared in an unprecedented television ad to support her husband.

Inouye, who had lost an arm in combat in World War II and been awarded the Medal of Honor for his heroism, was shocked by the allegations. He had never met an enemy like Reed before. Indeed, Hawai'i had never experienced a politician like Rick Reed.

Reed's accusations did have some effect. Although Inouye was reelected, he garnered only 58 percent of the vote—a near-landslide in the eyes of most politicians, but far below the 70-plus percent he had averaged in his past elections.

In 1994, Reed left Hawai'i and returned to his home in the state of Washington.

During my first term as governor, I received a telephone call from Hemmings, who had been Pat Saiki's lieutenant governor running mate in the 1994 election. He wanted to meet with me and discuss an idea he had. I was surprised by his call, but agreed to meet with him at my office at the State Capitol.

"Ben, you and me, we're both alike. You're a Kalihi boy; I'm a Kaimukī boy [a blue-collar neighborhood in East Honolulu]. I'm through with politics … I'm not going to run again … but I need a small favor."

No, I thought, *we're not quite alike.* Hemmings was a member of the exclusive Outrigger Canoe Club; my father worked there as a waiter, and except for the kitchen and employees' locker room, I never saw the inside of the club. About the only thing we had in common was that we were both local boys, born and raised in Hawai'i—otherwise we came from different worlds.

"After all the things he said about you, why are you going to meet with him? There are so many others who want to meet with you besides Hemmings," Nekoba asked.

But I had heard that before Gov. George Ariyoshi retired, Hemmings had met with him and apologized for his remarks about the "machine" and the "old boy network." (The meeting was private, of course, and the public never knew about his apology.) Besides, I had won—the election was over. And given the state's depressed economy, I was open to listening to any person who had a good idea.

"Ben, I have an idea for a restaurant with a surfing theme," he explained. In many surfing circles Hemmings was thought of as the father of modern surfing in Hawai'i. As he explained his idea, I thought the concept was a good one. Of course, I knew nothing about the restaurant industry, except that I had been told it had one of the highest failure rates in business.

"Sounds interesting," I said. "How can I help you?"

"Well, I want to lease the site of the old Captain's Galley restaurant from Sheraton."

"You mean the one in the Moana Hotel?"

"Yeah, it's a perfect site. Right next to the beach, Duke's [Duke Kahanamoku's] statue, all of the surf racks and the beach boys."

"Why do you need me?" I asked.

"I want to discuss the idea with Stanley Takahashi," Hemmings said. Takahashi was executive vice president and COO of Kyo Ya Corp., which owned the Sheraton Waikiki, Moana-Surfrider, Royal Hawaiian and Princess Kaiulani hotels.

"Why don't you just call him yourself? I'm sure he'd be interested in learning more about your idea."

"Well, I'm a Republican and he's a Democrat." (Indeed, Takahashi, who had graduated from Farrington a decade before me, was one of the few Democrats among top-level hotel executives.)

"Yeah, but so what? Stanley is a businessman."

"Well, I don't know him personally, and I'd appreciate it if you would call him and set up a meeting for me," Hemmings replied.

Why not? I thought. The economy was depressed, and Hemmings' idea sounded like it had potential.

With Hemmings sitting there in front of me, I asked my secretary to put in a call to Takahashi. Takahashi took my call, and I explained Hemmings' idea and asked if he would meet with him.

"Governor, we already have some long-term plans for the site," Takahashi replied.

"Well, could you meet with him?" I asked.

"I'll meet with him if you want me to."

"Yeah, I'd appreciate it, Stanley," I said, nodding affirmatively at Hemmings.

"Okay, have him call me," Takahashi replied.

Hemmings' idea apparently never got off the ground. In 2000, however, he decided to run again and was elected to the State Senate.

It didn't take long for me to learn that it would be business as usual. When in December 2001 the Governor's Committee on Long Term Care issued a report recommending a long term program called "Care-Plus," Hemmings denounced it publicly as a "fraud." The committee, chaired by my wife, Vicky, included unpaid respected private citizens and professionals who had worked for nearly a year to develop the proposal. Vicky took Hemmings' accusations in stride but felt badly for the others, who were hardworking volunteers.

"To disagree with us is one thing but to dismiss our work as 'fraud' … why would anyone want to serve [on a board or commission] if they're treated like that?" she asked.

Why indeed? Politics can be a rough game—one too often sprinkled with paradox and contradiction. Unlike the private sector, where one has greater leeway in deciding whom he or she will work with, the political arena requires its players to routinely and repeatedly interact and seek compromise to get things done.

As one veteran legislator put it to me while I was still a freshman legislator, "Ben, ours is a business where you must learn how to forgive the guys who tried to screw you on one day—because you may need their support the next day. Learn how to forgive—but don't forget." ❖

CHAPTER TWELVE

A-Plus for Island Kids

Latchkey Children

I n July or August 1989, Governor Waihee asked me to meet with him and then-Superintendent of Education Charles Toguchi.

"Ben, Charlie found out that Frank [Fasi] is developing an after-school program which he will begin before the 1990 election," Waihee said.

"Yeah, one of my staff members told me that someone from Fasi's staff called asking for information about the schools. When he asked what it was for, the person told him that the City was developing an after-school program," Toguchi said. "They plan to outsource the service to private providers and operate the program in the City's parks."

I could tell Waihee was mulling over whether Fasi was thinking about running for governor again. I didn't think Fasi would run, as he had just been reelected as mayor in 1988; moreover, the 1978 "resign to run" constitutional amendment would require him to resign as mayor. But Fasi—who once professed that he had decided to run for mayor (against John Wilson) at the last minute because he had a religious epiphany urging him to do so the night before—was notoriously unpredictable.

"Charlie, how big is this latchkey kid problem?" Waihee asked.

"Huge," Toguchi answered. "At the end of every school day thousands of children roam the libraries, the parks and other places where they are unsupervised and at risk of running into drug dealers, pedophiles ... getting hurt ... all kinds of problems."

"So what have we [the State] done about it?" Waihee asked, as if he was surprised the issue had not caught his attention earlier.

"Nothing much, both the City and State have pretty much left it to the private sector to provide after-school services. But at anywhere from $70 to $125 a month per child, many families can't afford it. It's not uncommon for a family to place their youngest child in a private program but not the two older ones, because they could not afford to pay for all three," Toguchi replied.

Waihee turned to me and asked, "Which department has jurisdiction over this?"

"That's the problem," I said; "it's not clear. I think some in the DOE see after-school care as babysitting … they don't think it's their kuleana [responsibility]. DSSH [Department of Social Services and Housing] doesn't think it's theirs, either."

"Charlie, Fasi is going to use the City parks for his program. Why can't we use the schools for after-school programs? The schools are so underutilized—it seems such a waste of taxpayers' money," I said.

"As a matter of policy we leave that decision to the school principal. Politically, the principal would be asking for trouble if he allowed a private provider to use a teacher's classroom. Most teachers feel very territorial about their classrooms, and principals, being former teachers, know this very well," Toguchi replied.

"Well," I said, "one of the biggest problems for parents who want their kids in an after-school program is transportation. Many parents can't just take off from work to take their kids to the program. And it's a major cost item for the provider to provide for pick-up service. If we can use the schools and restrict enrollment in our program to the kids from the school then we eliminate the transportation problem."

"Would you support using the elementary school facilities for an after-school program?" Waihee asked Toguchi.

"If it benefits the kids, of course."

"What about the BOE [Board of Education]—do you need their okay?" Waihee asked.

"Yes—but most of them will go along if they are convinced the program will help the kids."

"How will they hold up if the principals and teachers start complaining?" I asked.

"A few board members may play politics, but the majority will do the right thing," Toguchi replied.

"Okay, why don't you two guys put the program together and maybe we can start with a pilot program in a few schools," Waihee said.

"John," I protested mildly, "I would rather not do a pilot program; there's a place for pilot programs—but this is not one of them. If we use their classrooms, the teachers will resent it, and even if the program works well for the kids in one school, we'll have a tough time expanding it to the others. I've seen more good programs die because they started as pilot programs. If we come up with a good proposal, let's just go for broke—put a program in every elementary school."

"Charlie, how many elementary schools are there in the DOE?" Waihee asked.

"About 140 or so statewide."

"How do you feel about going statewide rather than a pilot program?" Waihee asked.

"Well, there will be difficult logistical and staffing problems we have to resolve, but I agree with Ben that there will be growing opposition … if we're going to do it, let's go statewide," Charlie Toguchi replied.

"You have a date in mind for the program to begin?" Waihee asked me.

"Yeah—right after the Christmas vacation, in January or February," I replied, smiling.

"That's only six months from now," Waihee said. "Charlie, is that realistic?"

"It'll be tough. I don't know if we can do it in every school by January, but I think we can do a lot," Toguchi replied.

"John, there's no money in the State budget for this, unless we can divert funding from other programs. You'll have to ask the Legislature for an emergency appropriation to fund the program," I interjected.

"Yeah, I'll have to sell the idea to the Speaker and the president. Right now I don't have anything specific to sell—so you guys develop the program and we'll go from there," Waihee replied.

"Charlie and I will get it done, if not in all the schools, most of them by January," I said.

Waihee smiled. "You have a name for the program?" he asked.

"Yeah, how about calling it the A-Plus After-School Program?" I replied, the name coming literally off the top of my head.

"A-Plus? Sounds good," Waihee replied.

Later, after Waihee left, I looked at Toguchi and asked, "Was I out of line in promising to open in January or February?"

"No more than you've ever been in the past," Toguchi replied with a laugh.

"Amazing, isn't it, what a little competition can do?" I said. "If we're lucky we'll have a nice present for the kids—and for our friend in City Hall—early next year."

Waihee formalized the project by establishing a Governor's Subcabinet, which I chaired. It included two members of Waihee's Cabinet—one from the Department of Social Services, the other from the Office of Children and Youth. Both, however, were reluctant and critical from the start—not of the need for an after-school program but of the "way" we were developing it. More input, they said, was needed from the private-sector providers and educators. *What*, I thought to myself, *do they expect the private providers to say about a State program that could take away children already enrolled in their programs?*

I wasn't about to turn over the development of the program to an informal, ad hoc process that would have amounted to a one-sided town hall meeting where detractors would nitpick the proposal to death. The need for after-school care was great, but the opposition was better organized and politically more influential than the parents, who at this stage knew little about the proposal. As often happens, there was virtually no one to speak for the latchkey children except for the politicians who understood the need for the program. If anyone had something to say about the program, they could testify when it was formally presented for public hearing to the Board of Education or the Legislature.

Eventually, the skeptics backed off. The Subcabinet devolved to two working members: Toguchi and me, assisted by our staffs. With the target date for starting the program only six months away, there was a lot of work ahead. We had to persuade the legislators, BOE members and educators that this was an important program. Time was of the essence.

Growing up in Kalihi back in the '40s and '50s, I was a latchkey kid during most of my childhood. My father worked a split shift at the Outrigger Canoe Club; he'd leave for work early in the morning and return home between 9 and 10 p.m. Ken and I were home alone a lot. But things were different back then. At that time Kalihi was a safe place to grow up. Neighbors knew and helped each other. Our doors were rarely locked at night. I was more afraid of ghosts than I was of strangers.

The biggest difference was drugs—there was no drug problem back then. Alcohol, yes, but no drugs. In 1989, the latchkey kids were at greater risk and faced far more serious challenges than the kids I grew up with.

Within a week, my staff came up with some preliminary findings. They estimated that out of approximately 60,000 elementary school children, nearly 30,000 were unsupervised and literally roaming the streets after their regular school classes ended; the rest were either enrolled in private after-school programs or had after-school care on an ad hoc basis: They were staying with grandparents, relatives, babysitters or friends of the family or were being picked up by their parents.

The numbers staggered me. All these unsupervised kids, loitering on the school grounds, in parks, libraries, and shopping centers—were put at risk of getting hurt, of encountering drug addicts, pedophiles or worse. *How did we let this happen?* I asked myself.

After the staff left, I said to Nekoba, "Lloyd, this project is the most important thing I've worked on ever since I got into politics. We got to make it work. I'm not about to stand for anyone screwing it up—make sure the staff understands that."

"Oh, they know it. They're jacked up about this project," he replied, "but Charlie told me that some of the higher-ups in the DOE are already giving him some shit."

"Like what?" I asked.

"Well, some don't think it's the DOE's responsibility ... they feel it's like babysitting, it's not education so it's not part of their mission," he replied.

"You know, Lloyd, these people are always complaining that the kids have a hard time learning because of their screwed-up family lives ... and now they say what happens to the kids after school is not part of education?"

"Well, there are others who are worried about the logistics, the funding and the opposition from principals and teachers about using the school facilities," Nekoba continued, "and even Charlie's personal staff have doubts about the project."

"What did Charlie say?" I asked.

"He read them the riot act. He told them, 'Don't tell me why we can't do it—

I want you to tell me how we can do it!'" Nekoba chuckled.

"Yeah, we're lucky Charlie is the superintendent and not some bureaucrat who's afraid to rock the boat," I replied.

Charlie Toguchi

Toguchi and I had been drawn together when we served in the Senate. We stood for many of the same causes and voted alike on many issues. Even when we differed and engaged in lively debates against each other there were never any hard feelings; it never affected our friendship because we knew we were both doing what we thought was right.

"Misery loves company," as the old cliché goes, and during the time we spent together as dissidents a bond of trust and respect developed between us. Besides his family, nothing was of greater priority for Charlie Toguchi than the education and well-being of our kids. Given his life experiences, I was not surprised.

Toguchi's basic values were shaped during his childhood in rural Windward Oʻahu. His father taught him a few things about honor and principle. Once his oldest sister told him about an incident that had happened on Maui before Charlie was born. Their father had stayed home from work on the sugar plantation because he was sick. A plantation luna (overseer, or foreman) came looking for Charlie's father. Back then, the lunas rode horses, and some carried whips. This luna—"a big Portuguese man," as Toguchi's sister described him—rode his horse onto the front porch of their small plantation house and began shouting Charlie's father's name, demanding that he come out.

The sight of the luna and his horse on their front porch was more than Charlie's father could bear. "As sick as he was, my father was outraged when he saw that luna ride his horse onto our porch. He got out of bed, yanked the luna off the horse, threw him off the porch and kicked the shit out of him. The next day, my father was fired. When he lost his job, our family lost the right to rent the plantation house. There were no jobs for him on Maui and they had to move to Oʻahu, where I was born."

Born and raised in rural Kahaluʻu on Oʻahu, Toguchi was a kolohe (mischievous) kid. Once, when his elementary school principal disciplined him by whacking his behind with a wooden paddle and twisting one of his ears, Toguchi got even by sneaking into the principal's backyard and stealing some of his watermelons.

He is the only person I know who was attacked by a monkey. Toguchi took a school bus to his elementary school. Whenever the school bus stopped in front of one particular house to pick up more kids, Toguchi would tease a pet monkey that was kept in a cage on the front porch. Eventually, the monkey went berserk each time he saw Toguchi.

One day, as he was teasing the monkey, Toguchi was surprised to see the cage door was wide open. On hearing Toguchi's voice, the little primate took one look at him, bolted out of the cage, bounded through the street and leaped through the front door of the bus. He stormed past all the other horrified kids, cornered Toguchi in the rear of the bus, hopped on his head and, in a fit of screeching fury, unleashed a vicious onslaught of bites and clawing that rearranged Toguchi's hair and parts of his scalp, leaving his head a bloody mess. Even as a kid, however, Toguchi needed to save face—he was, after all, Okinawan. So the next day, his head and hair discolored by dabs of iodine applied by his mother, he continued tormenting the poor animal—only from then on, he made sure the cage door was closed.

After high school, in 1967, Toguchi got his teaching degree from California State University at Long Beach. While studying for his master's degree, he taught at John Muir Junior High School, an all-black school in South Central Los Angeles. It was a defining experience for him. He remembered:

"The conditions those kids were growing up in were terrible. Worse than anything I ever saw in Hawai'i. Once this haole teacher and I pitched in money to buy a new pair of shoes and clothes for this poor black kid who always wore old, tattered clothing to school; the next day the kid came to school with bruises on his face, dressed in his old clothes and shoes. He told us that his mother didn't believe that a white person would buy new clothes and shoes for him. So we went to the kid's home and explained everything to his mother. 'Why would you do this? What do you want?' she asked. Life there was not like it was in Kahalu'u, where people were helpful and trusted each other."

One day, the school principal asked Toguchi to work with a student who had flunked the year before and was on the verge of doing so again. He was older than his classmates and big, standing over 6 feet tall and weighing about 220 pounds. This strapping boy-man was the unofficial "bull" of the class, if not the school. Like many of the other students, the boy came from a single-parent family. His brothers and sisters had different fathers. The family was living in run-down public housing and subsisted on welfare. Toguchi said:

"He was a big, tough kid, but I sensed he was good inside and had the potential to become a better student. I began spending more time with him and one morning, I saw him in the parking lot and I gave him the key to my classroom and asked him to open it for the class while I was in the administration office checking my mail. Attached were the keys to my car, locker and home. He was surprised that I trusted him, but he did it, and after that I would find him waiting for me each morning in the parking lot. After awhile, I knew that we hit it off, and so one day I asked if he would like to go fishing. He had never fished before. In fact, he had never been near the ocean. So one Saturday I took him to the pier at Redondo Beach, where I taught him how to use the fishing gear and how to fish. By then, he had really opened up to me and told me a lot about himself and his family. *It's a wonder,* I thought, *that this kid is not in jail.* At school, he helped me keep the class in order. Whenever one of the other kids misbehaved, he would tell them to 'shut up' from his seat in the back of the room. They all listened.

"I was finishing up graduate school, and so one day I told the class I would be returning to Hawai'i after the end of the school year. The next day the kid asked to meet with me after school. We met and he asked me if he could speak to Elaine [Toguchi's wife]. I asked him why and he said he wanted to ask her if it was all right for him to go to Hawai'i with us. I was stunned, at a loss for words. Finally, I explained that he couldn't come because he was still a minor and that he should stay in L.A. to help his family. By then he was teary-eyed and just nodded his head as if to say he understood. It broke my heart to see him like that. I gave him my address, but after I left for Hawai'i I never heard from him again."

Once back home, Charlie Toguchi was hired as a teacher at Castle High School in Kāne'ohe and got active in the teachers' union (HSTA). During the 1973 teachers' strike, he was a strike captain running the picket line. One teacher told me that Toguchi was really aggressive during the strike, encouraging the picketers, and when other teachers crossed the picket line he'd say a few choice words to them.

Toguchi was a strong supporter of his fellow teachers, but with him the kids always came first. "What's good for the teachers is not always good for the kids," he once told me. I never forgot it; it told me where his heart was.

Charlie Toguchi was the best person to help me put the A-Plus program together. I felt confident we were going to get the job done.

A-Plus Takes Off

Aside from the political obstacles we encountered, the logistics of setting up a statewide after-school program were mind boggling. Our staff estimated we needed hundreds of employees to operate the A-Plus program in all the elementary schools. We decided to offer the top-level jobs, which paid more than three times the minimum wage, first to teachers (both active and retired). We knew many teachers took low-paying part-time jobs to supplement their incomes and others continued to work after regular hours, some into the later afternoon. Our big task was to encourage these teachers to take the A-Plus jobs. The lower-level jobs would be offered to people with no teaching experience (parents, college students and high school seniors).

The latchkey-child problem was one that was pervasive but somewhat invisible. Few legislators understood its magnitude. We went to great lengths to educate them, to give them as much information as we could to help them understand the risks the children faced.

Disputes over turf are always problems in politics. It didn't take long for criticism to surface. One BOE member, Francis McMillan, angrily asked, "Since when is the lieutenant governor in charge of public education?" Russell Blair, a State senator, alleged that the proposed A-Plus program was illegal because we had not gone to the Legislature for statutory authority. Rod Tam, a State representative, argued that we needed to go to the Legislature for an emergency appropriation and that it would be illegal for us to use current DOE funds for the program.

McMillan's complaint was pure pique, but Blair's complaint worried me. I had assumed the BOE had the authority to adopt the program. I turned to my staff.

"Wayne, is Blair right?" I asked Wayne Kimura, one of my analysts.

"We're looking at it," Kimura replied.

"Well, look hard. I want you to find something—a rule, regulation or law which authorizes what we are doing," I said. "Otherwise, we'll have to ask the Legislature to pass a new law, which means that the project will be delayed or killed."

The next morning, my three analysts, Kimura, Janet Kawelo and Neil Miyahira, walked into my office with smiles on their faces.

"We found a law passed in 1972 which authorizes the DOE to develop child-care programs," Wayne said.

"Great," I replied.

"But it's intended for the DOE to develop 'pilot programs,'" Kimura said.

"Does it define a pilot program?" I asked.

"No," he said.

"Good, A-Plus will be the biggest pilot program in state history," I said, grinning.

"What about the funding—do we need an emergency appropriation from the Legislature?" I asked.

"No, the law is broad enough to authorize the DOE to use current operating funds," Kimura said.

"But we think you should ask the governor to request an emergency appropriation anyway," Kawelo said.

"Why?" I asked.

"Well, from what we've heard from some of their staff, many legislators feel left out; they want to get involved in some way," she replied.

"Yes, you know that the entire House and half of the Senate will be running for reelection in 1990.... I think they would like to claim some credit for A-Plus," Miyahira added.

A few months earlier, I had been worried about having to persuade the legislators to grant an emergency appropriation for A-Plus. Now it was apparent to most of them that there was growing public support for the program. Politically, it made sense for them to support the program.

Often, staff members play an important role in picking up this kind of information. Most politicians are only as good as their staffs. Kawelo, Miyahira and

Kimura joined me in 1980 when I chaired the Senate Ways and Means Committee; they were sharp, politically savvy, highly ethical and very loyal. All three would stay on with me until I retired from public office in 2002.

On February 4, 1990, the A-Plus program opened in all public elementary schools. The initial enrollment was approximately 15,000 latchkey children statewide. Parents paid $30 per child per month. The State subsidy per child per month was approximately $25. Within a few months, enrollment reached more than 20,000. In two years, it grew to nearly 28,000.

A-Plus was not a babysitting program; it provided a curriculum of homework, enrichment programs and physical education. Innovation was stressed, and many A-Plus staff developed unconventional methods in carrying out the curriculum.

Surveys indicated that, for the first two consecutive years, the parents gave A-Plus a resounding 96-percent approval rating for quality and affordability. A-Plus was a big hit with the children as well, and many parents shared anecdotes about their children preferring A-Plus to their regular school.

We had completed the A-Plus program in six months. And its enormous success with the parents and children left me with a feeling of great satisfaction.

"Isn't it interesting that some of our worst critics are now working in the program?" Toguchi said, grinning. Indeed, in nearly every school the principal, the vice principal or one of the teachers had taken on the job of running the A-Plus program.

Unrestricted by DOE regulations, many A-Plus staff developed innovative enrichment programs. One principal who ran her school's A-Plus program told of how she got some of her shy immigrant students to open up by having them participate in a Broadway-type play.

Despite A-Plus's success, there was still a residue of resentment among some teachers who felt slighted that the program had been imposed on their schools. And I also heard from some private providers who were upset over losing children to the A-Plus program. One angry private provider from Maui wrote me a scathing letter. It was unfair, she wrote, for her to have to compete against a State-subsidized after-school program. She had been a long-time supporter but vowed she would never support me again.

I understood why the woman was angry. She had a lot of hard work and money invested in her business. Now her own government had established a program that threatened her livelihood. Sixteen years in public office had taught me that there are times when the government's attempt to help the many may hurt the few. This was one of them. I had no answer for this angry citizen. ❖

CHAPTER THIRTEEN

Economy in the Doldrums

Japan Catches a Cold

There was good reason to expect that Hawaiʻi's economy would continue to grow. Since November 1987 the unemployment rate had remained below 3 percent, reaching a low of 1.6 percent in August 1989. In December 1990, the month I was sworn in to my second term as lieutenant governor, the State Department of Labor reported a 1.9-percent unemployment rate. But three events revealed the greatest weakness (and truth) about Hawaiʻi's tourism-dominated economy: It was shaped mainly by national and world forces beyond its control.

The 1991 Gulf War had a devastating impact on world tourism. People simply stopped traveling. Within weeks of Iraq's invasion of Kuwait in August 1990, Hawaiʻi hotel-room occupancy began declining as groups and individuals cancelled their bookings. The rapidly thinning pedestrian traffic on Waikīkī streets attested to the war's impact.

The war aggravated the ongoing Mainland economic recession. In 1992, President George H.W. Bush had found out that leading the nation to victory in war was no guarantee of victory at the polls. Angered by and suffering from the poor state of the national economy, the American voters rejected Bush's bid for reelection. "It's the economy, stupid," was the catchphrase when William J. Clinton, the comparatively unknown governor from Arkansas, was elected as the 42nd president of the United States.

California was the hardest hit of all the states. In 1992, it was reeling as businesses closed or left the state and thousands of workers lost their jobs. The economy was so bad that the State government was paying its workers with IOUs.

I found it difficult to imagine that the Golden State—with the fifth-largest economy in the world, bigger than those of England and France—had fallen to such a low. This spelled trouble for Hawaiʻi tourism. Previously, the annual total of California visitors to Hawaiʻi had been more than that of all the other states combined. Soon, westbound tourist traffic to Hawaiʻi fell dramatically and would remain flat for nearly a decade.

However, nothing had a greater impact on Hawaiʻi's economy than the Japanese recession. "When Japan catches a cold, Hawaiʻi gets the flu" was an old joke.

There was much truth to it.

For decades, Japanese investment in Hawai'i had played an important role in the state's economic growth. When Japan emerged as a world economic super-power during the 1980s, Japanese investment accounted for nearly 90 percent of all outside investment in Hawai'i. According to a 1989 First Hawaiian Bank report, Japanese investment accounted for $9 billion, or 45 percent of Hawai'i's $21 billion gross State product.

In 1988, an all-time record 6 million tourists visited Hawai'i, and 20 percent were Japanese. The Japanese tourist was an ideal visitor. Compared to Americans, the Japanese could be relied upon to obey our laws more, pay greater deference to the Hawaiian culture, litter the environment less and on average outspend Americans by a margin of $120 to $600 a day.

Like many State and business leaders, I saw Japanese investment as a form of economic diversification: If the Mainland economy went bad, Japanese investment would offset the losses. This had proved to be the case during the 1980s. When the Mainland U.S. went into a recession, Hawai'i hardly seemed affected.

By almost any measure, the growth of the Japanese economy in the 1980s seemed phenomenal. The Japanese, perhaps the only people in the world who can boast without appearing to, held up their economy as the ideal model for the rest of the world.

Given Japan's success, it was hard for Americans to argue. Japan's economy was soaring. America's was in recession. Japanese automakers were thrashing American automakers in the U.S. and world markets. While the Japanese boasted that their corporations provided lifetime employment for their employees, hundreds of thousands of American autoworkers, many of them middle-aged long-time employees, found themselves being laid off.

American congressmen took out their frustrations by wielding sledgehammers and smashing Japanese cars in front of the Capitol lawn. Japanese business and political leaders responded by taking some very un-Japanese potshots at Americans.

In 1986, Prime Minister Yasuhiro Nakasone attributed Japan's success to the country's not having ethnic minorities. Nakasone, considered a friend of the U.S., later clarified his gaffe, stating that he meant to congratulate the U.S. on its economic success *despite* its "problematic" minorities.

In 1993, Prime Minister Keichi Miyazawa added insult to injury when he attributed American economic problems to laziness: "I suspect that American workers have come to lack a work ethic. They do not live by the sweat of their brow."

Nakasone's and Miyazawa's uncharacteristically blunt words echoed what many Japanese felt about America. Nearly a half-century after World War II, Japan had emerged as an economic superpower. To Japanese leaders like Shintaro Ishihara, author of the proudly nationalistic book *The Japan That Can Say No: Why*

Japan Will Rise Among Equals, Japan had been subservient to the United States too long. Ishihara and co-author Akio Morita, Sony Corp. founder and CEO, wrote that Japan was America's equal, although a reader might easily have concluded that they really meant that Japan was superior, at least economically.

The authors berated America for racism and argued that the atomic bomb had not been used on Germany because Germans were white and Japanese were not. They asserted that nations colonized by Japan have been far more successful following liberation than those colonized by the United States. They argued that Japan was equal to the United States; that it should have its own defense forces; that its computer technology was superior to that of all other countries and should be used as a negotiating tool; and that Japan would be the most influential power in dealing with Asian nations.

The book provided an insight into something American economists never seemed to mention when they analyzed Japanese investment in the United States—Japan's growing nationalism. This should not have surprised any American who paid attention to Japanese politics, which I had not.

Most American readers reacted defensively and with anger. Initially, I was taken aback by the tone of the book. But later, as I reread it, I dismissed some of its factual errors and attained a better understanding of its themes. I learned that Ishihara, who was one of Japan's most outspoken nationalists, was the principal author. Grudgingly, I developed a respect for him. Compared to the stiff, boring official protocol shown to me whenever I visited Japan in my capacity as a State legislator and later as lieutenant governor, his candor was refreshing to me. I thought the criticism of racism in America was like the pot calling the proverbial kettle black; Japan, after all, is probably the most ethnocentric nation in Asia, if not the world. I agreed, however, with most of Ishihara's ideas about Japan's sovereignty.

Ishihara seemed very much like an American politician in his manner: blunt and outspoken. He had been a prominent novelist and adventurer before becoming a political leader. He was a big man, broad shouldered and nearly 6 feet tall. He was charismatic and, as brilliant as he was said to be, I sensed that it was his iconoclastic style that made him so popular with the Japanese people.

When I visited him in 2001, he was the governor of Tokyo. He greeted me warmly, dispensing with the customary bow, and shook my hand firmly. I had brought a copy of his book with me. I told him that I had been wondering how many of his predictions had come true since its release in 1991. He chuckled and jokingly lamented the way Morita had ducked for cover after the book was criticized by angry Americans, but noted that he was pleased overall with how Japan had evolved over the past decade. He loved Hawai'i and visited with his family annually for many years. He was a big fan of Nina Kealiiwahamana, one of the great singers of Hawaiian music. He expressed concern over the changes he noticed in Hawai'i. "Too much Japanese investment," I said jokingly. He smiled.

The Japanese began to show the hubris that often develops with long-term success. During the 1980s, Japanese investors seemed arrogant and reckless in their zeal to acquire American real estate. They were offering inflated prices that landowners found hard to turn down for American trophy properties.

Week after week on the Mainland, the news media reported the sale of American landmarks such as the Rockefeller Center and the Pebble Beach Golf Course to Japanese investors, who seemed to have endless supplies of money.

Paying high prices for real estate was not new to Japanese investors. In Tokyo, real estate prices were so high that some Japanese banks offered multigenerational mortgages (unheard of in the U.S.) to buyers. To Japanese investors the depressed American real estate market must have seemed like a fire sale.

The Japanese were paying prices that were so outlandish they flew in the face of common sense. *Surely*, I thought, *their American business advisers, if they have any, must have told them they were paying too much.* The Japanese explanation usually included talk about the "long term" and the "Japanese way." Whether it was intended or not, buying up American properties as they did strongly suggested that Japan was the equal of its former conqueror and occupier.

By 1990, however, the Japanese bubble economy had burst, and Japan slowly descended into a serious recession. Soon Japanese investors were unloading their U.S. properties, and Americans were buying them back at huge discounts.

In the mid-1990s, for example, a prominent kama'āina family that had sold a piece of property to a Japanese corporation for $15 million a few years earlier bought it back for $6 million. Another example was the Hemmeter Building, located across from the State Capitol. It had been purchased by a Japanese corporation for more than $80 million. In 2000, the State purchased the building from the financially strapped corporation for $22.5 million. Today, the building, which has long been designated a historical landmark, is the home of the Hawai'i State Art Museum. If anything, the Japanese recession, which is still lingering at this writing, proved that there is no "Japanese way," that the basic laws of economics are universal in their application.

The Gulf War nearly emptied the streets of Waikīkī, but, as with past economic downturns, recovery from the war's impact was fairly quick. The Japanese recession, however, inflicted at least seven years (1990-97) of economic stagnation on Hawai'i, the longest economic downturn in Hawai'i's history.

As Hawai'i's economy sagged, capitalism's "invisible hand" began to take its toll: Many small businesses struggled to stay afloat, and eventually many that were weak, undercapitalized and inefficient began to flounder and fail. Hotel-room occupancy declined, and room rates were lowered in a desperate attempt to attract tourists.

Japanese investment in Hawai'i dwindled from $9 billion in 1989 to less than $1 billion in 1997.

Construction, which had been one of the pillars of Hawai'i's past economic growth, fell off rapidly. As construction projects were completed and new ones cancelled, thousands of construction jobs disappeared. Around 1990, the construction workforce was at a high of 33,000, but by 1997 it fell to less than 22,000. Hundreds, if not thousands, of Mainland construction workers who had come to Hawai'i during the Mainland recession returned to the Mainland where there was more work. Many local workers found themselves scrambling to make ends meet and avoid repossession of their cars and foreclosure on their homes.

State and county officials have been accused of having being in a state of denial during those years. It was a fair criticism. But politicians were not the only ones in denial; so were most of the State's economists, many business leaders and the public as well. The Japanese had been successful for so long that many believed they could do no wrong.

The reaction of the Hawai'i Visitors Bureau was to ask the Legislature for an additional $1.9 million over its usual budget allocation for increased marketing. Waihee and the Legislature responded by appropriating $6 million. Increased funding for marketing was about the only thing the State could do for Hawai'i's sagging tourism industry.

The appropriation was more symbolic than anything else; the State had to do something to show it supported Hawai'i business. However, even if the $6 million had been $60 million, it still would have made little difference. The reality was that there was nothing the State could do to reverse what was happening to the Japanese economy.

Like most of Hawai'i's government and business leaders and economists, I assumed that history would repeat itself and the economic downturn would be short. Everyone who counted expected a quick turnaround, but it was not to be.

Government Spending

Despite the downturn, in 1994 the State had a $500 million fund balance (down from $1.1 billion in 1991), which was the margin by which revenues exceeded expenditures at the time. This is commonly referred to as a "surplus."

Rather than opt for the tax rebate mandated by the State constitution, Waihee chose to spend down the fund balance and squirrel some of it away as special funds that did not count against the expenditure ceiling. Years later as governor I would tap into these special funds to balance the State budget.

Waihee has been criticized for wasting the $500 million surplus. The truth is that he spent it down on what he deemed were important public needs. He spent $138 million in a partial settlement of the State's ceded-lands dispute with the Office of Hawaiian Affairs and approximately $200 million to buy land for future State housing projects, mostly in Kapolei, the designated Second City.

Unfortunately, most people knew little about the ceded-lands dispute, and buying land in Kapolei with money from the airport fund created a controversy when the federal inspector general ruled it illegal and the State had to reimburse the airport fund with money from the general fund.

Given the poor economy, spending down the surplus made sense if it created jobs and stimulated more economic activity. But the settlement with OHA and the $200 million in land banking did not create the quick, short-term job relief and spending needed at the time. Waihee was not oblivious to this; at his request, the Legislature had approved a $1 billion appropriation for capital improvements to help boost construction.

However, it was the $500 million cash surplus that caught the public's attention. Had Waihee instead used it on nonrecurring costs such as repair and maintenance of the public schools or the University of Hawai'i, for which there was greater support, it is likely the public would have looked on his spending more favorably.

As the economy grew worse, the inevitable search for scapegoats began. Increasingly, businesses, goaded by opportunistic Republican politicians, saw State government as the main cause of their troubles. This struck me as hypocritical, since State laws had basically been the same during the many years businesses had flourished.

In a short time, there was growing criticism against Waihee for increasing the size of the State government. There was more than a grain of truth to this criticism. Between 1986 and 1994, every State department had experienced an increase in personnel; in some, the number of new employees reached double digits.

Ariyoshi had been a frugal manager and had kept a lid on State spending. Waihee, however, was an activist governor. As a college student on the Mainland, he had been actively involved in community organizations serving the urban poor. The experience had a profound impact on his view of the role of State government.

Among the new programs he established were the Community Mental Health Program and Med-QUEST. Med-QUEST was designed to provide managed health-care services to the unemployed poor. Launched in 1994, the program, which would serve 160,000 people, required more than 100 new workers to implement.

Further, the federal courts had issued a number of adverse rulings that required the State to correct the poor conditions in the State prison and mental hospital as well as provide appropriate services to children in special-education programs. The problems could often be traced to understaffing.

Fiscally, I tended to be conservative, but I believed strongly, as former New York Gov. Mario Cuomo once said, "We should have only the government we need—but all the government we need." Waihee's new social programs deserved support because they were intended to do what State government should do—help the poor and the needy.

There was, of course, waste and inefficiency. The two biggest contributors were the restrictions in the collective bargaining contracts and the so-called "warm-body" policy, which, as I explained earlier, over the long term was akin to "featherbedding" and virtually assured that no one would ever be laid off.

Waihee was very generous in granting departmental budget requests for additional staff. This was a mistake. I had learned when I served as chairman of the Senate Ways and Means Committee that department heads had a naturally narrower perspective than the governor and tended to submit inflated budget requests, fully expecting they would be trimmed down later. It was the governor's responsibility to shape the final budget.

During my first term Waihee and I had worked well on the projects he assigned to me. But, as had likely been the case with every lieutenant governor before me, I had no input in developing the State administration's budget or setting its policies for the State government. In eight years, I attended no more than a handful of Cabinet meetings.

I did have control over one office: the Office of the Lieutenant Governor. "Lloyd," I said in 1990, "when my term ends in 1994, I want to leave this office with fewer employees than it had when we started in 1986." In 1994, I took some satisfaction in pointing out to critics that mine was the only State office that had not experienced any staff increases in eight years.

Waihee had treated me fairly, and I appreciated it. During our first term, I refrained from criticizing him or his Cabinet, even when I disagreed strongly. But my first duty was to the State and its people, not to the governor or any other politician. In 1991, a series of troubling events unfolded that pitted loyalty against duty.

Sharon Himeno and the ERS Controversy

Prior to 1989, State law had limited real estate investments to 5 percent of the Employment Retirement System (ERS) trust. Past attempts to increase the ceiling from 5 percent to 10 percent had been rejected on the grounds that real estate investments were high risk and should be kept at a minimum. But there were some who felt the ERS should invest in Hawai'i's real estate market. In 1989, the Waihee administration succeeded in persuading the Legislature to increase the ceiling to 10 percent. It made good economic sense for the ERS to invest more heavily in real estate, Waihee said. Indeed, that same year, the ERS began investing in more real estate than ever before.

Late in 1991, retired Supreme Court Justice Edward Nakamura caused quite a stir by resigning from the ERS board, to which he had been appointed only a few months earlier, saying he could not be a party to the misuse of ERS funds for real estate investments.

Nakamura resigned after a majority of the ERS board approved the $31 million purchase of Wood Ranch, a California golf course. The purchase was proposed by Rodney Inaba, a real estate developer and the friend of ERS board member Gordon Uyeda, who was himself a realtor. Inaba was a controversial figure. One of the few Asian members of the once all-haole Waikiki Yacht Club, he reportedly ran up the Japanese flag on his yacht to express his displeasure with club policies or haole members he did not like.

(One member, Robert Hall, was so infuriated by Inaba's in-your-face style that one day, in a fit of rage, he pulled out a pistol and shot Inaba. Fortunately, Hall was inebriated and Inaba sustained only a leg wound. Four others suffered minor wounds from stray bullets. Hall had the presence of mind to hire David Schutter, Hawai'i's top criminal defense lawyer. Schutter pulled off one of his courtroom miracles, persuading the jury to acquit Hall of attempted murder charges on the grounds that the wine Hall had drunk prior to the shooting contained a substance that caused a chemical imbalance, altering his judgment.)

Nakamura's resignation brought to light a series of questionable real estate deals previously approved by the ERS board. There were two political insiders involved in the real estate transactions: Sharon Himeno, wife of Attorney General Warren Price, and Yukio Takemoto, who as director of the Department of Budget and Finance sat on the ERS board as an ex-officio voting member.

After the real estate investment ceiling was raised to 10 percent, the law firm of Okamoto Himeno & Lum took over the legal work for ERS real estate investments that had been previously done by the attorney general's office. Himeno was the daughter of developer Stanley Himeno. Ken Okamoto was the husband of Sandy Himeno, Price's administrative assistant and Sharon's sister. Between 1989 and 1992, Okamoto Himeno & Lum were paid more than $600,000 by the ERS.

Takemoto persuaded the ERS board to hire the real estate firm Marcus & Associates, whose chairman, Marcus Nishikawa, was his good friend, as its real estate agent.

The most egregious real estate deal came in 1989 when the ERS financed a proposal by Stanley Himeno to buy Centrepoint, a California warehouse complex. Because Sharon Himeno was a director of her father's company, there was an obvious conflict of interest, and Hoe Yap and Sugimoto—Waihee's former law firm—was hired to do the legal work.

At some point, the ERS was persuaded to buy Centrepoint from Stanley Himeno's company. Ernst & Young, a CPA firm that had done work for Himeno, appraised the property for the ERS board at $26.2 million. The ERS offered Himeno's company $26 million. Himeno quickly accepted, and the sale was closed. A short while later, the ERS trustees learned that Himeno had bought the Centrepoint property for only $23 million and had arranged for back-to-back closings. Thus, Himeno had borrowed the $23 million from the ERS to buy Centrepoint and then sold it to the ERS for $26 million, making a $3 million profit in a matter of minutes.

This was the kind of deal that Nakamura found objectionable. Given the players involved in each ERS real estate transaction, it seemed the chances of dealing with the ERS board were very good for those with the right connections.

Like most people, I learned of this after Nakamura resigned. His resignation proved damaging to the administration. I felt troubled by it but said nothing publicly.

In February 1993, Waihee nominated Sharon Himeno to the Hawai'i Supreme Court. I was stunned. Considering the controversy stirred up by Nakamura's resignation, I found the appointment inexplicable.

I had no problems with Waihee appointing a political insider like Himeno to the Supreme Court. Every governor (and president) wants to leave behind a court which shares his or her judicial philosophy. In fact, America's history is replete with examples from John Adams to Franklin D. Roosevelt and, most recently, George W. Bush's attempts to "pack the court."

In Himeno's case, the crucial question was whether she was the best-qualified person for the job.

Soon it became clear that she was not. By most accounts, she was considered an average lawyer. She had not authored any scholarly legal writings by which her legal scholarship could be evaluated. And she was only 36 years old—to me, much too young to have acquired the kind of meaningful life experiences I wanted to see in a Supreme Court justice.

Sharon Himeno was clearly a political insider. Both she and Warren Price had served as co-chairs of Waihee's political campaign. Waihee had appointed Himeno to the Land Use Commission and subsequently to the Land Board—the two State entities that are critical to land development in Hawai'i. Himeno had furthermore parlayed her political connections into getting her law firm selected to provide legal work for the ERS board, earning lucrative fees.

Daughters (and sons) should not be punished for the sins of their fathers. Nevertheless, she was a director of her father's company. Himeno's father's deal with the ERS was not illegal, but given her connections to some members of the ERS Board and the governor, it fueled the impression that she was a "player" in the world of politics—and one who would use her political influence for her own purposes.

There was one other reason—which I never mentioned publicly although it troubled me greatly—that I opposed her appointment: Himeno had failed to protect the governor from his own misjudgment. Waihee is one of the most astute politicians I know, but on Himeno's appointment he badly misread the public and the Senate.

Himeno should have known her nomination would be a hard sell for the governor. Had she been thinking about him and the legacy he would leave after his final term, she would have refused the appointment or asked that her nomination be withdrawn when it became apparent there was strong opposition. Governors are human and have moments when they suffer lapses in judgment. One of the roles of those who have the governor's confidence—the members of his or her so-called "kitchen cabinet"—is to advise the governor against his missteps. Himeno's failure to protect Waihee suggested she did not possess the wisdom one would expect from a member of the State's highest court.

For most lawyers, the thought of one day bringing a case before a justice whose confirmation they opposed can be intimidating. The Hawai'i Bar Association Committee added to those fears by voting 12 to 4 to support Himeno's confirmation. A few young lawyers, however, led by attorney James Bickerton, began soliciting signatures for a petition to oppose Himeno's nomination. Not surprisingly, they were having a difficult time getting other lawyers to sign.

For several days, I struggled with the thought of openly opposing the nomination. I did not want to hurt Waihee, who had treated me fairly and with whom I had developed a good personal relationship. Moreover, I had a high regard for Warren Price, and I knew that my cordial relationship with him would be damaged if I opposed his wife. But after much soul-searching, I decided to speak out. Loyalty should never trump duty.

I was scheduled to speak to the Maui Rotary Club in Spreckelsville on February 17, 1993. The night before, I decided to speak about the Himeno nomination and the judicial selection process. I struggled writing the speech, feeling as if I was walking on eggshells. Finally, at about 3 in the morning, I finished it, satisfied that it expressed my feelings on Himeno without being disrespectful to Waihee. The speech was covered by *Star-Bulletin* reporter Richard Borreca on February 22, 1993:

> Lt. Gov. Ben Cayetano today called for a new process to appoint judges, saying the nomination of private trial attorney Sharon Himeno to the State Supreme Court raised more questions than it answers.
>
> … Cayetano did not endorse Himeno, and he devoted a third of his speech to detailing her close political connections to Waihee and the Democratic establishment.…
>
> She is an acknowledged member of the governor's kitchen cabinet and close personal friend.…
>
> She is the godchild of the sitting chief justice of the State Supreme Court.…
>
> Her law firm received lucrative legal work from the $4 billion State employee retirement system and had represented numerous businesses that do business with the State.
>
> The key question is whether the nominee—in spite of her political connections—is the best qualified to serve on the court.… If she is not, then her political connections take greater significance.
>
> Cayetano called the courts a "last refuge for justice, where

decisions should be free of politics.

"The public deserves to have the most capable legal talent sitting on the Supreme Court ... It is not just a matter of finding people who are intelligent. It is a matter of finding individuals who demonstrate they possess wisdom and fairness, strength of character, depth of experience, maturity and compassion."

The reaction was strong. I received dozens of telephone calls, most of them from lawyers. One of the organizers of the petition told me that my speech had broken the dam and that more lawyers were signing the petition. Even strong supporters of the governor called to express their agreement and lament the appointment.

When queried by the news media about my speech, Waihee was gracious. "We have a relationship where we are free to express our convictions.... As has been the case in the past, he occasionally states a position that I may disagree with, and I don't have a problem with that," he said.

At the Senate hearing the next day, the testimony supporting Himeno from lawyers, friends and law groups was reported as "overwhelming."

Within a few days, however, opposition to the appointment was spreading statewide. At a community meeting in Mānoa, nearly 100 residents, most of them older Japanese Americans, met with State Sen. Ann Kobayashi and Rep. Brian Taniguchi and unanimously opposed Himeno's appointment. Kobayashi described the residents' mood as "not only a feeling of outrage but of embarrassment."

In an unprecedented move, the University of Hawai'i Professional Faculty Forum, representing all 10 UH campuses, went on record to oppose the nomination.

In a significantly damaging blow to Himeno's nomination, two well-respected veteran trial lawyers, Ed Nakamura and Richard Stifel, stepped forward in opposition. Stifel, who was Himeno's supervisor in the litigation section of the law firm of Goodsill Anderson Quinn, was considered one of the deans of Hawai'i's insurance defense trial lawyers. Ill with terminal cancer, Stifel telephoned Bickerton, whom he had also supervised at the Goodsill law firm, and asked him to bring the petition to his hospital room so he could sign it. Word that the dying Stifel had signed the petition prompted former Supreme Court justice Ed Nakamura to sign as well.

According to Bickerton, my Spreckelsville speech and the opposition of Stifel and Nakamura were the two big factors that broke the ice and encouraged more lawyers to step forward to oppose Himeno's confirmation. A few days later, Bickerton told the news media that he expected more than 300 hundred lawyers to sign the petition.

On February 22, 1993, Senate President James Aki told the news media that the Senate would reject Himeno's nomination. There were already 13 votes against the nomination. "The 13 are solid and there is a possibility of four more negative votes," said Aki, who also said he would urge Waihee to withdraw the appointment.

Himeno, of course, could have spared the governor much grief by taking it upon herself to withdraw. She did not. Waihee, who had been urged by some of his key Cabinet members to pull back Himeno's nomination, would do so only if Himeno asked him. She did not, and Waihee, who by then must have known the votes weren't there, not surprisingly stood by her. The Senate responded by voting 17 to 7 to reject her appointment.

The Senate vote was an embarrassment for Waihee, but it wasn't over. The antics of Himeno and Yukio Takemoto at the ERS had caught the attention of a reform-minded State senator from Hilo, Richard Matsuura. Matsuura, who had spent two years in India as a missionary for his church, was highly idealistic.

In May 1993, the Senate established an investigative committee chaired by Matsuura to investigate the Waihee Administration's procurement practices and its actions at the Employees Retirement System. After Senate staffers tried to question witnesses at their homes, an angry Waihee called the investigation a "witch hunt" that was "reminiscent of McCarthyism."

I had been very concerned with how the ERS board was conducting its real estate transactions, but the procurement issues were complicated and unclear. Moreover, in the aftermath of the Senate's rejection of Himeno in February, *Honolulu Advertiser* reporter Ken Kobayashi wrote a story in which he raised the question of whether I was trying to distance myself from Waihee to better my chances in the upcoming 1994 gubernatorial election. As usual, the news media never gave any politician credit for acting out of principle. However, I did not want to add any more fuel to that kind of speculation. And so I decided that as much as possible I would not comment on the Senate investigation.

At the center of the ERS real estate deals and the procurement issues was Waihee's finance director, Yukio Takemoto. Takemoto was part of a cabal of young professionals who seemed to think nothing of doing favors for friends as long as they weren't illegal. Himeno and Takemoto had done tremendous damage to Waihee's public image in February. And now in April 1993, the controversy was dredged up again. Takemoto was the central figure of the Senate investigation. I was disgusted and angry but said nothing publicly. Finally, a reporter buttonholed me one day and asked for my opinion of the Senate investigation. "The governor," I replied tersely, "should fire Takemoto." It was my only public statement about the investigation.

Eventually, the public pressure generated by the Senate hearings proved too much, and Takemoto, unlike Himeno, spared Waihee further grief by resigning, asserting firmly that he had done nothing wrong. (Takemoto would land on his feet. He was quickly hired by the Bishop Estate at a salary twice what he earned as a State director.)

Looking back, I often wondered how different it might have been if Waihee had appointed Warren Price instead of Sharon Himeno to the Supreme Court. The older, more mature Price was respected by his peers, had established himself as a fine trial lawyer, had been a good attorney general and shared Waihee's judicial philosophy. He would have been easily confirmed, and there would have been little, if any, controversy.

(Years later, I found out that Waihee, with less than two years left in his final term, wanted badly to appoint the first woman to the Hawai'i State Supreme Court. That would have added a nice touch to his legacy. Unfortunately, he nominated the wrong woman.).

If Waihee was angry or disappointed with me, he never showed it. Our relationship remained cordial and respectful. He had accomplished much as governor, particularly in the area of social services for the poor and disadvantaged. And, as Bud Smyser had written, he had done more for the Hawaiian people than any other governor. But the Himeno-Takemoto controversies were blots on his record. History, of course, will be the final judge of his governorship.

As the 1994 gubernatorial election got closer, I was pleasantly surprised to get Justice Nakamura's support. I felt honored to have such a highly respected and dedicated public servant behind me. He would join Frank Padgett, my former boss and also a former Supreme Court justice, in a television ad endorsing my candidacy. During one of our conversations, Nakamura revealed his feelings about the ERS controversy and concerns about the Democratic Party: "These young Democrats forget where they came from, they're no different from the haole Republicans we kicked out in 1954 ... and I'm upset and embarrassed that most of them are Japanese." ❖

CHAPTER FOURTEEN

Dad

The Move to Mililani

I n January 1991, Lorraine and I separated. She moved to Mission Viejo, California, to stay with relatives. Nearly three years of marriage counseling and several failed attempts at reconciliation would follow. In 1996, after a six-year separation, our 38-year marriage ended in divorce. I had been 18 and she 17 when we married in 1958. I had spent a lot of time trying to save the world, but I could not save my marriage. With Lorraine gone, Brandon and Janeen out on their own and Samantha a sophomore at the University of Washington, Dad and I were living alone in our Mililani home, which was little more than a year old. We had used the equity in our Pearl City home and our savings to buy a lot and build on it in Mililani. It was supposed to be our final home. I expected we would live out our lives there. But it was not to be.

After Dad retired in 1972, I had invited him to live with us. His retirement income was not much—about $1,000 a month, $898 from Social Security and a mere $105 from his union pension after 10 years at the Flamingo Hilton in Las Vegas. He'd have a tough time making it alone. It didn't matter. I wanted Dad to live with us, to be with his grandchildren again. Besides, I was his oldest son, and it was only right that I take care of him.

Dad enjoyed playing cards, usually with a small group of retirees. Four or five times a week, he would take the bus from our home in Pearl City to ʻAʻala Park in downtown Honolulu, where he'd either go to a nearby pool hall or play cards at the outdoor tables near the canal. His friends were elderly Filipino men, most of them bachelors whose families were still in the Philippines. In the 1970s, ʻAʻala Park was a relatively safe area; the drug addicts, dealers, pimps and prostitutes had not yet proliferated to the levels of today.

His senior-citizen bus pass—one of Frank Fasi's better ideas—gave him mobility. With it, he could go wherever the bus went. In Pearl City, the bus stop was about a block away.

I could tell when Dad lost most of his money. He'd stay at home and wait until his checks came in. Then he'd go to ʻAʻala Park again. He never asked me for money to play cards, although there were times when I'd give him some because I knew he got restless staying home. When he won, he'd usually come home with something, almost always food—roast pork, Chinese noodles or fresh fish from Tamashiro Fish Market in nearby Pālama.

Dad was not the type to join a senior citizens' club. Several times when I suggested it, he'd laugh and say, "Oh, son, I feel silly there. I no like that kind singing and dancing." Once I took him to a senior citizens' club in Pālama, and I could tell immediately that the sight of elderly men playing 'ukuleles and singing with elderly women dancing the hula was not Dad's cup of tea.

He loved to watch boxing. Before I left for Los Angeles in 1963, he and I would go to nearly every boxing match that was held at the old Civic Auditorium. After he retired and moved in with us, I'd often remind him when there was boxing on television, and tape-record it for him to watch later. At times we would watch together.

Our new home in Mililani was not convenient for Dad. Unlike in Pearl City, where there was a bus stop right around the corner from us, our Mililani house was in a gated community, a long walk to the nearest bus stop. After we moved there, Dad frequently got home near midnight, and several times he got home near mid-morning. Once when I asked why he was so late, he replied, "Oh, my friend drop me off." Eventually I found out there was no "friend"; Dad was just having a hard time remembering how to get home and kept getting lost.

Dad was in good physical shape for an 82-year-old man, but I was concerned that the walk was too long for him, especially at night. I began juggling my schedule so I could drop him off at 'A'ala Park in the morning and pick him up in the early afternoon.

Dementia

It got harder because I got busier. In late 1991, for example, Waihee asked me to chair the Governor's Task Force on Education Governance. The task force, which was comprised of legislators, a few members of the Board of Education and private citizens, held hearings on every major island. To my surprise the hearings were usually packed with people and often ended late at night. When I went to Neighbor Island hearings I'd almost always have to stay overnight. The burden fell on Ken to watch Dad while I was gone. Ken would pick him up, fix dinner and keep him company, but he did not stay overnight.

Nevertheless, Dad seemed to be getting along well. But one night in mid-1992, at about 1 a.m., I was awakened by a telephone call from the police officer in charge of the Wai'anae Police Station.

"Is your father named Bonifacio?" he asked.

"Yes …" I replied anxiously.

"We found your father walking on the road near Mākua Beach."

My heart sank. "Is he all right?" I asked anxiously.

"Yes, but he is a little disoriented."

"What happened?" I asked.

"Apparently, he was robbed by some men and left at Mākua."

"Mākua? My God!" I said. "I'll be right there."

A dozen thoughts streaked through my head as I sped off to Wai'anae. *Mākua Beach? How did he get there?* I'd been to Mākua late at night with some friends when I was in high school. It was a remote, desolate area located at the western tip of O'ahu, where the two-lane highway ends and becomes a gravel road. The nearest home was a few miles away. There were no streetlights. At night the area was pitch dark. During high tide, the ocean water sometimes overflowed the road in certain places. It was a place where car thieves stripped stolen cars and left the chasses or people dumped used refrigerators, stoves and other junk. It was a place where crimes were committed and bodies dumped. Mākua was not a safe place for anyone, much less an elderly person, to be alone late at night.

When I got to the police station, Dad was sitting on a bench, a Band-Aid on the left side of his forehead.

"Daddy, are you okay?" I asked anxiously.

"Oh, I'm fine, son," he replied, grinning slightly. I turned to the police sergeant, a tall, wiry Portuguese-Hawaiian man standing next to Dad.

"He's got a small bump on his head ... we had one of our paramedics look him over, and it looks like he's okay."

"What happened?" I asked.

"One of our officers patrolling the area found him walking on the gravel road by the beach. Your father told him that some guys offered him a ride home and instead they took him way into Mākua. They took his wallet and his wristwatch. The only thing they left him was his senior-citizen bus pass; that's how we figured out he was your father. We got your telephone number through the telephone company's operator."

"Did they beat him?" I asked, pointing to Dad's forehead, anger welling up in me.

"Well, your father said that they didn't and that he fell down. At this point we don't know, because he seems disoriented."

"Are you going to investigate this?" I asked.

"We don't have much to go on. Your father hasn't been able to tell us much."

Turning to Dad, I noticed there was sand in his hair. "Daddy, how come you have sand in your hair?" I asked as I brushed some off with my fingers.

"Oh, son, I fall down by the beach," he replied, smiling sheepishly.

Those bastards, I said to myself, feeling even angrier as I imagined Dad walking lost in the pitch-darkness trying to find his way out.

Later that morning, I took Dad to his doctor. I told him about the incident and Dad's increased forgetfulness, that our move to Mililani seemed to have made it harder for Dad to get home by himself and that he seemed confused at times.

He examined Dad and found him in good health. "Your father is at the age where they can become forgetful and more easily confused. He may have a mild case of dementia," the doctor said.

"Is dementia the same as Alzheimer's disease?" I asked.

"Alzheimer's is a form of dementia," he replied.

"What causes dementia?" I asked.

The medical profession, he explained, understood the main cause of dementia, the erosion of brain cells. "We can tell you what the causes and symptoms are, but we have no good answers on how to treat it. From what you've told me I think your father may have a mild case. He may forget things but he still recognizes you and your brother and can converse lucidly with you."

"Will it get worse?" I asked.

"Probably. Except for rare cases, dementia is irreversible. But if you can keep your father fairly free from stress it would help. With care, your father may be able to live out his life in reasonable comfort at home."

"Do you think what happened to him at Mākua will affect his condition?" I asked.

"That's the kind of stressful experience that may make it worse. We'll have to wait and see."

Over the next three or four months, Dad's mental condition began to deteriorate. One morning, as I was getting ready to leave for the office, I noticed the front door was wide open and Dad was gone. My security driver, who was parked outside waiting in the State car, told me he saw Dad walking out the gate. I got into the car and asked my driver to drive by the bus stop so I could pick up Dad. He wasn't there. I saw the bus arrive at the stop, so I knew Dad was not on it. We drove through the neighborhood. After 10 or 15 minutes, I saw Dad. His brow was wet with perspiration. He was lost. I got out of the car to get him. An elderly Japanese man who was out in his yard called over to me.

"Hello, Mr. Cayetano, is your father all right?" he said.

"Yes," I replied.

"Oh, good. You know, I've seen him walking by here several times. At first I thought he was just taking a walk, but later I thought he looked like he was lost," the man said.

Yes, Dad was lost. In trying to find the bus stop, he had taken a wrong turn. The neighborhood had become a maze for him. When I found him he seemed exhausted and dehydrated.

It would not be the last time Dad got lost in the neighborhood. One evening he walked out of the house while I was taking a shower. He left at about 8 p.m., but I did not notice until I went to his room an hour later. I hurried out of the house and looked down the street, but he was nowhere to be seen. I telephoned Ken immediately, then got in my car and drove around the neighborhood. Ken drove over and we searched different areas. While Ken continued to look, I went home and telephoned the Wahiawā police and reported Dad as a missing person. I asked Ken to wait at my house while I drove to ʻAʻala Park to look for Dad.

Around midnight I got a telephone call from the police. They had found him. A police officer had seen him walking aimlessly in another part of Mililani a few miles away from our home. I telephoned Ken and told him the news. I told him not to come over and to get some sleep. He came over anyway.

Subsequently, Dad got lost three or four times in the Mililani area. The Wahiawā police came to know him well. He wasn't the only senior citizen they had on file; there were several others who often got lost. The police were great, very professional, understanding and patient.

Then came the time when Dad made the 6 o'clock news. That day, I had left him at home alone. Ken had taken off from work for an appointment with his doctor. He agreed that after his appointment he would check on Dad and stay with him until I got home.

I was at a luncheon and had asked my security officer to call my home to check on Dad, or "Grandpa," as they referred to him. No one answered the phone. Finally, I got in touch with Ken. He was at my house. When Ken had gotten there earlier that morning, Dad was gone and the front door was wide open. It was now clear to me that we could not leave Dad alone even for a few hours.

Ken said he was going to drive through the neighborhood to see if he could find Dad. After the luncheon I cancelled my appointments and headed home. We drove through the section of the neighborhood where Dad had gotten lost before, but he wasn't there. Finally, I telephoned the police and reported Dad missing.

Time is critical when an elderly person is reported missing. As a matter of policy, the police issue an "APB" or "all-points bulletin" after a number of hours (I think it is six) have passed. And so Dad, along with his photo, made the 6 o'clock news. Around 9 p.m., I got a call from the police. Someone had reported seeing Dad walking around in Pauoa, and the police picked him up. Pauoa is more than 20 miles from our home.

"Congratulations, Daddy, you're famous now; everyone knows who you are," I said with a chuckle as I hugged him.

"How did you get from Mililani to Pauoa?"

"Oh, I use my bus pass," he said with a slight grin.

I decided to limit Dad's mobility. The bus pass was a great service for senior citizens, but not for those suffering from dementia. I persuaded Dad to let me hold his pass.

By this time it was clear that Ken and I should consider placing Dad in an adult day care center or, as a last resort, a residential adult-care home. I was reluctant to put Dad in a residential care home. He had lived with me for more than 20 years, and I couldn't bear to shuttle him off to live with strangers. I suggested to Ken that we enroll him in a day care center and take turns picking him up after work. Moreover, Samantha was returning home for the summer, and she could help out. Ken agreed. The care home would be a last resort.

Over the next few months, Dad's condition slowly worsened. One morning at about 2 a.m., I heard voices coming from Dad's room. The door was slightly open and I peeked in. Dad was the only one in the room, and within a few moments I realized he was having a conversation with Mom—a one-way conversation, of course, since Mom had died in 1978.

"Daddy, who are you talking to?" I asked, as I opened the door fully.

"Oh, your mother…." he said before catching himself. "Oh … I was just talking *about* your mother." For a moment he had an odd look on his face. He even sounded different, almost mischievous. It would not be the last time he would be delusional.

Later that day, I telephoned Ken and told him what had happened. Ken added that he had noticed Dad's personal hygiene had deteriorated.

All of his adult life, Dad had been fastidious about his grooming, his dress and appearance. Now he was losing even that.

"I think we just have to help him by reminding him to do those things," I replied.

"You remind him; he listens only to you. Whenever I do it, he gets annoyed with me," Ken said.

It was true. Dad tended to ignore what anyone else in our family told him. So a new part of my daily routine was to remind Dad to take care of his personal hygiene, as if he was a little boy again. There were some light moments.

There were times when Dad would pretend to bathe by just running the shower. Eventually I caught him at it when he walked out of the bathroom still fully clothed. Thereafter I had to stand outside the bathroom and threaten to watch him shower to get him to do it. Once, he emerged from the bathroom with his head still lathered with soap. He looked as if he was wearing a hat of some kind. When we saw him, Samantha and I broke out in laughter.

A year earlier, Dad had been in remarkable physical condition for someone his age. But his numerous wanderings, sometimes for hours, and the stress he experienced had drained him physically and mentally. He had become noticeably weaker and tired easily.

Samantha had helped us get through the summer, but in early August 1992, she left to begin her junior year at the University of Washington. Without his bus pass, it was harder for Dad to get around. Moreover, he tired more easily, and it was difficult for him to walk long distances. There were no major incidents, and Dad would continue to live with me through the 1992 holiday season. In March or April 1993, I enrolled him in an adult day care program in nearby Wahiawā.

The center was operated by a church. The premises were clean, and the people who ran it seemed caring and competent. I hoped that this arrangement would allow us to keep Dad home.

After only a month in the day care center, however, a staff person told me that they could not care for Dad anymore; he needed a higher level of care. There were no other options but to place Dad in a residential adult-care home. After a wait of several months, we found a vacancy at a care home in Pearl City. The home was clean and, according to the Department of Human Services, the caregiver had a good record of caring for her "residents" (they were never called "patients"). The care home was only a half-mile away from our former home in Pearl City, and only a 10-minute drive from both Ken's and my homes. Dad would be one of five residents who lived there.

The adult residential care home program is a by-product of the policy adopted in the 1960s to deinstitutionalize services for the elderly and mentally ill. It was seen as a more humane and compassionate and less costly way of providing services by nonprofessionals to adults who needed a certain level of care.

Back then, the overwhelming majority—perhaps 95 percent or more—of the adult residential care home operators were Filipino immigrants. Operating a care home entailed sacrificing the privacy of one's home—a sacrifice few locals were willing to make. Nor was it lucrative. Clearly, the operators were underpaid, although there was no doubt that the program was indispensable for families of all ethnic groups who were unable to afford private nurses or expensive home care.

Ken and I visited Dad as often as we could. I visited at least once a week; Ken was there more often, usually stopping by after work. The care home operator seemed very diligent. During the first couple of months, Dad seemed to be doing fine. But by the third month, he had become restless and increasingly incontinent.

The holiday season was tough for all of us. Ken told me that each time he visited Dad, he asked Ken to take him home. He never said it to me. On several occasions, Dad tried to leave the care home, but each time, the care home operator dissuaded him from doing so.

Several days before Christmas, I got a telephone call from a former neighbor, who lived a half-block from our old home in Pearl City.

"Mr. Cayetano," she said, "your father was just taken by ambulance to the hospital."

"What happened?" I asked.

"Well, I saw him walk past our house several times; he seemed lost. And then he stumbled onto our driveway and collapsed. I rushed outside to help him, and he looked like he was really dehydrated. He was breathing hard and seemed very weak and disoriented, so I called the ambulance. One of the paramedics told me he thought your father suffered a stroke."

"Thank you so much for helping him," I said.

"I hope he'll be all right," she replied.

I telephoned Ken and rushed to the hospital. Ken, who worked in the immediate area, got there before me. "The doctor said Dad had a stroke," Ken said. "It looks like he'll be all right, but they'll know for sure after they run all these tests. He's going to be here for a while."

A few days later, Dad's doctor told us that the stroke itself was mild but that Dad had developed a respiratory infection which he feared might lead to pneumonia. From the sound of Dad's cough, I could tell he was congested.

They had tied restraints on both of his hands to prevent him from removing the tubes that had been inserted up his nose and down his throat to help aspirate him as needed. When we visited, Dad would often motion us to have the tubes removed. He was clearly uncomfortable with them.

On New Year's Eve, I visited Dad at about 8:30 p.m. Ken had been there for a couple of hours and left shortly before I got there. The tubes in Dad's throat and nose made it difficult for him to speak, so I did most of the talking, and he would either smile or nod in response. I told him his favorite story: the one Mom had told me about the time he and his Filipino friends were attacked by a gang of local boys near Maunakea Street and how Dad was the only Filipino still standing, slugging it out, when the cops finally arrived. I had relived this story dozens of times with Dad in the past and it always delighted him—it was a badge of his manhood. This time it was clear he didn't remember much of it.

Finally, around 10:30 p.m., I got up to leave. "Daddy, I have to go now. Tomorrow I'll come back and we can watch football on TV, okay?" I said as I squeezed his hand. He smiled and nodded.

As I stepped out of Dad's room, I noticed there were only two nurses on duty, both seated at the nurses' station. Usually, there were at least five or six. That night the floor was eerily empty. I stopped at the nurses' station.

"Nurse, my father's congestion seems worse; would you check on him and see if he needs to be aspirated?" I asked.

"Oh, yes, we aspirate him every two hours, but I'll check on him in a few minutes," she replied.

"How do you know when it's time to do it?" I asked.

"There's a light on the master panel which goes on," she said, pointing to the panel.

"Where's everyone? Usually there are at least five or six of you," I asked.

"It's New Year's Eve ... I guess some of them took off," she replied.

"Well, please check on my father," I reminded her.

"Don't worry, I'll do it in a few minutes," she replied.

I drove home and went straight to bed.

At about 8 the next morning I received a telephone call from one of the resident doctors on duty at the hospital.

He was sorry, he said, to inform me that Dad had passed away early in the morning. I was stunned. I had just spoken to Dad the night before. Except for his congestion, he'd seemed stable. How could this have happened? How did he die? I asked. He had died from asphyxiation, the doctor said. It was a polite, clinical way of saying that Dad had suffocated on his own vomit. He was 85 years old.

Three or four days later, someone from the hospital called and asked if I would drop over to sign the Medicaid application that had been filled out for Dad so they could process it. The image of Dad, hands tied to his bed, struggling for breath when help was only a few yards away was still fresh in my mind. I had not intended to say anything, but the call upset me. I took a deep breath and calmly expressed my displeasure about the lack of nurses on the floor that night. I said I wanted to see the hospital record to determine the times Dad had been aspirated before I signed anything. They never called me back. Like most Asian immigrants, Dad frowned on asking for welfare. Death spared him from being the first in the Cayetano family to do so.

I once read a news account about a son in Chicago who was arrested for chaining his elderly father in the bathroom before he left for work. The story provoked quite a discussion among my staff, who were all disgusted that a son could treat his father so cruelly. After struggling for more than two years to care for Dad, however, I felt the situation must have been more complicated than the news media reported. The son must have loved his father; otherwise he would have abandoned him as others have their parents. Perhaps he couldn't afford a nursing home or got no help from his siblings. He must have been desperate. I wondered what I would have done if I had been living with Dad in a big city like Chicago. ❖

CHAPTER FIFTEEN

Governor

The 1994 Primary

Until I was reelected as lieutenant governor in 1990, I never gave serious thought to running for governor. My political goals were short term. I rarely looked beyond the term I was serving. Ever since my election to the State House in 1974, I had treated each term as if it would be my last. I believed that holding public office was a great privilege, but I did not covet the office.

I knew of others who developed ambitious plans for higher office. They usually had one thing in common—they walked gingerly when it came to making tough political decisions, at times compromising their core beliefs to ensure their political survival or gain. For me, that was too high a price to pay for holding public office.

Jack Seigle, who had masterminded our come-from-behind win against Eileen Anderson in 1986, thought I could win. "I think the time is right," he said. "You've won every one of your past elections because you've been able to get good support from the different ethnic groups. In fact, you are one of the few [Filipino-American politicians] who's been able to get strong AJA support. That vote along with the Filipino vote will give you a good shot at winning the Democratic primary. Frankly, I think you should go for it. I don't think things will get any better for you," Seigle concluded.

As Seigle spoke, I recalled Mike Tokunaga's words after Waihee and I won the 1986 election: "Ben, we AJAs had our chance with Ariyoshi, now it's the Hawaiians' turn with Waihee—you be patient ... the Filipinos will have their turn next time."

I had been patient. I had supported Waihee on most issues and opposed him on a few big ones. But unlike some past lieutenant governors, I did not run against the governor, nor had I harbored any intention of doing so. I liked Waihee, and he had treated me fairly.

Furthermore, I was about as well qualified as Ariyoshi and Waihee had been when they ran for governor. I had served 12 years in the Legislature and had held important posts such as chairman of the Senate Ways and Means Committee and majority policy leader. And I had a record the public could scrutinize, including my investigation into the heptachlor milk crisis and the founding of the popular A-Plus After-School Program.

If I ran, I would have the best political analyst in Hawai'i. Seigle, a tall, urbane haole who always looked as if he could use a suntan, had been recommended to me by banker Walter Dods for the 1986 election. Seigle had established himself as the dean of Hawai'i's political consultants, working closely with the renowned national political consultant Joe Napolitan to strategize remarkable come-from-behind election victories for Jack Burns and George Ariyoshi. Seigle and Napolitan had never lost a governor's election in Hawai'i. In 1968, Napolitan had helped Hubert Humphrey erase a 17-point deficit, only to lose to Richard Nixon in the closest presidential election in American history. My win over Eileen Anderson in 1986 gave me a firsthand look at Seigle's political skills.

Looking over the potential Democratic competition, I felt I had a good shot at winning the primary. In 1992, I decided to run. My feelings had evolved to the point that I *wanted* to be governor. I remained as idealistic about my political beliefs as I had been when I was first elected in 1974, but it was more than that. Deep in my gut I did not think any other Democrat could beat either Frank Fasi or Pat Saiki.

Charlie Toguchi had resigned as superintendent of education to be my campaign manager. He and I were close friends, and I knew from our days in the Senate that he had great political instincts, was tough in a fight—and, most important, was honest to the core. Toguchi hit it off well with Seigle and Napolitan, and a strong bond of trust and respect developed between among them. The three would plan the strategy for our campaign.

A poll taken by Seigle in 1992 reinforced what the polls we took for the 1990 election had shown: I was rated high marks for independence and honesty, while on the other hand, I was seen by too many as arrogant and brash. In other words, although many voters did not like my style, the majority thought I was a man of good character.

"The voters often consider a candidate's character much more important than his position on issues, especially for the higher offices. That's why Fasi could never win the big race; the majority of the voters did not trust him to be governor," Seigle said. "In your case, some voters may not like you, but most trust you."

"Who was it that said, 'It is better to be feared than loved because love can be easily taken away'?" I joked, paraphrasing Machiavelli's famous words.

"How much do we need to run a competitive campaign?" I asked.

"About 3 million," Seigle answered. "Fasi and Saiki will outspend you [they did]. But we can even things by out-organizing them. The labor unions can help us make up the difference."

"It'll be tough to raise that kind of money," I said.

"Yeah, but if you win the Democratic Primary, the money will come," Seigle replied. "Try to get out front early in your fundraising. If you have a good-sized campaign kitty by 1994, you might scare off other Democrats."

"Right."

"How do your kids feel about your separation from Lorraine? Are they angry? Will they help in the campaign?" Napolitan asked.

"I think they saw it coming, and they hope we can work it out. I haven't been the best father in the world, but they'll be there for me. They always have been. In fact, Samantha is giving up going through the formal graduation ceremony at the University of Washington to come home early to help in the campaign."

"Good. Your family story has always been a big asset in the past, and we have to use it for the campaign," Napolitan replied.

"Ben, a big problem for us is that most people know you mainly from what they read and see on the news. We need to tell them your life story, show the softer side of you. I want to do a half-hour video of you and your family—like we did for Burns [*Catch a Wave*] and Ariyoshi [*The Boy from Kalihi*]. It'll cost a few bucks, but I don't think we can win without it," Seigle said.

"How much will it cost?"

"To produce it, buy television time and bring in Harry Mulheim from San Francisco to help write the script—between $300,000 and $400,000."

"That's a lot of money," I said.

"Yes, but we know it works; it did for Burns and Ariyoshi. Joe and I think it's crucial for your campaign."

"By the way, what is Waihee going to do? Will he help or will he put up someone to run against you?" Napolitan asked.

"I think he'll play it pretty straight and stay neutral in the primary," I responded.

"Let's hope so."

By the end of 1993, we had raised more than $750,000. It was a good start and a good sign that there was support for us out there.

At the time, no other Democrat seemed seriously interested in running. On the other side, the opposition seemed formidable: Frank Fasi, who served as Honolulu's mayor for more than 20 years, would run as an independent (Best Party), and former U.S. Congresswoman Pat Saiki would be the Republican nominee. The two were tough, experienced and smart. I was looking forward to the election.

Early polls showed Saiki holding a big lead. I was in second place, about 30 points behind her, and Fasi was in third, a few points behind me.

There was little difference in our positions on issues. Whether it was education, health care or other social issues, we all sounded alike. To be sure, there were some controversial issues such as same-sex marriage, Hawaiian sovereignty and the economy, but they would not fully emerge until after the 1994 election.

This election would not be about issues.

No one knew Frank Fasi better than Seigle and Napolitan. They had tangled with him several times in the past and beaten him each time. "Focus on organizing, fundraising and getting your message out," Napolitan advised me. "At some point, Fasi will probably have to attack Saiki to move up from third place."

Meanwhile, they wanted me to stay away from getting into controversy and confrontation. "Everyone knows you're a fighter, Ben, but we need to show them you are also a reasonable and compassionate man," Seigle said, grinning.

"Yeah, I don't know if that's possible," Napolitan joked.

We had hoped to get through the Democratic primary without opposition but in July 1994, Jack Lewin, who was Waihee's director of the Department of Health, entered the race. Lewin, I thought, had been one of Waihee's best Cabinet members. Like most haole Democrats in Hawai'i, Lewin was an unabashed liberal. He was the brains behind Waihee's Med-QUEST and Community Mental Health programs. In 1989, Lewin and I were part of a Hawai'i delegation that traveled on a goodwill trip to Israel. During the 10 days we traveled together, I got to know him better. He was articulate, energetic and bright. I had a high regard for him.

There were rumors that he was going to run for governor. I asked him about it. Initially, he told me he was not going to run, only to change his mind a week later. There was talk that he had been urged to run by some of Waihee's close supporters, among them Warren Price and Sharon Himeno. Waihee himself stayed neutral.

It didn't matter. I knew Lewin would be a tough opponent, but I felt confident that I would beat him. I believed my time had come.

"Well, Ben, unless you do something crazy, you should beat him in the primary," Seigle said. "Just be careful what you say about him, because if we can't get him to help us in the general election, we need to at least keep him neutral." That would be easy because I liked and had high respect for Lewin.

On September 20, 1994, I defeated Lewin and four others with 57 percent of the vote. Some of our supporters had been worried that the primary election would sap resources we would need against Fasi and Saiki in the general. As it turned out, the contested primary with Lewin charged up our supporters. With only six weeks between the primary and the November general election, our primary victory gave us much-needed momentum—a head start—over Fasi and Saiki. As they were mustering their campaign workers, our supporters hit the ground running. And Seigle was right—after winning the primary, the money came; we managed to raise the $3 million needed to run a strong campaign.

Mazie Hirono, a former State representative, had won the Democratic primary for lieutenant governor. Hirono had come to Hawai'i from Japan when she was five. She was raised by her mother, attended public schools and graduated from the University of Hawai'i and Georgetown Law School. As a legislator, she had developed a reputation as a strong advocate for consumers. Ethnically, she was a perfect foil to Saiki.

Fasi's running mate was Danny Kaleikini, one of Hawai'i's most popular entertainers. Danny, who had never run for office before, had a great sense of humor. Once a reporter asked him if he and Fasi won the election, what would he do as lieutenant governor if Fasi had a heart attack? After a short pause, Danny said jokingly, "I'd call 911!" prompting laughter from the reporters.

Fred Hemmings was Saiki's running mate. It was an odd pairing. Saiki was a liberal-moderate Republican; Hemmings was a wannabe Newt Gingrich conservative. From our point of view, Hemmings was the perfect choice.

Playing Hardball

Just as Napolitan had predicted, Fasi ran a negative attack campaign against Saiki and me. Fasi always ran hard-hitting campaigns, but his 1994 campaign was particularly nasty. Perhaps it was because he realized that, at age 74, he was facing his last real chance to achieve his longtime dream of becoming Hawai'i's governor in the 1994 election. He was unpredictable. Once, he publicly challenged me to a push-up contest. Even at his age, Fasi had the physique of fitness guru Jack LaLanne. Naturally, I joked my way out of it.

Before resigning as mayor in July 1994, as he had to do in order to run for governor, Fasi decided to fire Jeremy Harris, the City managing director. Fasi had hired Harris, a former Kaua'i County councilman, after Harris was defeated by Tony Kunimura in Kaua'i's 1984 mayoral election. By law, Harris, as managing director, would become acting mayor once Fasi resigned. Thereafter, a special election for a new mayor would be held during the September primary election.

Harris saw this as an opportunity to get back into politics. As acting mayor he would have an advantage over his opponents. But a problem arose that upset Fasi. Harris was trying to recruit City workers and others who had been part of Fasi's campaign organization and were needed for Fasi's gubernatorial campaign. Fasi warned Harris several times not to do it anymore. When Harris persisted, Fasi called him in to tell him he was fired. One account of that meeting portrayed Harris weeping and begging Fasi not to fire him. Another—an apparently embellished version—had Harris not only weeping and begging but hugging Fasi at the knees like Carlo Ricci pleading with Sonny Corleone in the movie *The Godfather*.

A few years after I was elected, I asked Sam Callejo, who had joined my administration as the director of the Department of Accounting and General Services, about the story. Callejo had been Fasi's deputy managing director and had campaigned for Fasi against me. But he was highly respected for his honesty, loyalty and professionalism (Fasi had an excellent Cabinet), and I offered him a Cabinet post.

"Sam, is there any truth to the story?" I asked.

"Well, Harris did not get on his knees and wrap his arms around Fasi's legs," Callejo replied, grinning, "but he did cry and beg to keep his job."

"How do you know?"

"I was there," Callejo said.

"What did Harris say?"

"He went on and on about how if Frank fired him it would hurt his campaign for mayor in the special election and pleaded with Frank for another chance. It was embarrassing."

"What did Fasi say?"

"Well, Frank felt sorry for him and kept him on, which turned out to be a big mistake."

"Why?"

"The day Frank resigned as mayor, he met with the Cabinet and thanked us for our support, and then later the Cabinet walked over with him, Joyce [Mrs. Fasi] and their kids to your office [the Office of the Lieutenant Governor] to show our support as he signed his nomination papers."

"Yeah, I was there to greet him," I reminded Callejo.

"Well, while we were grouped around Frank and Joyce for photos, someone noticed that Jeremy was the only Cabinet member not there. When we got back to City Hall, we were shocked to find that Harris had already moved into Frank's old office and Frank's personal belongings had been put in cardboard boxes piled up in the hallway!"

"The body wasn't even cold and the guy moved in," I chuckled.

"I don't think Frank ever saw the inside of that office again," Callejo said.

"When Harris became acting mayor, why didn't you move up to become managing director?" I asked.

"Harris told the corporation counsel there was no need for a new managing director, that he would serve as both acting mayor and managing director. The guy didn't like me because I had questioned some of the things he done as MD, so I remained as deputy managing director," Callejo replied.

Then he asked me, "Did you ask him for support after he won the mayor's election?"

"Yes, I did, but he told me he had to stay neutral."

"Did he say why?"

"Yeah, he told me that after he lost the mayor's race on Kaua'i, he was devastated emotionally and couldn't get a job. And because Frank hired him when no one else would, he said he owed it to Frank to stay neutral. I understood that kind of loyalty and accepted it at face value," I explained.

"Well, if Jeremy won the mayor's election, we all expected him to help Frank, but after he won, he never did," Callejo said.

"Yeah, I'm not surprised. Our supporters on Kaua'i know him like a book—they told me the guy couldn't get a job because no one could trust him."

Fasi had campaign ideas of his own. Using his daily radio program, he repeated unsubstantiated rumors about my personal life. These were cheap shots that even the news media ignored. On one broadcast, however, Fasi accused me of trying to bribe the owner of an Italian restaurant located in one of the Nauru Towers near Ala Moana Beach Park. This I could not ignore. We quickly called a press conference, and I challenged Fasi to join me in submitting to a lie-detector test given by the FBI. Whoever failed the test would promise to drop out of the governor's race. For once, Fasi was at a loss for words; the restaurant owner said Fasi had misunderstood him, and that ended the matter.

Fasi then turned on Pat Saiki. Using a technique called "morphing," Fasi produced a television spot that showed a photo of Saiki slowly evolving into a photo of Larry Mehau, a close friend and supporter of Saiki and Andy Anderson. Mehau had long been accused by malcontents like Charles Marsland and Rick Reed of being the "Godfather" of organized crime in Hawai'i. Fasi had no love for Mehau, who had helped Ariyoshi beat him in the 1974 election.

When Seigle and Napolitan saw Fasi's morphing ad, they both shook their heads. "The man has lost it," Seigle said.

Napolitan, who looked as if he wanted to dance a little jig, chuckled, "Ben, stay out of it; don't get in a fight with either one; let them beat each other up."

Despite protests from the Saiki camp, Fasi kept on running the morphing ad. Andy Anderson, who had had an off-and-on relationship with Fasi for more than a decade, was reported to be furious and vowed to take Fasi down. Fasi's ad was outrageous and unfair—but the Saiki response was weak.

As Saiki's campaign began to falter and I gained on her, her camp launched a television and newspaper ad attacking me for "blaming the rape victim" in a speech I had given during floor debate on a bill that would have increased the penalty for rape. Unfortunately for Saiki, they violated the first rule of negative campaigning: The accusation must be true. It was not. The League of Women Voters, which played a watchdog role over elections back then, analyzed my floor speech and concluded that my remarks had been taken out of context. A similar conclusion was reached by the *Honolulu Advertiser*. For our part, Mazie Hirono gave a strong but measured reply.

Saiki herself did not respond, leaving that task to GOP lawyer Rich Clifton, who would later be rewarded for his fidelity with an appointment to the U.S. 9th Circuit Court of Appeals. My floor speech "spoke for itself," Clifton said with a straight face. The ploy had fallen flat.

The Democratic Party did our heavy work. By law we were prohibited from getting involved in any way with the Democratic Party campaign strategy. But Saiki's congressional voting record was an easy target for the Party's strategists.

Saiki had voted against increasing the federal minimum wage. She explained her vote by stating that she would have voted for another bill to increase the minimum wage but it had been deferred and that she voted against the new bill because the proposed increase was too high and would hurt small business. Democratic Party researchers found that the difference between the two proposals turned out to be an amount equal to the price of a cup of coffee. It made for a great television ad.

"For the price of a cup of coffee Pat Saiki voted against increasing the minimum wage—and against Hawai'i's working people," the ad stated, as it showed a cup of coffee and a hand dropping a few coins around it. Voting against the minimum wage played well in Washington, D.C., Republican circles, but not in Democratic Hawai'i. Saiki had toed the Republican Party line on the minimum wage bill, and it came back to haunt her.

A month before the general election, Seigle began running *Reach for the Moon*, a 30-minute video about my life. Harry Mulheim had sketched a rough script but decided to let the people speak unscripted. It worked well and gave those who spoke credibility.

My three kids spoke about our family and friends, and supporters like Frank Padgett, Mike Tokunaga, Ed Nakamura and Auntie Aggie Cope, a highly respected leader in the Hawaiian community, gave testimonials endorsing me.

Watching and hearing my kids pour their hearts out moved me emotionally. I was proud of them. After the lights went on I could tell that Charlie Toguchi and the others had been touched also. I knew the video would have an impact on whoever saw it.

Seigle was delighted. "I think it's the best one we've ever done," he said. "It may not change the minds of the people who don't like you, but for the ones who are still undecided it'll reveal another side of you that most know little about."

Reach for the Moon gave our campaign the boost it needed to turn the corner. It inspired our supporters to ramp up our efforts and raise more money for additional television time. Hundreds of copies were made for supporters to use at coffee hours and meetings throughout the state.

Two weeks before the November general election, our polls revealed we had overtaken Saiki, who fell back into second place and seemed to be fading. Fasi was gaining on her. Meanwhile, he had set the tone of the campaign with his negative attacks. Moreover, at the last minute he had bailed out of the only televised statewide gubernatorial debate, denying the people the opportunity to hear us on the issues. Not surprisingly, the election turned more on character, leadership style and integrity than on issues.

On November 6, 1994, Hirono and I were elected with 35.8 percent of the vote; Fasi and Kaleikini finished second with 30 percent and Saiki and Hemmings came in third with 28.6 percent. We had run a textbook campaign.

The Budget Crisis

Brandon, Janeen and Samantha held the ceremonial Bible on which I placed my left hand as I was sworn in as governor by Supreme Court Justice Simeon Acoba. I could tell they missed having Lorraine there, but I knew they were also proud of the moment—December 5, 1994 was a memorable day for the four of us.

The grueling election had left me almost totally exhausted, both physically and emotionally. But there was little time to rest. The first things to do were to complete the hiring of my Cabinet and to analyze the fiscal condition of the State government.

I wanted the best talent we could find to work in my administration. We put out notices inviting the public to apply for the available positions. By late November, we had received hundreds of applications, including a few from the Mainland.

The biggest obstacle was the pay. It was woefully low compared to pay in the private sector. Many good applicants wanted to serve but dropped out because they could not afford to do so. (In 2007, the annual salary of a State director remained unchanged; meanwhile, since 1994, the legislators, through a so-called "Legislative Salary Commission," had increased their own salaries and perks.)

I unintentionally ended up hiring more women to serve as directors and deputy directors in my Cabinet than any previous governor. Diversity is important to me. All other things being equal, I will consider gender and ethnicity. But I don't believe in quotas. I hired these women—most of whom I had not known previously—because they were the best qualified. Among them was Margery Bronster, who became the first woman to serve as State attorney general.

I was lucky. The caliber of the people who joined my administration was truly impressive. Many had left well-paying jobs and, as I would eventually learn, had joined me out of idealism, motivated by the thought of giving something back to the community.

On January 23, 1995, the third Monday of January, as required by law, I was scheduled to give my first State of the State address to the Legislature. But on Friday, our budget analysts reported some shocking news: Because of lower-than-expected revenues and recurring "emergency appropriations"—which should have been but were not included in the State Budget Bill—the general-fund deficit was estimated at $250 million instead of $150 million.

The revelation caught us by surprise. We had not prepared the budget bill. By statute, the budget (both biennial and supplemental) is submitted to the Legislature 30 days before the start of each regular session, roughly mid-December. However, it takes at least two to three weeks to assemble and print the budget document. Consequently, all of the policy decisions and the governor's messages were made by the outgoing governor around the end of November.

As the incoming governor, I could have stopped the printing process and attempted to modify the bill, but that wasn't practical, since it would have given us only about two weeks to develop a new budget and almost no time to print it.

That weekend I rewrote my State of the State address (my earlier draft had mainly been about the policies and programs I had pledged to carry out during the campaign), focusing almost exclusively on the extent of the fiscal crisis faced by the State government. "No governor, no Legislature since statehood has faced a financial crisis of the magnitude and severity that we face today," I said somberly.

I further said we would implement a new, stringent fiscal policy to get the government back on sound financial footing and explore ways to revive the economy.

First Hawaiian Bank's Leroy Laney had been the lone voice among state economists warning everyone who would listen that Hawai'i was already in or would soon be heading for a recession. Laney had been in Hawai'i for only five years; perhaps his not having experienced the state's quick economic recoveries in the past helped him see things more objectively than his colleagues. I joined the growing number of government and business leaders who no longer needed to be convinced that Laney was right.

As the economy got worse, the search for scapegoats began. More business-people blamed the State government for their problems. The State was a convenient scapegoat for business woes during troubled economic times. Grumblings about high taxes, over-regulation, big government and so on were complaints I had heard before.

There was no question that the State government had grown. In fact, from fiscal year (FY) 1987 through FY 1995, State general-fund expenditures grew from $1.6 billion to $3 billion, an average of about 8.3 percent a year. During that period, every State department had grown except mine.

However, I was not concerned as much with the size of the government as with its efficiency in delivering needed services to the people. I believed that the majority of citizens shared my concerns. Ask the so-called "man on the street" if he believes the State government is too big and he is likely to say "yes." Ask him if the State should spend more money for services such as public education or programs to help the poor and needy, and he is likely to agree again, with the qualification that the money be spent "wisely."

To get the government on sound footing again, I ordered a temporary freeze on spending; new positions and the filling of vacancies created by retirement or resignations were put on hold, as were cost items such as discretionary travel and purchases of new equipment. By law, the governor has the discretionary power to restrict spending. Unlike a veto or line-item veto, the governor's restriction of an appropriation previously approved by the Legislature is not subject to an override. To the consternation of some legislators, I restricted millions in appropriations they had approved.

Within the year, we had eliminated 20 boards and commissions and 15 non-essential programs and streamlined another 60 to improve efficiency. We also cut red tape. By 1996, the State, working with the private sector, had adopted measures that cut the time it took to build a public school by one third. That same year, we hired private engineers and consultants to assist State workers in processing permits and dramatically reduced a backlog of approximately $400 million worth of projects awaiting clean-water permits from the Department of Health.

These were merely short-term adjustments, though. What was needed was a major restructuring of State government and a change in the culture that had permeated it for decades. Civil-service reform became a high priority; we would develop and submit legislation to help achieve it in the next legislative session.

The civil-service system was established in the late 1880s to create a professional workforce that was competent, stable and free of political cronyism. The milestone reform was welcomed by a public that had grown tired of government by political patronage, in which many jobs, from the top to the bottom of government, were given to the supporters of the victorious politician regardless of their qualifications or competence, resulting in wholesale changes in personnel with each election that disrupted the delivery of services to the public.

To that end, civil service has succeeded. Today, the practice of political patronage still exists, but it is limited mainly to the politician's office staff or to a governor's or mayor's Cabinet. The basic core of the government workforce is professional and competent, and its tenure under civil service assures a stable delivery of government services regardless of the election results.

In some parts of the world—Hong Kong and Singapore, for example—civil service continues to be a meritocracy in which a worker's status is determined largely by his or her competency. This is no longer true in the United States.

With the advent of collective bargaining for public employees, American civil service, while basically free from political influence, has evolved into a system in which seniority has priority over competence and performance.

Like most of the governors I've met, I believe that the civil-service system is obsolete. It should be reinvented, reformed or abolished. In a fast-changing world, it hinders the ability of the government to adapt to the economic, political and social changes that affect the well-being of the people. It holds few rewards for good workers, makes it difficult to get rid of bad ones and makes it an agonizingly long process to hire new ones. That civil service continues to exist in its current form is a testament to the resistance of those in the system to change.

There was no better example of the need for reform than our attempt to initiate the first reduction in force (RIF) in the history of our State government.

Given the gloomy long-term economic forecast, I had no choice but to reduce the State's workforce. There would be no warm-body policy. Earl Anzai, my director of Budget and Finance, after exhaustive consultations with the other department heads, had identified 1,300 positions that were deemed low priority. The thought of laying off that many people in a depressed economy bothered me greatly.

I need not have worried. After a month of consultations with the public labor unions, we realized that the RIF would result in the termination of many fewer.

In one unforgettable case, we decided to eliminate a $70,000-a-year position. The worker who lost that job "bumped" (took over the job of a worker with less seniority) someone who had been paid $40,000 a year and continued to receive his $70,000 salary. Bumping is common in State governments but, unlike, in the federal government, which sets a time limit (18 months) on the senior employee's right to maintain his old salary, there is no time limit for Hawai'i State employees. Bumping was great for the senior employee, but paying a worker nearly twice what the job was worth was hardly conducive to promoting efficiency and productivity in State government.

I watched in amazement as the number of permanent civil service employees we could actually eliminate dwindled from 1,300 to approximately 150. Most of the employees we laid off were "exempt" (temporary) workers who were not protected by civil service or collective bargaining. When Anzai asked me if I wanted the staff to calculate the actual savings from the RIF I told him not to bother; I knew it would be far less than we had expected.

Nevertheless, by 1996, mainly through retirement, resignation and a freeze on new positions, we had managed to reduce the number of full-time State workers by 3,000. This was a temporary respite; as the state's population increased, so would the demands on public schools, hospitals and other social programs.

Trouble at the University

During the 1994 campaign, I had pledged to give public education my highest priority, and I felt obligated to do so as governor. The Department of Education (DOE) accounted for 39 percent of the operating budget, the University of Hawai'i (UH) approximately 13 percent. Combined, both departments accounted for 52 percent of the State general fund operating budget. Rather than cut the budgets of both departments, I decided to spare the DOE. This meant that the University and all of the other State departments would have to bear what would otherwise be the DOE's share of the budget cuts.

Besides the DOE, UH is the only State system that is not under the governor's direct control. UH is governed by its board of regents. Apprised of the State's fiscal crisis, the University's regents and president accepted grudgingly that, under our budget allocation, the University would sustain a $50 million reduction over two years. To soften the budget cuts, the regents announced they were considering a tuition increase.

While many faculty members were upset with the cuts, there was an outspoken minority who accused me of betraying my campaign pledge to support public education. UH students, learning of the proposed increase in tuition, joined the faculty in protest.

I was frustrated by the criticism. If there had been enough revenue to spare the University from budget cuts, I would have. It was that simple.

Moreover, there was no political support for a tax increase to make up for the revenue shortfall; if anything, most legislators believed, as I did, that a tax cut was necessary to help revive the economy.

As governor I could reduce the UH budget, but it remained for the president and the regents to develop the specifics of the University's operating budget. I believed there was fat in the UH budget. What was needed was leadership from the president and regents to find and purge it.

The bright side of a bad economy is that it is probably the best time to make serious reforms. It was time for the University to get serious about implementing the "selective excellence" policy set forth in its master plan. That is, UH should not attempt to be all things to all people, but instead should strive for excellence in certain disciplines. Implementing this policy meant making difficult choices and initiating change.

UH President Ken Mortimer had set up a blue-ribbon task force to determine the University's priorities. Its primary recommendation was the abolishment of the John A. Burns School of Medicine and the William Richardson School of Law. Politically, this recommendation was unacceptable. In the eyes of most Hawai'i politicians, past and present, Democrats and Republicans, the two professional schools were not only a source of great pride but were also crucial to the University's development and stature. My vision of Hawai'i's becoming the premier healthcare center in the Pacific could not be achieved without a first-rate medical school. The task force's report was seen as the result of University politics and dismissed accordingly.

Furthermore, a report by the legislative auditor had concluded that many of the tenured faculty were not working the full class hours required per semester under their collective-bargaining agreement. This meant that lecturers had to be hired to make up the hours not worked. The report was disputed by the faculty and its union. But it lent credence to the belief—shared by some of the regents I appointed—that the University could do more to streamline its operational costs.

For a major research university, the UH had then (and still has today) one of the lowest student tuitions in the nation. One national magazine ranked UH as a "bargain." Tuition accounted for approximately 15 percent of the cost to educate a full-time student; the remaining 85 percent was paid for out of the State's general fund. The regents' announced tuition increase, while causing great consternation among the students, was long overdue.

The University is the intellectual heart of our economy and the state's only public university; there is no doubting its importance. But my decision to spare the DOE from budget cuts meant that UH, like all of the other State departments, had to carry a bigger share of the cuts. For better or worse, this was the course of action I would follow for the full eight years of my governorship.

In late October 1995, I was told that a demonstration was planned by University faculty and students to protest budget cuts. The demonstrators planned to march the 2.5 miles from the University to the State Capitol, where a rally would be held. One of the student leaders called my office to invite me to address the crowd. My staff had mixed opinions as to whether I should speak or have someone speak on my behalf.

"Well, they assured me the demonstration would be peaceful. Besides, it's an opportunity for me to get more information out to the public," I explained.

"But you won't have good news for them; things are actually getting worse. We may have to cut UH even more," Anzai said.

"I know, but what will people think if I don't show up? I have no choice but to accept," I said.

"I guess so. But just remember, it's the messenger bringing the bad news who usually is the first to get shot," Anzai joked.

On October 31, 1995, a crowd of between 3,000 and 5,000 faculty, students and staff marched to the Capitol and gathered at the west end of the lawn, where a small stage for the speakers had been set up.

As I walked toward the stage, I noticed that some demonstrators were carrying signs. One read, "Uncle Ben, You Sold Out"; others were less flattering. It appeared that minds were already made up. I got the feeling I had been set up. As I continued toward the stage, a student stepped out of line and waved his sign in my face. I grabbed his arm, brushed the sign aside and uttered a few choice words to him. From some of the smirks and angry looks on the faces of the demonstrators, I got the feeling this was not going to be a good day for me.

About halfway to the stage, Anzai hurried up from behind me.

"What did you say to that kid?" he asked.

"Why?"

"The kid looked shocked. He kept saying, 'Did you hear what he said to me? Did you hear what he said to me?'" Anzai said, grinning.

"Yeah, well, when he stuck that sign in my face, I grabbed his arm and told him quietly to 'kiss my ass,'" I replied.

"He'll never forget it," Anzai said, trying to stifle a laugh.

"Yeah, that's the idea," I grinned as we reached the stage.

"Keep your cool," Anzai said, his expression now serious.

As I stepped up to the microphone, I could feel the tension in the air.

The next day, November 1, 1995, *Honolulu Advertiser* reporter Bill Kresnak described what happened at the rally:

Angry University of Hawai'i students, faculty and staff yelled obscenities and shouted down Gov. Ben Cayetano as he tried to speak at their "Death of Education" rally yesterday protesting UH budget cuts.

… Holding signs that read "Uncle Ben, You Sold Out" and "We Will Vote, We Will Remember," the students, faculty and staff booed and swore when the governor stepped to the microphone.

Cayetano tried to explain that he cut the UH budget as little as possible. But, he said, all State departments must make sacrifices to deal with the State's fiscal crisis.

Cayetano gave up trying to address the hostile crowd. State law-enforcement officers formed a human barrier to whisk him away from the rally, across Beretania Street and to Washington Place, the governor's mansion. Some of the rally crowd followed, shouting more obscenities.

"I saw your security guys carrying you across the street; what happened?" Anzai asked after the rally, a big smile on his face.

How absurd it must have appeared. My two security officers, Matt Mokiao and Joe Sniffen, both about the size of NFL tackles, had actually lifted me off the ground and carried me off. Seconds before, a portly woman in her late 30s or 40s, wearing dirty jeans two sizes too small, her face beet red, came rushing up from behind me, and as I turned she screeched out a very loud "fuck you" and threw something that hit me right between my eyes. My adrenalin was so high at the time I couldn't tell if I had been injured. *Was it a rock, another water bottle?* I looked at the ground and saw a crumpled plastic cup! I was reaching down to retrieve it, fully intending to stuff it into the big hole that passed for the woman's mouth, when Mokiao and Sniffen pulled me across the street.

The sardonic humor of the incident provided me some relief. I was very disappointed, however, in the way the rally had turned out. Among the crowd were many of the most highly educated people in the state and the so-called "next generation" of young leaders. I had hoped they would at least allow me to speak.

Over the next few days, I received phone calls from a few faculty members apologizing for what had happened, as well as an invitation to make a presentation on the State's fiscal condition to a group of faculty and students on the UH campus, which I accepted. It was a totally different atmosphere. Accompanied by Anzai, Susan Chandler and Seiji Naya, both former UH professors who were members of my Cabinet, we gave a report of the budget crisis and then opened the floor for questions. The session was tense but cordial. Most of the faculty and students asked good, hard questions, and we gave them candid answers. But by the end of the session, I had made little difference. To the majority of the faculty members, the University was the most important thing in the world, and they were at a loss to understand why its budget was being cut.

I was no stranger to faculty-student demonstrations; I had experienced and taken part in a few at UCLA and Loyola Law School during the late 1960s. Not only civil rights and the Vietnam War were hot issues; I had also taken part in protest rallies in which faculty and students excoriated Reagan for making huge cuts to the University of California system. In October 1995, the irony of my situation became apparent to me. ❖

CHAPTER SIXTEEN

Balancing the Budget

The Cuts

Her name was Kathleen Rhodes. She worked for United Self Help, an organization established and operated by and for people with mental health disorders. United Self Help assisted them in much the same way Alcoholics Anonymous did alcoholics: providing counseling and training on coping and problem-solving and serving as advocates in the political arena to advance the causes of people with mental disorders.

Rhodes herself suffered from severe depression. She was an assistant to Randy Hack, United Self Help's administrator; she was also the editor of the group's newsletter. It was said that she was a former reporter for the *Washington Post.*

In October 1995, United Self Help's annual State subsidy was cut from $300,000 to $50,000. Hack told Rhodes that, because of the budget cuts, he had to terminate her job. The job did not pay much, but helping others helped her deal with her own depression. She was crushed, fell into a deep depression and had to be hospitalized.

In her final newsletter she informed the readers that she would no longer be able to serve them because she had lost her job. Ominously, the newsletter was bordered in black.

On October 23, 1995, a week before UH's "Death of Education" rally, Rhodes walked to the H-1 freeway and leaped into the path of oncoming traffic.

The news media gave extensive coverage to the debacle of the UH rally, complete with photos and a lengthy article. Rhodes' suicide was covered in a short, two-paragraph story. Twelve years later, the story still sticks in my mind. Not because I felt I was responsible for her death—although the thought entered my mind—but because Rhodes was a sad, poignant example of a political truism: Those who fare worst in the political system are those who have little or no political power.

Business, labor unions, religious and most other special-interest groups all have the power of resources, organization and influence; the poor and needy have only the collective conscience of their elected public servants.

There is a difference in the perspectives of legislators and a governor in dealing with these issues.

An example is the case of Gov. Bob Riley of Alabama. Riley, a three-term conservative Republican U.S. congressman, who boasted he had never voted for a tax increase, was elected governor of Alabama in 2002. Shortly after he took office, Riley startled his fellow Alabamans by proposing a $1.2 billion tax increase, the biggest in Alabama history. Faced with a $675 million State budget deficit, Riley opted to increase taxes rather than cut programs. It was, he said, "the Christian thing to do," pointing out in his public statements that some of the tax burden on the poor (Alabama taxed personal income as low as $5,000) should be shifted to the wealthy.

The Democratic-dominated Alabama Legislature approved Riley's tax proposal, and the issue was put before the voters for approval. Conservatives were shocked by Riley's flip-flop. The Alabama chapter of the Christian Coalition waged a strong campaign to defeat Riley's proposal. Even out-of-state conservative politicians such as Dick Armey traveled to Alabama to campaign against it. According to news accounts, Alabama liberals and moderates were delighted; conservatives were dismayed.

Riley's proposal was defeated. Praised by *TIME* magazine and other national publications for his courage, Riley was, interestingly, reelected in 2006, soundly defeating his Republican and Democratic opponents in the primary and general elections.

Some arch-conservatives reacted as if Riley had lost his mind. Far from it: The conservative former congressman had discovered that the view from the governor's seat is far different than the view from a congressman's.

In Hawai'i, there was no political support for a tax increase to avoid the drastic cuts. Moreover, I believed that a tax cut was needed to give taxpayers and businesses some relief. When I was chairman of the Senate Ways and Means Committee in 1980, I proposed a major tax-relief program. The plan was designed to shift some of the tax burden from residents to tourists and nonresidents, either by a tourist tax (none was in effect at that time) or by increasing the general excise tax, of which approximately 25 percent was paid by nonresidents and tourists. The plan passed the Senate but died in the House, as the governor also opposed it. In 1997, I asked my staff to review the 1980 plan and develop a new revenue-neutral tax-cut plan that I hoped we could submit to the 1998 Legislature.

Ever since I had been elected to the State House in 1974, I had been a steady supporter of most of these human-service programs. In 1995, as governor, however, I had little choice but to cut their budgets. It saddened me when I saw the looks of disappointment and hurt in the eyes of those with whom I met. For many years, they had been able to count on me to support their programs, and now I had to let them down. In 1995, my budget decisions subjected private human-service programs such as United Self Help and others providing assistance to victims of domestic violence, alcohol and drug addiction to huge budget cuts. Unable to obtain private funding because of the depressed economy, some programs simply closed their doors.

At a time when workers in the private sector, at least the lucky ones who still had jobs, were compelled to accept wage freezes or agree to wage-cut concessions, and with State departments being ravaged by budget cuts, giving pay raises to State workers seemed inappropriate. But the State's mandatory arbitration law produced arbitration awards for the Hawai'i Government Employees Association and the United Public Worker's Union (UPW) and prompted contract agreements with the Hawai'i State Teachers Association (HSTA) and the University of Hawai'i Professional Assembly.

Our get-tough budget policy had produced savings. Most of it, however, went to pay the hundreds of millions of dollars in pay raises for State workers. Under the circumstances, the collective-bargaining agreements were a fact of life, a bad hand with which our administration had to live.

People were hurting economically all over the state. As job losses mounted, the unemployment rate in late 1996 reached 6 percent, a sharp upswing from the low of 1.9 percent in January 1990.

For the State government, the stark reality was that the decline in tax revenues was likely to get worse as real estate foreclosures and bankruptcies rose to record heights, as small businesses struggled to survive and certain segments of the economy, such as construction, experienced huge unemployment.

Never was the nexus between State services and the economy more clear: Simply put, if tax revenues decline because of a poor economy, so does the capacity of the State to help the poor and needy.

There was no quick fix for the economy. Basically our approach was fourfold: (1) reform State government to greater efficiency, (2) support core industries, (3) reduce or remove barriers to doing business and (4) diversify the economy.

Thus, in 1995-96, for example, working with the Legislature we reduced workers' compensation premiums by about 30 percent and no-fault auto insurance premiums by 30 percent; we shored up tourism by providing more funding for marketing, particularly for the Japanese market; and, to jump-start construction, the Legislature approved my request for a billion-dollar capital-improvement budget, mainly to improve and build new facilities for the public schools and the University of Hawai'i.

Economic diversification was a high priority. To explore the feasibility of spawning high-tech and biotech industries in Hawai'i, I met with the CEOs of companies in Silicon Valley. I was optimistic about the potential of Hawai'i to become the premier healthcare center of the Pacific and visited with officers of the Mayo Clinic and M.D. Anderson Cancer Center. (These visits were highly educational and would lead to milestone legislation such as Act 221 (tax credits for high-tech and biotech companies) and the construction of the new medical school in Kaka'ako.)

In 1996 and 1997, the economy continued to deteriorate. The complaints and pleas for help from the desperate business community were growing in intensity and anger.

By late 1997, national Republican political analysts were already predicting the Republicans would win Hawai'i's governorship in 1998. One of them, Charles Cook, noted that he had never seen an incumbent governor with such high negative ratings as mine get reelected. Hawai'i Republicans, tasting blood, shunned bipartisanship and took advantage of every opportunity to blame Democrats for the poor economy.

They got help from the Mainland.

In 1997, *Forbes* magazine wrote a scathing article criticizing Hawai'i as a poor place to do business, titling its story "The People's Republic of Hawai'i."

The title said it all. *Forbes* was not an objective magazine; its president and editor-in-chief, Steve Forbes, son of Malcolm Forbes, the magazine's founder, was an ultraconservative. Considered in some circles a bit eccentric, Forbes was a strong proponent of the flat income tax, which even conservatives such as Ronald Reagan and Barry Goldwater thought unfair and extreme.

The writer of the *Forbes* article made it a point to interview key Republicans in Hawai'i but never contacted me or anyone in our administration to find out what had been done to improve the business climate. It would not have made a difference, of course, as the article was clearly politically motivated.

When a reporter asked me to comment on the *Forbes* article I ignored the advice of my communications staff, who suggested I say something "gubernatorial-sounding," and instead dismissed the article for what it was: a Republican hit piece. I wasn't about to give credence to an article that compared Hawai'i to "the People's Republic." Moreover, I considered the *Forbes* title a not-too-subtle ethnic slur.

The local Republican Party was now firmly in the hands of conservatives; the Religious Right; and Linda Lingle, the mayor of Maui, who was the GOP's anointed candidate for governor in 1998. They seemed unperturbed by the *Forbes* slur. In fact, Steve Forbes, who ran against Bob Dole for the GOP presidential nomination in 1996 and against George W. Bush in 2000, seemed to be a favorite of the local Republican Party, as in both years he was invited to Hawai'i to deliver his ultra-conservative message.

In June 1998, the *Economist* published a critical story about Hawai'i as a "lousy place to do business" and described our reforms as "not painful enough to jolt Hawai'i out of its love of the status quo."

I took the criticism to heart. The *Economist* was a well-respected British journal and, although it had not interviewed anyone in our administration, it seemed to have done its homework on Hawai'i. I didn't agree that Hawai'i was a "lousy place" to do business. After all, many businesses seemed to have done quite well over the previous two decades of continuous and prosperous economic growth.

I got so tired of and irritated at being told by obnoxious businessmen that they could do better on the Mainland. I'd ask them, "When are you leaving?"

But I agreed with the *Economist* that our "reforms were not painful enough" and had not brought about the full extent of change we had hoped to achieve. The Legislature, under heavy pressure from the public-worker unions, had rejected our civil service reform bills. Legislative leaders urged me to pursue the reforms through collective bargaining.

Bold Proposals

In the summer of 1997, I established the Economic Revitalization Task Force (ERTF) to develop a strategy for restructuring Hawai'i's economy. The ERTF's objective was to propose strategic long-term reforms that would improve Hawai'i's economic infrastructure.

Unlike the Mainland task forces, which tended to include only business leaders, the ERTF's membership was much more diverse. To encourage buy-in of ERTF recommendations, I invited leaders from business, labor unions and universities, as well as the Speaker of the House, the Senate president and the publisher of the *Honolulu Advertiser*, Hawai'i's largest daily newspaper.

The *Honolulu Star-Bulletin*, Hawai'i's second-largest daily newspaper, had been invited to participate but had declined. I was not surprised. The *Star-Bulletin*, founded in 1882, had long been considered a Republican newspaper. With polls showing that the Republicans had a virtual lock on winning the 1998 gubernatorial election, it was understandable that the *Star-Bulletin* editors wanted no part of an ERTF established by a Democratic governor.

The ERTF members were a diverse group not only in occupation but also in ideology. Hotelier Richard Kelley, for example, was a Republican conservative, while labor leader Russell Okata was a liberal Democrat. Tom Leppert, a moderate Republican and CEO of Castle & Cooke, a subsidiary of Dole Corp., was selected to serve as the task force's facilitator.

The preliminary staff work spanned a six-week period, during which five working groups were established to develop recommendations that were submitted to the Task Force. Public input was solicited through comment sheets and email. The recommendations covered five economic categories: (1) education and workforce development, (2) taxation, (3) business climate, (4) role of government and (5) economic development.

On October 20 and 21, 1997, the ERTF met in closed meetings to discuss the recommendations. The members agreed that each recommendation had to meet two conditions: It had to be bold or, as Leppert put it, something that "flew at the 30,000-foot level," and it had to be feasible, something that could be implemented quickly and not take years to gain public approval. The members also agreed that the ERTF would submit its recommendations as a package, developed by consensus. No recommendation would be submitted without unanimous consent. There would be no minority report.

During the two-day meeting, I was impressed with the spirit of cooperation and free exchange of ideas. The discussions were cordial and respectful. I felt, as I believe the other ERTF members did, that the two days presented an historic opportunity to make significant reforms that would benefit not only business but the average citizen as well. There were no ideologues on the ERTF—at least not for those two days.

The ERTF made a number of recommendations, among them that the Transient Accommodations Tax (TAT) would be increased from 6 percent to 7 percent, 3 percent of the revenue of which would be dedicated to marketing tourism, overseen by a 7- to 11-member board (later named the Hawai'i Tourism Authority); government officials would have limited time periods in which to approve or disapprove petitions and licenses, which would otherwise be approved by default; the State Land Use Commission would be abolished, and land-use decisions would be left to the counties; four county-level boards, appointed by the governor, would replace the elected State Board of Education; and the University of Hawai'i would be given autonomy from the State government, giving it a quasi-public corporate status.

The ERTF's tax-reform proposal was clearly its boldest and most far reaching. Critics had labeled Hawai'i a "tax hell." Given that the State government assumed responsibilities normally carried out by cities and counties on the Mainland, the State personal income tax was understandably high. At 10 percent, it was one of the highest in the nation. Real property taxes, on the other hand, were among the lowest in the nation. Nevertheless, tax reform was sorely needed, if for no other reason than to change the perception that Hawai'i was a tax nightmare and a poor place to do business.

Every member of the ERTF agreed that taxes should be reduced. But Russell Okata and Gary Rodrigues, the two public-worker union leaders, argued that the tax reform should be "revenue neutral"—i.e., theoretically, at least, there should be no loss of tax revenue. To address their concerns, a tax scheme was designed to provide tax relief to Hawai'i taxpayers by shifting some of the burden to tourists and nonresidents through the general excise tax, the State's biggest generator of revenue.

The final proposal called for an increase in the general excise tax from 4 percent to 5.35 percent, accompanied by a reduction in the State personal income tax from its 10-percent top margin to 7 percent and, after three years, to 6 percent. The approximately 25 percent of general excise tax revenues generated by tourists and nonresidents made up for the 4-percent loss of personal income tax revenue. To abate the impact of the increased general excise tax on local residents, each would be entitled to receive a tax credit. In addition, the corporate income tax would be cut in half. According to ERTF staff calculations, the tax burden of every Hawai'i family would be reduced under the ERTF tax package. Every member of the ERTF, which included some of Hawai'i's respected Republican business leaders, believed it was the kind of bold proposal needed to reshape Hawai'i's tax structure.

The problem with the tax-reform package was that it was complicated, and one had to understand how all of its components worked together to understand its benefits.

The Republicans had not won the governorship since 1962, when Democrat John A. Burns defeated the Republican incumbent William F. Quinn. Faced with their best chance to win the governorship in 36 years, the Republican leaders weren't about to hamper their chances by allowing the ERTF proposals to succeed.

We expected that there would be full debate on the ERTF proposals. We realized it was the ERTF's responsibility to go out and seek the approval of the community and the Legislature. Therefore, a team of ERTF members led by Tom Leppert was designated to present the proposed ERTF proposals to the general public. Bankers Walter Dods and Larry Johnson agreed to raise money for a media campaign to promote the ERTF package.

The strategy of Republican critics was simple: attack and isolate the increase in the general excise tax without mentioning the reduction in the personal income and corporate taxes. Half-truths have long been used to distort real truths and spread confusion, and the Republican campaign against the ERTF proposal was a classic case.

Leppert took the lead for the ERTF and spent countless hours meeting with small-business leaders to explain the tax proposal. Meanwhile, Republican legislators, led by conservative Sens. Sam Slom and Fred Hemmings, spearheaded the GOP's campaign of misinformation.

Leppert was articulate, intelligent and indomitable. He strongly believed the tax proposal would be good for Hawai'i, but the Republican attacks created a great deal of confusion and uncertainty. There were many Republican businessmen who, like fellow Republican Richard Kelley, understood the ERTF tax proposal but, unlike Kelley, were more interested in restoring Republican political power than the economy.

The ERTF proposal was the final product of the Democratic and Republican ERTF members, who had set aside their political differences to bring about needed economic reforms. In 1998, the ERTF became too much of a risk for Democratic legislators, the majority of whom faced reelection campaigns less than a year away. The House, under Speaker Joe Souki, was still holding firm, but the Senate, under Norman Mizuguchi, had begun to waver. Privately, I knew we had lost the public relations battle. My heart went out to Leppert and the other

ERTF members who had attended meeting after meeting and spent countless hours trying to explain the proposal.

About two thirds of the way through the 1998 legislative session, Sens. Roz Baker and Carol Fukunaga, the co-chairs of the powerful Senate Ways and Means Committee, met with me. Mizuguchi was seeking a compromise. Baker told me that the Senate was willing to pass a reduction in the State personal income tax without raising the general excise tax. With the Senate backing down, it was time to consider a compromise.

"How much do you propose to reduce the personal income tax?" I asked Baker.

"From 10 to 9 percentage points," she replied.

"One percentage point? Senator, it's so manini that the Democrats will be ridiculed all over the state," I replied incredulously.

"Well, if the tax cut is too big it will impact State programs," she replied.

"Yeah, but the economy needs a shot in the arm—a big one. I'm sorry, but I can't accept 1 percent. Frankly, I'll veto the bill," I said.

"What would you accept?" she asked, apparently having anticipated my answer.

"At least by 2 percentage points—that's a 20 percent tax cut—but more, if possible," I replied.

"We'll discuss it with the president and the Senate caucus," she said.

"Senator, a 1-percentage-point decrease will have no impact on the economy and will become a public relations disaster for Democrats. If we're going to cut taxes it should be something meaningful; otherwise, let's not do it at all."

With the 1998 election looming, there was great pressure on the Legislature to come up with some kind of meaningful tax reform. Given Senate President Norman Mizuguchi's close relationship with the HGEA, I assumed that he was caught in a bind: On the one hand, he knew it would be a political disaster for Democrats if tax reform failed; on the other hand, he wanted tax reform that was acceptable to the unions.

I had heard, however, that there were seven Democratic senators who were opposed to the proposed 1 percentage point—they wanted a bigger tax cut or none at all. The regular legislative session had expired; the session had already been extended once. I had heard that Mizuguchi and the Senate majority Democrats wanted another extension of the legislative session to work on their 1-percentage-point tax-cut bill and persuade the seven Democrats to support it.

When the seven dissenting Democrats got wind of the move for an extension, they sent me a letter, signed by them and two Republicans, urging me not to grant another extension unless there was meaningful tax relief.

Under Hawai'i law, unless both the House and Senate mustered a two-thirds majority, only the governor could grant an extension of the legislative session.

I called Randy Iwase, who was taking the lead for the dissenting Democrats. Iwase was a close friend, honest, idealistic and smart.

"We don't like it," Iwase said. "One percentage point is too little."

"Are your guys solid in opposing an extension of the session?" I asked.

"Oh, yeah. One percent is ridiculous. It doesn't really help the working-class people," Iwase replied.

"What about the two Republicans, Whitney Anderson and Sam Slom?" I asked.

"On the extension, they are solidly with us," Iwase answered.

I did announce I would not grant any further extensions unless we could agree on more tax relief, which satisfied most of the Legislature and kept a frustrated Speaker Calvin Say from breaking off talks altogether, as he had been considering doing.

The *Star-Bulletin* described our tax proposal:

> Cayetano's initiative expands all income-tax brackets, lowers the tax rates for each bracket and creates a lower-income tax credit by abolishing the food-tax credit, which Cayetano has long believed was unnecessary for middle- and upper-income taxpayers.
>
> Under Cayetano's plan, a family of four with an adjusted gross income of $35,000 a year will save $1,152 over four years. For a family of four earning $50,000, the savings will be $1,893.

> House and Senate conferees accepted the plan 50 minutes before a midnight deadline.

Under the bill that was approved, the State personal income tax was reduced from 10 percent to 8.25 percent, a 17.5-percent reduction overall. This was not the kind of bold proposal I (and ERTF members) had envisioned; nevertheless, it was something of which the Democrats could be proud. It put money into the pockets of people. In fact, it turned out to be the biggest reduction in State income taxes in the nation, drawing grudging praise from the conservative CATO Institute.

At a National Governors Association meeting the following year, I heard Michigan Gov. James Engler, who at the time was considered a potential presidential candidate, speak proudly about the tax cuts approved in Michigan. Engler, a big, rotund man, beamed as he explained how his tax cuts would save Michigan taxpayers about a billion dollars. As I listened, I realized that Hawai'i's State personal income-tax cut was really significant. It would save the taxpayers $750 million; combined with the other tax-relief measures passed in 1998, the savings was estimated at about $1.2 billion. Michigan's population was about 10 million people; Hawai'i's, 1.2 million. By comparison, Hawai'i residents had fared far better than their Michigan counterparts.

Lingle and some Republicans attacked the final tax cut as too little. That the tax cut was approved while the economy was still struggling was quite an achievement.

The Payroll Lag

By late 1998, some of the state's economists stated publicly that the state's economy was beginning to rebound. Our billion-dollar capital-improvement program was beginning to create more construction jobs. Even as student enrollment in our public schools increased and welfare cases, fueled by high unemployment, rose by 20 percent, we managed to keep the growth of State government down to less than 1 percent. Moreover, and perhaps most significantly, the business community had been purged of the weaker companies, and many businesses had become more efficient and productive.

In 1998, I asked Joe Nicolai, a good friend and principal of JN Chevrolet, how his company was doing. "Ben, we had a good year in 1997 and we're having a record year in 1998. We're selling a hell of a lot of trucks."

"That means more construction workers have jobs," I replied.

"Right, construction workers are among our biggest customers for trucks," Nicolai replied.

"How're the other car dealers doing?" I asked.

"Ben, if any car dealer is not doing well it's their own fault," Nicolai replied.

The economy was slowly getting better. In fact, according to Paul Brewbaker, senior economist for Bank of Hawai'i, real personal income growth began rising once again in 1997, a sign of recovery. Economists, of course, are trained to notice these signs, but the unemployed and those on the verge of bankruptcy are usually not. At the time, for most people nothing had changed for the better.

When the economy begins to recover there is a significant lag time before the State starts to realize an increase in tax revenues. Since most people are concerned foremost about economic issues, the lag can have significant political consequences.

Indeed, a good example was the 1992 U.S. presidential election. Most political analysts attribute President George H.W. Bush's loss to Bill Clinton to the poor national economy. On the other hand, in that same year most economists saw the signs of a strong economic recovery. If the election had been held a year later, perhaps the outcome would have been different. But full economic recovery would come too late to help Bush in 1992.

I knew that I would be put in the same situation during the 1998 election. *How*, I wondered, *will the economy affect the election?*

In July 1998, we were still struggling with balancing the State budget. Since 1996, we had come up with several proposals to avoid massive layoffs of State workers. To deal with the problem of arbitrated pay raises, we proposed reducing the workweek to 35 hours but continuing to pay the workers for the regular 40 hours. UPW leader Rodrigues supported the idea, but it got a mixed reaction from others. Another idea was to shorten the hours of State workers simply by shutting down the State government at certain times. The legality of this idea was challenged, and it was abandoned.

Finally, we settled on the "payroll lag." Earl Anzai developed the idea in 1996. The concept was simple: By delaying the payment of one State paycheck into the next fiscal year, Anzai estimated it would give the State a $51 million cushion. It meant we could avoid cutting the budget another $51 million.

The Republicans denounced the idea as an accounting gimmick and attacked my administration for not facing up to the State's real fiscal problems. "Yes, it's an accounting technique that businesses do all the time to gain tax advantages for their companies," I replied. "Besides, if the Republicans want me to cut the budget further, tell them to submit a list of programs they want to see cut," I added.

A bill we submitted to give us the legal standing to implement the idea was approved by the House but rejected by the Senate in 1997. I wasn't surprised; Mizuguchi and other Senate leaders were closely aligned with the HGEA. "Senate says Gov has to negotiate payroll lag," read one newspaper headline. The negotiations began.

We provided extensive briefings on the State's dire fiscal problems to each union. A two-week delay would be too long, union leaders advised us, and the lag was negotiated first to a five- and finally to a one-day delay.

Every public-worker union agreed to the payroll lag except one—the University of Hawaii Professional Assembly (UHPA). Not only did UHPA oppose the payroll lag, it sued in court for an order enjoining the State from implementing it against UHPA members. The payroll lag, UHPA argued, would be a breach of its current contract with the State. The injunction was granted.

It was a legal argument that every one of the public-worker unions could make but didn't because their leaders understood that the payroll lag wasn't about legal rights; it was about being practical, about showing some compassion and empathy by giving the State breathing room in which to restore some of the budget cuts suffered by organizations and State programs for the poor and needy.

UHPA's action was seen as selfish even by other union leaders. HGEA leader Russell Okata stated publicly that HGEA would not join UHPA's lawsuit. "If there is a RIF," Okata said grimly, "UHPA's members should be the first to be laid off."

The thought that UHPA's leaders might have been thinking about renegotiating their contract with the State as a condition for accepting the payroll lag occurred to me, and I stated publicly that the State would not agree to reopen contract talks unless the payroll lag was accepted.

"The State custodians, secretaries, clerks, engineers and nurses understood the payroll lag; they don't like the inconvenience of a late paycheck, but they were willing to help, but not UHPA, not the damned faculty," I said angrily to my staff.

"I think it's more UHPA's leadership and not the faculty; they don't seem to know anything about the State budget," Lloyd Nekoba replied.

"Oh, really? They know enough to take potshots at me for cutting the UH budget," I said, recalling the Death of Education rally, "but when it comes to asking them for a little help—so we can restore some of the cuts we made to the human-service programs for the poor—they sue us!"

"The UHPA leaders are not like guys like Russell and Gary [Rodrigues, of UPW]. Gary and Russell are local, they understand, but the UHPA guys are from the Mainland; they look at things different," Nekoba replied.

"They live in another world … so damned self-centered," I added.

"But you know … Neil [Abercrombie] said the faculty really doesn't understand the politics of the process, most of them are naive and they just want to do their work," Nekoba added.

"Listen, Lloyd, these are the people who teach our kids what government is all about. They pontificate to their students all the time about ethics, about values—they *should* understand what's happening to the State better than the janitors who clean their classrooms! And it angers me when I think that they got their pay raises long before those janitors!" I said tersely.

"I read where UHPA is claiming the State already lags the faculty's pay because although the faculty works only 10 months in a year, they are paid over a 12-month period," Nekoba said.

"That's bullshit. The reason they get paid over a 12-month period is so that they get health insurance coverage over a full year and not just 10 months. This was something the faculty wanted, and it was agreed to by the State a long time ago. Musto [UHPA's executive secretary] knows the truth and yet he continues to mislead UHPA's members."

"Well, Alex Mallahoff [UHPA's president] has been saying it," Nekoba said.

"You know, Mallahoff is a nice man and I've been told he is a world-renowned scientist, but when it comes to his union's history and collective bargaining, he's a duck out of water," I sighed softly.

"You realize we need UHPA's endorsement in 1998; Lingle is going to be tough to beat," Nekoba said, concerned about my deteriorating relationship with UHPA.

I was beyond caring. "Lloyd, I don't give a damn. The way things are going right now, I won't be surprised if they go Republican [they did]. But if they do, we'll win without them."

"Yeah, but go easy on the faculty. You know you still got friends there who've supported you for a long time," Nekoba said, "and they'll continue to support you."

"Yeah, but they're different from this crowd that's heading UHPA," I said,

~~feeling regret over my indiscriminate criticism of the faculty.~~

"By the way, Neil called from Washington earlier today," Nekoba said.

"What did he say?"

"After I briefed him on what's happening with you and UHPA, he laughed and told me to ask you if you are deliberately trying to make your reelection 'close,'" Nekoba said, grinning widely.

"Ah, I needed that," I replied, chuckling at Abercrombie's little joke. ❖

CHAPTER SEVENTEEN

On Native Hawaiians

Ceded Lands

I n July 1996, State Circuit Court Judge Daniel Heely issued an oral ruling that under Act 304 OHA was entitled to 20 percent of the gross revenues from all ceded lands. In October 1996, Heely issued his written order. The ruling caught me, and many State officials, by surprise. In a January 13, 1997, article, the *Star-Bulletin* described Heely's ruling:

> He [Judge Heely] cited the federal government's apology for the illegal overthrow of the Hawaiian kingdom, and invoked a State law allowing him to "contemplate and reside with the life force," and consider the aloha spirit—"the essence of relationships in which each person is important to every other person for collective existence."
>
> "The court cannot conceive of a more appropriate situation in which to attempt to apply the concepts set forth in the Aloha Spirit law," he said, "than ruling on issues that are directly related to the betterment of the native Hawaiian people."

With those ideals, Heely sparked the latest controversy over the ceded lands, 1.2 million acres of property in all four counties, comprising about 43 percent of the Islands' area. Native Hawaiians hailed the ruling as "historic," recognizing the legitimacy of their legal claims to the lands.

I had known Heely from the days I practiced law. He was a good judge, respected for his intellect and sincerity. His wife, Patricia, was part-Hawaiian and a graduate of Kamehameha Schools. One judge described Heely's chambers as reflecting "a strong sense of family and 'Hawaiianness.'" His ruling in the OHA case was one of his final decisions as a Hawai'i judge before he, his wife and their six children moved to the Mainland, where he had accepted a position as an administrative judge with the federal government.

Heely's reference to the Aloha Spirit law and the 1993 U.S. Apology Resolution, neither of which was relevant to the disposition of Act 304, suggested strongly that he was affected by his sincere and deep desire to help Hawaiians. I disagreed with his ruling; as imperfect as Act 304 was, unlike its predecessor, Act 273, it included a revenue formula that indicated the Legislature did not intend for OHA to be paid 20 percent of the gross revenues from all of the ceded lands. My personal feelings were irrelevant, of course. Pending the Hawai'i Supreme Court's ruling on the State's appeal, it was clear to me that the State's interests would be best served by a quick settlement that was fair to both sides.

The impact of Heely's ruling was profound. It was the first affirmation by a State court that under State law (Act 304) OHA was entitled to one fifth of the *gross* revenues from the ceded lands, which meant the State would not receive any offset for the billions of dollars it had invested in enhancing the value of the ceded lands since annexation. The thought of the State paying one-fifth of the gross revenues derived from its hospitals, the University, the affordable rental housing projects and the airport special fund seemed unreal, to say the least.

The State is not in the business of making profits. Its hospitals, affordable rental housing projects and the University—like virtually every State service—are heavily subsidized with tax dollars. The State had invested billions of dollars in developing its airport system, but under *Heely,* it was required to pay OHA without receiving any discount or credit for the hundreds of millions of taxpayer dollars it invested in building the airport.

We're in the middle of the worst recession in State history, cutting social programs to balance the budget, arguing with the unions over pay raises and civil-service reform—and now this, I thought.

For many Hawaiians, *Heely* confirmed the justness of their cause. It heightened their expectations and inflamed their emotions. The reaction of OHA trustee Rowena Akana, quoted in an October 1996 issue of the *Star-Bulletin*, was typical:

> Among other changes, Cayetano wants to specify that the law applies only to raw land, and not land with improvements. OHA Trustee Rowena Akana sees an effort to create a "smokescreen," diverting attention from the State's irresponsible spending habits and inability to make good on its obligations.
>
> "What is the difference between the Cayetano administration and the federal government and their treatment of the American Indians?" Akana asked. "What is the difference? Is this what American justice is all about?"

Heely came as a shock to many legislators, evoking mea culpas from some key legislators who had voted for Act 273 in 1980. In a 1997 interview with the *Star-Bulletin*, House Finance Chairman Ken Kiyabu said, "I know there was some concern about what the long-range effect was going to be, but we didn't have any numbers at the time."

In the same interview, former Republican State Sen. Andy Anderson—

who in 1980 had praised Henry Peters in a Senate floor speech for muscling the Senate into approving Act 273 and had grandly proclaimed before a gallery packed predominantly with Hawaiians that "it was about time the Hawaiians won one"—explained lamely, "As I recall, most of the projections at that time were on ag land, and those numbers made sense ... nobody had the foresight to apply it to other than ag lands."

Anderson's words irritated me. In 1980, there had been Democratic and Republican senators who expressed their fears that the 20 percent was open ended and its fiscal impact would extend beyond agricultural lands. Anderson, whose ambitions for higher office were well known, wasn't listening; he was too busy grandstanding to the audience in the Senate gallery.

Heely brought back memories of the hard and at times bitter fight between the House and the Senate over Act 273. Its passage had been a great personal victory for Peters, who had fought tenaciously for it. Given full rein by Speaker Wakatsuki to negotiate the State budget, Peters had bottled up important bills in the House Finance Committee, to the embarrassment of committee chairman Ted Morioka. The unspoken message was clear: Unless the Senate agreed to approve Act 273, the other bills would die.

With the passage of Act 273, Peters became a champion of the Hawaiian people, a role he would play again in the early years of his Bishop Estate trusteeship. I was tagged as "anti-Hawaiian," a label used by some OHA trustees and Hawaiian activists who had little aloha for anyone who disagreed with them.

In 1983, OHA filed its first lawsuit against the State, claiming 20 percent of a settlement the State had reached with a private party in an illegal sand-mining lawsuit. In 1984, OHA filed another suit, this time claiming 20 percent of the revenues from the State hospitals, affordable public rental housing, University of Hawai'i and duty-free concession at the Honolulu International Airport and Waikīkī outlets.

Ariyoshi was governor at the time, and he held firm against OHA's demands. Waihee, who was lieutenant governor, once told me that former State Sen. T.C. Yim, the director of OHA, offered to settle all of OHA's claims for land and a few State buildings in Kaka'ako. Ariyoshi rejected the offer.

In *OHA v. Yamasaki* (1987) the Hawai'i Supreme Court gave the State relief from OHA's claims when it ruled that the revenue formula in Act 273 was too vague to enforce and suggested that it raised a political question that should be resolved by the Legislature.

Despite the clear message from the Supreme Court, it took the Legislature nearly three years to act. In attempting to clarify Act 273, it passed Act 304 (1990), which attempted to define "revenue" and distinguish between revenues derived from the use of ceded lands which were "sovereign" in nature and to be retained by the State (public schools, hospitals, etc.) and those that were "proprietary" (commercial development), from which 20 percent could be paid to OHA. Nonetheless, disputes between OHA and the State over the 20-percent allocation continued.

In 1993, Gov. Waihee reached a partial settlement with OHA, in which the State paid $134 million. OHA had rejected Waihee's demand for a global settlement of the ceded-lands claims.

In 1994, Waihee's final year as governor, OHA filed a number of suits against the State. In one, it claimed it was entitled to 20 percent of rental housing, hospital-patient services and interest-income receipts as well the lucrative duty-free concessions at the airport and in Waikīkī. In another suit, OHA successfully got a court order enjoining the State from transferring ceded lands to the State's housing agency to complete public housing projects on Maui and the Big Island, in which the State had already invested tens of millions of dollars.

These disputes raised serious questions as to whether the State could transfer ceded lands for any public purpose. Title companies refused to issue certificates of clear title for joint State and private-sector housing projects in which the State provided lands for the private sector to develop. Moreover, the State's bond rating was being negatively affected, because it was routinely forced to disclose the pending litigation to prospective bond buyers.

Fierce lobbying by OHA and Hawaiian groups defeated every attempt by the State administration to get relief from the intimidated Legislature.

By the time I became governor, it was clear to me that the best course of action for the State was to seek what lawyers call a "global" settlement (a final settlement of all claims) with OHA that was fair to both sides. The time for debate about Hawaiian history had long passed; like it or not, Act 304 was the State law, and it was my duty to execute it.

Former State Sen. Clayton Hee had been chairman of the OHA board of trustees since 1991. Unlike some of the more vocal Hawaiian leaders, Hee was not an ideologue. As the only trustee with legislative experience, he knew what it took to operate the State hospitals and other facilities. We had become close friends when we served in the State Senate together, for which his Hawaiian detractors would label him a "sellout." But Hee was secure in and passionate about his Hawaiianness. A graduate of Kamehameha Schools, he was one of the few young Hawaiian leaders who could speak the Hawaiian language fluently. In later years, he would be instrumental in setting up the Hawaiian-language master's program at UH-Hilo.

Hee had a lot to do with the filing of OHA's lawsuits against the State. He was a tough negotiator. He also knew that the Legislature tended to be reactive and that, at some point, it could be pressured by an aroused public to repeal or amend Act 304 as easily as it had passed it. He wanted to work out a settlement as much as I did.

There was a lot of preparatory work to be done. My staff had none of the information on which Waihee had relied in agreeing to a $134 million settlement with OHA in 1993. We had to start from scratch. Hee and I agreed to set up negotiation teams to do the research we would need to develop an equitable settlement.

In 1996, we made the first settlement offer to OHA: The State would pay $151 million in cash and transfer 20 percent of the ceded lands to OHA, which meant OHA would get 100 percent of the revenues from those lands.

Hee liked the idea. Which ceded lands would be included in the 20 percent would be the subject of further negotiations. Unlike some of the other trustees, Hee was practical and results oriented. He already had some income-generating parcels in mind, among them the site of the Waikīkī Yacht Club, the Gold Bond Building on Ala Moana Boulevard and the marina at Sand Island.

With Hawaiian activists still celebrating the Heely ruling, I knew Hee would have a tough time selling the State's offer to the other trustees. *Heely* worried me, and I was prepared to offer a higher cash payment to settle the dispute. Just before Hee walked out of my office, I said: "Clay, if it helps, we'll throw in all of the ceded lands on Moloka'i. Just imagine—combined with the homestead lands, OHA can have its own county." I sounded as if I was joking, but I was dead serious. "But it has to be a global settlement. I want to put this issue to rest once and for all," I reminded him.

"If the offer is right, then we [OHA] will cut the umbilical cord and stand on our own feet," he replied, still smiling.

Not surprisingly, the OHA trustees rejected the offer despite the efforts of Hee and OHA attorney James Duffy, who had argued that OHA could still negotiate for a larger amount of cash but that the State would not agree to anything but a full and final settlement.

That was the deal-breaker. OHA would not agree to a global settlement. The Heely decision had given OHA tremendous bargaining power.

"Well, that was the opener. We'll review the information, and if it's justified, we can sweeten the pot," I told our negotiating team.

In October 1997, however, Hee stepped down as chairman of OHA. Long-time activist Adelaide (Frenchy) DeSoto, a former Hee supporter, replaced him. DeSoto had been at the center of the turmoil that had plagued the OHA board for years. Trustee Rowena Akana had harsh words about her: "When she storms out of meetings at the Legislature, when she calls legislators names, flips the bird at constituents—I mean, I shudder to think of where our office will be," Akana said.

I took Akana's words as more than just a criticism of DeSoto; they were an indication of how chaotic things were at OHA.

DeSoto was a big, charismatic woman well known for her acerbic tongue. She seemed to be perpetually angry and was quick to retreat into populist rhetoric to incite rather than inform her audience whenever she was short on facts. From past experience, I knew it would be difficult to work with her.

DeSoto, along with Waihee, was considered one of the founders of OHA. I never doubted her commitment to improving the lives of the Hawaiian people, but she used every political ruse at her disposal to make a point or get her way. Once, while visiting Queen Lili'uokalani's bedroom at Washington Place, DeSoto told my wife, Vicky, that a former governor had ordered the legs of the queen's bed cut shorter to make it easier for his kids to climb onto it. Vicky was shocked. The former governor DeSoto mentioned was Bill Quinn. Vicky could not believe that Quinn would do such a thing. Neither could I.

This was the kind of story that would anger most people, Hawaiians and non-Hawaiians. To those like DeSoto, who were predisposed to blame haoles for all the suffering of Hawaiians, there was no need to check the truth of the story—it was just another example of the haoles' long list of sins against the Hawaiians.

Later, Vicky asked Jim Bartels, the executive director of Washington Place, if DeSoto's story was true. Bartels, who for many years had been the curator of the historic 'Iolani Palace and was highly respected as an expert on Hawaiian history, told her that it was an old rumor that had been passed on since statehood; not only was it not true, it was, in fact, the queen herself who had ordered the legs of the bed shortened to make it easier for *her* to get onto it.

Apparently, a majority of the OHA trustees shared Akana's concerns: Within the year, Akana replaced DeSoto as OHA chairperson. In a little more than a year, OHA had had three chairpersons.

On March 31, 1999, after being briefed by our negotiating team, I authorized an offer of $251.3 million in cash and one-fifth of the State's ceded lands. Except for increasing the cash settlement from $151 million to $251 million, the terms were identical to our 1996 offer: OHA would get 20 percent of *all* the ceded lands—approximately 365,000 acres—rather than 20 percent of the income; and 100 percent of the revenues from its the lands, which they were free to develop and control. I was optimistic. As in 1996, I was open to renegotiating a higher cash settlement, but only if OHA agreed to a final settlement of all of its claims under Act 304.

On April 1, 1999, OHA countered with a $309.5 million offer. On April 16, 1999, before the State could respond to its earlier offer, OHA made its final offer: It would settle for $304.6 million and any ceded lands with a revenue stream of $7.4 million. Nothing was mentioned about a global settlement.

That week I instructed our negotiating team to break off further talks with OHA. Once again, the deal-breaker was OHA's refusal to accept a global settlement. Five years of negotiations had produced nothing.

Only Hee seemed to realize the cost of OHA's rejection. A newspaper story read: "Hee, in hindsight, said last week OHA should have taken the State's final offer as a 'bird in the hand.' If it did, OHA's native Hawaiian trust could be worth close to $1 billion today, and OHA would have a land trust about three times the size of Molokai and bigger than that of Kamehameha Schools."

"No sense fooling around anymore," I told Sam Callejo, my chief of staff and head of the State's negotiating team. "They [OHA] seem so terrified of a global settlement they just don't mention it—as if we never brought it up. From now on, we'll leave it up to the courts or the Legislature to resolve the issue."

"It's hard to understand why they didn't go for it. By giving OHA 20 percent of the ceded lands it meant they would be entitled to 100 percent of the revenues from those lands. They would have discretion to develop those lands as they saw fit—a great opportunity to increase the revenue stream," Callejo said.

"Well, many Hawaiians have an entitlement mentality. [OHA trustee] Haunani Apoliona was quoted in the *Star-Bulletin* as saying they rejected our offer because as trustees they could not agree in good conscience to a final settlement that would end the entitlements. A final settlement creates certainty. In this case it meant that once the State settled with OHA and gave them 20 percent of the ceded lands they were on their own. The self-righteous rhetoric about self-determination comes easy, but when the opportunity to end their dependency on the State becomes a reality they back down. That's the kind of thinking that prevented Waihee from getting a final settlement in 1993," I said.

"Well, the Legislature can fix this mess, but they are too worried about angering the Hawaiians," Callejo added.

"Yeah, and ever since [State Rep.] Ed Case tried and got his 'ōkole kicked, no one else is inclined to do anything. Do you folks remember what happened to him?" I asked my staff.

"Well, hundreds of very angry Hawaiians showed up to demonstrate against Case's bill. They made it very personal by hanging him in effigy," someone chuckled.

"Actually, Case's bill sounded pretty good."

"The big problem was that, although Case is a local boy, they treated him like a Mainland haole."

"Well," I interjected, "unless OHA gets a court order forcing the State to pay the 20 percent we'll just wait for the Supreme Court to rule on *Heely*. As time passes, let's hope the public will gain a better understanding of what's at stake if *Heely* is affirmed. My guess is that, at some point, the public pressure will force the Legislature to either amend or repeal Act 304. Meanwhile, unless OHA has a change of heart, we'll just sit it out."

And this was what we did—until things came to a head once again.

Waihee and the Hawaiians

The drive for greater Hawaiian political power took a giant leap forward in 1986 when John Waihee was elected governor. By then, politics overshadowed culture in the Hawaiian Renaissance. Hawaiian activists, who tended to be young, confrontational, angry and skeptical of anyone in State government, ascended to power within Hawaiian organizations, replacing the old leadership.

Most Hawaiians had high expectations of Waihee. As governor, however, Waihee wore a different hat; he was governor of all Hawai'i's people and duty bound to act accordingly. Inevitably, Waihee fell out of favor with ("was vilified by" may be more accurate) some of the radical Hawaiian activists, whose insatiable demands no governor could realistically satisfy.

In truth, Hawaiians fared very well during Waihee's two terms as governor. Indeed, by the end of his final term in 1994, Waihee had committed the State to paying OHA and the Department of Hawaiian Homes nearly a billion dollars, without so much as a whisper of objection from the Legislature.

OHA received more than $200 million in settlement and annual payments from the State, $134 million of it from the partial settlement in 1993. A $600 million agreement was negotiated successfully between the State and the Department of Hawaiian Homes to settle claims of past mismanagement of the Hawaiian Homes programs. This novel settlement was a measure of Waihee's political skills. It was as if the U.S. Bureau of Indian Affairs had sued and settled with itself to make up for its alleged past mismanagement.

But with Peters and Wong having left the Legislature for Bishop Estate trusteeships, Waihee's chances of getting $600 million through the regular legislative budget process were highly unlikely. By negotiating a settlement first and then requesting the appropriation, Waihee had made it difficult politically for the predominantly non-Hawaiian Legislature to disapprove the request.

The settlement was literally a slap in the face of past DHHL directors, all of whom were respected Hawaiian leaders such as Hoaliku Drake and Billy Beamer. The innuendo that their leadership had failed was unfair. As I saw it, historically DHHL's biggest problem was not a lack of land—it had plenty—but inadequate funding with which to develop homestead lots with the infrastructure necessary for housing. Consequently, DHHL could never provide enough house-ready lots even to make a dent in the growing backlog of Hawaiians waiting to be assigned them. Waihee, whose father had died after waiting futilely for several decades to be assigned a lot, was all too familiar with the problem. The $600 million settlement was his way of dealing with it.

The formal signing of the settlement agreement carried over to my first term. It was already a done deal. Given the circumstances, I had no reluctance about signing it.

In 1991, the Legislature had enacted Act 323, which allowed individual beneficiaries to recover actual out-of-pocket monetary losses for past breaches of the Hawaiian Home Lands Trust between August 21, 1959 (Statehood Day) and June 30, 1988. The act was unusual, allowing for stale claims that under ordinary civil law would be barred by the statute of limitations.

The law established an Individual Claims Resolutions Panel whose members were appointed by the governor and approved by the Legislature to review individual claims and make awards of monetary damages as it saw fit; it also waived the State's sovereign immunity to allow the individual claimants to sue the State for damages.

The claims panel seemed to follow the Hawaiian practice of hoʻoponopono ("making right") rather than a structured Western dispute-resolution process. By August 1995, 2,800 beneficiaries had submitted 4,327 claims for damages. The panel recommended damage awards amounting to nearly $18 million.

To me, Act 323 was bad law. Allowing claims as old as 40 years to be made against the State was bad policy. There are sound reasons for a statute of limitations: Memories fade, witnesses die or can't be found, records get discarded or destroyed. Thus, the process followed by the claims panel turned almost solely on the testimony and proof submitted by the claimant. There was also a built-in conflict of interest—the governor had appointed the panelists to administer a law he proposed. Fortunately, the law had been set to expire in 1999. That year, I instructed the attorney general to let it expire. If the Legislature had approved an extension, I would have vetoed it.

To boost DHHL's inventory of land, Waihee ordered the transfer of more than 16,000 acres of State land to the Department of Hawaiian Home Lands for homestead use.

At the University, Waihee secured funding to build a new $7.5 million center for the Hawaiian Studies Program at UH-Mānoa. The center was later named the Kamakakūokalani Center for Hawaiian Studies after the distinguished educator and Native Hawaiian leader, Gladys Kamakakūokalani ʻAinoa Brandt.

Had I tried to do as much for Filipino Americans or George Ariyoshi for AJAs we would have been severely criticized. But Hawaiians were special; they were the state's indigenous people and, like most non-Hawaiians, I wanted to help uplift their lives.

Meanwhile, on the federal level, history was made when on November 6, 1990, U.S. Congressman Daniel Akaka—brother of the beloved Rev. Abraham Akaka—became the first Native Hawaiian elected to the United States Senate.

However, no single event demonstrated more clearly the depth of emotions felt by Hawaiians than the commemoration—called ʻOnipaʻa (steadfast, resolute)—of the 100th anniversary of the 1893 overthrow of the Hawaiian monarchy, which took place January 13-17, 1993.

I was seated next to Waihee at the somber opening ceremony. As the kahu (priest) chanted the pule (prayer), Waihee leaned over and said softly, "Ben, I ordered the American flag lowered—only the State flag will fly, at half mast, over State buildings for the next five days."

I never felt that how one treated the American flag was a measure of one's patriotism or love of country, which is why I do not believe flag-burning should be a crime. Nevertheless, I was momentarily taken aback by Waihee's words.

"That's bound to anger some people," I said in a hushed voice.

Waihee nodded, but his demeanor and body language suggested that this was something he felt he had to do (his press secretary had advised against it, I later learned). Every politician has moments when conviction trumps political considerations, and for Waihee this was a big and meaningful one, an expression of his leadership as a Native Hawaiian. It took guts, and I respected him for doing it.

The symbolism was poignant. A century had passed since the 1893 overthrow; the Hawaiian kingdom was gone, now a footnote in the pages of world history. *Surely,* I thought, *the United States, the world's greatest, richest and most powerful nation, will survive without its flag being flown full mast over State buildings for five days.*

The next day, Waihee received a hand-delivered letter from U.S. Sen. Dan Inouye, who wrote that it was a mistake to lower the American flag and urged Waihee to raise it to full mast again. According to Clayton Hee, who was with Waihee at the time, Waihee read the letter, showed it to Hee and then, without comment, "rolled it up and put it away in his desk." Inouye was disappointed. The American flag was not raised again until the five-day commemoration was over. Others were not as polite as Inouye and expressed their feelings in a deluge of angry telephone calls, faxes and letters.

During Waihee's eight years as governor, the Hawaiian flag was the only flag that flew over 'Iolani Palace. After I became governor in 1994 I continued the practice—a token to the memory of the monarchy. Gov. Linda Lingle has continued the practice as well.

Growing Pride, Growing Power

The 100th commemoration of the overthrow was just the first in a series of important events that made 1993 a milestone year.

On May 7, at Maui's Palauea Beach, I watched, along with nearly 1,000 other people, many of them Native Hawaiians, as Waihee and Deputy Assistant Secretary of the Navy William J. Cassidy, Jr., signed two documents, one written in English and the other in Hawaiian, consummating the formal agreement to return Kaho'olawe to the State government within 10 years. (In October 1990, President George H.W. Bush had ordered a halt to the use of Kaho'olawe by the U.S. military for bombing and artillery practice.) It was a somber yet emotional ceremony for many who were there. In contrast to the chest-thumping pride expressed by many of the younger Hawaiians, I saw tears in the eyes of some of the kūpuna (native elders).

On November 11, President Bill Clinton approved a federal law appropriating $400 million to remove unexploded ordinance from the island and plan for its return to the State. "Hawai'i is whole again," Waihee said proudly, expressing a view held by not only Hawaiians but the majority of the public as well.

On November 23, 1993, Clinton approved a congressional joint resolution by which the United States government formally apologized for the illegal actions of U.S. diplomat John Stevens and USS *Boston* Capt. John Wiltse for their roles in the 1893 overthrow of the Hawaiian monarchy. (Inouye had garnered some of the votes for the passage of the resolution by promising it would not be used to argue for Hawaiian sovereignty. Whatever Inouye's intentions, there was no way he could hold anyone but himself to that promise. Since the passage of the resolution, Hawaiian activists regularly refer to the apology as proof of the U.S.'s guilt in the overthrow.)

In October 1992, Matsuo Takabuki's resignation marked a turning point in the history of the Bishop Estate. Takabuki, whose appointment in 1971 had set off a firestorm of protests by Hawaiians furious that an AJA had been appointed, was arguably the most skilled trustee in the estate's modern-day history. He was the guiding force behind the estate's investment strategy and the architect of its profitable Goldman Sachs investment. Resented when he was first appointed, he was honored by Hawaiians when he retired.

With the appointment of Lokelani Lindsey in 1993, all five trustees of the estate, America's richest and largest charitable trust, were Hawaiian. Only one of the trustees, Oswald Stender, a former chief executive officer with the Campbell Estate, had any business experience. The other four were politically connected: Myron Thompson, Henry Peters and Dickie Wong were all steeped in politics—the latter two were the former House Speaker and Senate president, respectively—and Lindsey, an educator, claimed to be Waihee's first cousin.

Hawaiian activist organizations had flourished since 1978. According to one observer, by the mid-1990s as many as 300 had been formed. Among the most prominent was Ka Lahui (1987), an activist group claiming 8,000 members and dedicated to achieving a sovereign Hawaiian nation, which was founded under the leadership of two outspoken and militant activist leaders: Mililani Trask, a lawyer, and her sister, Haunani Trask, a professor at UH. The 7,000-member 'Ohana Council, led by the charismatic Bumpy Kanahele, was another large and powerful group that often showed up in the news.

In January 1994, the 'Ohana Council, citing international law under Kanahele, proclaimed the birth of the Independent Sovereign Nation of Hawai'i. Kanahele, who was over 6 feet tall and weighed at least 300 pounds, stood in great contrast to the mercurial Trask sisters. A former producer of reggae music, he was not college educated. Moreover, he had served time in prison for violations of State and federal law, most of which were related to his political activism (I pardoned him for the State violations). But he was self educated and smart and had a disarming, almost self-effacing but effective way of arguing for Hawaiian causes.

When I became governor in December 1994, Hawaiian political activism was in full stride, stronger and more militant than ever. There was obviously great pride among Hawaiians, especially among the young, as they wielded their growing political power in trying to shape issues important to them.

But by then, hubris, arrogance, hypocrisy and racism had made inroads into the Hawaiian movement and would take a toll in eroding the once-widespread pool of support expressed by non-Hawaiians on Hawaiian issues in the 1978 election.

The 1978 constitutional amendment that created OHA was narrowly ratified by the voters in the November general election. Voters had only three months to evaluate the amendment. Arguably, most had only a vague understanding of the possible ramifications of an Office of Hawaiian Affairs. I was among them. (Besides, I was running for the State Senate at that time, and winning that election was foremost in my mind.) Many non-Hawaiians, I believe, voted for the amendment mainly out of empathy for Hawaiians. Without their votes, OHA would not exist today.

Early polls revealed that a majority of every local ethnic group was generally supportive of new laws or programs that would help the Hawaiians better their lives. Japanese Americans were the most supportive of all the ethnic groups.

This widespread support among locals was not surprising. Unlike the haoles, most locals grew up with Hawaiians; their children attended the same public schools, they played and worked together, they were friends and neighbors and increasingly married into each other's families.

But many Hawaiian activists seemed either to take the support of local non-Hawaiians for granted or, caught up in their own often-angry rhetoric, to dismiss it entirely, perhaps due to the absence of debate on or criticism of Hawaiian issues by politicians and academics. Regardless, most of the major changes Hawaiian activists sought were not possible without the support of the local community, a point many would soon ignore.

There was no better example of the importance of broad community support than the struggle for the return of Kaho'olawe. Hawaiian activists had played an important role, to be sure, but the reality is that the return of Kaho'olawe would not have been possible without the efforts of Govs. Ariyoshi and Waihee, the State Legislature and Hawai'i's congressional delegation. Kaho'olawe continues to be a testament to what can be accomplished when cooperation rather than polarization prevails.

Politics has its own version of Newton's Laws of Physics. For every action there is an opposite (albeit not always equal) reaction; for every reform or change there are consequences. As history has repeatedly shown, even the most well-intentioned voters ultimately will be guided mainly by their personal interests—how they and their families are affected—in responding to proposed or actual changes.

In the aftermath of the Civil Rights Movement, for example, white voters who initially supported equal rights for black Americans were opposed to court orders that required their children to be bussed from their neighborhood schools to predominantly black schools. Requiring open and equal admissions to the nation's public universities was something most Americans could support, but bussing children from the relative comfort and safety of their neighborhood schools proved to be too high a political price to pay. Children, I believe, should never be used to make a political point under such circumstances.

By the mid-1990s, Hawaiian activists had given the general population much to think about. For example, OHA's string of lawsuits against the State for 20 percent of the gross revenues from ceded lands turned out to be a public relations disaster, as non-Hawaiians slowly realized the cost of meeting OHA's demands. Further, OHA's opposition to giving the State any credit for the cost of developing income-generating facilities located on ceded lands left the impression that the trustees were unfair and unreasonably demanding.

After the Heely decision, the attitudes of the trustees hardened. The contemptuous words of activist attorney Hayden Aluli manifested an attitude I could sense in many Hawaiians: "Frankly, 20 percent is too cheap," said Aluli. "If Hawaiians had control over their resources and lands, we would be charging the State rent, okay? And that's the way it is, period."

As one visibly upset legislator bluntly put it: "After *Heely*, they think they got the State by the balls, and they're going to squeeze for as much as they can get."

Hawaiian activists found most legislators open to their requests. The Legislature, for example, approved new laws that defined "gathering rights" and provided protection for ancient burial sites and remains uncovered during construction. But legislators who offered legislation that proposed to balance the interests of Hawaiians and the general population were often treated with contempt and disdain.

When State Rep. Ed Case introduced a bill to resolve the ceded-lands dispute, he was excoriated by Hawaiian activists and hung in effigy. Case, a local-born haole and a Democrat, had acted with good intentions. "I was the wrong messenger; I looked too haole," Case later recalled with a chuckle.

State Sen. Randy Iwase, who introduced a bill to clarify the Hawai'i Supreme Court's decision in a case regarding customary and traditional gathering rights, was jeered and booed as he attempted to speak to a crowd of hundreds of Hawaiians. "Go back to Japan," someone in the crowd shouted at him. Iwase, who was born and raised in Hawai'i and has relatives of Hawaiian blood, was furious.

"I thought, if that's how they felt then they got no chance of success," Iwase told me. "You know, Ben, we AJAs don't say much publicly but we know what happened to the monarchy, and we want to help make things right for the Hawaiians. I don't understand why they make it so tough for us—if they keep this up they are going to get nowhere."

In February 1994, when the State was mired in the worst recession since statehood, 100 members of The Nation of Hawai'i (formerly the 'Ohana Council) held a demonstration in Waikīkī, distributing leaflets to tourists that read "Tourists go home" and "Your visit and stay in Hawai'i assists the illegal state of Hawai'i!"

This caused much consternation, among not only tourist industry leaders but also thousands of hotel workers—most of them inclined to support Hawaiian causes—who were worried about their jobs.

If there were voices of moderation they were drowned out by the incendiary, angry rhetoric of radical activists like Haunani Trask. On the final day of the January 1993 commemoration of 1893 overthrow, Trask shouted defiantly to an estimated crowd of 15,000: "We are not American! We are not American! We are Hawaiian!"

When she was not denouncing her country and disclaiming her nationality, Trask was quick to attack those who disagreed with or offended her. A haole University student named Joey Carter once wrote an op-ed article for *Ka Leo*, the University's student newspaper, in which he argued that he was offended by the manner in which the term "haole" was used. Trask blasted him, ranting that if he did not like the word "haole" he should return to the Mainland. When a few professors criticized Trask for trying to intimidate the student, she attacked them as well, pointing out that the faculty was "85 percent haole." Trask was an expert in shutting up her few haole critics by making them feel guilty for being haole, a technique described by novelist Tom Wolfe as "Mau-Mauing" when used by African-American activists. When she was accused of racism, Trask replied that it was impossible for her to be a "racist" because she "had no power." When it suited her purpose, she was a classic sophist.

Trask was intolerant of the opinions of the few educators who dared to openly disagree with her. When libertarian Ken Conklin, an outspoken opponent of Hawaiian sovereignty, was hired by the UH as a lecturer, he complained that some Hawaiian students had tried to intimidate him into not teaching his class. Rather than support the lecturer, at least for the sake of free speech, the dean in charge caved in to the opposition, and the class was cancelled. Trask said that she was glad Conklin felt intimidated.

"If you think the United States is good ... take my class," Trask had dared students. At the time, Trask was the director of the Hawaiian Studies Program. Her words spoke volumes about the level of scholarship that went into the Hawaiian history that was being taught there. Trask's longtime haole boyfriend, UH professor David Stannard, echoed the sentiments of Trask and her equally mercurial colleague, Lilikala Kame'eleihiwa, when he publicly dismissed the earlier interpretations of Hawaiian history by haole scholars as the works of racist old white men. (When asked to comment on the September 11, 2001, terrorist attacks, Trask revealed her total lack of sensitivity for the victims when she said, "The chickens have come home to roost.")

I first heard of Lilikala Kameʻeleihiwa while I was in the Legislature. While arguing against the building of the H-3 freeway, Kameʻeleihiwa wished death on those who worked on it. Later, two workers were killed and scores injured. Some UH regents complained that Kameʻeleihiwa would threaten them when she did not get her way. "We will make all of you resign," she once said to the regents.

The Kamakakūokalani Center for Hawaiian Studies was named after one of Hawaiʻi's most respected citizens—the distinguished educator and native Hawaiian leader, Gladys Kamakakūokalani ʻAinoa Brandt. I had the pleasure of knowing Mrs. Brandt, or "Aunty Gladys," as she liked to be called. She was a dedicated public servant at heart. When I asked her to serve temporarily as an OHA trustee in 2000, she smiled and replied, "Ben, you are a rascal." At age 95, this remarkable kupuna stepped forward once again to serve the Hawaiian people and brought a measure of civility to the way the trustees did business at OHA. Her greatest legacy was co-authoring "Broken Trust," the 1997 essay that led to the reform of the Bishop Estate. Unlike Trask and Kameʻeleihiwa, Aunty Gladys was from the generation of Hawaiians that believed feeling Hawaiian was as much about what was in the heart as it was about the blood in the veins. She was one of a kind.

That Trask and Kameʻeleihiwa controlled the center named in Brandt's honor boggled my mind. They had done a disservice to her honored name. They had turned the center into a forum for teaching their revisionist views of Hawaiian history rather than an institution that taught its students how to think critically, to be open to other points of views and to search for the truth, whatever it might turn out to be.

I believe deeply in free speech, but Trask, Kameʻeleihiwa and others like them taught people how to *hate*; that was the big difference between them and activists such as Bumpy Kanahele, who were just as passionate in their beliefs for Hawaiian sovereignty but were not so divisive. It was hard for me to stomach that Trask and Kameʻeleihiwa were operating at the taxpayers' expense while I was forced to cut social programs for the poor.

In 1996, two events should have caused the OHA trustees to reflect on the strategy of their negotiations with the State. First, the U.S. Department of Transportation's inspector general notified the State that paying $30 million to OHA from airport revenues did not comply with federal law. The following year, Congress passed the Forgiveness Act, which exempted states from having to repay the federal government for using airport revenues for non-airport purposes, but prohibited such use in the future. Hawaiʻi's was forgiven for using $28 million in airport revenues to pay OHA.

Inouye, who voted for the Forgiveness Act, assured OHA: "The airports continue to sit on ceded lands. The State's obligation to compensate OHA for use of the land ... should also continue. The only difference would now be the source the State draws upon to satisfy its obligation." In other words, Inouye suggested, although it was illegal under federal law for the State to pay OHA from airport revenues, it should pay OHA a like amount from other sources, namely the State's general fund. I was surprised by Inouye's statement; apparently he had misread Act 304, which provided that if any of its provisions conflicted with federal law the entire act would be declared null and void and OHA's demands for the 20 percent mooted. The reversal of *Heely* meant that there was no statutory formula by which to pay OHA anything.

The attorney general had notified the Hawai'i Supreme Court of the new Forgiveness Act shortly after it became law, but nearly four years passed before the court finally issued its ruling on *Heely*. Earlier, the court had stated that the ceded-lands dispute was a political question that should be resolved by the Legislature. In turn, the Legislature, reluctant to deal with such a politically charged issue, looked to the State administration to negotiate a settlement with OHA. But as long as *Heely* was left unresolved by the Hawai'i Supreme Court, our negotiations with OHA got nowhere. In 1999, after five years of fruitless negotiations, I instructed State negotiators to terminate the talks.

In March 1996 a few months before Heely's decision, a Big Island rancher named Harold "Freddy" Rice requested an application to vote in the upcoming OHA election and was turned down by the county clerk, who informed him that, by law, only Hawaiians were permitted to vote in the OHA election.

Rice was not a Mainland haole new to Hawai'i. He had been born and raised on the Big Island, and his family traced its roots in Hawai'i to the 1800s. Among his good friends were many Hawaiian paniolo (cowboys). One of my Big Island supporters who knew him described Rice as an honest man. "Freddy is the kind of guy who will do something out of principle. If he believes something is not right, he'll try to fix it," he told me.

On April 25, 1996, Rice sued the State and OHA in federal court, alleging that the OHA Hawaiians-only rule violated the 14th and 15th Amendments to the U.S. Constitution.

On May 6, 1997, U.S. District Court Judge David Ezra ruled against Rice, holding that the Hawaiians-only voting restriction was based "upon the unique status of Native Hawaiians" and was proper because Hawaiians are OHA's only direct beneficiaries.

By then the Rice case had been brought to my attention by Attorney General Margery Bronster. My own view was that Ezra had made a close call. He seemed to have equated OHA's legal status with that of the American Indians, an argument for which I thought there was little evidence. OHA, after all, was a State agency created by State law.

On June 22, 1998, the 9th Circuit Court of Appeals affirmed Ezra's ruling, holding that the OHA voting restrictions were "not primarily racial, but legal and political" and "rooted in historical concern for the Hawaiian race." Rice then filed an appeal to the U.S. Supreme Court.

I took no comfort in the 9th Circuit's ruling. It was common knowledge among Hawai'i lawyers that the 9th Circuit had the reputation of being the nation's most liberal appellate court. In fact, some legal scholars described it as a "runaway court." Our research revealed that no other federal appellate court has been over-ruled more than the 9th Circuit. In its 1996 and 1997 sessions, the U.S. Supreme Court reversed 27 of the 28 cases it considered from the 9th Circuit, and 17 of those cases were overturned by unanimous decisions. When liberal justices such as Stephen Breyer and Ruth Bader Ginsburg joined the conservative and moderate justices in unanimously overruling the 9th Circuit, it said much about the Supreme Court's disrespect for 9th Circuit rulings.

While OHA trustees took heart in the favorable rulings of Ezra and the 9th Circuit Court of Appeals, I shared the attorney general's concern about the U.S. Supreme Court. As much as I thought both Ezra and the 9th Circuit rulings stood on weak grounds, if the Supreme Court declined to hear Rice's appeal that would end the matter and OHA's Hawaiians-only voter restriction would stand. If the Court agreed to hear Rice's appeal it would be a crapshoot.

"Governor, if the Supreme Court decides to hear *Rice* we may be in trouble," Bronster told me.

"I know. Keep me posted, and just make sure your people are ready for it," I replied.

As it happened, though, it took two years for the case to get that far—and there was much to engage our attention in the meantime. ❖

CHAPTER EIGHTEEN

The Bishop Estate

"Modern-Day Ali'i"

Theonly thing that's changed at the Bishop Estate is the complexion of the trustees' skins," a part-Hawaiian friend said to me after the Supreme Court justices appointed Waihee's political confidant Gerard Jervis to replace retiring trustee Myron Thompson in 1994.

Bishop Estate, created by the will of Princess Bernice Pauahi Bishop when she died in 1884, was one of the nation's wealthiest charitable institutions. With an inventory of approximately 350,000 acres of land, it was also the State's largest private landowner. But after the U.S. Supreme Court upheld the 1967 Land Reform Act in 1984, the seemingly endless stream of cash from the mandated sales of its residential leasehold lands made Bishop Estate the nation's wealthiest charitable trust. In 1995, the *Wall Street Journal* estimated the trust's endowment at $10 billion—greater than the endowments of Harvard and Yale.

The sole beneficiary of Bishop Estate Trust is Kamehameha Schools. It was founded in 1887, first as a school for boys, and since then tens of thousands of Hawaiian boys and girls have graduated from it, many going on to become leaders in politics, business, labor and the professions. With its considerable economic power and vast land ownership, as well as the influence of thousands of loyal Kamehameha alumni, Bishop Estate has become a powerful force in Hawai'i politics.

The estate was created nine years before the overthrow of Queen Lili'uokalani and the Hawaiian Kingdom in 1893. Its trustees were appointed by the justices of the Kingdom's Supreme Court, as set forth in the princess's will. After Hawai'i's annexation by the United States in 1898 there was no legal reason for this practice to continue, but it did, for 116 years, until in 1999 it came to an end.

The continued involvement of the Supreme Court justices after 1893 stemmed in part from a genuine desire to honor the legacy of the princess, who was one of the most beloved of the Hawaiian ali'i. The princess's love for the Hawaiian people, expressed through her efforts to educate poor and orphaned Hawaiian children, made her one of the most admired and respected ali'i in the eyes of the non-Hawaiian community as well.

Originally I had hardly given a second thought to the potential legal problems of the Supreme Court's involvement in the selection of trustees, but gradually

372

my feelings on that issue evolved from indifference to concern. In 1982, the justices appointed one of their own—sitting Chief Justice William Richardson—as a trustee. Justice Herman Lum, who had urged Richardson's lateral move from chief justice to trustee, then succeeded Richardson as chief justice. In hindsight, the move was as blatantly arrogant as the conflict of interest was obvious. It wasn't as clear at the time. The story that Lum had set up the appointment for Richardson was anecdotal, but it was known that the other three justices had agreed to the appointment without dissent and had made an exception to the mandatory age-70 retirement rule by allowing Richardson to serve until age 73. Although the move raised some eyebrows—there was some grumbling but no open dissent among senators (of whom I was one)—Richardson, who is part-Hawaiian, was seen as an overdue appointment by most Hawaiians, and Lum, whose elevation to chief justice was unanimously confirmed by the State Senate, was well qualified to serve as chief justice.

Most lawyers, particularly the younger ones, looked up to the Supreme Court, perhaps because while they had been in law school they had studied cases that presented Supreme Court justices at their finest in terms of intellect, ethics and dedication to the law. However, the Richardson-Lum move made me think more deeply about the Bishop Estate trustee appointment process. Thereafter, I joined the growing ranks of lawyers who saw the court's continued involvement as boding nothing but trouble for its integrity and the public's confidence in the Judiciary.

The Richardson-Lum move caused many to consider the propriety of the court's involvement. Supporters argued that the practice was proper because the justices were acting as individuals and not as justices. I found this rationalization embarrassing. Clearly, the five individuals were authorized to appoint trustees only because they were Supreme Court justices. Moreover, even a first-year law student could envision the eventuality that the justices would be called upon to rule in cases—as they later were and did—involving trustees they had appointed.

The biggest issue and the root cause of the ethical and political problems plaguing the Bishop Estate, particularly from the 1980s through 1999, was the lucrative trustee compensation. Trustee "fees," as they were called, were determined by State law. The law was intended to put a ceiling on the fees, which were derived mainly from real estate sales. But the framers of the law did not foresee the multi-hundred-million-dollar sales of Bishop Estate lands compelled by the 1967 Land Reform Act. According to data provided by Professor Roth, fees in 1980 were $125,014 per trustee, increasing to $240,787 in 1984 and skyrocketing to $926,487 in 1987. No other charitable trust in the nation paid its trustees such exorbitant fees.

I was still a member of the State Senate (1978-1986) when I first saw Pearl Richardson testify at a public hearing on a bill intended to reduce the compensation of the Bishop Estate trustees. Remarkably, she was the sister of William Richardson, the former chief justice and lieutenant governor who was currently serving as a trustee. *That takes courage*, I thought—or extreme sibling jealously, some trustee supporters whispered. I was eager to hear what she had to say.

She was a slightly built Chinese-Hawaiian woman who bore a strong resemblance to her well-known brother. Indignant, eyes flashing, the feisty and articulate woman gave the trustees what amounted to a public scolding and urged the legislators to approve the bill. She argued that the trustees' compensation was a "disgrace" and a "disservice" to the trust's beneficiary. Trustees for most charitable trusts, she pointed out, usually served without any kind of remuneration except for travel and other out-of-pocket expenses.

The hearing room was packed with people, mostly Hawaiians, and the ubiquitous news media. During Richardson's testimony the quiet in the warm, stuffy room was broken only by an occasional muffled cough and the heavy breathing of a very overweight, perspiring man who, like the rest of the audience, was transfixed by the proceedings.

Richardson said publicly what other Hawaiians complained about privately. Her heartfelt testimony persuaded me she was right. But one need not have been Hawaiian to wonder how the trustees could justify the kind of money they were being paid. The excuse, propounded mainly by Henry Peters, that the previous haole trustees had been similarly compensated meant nothing. Takabuki and Richardson, after all, were leaders of the 1954 Democratic Revolution; they were expected to be progressive and make positive changes. The old joke about the haole missionaries—"they came to do good, and they did very *well*"—seemed applicable.

I was surprised by the strong support the trustees received from Hawaiian organizations such as the Kamehameha Alumni Association, the Hawaiian Civic Club and others. I had assumed that other Hawaiians would come forward as Pearl Richardson had. But at the public hearings I attended, she was the only one.

A longtime friend, who was part-Hawaiian, a Kamehameha alumnus and college educated, explained, "Ben, Hawaiians have almost a spiritual connection to the legacy of the princess. And we get very concerned any time the government starts poking its nose in Bishop Estate business."

"But I've heard a lot of Hawaiians complain about the trustee compensation, even you," I said.

"Yes, but that's for Hawaiians to deal with. You know, Ben, the last time the State got involved with Bishop Estate, it passed the Land Reform Act, which today is forcing the estate to sell its residential leasehold lands. Now, intellectually I can understand the social policy behind it, but as a Hawaiian I have a hard time emotionally dealing with it."

"But don't you think the trustees can use all of that cash that's coming in and get better returns on investments? Bishop Estate is land rich and cash poor," I said, resurrecting an old argument.

"Yeah, that's what the trustees of Lunalilo Trust thought. They sold trust land, including the prime lands at Diamond Head and other places, and then they lost everything in the stock market. Today, the only land the Lunalilo Trust owns is the five acres the old folks' home is on—only five acres left!" he replied, grimfaced.

I had touched a nerve and felt it wise just to listen.

"You grew up in Kalihi; you know how much that school on Kapālama Heights means to Hawaiians. Kamehameha is the princess's great legacy, and that's why many Hawaiians look up to the trustees. Some Hawaiians see them as modern-day aliʻi. Look, Ben, many Hawaiians believe the Bishop Estate's biggest problem is not the trustees; it's the government. Today the State wants to fix the trustee compensation—what's next? If something bad happens to Bishop Estate, the school will suffer, Hawaiian kids will suffer.... Stay away from Bishop Estate ... politically it's not worth it for you."

At the time, it seemed that there was a chance the committee would approve the bill to reduce compensation and send it to the full Senate for approval. But the bill had been written to apply to private trusts generally. Consequently, it was opposed by representatives of other trusts who argued that, if approved, the bill would unfairly and unreasonably infringe on the operation of their respective trusts. Their arguments were persuasive, and the bill was deferred for further study.

The following year, a similar bill was introduced. Mrs. Pearl Richardson testified again. It seemed as though the new bill had the support in the committee to move it to the Senate floor for a vote, but it was deferred once more.

I later found out that, while Richardson openly urged legislators to approve the bill, a trustee had negotiated a behind-the-scenes agreement with key legislators to "kill the bill and let us [the trustees] 'police' ourselves, and we'll reduce our compensation." The bill was killed.

The trustees did police themselves, for a while. In 1987, each trustee was entitled to $1,038,455, but waived $111,968, earning $926,487 for the year. In 1988, they were entitled to $1,545,510 but waived $906,416, earning $648,094 each. In 1993, the trustees' fees increased to $823,974, rising further in 1994 and 1995 to $915,238 and $938,047, respectively, with no waivers.

Allowing the trustees to police their own compensation missed the point. The real issue was whether the trustees of a charitable trust should be paid fees at all and, if so, how much? Furthermore, the trustees' duty of loyalty prohibited their paying themselves more than the value of their services. This was subjective, of course, but I doubted there were many people who believed the trustees had earned what they ultimately paid themselves. After all, it was the 1967 Land Reform Act—which the Bishop Estate trustees had fought against all the way to the U.S. Supreme Court—that compelled the sale of trust lands and thus ironically generated such high fees for the trustees.

Moreover, in Hawaiʻi, none of the trustees of private schools such as Punahou, ʻIolani and Mid-Pacific were compensated. Nor were the trustees of prestigious

Mainland universities such as Harvard, Yale and Stanford. What was the justification for treating the Bishop Estate trustees differently?

Undoubtedly, the question troubled the trustees. By the mid-1990s, they could no longer point to the State law setting their fees as an excuse when the public was able to figure out that they were at the same time working behind the scenes to kill attempts by legislators to reform the law. When Peters was appointed trustee in 1984 he was the Speaker of the House. Wong had been president of the Senate when he was appointed in 1992. The two trustees still had enough influence in the Legislature to stop the bills. Moreover, Peters had doled out jobs and contracts to at least a half-dozen legislators, among them Sen. Milton Holt and House Speaker Joseph Souki.

To justify their compensation, the trustees had adopted the so-called "lead trustee" system, in which each trustee was assigned a specific area to manage. The idea, I learned from Attorney General Margery Bronster, had been started earlier by Matsuo Takabuki, who was designated lead trustee for asset management. Takabuki demonstrated considerable skill in managing and investing the trust's assets. Some of his investments were very successful, and eventually three of the other four trustees relied so heavily on his recommendations that Takabuki pretty much called the shots. Only trustee Hung Wo Ching, himself a highly successful businessman, questioned Takabuki's judgment, even suing Takabuki to stop a particular investment.

After Takabuki retired in 1993, the remaining trustees liked the lead trustee idea so much they continued it. This time, however, all five trustees were designated "lead trustees" for different areas. Lokelani Lindsey was designated lead trustee for education and communication, Peters for asset management, Wong for governmental affairs, Jervis for legal affairs and Stender for alumni relations. As lead trustees they saw themselves as the equivalent of corporate CEOs and therefore entitled to be compensated as such. Stender was the only trustee with actual experience as a corporate CEO. His assignment as lead trustee for alumni relations was a reflection of board politics rather than sound business judgment.

The lead trustee system was strikingly similar to the committee system of the State Legislature, in which committee chairmen often decided what bills their respective committees would consider for passage to the House or Senate. I was not surprised; Takabuki, Peters and Wong were all former legislators (Takabuki was a City councilman). However, Bishop Estate was a trust, and the idea of putting one trustee in a position of dominance over the others was such an obvious breach of the trustees' fiduciary duties that I wondered whether it had been reviewed by the estate's many high-priced attorneys or whether it had been concocted by the trustees themselves. At least two—Gerard Jervis and Oswald Stender—should have known better. Jervis, after all, was a lawyer and Stender a former Campbell Estate CEO. But both went along.

The ambivalence of Hawaiians regarding Bishop Estate puzzled me. I recalled how, during the controversy over the OHA ceded-lands bill in 1980, a veteran senator had told me he had learned to stay away from Hawaiian issues because "they can't make up their minds about what they want." It was more complicated than that, of course, but in 1980 I had been on the wrong side of the OHA bill and experienced how emotional Hawaiians could get over such matters. It did not feel good to be typecast as "anti-Hawaiian." *It's no wonder*, I thought, *there is an unspoken understanding among many legislators that the Bishop Estate is the exclusive business of Hawaiians and not the State.* I decided that if the Hawaiians did not care how the trustees ran Bishop Estate, neither would I.

Thereafter, except for my role in lobbying unsuccessfully for the governor's proposed leasehold conversion law for condominiums and townhouses in 1989, I reacted but did not take any affirmative steps on issues that directly affected Bishop Estate.

The Dispute Heats Up

Nearly a decade later, in March 1997, I was invited by Michael Chun, Kamehameha Schools' popular president, to attend the 75th Kamehameha Song Contest. I knew there was trouble brewing at Kamehameha Schools. Disputes had arisen between Chun and the faculty on one side, and the trustees, Lokelani Lindsey in particular, on the other. I had never been invited to the song contest before and wondered whether Chun's intent was purely social. Nevertheless, I looked forward to the event.

The Neil Blaisdell Center was packed with a standing-room-only crowd. Among the 8,000-plus audience were 1,500 to 1,600 Kamehameha freshmen, sophomores, juniors and seniors. The classes competed with each other by singing Hawaiian songs a capella in the Hawaiian language. The contest was a showcase of school pride and the culture of Hawaiian music. It was a singular event that commanded the audience's attention for several hours and had became so popular with the general public that it was televised.

I shortly found out that the dispute at Kamehameha was far more serious than I had thought. When the trustees were introduced there was only light, tepid applause by the students (I learned later some had actually booed during rehearsal, prompting a stern warning from Lindsey and Wong). But when Chun, who had emerged as a sympathetic figure in the dispute, was introduced, he received a rousing, standing ovation and cheers led by the students that were so prolonged I felt embarrassed for the unsmiling trustees. I wondered whether the television audience noticed the stark contrast in greetings. As I watched Chun, who was obviously touched by the outpouring of warmth, I had no doubt whose side the students were on.

By May, the dispute had become more public. The Kamehameha faculty, fed up with Lindsey's micromanaging and intimidating style and realizing that Chun was not then inclined to take her on, formed Na Kumu o Kamehameha (the Teachers of Kamehameha). Meanwhile, alumni, parents of students and others equally concerned about the deteriorating situation at the school formed Na Pua a Ke Ali'i Pauahi (the Children of Princess Pauahi) to air and resolve their differences with the trustees.

The makeup of the two groups stood in contrast to the militant activists from Ka Lahui and other sovereignty organizations. The membership of Na Kumu and Na Pua included Hawaiians who had distinguished themselves as leaders in the community at large, professionals and parents, as well as many alumni who were otherwise unlikely to join demonstrations of any kind. Some of the names comprised a virtual "Who's Who" list of the Hawaiian community.

But there was a dearth of Hawaiian attorneys. Some were representing the individual trustees, but where were the others, I wondered, the ones who didn't hesitate to sue easy targets such as the State, developers or anyone else on the wrong side of Hawaiian issues?

It remained for Beadie Dawson, a part-Hawaiian graduate of Punahou, who in her 50s had returned to school and earned a law degree from the UH law school, to step forward and represent Na Pua. While Hawaiian men such as Roy Benham, Fred Cachola and Jan Dill were involved in the protest movement, strong Hawaiian women such as Dawson and revered kūpuna Gladys Brandt and Nona Beamer, as well as women who did not usually join in demonstrations, such as Toni Lee, assumed highly visible and prominent roles in the leadership of Na Kumu and Na Pua. Nothing, I learned as a legislator, riles up women more than threats to children or their education.

Lindsey was the primary object of the protesters' anger. She was a stout part-Hawaiian woman who looked more haole than Hawaiian. On the few occasions I met her, she struck me as warm and gregarious. She was a former physical education teacher who had earned a master's degree in education, served as the principal of three schools in four years, and for nearly 11 years been deputy superintendent of education for Maui.

She had been somewhat controversial as deputy superintendent. She was unpopular with the Maui principals, who unanimously complained about her leadership style. In 1986, the principals wanted new Superintendent of Education Charles Toguchi to replace Lindsey, but Margaret Apo and Darryl Aiona, the two Hawaiian members of the Board of Education, urged Toguchi to keep her on. Although wholesale changes in deputies are common with new superintendents, Toguchi, noting that Lindsey was the only Hawaiian among his 21 deputies, agreed to keep her on his team.

I got the impression that Lindsey was an emotional, somewhat hyperactive person. According to one story, when Lindsey received her first monthly trustee's paycheck, she pranced around the board room whooping giddily while holding her check for $75,000 up over her head (she earned $85,000 annually as deputy superintendent), giving her bemused fellow trustees a humorous and revealing insight into her penchant for quirky behavior. Ignoring this as a potential sign of things to come, the four other trustees agreed to appoint Lindsey "lead trustee" for education, a role she undertook with great enthusiasm. Lindsey's critics portrayed her as a martinet, tyrant, manipulator and micromanager; later she was labeled "paranoid," "crazy" and "evil" by co-trustee Stender.

As angry as the protestors were, however, they did not seek the removal of the trustees—that would come later; at this point they wanted to meet with the trustees to air out and resolve their grievances using the process of ho'oponopono, or mediation, to make right. After agreeing to meet, Wong, who was acting as spokesman for the trustees, inexplicably changed his mind and stated there would be no meetings with the trustees. The trustees had circled their wagons. It would prove to be a fatal mistake.

I wondered why Lindsey had behaved in a way that provoked such anger. But the din of the controversy was so great that her side didn't get heard. I found out subsequently that Lindsey blamed Chun, who was not an educator, for what she believed was a precipitous decline in Kamehameha's academic performance.

Apparently, Lindsey had hired an expert to evaluate and report on the quality of Kamehameha's education. The report concluded that there had been a decline in the reading and math scores of students who were admitted during Chun's presidency, that more than half of Kamehameha's students failed to make the minimum SAT scores required for admission to the University of Hawai'i (some of the state's top public high schools fared better), and that the SAT scores lagged far behind those of students from rival private schools 'Iolani and Punahou. As a former DOE deputy superintendent, Lindsey should have known that the comparison was unfair, as both 'Iolani and Punahou select only the top students from all ethnic groups, whereas Kamehameha was limited to selecting from a smaller pool of only Hawaiian students.

Nevertheless, Lindsey expected better and was enraged by the SAT scores. Moreover, she found there was little accountability for the costs of operations. In one instance, hundreds of thousands of dollars' worth of computers were missing and could not be accounted for. Lindsey demanded that each teacher produce an accounting of his or her equipment, and she pledged to the other trustees that she would "turn things around in five years."

Lindsey also criticized Chun personally, alleging that he had spent hundreds of thousands of dollars without authorization from the trustees. In one instance, Lindsey alleged, Chun's wife, Bina, placed an order for $600,000 worth of new koa furniture for the president's residence that Lindsey later cancelled.

If Lindsey's allegations were true, it would be grounds for the trustees to fire Chun. Chun was an engineer, not an educator. He had been a member of former Mayor Eileen Anderson's Cabinet but had not distinguished himself from other Cabinet members. However, as one writer described him, Chun was "Mr. Kamehameha." While a student at Kamehameha, he had been one of the school's great athletes, earning state and national honors as an end on the football team, an outstanding student, a member of the National Honor Society and the student body president of the boys' school. Handsome, charismatic and friendly to all, Chun also understood the nuances of Hawai'i politics very well.

But Chun's reaction to the growing controversy was to hunker down, and for good *personal* reasons. If Chun took on Lindsey and the other trustees, win or lose he was likely to lose his job. As president, he lived like a modern-day ali'i, with a six-figure salary, generous expense accounts for himself and his wife, a home, a car and other perquisites. Moreover, Chun served as a paid director on the boards of Bank of Hawai'i, Alexander & Baldwin and Matson Navigation Co. All told, as Kamehameha's president, Chun was receiving a salary and benefits package that nearly equaled a trustee's annual compensation.

Chun's inaction was criticized by some Hawaiians. At a meeting I had with Gladys Brandt regarding OHA, our conversation drifted to Bishop Estate and Chun. A disappointed Brandt told me she had scolded Chun for remaining silent. "You are the president; why don't you act like one?" she said she had asked him. The crisis at Kamehameha could have been a defining moment for Chun, in which he could have shown leadership worthy of his position. Instead, he offered only a modest response when the protest movement evolved from a desire for ho'oponopono to a demand to remove Lindsey and one or more of the other trustees. When he was needed to vouch for his angry and demoralized faculty, he sadly let the moment pass.

I wondered why the trustees didn't fire Chun. Clearly, it was their prerogative. But emotions got in the way. If Lindsey wanted to fire him she would have had to persuade Peters. Peters took pride in claiming that he was responsible for Chun's becoming president. He would later tell people privately he was disappointed in him. But Peters, who could be a terror to his enemies, was a soft touch when it came to his friends. He could not bring himself to fire Chun. Ironically, it would be Peters who would lose his job, while Chun would keep his.

It was left to Lindsey to find ways to control Chun and get Kamehameha up to speed academically. The academic expert's report suggested that there were, in fact, academic problems at Kamehameha. If that were true, one could hardly blame Lindsey for being upset. Unfortunately, she went ballistic, like the proverbial (and angry) bull in a china shop. Lindsey's criticism of Chun regarding Kamehameha's academic shortcomings was in fact an attack on the faculty. She showed her contempt for some of the teachers by openly calling them incompetent or worse. She was bumbling and at times verbally abusive and intimidating to administrators and faculty she thought opposed her. Moreover, she did not come with "clean hands," as she, too, was found to have used Bishop Estate employees for her personal projects.

Ultimately, the academic issues took a back seat to Lindsey's abrasive personality and her treatment of the faculty and a few unlucky administrators. Later, I learned that she had gotten into an intensely personal feud with co-trustee Stender, driving the normally mild-mannered man to file a lawsuit to have her removed as trustee.

At this point, the thought of State intervention was the furthest thing from my mind. As far as I was concerned, the highly charged dispute between the trustees and faculty was an internal matter that should be resolved by the parties involved. Under the princess's will, the trustees were the final authority on the policies adopted for Kamehameha Schools. Moreover, the fact that many people disagreed with the trustees did not mean they had breached their fiduciary duties.

I had never practiced trust law, but I understood enough to know that it allows trustees a great deal of leeway in making decisions, even mistakes in judgment, if, acting as "prudent trustees" would, they believed they were acting in the best interests of the trust and its beneficiaries. At this point, I saw no need for the State to investigate what appeared to be a nasty spat between the trustees and the Kamehameha faculty. Besides, special investigations were costly, and 1997 was a time when I was cutting the budgets of State departments, including the Department of the Attorney General. Economic recovery, State government fiscal issues and collective bargaining were foremost in my mind.

"Broken Trust" and the State Investigation

On August 9, 1997, however, everything changed. The *Star-Bulletin* published "Broken Trust," an essay authored by five individuals who accused the trustees of arrogance, cronyism and breaches of their fiduciary responsibilities. "Broken Trust" became a sensational news scoop for the *Star-Bulletin*.

The driving force behind "Broken Trust" was University of Hawai'i law professor Randy Roth, a Mainland haole who had come to Hawai'i in 1980s to teach trust law. I was wary of Roth. I had first met him after he won a bid for a dinner at Washington Place that Vicky and I had donated to a charity auction. At the dinner, Roth and his gracious wife struck us as very friendly and personable. We enjoyed their company. Later I learned that he was a key political insider to Maui Mayor Linda Lingle, who was already gearing up to run against me in the 1998 gubernatorial election. I assumed that Roth had bid $800 for the opportunity to size me up. "Well, I guess I didn't impress him," I joked to Vicky afterwards.

The co-authors of "Broken Trust" had alleged that the appointments of Bishop Estate trustees were politically manipulated. Except for Stender, the trustees were all Democrats, as were almost all of the other so-called "manipulators" such as the Supreme Court justices (the chief justice was a Republican), members of the Judicial Selection Commission and the governor. Roth must have anticipated that "Broken Trust" could lose its effectiveness if it was seen as another partisan political screed, and it might well have been depicted that way. In 1997, the spirit of bipartisanship was literally non-existent in Hawai'i. The polarization that divided the U.S. Congress along party lines was rampant throughout the states, and Hawai'i was no exception. Hawai'i Republicans, anticipating certain victory in the 1998 gubernatorial race (I was written off as dead by some national political observers), were on the attack; the Democrats were on the defense. If Roth had been the only author (which, in fact, he essentially was), "Broken Trust" might well have been a three- or four-day media event that would eventually have been forgotten.

But Roth persuaded four distinguished Hawaiians to share authorship: two Democrats, a Republican and a man of God, who were respected not only in the Hawaiian community but in the community at large: Gladys Brandt, the first woman principal of Kamehameha Schools and a former chairperson of the University of Hawai'i Board of Regents; Walter Heen, a former City councilman, State Circuit Court judge, U.S. Attorney and prominent member of the Democratic Party; Monsignor Charles Kekumano, a retired and highly regarded Catholic priest; and Samuel King, a sitting judge of the U.S. District Court, a prominent Republican who had once run unsuccessfully for governor and whose father was a former Bishop Estate trustee and Territorial governor. The four gave "Broken Trust" great credibility (I later learned that even former Supreme Court Justice Edward Nakamura, a leader of the 1954 Democratic Revolution, was helping Roth). The article could not be ignored. The UH law professor had pulled off a remarkable feat and, as it turned out, performed a valuable public service.

While mulling over the import of "Broken Trust," I recalled a lecture by my trust professor at Loyola Law School in which he stated that "under trust law the end result is not always as important as the process the trustee followed to get there … and in getting there the trustee must act as would a 'prudent trustee.'"

"Broken Trust" included allegations of breaches that put the controversy at Kamehameha in a context that could not be ignored. It was no longer just a faculty-versus-trustee dispute. The trustees seemed out of control. Under the circumstances, I felt it was the State's duty to find out what had happened and why, and, if necessary, to take appropriate legal action.

Bronster briefed me on the scope of my statutory authority over such matters. Hawai'i law provides that "(t)he attorney general shall investigate alleged violations when directed to do so by the governor or when the attorney general determines that an investigation would be in the public interests." According to Bronster, Stender had expressed his concerns about the other trustees to her "a long time ago," when he happened to be seated next to her on a return flight from the Mainland. It was the first time I learned of their discussion.

Stender apparently had been expressing his concerns about his co-trustees to everyone he deemed important and influential. But if he thought the other trustees had breached their fiduciary duties, at the very least he should have brought it to the attention of the probate court, which had the discretion to look into the matter itself. I wondered why it had taken a chance meeting for Stender to disclose his concerns to the attorney general, the only State official designated by law to investigate alleged breaches of trust, and why I had not been informed about his allegations. Was Bronster concerned I would not support an investigation because I knew Peters and Wong? After all, if I hadn't approved I could have cut off the funding she would need to do a decent job. But these thoughts passed quickly. They didn't matter; time was being wasted, and I directed Bronster to start the investigation as soon as possible.

When I appointed Margery Bronster as the State's attorney general in 1994, she became the first woman to hold the post. I had not met her before I interviewed her for the position. Subsequently, I learned that she had graduated from Brown University in 1979 and from Columbia University Law School in 1982. While practicing law in New York she met her husband, Hawai'i-born Mark Fukunaga, who was also practicing law there. They moved to Hawai'i, where she joined a major law firm in 1989 and Mark became CEO of his family's highly successful business, Servco Pacific Corp.

Bronster had excellent professional credentials. But lawyers with excellent résumés are a dime a dozen. Integrity, compassion, courage and loyalty were personal traits I thought were essential in a good attorney general. I had a gut feeling that she possessed those qualities. Moreover, the fact that she was a Jewish-American woman who had majored in Chinese at Brown, spoke Mandarin and had married a Japanese American said much about her as a person.

Taking on the Bishop Estate trustees was one thing, but taking on the Supreme Court justices as well was not for the timid. Bronster, after all, would return to private practice one day and perhaps find herself with cases before the Supreme Court. But when I asked her to investigate, she agreed without hesitation.

Bronster said she would need additional funding for the investigation, perhaps as much as $200,000, as I recall. That was a lot of money, especially in those hard times. But just as it had been for me, "Broken Trust" was the tipping point for many legislators. I was confident they would support my request for additional funding, even those who were close to Peters and Wong. Politically, they could not afford not to. The funds would be there, I assured Bronster.

On August 12, 1997, I announced publicly that I had directed the attorney general to conduct a formal investigation. "Broken Trust," Roth would write later, had brought the issues to "critical mass." Indeed it had, and the unspoken rule that the Bishop Estate's business was the exclusive business of Hawaiians no longer applied. The Hawaiians at Kamehameha wanted the State's help, and they would get it. From that day and for the next two years, at least, the Bishop Estate became the State's business.

"Broken Trust" included two specific allegations that appeared to be prima facie breaches of fiduciary duty:

(1) Some of the trustees (including former trustees) had made personal investments of roughly $2 million in a Texas methane gas deal in which the estate also invested $85 million. The deal went sour and Bishop Estate lost $65 million. This seemed obviously improper because the trustees' personal investments could have colored their judgments on whether the trust should invest more money or cut its losses and get out.

(2) Peters had negotiated for the other party in a multi-billion-dollar golf course deal involving the Bishop Estate. If this was true, there was no way Peters could justify his actions as a trustee.

I took no pleasure in ordering the State's investigation. I had served with Peters and Wong in the Legislature, and, despite some hard-fought political battles I'd had with them, I had a cordial relationship with both. I also knew how tough they could be. Based on their responses to the protests by the Na Kumu and Na Pua groups, I anticipated a terrible legal and political battle ahead.

To avoid any appearance of conflict of interest, I told Bronster that, although I wanted to be kept informed of the investigation's findings, I would not get involved in the scope and manner in which she investigated the issue. My friendship with Peters and Wong and the obvious political ramifications of the upcoming election made it important for me to maintain a hands-off approach. In the event I was subpoenaed to testify at a deposition or a trial, the public needed to know that I had not tried to influence the investigation in any way.

November 1997 brought more bad news for the trustees. On November 27, the *Star-Bulletin* published "Broken Trust II," which accused Lindsey of trying to intimidate teachers and administrators who openly questioned her methods and took her to task for what seemed like a particularly troubling interrogation of a student leader. Like "Broken Trust," "Broken Trust II" was co-authored by five respected individuals, all of them distinguished educators: Gladys Brandt; UH professor Isabella Aiona Abbott; Winona Rubin, former director of the State Department of Human Services; Nona Beamer, a revered former teacher at Kame-hameha; and Roderick McPhee, president emeritus of Punahou School. McPhee was the only haole; the other four were Native Hawaiians.

Earlier, on November 17, court-appointed master Colbert Matsumoto had released his preliminary report on the financial affairs of Bishop Estate. From a legal standpoint, Matsumoto's report was devastating, providing specific evidence of wrongdoing by the trustees. Among the most serious were his conclusions that the trustees had not complied with the law and the princess's will, that some had made private investments despite obvious conflicts of interest and that the lead trustee system adopted by the trustees was itself a violation of basic trust law.

Furthermore, Matsumoto found that, contrary to the trustees' claims of returns on investments, the estate had actually lost $135 million. Apparently, the loss had been masked on the estate's tax returns by an infusion of cash, mainly from the sale of residential lease lands prompted by the 1967 Land Reform Act. Although Matsumoto concluded that the misrepresentation was not deliberate but rather an example of the trustees' inattention to details, the finding was particularly damaging. It cast a cloud over the trustees' credibility and highlighted their poor investment decisions.

One could only wonder what impact the losses had had on the trustees' decision to cut educational programs. One casualty was former trustee Myron Thompson's outreach programs, a well-intended effort to extend the estate's resources to Hawaiian children who were not lucky enough to be among the 3,000 students admitted to Kamehameha Schools.

Shortly after Thompson retired, the new trustees dismantled his outreach programs, firing 171 outreach workers who were part of Kamehameha's preschool, tutoring and parenting programs for Hawaiian children. Studies on early childhood education were also terminated. Some questioned the effectiveness of these programs. I did not know how effective they were, but I was a strong believer in early childhood education and tutoring for disadvantaged children. Generally, educators, psychologists and psychiatrists supported the programs. Moreover, some of the programs had attracted national attention, and experts from other states had visited Kamehameha to observe how the programs were operated. Apparently, the trustees disagreed on the value of the programs. They had a long-term, more ambitious and costly vision—to build Kamehameha Schools on the Neighbor Islands. Meanwhile, there would be virtually no outreach benefits for thousands of needy Hawaiian children.

As a court-appointed master, Matsumoto's findings were considered prima facie evidence, which meant that, unless rebutted by the trustees in court, the court would accept them as proof of fact. If Matsumoto's findings held up, they would provide more-than-ample grounds to remove any or all of the trustees. The trustees, of course, were entitled to due process—a full-blown trial. Using trust money, the trustees had literally unlimited resources with which to hire the best lawyers in Hawai'i, if not the nation. A trial would be difficult and lengthy and cost millions in legal fees.

I had first met Matsumoto when I ran for the State Senate in 1978. He showed up at my campaign headquarters one day, head shaved after living like a monk at a dojo in Kalihi Valley, and volunteered to help in the campaign. Our friendship grew. He served as my committee staff attorney for two years and then left for private practice.

Matsumoto was born and raised on Lānaʻi, where most of the approximately 2,500 residents, his parents among them, were Filipino and Japanese plantation workers. It was quite an achievement for a kid from Lānaʻi to become a lawyer. Matsumoto had just started his own law firm when he was appointed as master for the estate. From a business point of view, he needed to make friends, not adversaries—at least not any as powerful as the Bishop Estate trustees.

A few former court-appointed masters had raised concerns about the Bishop Estate, but their reports had amounted only to cursory reviews. Matsumoto felt that the integrity of his report was a test of his character. After doggedly analyzing the estate's records, Matsumoto produced a preliminary report of such depth and candor it stunned the estate's lawyers and probably everyone who read it.

Despite our close friendship, I made it a point never to question Matsumoto about his report on the Bishop Estate while the investigation was going on. It would have been pointless, anyway, as I knew he would not have given me or anyone else information unless he had been cleared to do so by the court.

Matsumoto's report had uncovered what Roth would later describe as a "world record of breaches." The report was excellent but covered only three years (1994-1996). As a matter of common practice, the court generally does not permit the reevaluation of the reports of past court-appointed masters. But Peters and Stender had become trustees in 1984 and 1989, respectively, and more information was needed about the years before 1994. Bronster's investigation would be more extensive. She began by issuing subpoenas to gather facts, a process known in legal terms as "discovery."

The news media needed a hero, but the low-key, unassuming Matsumoto, who when he was required to respond to news media questions gave short answers without editorial comment, did not fit the bill. However, the self-assured, personable and articulate haole woman from New York did.

Once the investigation got underway, the news media began depicting Bronster as the people's champion. The *Star-Bulletin*, whose editors could hardly hide their glee over scooping "Broken Trust" literally from under the nose of their rival, the *Honolulu Advertiser*, ran favorable stories, flattering photographs and supportive editorials about Bronster.

She needed all the support she could get. The trustees had hired local trial lawyer William McCorriston to lead a team of lawyers from half a dozen top law firms to represent them in the investigation. McCorriston was considered one of the top trial lawyers in the state. His clients included former mayors Frank Fasi and Jeremy Harris.

McCorriston met Bronster head-on in court. When Bronster subpoenaed Bishop Estate or trustee records, McCorriston filed legal motions either to delay or to object to providing them. He appealed adverse court rulings. The court battles between the two often got personal, and the news media gave them wide coverage.

At Bishop Estate's expense, the trustees paid millions in legal fees for the services of McCorriston and the other attorneys. Rather than trying to work out an agreement with Bronster to safeguard the estate's proprietary and other sensitive material, McCorriston, perhaps on the instructions of his clients, had declared war on the State.

A big part of McCorriston's strategy seemed to be to delay the legal proceedings until after the 1998 gubernatorial election. A few national political observers had literally written my political obituary and predicted that my Republican opponent, Maui Mayor Linda Lingle, would win Hawai'i's governorship in 1998. A new governor would likely result in a new attorney general. It was that simple.

However, by stonewalling Bronster at every turn, McCorriston was creating the public impression that the trustees had something to hide. It seemed that the trustees, McCorriston and their other lawyers were totally unaware that, below the public radar screen, Internal Revenue Service agents conducting an ongoing audit of Bishop Estate were undoubtedly watching the action with great interest.

One trustee understood the bigger picture. Stender wrote a memorandum to the other four trustees stating that he was puzzled by McCorriston's tactics, that the trustees should be cooperating with the attorney general to find out if there was anything wrong and, if so, how best to correct it. "Are we engaging the services of these attorneys to protect the legacy or the trustees?" he concluded.

Stender's memorandum helped distance him from the other trustees, creating the impression that he was the "good guy" among the group. I had a gut feeling that Stender had been advised by someone to write what local lawyers call a "cover-your-'ōkole" memorandum. Obviously, McCorriston and the other attorneys were unlikely to advise Stender to write a memorandum that would help his image at the expense of the other trustees.

My intuition about Stender's memorandum was confirmed somewhat when, two years later, on June 23, 1999, investigative reporter Bob Rees wrote an article ("The Land of Oz: There's a hidden history behind Oswald Stender's efforts to topple the Bishop Estate") in the *Honolulu Weekly*. Rees concluded, "Stender may seem to have stayed above the fray. In reality ... he had his own conflicts, allegiances and self-interested motives."

Although Rees had written some scathing articles criticizing my administration, I considered him the best investigative reporter in Hawai'i. Once, when I thought he was wrong in one of his articles, we met and aired our differences. He was tough but fair and honest. I trusted him to do what he thought was right. (Rees died of cancer in 2006.)

Relying on court documents mainly from the Stender-Lindsey lawsuit and other sources, Rees pointed out that Stender adopted a practice commonly used by politicians—he had his own "focus group" to advise him on how he should respond on certain issues. The group included Doc Stryker of Stryker Weiner Associates, one of Hawai'i's top public relations firms.

In one instance, after meeting with the group, Stender reversed himself publicly on his prior agreement with the other trustees to terminate Thompson's outreach programs. Smarting from the public outcry over the termination of the programs, the other trustees were furious with Stender, prompting an enraged Jervis to write a memorandum blasting him for going back on his word.

After another meeting with his focus group, Stender was moved to write a letter to the *Honolulu Advertiser* urging its editors to withdraw an interview he had given to reporter Greg Barrett. Stender's explanation that he "was concerned how the story would affect the trustees" seemed at odds with his maneuvering against them.

Apparently, Stryker was Stender's key adviser and had shaped a public relations strategy for him. Stryker was so influential that when Stender was subpoenaed by the attorney general to produce records, he asked Stryker what material he should or should not produce.

"By October 1997," Rees wrote, "Stryker advised Stender to be like Abe Lincoln. Lincoln, noted Stryker, did not position himself as anti-South or anti-slavery. He positioned himself as for the union.... [Hawaiians] desperately need a symbol of goodness, generosity, unselfish dedication."

Rees' article cast Stender in a different light. Apparently, Stender's flip-flopping was the result of his heavy reliance on his focus group. Peters and Wong were not the only politicians among the trustees; Stender was pretty good at politics himself.

Stender's ire stemmed mainly from his confrontations with Lindsey. Taking the side of the faculty and Chun was a politically correct move, but Stender had no answer to the report on Kamehameha's academic problems that had provoked Lindsey's micromanagement and usurping of Chun's powers. Apparently, Stender had missed so many trustee meetings that he later admitted he was unaware of Lindsey's memorandums regarding the problems at the school, and conceded that he might have reacted differently had he read them.

Lindsey had also asked Bishop Estate attorneys for an opinion on whether Stender had committed a breach of fiduciary duty when, as a principal member of a hui (partnership), he was negotiating to buy Maui Land and Pineapple Co. at the same time Bishop Estate was looking into buying the same company. Not surprisingly, the law firm, Cades Schutte, which throughout the years was paid millions in fees by the estate, opined by letter that it was "inconclusive" whether there had been a breach. Also not surprisingly, Stender was furious. A war had started between him and Lindsey that would eventually result in Stender's filing a lawsuit to remove Lindsey as a trustee. He eventually won.

Stender emerged from the debacle at Kamehameha as a folk hero of sorts in the Hawaiian community and perhaps even in the community at large. In fact, his status had risen to such a high level that, in a subsequent commencement speech, a grateful Chun, whose job Stender helped save, compared him not to Lincoln but to Kamehameha the Great.

But Stender could not claim folk-hero status or "clean hands" when it came to the two dozen or more alleged breaches of trust uncovered in Matsumoto's reports. He had served as a trustee since 1989, longer than Jervis, Lindsey and Wong. For the time he served, he was just as accountable as the other trustees for the alleged breaches.

Stender had asked whether the trustees were looking for the lawyers to safeguard them or the trust, but apparently that question had not occurred to him in 1995, when he joined the other trustees in the most egregious of the breaches, spending a million dollars in trust funds to hire lobbyists to stop Congress from passing the Internal Revenue Service's proposed "intermediate sanctions" law.

The proposed law, supported overwhelmingly by charitable trusts throughout the nation, benefited the trusts because it gave the IRS the option of imposing sanctions against individual trustees who breached their fiduciary duties rather than imposing the only sanction available to the IRS under the old law, which was to revoke the tax-exempt status of the trust. If there was a reasonable rationale for the trustees' actions, they never explained it publicly. Clearly the trustees had put their personal interests above those of Bishop Estate.

Stender's successful lawsuit to remove Lindsey as a trustee demonstrated the extent to which he would go when provoked. But Matsumoto found nothing that indicated Stender had objected to the breaches uncovered in the report that occurred during his time as trustee. He may have grumbled privately to the members of his focus group, his friends and associates about the actions of the other trustees, but there is nothing on record to indicate that he did anything except go along. Perhaps part of the problem was that Stender missed about 25 percent of the trustee meetings while tending to his many other business interests. If he thought the other trustees had breached their fiduciary duties, his silence and inaction were themselves breaches of his duty as trustee.

McCorriston had attacked Matsumoto's preliminary report as incompetent, inaccurate and politically motivated to help me get reelected. McCorriston was a tough trial lawyer who would do almost anything to win. But I took his personal attacks on Matsumoto and, later, Bronster, and his accusation of politics as a strong indication that he knew the facts were not favorable to the trustees. His tactics brought to mind the oft-used aphorism: "If the law is on your side, pound the law. If the facts are on your side, pound the facts. If neither is on your side, pound your opponent."

From the news accounts of the court battles, it appeared that Bronster was being outgunned. A veteran trial lawyer observing the court action told me that McCorriston was "running circles" around Bronster and her deputies. Another trial lawyer described the courtroom performance of one of Bronster's deputies as "green, inexperienced."

Perhaps. The legal system is replete with rules that may be used to delay any lawsuit and discourage or demoralize the other party by driving up the costs. This was a tactic used commonly by insurance companies and big corporations against ordinary citizens who have the temerity to sue them. McCorriston was very skilled at using such tactics.

Bronster, however, was winning the public relations battle. McCorriston had a few problems: First, his clients were not sympathetic figures. The public is not inclined to feel much empathy for less-than-forthcoming millionaire trustees who get into fights with teachers. Second, the news media was clearly on Bronster's side. The *Star-Bulletin* depicted her as a modern Joan of Arc. Whatever missteps she made in court were glossed over in news reports. It didn't matter; the public was looking for someone to do what was right, and Bronster was beginning to look like that person.

McCorriston's cry of politics cut both ways. Hoaliku Drake, Henry Peters' mother and a longtime Democrat, had supported me in the 1994 election. But in 1997 she joined Republican Linda Lingle's campaign as one of her campaign co-chairs. Lingle said literally nothing on the Bishop Estate investigation, and few knew where she stood on the issue. A Lingle victory in the 1998 election would mean a new governor and a new attorney general.

I held Drake in high regard. She had served the public with distinction as the director of the Department of Hawaiian Home Lands under Ariyoshi. But, in 1997, she was leading counterdemonstrations against Na Kumu and Na Pua and in one instance was quoted as admonishing the protestors for "biting the hand that feeds you." It saddened me to see her out there, but she did what good mothers do: She stood by her son.

There is almost always a price to pay in political controversies, and I hated the price I was paying with Drake. If there was one consolation it was that Drake's sister, Agnes Cope, or "Auntie Aggie," as everyone called her, continued to stand by me. Auntie Aggie had known my Aunt Rachel and my mother. She had babysat me a few times when I was growing up in Kalihi and had often referred to me as her hānai (adopted) son long before I became governor.

Both sisters were loved and respected in the Hawaiian community and by the non-Hawaiians who got to know them. Auntie Aggie was featured in one of my television campaign advertisements during the 1994 campaign. When during the 1998 campaign a mutual friend asked Auntie Aggie why she continued to support me even though her sister did not, she simply smiled and said, "Sisters sometimes differ." I never forgot it. ❖

Chapter Nineteen

Victory from the Jaws of Defeat

Running against the Economy

As my first term drew to a close, a number of hot, complicated political issues remained unresolved, among them negotiations with OHA over ceded-lands revenues, reform of the Bishop Estate, civil service reform, restructuring the State government and collective bargaining. We began other initiatives as well, such as a lawsuit against the gasoline companies for fraud and collusion and the privatization of government services. I needed another term to resolve these issues. The 1998 election would be my eighth and most important.

The biggest issue remained the economy. In 1998, several economists noted there were signs that Hawai'i's economy was recovering. But while certain business sectors had experienced positive growth—automobile sales, for example, were robust—it was not apparent to most of the general public. The specter of record filings of foreclosures and bankruptcies from 1995 through 1997 still haunted struggling businesses and worried workers.

Early polls showed that my approval ratings with the public were declining while those of Honolulu Mayor Jeremy Harris and Linda Lingle were rising. When pressed by the news media for comment I gave the usual responses: "The only poll that counts is on Election Day," "This is not a popularity contest" and so on. Actually, I was very disappointed. Any politician who claims he doesn't care what the public thinks of him is being disingenuous.

The Republican attacks on our economic proposals had caused uncertainty and confusion. By the end of the 1998 legislative session, however, most of the ERTF proposals had been approved in one form or another. Our challenge in the election would be to make clear to the voters that we had taken significant, positive steps toward improving the economy. I knew that some of my decisions had upset many people. I could only hope that by Election Day, enough voters would have realized what we had achieved to provide the margin I needed for reelection.

I had been down this road before. As a legislator and later as lieutenant governor, it seemed as if I had been involved in virtually every controversial issue that arose. Veteran legislator Tony Kunimura once chided me about fighting every battle, big or small. "Pick the big ones and forget the manini ones," he said. It was all a matter of perspective; there were times when a small battle involved a big principle.

Controversy creates detractors, and I had more than my fair share of them. I was so overwhelmed when I was elected to the State House in 1974 (I was a big underdog) that I pledged to myself I would say and do what I thought I should regardless of the political consequences. Living up to that promise was a major challenge throughout my political career.

But I learned early that the most effective form of politics was getting (or trying to get) the job done. High public approval ratings do not necessarily convert into votes. When I ran against Eileen Anderson in 1986 and Pat Saiki in 1994, both women had public approval ratings in the high 70s and 80s; mine were in the mid-50s. In the so-called "horse-race" match-ups, our early polls showed that Anderson had a 28-percent lead over me, while Saiki had 34 percent. Ultimately, I won both elections by comfortable margins.

However, the public mood was different in 1998 than it had been in 1986 and 1994: Many people were hurting economically and were desperate for relief. Politically, it was not a good time to be an incumbent, particularly an incumbent Democratic governor. In fact, a few Mainland political observers predicted that Hawai'i would have a Republican governor for the first time since 1962. Prompted by early negative polls, some Democrats feared I was likely to be beaten by Lingle and looked for other Democrats to challenge me in the primary.

Jeremy Harris

Mayor Jeremy Harris emerged as a potentially formidable challenger. I didn't know much about him except that he was from Delaware and had first moved to Kaua'i to teach at Kaua'i Community College. He was elected as a delegate to the Constitutional Convention in 1978 and, in 1979, became the first Mainland haole elected to the Kaua'i County Council. Harris unsuccessfully challenged Democratic Mayor Tony Kunimura in the 1984 Kaua'i mayoral primary election. Honolulu Mayor Frank Fasi, who had quit the Democratic Party, saw Harris as a political comer and offered him a job in his administration. By 1994, Harris had become Fasi's managing director, the City & County's highest Cabinet post.

Harris had a lot going for him as Honolulu's mayor. Like Lingle's, Harris' approval ratings were high. He was well educated, young, articulate and smart. His biggest political asset was that, as one of the few haole Democrats holding a major public office, he could draw haole votes.

He showed his drawing power in the 1994 special election for mayor when he soundly beat fellow Democrat and City Councilman Arnold Morgado in the general election. Morgado had outpolled Harris in the primary, but fell short of the 50 percent-plus required by law for victory. A runoff was required in the general

Top: On a post-9-11 visit to New York City, Governor Ben presents Mayor Rudy Giuliani with a lei of dollar bills from Hawai'i schoolchildren, a check for $125,000 from Island businesses and community groups, and an invitation from Hawaiian Airlines and Hawai'i hotels to free Hawaiian vacations for 1,200 rescue personnel or their surviving spouses or parents. Bottom: Idaho Governor Dirk Kempthorne turns the gavel over to Ben as he succeeds Kempthorne as chairman of the Western Governors Association for 1999.

Top: Five Hawai'i governors are represented in a historic photo opportunity (left to right): Ben and Vicky, John and Lynne Waihee, George and Jean Ariyoshi, Judge James Burns and wife Emme Tomimbang (representing James' late father, John A. Burns), and Bill and Nancy Quinn. Bottom: Ben and Vicky greet Japan's Prince Norihito and Princess Takamado at Washington Place as former Gov. Ariyoshi (left) looks on.

First Lady Vicky greets Tadao Chino, chairman of the Asian Development Bank, at Washington Place. According to Chino, the ADB conference held in Hawai'i was the most peaceful and successful meeting in the bank's history.

Top: Governor Ben and Vicky pose with schoolchildren on Ni'ihau, the only privately owned island in Hawai'i, home to a diminishing population of some 200 Hawaiians and part-Hawaiians who speak the Hawaiian language fluently. Bottom: The controversial trustees of the Bishop Estate (left to right): Lokelani Lindsey, Henry Peters, Dickie Wong, Oswald Stender and Gerard Jervis.

University of Hawai'i professor Haunani Trask (left) and other Hawaiian activists protest Governor Ben's appointments to the Office of Hawaiian Affairs in 2001.

Top: Ben and Vicky meet Rolling Stones (left to right) Ron Wood, Mick Jagger, Keith Richards and Charlie Watts at the Kāhala home of Sony founder Akio Morita. Bottom: First Lady Vicky, guests and Cabinet members react as Governor Ben pokes fun at University of Hawaiʻi president Evan Dobelle (second row, second from left) during his 2001 State of the State Address.

Top: Governor Ben debates Republican challenger Linda Lingle during the 1998 gubernatorial campaign, in which he overcame June's 22-point deficit to eke out a narrow victory in November. Bottom: Ben convenes an emergency meeting with political, business, labor and community leaders to forge a post-9-11 recovery strategy for Hawai'i. Lieutenant Governor Mazie Hirono is seated to the governor's immediate right.

Top: University faculty and students demonstrate during the April 2001 strike. Bottom: Governor Ben, Congressman Abercrombie and U.S. Senators Akaka and Inouye listen somberly as newly elected Republican Governor Linda Lingle gives her inaugural speech in 2002.

election. Harris scored a resounding win, with 67,670 votes to Morgado's 58,018. Harris' win was a reprise of the 1959 Tsukiyama versus Long election in which local Democrats—mostly AJAs—voted for haole Democrat Oren Long while many haole Republicans abandoned their fellow Republican Wilfred Tsukiyama to vote for Long. In the flush of victory, Harris was a man on the move. He apparently began considering a run for governor as soon as it became obvious that my approval ratings were falling.

Harris' betrayal of Fasi left me with mixed emotions. On one hand, it was delightfully funny to hear that Fasi had returned to his office to find that his former protégé had moved in and left Fasi's personal belongings in boxes stacked outside the office door. Having been the target of some of Fasi's past shenanigans, I was amused by the irony of his getting a taste of his own medicine. He had taught Harris well.

On the other hand, the story revealed a side of Harris that was unflattering; he had reneged on his promise to endorse Fasi. In my eyes, Harris had some serious character flaws. Trust, loyalty and keeping one's word are of critical importance in politics, where much is achieved on the basis of interpersonal relationships. Harris had broken his word to Fasi—"the only person who would give me a job" after he lost the Kaua'i mayoral election, Harris once told me. But while Harris might have savored his moment of revenge against Fasi for trying to fire him, the story evolved into one that would be repeated for years to all who would listen, portraying Harris as untrustworthy and loyal to no one. (Fasi, true to his Sicilian roots, tried to get even by running against Harris in the 1996 mayoral election. Unfortunately for Fasi, Morgado was also running and split Fasi's vote. Harris won easily.)

Most politicians appreciate positive publicity. Harris craved and cultivated it. Eventually, I saw him as a tireless self-promoter who would seize or create every opportunity to get his name in the news. As long as his antics did not hurt anyone, including me, I had no problem with them. But Harris' penchant for publicity not only became obvious—news reporters joked about it—at times it clouded his judgment.

In July 1995, the Honolulu Fire Department conducted two highly publicized searches for hikers lost in O'ahu's towering Ko'olau Mountains. The first, in early July, was for a young man named James Pantelioni, who had been missing for three weeks. Pursuant to the Fire Department's rescue protocol, the search was discontinued after three days. However, the man's mother came to Hawai'i from the Mainland and met with Harris, who in a subsequent televised press conference announced he had ordered the search extended.

At the same time, the Fire Department began a second search for two BYU-Hawai'i students, Eric Jones and Wade Johnson, who were reported missing while hiking in the Ko'olau Mountains near Sacred Falls. The two young men had started their hike on July 15, but, because of bad weather, they were unable to hike out again. Before leaving, they had given a map to friends with the details of their planned hike and a helicopter pickup site if they had not returned by July 17. On the day that the men were reported missing, the Fire Department was notified and a rescue helicopter was able to pick up Jones at the pre-designated site. (On July 16, Johnson, who was related to the wife of BYU-Hawai'i's president, had decided to attempt hiking down the mountain himself and was not picked up.)

On July 18 or 19, Charles Toguchi, my chief of staff, told me that we had received a telephone call from Harris' office. Harris had extended the searches for Jones and Pantelioni and wanted to know if I was willing to call out the Hawai'i National Guard to assist the Fire Department.

Calling out the National Guard would be clearly inappropriate. As governor, I was commander in chief of the National Guard, but, aside from providing for the defense of the state in times of war, terrorist attacks or riots, I was authorized to deploy it only for emergencies caused by natural disasters such as hurricanes, floods or tsunamis. A hiker lost in the mountains is a tragedy, but hardly qualifies as a state emergency.

Before responding to Harris' request, I decided to discuss the matter with Maj. Gen. Edward Richardson, adjutant general of the Hawai'i National Guard. Richardson, who is a second cousin to former Bishop Estate trustee and Chief Justice William Richardson, was the first Hawaiian to command the Hawai'i National Guard.

A graduate of Kamehameha Schools and the University of Hawai'i, Richardson had served as a fighter pilot during the Vietnam War. He was highly respected by the guards and the regular military, and under his leadership (1991-2000) the Hawai'i National Guard became one of the finest guard units in the nation. I held the soft-spoken Richardson in high regard. He was the only first-line Cabinet member from the Waihee administration that I reappointed after I became governor in 1994.

Richardson walked into my office with a concerned look on his face. He had been briefed in advance.

"General, we got a telephone call from the mayor's office," I said. "The mayor asked whether I would be willing to call out the National Guard to assist the Fire Department in the searches for the missing hikers."

"Governor," he replied, choosing his words carefully, "I can't agree to it. My soldiers are not trained to do rescue work in the mountains. To continue the search for the hiker who has been missing for three weeks doesn't make sense. That man is very likely dead, and if the wild pigs got to him his body will never be found. In this kind of weather, it's irresponsible to risk the lives of the living to recover the body of someone who is probably dead.

"As for the second search, the one for the BYU student, the terrain in that area is highly vegetated and dangerous. It's steep; the altitude may be as high as

2,000 feet. To get there, the Fire Department's rescue squad rappels its men down from the helicopter. Our guardsmen are not trained or physically fit to do that kind of work."

"General," I said, "no need to worry. I wasn't going to call out the Guard. But if Harris makes his request public and the news media asks me why I turned him down, I wanted to have gotten your opinion before I gave my reply."

A few days later, on July 21, 1995, tragedy struck: A Honolulu Fire Department rescue helicopter, attempting to lower two specially trained Honolulu police officers in a basket onto a mountain to search for one of the missing men, was buffeted by strong winds and crashed into the side of the mountain, killing the two officers and the pilot.

I was shocked. Later, when I learned more details of the search, I got angry. Richardson had described the terrain accurately. It was treacherous, highly vegetated and steep, varying in altitude from 1,600 to 2,000 feet. Over a period of five days, rescue personnel had been sent in intermittently, rappelling from helicopters into the area. The weather had been so bad that at times the helicopters could not pick them up, leaving them to hike out.

According to one news report, a few minutes before the crash, the Fire Department's dispatcher had radioed the pilot, warning him that the weather was worsening and imploring him to return to base. Eyewitnesses on the ground said the basket carrying the two police officers was swinging dangerously back and forth before the helicopter disappeared into the clouds and crashed.

At a press conference, Leonardo Altillo, the assistant fire chief, took full responsibility for the tragedy. The weather had been bad for four or five consecutive days, with rain and high winds. I found it hard to believe that an experienced professional like Altillo would advise Harris to extend the searches in such conditions. Harris was not present at the press conference. When questioned by the news media later that day, he limited his remarks to praising the dead men as heroes and speculating as to how the accident had happened.

None of the reporters asked Harris why he had extended the search for a man who had already been missing for three weeks, or why he had continued the search for the BYU student in such treacherous weather.

Three days after the accident, Harris was blaming the hikers for being "irresponsible" and not taking precautions or planning their hikes. He also complained about the high cost of rescue missions. In fact, the two BYU-Hawai'i students had—quite responsibly, I thought—taken the precautions of leaving a map with friends, setting a date by which to call the Fire Department and designating an area for a rescue helicopter pickup.

Few people outside of my office knew that Harris had asked me to call out the National Guard. His request left me with a different perspective on his behavior than that of most people. I concluded that Harris had been so caught up in the publicity of the two rescue events and was so intent on emerging as a hero of sorts that he had thrown caution to the wind and extended the searches, apparently indifferent to the risks faced by the rescuers.

Throughout the aftermath of the crash, including lawsuits filed by the police officers' and pilot's widows, Harris maintained that he had relied on the advice of the Fire Department. He gave an amazing performance, managing to deflect accountability for the accident onto everyone but himself. In my eyes, the assistant fire chief had fallen on his sword for Harris.

Regardless of any advice he had received from Altillo or other fire rescue personnel, the final decision to extend the searches was Harris'. Presidents, governors and mayors are expected to make tough decisions. If things go well, they may get credit; if not, they shoulder the blame. It comes with the job.

"Should I give the story about Harris and the National Guard to one of the reporters?" my press secretary asked.

"No. I'm sure it would make a good story and Harris would come out of it smelling like shit. But there's been enough bad news about this tragedy. There are a lot of people grieving; let it be."

The helicopter crash had widowed three women and left their children fatherless. The lawsuits were settled out of court. Neither James Pantelioni nor Wade Johnson was ever found.

Over the next few years, Harris resorted to a number of antics designed more for publicity than substance. In one instance, he inserted himself into the debate on prison overcrowding. Harris instructed City architects to design and build a model of new prison facilities. In a subsequent press conference, complete with renderings and PowerPoint presentations, Harris presented the model as his answer to the problem. Like everyone else, I found out about the project through news reports.

"What is wrong with this guy?" I asked my staff, exasperated. "The prisons are under State, not City, jurisdiction."

Prison overcrowding was a major issue. But Harris had wasted City time and money to develop a non-solution. The real challenge was selecting a site for the prison, not the design of the facilities. Selecting a site, of course, was fraught with political risks. Every site I selected was met with fierce community opposition. At a public hearing for a proposed prison on the Big Island, people traveled for miles to testify against the proposal. I was booed and heckled (it was not the first time), and legislators who represented those communities quickly joined in the opposition, blocking my requests for funding. Our inability to find a place to build a new prison was the major reason we were sending prisoners to private prisons on the Mainland. The problem of selecting a new prison site remains unresolved today.

These experiences shaped my thinking about Harris as a person and a politician. Interpersonal relationships based on trust and credibility were needed to get things done. I had amiable working relationships with the mayors of the three other counties, including Linda Lingle on Maui. There was much Harris and I could have done for the public by working together. Had he asked for help, I certainly would have considered it. He never did. My relationship with him was cordial but guarded.

The news media had played up Harris as a potential challenger. At the State Democratic Convention in May 1998, U.S. Sen. Dan Inouye, apparently concerned that a primary battle between Harris and me would hurt the Democratic candidate in the general election against Lingle, asked to meet privately with both of us.

Inouye is respected for many reasons, but a big reason among Democrats is his unwavering loyalty to Democratic candidates. When, for instance, Burns and other top Democrats were surreptitiously supporting Republican Andy Anderson against Democrat Frank Fasi in the 1968 election for Honolulu mayor, Inouye openly supported Fasi.

We met with Inouye in his hotel room. Media accounts of the meeting—I have no idea how they found out about it—generally portrayed Inouye as the Democratic guru reading the riot act to Harris and telling him to stay out of the Democratic primary. Inouye is a powerful force in Hawai'i politics, but I have never known him to throw his political weight around. The depiction of Harris as being forced out of the running was a creation of reporters who believed that the Democratic Party was a monolithic entity, with the old boys meeting in smoke-filled back rooms to groom and anoint favored Democrats for public office. Independent Democrats such as Abercrombie, Harris, Mink and Fasi anointed by the so-called "old boys"? It was hard not to laugh at the thought.

Our meeting with Inouye was brief and to the point. "I don't have to tell you two guys that a bitter primary can hurt us badly in the general against Lingle," Inouye said.

"Well, I'm running for reelection, so it's up to Jeremy. Jeremy, you can't beat me in the Democratic primary," I said, turning to Harris.

"That's not what my polls say," Harris retorted sharply.

"Well, then you should run," I said, daring him. (Harris' polls showed him with a slight lead, 38 percent to 36 percent, with 24 percent undecided. Napolitan and Seigle were confident most of the undecided votes would be mine and I would beat Harris easily. I felt the same way.)

"Maybe I will," Harris replied.

Inouye, who had probably figured out by then that there was nothing more to discuss, said, "Well, I hope you two will talk it over and work something out."

After two years of putting up with his antics, I was fed up with Harris. As he walked out of the room, I turned to Inouye and said, "That guy's such a liar."

"Well, Ben, just remember this—he's *our* liar," Inouye replied.

On the final day of the convention, Harris, relying on the advice of his pollster and confidant, Don Clegg, relented and announced that he would not run. Harris told the news media and convention delegates that, for the sake of party unity, he would support me. He had little choice. Given our respective personalities and styles, it would probably have been a contentious and bitter campaign that would have drained the resources of both of us and left the supporters of the loser reason to be angry at the winner. Harris was young, and it was wiser for him to cultivate my supporters and wait for the 2002 gubernatorial election.

The issue settled, Harris and I made the obligatory speeches about setting aside our differences and promoting party unity. Inouye closed the convention with a rousing speech urging Democrats to unite and take the fight to the Republicans in November.

A month or two after our meeting with Inouye, I was told that Harris wanted to get actively involved in our campaign and was willing to speak at places I could not cover. If he had been any other Democrat I would have been overjoyed. It was one thing for Harris to endorse me, but actively getting involved was another. I did not delude myself into believing that he had become a fan of mine. He was acting out of self-interest, with an eye toward the 2002 governor's election. It was a measure of his ambition that he had already started his campaign. I was reluctant to let him get involved, because I did not want to give him an edge over Lt. Gov. Mazie Hirono in 2002.

Meanwhile, there was still a lot of unfinished business. Working closely with Ed Cadman, the new dean of the John A. Burns School of Medicine, and UH President Ken Mortimer, I persuaded the Legislature to approve my request for preliminary engineering and design funding for the new UH Medical School and Research Center in Kakaʻako.

Another of my priorities was to build a new campus for UH-West Oʻahu, which for more than 20 years had operated out of old one-story wooden buildings at the site of Leeward Community College in Waipahu. The new campus, I believed, would provide greater access to educational opportunities to Leeward residents and serve as a catalyst for the growth of Kapolei, just as UC-Irvine had for the city of Irvine, California.

And there was also the unresolved ceded-lands dispute with OHA. I had negotiated hard for a settlement that was fair to both Hawaiians and non-Hawaiians. Based on Lingle's public statements, I was convinced that she had little understanding of what the ceded-lands dispute was all about and that she would be guided more by politics than substance in seeking a settlement with OHA that was justified and fair to the people of Hawaiʻi.

Obviously, I would have no influence in trying to resolve these issues if I was not reelected.

"Ben," Napolitan said, "winning is an 'addition,' not a 'subtraction,' game. We want to add voters to your side, not subtract. You've already angered UHPA and now they're supporting Lingle."

"Screw 'em, we'll win without them," I said. "I cut welfare and social programs to pay for their pay raises, and all they do is complain. Those professors are the best-educated people in the state; they're better equipped to take care of themselves than the people on welfare. And more than anyone else they should understand the state's fiscal problems; if we had the money I'd give it to them, but we don't, and they just don't get it."

"Well," Napolitan cut me off with a grin (he had heard me vent about UHPA before), "the last client I had who had that attitude got his ass handed to him by the voters. Now who else are you going to add to that list besides UHPA? Add any more and you'll be back practicing law after November."

"No, I'll just become a consultant like you, Joe," I chuckled, realizing I was losing the argument.

"Ben," Seigle added, "Harris has a pretty good organization, especially in Chinatown, where he has strong supporters and we don't. We could use his help."

This was the part about politics I didn't like.

Politics makes for strange bedfellows, it is often said. At times, circumstances require rivals to band together to defeat a common foe. In 1998, the common foe for Harris and me was the fast-rising Republican Linda Lingle. Harris was already seen by many as the Democratic front-runner for the 2002 governor's race. Obviously, it was in his best political interests that I beat Lingle in 1998 and clear the way for him to run in 2002. It was in my interests that I not offend disappointed Harris supporters; we needed their support for what would be the toughest election of my 28 years in public service.

By the end of the election, having watched Harris campaign and interacted with him on some issues, I concluded that Harris, not Hirono, was the Democratic Party's best hope to retain the governorship in 2002. He was very bright, articulate and knowledgeable about City and State matters; he was a terrific campaigner and would handle Lingle easily in a debate—and he was haole. My decision to support Harris for governor in 2002 had little to do with what I thought about the man as a person—it was all about Hawai'i's changing demographics, and winning.

Two of my three campaign chairs were former Republicans. Ann Kobayashi became a Democrat while serving in the State Senate after the Religious Right took control of the GOP. Kobayashi and I were good friends from our days in the Senate. She was honest and smart. I had gotten to know Rick Humphries shortly after the 1994 gubernatorial election, when he served as treasurer for my Republican opponent, former Congresswoman Pat Saiki. That Humphries, a local-born haole, Punahou graduate, successful businessman and long-time moderate Republican had left the GOP was symptomatic of the party's transformation. (The third chairperson, Mike McCartney, was a former Democratic State senator.)

The Graying of the Party

The Democratic Party was changing, too. More than anything else, it was aging. The generation of World War II AJA veterans and union workers who had led the 1954 revolution was in its early 70s. At rally after rally I saw a sea of gray and white hair in the audience. I wondered whether that generation of Democrats, which had been such a force in Hawai'i politics since 1954, could help us carry the day in 1998 as it had done in countless past elections.

Democrats were victims of their own success. For many, the struggle for social and political equality had opened the doors to better lives. Democratic parents were able to provide their children with better education, greater economic opportunities and expanded social mobility. But there was a political price to pay. As union leader Richard Dumancus once lamented, "We Democrats have been so successful that we spoil our kids, give them everything we never had; they don't know what it means to sacrifice, and now we've created a bunch of Republicans."

Hawai'i's demographics were changing. According to the 1990 federal census the four major ethnic groups were Caucasians, 33 percent; Japanese Americans, once the largest segment, a distant second at 22 percent; Filipinos, Hawai'i's fastest-growing ethnic group, 15 percent; and Hawaiians and part-Hawaiians, 13 percent.

A poll we took in June 1998 showed Lingle leading me by 22 percent. I did the best with Japanese-American and Filipino-American voters. Lingle's main support came from local and Mainland haoles and Hawaiians. In an ominous sign of my political standing with the voters, Lingle had a slight lead over me among union members.

Napolitan and Seigle called a meeting to discuss the poll. Barbara Ankersmit, our pollster, explained the poll methodology. Napolitan then gave a detailed and sobering analysis of the results.

"Well, here's the bad news," Napolitan began. "It's incredible, but the voters seem to know virtually nothing about what the governor has accomplished over the past three and a half years." In fact, when voters were asked to name my "major accomplishment," most didn't know much about my record, but my getting married to Vicky got the most votes (7 percent). I was a bit embarrassed, to say the least.

Napolitan continued, "The governor's job rating is abysmal: 23 percent positive, 75 percent negative. Lingle's numbers are 53 percent positive, 30 percent negative. His favorable/unfavorable ratio is a modest 47/44; Lingle's is an impressive 66/10.

"About three-quarters of the voters give the governor a negative rating on the way he has handled state problems.

"Voters think Lingle brings a fresh face, a new vision, new ideas, honesty and integrity to State government. But here's the *good* news: Virtually no one can identify any of Lingle's specific plans or accomplishments. Overall, 74 percent of those planning to vote for Lingle are doing so because of disappointment with the economic situation and the governor; only 25 percent give positive, pro-Lingle reasons to vote for her.

"What she is saying is, 'Conditions are terrible. That's Ben's fault. Vote for me and I'll make the changes you want.' But nobody knows what these 'changes' are. She deals only in generalities.

"There are two possible reasons the poll numbers are so bad. Either the governor is doing a lousy job as governor and the voters know it—or the governor is doing a good job and voters don't know it. Obviously, we all think he's done a good job. But frankly, in all of my years of consulting, I've never seen a situation where there has been such a breakdown in communications between a governor and the voters. We need to fix that.

"So here's what I propose. Get on television as quickly as possible and stay on as long as necessary. Raise more money for television and, if necessary, cut the campaign budget for other things and use the money for our television spots. Jack [Seigle] and Phil [Wood] will produce the television spots highlighting the governor's accomplishments. That big tax cut should be in the first spot that we air. I'm amazed that it's supposed to be one of the biggest State income tax cuts in the nation—and yet our poll shows few voters know about it.

"Now, there are other positives—the poll shows that 68 percent of voters still believe the Democratic Party is closer to the mainstream of Hawai'i voters; only 19 percent think the Republican Party is. And while many voters don't like the governor and blame him for the lousy economy—60 percent of the voters still believe the governor is 'a person of high integrity.'

"We need to remind the voters that Lingle is a Republican, just like we did with Pat Saiki in 1994. And we've got to soften the governor's image. Too many people see him as a hard man; some call him arrogant, brash. The Republicans are trying to portray Lingle as a 'nice and warm' person and the governor as 'not nice and unfriendly.' Those who know him know this is not true—otherwise Vicky wouldn't have married him. Unfortunately, because he is so serious that's the way he comes across. So we need to stress the family side of him. Vicky has agreed to do some soft, family-type television spots. She's articulate, pretty and comes across very well on television. She'll remind the voters that the governor has a spouse and family; Lingle doesn't. To some voters it may make a difference.

"Now all of this stuff stays in this room. The last thing we need is for our own poll results to leak out and discourage our campaign workers. Any questions?"

There was a long silence. Finally, Bert Kobayashi, our chief fundraiser, broke the ice: "Yeah, should I make arrangements now to move my family and business to Guam?"

Everyone laughed.

"We've been down before; we just have to work hard," someone said.

"Harder than ever," someone else said.

Napolitan was right about our communication breakdown. It wasn't my staff's fault. Often, I'd ignore their advice about using the bully pulpit to tout our programs. Instead, I held regular weekly press conferences in which I engaged the news media in candid dialogue on the issues of the day. My staff issued press releases on things we had done or were trying to do, but I limited my speaking engagements to organizations like the chambers of commerce and business groups.

I had not realized how bad things were.

"Joe," I said, "our opposition research investigation came up with some good stuff on Lingle. Shouldn't we go after her?"

"It's too early," Napolitan replied.

"Well, I'm beginning to feel like a damned piñata," I said. "Hardly a day goes by without Lingle and other Republicans attacking me. It's frustrating, because they use half-truths and blame me for crap I had no control over. I'm surprised they don't blame me for the Gulf War or for screwing up the Japanese economy."

"According to our opposition research report, Lingle is no Mother Theresa. She's been held in contempt of court; she's had federal and State tax liens filed against her for nonpayment of taxes; she hired her lawyer ex-husband to represent her in a lawsuit and paid him about $100,000 in County money, and the Hawai'i Supreme Court ruled it was illegal for her to do so; when the County made a mistake in issuing a zoning permit to a developer she tried to cover it up by having the County buy the project, and the developers walked away with a $1.4 million profit; and there's the pollution at Mā'alaea Bay, where the boat owners are pissed at the County....This is stuff we know to be true."

"Ben," Napolitan said, "I think it's okay for you to use that material in your speeches, but I don't think the time is right to do it on television. Right now we should use our television money for the positive stuff. And if we do go after her we have to be careful. Running a negative campaign against a woman can backfire."

"Yeah, but our negative television ads against Eileen Anderson in 1986 made a big difference in that campaign ... telling the truth works," I said, turning to Seigle (Napolitan had not been involved in that election).

"But this campaign is a little different," Seigle replied. "We're concerned about losing Japanese voters, especially the women, who don't like negative campaigning. A lot of them are undecided Democrats who like Lingle. We need to get them back on our side. Remember your base is mainly Filipino and Japanese voters. We get those voters back, and you'll win."

"Negative campaigning works if it's the truth. I learned that from you two guys ... so what's wrong with hitting her back when she makes these wild statements? Lingle will say anything her PR people dream up, even if it's wrong or untrue," I said.

"Ben," Napolitan said, "right now we need to first persuade the voters that your accomplishments far outweigh hers and that you're the best person to lead the state over the next four years. You've done a lot, and it blows my mind that most voters don't know much about it. A lot of voters don't want to vote for you right now, and she's the only alternative and they like her. We'll be much more effective in attacking Lingle *after* we've succeeded in improving the voters' perception of you. So first we push you up, and then we knock her down. Now that's our opinion, but you're the candidate, so the final decision is yours."

I considered Napolitan and Seigle the best in the business. Both were strong Democrats, and they had never lost a governor's race in Hawai'i. Our relationship went beyond politics; over a span of three elections we had become friends. I trusted them completely, and as much as I wanted to take the offensive against Lingle, I deferred to their advice. At this point, our campaign would remain positive.

"Ben, smile more—even if it cracks your face," Napolitan said with a laugh.

On September 20, 1998, Hirono and I easily won our primary elections. In the Republican primary, Lingle defeated Fasi, while Stanley Koki, a Japanese-American businessman and avowed born-again Christian, won the GOP race for lieutenant governor.

Although we were running in different primaries, the media made much of Lingle outpolling me, 109,399 to 96,019. Fasi, Lingle's opponent in the GOP primary, got 48,671. Fasi had little credibility with Republicans, and we assumed that most of his vote was due to crossover Democrats and independents. The question was how those votes would divide up in the November general election. Meanwhile, news columnists and political analysts began juggling the numbers, and most concluded that Lingle had a significant edge over me going into the general election.

Interestingly, I outpolled Lingle 14,635 to 10,190 on Maui, where she had served as mayor for eight years. When asked for a comment by a reporter, co-chair Ann Kobayashi replied, "Do people on Maui know something that O'ahu doesn't?" The election results seemed to confirm the findings of our June poll: Outside of Maui County the voters didn't know much about Lingle.

I first saw Stanley Koki at a Senate public hearing in the mid-1980s. Koki testified regularly in support of anti-drug and anti-pornography bills. He had been a drug user. "I tried them all," I recall him saying at one public hearing. His drug use, he said, had hurt his family, his business, his friends and himself. Along the way, he experienced a religious epiphany that helped him straighten out his life and achieve success in his business. He had become a born-again Christian. It was a touching story. But Koki concerned me; he seemed punitive and unduly harsh and opposed laws intended to rehabilitate and treat rather than punish. I got the feeling that, to Koki, religion seemed like the only sure answer to people's problems.

In another election at a different time, Koki would probably have been considered a liability, at least in progressive Hawai'i. But 1998 was no ordinary election. The Hawai'i Supreme Court's decision in *Baehr v. Lewin* (1993) ordering a full retrial by the Circuit Court on the question of whether the State had a compelling interest in denying same-sex couples marriage licenses had attracted national attention. At the trial three years later, *Baehr v. Miike* (1996), Circuit Court Judge Kevin Chang ruled that the State had failed to prove it had a compelling interest to justify not issuing a marriage license to a same-sex couple. Chang's decision sent shock waves throughout the state and the nation, and religious organizations from the Mainland joined local organizations in a campaign to pressure the Legislature into passing a law banning same-sex marriage in Hawai'i.

Early polls indicated 70 percent of the public opposed same-sex marriage. Not surprisingly, religious groups such as the Catholic Church, the Mormon Church and Religious Right organizations invested considerable resources in supporting the same-sex marriage ban.

But it was the evangelicals from the Religious Right who dominated the emotionally charged legislative public hearings. Representatives of the other religious organizations were literally ignored as the news media focused almost entirely on the Religious Right. These zealots aggressively buttonholed legislators, many angrily demanding that legislation banning same-sex marriage be passed immediately and warning legislators against entertaining compromises such as "domestic partnerships," which were dismissed as a "deception" for gay rights. State Rep. Len Pepper, one of the few who had the courage to explore alternatives, told me later that on several occasions he felt "physically intimidated" for the first time in his political career when he found himself surrounded and confronted by angry people who demanded that he support a ban on same-sex marriage.

No individual influenced the course of the same-sex marriage debate in Hawai'i more than Mike Gabbard. Gabbard, a haole-Samoan born in American Samoa who had moved to Hawai'i in 1977, had been a devotee of Krishna. He, along with former State Sen. Rick Reed, for whom he had worked as an aide, were disciples of Chris Butler, a former Krishna follower who was the guru of a sect he had founded in Hawai'i.

By most accounts, Gabbard was a nice person. He was well educated, holding a master's degree in community college administration from Oregon State University. But when it came to homosexuality, it was clear that he was an outright homophobe. Gabbard blamed gays for everything. "I believe," he once said, "that all of our problems—be they environmental, crime, health, economic, wars, etc.—can be traced to people holding on to and living by [a] hedonistic and therefore selfish worldview"—i.e., homosexuals. He had no problem stooping to inflammatory statements to demean homosexuals: "[I]t is not a good idea," he said once, "to be inserting penises … into the anus/rectum because these excretionary organs are designed specifically for eliminating things, not putting things into them."

Gabbard sat on the board of directors of an ad hoc group that called itself "Save Traditional Marriage '98" (STM '98). During the election, STM '98, financed by the Catholic and Mormon churches as well as the Religious Right, ran anti-same-sex marriage television ads, some suggesting that gay marriage could lead to "unnatural" alliances (bestiality, for example); others warned that legalizing gay marriage would lead to teaching about the gay lifestyle in the public schools.

While the Catholic priest who was on STM '98 defended the television ads, saying they were not meant to be "homophobic," Jennifer Diesman of Rosehill and Associates, the media consultants who produced the ads, was brutally blunt: "Some may find them [the ads] insensitive or hard-hitting. Sometimes the ends justify the means."

I knew virtually nothing about the Mormon Church, but, as a former Catholic—like most Filipino Americans, I was baptized one—I could hardly believe that the Catholic Church would allow itself to be sucked into such a mean-spirited strategy. The Christian values of compassion and tolerance were being thrown out the window. Fear and intolerance were promoted, making a civil and rational discussion of the issue virtually impossible. The imprint of Mike Gabbard—Hawai'i's most notorious homophobe—was implicit in STM '98's ads. It was not the Catholic Church's finest hour.

(Gabbard later parlayed his notoriety into a political career. After a stint on the Honolulu City Council and an unsuccessful run for Congress, he was elected to the State Senate in 2006. In 2007, he turned Democrat, causing a half-dozen Democratic Party regulars to resign in protest. Gabbard apologized to Democratic Party leaders for those he "may have offended." Some say although he remains opposed to same-sex marriage, his interaction with Democrat politicians has softened his anti-gay feelings. Whether he is sincere remains to be seen.)

In 1996, Religious Right conservatives targeted legislators who had the courage to consider alternatives to banning same-sex marriage outright. Sen. Rey Graulty, a devout Catholic, and State Reps. Devon Nekoba, Len Pepper and Jim Shon—all Democrats—were among those defeated.

To many Democratic legislators, the message of the 1996 elections was clear: Ban same-sex marriage or else. Some legislators hung religious symbols on their office doors or walls to indicate where they stood on the issue. Others organized prayer meetings. Some, no doubt, did it out of their own religious convictions, but there were a few who I doubted ever saw the inside of a church. Others took the easy way out, deciding there was no need to consider alternatives, no need to compromise, no need to *think*—just vote against same-sex marriage.

I had supported "domestic partnerships" in 1994 and reiterated my support of them in 1998. The controversy caused me to wonder again why the government was in the marriage business in the first place. "Separation of Church and State" is a bedrock principle of our democratic government, but the State laws governing marriage contradict that principle, one of many such contradictions that have become entrenched in our system of government.

I never considered religion and a belief in God as intertwined. Religion is a creation of men. Marriage is a creation of religion. So why was the State involved in the business of marriage? For legislators to argue that the State should pass a law to "preserve the sanctity of marriage" and, in virtually the same breath, affirm their commitment to "separation of Church and State" was hypocrisy.

There were reasonable arguments based on social policy grounds rather than religion for maintaining traditional "marriage." (The prohibition of polygamy in Utah is an example.) But few made them. I did not believe that marriage was a right guaranteed under the State constitution. I saw it as a "privilege" subject to State regulation by general law. Privileges are generally seen as lesser rights that are determined by the Legislature. There were compromises available. Recognizing domestic partnerships was one of them.

Religious Right conservatives and homophobes like Gabbard angrily attacked my support of domestic partnerships as a "deception" to give gays marital rights. Lingle also supported domestic partnerships, but they could hardly attack the standard-bearer of the party they now controlled. Polls indicated that, although nearly 70 percent favored a ban on same-sex marriage, a majority also supported treating homosexuals equally in all other matters.

By mid-September, a new poll revealed that we had cut Lingle's 22-percent lead to 7 percent (47-40). The Japanese Democrats were coming home and, in a dramatic shift, the majority now supported me. I continued to enjoy a big lead among Filipino voters. The Neighbor Islands—traditionally Democratic—were shifting in our favor. I had a 20-percent lead on Kaua'i, and trailed Lingle by 4 percent on Maui and 10 percent on the Big Island. Don Clegg, Harris' pollster, described the voters who had flirted with the idea of voting Republican only to return to the Democrat fold as "bungee-cord Democrats."

"Lingle's got a big lead over you with the white voter," Napolitan said, interpreting the poll results. "Right now you're getting about 22 percent of the white vote, and I doubt you'll get any more than that … so we got to get the Democrats—especially the Japanese voters—to come back in greater numbers than they are now. We need about 65 percent of them." (Unlike Seigle, Napolitan never used the word "haole" or "Caucasian.")

Surprisingly, I was doing better among women than Lingle. Seigle attributed it in part to Vicky's presence in the campaign. "She's helped soften your image," he said. "She's proving to be a strong force for us on television. Joe wrote a special television ad called 'My Husband' in which she talks about you. It's powerful."

Meanwhile, except for UHPA, nearly every labor union representing the private sector and government had endorsed me. A common misperception is that union workers vote in lockstep with their leaders. The reality is that their voting pattern—at least in Hawai'i—closely tracks the vote of the general public. But unions can provide manpower for campaign workers and use newsletters and phone banks to educate their members about the politicians they've endorsed.

The Sierra Club endorsed me as it had done in 1994. This was a good endorsement. Given the Sierra Club's reputation for confronting the State and County governments on environmental issues, no one could reasonably argue that it would endorse a candidate who was allegedly a leader of the so-called "old boys network." Furthermore, it helped highlight that our environmental record was better than Lingle's, which, among other things, included a controversial dispute with the Federal Environmental Protection Association (EPA) over the pollution of the Māʻalaea Harbor caused by runoff from a construction project that had been approved by Maui County officials.

Gladys Brandt—"Aunty Gladys"—had organized a group of Hawaiians, many of them leaders in the ongoing protest against the Bishop Estate trustees, to do a television spot and newspaper ad endorsing me. My dispute with OHA over the ceded-lands revenues had alienated many Hawaiians. If anything, Aunty Gladys's endorsement helped stabilize our Hawaiian votes.

In mid-August, the campaign got ugly. At a Lingle campaign rally in Hawai'i Kai, a haole man who appeared to be in his late 50s or mid-60s, wearing a *Lingle for Governor* T-shirt, got up before nearly a thousand Lingle supporters and asked Lingle if she was gay. Lingle denied it, eliciting loud applause from the crowd. The television news crews and newspaper reporters were covering the event, and it made the late evening news; on the following day the story got heavy coverage in the newspapers and again on television news. A campaign worker we had sent to check out the event reported later, "It was a setup. Lingle's a great actress."

Our people began speculating why the Lingle campaign had staged the event. Seigle believed that Lingle's public relations people had done it to preempt any talk about the longstanding rumors regarding Lingle's sexual orientation. "They made a big mistake bringing it up. Now more people will be talking about it," Seigle said.

"Maybe they were trying to assure Koki [supporters] and the Religious Right conservatives in her campaign that she is straight and not gay," someone quipped.

Rumors about the personal lives of political candidates are a fact of life. During the 1994 gubernatorial campaign, Fasi had spread rumors about me on his radio program. A reporter once asked me if I wanted to respond. "Too bad dueling is illegal," I replied with a smile. After the election, a reporter told me that his station had received several rumors about my personal life, but, without any proof offered, they refused to report them. I wonder how the news media would handle it today.

Months earlier, Seigle and Napolitan had warned our campaign workers to stay away from the rumors about Lingle. "Don't even go there," Napolitan had warned. "It's dirty campaigning, and, even if true, it will backfire."

During the last week of August, Bob Awana, Lingle's campaign manager, called a news conference and accused our campaign of spreading the rumors about Lingle's sexual orientation. (Awana was Eileen Anderson's campaign manager in 1984 when, after only one term, she was defeated by Frank Fasi.) Ann Kobayashi, one of my co-chairs, responded strongly, denying the accusation and demanding that Awana produce proof. Awana came up with a copy of an unsigned letter—described as "rambling" by one reporter—that he alleged came from my campaign. When asked for proof, Awana replied that his "management sense" led him to that conclusion. (For stunts like this Lingle paid Awana's consulting company, Norfolk Consulting, nearly $100,000.)

After it became apparent that his ploy was going nowhere, Awana began backpedaling, saying: "If the Cayetano campaign says it is not behind the spreading of these rumors, then we accept that—period."

But Ann Kobayashi would have none of it. "Why didn't they accept our word before? What has changed?" Kobayashi asked in an interview with *Star-Bulletin* reporter Mike Yuen. Angered, she demanded an apology, stating that Lingle and Awana "have been caught in a lie and now they want the issue to go away.… This shows the type of campaign they run. They charge something, smearing people, and then run. For me, the smear is still hanging over us." In all the years I had known Ann, I had never seen her as indignant.

Seigle, delighted by Kobayashi's angry reply, could only chuckle. "Boy, did Awana blow this one," he said.

The Power of the Press

Even in an age dominated by television, the newspapers still remained powerful shapers of public opinion, especially during elections. The Republicans complained a lot about the power of the unions. But any advantage I gained from the union endorsements was offset by the power of the press. Lingle received the endorsement of every newspaper in the state. Theoretically, newspapers try to keep their editorial stances from creeping into their regular news reporting. Some newspapers try to get around this self-imposed ethical standard by withholding their editorial endorsements until the last week before the election. In 1998, there was no better example than the *Honolulu Star-Bulletin*, the state's second-largest daily newspaper.

On Oct. 12, the *Star-Bulletin* began a four-part series entitled "State of the Unions," which seemed to focus mainly on whether the unions in Hawai'i were too powerful. On the final day, the *Star-Bulletin* ran an editorial concluding: "If the people of Hawai'i want to take back their government from public employee unions, they will vote for candidates who put the people first and are willing to fight the unions."

The joke circulating among our campaign workers was that, since the *Star-Bulletin* did not name the "candidates who put the people first and are willing to fight the unions," I had a shot at getting the endorsement, as my disputes with the unions were usually front-page stories and no one could recall when Lingle had ever fought a union.

The editorial reminded me of an anecdote Waihee had shared with me about Lingle's actions during the 1994 HGEA strike, when she was mayor of Maui. Waihee had met with the four county mayors to discuss the three-week-old strike. "I told the mayors that the strike was unraveling and that if we held the strikers out for another week or two the strike would probably fall apart. I asked each mayor how he or she felt about holding them [the strikers] out for another week. They all agreed, and Lingle was the most vocal about it. 'Yes, yes, let's keep them out longer,' she said. Later, I found out that, after our meeting, she had gone to the picket lines, was seen shaking hands with the strikers and overheard encouraging them to 'hang in there,'" Waihee told me, shaking his head and grinning.

On October 26, a week before the general election, the *Star-Bulletin* began publishing the results of poll taken by a Maryland polling company. The first installment was headlined, "Lingle Still Popular," and reported that Lingle had a favorable rating of 53 percent to my 35 percent, an 18-percent difference. The *Star-Bulletin* had been publishing these "favorable-unfavorable" polls since June 1998.

Many voters mistakenly believe that favorable-unfavorable ratings translate into votes. Experienced politicians and pollsters know that they don't. Standing alone, however, the 53 percent-35 percent suggested to the average voter that I could be trailing Lingle by 18 percent. This would be cleared up, I thought, when the *Star-Bulletin* published the head-to-head or so-called "horse-race poll," which measured how Lingle and I would match up if the vote were taken that day.

The next day, the *Star-Bulletin* published another poll result with the headline, "Voters Like Lingle's Ads Better," but still no horse-race poll.

On October 28, the *Star-Bulletin* published the poll results on the economy. One of the questions asked who or what was to blame for the state of Hawai'i's economy.

The choices given were "The Legislature," "Gov. Cayetano," "John Waihee," "Business executives," "Unions" and "Other/Don't Know." The most recent results showed slightly less than a third believed I was at fault, slightly more than a third thought it was Waihee and 21 percent believed the Legislature was to blame.

Boiled down to its bare essentials, the question assumed that the poor economy could be attributed to Waihee, me and/or the Democratic Legislature. Whatever the editors' intent, had they asked any of the economists who endorsed Lingle in 1998, they would have learned that the premise of the question was flawed.

Eight years later, in October 2006, *Star-Bulletin* columnist Richard Borreca interviewed economists Carl Bonham and Paul Brewbaker about factors that influence the state's economy. Borreca asked Bonham, a UH economics professor who had endorsed Lingle in 1998 and who was the executive director of the University of Hawai'i Economic Research Organization, how much influence the State government had on Hawai'i's economy.

Bonham replied, "Hawai'i's economy reflects national and international decisions, not local decisions." He added, "Neither Lingle nor Cayetano before her can take credit for the Hawai'i economy. The external factors—such as strength of the U.S. economy, declining interest rates, offshore investment in Hawai'i real estate and, of course, tourism and military—are simply too large and move in their own directions."

Brewbaker pointed out that Hawai'i's economy had begun to improve in 1997, not 2003, when Lingle had become governor. "Real Hawai'i total personal income began growing in 1997 ... the current expansion is about 10 years old, not four years." He continued, "Lingle and Hawai'i were helped by the 'lagged effect' of improved economic conditions they inherited."

In 1998, there was little disagreement among Hawai'i economists that the external factors affecting Hawai'i's economy were (1) the 1991 Gulf War, (2) the Mainland recession, and (3) the deteriorating Japanese bubble economy. No local politician, Republican or Democrat, had any control over these factors. Yet the *Star-Bulletin*'s poll question assumed the contrary, and the results fit nicely with the Republican strategy of blaming the Democrats for the state's poor economy.

It was clearly appropriate for Lingle and the Republicans to hold me accountable for the State government's fiscal problems and the local business climate, but to blame me or any other politician for being *the* cause of the state's poor economy was misleading. That Lingle went out of her way to blame me told me two things: Either she didn't understand how external factors affected the economy and just did what her public relations people advised her to do, or she understood but wasn't above twisting the truth to win.

Politically, it made no sense for me to argue about the impact of external factors on Hawai'i's economy: It would appear as if I was trying to evade taking responsibility. "Don't waste your time trying to explain it, Ben; it's a losing proposition. Just suck it up and tell the voters about your record and about the signs that the economy is getting better," Napolitan suggested.

On October 30, the *Star-Bulletin* published the poll results on whether or not a constitutional convention should be convened.

On October 31, it published the final poll results on same-sex marriage.

After five days the *Star-Bulletin*'s poll results had shown that: (1) Lingle had an 18-percent higher favorable rating than I did, (2) people liked her television ads better than mine, (3) people did not favor holding a constitutional convention, and (4) people were opposed to same-sex marriage. But where was the *Star-Bulletin's* horse-race poll?

Probably tucked away in a safe at the Star-Bulletin *somewhere*, I thought.

On October 31, *Star-Bulletin* editor David Shapiro explained the paper's rationale for not publishing the horse-race poll: "Horse-race polls … spawn endless conjecture about who's winning, a meaningless question that has little to do with the issues that drive elections…. Trying to measure who's winning before Election Day is as pointless as speculating about who's winning a sumo match while the sumotori are throwing salt around before stepping into the ring."

This reasoning also applies to measuring candidates' favorable-unfavorable ratings; and how meaningful to the election is measuring which candidate's television spots voters liked best? The same technical flaws that critics say make horse-race polls speculative or unreliable apply to the questions asked in any poll. Why, then, should the *Star-Bulletin* publish any polls at all?

Polls are only as good and reliable as the people who take them and the methodology used. Many forget that a poll is but a snapshot of how people feel at the moment they are polled. During the 1994 gubernatorial election, the *Star-Bulletin's* last horse-race poll had showed me winning by 4 percent, Saiki in second place and Fasi trailing Saiki by 11 percent. Our poll showed me winning by 7 percent, with Fasi in third place and coming up fast and Saiki in second but fading badly. The final result was that I won by 6 percent, Fasi was second and Saiki third. These results were clearly predictable to an expert who knew how to interpret the trends of the last polls taken.

From September 23 to November 2, 1998, Barbara Ankersmit and Don Clegg were taking "rolling polls," which were taken daily of groups of between 150 and 200 people. Although the samples were small—too small for a single poll—over the long run these polls were very accurate. By early October, our rolling polls showed we were in a nip-and-tuck race with Lingle—we had cut her lead to even and at times had even spurted ahead.

In a race that we believed was virtually a dead heat, the *Star-Bulletin's* decision to publish the favorable-unfavorable results but not the horse-race results left the impression that Lingle had an 18-percent lead. Since June 1998, the *Star-Bulletin* had published a number of polls showing that Lingle's favorable ratings were significantly higher than mine. Elections are not supposed to be popularity contests, but the *Star-Bulletin's* treatment of its poll results made the race between Lingle and me seem like one. Close races are often determined in the last few days of the election. Voter perceptions of the candidates are crucial. While the phrase "everybody loves a winner" is a cliché, it became one because it is a hard truth that has been verified repeatedly by experience. The *Star-Bulletin* had created the misleading impression that Lingle was far ahead of me, that she was a sure winner.

We had no complaints with the *Advertiser*, which had endorsed Lingle but treated us fairly. Other smaller newspapers such as the *Maui News* (which had been a cheerleader for Lingle throughout her years as Maui's mayor) and *West Hawaii*, Kona's biggest newspaper, were such ardent advocates for Lingle that the theoretical line separating editorial policy from news reporting was literally nonexistent.

Two national publications, *Forbes* magazine and the *Wall Street Journal*, both with long histories of supporting Republicans, published timely articles blaming Democrats for Hawai'i's poor economy. *Forbes*, whose enigmatic publisher, Steve Forbes, had run for president, was the magazine that had once referred to Hawai'i as the "People's Republic of Hawai'i." John Fund, the *Wall Street Journal* reporter, was a well-known and avowed conservative. Both articles had one thing in common: The writers interviewed and quoted only Hawai'i Republicans, giving conservatives like Sam Slom an exclusive forum. With every newspaper in the state, along with *Forbes* and the *Wall Street Journal* supporting her, Lingle got widespread favorable print coverage she couldn't buy.

On October 30, 1998, the *Honolulu Advertiser*'s horse-race poll showed Lingle ahead of me 42 percent to 38 percent with 19 percent undecided. With a margin of error of 4.5 percent, the poll was comparable to ours. The high number of undecided was a good sign, as experience had shown that most of those voters were locals who usually favored the incumbent.

On October 12, I received a memorandum from Napolitan warning, "The election may very well hinge on how well you do in the two televised debates."

He pointed out that Lingle came off as warmer and friendlier than I did, but that I had solid experience and accomplishments under my belt while her plans lacked substance. He added, "Under your gruff exterior, you are a warm and sympathetic person; under her glowing cheeks beats a Republican heart of stone."

He directed, "Our debate team has got to develop the roughest, nastiest, most infuriating questions to ask and you've got to learn how to handle these with a smile on your face even though you may really feel like tearing out the throat of the person who asked the question...."

"If you bleed in the mock debates, that's fine; better bloodshed there than dripping out of the television screen on October 16."

Attorney General Margery Bronster led our debate preparation team, which also included Jennifer Goto-Sabas from Inouye's office; Chuck Freedman, Waihee's former director of communications; and Joan Bennett, a public relations consultant. Bronster delighted in cross-examining me (I jokingly reminded her that I had appointed her); it was grueling and at times fun. After two evening practice sessions I was about as ready as I could be.

Lingle was a skilled speaker, but we had noticed some weaknesses. It was obvious she was overconfident. It was equally obvious she was not as familiar with state issues as I was. Once during the campaign she proposed eliminating the Department of Business, Economic Development and Tourism (DBEDT). DBEDT, she argued, was in part to blame for the state's economic woes; eliminating it would save hundreds of millions of dollars. This zany line of reasoning would have justified abolishing the U.S. Department of Defense because it had failed to prevent the December 7, 1941, attack on Pearl Harbor.

The first televised debate was held on October 16. After the debate, when I returned to our campaign headquarters, our workers were cheering and whooping it up. A UH political scientist was quoted in the *Advertiser* as calling the debate a "draw." *A good sign*, I thought, as most of the UH faculty were supporting Lingle. I was satisfied with my performance.

In an October 22 interview with *Star-Bulletin* reporter Richard Borreca, Lingle revealed her attitude on our debates: "The debate is no big deal.... Some people may approach them with trepidation, but I enjoy it," she said.

Unlike Lingle, I felt a little trepidation prior to both debates—the same kind of feeling I felt many times when I made an opening statement to a jury, the slight nervousness I experienced when as a kid I was about to get into a fistfight—a nervousness that disappeared once the first punch was thrown.

During the second televised debate on October 26, Lingle acted as if she was following a script. She had not learned anything from our first debate. During both debates she responded vaguely to questions from the panel of reporters. Her evasiveness made our "Where's the beef?" television ads very effective. The second debate made it clear that she was not as familiar with the issues as she had boasted.

Later, I learned that after one of the debates, Lingle and her debate coach, Al Hoffman, who in a pre-debate interview was quoted as saying, "We'll hold him accountable for the economy," got into a loud and heated shouting match in the television station's parking lot. Apparently, she blamed his coaching strategy for her robotic performance.

People who did not watch us debate had to form their opinions mainly from what they saw on the television news or read in the newspapers. A story on the debate written by the *Star-Bulletin*'s Richard Borreca quoted a well-known Republican named Peggy Ryan as saying, "The man is a dreary dolt. I predict a Lingle victory." *Why*, I wondered, *did Borreca include in his story a comment that amounted to no more than an ad hominem attack?*

But I must have done better than Ryan imagined; our post-debate polls showed that we had wiped out Lingle's September 7-percent lead. Since June, we had slowly been chipping away at what had once been her 22-percent lead. We were now in a statistical tie. (Later, in a post-election interview, Don Clegg would tell the *Star-Bulletin* that "the tide turned after the second debate.")

For most of October, the Democratic Party's Coordinating Campaign (chaired by Jeremy Harris) and the labor unions were running television and print ads attacking Lingle's economic plans and her ties to Newt Gingrich and the conservative Republicans who had taken over Congress in 1994, defeating 10 of the 11 Democratic governors who were up for election (I was the only one who survived). Her "It's time the Republicans took back the state" speech, which had elicited loud cheers from Republicans, was used in the Democratic and labor union ads against her.

One of the most effective television ads was the "Neva [never] Happen" ad run by the carpenters' union. The 30-second ad was designed to rebut the so-called "Maui Miracle." Maui was the county least affected by the State's economic slump, for which Lingle took full credit. The ad showed an unemployed carpenter, in his early 30s, with his young son. Speaking in pidgin, the carpenter said, "She wen promise us work and we wen endorse her—but it neva happen." The ad—designed to appeal to local voters—was a powerful attack on Lingle's claim of the Maui Miracle.

When I asked Walter Kupau, the fiery leader of the carpenters' union, why the union was endorsing me after it had endorsed Lingle when she ran for mayor, he replied, "That was for mayor. We think you've been a good governor. Besides, she talks a lot, makes promises ... but can't deliver. A lot of my boys on Maui are still on the bench [not working]."

About 10 days before the November 3 general election, Seigle called for a meeting. Charlie Toguchi, Bert Kobayashi, Bob Toyofuku (an attorney running Hirono's campaign) and our co-chairs met with Seigle at our campaign headquarters.

"I just found out that Lingle has been canceling a lot of her television buys," Seigle said.

"Why would she do that?" someone asked.

"The word I got is that she is certain she's going to win."

"Really? What makes her think she's got it in the bag?"

"Well," Seigle replied, "I've been told that she's using a Mainland pollster out of Virginia or Maryland and her polls show her with a more-than-10-percent lead. Now, I think that's way off. I've talked to Barbara and Don, and they both feel very confident about our polls."

"What do you think we should do about it?" I asked.

"I called Joe [Napolitan] in New York this morning, and we both agree that if we have the money we should buy up the time slots she's giving up before she realizes her polls are wrong and tries to buy them back."

"How much are we talking about?"

"About $400,000."

I turned to Kobayashi. "Bert, how much do we have left for television?" I asked.

"Nothing; we already spent it for our television ads," Kobayashi replied.

"I think if we give up some of our newspaper ads, radio spots and other media costs, we can save perhaps $100,000 or so," Seigle said.

"Hold off on that; I think if I show people our poll results, we'll be able to raise the money, but it'll take some time," Kobayashi said.

"Well, the stations require payment up front, so we'll advance the money to buy the spots, but, Bert, I want your word that, win or lose, you'll help raise the money to pay us back."

"You got it," Kobayashi replied. Nothing else needed to be said. With Bert a handshake was enough. Those who knew him trusted him. (Armed with our latest polls showing that the election was a dead heat, Kobayashi was able to raise the money in a week.)

"Jack, how could her polls be so way off from ours?" I asked.

"The problem with using Mainland pollsters is that local people are very reluctant to answer questions from someone with a Mainland accent who often has a hard time pronouncing local names. Now, local pollsters deal with this by using a certain weighting formula to measure the votes of people from certain ethnic groups. And our weighting formula is based on years of experience and trial and error. Mainland pollsters often don't have this expertise. With the exception of Peter Hart [a nationally renowned Democratic pollster of the 1970s] for Jack Burns' campaign, I've always used Barbara [Ankersmit], who Hart himself recommended. Barbara has called every one of your statewide elections within 1 to 2 percent."

An advantage of using a Mainland pollster is that he or she provides greater security than local pollsters, who use local people to ask the poll questions. The disadvantage is that accuracy is sometimes compromised for security.

"Okay, let's go for it," I replied, delighted at the thought of our television ads dominating prime time while Lingle's were running on the *Late Show.*

Later that day, Seigle bought every prime-time television slot the Lingle campaign had cancelled. (After the election, the Lingle camp claimed that it had cancelled her television ads for the final week because it was trying to adhere to the campaign spending law. This was shibai and revealed Lingle's penchant for putting a positive public relations spin on everything—including a loss. The truth is that Lingle was not eligible for campaign spending matching funds for the general election. Unlike the primary election, in which she agreed to follow the campaign-spending limit, she was under no obligation to do so in the general election. Conventional political wisdom is to spend every dollar for the campaign. A technically successful campaign is one that has little money left at the end. The objective in an election, after all, is to win, not save money. Lingle's decision to cancel her television buys was another indication of the hubris that permeated her campaign; plus it also revealed the folly of using a public relations firm (Communications Pacific) that had no previous experience in running a statewide political campaign.)

In the final days of the campaign, things got nastier. On November 1,

Republican State Sen. Sam Slom issued a press release claiming that Vicky's and my purchase of a 2.6-acre lot in 1997 indicated that I had expected to lose the election. The press release was covered in a *Star-Bulletin* story. "Mr. Cayetano has made prudent retirement plans for life after November 3, when Linda Lingle will be elected Hawai'i's first woman governor," Slom was quoted as saying. He also "scoffed" at those who hinted that my moving into the neighborhood might depress property values.

Anyone who thought Slom was merely engaging in light humor was likely to be disabused of that notion on November 2, when a pro-business ad hoc group called the Hawaii Coalition of Small Business Owners ran a three-quarter-page newspaper ad in the *Star-Bulletin* criticizing our land buy, stating "Ben, your deeds speak louder than your words."

Neither Slom nor the ad hoc group alleged that we had done anything illegal (we had not). They just wanted the voters to know that we had purchased an expensive lot at a time when the economy was still struggling to recover.

It was a cheap shot aimed primarily at Vicky, who, according to Seigle and Napolitan, had become an influential force in our television campaign. Not only was she great in our television ads, she was enthusiastically received as she traveled throughout the state speaking for me. She had spearheaded a "Women for Ben" campaign, persuading 1,000 women to sign a full-page endorsement ad and organizing a luncheon attended by 300 to 400 women, including some who had not yet decided how they would vote.

I declined to comment, but Vicky responded. "It [the land] is an investment for the future of my two children, and my husband supports it fully," she said, her voice trembling with emotion. "His [Slom's] words," she continued, her voice now firm, "are truly thinly veiled racist remarks that you have heard in the past and even now on the Mainland, when people, minorities, try to move into areas that they normally don't reside in." It was straight from her heart. When it came to family—my wife was a fighter. I was proud of her.

Seigle just shook his head. "I think it's going to backfire, especially with local people. Despite all the years he's been living in Hawai'i, Slom still doesn't understand local people."

In a post-election interview, Don Clegg stuck the needle in further. "I was certainly going to thank Gene Ward and Sam Slom for all of their assistance," he quipped to a reporter. "I think the Sam Slom ad ... was a definite plus for us and lost her [Lingle] votes." (In 2008, I learned that Kitty Lagareta, Lingle's media consultant, had advised Lingle to stay away from getting involved in running the ad and Lingle had agreed. Thus it was left to Slom to organize the ad hoc group to pay for and run the ad, which of course, he did.)

About a week before the election, Charlie Toguchi asked me to meet with Raynette Kamaka and Carol Toguchi, our two front-office receptionists. "Ray, tell the governor what happened," Toguchi said.

"Well, a man came into the office with two women and he pointed to my desk and told one of the women, 'You're going to be sitting there.' Then he pointed to Carol's desk and told the other woman that she was going to be sitting there."

"What did the guy look like?" I asked.

"He was haole, middle-age."

"And the two women?"

"They looked local, mixed."

I looked at Charlie and smiled. "Ray," I said, "if that man comes in again, you and Carol tell him that I gave permission for him to go into my office to measure the drapes, okay?"

Toguchi looked at me. "They smell blood. They think they're going to win. The only way to shut these people up is for us to beat Lingle."

"Yeah, this election is not only about the economy, it's about political power. They want a Republican governor—but they're going to have to wait a little longer—because it's not going to happen on my watch. You know, Charlie—I just love it when they take us cheap."

On Election Day, Barbara Ankersmit and I met privately. "Governor, my poll indicates the race is very close. I think you'll either win or lose by 1 percent," she said calmly. "Our final poll shows you ahead 44 percent to 43 percent—a statistical tie."

Ankersmit told me she felt we had the momentum and that I would win. Don Clegg, I found out later, thought I would lose by 3 to 4 percent, but agreed with Seigle that I should not be told. I knew it would be close, but there was nothing left to do but vote, thank our campaign workers, try to relax and await the evening television news for the final results.

Napolitan called from New York to wish me luck. An Italian American in his early 70s, with a shock of white hair, he had a great sense of humor and a trove of great political stories and bawdy jokes. But in the presence of women, he was always a gentleman. He was short, about 5 feet 4 inches, and traced his family roots to Naples, Italy. I kidded him about how the thing I remembered most about my first trip to Italy was that I had never seen so many short white guys in my life. Once, I asked him if he was Sicilian—and got a humorous, tongue-in-cheek lecture about my not being able to figure out that he was a "Napolitano." Vicky and I admired him and loved being around him.

"Ben," he said, "we've made a hell of a comeback. I think we'll beat her tonight, but, then, I thought Hubert Humphrey would beat Richard Nixon in 1968. [As one of Humphrey's consultants, Napolitan had helped devise the strategy that erased Nixon's 17-percent lead only to fall short in one of the closest presidential elections in history. 'Another week and Humphrey would have won,' he had lamented.] Whatever happens tonight, just remember to be gracious."

"Well, Joe, if I lose I'll do something real classy. I'll stand on the corner of King and Bishop Streets and shout, 'The people have spoken—those bastards!'"

He laughed and told me another one of his jokes.

Victory

I was cautiously confident. I thought about the seven elections I had gone through; about my 24 years in public service and what I had done or tried to do for what I believed was in the public's best interest. Would I have any regrets over some of the hard decisions and compromises I had made as a legislator and in my first term as governor?

If I lost I knew that I would have enduring regrets about the cuts I had made to social programs that served the poor and needy. If there was one reason I wanted to be reelected it was to restore those services. That night I swore that, if I was reelected, I would not compromise services to the poor and needy for the sake of business, labor unions or the special-interest groups that feed off the State coffers.

At about 7:30 p.m. the first voting printout showed that I was leading Lingle by 1,523 votes. It was a good sign. Fasi dropped by our campaign headquarters about that time and was interviewed on television. "He's going to win," Fasi said; "I thought he would be behind at the first printout, but since he's ahead at this point, there's no question he is going to win." As lieutenant governor, I had run the elections for eight years and was familiar with voting trends. I thought Fasi was right.

By the third printout, my lead had increased to a little more than 12,000 votes. Our campaign workers were whooping it up at our headquarters. I asked Lloyd Nekoba to check whether all of the votes were in. Nekoba checked with the voter central and told me all the votes had been counted. We headed for the headquarters. Vicky and I got on stage, and I declared victory.

It was premature.

About five minutes later, Harris rushed into our campaign office. He looked worried and said excitedly, "Kona didn't come in—the Kona vote is not in!" He looked as if *he* might be losing the election!

Seigle looked at me and said calmly, "I don't think her Kona vote can overcome a 12,000-vote lead." Kona was predominantly haole. Our polls showed I was getting about 22 percent of the haole vote statewide. In Kona, however, it was probably closer to 10 percent. Bob Toyofuku, who was Hirono's campaign strategist, analyzed the returns and estimated that, depending on the voter turnout, we would still win by approximately 7,000 votes. When the Kona votes were finally counted, my 12,000 lead had been cut to 5,253 votes, or 1.3 percent of the total ballots. We had gotten clobbered in Kona. In one precinct I was beaten by a margin of 1,400 to 112 votes. But it didn't matter; all I needed was one more vote than Lingle.

The 1998 gubernatorial election was over.

Lingle didn't take her loss well. Her reaction brought Napolitan's words to mind: "Under her glowing cheeks beats a Republican heart of stone." While the news media cast Lingle in an emotional, sympathetic light, the discerning person might have noticed she gave no concession, no congratulatory remarks; she made no offer to set aside differences and work together for the common good.

Instead she complained: "My one disappointment in the campaign is the way Gov. Cayetano tried to divide people, between parties, between labor and management, between newcomer and kama'āina."

Even at the end, she remained true to form—blaming everyone else but herself for her defeat. She took no responsibility for her lack of preparation for our televised debates or for her decision to cancel her television ads in the final two weeks of the campaign or for committing one of the biggest sins in political campaigning—underestimating your opponent.

As far as I was concerned, her complaint was a case of the proverbial pot calling the kettle black. Elections are all about making choices. Robust debate and probing discussions tend to divide voters along ideological and personal lines. The reality is that elections naturally divide people and parties; it is inherent in the process, and those who believe otherwise are naive.

Divide people? When Lingle exclaimed to her GOP faithful, "It's time for Republicans to take back this state!" she caused Democrats who remembered what it was like when the Republicans ran things in Hawai'i to have second thoughts, and many came back home to support me.

When the Republican-oriented *Star-Bulletin* published a four-part series exploring why unions were so powerful in Hawai'i and followed up with an editorial in which voters were urged to "take back their government from public-employee unions," it was a clarion call for union leaders and their members to unite and get out the vote for Democrats who were not hostile to the cause of unionism.

When newcomers—including some of the editors of the newspapers that endorsed Lingle—dismissed the words "local values" as a racist code for "non-white," it upset locals who viewed those words as a metaphor for the local culture that sets Hawai'i apart from the rest of the world. Some Mainland haoles like Barbara Ankersmit, who came to Hawai'i in the late '60s, understood what "local values" meant—and realized that they were matters of the heart, not place of birth or skin color or manner of speech. Mainland haoles like Sam Slom and the newspaper editors just didn't get it.

On election night, I extended my hand to Lingle in an earnest plea to set aside our differences and work together for the common good. She spurned it, responding instead with complaints about my dividing people. I wasn't surprised. It had been a tough loss for her.

On November 5, two days after the general election, State Republican

Party executive director Jess Yescalis, a self-proclaimed protégé of Republican political consultant Lee Atwater, who had been sent to Hawaiʻi by the National Republican Party to help strategize Lingle's campaign, announced, "The fight [for 2000] starts today."

On December 7, 1998, in my inaugural speech, I extended my hand once again:

"To those who did not support me in the election, I welcome your wisdom. I welcome the energy and commitment you displayed which made the election such a hard-fought and close one. To you I pledge an open mind to your ideas, to your sincere desire to work together for the common good."

The Republican response was to float the idea that the Democrats had committed voter fraud and somehow rigged the election in my favor. On November 23, Democratic Party Chairman Walter Heen, noting that there were 157 votes disqualified because of over-voting in District 44 of the State House, filed a motion requesting that the Supreme Court invalidate the election results in which Republican Emily Auwae defeated Democratic incumbent Merwyn Jones by a mere 21 votes. The court did not invalidate the election but instead ordered a recount. Apparently, there had been a glitch of some kind in one of the electronic voting machines being used for the first time.

Having no legal grounds to challenge the results of Lingle's defeat, the fertile minds of her public relations advisors and advisors like Bob Awana saw the court-ordered recount of Auwae's election as an opportunity to smear the entire election as a fraud.

Meanwhile, amid growing speculation that there were other defective electronic voting machines among the nearly 400 or so that were used statewide, the State Senate, led by Democrat Colleen Hanabusa, whose Senatorial district included District 44 of the State House, passed a resolution requesting that Marion Higa, the legislative auditor, oversee an electronic recount of the entire election.

Whatever the results of the electronic recount, they would not change the official results of the election. But thoughtful senators like Avery Chumbley of Maui and Matt Matsunaga, who co-chaired the Senate Judiciary Committee, believed a recount was necessary to quell the notion that the election had been rigged and "restore public confidence" in the system.

Bob Awana, Lingle's campaign manager, told reporters that he was aware of 34 instances of voter fraud—specifically, of aliens voting in the election. When an *Advertiser* reporter actually investigated, he found that Awana's allegations were spurious. The falsehood was compounded when Republican State Rep. Barbara Marumoto wrote a letter to the *Advertiser* asserting there had been "illegal" voting.

Not to be left out, Sam Slom's girlfriend, Malia Zimmerman, who at the time was a reporter for *Pacific Business News* (*PBN*), wrote a story recycling charges made by Republican State Rep. Mark Moses that aliens had been allowed to vote in the 1994 election. "The state is no stranger to voter fraud," she wrote. "It was clearly proven in 1994, according to Mark Moses."

The truth is that Moses' charges that the Immigration and Naturalization Service (INS) had confirmed that up to 30 percent of the voters in some districts in the 1994 election were aliens were false—they had been refuted by INS director Don Radcliffe in a letter in 1996.

In another *PBN* story Zimmerman cited an unnamed "Chinatown bookie" as her source for the charge that "the fix was in" and the election was somehow rigged for me to win. *PBN* had a long history of supporting Republicans, but I was surprised that it would run such crackpot stories. (Apparently, Zimmerman's brand of journalism troubled *PBN*'s editors, as she was subsequently fired.) Lingle herself contributed to the smear when she—while claiming to have "moved on" after her loss—described the complaints of voter fraud as "well documented."

I experienced many wild charges in my eight elections, but the falsehoods that "aliens" had voted in the 1998 elections angered me. There was no doubt that by "aliens" the three Republicans meant Filipino aliens. The obvious innuendo was that the aliens had voted for me. These lies were racist and demeaning to the Filipino community.

Finally, on March 15, 1998, the recount of the November 3 general election was completed. The State and federal governments accepted the results. Marion Higa, whose office conducted the recount, concluded: "The election had integrity. No credible evidence has been presented to demonstrate fraud." The recount, however, was a little late. Like all political smears, the Republican smear of the 1998 gubernatorial election could never be completely erased.

Lingle's defeat was a bitter pill for even the National Republican Party to swallow. On February 27, 1999—four months after the election—GOP National Committee Co-Chairman Patricia Harrison told a Lincoln Day dinner audience in Fort Lauderdale, Florida, that Hawai'i's "Democratic machine" had committed an anti-Semitic smear (Lingle is Jewish) by spreading the word that, if Lingle won, "Christmas in Hawai'i would be abolished."

It was that kind of an election. ❖

CHAPTER TWENTY

Bishop Estate: Round Two

"Now the [legislative] session is the Bronster session."
Sen. *Norman Sakamoto, April 28, 1999*

The Vote on Bronster

Meanwhile, as the election controversies swirled around us, Margery Bronster's investigation of the Bishop Estate trustees continued. Bronster's self-assuredness and aggressive style provoked anger and resentment among the trustees and others. She pulled no punches in her public statements about the trustees and their lawyers. She was playing hardball—a rough game at which, I knew from personal experience, trustees Peters and Wong were experts.

Her detractors knew that once I was reelected, I would reappoint Bronster to a second term as attorney general. They also knew that before Bronster could assume a second term she would have to be confirmed by a majority of the State Senate, where she was still well connected.

Even among my Cabinet members, Bronster had stepped on some toes. Many of my Cabinet directors and deputy directors were attorneys themselves, and a few, like Mike Wilson, who headed the Department of Land and Natural Resources and chaired the Water Commission, and Larry Miike, the lawyer and physician director of the Department of Health, disagreed strongly with some of the legal opinions Bronster issued that affected their respective departments. Overall, however, she was held in high regard by the Cabinet. Bronster was honest, smart, tough and loyal. She was no sycophant.

Bronster's investigation of the trustees, which started in August 1997 and continued unabated during the 1998 election, turned up some damning and embarrassing information regarding the trustees' actions. By April 1999 she had uncovered a growing number of facts that exposed how the trustees had mismanaged trust assets, abused their powers as trustees, squandered trust money and used Bishop Estate staff to develop questionable relationships with State politicians—actions that could endanger the estate's tax-exempt status as a charitable trust. Peters had served the longest among the trustees, and the investigation revealed how politicians and ex-politicians he favored had benefited by his largesse with trust money.

The most flagrant example was former State Sen. Milton Holt, who had been hired by the Bishop Estate after he lost his bid for reelection in 1996. Holt had misused his Bishop Estate credit cards to run up thousands of dollars in bar tabs, lunches, dinners and other unauthorized expenses. Unknown to the other trustees, Peters had instructed the estate's accountants to pay the expenses. When Holt's transgressions were discovered by the other trustees, who then demanded that Holt reimburse the estate, Peters arranged for Holt to be paid "bonuses" in the exact amount of the unauthorized expenses, including payment of all federal and State taxes owed. There were rumors of Holt's drug use and charges of domestic violence that led to his divorce—it was no secret among politicians that Holt's personal life was in shambles. For those who had served in the Legislature with Holt, as I had, his fall from grace was truly sad. The Kalihi-born Kamehameha and Harvard graduate, who had once been considered by many political observers to be the most promising all of the young Hawaiian politicians, was in a freefall to disaster. I had no doubts Peters was trying to help Holt, but he had no authority to squander trust funds in doing it.

Another legislator who benefited was State Sen. Marshall Ige, a fawning disciple of Peters'. Ige was being investigated on charges that Bishop Estate had helped him erase a campaign debt of approximately $18,000 owed to a printing company by having another firm that had extensive no-bid contracts with Bishop Estate pay the printing company for bogus services in the exact amount of Ige's debt.

Elected to the State Senate in 1996, Ige's arrogant response to the investigation of his activities was to demand that the attorney general disclose the details of a $480,000 contract she had awarded to an investigative firm for the Bishop Estate investigation. Egotistical and obnoxious, Ige made it clear he was going to vote against Bronster's confirmation, and he ignored my request to recuse himself from voting.

As the attorney general's investigators uncovered more proof of his wrongdoing, Ige played the role of victim. In a shameless display of self-pity, he compared his plight to that of Japanese Americans who were politically disenfranchised and interned during World War II: "I have told my family that I now know how many of the AJAs felt during the war. Being prejudged by a group with power, resulting with no due process."

By the first week of April 1999, I knew Bronster's confirmation was in jeopardy. While my chief of staff, Charles Toguchi, was lobbying senators to support Bronster, I called on a few senators myself to find out the concerns of those who were either opposed to or undecided on Bronster's confirmation. There were some legitimate complaints, but none seemed to justify rejecting her. No one questioned her character or integrity. I knew, however, that Peters, Dickie Wong and Larry Mehau were lobbying their supporters to oppose her. (Wong admitted as much in a subsequent deposition taken by the attorney general.)

Still, a few days before the confirmation vote, we counted 14 senators (she needed 13) who said they intended to support Bronster. When the HGEA announced it would oppose her because it disagreed with some legal opinions she had issued relating to privatization of State services and the vote on the Constitutional Convention, my concerns grew worse.

The final vote was 11 to 14 against Bronster. Three of the senators we thought we could count on had flipped at the last minute. Among them was Senate President Mizuguchi, who cited the HGEA opposition as the reason for his "no" vote. Although it was not a hard-and-fast rule, the Senate president was expected to support his committee chairmen. Understandably, Mizuguchi's "no" vote had angered Sens. Avery Chumbley and Matt Matsunaga, the co-chairmen of the Senate Judiciary Committee who had recommended strongly that Bronster be confirmed.

The anti-Bronster forces had won a pyrrhic victory. A firestorm of protests by angry voters broke out. Bronster's high-profile investigation had already won her widespread public support. A post-confirmation poll indicated that four of every five persons polled believed that Bronster's ouster was "political."

Among the 14 "no" votes were those of four freshmen senators led by Sen. Colleen Hanabusa. A freshman herself, she represented the predominantly Hawaiian Waiʻanae-Nānākuli area and seemed dismissive of the public cry of "politics."

"It's a lot easier to believe a deal was cut. It's a lot easier to believe someone else was influenced than to believe that someone actually studied the issue ... [t]he estate is an easy object to hate, especially in some communities," she said, leaving me to wonder why she had singled out the estate rather than the trustees as the object of the public's ire.

The reasons for Hanabusa's vote were a bit more complicated than she would admit. It was well known that Hanabusa had had an earlier run-in with Bronster in a controversy over reports that voting machines had malfunctioned in one of Hanabusa's senatorial voting precincts in the 1998 election. Hanabusa was purportedly angered over remarks Bronster had allegedly made about the education level of the voters in her precinct (Bronster denied making the remarks).

But Hanabusa had other reasons to oppose Bronster's confirmation. Henry Peters and his influential mother, Hoaliku Drake, who had organized public demonstrations in opposition to Bronster's confirmation, were both supporters who lived in her district. Politically, that alone would have been reason enough for her to vote against her. But, as the *Honolulu Advertiser* would later disclose, Hanabusa had a close relationship with developer Jeff Stone, whose sister was married to Bishop Estate trustee Dickie Wong and who, along with Peters and Wong, had been indicted by a grand jury convened by Bronster. As the attorney general's investigation would later reveal, prior to the confirmation hearing, Hanabusa had met privately with Larry Mehau and Wong. When confronted by a reporter, Hanabusa confirmed that the meeting had taken place, but, in a remarkable lapse of memory, she could not remember if Bronster's confirmation had been discussed.

Senate Judiciary Co-Chairman Matt Matsunaga had no quarrel with Bronster and saw her in a different light: "I think that Margery represented courage and change, and I think people believed that a vote against Margery was a vote against standing up for what you believed in," he said. Matsunaga had described the situation almost perfectly. Perception is reality in politics. For a host of reasons—unfavorable news media coverage was one—the trustees were seen by many as self-dealing, overpaid, corrupt and arrogant. Bronster, on the other hand, had received effusive public praise and was seen as a modern-day Joan of Arc.

In an unprecedented move, the State Central Committee of the Hawai'i Democratic Party, headed by Democratic Party Chairman Walter Heen, a co-author of "Broken Trust," issued a resolution expressing its "disapproval and disavowal" of the senators who had voted against Bronster's confirmation:

"Those senators performed a disservice to the general public, contravened the philosophy and principles of democratic governance and caused the Democratic Party embarrassment and a loss of public confidence ... such actions have undermined the credibility, integrity and honorable traditions of the Democratic Party."

I thought that the State Central Committee's resolution was over the top. The anti-Bronster senators had not "contravened the philosophy and principles of democratic governance"; there was nothing wrong with *how* they had used the process, although many found the final *result* objectionable. It was that result that had set off the most effective check and balance in any democratic form of government—voter outrage.

In the 2000 election, the most notable target of angry voters was Marshall Ige. In a startling case of self-deception, Ige decided to run for reelection. With a growing number of criminal charges hanging over his head, Ige's candidacy was a gift to the Republicans. He was defeated soundly in the primary by former Republican-turned-Democrat Sol Naluai, who in turn was trounced by the affable Republican Robert Hogue, a well-known sportscaster, in the 2000 general election.

In 2001, Ige was convicted on charges of failing to report campaign expenditures. Moreover, in a separate case involving a California couple seeking a pardon for their daughter and some farmers, he was convicted of fraud, extortion and other charges in January 2002. The last time I saw Ige he was clad in brown overalls as part of a prisoner work crew cleaning the yard at the governor's residence at Washington Place.

Apparently, most voters blamed the Democrats for Bronster's ouster. Moreover, the fact that four of the five Bishop Estate trustees were Democrats (Stender was a Republican) prompted voters to take their ire out on all Democrats. I found this ironic, as it was a Democratic administration that was trying to clean things up. Nevertheless, Republicans gained seven new State representatives and one

State senator in the 2000 election.

The four freshmen in Hanabusa's group—Jonathan Chun (Kaua'i), Jan Yagi-Buen (Maui), David Matsuura (Big Island) and Bob Nakata—were all defeated in 2002. Another casualty was Whitney Anderson, the lone Republican senator (there were only two Republicans in the Senate) to vote against Bronster, who was defeated in the Republican primary.

Months before the primary, another anti-Bronster senator, Brian Kanno, having read the tea leaves in his district, mailed a groveling pre-election letter of apology to more than 20,000 voters in his district, literally begging for forgiveness. Kanno's mea culpa saved him, although barely: He was reelected by a mere 79 votes over a virtually unknown, inexperienced Republican opponent.

Mizuguchi, after losing the support of Chumbley and Matsunaga, no longer had the votes to retain his Senate presidency. Perhaps with the memory of his barely winning reelection in 1994 still in mind, he decided to call it quits, retiring after 26 years in public office.

"A Personal Investment Club"

On April 28, 1999, the day Bronster's confirmation was voted down, the *Star-Bulletin* ran a front-page story headlined: "IRS Wants Trustees Out." The headline was later confirmed by the IRS.

"The planets finally lined up," court-appointed Master Colbert Matsumoto would say to me later. Indeed, a confluence of forces—the protests of the Na Pua and Na Kumu groups, Matsumoto's devastating Master's Reports, and "Broken Trust," the blockbuster essay that had spurred the attorney general's investigation—had combined to paint a sorry picture of mismanagement, abuse, corruption and greed at the Bishop Estate which the IRS could not ignore.

"They treated the estate as if it was their personal investment club," an IRS official was quoted as saying. Indeed, the trustees' reaction to the protests and the attorney general's investigation was to circle their wagons, ignore the grievances of the protesters and use their political muscle to oust Bronster, all of which turned out to be a resounding self-indictment of wrongdoing.

On May 6, 1999, only eight days after the State Senate rejected Margery Bronster's confirmation, Circuit Judge Bambi Weil Eden Hifo ordered the permanent removal of trustee Lokelani Lindsey. The next day, Circuit Court Judge Kevin Chang ordered a 90-day temporary removal of the other four trustees.

On August 20, 1999, Gerard Jervis became the first trustee to voluntarily resign permanently. He protested, however, that the decisions and practices of the trustees found objectionable by the IRS had occurred before he became a trustee or had been approved by the estate's attorneys.

Jervis had a point, of sorts. What he failed to mention was his biggest transgression as a trustee: On March 3, he had been caught by a hotel security guard engaging in a sex act with a female Bishop Estate attorney (I will not mention her name) in the men's restroom at the Hawai'i Prince Hotel in Waikīkī. When told by the security guard to leave the premises, Jervis inexplicably retorted, "Do you know who I am?" The shocked guard didn't know who Jervis was but dutifully reported the incident to the hotel manager. Tragically, the 39-year-old, married, Japanese-American woman attorney, apparently distraught, drove home, parked her car in her garage, closed the garage door and, with the engine still running, sat in her car to await the death that would end her shame. Later, police investigators found a credit card receipt in her purse, signed by Jervis, for dinner at the hotel the night before. A follow-up interview with the hotel manager uncovered the incredible story.

On March 11 a reporter was tipped off and asked Jervis about the incident. Later that day, Jervis purportedly tried to commit suicide by swallowing an unknown number of Valium pills. His suicide attempt failed and he fully recovered. Subsequently, investigators from the attorney general's office found evidence that Jervis had attempted to destroy all records at his Bishop Estate office that revealed his past activities with the deceased woman. The evidence was added to the attorney general's pending petition for Jervis's removal. His disgraceful behavior was by itself more than ample cause to remove him as a trustee.

On September 27, Oswald Stender resigned. On December 3, 1999, eight months after the Senate rejected Bronster's confirmation, Dickie Wong resigned. Ten days later, Henry Peters, who had vowed to take the IRS to court over its demand that the trustees resign, tendered his resignation.

November 25, 1994, had been a historic moment: When Gerard Jervis, a Waihee confidante and part-Hawaiian, was appointed as a trustee, all five trustees were Hawaiian. Five years later, by December 1999, all five had resigned under a cloud of abuse, mismanagement and corruption. The all-Hawaiian Board of Trustees was no more.

In April 2000 the attorney general issued a 20-page report detailing how Bishop Estate trustees had used staff to establish legislative teams to monitor the estate's interests at the Legislature. The staff would draft bills, amendments and committee reports, write floor speeches and plan political activities, such as door-to-door canvassing, sign-holdings and coffee hours, and direct fundraising for certain legislators. The records also revealed expenditures for dozens of lunches and dinners for favored legislators.

When asked about these findings, Peters argued it was appropriate to host legislators because it gave the trustees the opportunity to tell the estate's story. Such political tactics are commonly used to lobby politicians by for-profit corporations but are prohibited for charitable trusts like the Bishop Estate, which enjoy federal and State tax-exempt status. Knowing Peters as I did, I had no doubt that he believed he had done nothing wrong.

In May 2000, attorney Robert Richards, who was appointed master of the Bishop Estate by Circuit Court Judge Kevin Chang, issued a blistering report on the trustees and their lawyers. The *Star-Bulletin* quoted excerpts from Richards's report:

> "The conclusion of this master [is] that no stone would be left unturned by the trustees in attempting to silence their critics," Richards said. "There was ... the adoption of a 'destroy the opposition' strategy. There was a constant effort made, nearly always unsuccessful, to take steps to silence or discredit what was perceived to be the 'opposition,' whether that was an employee, a reporter, the attorney general, a judge or a master."
>
> Richards also noted that the former trustees and their law firms engaged in a "Herculean effort" to stall and avoid full disclosure in investigations by the attorney general and the estate's court-appointed master.
>
> In many cases, the retention of the law firms was approved by Nathan Aipa, the trust's then-general counsel. Aipa currently serves as chief operating officer.
>
> "There were monumental efforts made to keep trustee conduct from coming to light or, if it did come to light, to rationalize it," Richards said.
>
> "In fact, one can easily conclude, as this master has, that a strategy was adopted to obstruct the legal process, to delay wherever possible, to object wherever possible, to utilize so many lawyers and so many arguments that the opposition would be overwhelmed and would choose to give up. That did not prove true."

Bronster might have seemed vindicated by the trustees' resignation, but questions about her methods continued.

Some critics argued that she had been too high profile, that she had reveled in the publicity she was getting and should have followed Matsumoto's route of going through the Probate Court to get information. I sensed Bronster enjoyed the favorable publicity but disagreed that she should have gone through the Probate Court. Matsumoto, of course, was a court-appointed master and had no choice but to follow the Probate Court's procedure. As attorney general, Bronster was authorized to conduct the investigation as she saw fit. Had Bronster followed the Probate Court procedures, it would have been the court that decided what information could be released to the public, and when. The trustees' lawyers could have delayed the investigation through my second term. A high-profile approach was necessary simply because transparency and public awareness were needed to drive the reforms.

Bronster was aggressive in conducting the investigation, even suggesting to the Supreme Court justices that she might have to subpoena them and take their sworn oral depositions to get their individual recollections of their deliberations in selecting the Bishop Estate trustees. Reluctantly, the justices agreed to be interviewed, but only as a group. *How sad and embarrassing,* I thought. The court's conflict of interest in being involved in the trustee-selection process had put the justices in a bind: If they were acting as individuals in selecting a trustee, how could they disagree to be interviewed or subpoenaed and deposed as individuals by the attorney general? They couldn't, of course, and Bronster's agreeing to interview them en masse was a sop to their predicament.

Bronster's threat did not sit well with Justice Steven Levinson, who argued it was improper to force the justices to cooperate in the investigation. Levinson's argument that his status as a justice cloaked him with immunity for his actions as an individual only damaged the court's credibility. President Bill Clinton himself, after all, had not been immune from being subpoenaed and deposed by Congress for his affair with Monica Lewinsky. But Levinson, as I will write later, had good reason to worry about being subpoenaed and deposed.

From the beginning, I had had grave concerns about the criminal indictments against Stone, Peters and Wong. My experience as a criminal defense attorney made me wary of the potential for overzealous prosecution of individuals by the government. Bronster was an experienced civil attorney with little criminal law experience, as was her successor, Earl Anzai. She had assigned one of her deputies, Lawrence Goya, to handle the case. By all accounts, Goya had a good reputation as a former prosecutor. When I asked Bronster how she would deal with the potential conflict created by her office handling both the civil and criminal cases, she explained they would establish a "Chinese firewall" to avoid the conflict. I was not comfortable with her answer. The last time I had heard talk about establishing a Chinese firewall to avoid a potential conflict was from Sharon Himeno, whose nomination to the Hawai'i Supreme Court by Gov. Waihee was rejected by the State Senate.

Furthermore, the costs for the civil lawsuit and the investigation were running far higher than I had anticipated. Given that I was cutting spending and restricting legislative programs, it was inevitable that legislators would express concerns about the costs of the State's investigation and lawsuits against the trustees. Bronster seemed oblivious to this problem, which might have undermined her support from some legislators.

The State's theory was that there had been a kickback scheme involving Stone's (and his partners') acquisition of the high-end, 229-unit Kalele Kai condominium in Hawai'i Kai. Allegedly Stone and his partners got a sweetheart deal from the Bishop Estate trustees, from which they made huge profits. For Peters' and Wong's support of the acquisition, Stone allegedly arranged for a third party to buy Peters's two-bedroom for $575,000 and then allow Peters to buy a three-bedroom penthouse unit in the same building for the same price. Wong sold his Makiki apartment to Stone, who was his brother-in-law at the time, for $613,800, even though the attorney general's appraiser had valued the unit at only $485,000.

I was concerned that the State's two key witnesses, an appraiser named Patrick Keller and Stone's former attorney, Richard Frunzi, had both been convicted of other crimes and were serving time in jail. It is commonplace for prosecutors to rely on witnesses of dubious character to convict others of crimes, but great care has to be taken to prosecute such cases properly.

The attorney general made some serious procedural errors in presenting testimony to the grand jury. As a result of errors in the State's presentation of Frunzi's testimony, the grand jury's first indictments were set aside by Judge Michael Town. Town, a veteran and highly respected judge, ruled that Frunzi's testimony should have been excluded because of attorney-client privilege. Under Hawai'i law, in order for an attorney to testify against his client, the client (Stone, in this case) must first be given notice, by motion, of the State's intention to call the attorney as a witness against him. The notice is necessary to give the client fair warning to decide whether to assert his privilege to keep his lawyer's testimony from being used against him. The privilege does not apply in cases where the privileged matter involves the planning or commission of a crime. But it is up to the court, after weighing the facts, to decide, outside of the presence of the jury, whether the exception is applicable and the facts admissible as evidence.

Unfortunately for the State's case, the attorney general did not follow this procedural step. After Town set aside the first grand jury indictments on these procedural grounds, Bronster had the option of re-indicting the three men. The grand jury was again convened, and again it voted to indict. At the grand jury hearing, Goya called Nathan Aipa, the chief counsel for the Bishop Estate, as a witness. The attorney general believed that, because Aipa was the estate's and not the individual trustees' attorney, the attorney-client privilege did not apply and that therefore there was no need to follow the notice procedure. Town disagreed, however, ruling that the attorney-client privilege covered the individual trustees as well.

Ordering the attorney general to investigate was one thing, but it was clearly inappropriate for me to tell her *how* to conduct the investigation. Peters and Wong, after all, had both been friends of mine. Nevertheless, I expressed my concerns to Anzai about the viability of the criminal cases after Town had set aside the second indictments. Anzai, who was still trying to familiarize himself with the Bishop Estate investigation, replied that Goya thought Town had erred in dismissing the second indictments and that an appeal would be filed.

Again, Town's ruling was on procedural grounds, and the attorney general was free to seek another indictment against the defendants. The grand jury was reconvened and a third time voted to indict. Town dismissed the third indictments, ruling that Goya had withheld exculpatory evidence favoring the defendants by cutting off the testimony of one of the State's witnesses. Town's rulings were appealed to the Supreme Court. The Court, comprised of substitute justices appointed by the chief justice, issued a scathing opinion excoriating the attorney general's office for ignoring the proper procedure, attempting to withhold exculpatory evidence, repeatedly presenting the privileged testimony to the same grand jury and denying the defendants' rights of due process. The appeal was dismissed and no further indictments were filed.

As attorney general, Bronster was ultimately responsible for Goya's actions on the first and second grand jury indictments; she was no longer attorney general when the third indictment was issued. Regardless, procedurally, the criminal case had been badly mishandled, and the charges were never refiled.

Whenever I think about the Bishop Estate debacle, I often wonder how different things might have been if the trustees had met with the Na Pua and Na Kumu groups, listened to their concerns and given them the assurance that they would take action to resolve the problems at Kamehameha Schools. Instead, blinded by their enormous power, they acted as if they were ali'i rather than trustees.

Like most people, I hoped that the resignations of the trustees marked the end of the controversy and that the anticipated reforms would signal a new beginning for Bishop Estate. I had long believed that the root cause of the estate's problems was the enormous, unjustified trustee compensation, and I welcomed the new trustee-compensation schedule set up by the Probate Court. I hoped that the Supreme Court's decision to step out of the trustee-selection process would be permanent and that eventually the State Judiciary would get out of the selection process completely.

But I expected more changes, among them the termination of some highly paid employees and expensive lawyers who had put the welfare of the trustees before that of the estate itself. Remarkably, instead of holding them accountable and wiping the slate clean, the new trustees kept them on as if nothing had happened, stating—unconvincingly, at least to me—that the experience and knowledge of these people were invaluable to the estate. When the two court-appointed masters, Colbert Matsumoto and Robert Richards, recommended strongly that the trustees be surcharged as individuals to repay the millions of dollars they had squandered, the new trustees declined, explaining that it was a time for "healing."

The failure of the new trustees to "clean house" left me wondering whether the problems that vexed the old trustees and the Bishop Estate would emerge again one day when the passing of time had blurred the reasons the reforms were made in the first place. Ominously, in 2004, there had been a proposal by a court-appointed panel to increase the new trustee compensation from $97,500 to $165,000. Although the proposal was approved by the Probate Court, the new trustees wisely turned down the pay increase; one of the trustees reportedly pointed out it was not "politically appropriate" to accept it. One could only wonder whether the panel, the probate judge and the new trustees had learned any lessons from the Bishop Estate controversy. (In 2008, a consultant hired by the trustees recommended their pay be increased 150 percent. As of this writing the matter is still pending.)

Why the Hawaiians gave nearly blind deference to the trustees was not difficult to understand. I was told that Hawaiians had always paid respect to the old haole trustees, perhaps mostly out of pride in Kamehameha Schools and the enormous wealth of the Bishop Estate, but that the 1994 trustees were special: They were all of of Hawaiian blood and supposedly understood the needs and problems of the Hawaiian people better than the old trustees.

But disappointment and outrage replaced hope and pride as the Matsumoto reports and the attorney general's investigation revealed how the trustees had abused their authority and breached their fiduciary duties. The trustees not only acted as if they were ali'i; that is how they were treated by the Hawaiian people. Jan Dill, one of the leaders of Na Kumu, described this relationship in his Afterword in the 2006 book *Broken Trust* this way:

"In traditional Hawaiian culture, the relationship of the ali'i with the commoners was that of an unstated compact of common benefit. The chiefs enjoyed power because they committed themselves to caring for the larger community in a form of servant leadership. Part of the outrage in the Hawaiian community in the Bishop Estate battle was the violation of this relationship by the Bishop Estate trustees, the ali'i of contemporary Hawai'i."

The attorney general's investigation exposed a Hawai'i Supreme Court tainted by politics. The Court had already embarrassed itself in 1994 when it rejected the recommendations of a blue-ribbon committee it had set up to review the qualifications of applicants and develop a short list from which the Court would select an applicant to fill the anticipated retirement of Bishop Estate trustee Myron Thompson.

Gladys Brandt, who was appointed by the chief justice to chair the committee, told me that, after months of the committee reviewing the applications and finally selecting the finalists, when she met with the justices and presented the short list, one trustee of the justices (she would not tell me which one) asked, "Where's what's-his-name?"—referring to Waihee. "We [the majority of the committee] thought with Peters and Wong already serving as trustees, there would be too many politicians. When they rejected our recommendations, some of the members were furious and vowed never to serve the State again."

In the end, Waihee's closest associate, Gerard Jervis, was chosen. According to *Broken Trust*, written by UH Professor Randy Roth and federal Judge Samuel King, Justice Steven Levinson assured everyone, "Wait and see, Gerry Jervis will be a great trustee."

A Breach of Ethics

I did not know of Levinson's close friendship with Jervis until mid-July 1999, when the new attorney general, Earl Anzai, showed me copies of handwritten messages from Jervis' secretary's phone message book. The messages revealed a number of phone calls Levinson had made to Jervis. Bronster had mentioned the messages earlier, but seeing and reading copies of them for the first time stunned me. Among the half-dozen messages I was shown, there was one that said, "Good news! Call me, Steve." Another said, "Steve Levinson desperately needs to talk to you. Says to please call him tomorrow. Wants to share happy stuff about the school and other stuff because you're his good buddy."

The dates of the messages left little doubt that Levinson was providing Jervis with information about the Court's deliberations regarding Bishop Estate. These ex parte messages were an obvious and egregious violation of the Judicial Code of Professional Ethics that Levinson and all of the other justices had sworn to obey.

Like most lawyers, I wanted only the best justices to sit on the Supreme Court—those whose personal and professional ethics matched their high intellects. Upon learning of Levinson's ex parte communications, I was not only shocked but angry. I thought, *No wonder Levinson was so adamant* (Bronster had described his demeanor as "red-faced") *in opposing Bronster's request to interview the justices.*

"When the public learns about this, how can they still have confidence in the Court?" I asked Anzai. "How did a guy like this ever get on the Supreme Court?"

"Well, when Jervis was on the Judicial Selection Commission he reportedly had a big hand in getting Levinson appointed. But they say Levinson's pretty smart," Anzai replied.

"Earl, you and I know there is no shortage of smart lawyers in this town, but there seems to be a real shortage of lawyers who are ethical *and* smart."

Anzai just nodded in agreement.

"Look, this guy is not fit to sit on the Court. He may be smart, but as far as I'm concerned, acting like a messenger boy for Jervis was pretty stupid. Check when he is up for retention and make sure we oppose his retention for a second term."

By then my take on the Supreme Court was that it had become hopelessly political. I had no doubt that a judge of the Circuit or District Court would surely have been disciplined, but I sensed that neither the chief justice nor the Commission on Judicial Discipline would take any disciplinary action against Levinson.

"Let's see if we can get this guy off the Court," I repeated to Anzai.

But fate intervened. A month or so before his retention hearing in April

2002, Levinson's wife died. I knew that the authors of *Broken Trust* had already filed their opposition to Levinson's retention with the Judicial Selection Committee. Levinson's communication to Jervis would be an issue with the commission members. He would have to answer to them. Nearly three years had passed since I found out about Levinson's breach of ethics; time had assuaged my anger and, in my last year as governor, I didn't have the heart to pile more trouble on Levinson while he was still grieving over his wife's death. "Let the *Broken Trust* people handle it," I told Anzai. Levinson was retained by the Judicial Selection Commission for another 10-year term, and to this day he has never been disciplined for his ethical lapses.

Rice v. Cayetano

On March 22, 1999, another issue touching on Hawaiian rights came to the foreground of our consciousness. The United States Supreme Court agreed to hear the *Rice v. Cayetano* case. This was the case alleging that restricting voting in OHA elections to Hawaiians was unconstitutional.

As governor, I had sworn to defend the laws of Hawai'i. As a lawyer, I thought that the OHA restriction was a clear violation of the 15th Amendment. Moreover, I felt that because the Supreme Court had agreed to hear *Rice,* the odds were heavy that it was inclined to reverse the decision of the U.S. 9th Circuit Court of Appeals, which had upheld the restriction. We needed the best constitutional lawyer we could find to represent the State.

"Margery, see if we can get Lawrence Tribe to represent the State," I said to Bronster, who was still acting attorney general at the time.

Tribe, a distinguished professor of law from Harvard University, was considered one of the nation's premier constitutional lawyers. He had successfully defended the State's 1967 Land Reform Act (leasehold conversion law) in the Midkiff case. He was also one of the constitutional lawyers who represented Vice President Al Gore before the U.S. Supreme Court in the controversial Florida recount case in 2000.)

Tribe was not available, and the task of finding a top-notch constitutional lawyer to represent the State was left to Bronster's replacement, Anzai.

"I found a lawyer I think we should retain to defend the State in *Rice,*" Anzai said.

"Who is he?" I asked.

"John Roberts."

"What's his reputation?"

"Well, he was [Justice] Rehnquist's law clerk from 1980 to 1981. He was a special assistant to U.S. Attorney General William French Smith from 1981 to 1982 in the Reagan administration, and from 1982 to 1986 he served as associate counsel to President Reagan himself. From 1989 to 1992 he served as deputy solicitor general under President George H.W. Bush," Anzai replied, reading from a note.

"Sounds like he's a pretty strong Republican," I said.

"Yeah, but I was told he is considered a top-notch advocate. He's been before the Supreme Court many times and the justices know and respect him."

"Well, it's one thing to be an expert on constitutional law, but in oral argument some of those guys will put you to sleep. We need one who excels in oral argument, who will give the justices something to think about."

"Well, I think Roberts is the best available," Anzai replied.

"Yeah. Besides, with arch-conservatives like Scalia and Thomas on the Court, it may not be wise to get a liberal Democrat. So let's go with Roberts."

On October 6, 1999, the Supreme Court heard oral arguments in *Rice v. Cayetano*. I did not attend the oral argument in Washington, D.C., but Anzai was there. His report was not encouraging. "It doesn't look good," he said.

OHA Chair Rowena Akana attended the oral argument and was apoplectic over the questions asked by the justices. Obviously upset and forgetting for the moment the historical lessons of the American Civil War, she declared that "perhaps the idea would be to separate ourselves from the State immediately and declare ourselves a nation." Mililani Trask—the only OHA trustee who was an attorney—argued that the movement for sovereignty be accelerated. "[T]his Court will not recognize sovereignty for a Hawaiian nation," she said.

No reasonable, thinking person should have been surprised by the questions asked by the justices, I thought. Hawaiian leaders like Akana and Trask were surprised because they didn't respect the views of anyone who disagreed with them. "They don't listen to anyone but themselves, they sing only to the choir and that's not going to change," I said with exasperation to Anzai.

On February 23, 2000, the U.S. Supreme Court reversed the 9th Circuit Court of Appeals. Writing for the 7-2 majority, Justice Anthony M. Kennedy opined: (1) The State's OHA voting scheme violated the 15th Amendment's prohibition against race-based voting qualifications; (2) The Court rejected the State's argument that the legal status of Native Hawaiians was similar to that of the continental Indian tribes, noting that Indian tribes enjoy a unique status in American constitutional law which warrants exceptional legal treatment from Congress. OHA, the Court noted, is a State agency, not a quasi-sovereign entity like the Indian tribes. But even if Congress could lawfully treat Native Hawaiians as tribes, the 15th Amendment prohibited Congress from authorizing a state to create an OHA-type voting scheme.

Roberts had done a good job. The Court had limited its decision to the 15th Amendment and did not rule on the 14th Amendment arguments raised by Rice's attorneys. The decision, Roberts said, "could have been a lot worse ... the good news is that the majority's opinion was very narrowly written and expressly did not call into question the Office of Hawaiian Affairs, the public trust for the benefit of Hawaiians and Native Hawaiians, but only the particular voting mechanism by which the trustees are selected."

The narrowness of the decision, Roberts said, should limit further lawsuits against OHA and other Hawaiian entitlements. Roberts—who would be appointed by President George W. Bush as chief justice of the United States Supreme Court in 2006—could not have been more wrong. Within a week, John Goemans, one of the lawyers for Rice, announced that lawsuits would be filed to challenge the constitutionality of OHA itself. Other lawsuits, ranging from challenges to the admissions policies of Kamehameha Schools to the constitutionality of the Department of Hawaiian Homes, would follow.

While the State's lawyers mulled over the impact of the *Rice* decision, Justice Kennedy's dicta caught my attention. His words eloquently summed up the State's dilemma in trying to resolve the sovereignty issue:

"When the culture and way of life of a people are all but engulfed by a history beyond their control, their sense of loss may extend down through generations and their dismay may be shared by many members of the larger community. As the State of Hawai'i attempts to address these realities, it must, as always, seek the political consensus that begins with a sense of shared purpose. One of the necessary beginning points is this principle: The Constitution of the United States, too, has become the heritage of all the citizens of Hawai'i."

More worrisome for sovereignty advocates looking to Congress for legislation to give Hawaiians and Native Hawaiians the same legal status as American tribes was the Court's admonition:

"The State's argument [that Hawaiians and Native Hawaiians have the same legal status as Indian tribes] fails for a more basic reason. Even were we to take the substantial step of finding authority in Congress, delegated to the State, to treat Hawaiians or Native Hawaiians as tribes, Congress may not authorize a State to create a voting scheme of this sort."

To me, the plain meaning of the majority's words was clear: Whether or not Hawaiians were granted the same legal status as American Indian tribes, neither Congress nor the State of Hawai'i could authorize the use of any voting scheme that abridged the right to vote because of race or ancestry.

Justice Breyer, with Justice Souter concurring, was even more direct:

"I see no need, however, to decide this case on a basis of so vague a concept as 'quasi-sovereign'.... Rather, in my view, we should reject Hawai'i's efforts to justify its rules through analogy to a trust for an Indian tribe because the record makes clear that (1) there is no 'trust' for Native Hawaiians here, and (2) OHA's electorate, as defined in the statute, does not sufficiently resemble an Indian tribe."

I believe that the Supreme Court's ruling posed an insurmountable obstacle to the dream of Hawaiian activists for sovereignty. Since my first year as governor

I had remained open to the idea of some form of self-determination for Hawaiians. In my December 1998 inaugural speech I closed with a call for Hawaiians and non-Hawaiians to stand together and seek a fair resolution to the sovereignty issue. But the *Rice* decision and our failed negotiations with OHA caused me to rethink and change my position.

Personally, I had reservations about the quest for sovereignty. I was born and raised in Hawai'i and grew up with friends of every ethnic group, including local haoles. My mother's sister, Rachel, had married a part-Hawaiian named William Willing. Aunt Rachel and Uncle Billy had six children, two boys and four girls. The high number of interracial marriages was a big reason Hawai'i's diverse people lived in a harmony unmatched in the world. The thought of a Hawai'i in which a new government separated Hawai'i's people by race or ethnicity was foreign and unacceptable to me.

As governor, however, I had a duty to be open to the dozen or so variations on the idea of sovereignty, to weigh their pros and cons and, if it was in the best interests of the state and supported by the majority of the people, to find a way to help realize the dream held by so many Hawaiians.

But in my eyes, *Rice* had foreclosed any possibility of attaining the type of sovereignty sought by Hawaiian activists. Moreover, the debacle of the all-Hawaiian Bishop Estate trustees and the spectacle of OHA trustees reduced to political impotence because of their petty, personal infighting provided two worst-case examples of what a sovereign Hawaiian government might be like. As far as I was concerned, there was no justification to saddle the people of Hawai'i with another government.

In my opinion, further pursuit of sovereignty was like the quest for the Holy Grail—an exercise in futility, an impossible dream. It was time to move on and in the best interests of all of Hawai'i's people that we do so. "Forget sovereignty, save the culture," the late journalist Robert Rees wrote. I agreed wholeheartedly.

It was easier for a non-Hawaiian like me, of course, to close the door on the issue of sovereignty. But for Hawaiian activist leaders who had invested so much of their political and spiritual capital, their credibility and their resources in pursuit of sovereignty, it was too much to ask. Politically, it was difficult for any political leader—Hawaiian or non-Hawaiian—to argue that the drive for Hawaiian sovereignty should be abandoned. Besides, they were prisoners of the revisionist history they had taught to two or perhaps three generations of young Hawaiians: The plight of the Hawaiians was caused by the haole. Self-determination for Hawaiians was justified and would make things better.

The pursuit of sovereignty had assumed a life of its own.

The U.S. Supreme Court had not ruled in *Rice* on whether non-Hawaiians could run as candidates in an OHA election. Not surprisingly, in March 2000, a group of non-Hawaiians sued in federal court for an injunction that would allow non-Hawaiians to run as candidates in the upcoming OHA elections. On April 13, 2000, the Legislature responded by passing a bill (Senate Bill 2477 SD1) that would require all OHA candidates to be Hawaiian.

In light of the *Rice* decision, I thought the bill was unconstitutional. It seemed logical that if non-Hawaiians could vote in an OHA election they also should be allowed to run as candidates. I had little doubt that many legislators privately held the same opinion. Yet 75 of the 76 members of the Legislature (one legislator was not present)—Democrats and Republicans—voted to approve the bill. I had to decide whether I was going to veto the bill or let it become law.

"They must know that the bill has no chance of standing up in court—it's race based," I said to Attorney General Anzai.

"Yeah, but I think the bill is just a political statement to show support for Hawaiians and OHA," Anzai replied. "The *Rice* decision has really shaken up the Hawaiian community. Some of the leaders are really depressed."

"I wonder if I should veto the bill," I asked.

"I don't think that's a good idea. Technically, *Rice* left the question of non-Hawaiian candidates unanswered and the bill is probably unconstitutional, but your veto would just upset more Hawaiians. I'd let the bill go—let the U.S. District Court decide whether non-Hawaiians can run for OHA. Let someone else take the heat for a change."

"Well, as governor, I have a duty to defend and enforce the existing OHA law restricting candidates to Hawaiians only. But this new bill just restates what the current law already says—it's unnecessary. Now, under normal circumstances I'd veto the bill, but I think you're right; the Hawaiians are still reeling over *Rice*. If I veto the bill it would only aggravate the situation. No need for me to rile them up again or add to their misery."

"What if the reporters ask you whether you think the bill is necessary or unconstitutional?"

"I won't answer the question. I'll just say that the attorney general is analyzing the bill. Besides, where does it say that I have to answer every question the news media asks me?"

"They'll expect you to answer—you usually do."

"But not this time. How can I explain that this bill is political and has little to do with the reality of the law?"

Thus, Senate Bill 2477 SD1 became Act 59. Although it is totally unenforceable, it still remains in the Hawai'i Revised Statutes today, a political statement whose time has passed.

On August 16, 2000, U.S. District Court Judge Helen Gilmore granted a preliminary injunction that cleared the way for non-Hawaiians to run for OHA in the 2000 election.

Rice meant that the election of the OHA trustees was illegal. The attorney general opined that the eight of the nine trustee seats that had been filled by the election were technically vacant. The ninth seat was not affected because that trustee had been appointed (by me), not elected. A dispute followed when the eight trustees objected strenuously to the attorney general's opinion and refused to step down. Once again, the OHA trustees were mired in controversy.

In September 2000 all nine trustees resigned. Their supporters demanded that I appoint the former OHA trustees to fill the interim vacancies because they had been elected by the Hawaiian electorate. But OHA had been literally dysfunctional during most of my first term, beset with infighting, factionalism, political maneuvering and heated arguments that at times bordered on fistfights. Trustee Mililani Trask had caused a stir in 1999 when she called U.S. Sen. Dan Inouye "a one-armed bandit." No one had done more for the Hawaiians than Inouye, but Trask never directly apologized for her remarks. I was not about to reward Trask by appointing her as an interim trustee—nor did I appoint six other trustees.

I did appoint two of the trustees: Clayton Hee and Collette Machado, who at the time was the youngest OHA trustee. The other interim appointees were newcomers: Gladys Brandt, a former UH regent and educator at Kamehameha; Hannah Springer, a former OHA trustee; Dante Carpenter, a former State senator and mayor of the Big Island; Ilei Beniamina, a full-blooded native Hawaiian born on Ni'ihau and professor of Hawaiian studies at Kaua'i Community College; Nalani Olds, an entertainer; Nani Brandt, a Kamehameha alumna and teacher; and Charles Ota, a Japanese-American World War II veteran who had served with the famed 442nd Regimental Combat Team in Europe and was a former Maui County councilman and a successful businessman.

Hawaiian activists were furious that I had not appointed all of the previous OHA trustees to fill the interim vacancies. Not surprisingly, they again accused me of being "anti-Hawaiian." But allowing non-Hawaiians to vote and run in OHA elections actually strengthened the argument that OHA was not race based and therefore was constitutionally sound. In the heat of the moment, however, none of this meant anything to the Hawaiian activists, angered by my appointment of a Japanese American as an interim trustee. The uproar over Ota's appointment reminded me of the controversy that had erupted in 1971 when Matsuo Takabuki was appointed as the first Japanese American to serve as a Bishop Estate trustee.

Tough and outspoken at times, Ota, already in his 70s, was a strong supporter of Hawaiian causes. In a newspaper interview, Ota commented that, although his ancestry was Japanese, "I feel I have been Hawaiian all my life," a sentiment shared by many local non-Hawaiians. As I expected, Ota and Gladys Brandt, who was nearly 90, brought civility to the OHA Board. At the end of his interim term Ota ran for his OHA seat, and in 2000 he became the first non-Hawaiian to be elected as an OHA trustee.

On September 12, 2001, the Hawai'i Supreme Court overturned the *Heely* ruling, holding that the State law setting up payments to OHA was invalid because it conflicted with the 1998 Forgiveness Act, a federal law which bars the State from using revenues generated at airports to pay for ceded-lands claims. The *Heely* ruling, which held that the State government was obligated to pay OHA 20 percent of the *gross* revenues from the ceded lands (and by some estimates could have cost the State more than a billion dollars), had given OHA tremendous leverage in its settlement talks with the State.

When the Hawai'i Supreme Court overruled *Heely* it also invalidated the State law that set the formula for ceded-lands payments to OHA. With the State law invalidated, the Legislature was left with the old law, which the Hawai'i Supreme Court had ruled in a previous lawsuit was unenforceable. Thus, there was no formula for determining how much of the ceded-lands revenues should be paid to OHA. After *Heely* was overturned, I immediately suspended all ceded-lands payments to OHA.

Throughout the State's negotiations with OHA, *Heely* was a major concern. Indeed, it was a big reason for the State's generous settlement offers. Once the Supreme Court reversed *Heely* the urgency for a quick settlement was off. It was up to the Legislature to amend the old law or pass a new one.

Not surprisingly, the Legislature, mindful of the history of political difficulties experienced by past Legislatures in establishing a formula by which to pay OHA, decided to leave the old law in limbo. Instead, it decided to pay OHA an annual sum of $12 million. OHA, chastened by the *Rice* decision and the overruling of *Heely*, did not complain. Ironically, this was the method of funding OHA that Sen. Dennis O'Connor and I had proposed in 1980. As of this writing, the law is still unchanged.

Rice should have been a wakeup call for Hawaiian leaders. The chest-thumping and arrogant, racist rhetoric of extremists like the Trask sisters, Kame'eleihiwa and others had dominated the local news and opened a Pandora's box of problems for the Hawaiian people. Not only did the extremists motivate local residents like Freddy Rice to seek relief in federal court, they also attracted the attention of well-financed conservative Mainland groups dedicated to dismantling affirmative action programs for minorities, such as OHA. In an ironic twist of history, the conservatives were using the same arguments against the Hawaiians-only admission standards of Kamehameha Schools that liberals used to overturn the whites-only admission standards of private universities and colleges on the Mainland.

Nevertheless, OHA's top priority continued to be the pursuit of sovereignty. With literally no legislative oversight, OHA has continued its quest, spending millions of dollars for lobbyists, an office in Washington, D.C., and a costly television public relations campaign—monies which could have been otherwise used to address the Hawaiian community's real problems.

The Native Hawaiian Question

In response to *Rice,* U.S. Sen. Daniel Akaka introduced an amended version of the Akaka Bill. Basically, the bill proposed to reclassify Native Hawaiians to the same legal status as the American Indian tribes. In my view, reclassifying Native Hawaiians as a tribe would not change the *Rice* ruling forbidding federal and State governments from authorizing racial or ancestral voting schemes. The Akaka Bill was written so that if the section of the bill regarding election of an entity to represent the Hawaiian nation was declared unconstitutional, the other sections remained in effect.

I supported the Akaka Bill because I thought the reclassification might add a veneer of additional protection to long-standing and now at-risk federal entitlements for Native Hawaiians. Proponents believe that if Native Hawaiians are reclassified to tribe status, then Hawaiian entitlement programs should be given the same legal protection received by Indian entitlement programs. The viability of this theory is subject to debate, but it is one of the few options left to defend against the onslaught of lawsuits by conservatives seeking to dismantle Hawaiian entitlement programs.

Hawaiian activist leaders often speak in accusatory tones about the current ills of their community: Hawaiians suffer the highest infant death rate; the highest rates of serious mental and physical illness; the highest crime rate and rate of incarceration; the highest rates of drug addiction, alcoholism and domestic abuse; the highest number of welfare recipients; the lowest high school graduation rates and the lowest personal income. These claims are undisputed. But the unstated questions in the minds of many politicians, which none dared to ask publicly, were "Why do Hawaiians suffer so?" and "What are the Hawaiian leaders doing to help the Hawaiian people help themselves?"

We are all creatures of our upbringing, circumstances and culture. It is important for future non-Hawaiian and Hawaiian leaders in our state to make a concerted effort to understand and learn about the Hawaiian culture as they tackle Hawaiian-related issues. It is well worth understanding, for example, that just as the ancient Hawaiian commoners expected the ali'i to take care of them—the so-called "sense of entitlement"—so, too, do many contemporary Hawaiians look to the ali'i trusts and foundations to care for them.

The Bishop Estate, for example, is just one of a half-dozen trusts established by the ali'i to care for Hawaiian commoners. Others include The Queen's Medical Center, founded by Queen Emma and Kamehameha III to provide hospital services for Hawaiians; Lunalilo Home for the care of the elderly; and Lili'uokalani Trust and Kapi'olani Medical Center for Women and Children, established by Queen Esther Julia Kapi'olani. All these legacies were established by the diminishing Hawaiian ali'i to fulfill their obligations under the "unstated compact of common benefit" described by Jan Dill.

Various well-intentioned programs have sought to aid the Hawaiian community, such as the Hawaiian Homes Commission Act of 1920. Enacted by the U.S. Congress, the act entitled Hawaiian homesteaders to lease parcels of land for a dollar a year for up to 99 years (today, it is possible for a homesteader and his family to lease land for up to 199 years!). Such programs reinforced the old sense of entitlement, which still lingers today among many Hawaiians.

As distinguished historians such as Gavan Daws and Lawrence H. Fuchs have pointed out, a major obstacle in the economic and social development of the Hawaiian people has been their recurring urge to restore the past, to embellish the images of the ali'i, to see history as they want to see it rather than as it was. It is one reason Hawaiians have fallen behind while Hawai'i's Asians—driven by cultures that stress hard work and self-sacrifice and shun instant gratification for future gain—have moved forward. Of course, it has not been the place for any non-Hawaiian politician to say this. Ideally, one day a strong, charismatic Hawaiian leader will do so. Regardless, over time, future generations of Hawaiians will figure it out for themselves.

Hawaiian issues are complex, often so politically highly charged that many politicians shun them. But in the long run Hawaiian issues are far more important than economic issues. An economic downturn will end, no matter what the State does. But the manner in which Hawaiian issues are resolved could have a far greater, more lasting impact on the relationships between Hawaiians and non-Hawaiians and the common bond which holds Hawai'i's people together—the aloha spirit.

It is critical for Hawaiian and non-Hawaiian leaders to develop a sense of the limitations of what the State government can do to help Hawaiians—and of what Hawaiians must do to help themselves. An excerpt from Lawrence Fuchs' *Hawaii Pono* provides some guidance:

"The problem for Hawaiians, as is true for many Native American Indians, is that they are caught in a double bind. On the one side, it does not seem possible to change fundamentally the standards of success established by American culture for which traditional Hawaiian culture appears to be ill suited. On the other side, Hawaiians have no way to fight back against the domination of others except to exercise claims for wealth and power in the American cultural context. But the reparations for the overthrow of the monarchy called for in the Minority Report of the Native Hawaiians Study Commission, which importuned Congress in June 1983, while possibly alleviating some of the grievances of Hawaiians, would not touch their real problems. One can only hope that greater sensitivity to and appreciation of Hawaiian culture, along with more effective work with small Hawaiian children, will help those who wish to participate in American life to do so successfully without losing the knowledge and appreciation of their own past and that those Hawaiians who wish to live apart from mainstream American life according to the old ways will find the opportunity to do so in health and satisfaction." ❖

CHAPTER TWENTY-ONE

Second Term: Challenges and Triumphs

An Economy on the Rebound

"A year ago, few of our economic experts acknowledged even a hint of [economic] recovery. Today, all of them agree that Hawai'i's economy is in recovery. Some, like Bank of Hawai'i's Paul Brewbaker, believe that Hawai'i's economy is past [the] recovery [stage] and is now in the expansion stage. What a difference a year makes!" (State of the State Address, January 24, 2000.)

My words were a not-too-subtle jab at the economists who, having endorsed Linda Lingle, suggested that the election of a Republican governor would somehow turn the economy around, but remained silent through the 1998 election even though there were clear signs the economy was already growing. Not all were silent. Lowell Kalapa, an economist from the Tax Foundation of Hawai'i (an organization funded by business interests), apparently concerned that voters might believe my claim that the State would end 1998 with a $175 million surplus, predicted the government would face a $500 million shortfall! *Unbelievable*, I thought. I had long considered Kalapa a mouthpiece for the Republicans, but this time he had really stuck his foot in his mouth. Not surprisingly, when I beat Lingle and the $500 million deficit did not materialize, Kalapa was unavailable for post-election interviews.

In fact, according to Brewbaker and Dr. Seiji Naya, my director of the State Department of Business, Economic Development and Tourism (DBEDT), the economy had been slowly expanding since 1997. By January 2000, the state's jobless rate was at a six-year low. By June 2000, most of the private-sector economists agreed that the state's economy was up again. Leroy Laney, the only economist who had predicted the state's prolonged economic downturn when I assumed the governorship in 1994, agreed, stating publicly in August 2000 that the "economy was definitely improving.... We're seeing that everywhere."

Brewbaker agreed: "Retail sales were going off the charts at the end of last year. I really think we're in a very strong mode right now and it's going to surprise a lot of people."

By December 2000, the signs of economic expansion were undeniable, noticeable in virtually all indicators used by economists. The state's jobless rate, at 3.7

percent—down from 5.3 percent the previous year—was the lowest since 1992. Personal income growth was strong in 1999 and continued to be so through 2000. Bankruptcy rates were 20 percent less than in 1998. Building permits were up substantially, creating thousands of new construction jobs. Real estate growth was up by 16 percent over the previous year.

Many factors contributed to the state's economic recovery. Chief among them was the upsurge in U.S. Mainland tourism, which had more than made up for the decline in Japanese tourists. Tourism officials predicted a record 7 million tourists for 2000, topping the 1999 record. Moreover, six years of economic stagnation had taken their toll. Economic Darwinism had weeded out the weak and marginal businesses. The businesses that had survived were those that had adapted to the market, streamlined their operations, cut costs and taken steps to reform their infrastructure, making them more efficient and productive.

The complaints from businesspeople seemed never ending, but we had done a lot to improve the business climate. By the end of my first term in 1998, with the help of the Democratic-dominated Legislature, we had passed one of the biggest reductions in State personal income taxes in the nation, reduced workers' compensation rates dramatically (by 30 percent), approved a host of business tax credits, taken a big step in privatizing government services by turning over the operation and management of the State's Pālolo Housing complex to a private company, waived the landing fees for state airports for two years (saving the airlines $40 million a year), cut red tape, and kept the growth of State government to under 1 percent. Furthermore, our billion-dollar capital-improvement program spurred government construction, particularly for the public schools and every campus in the University of Hawai'i system, providing more jobs for contractors and construction workers and complementing the rise in construction in the private sector.

The State's biggest contributions were probably establishing the Hawai'i Tourism Authority (HTA) and more than doubling the annual subsidy to the visitor industry for marketing (from $25 million to $60 million)—on a population basis a subsidy greater than those provided by most states. Working with the Hawai'i Visitor's Bureau, the HTA's strategy of focusing on increasing Hawai'i visitor counts from the Midwest and East Coast, rather than just focusing on California and Japan, seemed to have paid off. The gains in Mainland visitors more than compensated for the decline in Japanese tourism.

A Republican governor would have had little luck getting these programs through the Democratic Legislature. The biggest opposition would have come from public-worker labor unions, which are wary of tax cuts and tax credits because they reduce State revenues, resulting in fewer State government jobs and less revenue for pay raises and employee benefits. They also generally oppose privatization. One union leader pointed out that Republicans favor privatization only for jobs that affect the poor, such as janitorial services, but not for services that affect the more affluent. We would discover this truth when the Republicans fiercely fought our attempts to privatize the Ala Wai Yacht Harbor.

If forced to choose sides between business groups (and the likes of *Forbes* and *The Wall Street Journal*) and unions, it would have been no contest: The Democrats would not have hesitated to support the unions. Too many business groups, while eagerly awaiting salvation by the anticipated election of Lingle, were unable to mask their visceral hostility and contempt for liberal Democrats and labor unions.

On the other hand, my proposals to help business and effect civil service reforms did not sit well with some die-hard Democrats and union leaders. "The governor is acting like a Republican," was a comment I heard often. That kind of talk bothered me. The unions had supported me in every one of my elections from 1974 through 1998. Furthermore, I was steeped in the history of the 1954 Democratic Revolution, and I knew the crucial role labor unions played in transforming Hawai'i from a territory controlled by a few to a modern American state that offered economic and social justice for working people.

As a legislator I had supported organized labor more often than not. However, I believe that collective bargaining works best when the parties' leverages are more equal. My experience as chairman of the Senate Ways and Means Committee in 1979-80 left me convinced that, as far as State government was concerned, the collective bargaining process had become too one-sided in favor of the unions.

In my first year as governor, this much was clear: If businesses did not recover, tax revenues would decline further and more State social services would be cut; the mandatory arbitrated and negotiated pay raises for State workers—averaging more than $300 million a year—were paid for the most part by the budgetary cuts I made to social service programs; and the State civil service system had morphed into near-obsolescence, impairing worker productivity and efficiency and rendering good management highly problematic.

I might have felt differently if I had still been one of the 76 members of the Legislature but, as governor, my perspective was broader. Unlike a legislator, whose primary duty is to represent the people in his or her House or Senate district, I had as my political constituents all of Hawai'i's people. The proverbial buck for the stewardship of the state stopped at my office on the fifth floor of the State Capitol. Whether an idea was Democratic or Republican meant little to me. If I thought it would help, I was open to it, and if it was doable, we'd try to do it.

Self-survival transcends ideology. In late 2001, for example, with California's economy reeling, the California Chamber of Commerce, hardly a liberal group, resorted to liberal Keynesian economics by proposing an initiative on the ballot calling for a $10 billion State capital-improvement bond issue to boost the economy. For hardcore conservatives, the proposed bond issue was undoubtedly ideological heresy, but for businesspeople trying to keep their heads above water, it didn't matter.

I am a liberal on most social issues but, again, my experience as chairman of Ways and Means taught me firsthand how inefficiency and waste adversely affect the State's ability to deliver services to the people, particularly the poor and needy. That experience more than any other shaped my fiscal conservatism.

Unlike most of the conservative Republicans, however, I was willing to spend money and even support raising taxes for as much government as was needed to help those who could not help themselves and to do what was needed to give all citizens an equal opportunity to pursue a better life for themselves and their families.

Most Republican conservatives simply wanted to reduce the size of State government for its own sake, arguing that if rich people got richer some of the new wealth would "trickle down" to the poor, leaving them, somehow, less poor.

Despite the unions' dissatisfaction with my policies and some of my decisions, every labor union except UHPA rallied behind Mazie Hirono and me—we could not have won in 1998 without their support. The Republican alternative had worried them. As one union leader warned, "If the Republicans ever get control [of the Legislature and governorship], one of the first things they'd do is repeal the State mandatory employee prepaid health insurance law." That was unlikely to happen under Republican Party moderates like Andy Anderson and Pat Saiki, who had often worked collaboratively with the Democrats when I served in the Legislature. However, conservative ideologues like Hemmings and Slom, who now controlled Hawai'i's Republican Party, would do it in a heartbeat if they had the votes.

At the time, Hawai'i had the only State mandatory prepaid health insurance law in the nation (in 1994, First Lady Hillary Clinton had used it as a model in her failed attempt to establish national health insurance). Few businessmen complained publicly about it—it wasn't politically correct to do so—but there was little doubt that employee health insurance was then and is still the biggest employee expense for Hawai'i's businesses.

Back then, I recall a Honolulu Chamber of Commerce poll showing that only 55 percent of the businesses polled (compared to 90 percent of the general population) supported the State's mandatory prepaid health insurance law. Mandatory prepaid health insurance in Hawai'i is bedrock social policy—a widely accepted social good for the greatest number—no different than workers' compensation or unemployment insurance. Anyone who wants to do business in Hawai'i must accept it as a cost of doing business in the state.

With the economy growing, I anticipated an upsurge in tax revenues that would allow us to restore the cuts I had made to social service programs and to increase funding for public education. During my first four years, a big part of the savings from cutting the cost of State government went to pay for employee pay raises and business subsidies—at the expense of the poor and disadvantaged. As I entered my second term, I vowed not to let that happen again.

However, I first awaited the Senate reorganization. It was important to know who the key players would be. With Mizuguchi's retirement in 2000, in January 2001, the 22 Senate Democrats—split in three factions—went through an intense reorganization. Apparently, the majority of Democrats engaged in some wild horse-trading (i.e., giving favors for votes) to stave off the bid of the ambitious upstart freshmen senator Colleen Hanabusa for the Senate presidency. Oʻahu Sen. Robert Bunda emerged as Senate president—a compromise wangled by veteran Sen. Donna Kim. Kim apparently found the thought of a young, bright, freshman female senator as president unacceptable. (Four years later, Bunda would be sent packing as Kim—who, for some reason, was embittered with him—joined in a coup that deposed him in favor of the now-acceptable Hanabusa.)

"A Government of Men not Laws"

Horse-trading has always been part of the legislative process, but from the 1990s to 2000 it seemed more widespread than ever—a sign that self-interest rather than public interest was foremost in the minds of politicians. The big problem is that it's likely to lead to legislators getting committee assignments for which they are ill suited in terms of ability, experience and training.

There was no better example than when Bunda assigned the enigmatic Rod Tam as chairman of the Senate Economic Development Committee. I had known Tam for nearly 10 years, and I didn't think he had what it took to run such an important committee.

When Earl Anzai, who was still director of Budget and Finance, heard about it, he reminded me that Tam had applied for one of 13 budget analyst positions with the Senate Ways and Means Committee when I chaired it in 1979 and was the only applicant who flunked the test Anzai (my committee clerk at the time) gave to all applicants for the position. It was Anzai's way of telling me that Tam was not one of the brightest minds in the Senate.

Once, Tam got Honolulu Mayor Jeremy Harris so angry that Harris publicly denounced him as the State's "worst legislator" and a well-known "laughingstock." Name-calling has long been somewhat of a sport in politics. But there was ample proof to support Harris' indictment. For example, when Tam served briefly as co-chairman of the Senate Education Committee under the Senate's new co-chair system, his lack of knowledge about public education was so startling that the teachers' union opposed his reelection (it supported his opponent Audrey Hidano instead) and, when Tam was reelected, his colleagues would not support his reappointment as co-chairman of the committee.

Tam was prone to doing weird things. Michael Wilson, who served as director of the Department of Land and Natural Resources during my first term (subsequently, I appointed him as a Circuit Court judge) told me about an odd encounter he had with Tam. One day, he got a telephone call from Tam summoning him to meet in his office immediately. Worried, Wilson, a local haole who was raised in Kailua, hurried over to Tam's office. Tam, who was sitting behind his desk, looked up at Wilson and began what Wilson later described as a "very strange" conversation:

"There's corruption at the Ala Wai [Yacht Harbor]," Tam told Wilson.

"What kind of corruption, Senator?" Wilson asked anxiously.

"Someone's killing the ducks."

For a moment, Wilson sat in silence, dumbfounded. "The ducks?" he finally blurted out.

"I have the proof."

"Where is it?" Wilson replied, relieved that it wasn't the kind of corruption he had feared.

"In my freezer."

"In your freezer?"

The incident seemed surreal, Wilson told me with a chuckle. It evoked memories of the scene from the Oscar-winning *Caine Mutiny,* in which the neurotic, strawberry-loving Capt. Queeg (played by Humphrey Bogart), of the Navy destroyer *Caine,* suffers a mental breakdown during a devastating hurricane while the ship is at sea. Queeg conducts a virtual witch hunt, insisting, "Someone stole the strawberries."

I never had any personal or business problems with Tam. At least I wasn't aware of any until the night of the 1998 primary election, when I discovered he had problems with me. Tam was opposed in the Democratic primary by an attractive, outgoing woman named Audrey Hidano. Hidano and her husband, Steve, owned a construction company. After trailing in the early voter printouts, Tam eked out a razor-thin 29-vote win over Hidano. When interviewed by television reporters about his narrow victory, Tam revealed that he had a bone to pick with former Gov. George Ariyoshi and me. The interview went something like this:

"Senator, 29 votes—that was a close call. You have any thoughts about it?" a television news reporter asked Tam.

"George Ariyoshi and Ben Cayetano are behind it—they put up Hidano to run against me," Tam replied, answering the question with an accusation, which I would learn later was a habit of his.

"Why?" asked the reporter.

"Because they're against me," Tam replied, or words to that effect.

I was perplexed. I'd had nothing to do with Hidano running against him. I hardly knew her. I had heard that Ariyoshi's son, Donn, was one of the co-chairmen of Hidano's campaign. Apparently, Tam had pronounced Ariyoshi guilty by association. In Tam's eyes, the father was guilty for the "sins" of the son.

In 1998, I had my toughest election ahead of me with "that woman from Maui," as someone described Lingle in a newspaper story. With pundits already

writing my political obituary, why in the world would I get involved in someone
else's campaign? *Maybe Tam was just exhausted that night,* I thought, giving him
the benefit of the doubt. Campaigns can take a lot out of candidates. Fatigue, sleep
deprivation—Tam's eyes showed that "1,000-yard stare"—often cause candidates
to make mistakes. I've made my share of them. That's the context in which I took
his remarks. Besides, I was feeling pretty good about my primary election win, and
Tam quickly faded from my thoughts.

A few days later, I asked Charlie Toguchi to talk to Tam. "It's probably just
a misunderstanding; I'll talk to him," Toguchi said. Toguchi and Tam had served
together in the House, and I knew Tam looked up to him. I was certain Toguchi
would straighten things out.

I was wrong.

There are all kinds of people in politics. Tam was one of those who was
totally obsessed with politics. Apparently, holding political office was the biggest
thing in his life. He campaigned incessantly year-round to safeguard his job.
It soon became apparent that anyone who tried to take it away from him was
asking for trouble. Ariyoshi was retired. *How lucky for him,* I thought. I wasn't
retired, and I would soon learn the lengths to which Tam would go to make life
miserable for me.

In January 1999, Senate President Norman Mizuguchi assigned Tam to chair
the Senate Committee on Government Efficiency and Operations. The committee
is considered the "Siberia" of the Senate, the committee of last resort, to which the
least competent allies or defeated rivals are assigned to minimize their influence
on legislation.

In February, a staff member told me Tam had introduced a bill that provided
for an audit of the governor's (my) family's household expenses. Our budget had
already been reviewed by the House Finance and Senate Ways and Means committees. *What's going on?* I wondered.

Then I found out about Tam's confrontation with Jim Bartels, the executive director of the governor's mansion, Washington Place. Bartels, now deceased,
was one of the nicest people one could ever meet. In his mid-50s, sophisticated,
soft-spoken and humble, Bartels was always respectful to public officials. He truly
believed that public service was a noble calling. One evening, Bartels found himself alone with Tam in one of the elevators at the State Capitol. It was an experience, he told me, that he would never forget.

"Good evening, Senator. I see you've been working late," Bartels said cheer-
fully, trying to make polite conversation. Brushing aside Bartels' warm greeting,
an agitated Tam, jabbing a finger at Bartels' chest, retorted: "I *know* her [Vicky's]
parents have been there [Washington Place] having dinner every night—and I'm
going to audit the governor's food bill!"

Startled, Bartels told Vicky about the confrontation. Knowing I had more important problems to worry about, Vicky kept the incident from me until I found out about Tam's bill to audit our expenses for food. Subsequently, I also learned from our personal security guards that Tam had been asking other guards for information as to who was visiting us at Washington Place. To curry favor with the guards, he even put $200,000 in the State budget to air-condition the guard kiosk at the State Capitol and to automate the gates at Washington Place (the gates were deliberately set for manual operation for security reasons). Later, the Senate Ways and Means Committee wisely deleted the funds from the State budget.

When I learned about Tam's shenanigans, I was furious. Confronting Bartels as he did was uncalled for and unprofessional. No responsible legislator would upbraid another's staff. And Tam's sneaking around trying to gather information about how often Vicky's parents—who were both in their late 70s and ate like birds—visited and dined with us was outrageous. This jerk was making whatever grudge he had against me very, very personal.

"I'm up to my neck dealing with the economy, angry Hawaiians and the labor unions—and I now have to deal with a neurotic in the Senate. He's pulling this crap to embarrass me by harassing Vicky and my in-laws. What's the matter with the guy? If that bastard wants a war, I'll give it to him!" I raged to Anzai.

"Cool head. You're the governor, you're supposed to the bigger man," he said with a smile and a twinkle in his eye.

"Don't give me that 'bigger man' lecture, Earl. If he went after your family like that, you'd be pounding the shit out of him!" I said, only half joking.

I had to talk Vicky out of testifying at the hearing Tam held on the bill.

"Oh, Ben," she said, "it's all right, I can handle it. Sen. Tam is entitled to review our budget."

"No, the only thing he deserves is a kick in the ass. Our budget was already reviewed by the Legislature. The guy's a nut and is out to make life miserable for us," I replied tersely.

I refused to let Vicky testify. I assigned Bartels to do it. As expected, he was very professional in giving his testimony. After presenting Tam's committee with our financial statement, Bartels concluded coolly, "The Cayetanos are the most frugal of all of the past first families since statehood." Most of Tam's committee members had either not attended or had walked out of the hearing. Except for the Republicans, everyone refused to sign the committee report, and the bill died in committee. The news media had apparently figured out Tam's motives and, to its credit, did not cover the hearing.

In January 2000 Tam made national news when he introduced a bill urging State workers to take a nap during their breaks. The bill also included a $600,000 appropriation for "free snacks" for the napping State workers. Talk-show hosts Jay Leno, David Letterman and others had a field day with Tam's bill on their television shows. *USA Today* gave it front-page coverage. One comedian joked that the bill was totally unnecessary because State workers were already napping on the job.

If Jimmy Wakatsuki or Dickie Wong had been running the Senate, Tam's bill would never have seen the light of day. But in 2000, the Senate organization was so fragile the leadership acted as if it were walking on eggshells trying to keep things together.

Tam's "snooze bill" (I think comedian Jay Leno gave it that moniker) got a big laugh from some of my Cabinet members. By then my opinion of Tam had deteriorated to the point where I was no longer amused by his zany antics.

But there was more to come.

In 2001, newly elected Senate President Robert Bunda assigned Tam to chair the Senate Economic Development Committee. Tam had control of one of the most important committees in the Senate. Bunda had paid a high price to get Tam to support him for Senate president. *Now*, I lamented, *Tam can do some real damage.*

On January 25, 2001, shortly after he had been assigned to chair the Economic Development Committee, Tam and his House counterpart, Lei Ahu Isa, spoke at a luncheon meeting held by the Hawai'i Venture Capital Association. Tam stunned the audience when in his rambling remarks he told the group, "There is no definition for high technology." Isa made matters worse when, asked to describe the role of government, she declared, "The role of government is to help redistribute wealth to the poor"—words that did not go over well with the audience.

Later, the chairman of the association told reporters that Tam was "incoherent" and that it was "disgraceful" that the Legislature had left the development of high technology in Hawai'i in the hands of "incompetent" people.

Venture capitalists are essential to the development of high technology and biotechnology anywhere. For six years, we had worked hard, collaborating with the private sector and some legislators to get Mainland venture capitalists interested in investing in Hawai'i high-tech and biotech startups. The embarrassing debacle at the luncheon did not help.

Later, in an effort to dispel the notion that he was incoherent, Tam slapped together and distributed to the news media a five-page article outlining his "goals and objectives" (his favorite phrase) for the industry in Hawai'i. To give it some credibility, Tam listed DBEDT director Dr. Seiji Naya as co-author—without Naya's permission.

Naya was highly respected in Hawai'i and Asia. He had come to Hawai'i as an 18-year-old member of a Japanese boxing team in the mid-1950s. Earl Finch, a prominent Mississippi businessman who had been something of a patron to the AJAs of the 442nd Regimental Team when the unit trained there, invited Naya to live with him and offered to send him to school. With Finch's help, Naya graduated from the University of Hawai'i in 1958 and went on to earn a Ph.D. from the University of Wisconsin in 1965. Along the way he boxed for

UH, becoming a two-time undefeated National Collegiate Athletic Association (NCAA) featherweight champion, and was selected as MVP of the NCAA tournament. For nearly 20 years he was the chief economist for the Asian Development Bank. Later he returned to Hawai'i to teach in the University of Hawai'i Economics Department.

Naya was horrified that Tam had listed him as co-author of the essay. According to Naya, Tam had called and asked a few questions about high technology. Apparently that was enough for Tam to bestow the title of co-author on him. I issued a scathing public criticism of Tam's unethical behavior in trying to take advantage of Naya's reputation.

"Go easy, most of our important bills are in his committee; piss him off and he's likely to kill them," Anzai (now attorney general) cautioned me.

As if I had to be reminded. Like it or not, Tam had control over some of our important bills. His committee had jurisdiction over our proposed aquarium, the science center and the high-tech and biotechnology park for startups. I decided to wait and see whether we could smooth things over with him. But what he had done to Vicky and my in-laws in 1999 was unforgivable—and unforgettable.

Potential in Kaka'ako

Midway through the legislative session, it was clear that Tam would hold all of our bills in committee, not even giving them a public hearing. I knew that would not change.

At risk was our project in Kaka'ako Makai, a 50-acre parcel of land located in Honolulu's 600-acre Kaka'ako district. Patterned in concept after the University of North Carolina's Triangle Park, the Kaka'ako Makai project included a new nine-acre campus for the John A. Burns School of Medicine (JABSOM) complex, to include a research facility that would stimulate the growth of a biotechnology industry in Hawai'i; a high-technology/biotech center for new startup companies; a $50 million aquarium and a science museum. Kaka'ako Makai was the largest parcel of unused State land in urban Honolulu. The new projects in Kaka'ako Makai would complement the University of Hawai'i's Ocean Marine Research Center already located at the site and the 30-acre Kaka'ako Waterfront Park, which had been developed by the Waihee administration.

I viewed the Kaka'ako Makai project as the catalyst for the development of the remaining 600 acres in Kaka'ako, most of it privately owned by two major landowners: Kamehameha Schools (a.k.a. Bishop Estate) and the Victoria Ward Estate. The proposal was grand and ambitious. The private sector, the University and organized labor all supported it.

Walter Dods, president of First Hawaiian Bank, was a major supporter. In an unprecedented move, Dods—the first banker from Hawai'i to serve as president of the American Bankers Association—pledged to raise $20 million from the private sector to help finance the $50 million aquarium. Victoria Ward's president and CEO, Mitch D'Olier, joined Dods on the fundraising committee.

With the private sector paying for 40 percent of the capital costs, I was optimistic that the proposed aquarium would succeed. Stand-alone aquariums usually lose money and require subsidies. But the Kaka'ako Makai aquarium would be surrounded by a critical mass of restaurants, shops, offices and condominiums, the science museum and the JABSOM complex, and it would be located just a few miles from the tens of thousands of tourists patronizing Waikīkī's 34,000 hotel rooms. Tourism officials, noting polls that showed a growing number of tourists felt Hawai'i fell short of expectations because there were few new attractions on O'ahu, supported the aquarium.

"This world-class aquarium will become to Hawai'i what the Sydney Opera House is to Australia," I declared hopefully in my 2000 State of the State address.

Kamehameha Schools, which owned land adjacent to Kaka'ako Makai, was supportive, retaining a well-known Mainland real estate development consultant to develop a plan for offices, shops and condominiums in the area. We had spent nearly three years studying, planning and negotiating successfully with Armstrong Produce, the lone lessee remaining in Kaka'ako Makai, to move its operations to a new location to make room for the JABSOM complex. Bishop Museum directors had already agreed to build their new science center in Kaka'ako Makai (the Bishop deal would later fall through when the costs of cleaning up the polluted soil at the site made it unfeasible).

Then, in February or early March 2001, Tam announced his proposal to build a multicultural center in Kaka'ako Makai. From the information available we knew of no plan or research that Tam had done—to me, the idea had come right off the top of his head. Tam's proposal would go nowhere but, for as long as he chaired the Economic Development Committee, our plans to develop Kaka'ako Makai would be at risk.

I cringed at the thought that nearly four years of hard work on the aquarium, the high-tech biotechnology park and the science museum—projects that were under Tam's committee's jurisdiction—would be wasted.

"If it were left to this guy to develop the economy, our kids would all end up working in hotels, selling souvenirs or dancing for tourists. I've had it with this guy," I said to my staff. Ever since the 1998 election I had not responded to Tam's shenanigans. Even after he went after Vicky and my in-laws I bit my tongue and immersed myself in dealing with other, more important issues. But now I wanted to send Tam a message. "Anyone know how to get in touch with Audrey Hidano?" I asked.

A deputy director position was open in the Department of Industrial Labor Relations (DILR). If she was qualified I wanted to offer the position to

Hidano. The business community had long seen DILR as a haven for organized labor. As a businesswoman, Hidano would give the department more balance. She could address business concerns about issues relating to OSHA and workers' compensation regulations. Meanwhile, Tam would wonder whether I was helping Hidano get ready to run against him again in 2002. This time I was hoping she would and, unlike in 1998, I would help her in any way I could. Hidano took the job and turned out to be one of the best deputies of my administration.

Fortunately, Tam's committee did not have jurisdiction over the proposed JABSOM complex, which, of all the Kaka'ako Makai projects, was our highest priority. Our research had shown that the complex could be an economic catalyst that would stimulate jobs, expand research and spur the growth of the biotech industry in Hawai'i. Many of these jobs would be highly skilled, well-paying, technical jobs, the kind that would help diversify Hawai'i's tourism-dominated economy and give some of our young people opportunities to remain in the state.

The vision for the new JABSOM complex in Kaka'ako had begun in 1999 when the University hired Dr. Edward Cadman from Yale to serve as the new dean of the medical school. Cadman, a trim, athletic man, and then-UH President Ken Mortimer visited me at my office at the State Capitol. An anticipated 15-minute courtesy call extended into an hour-long meeting as Cadman explained his vision for JABSOM.

Cadman struck me as a sincere, honest and humble person. I was impressed by the breadth of his vision for the medical school. After meeting and getting to know him, I knew he was the person to lead the medical school to greater heights. Mortimer had been equally impressed and had lured him away from Yale. In one of our later meetings, I suggested to Cadman and Mortimer that the new medical school should have a new campus, away from the main campus in Mānoa, to give it its own identity and special status. They agreed and I began searching for a site.

One day I called Cadman and Mortimer and told them I wanted them to look at a site in the Kaka'ako district. From the 10th-floor office of the Kaka'ako Development Authority, I pointed to a nine-acre parcel below and told Cadman, "That's where I want to build your new medical school."

"Wow, the site is breathtaking," he replied, somewhat startled.

"Just imagine, Doc, your students and faculty will have an ocean view," I said, jokingly.

"It's a great site—not far from the Mānoa campus and centrally located to most of the hospitals in Honolulu," he replied. Mortimer agreed.

I was inspired as I envisioned the JABSOM complex, the aquarium, the high-tech and biotech center, and Bishop Museum's science museum—all located within walking distance of each other in Kaka'ako Makai, and each contributing to the critical mass needed to spur economic growth in the entire Kaka'ako district. I was determined to make it all happen.

"Doc, I'll do all I can to get your new medical school built, but I want you to promise me something," I said.

"Sure, what is it?" Cadman replied.

"If we succeed in building it here in Kaka'ako, I want you to promise me you'll stay in Hawai'i and develop it into a world-class medical school."

"Governor," he said, looking me in the eye, "this new medical school will take 10, maybe 15 years to develop to its full potential—it will be my life's last work. I promise you I'll be here to see it through."

"Great. I'll be retired by the time the new school is built, but I expect to receive an invitation to the opening ceremonies." We both laughed.

Few bureaucrats impressed me, but Cadman was one who did. In an understated way, he was a big thinker. He was apolitical. On a personal level, we liked and trusted each other. From the day he agreed on the site for the new JABSOM complex, we worked with a sense of urgency to clear the site, get the approval of the Kaka'ako Authority commissioners, lobby the legislators for support and begin the design, planning and construction of the complex.

With less than two years left in my final term, I decided to step up our efforts to get legislative approval for funding and to begin construction of JABSOM. Although some legislators expressed concern about the estimated cost ($300 million), the Legislature approved $150 million for the first phase. Dr. Evan Dobelle, who had succeeded Mortimer as UH president, was very supportive of the JABSOM complex. I asked him if he could begin the construction before I left office. "Once they start construction the next governor can't stop it," I said.

"I'll take care of it," he replied. And he did.

In October 2002, a little more than a month before the end of my final term, preliminary construction of the John A. Burns School of Medicine complex began. Three years later, in the fall of 2005, the Medical Education Building opened; the Research Building opened that spring. Today, the $150 million complex is one of the most technologically advanced medical facilities in the nation, rivaling more renowned medical institutions around the world.

Sadly, on June 22, 2005, Cadman announced his resignation as dean of JABSOM. Cadman told the University regents that he had been diagnosed with a neurodegenerative disorder called primary progressive aphasia, an incurable, language-based dementia that affects the brain's ability to express thoughts verbally and sometimes in writing. He would remain at JABSOM and teach for as long as he could do so effectively. I was devastated by the news. It was such an undeserved fate for a brilliant and decent man.

Later that year, at a ceremony honoring him, Cadman gave his final remarks as JABSOM's dean:

"When I came to Hawai'i in 1999, there was a fledgling biotechnology industry and a desire by the State to strengthen the industry and diversify the economy. I articulated your vision for this industry. It is your vision, not mine. Embrace it, surround it and build it." In a slightly trembling, emotional voice, he concluded, "I love this school."

The Teachers' Strike

On April 5, 2001, Hawai'i's public school teachers and the University of Hawai'i faculty went on strike. Because Hawai'i's public schools are in a centralized system, the strike marked a historic first in the nation—the state's entire public education system was shut down.

Approximately 13,000 public school teachers and 3,100 University faculty were on strike. Nearly 185,000 public school students and 44,500 college students were affected. Thousands of parents who were scrambling to find child care for their children were upset and, in some cases, very angry because of the inconvenience to and disruption of their daily lives.

The two unions, HSTA and UHPA, had timed the strike to begin only two months before graduation. By the end of the first week of the strike, I began receiving emails and letters from high-school seniors, their tone becoming increasingly anxious about their graduation. It bothered me to see the students used this way.

"The governor's too hardnosed," some critics complained. I didn't think so. To me, collective bargaining was about more than pay raises and benefits. It was one way to improve what everyone agreed was an inefficient State government. It made little sense for the State to give pay raises and benefits without getting some concessions that would improve the quality of education in our schools and University. Otherwise nothing would change except the teachers' salaries.

I saw collective bargaining as a tool to "buy" reforms that could improve the public education system. Thus, the big question in negotiating the teacher and UH faculty contracts was not only affordability, but also whether the State got concessions from the unions that would improve the educational system.

In 1997, for example, I had agreed to increase teachers' salaries on the condition that the union agreed to a 10-day extension of the school year. The union rejected the State's proposal and threatened to strike. I instructed our negotiators to hold the line. I was willing to risk a strike over this issue.

Hawai'i had one of the shortest school years (total hours in class) in the nation. Students in Iowa's public schools, for example, spent the equivalent in hours of 20 more days in class than Hawai'i students. Our kids were at a clear disadvantage. Imagine the handicap Hawai'i students would have in taking a national test that covered subjects they had not had or completed in school.

Fifteen minutes before the strike deadline, a compromise had been reached: The union agreed to a seven-day extension. The teachers got a good pay raise and their students got seven more days of schooling. That, in my opinion, was true collective bargaining. It wasn't easy. It upset a lot of teachers, but we got something to help the kids. However, I paid a political price for it in the 1998 election.

In 2001, the HSTA had demanded a four-year (two years' retroactive) pay package that would cost $260 million. The only way the State could afford it was for me to cut the department budgets again. This time I warned HSTA that we could not spare the DOE from budget cuts as we had done during my first term. To head off the strike we offered a $93 million, two-year package. The offer was rejected. The unions announced they would strike the next day. I announced that if they went on strike the State would withdraw its $93 million offer and we would start again from ground zero.

The Senate was supposed to be the more mature, experienced body. It didn't act like it. Prior to the April 5 strike, the Senate had voted 14-11 to eliminate the State personal income tax cut scheduled to go into effect on January 1, 2002. Why did the Senate vote to repeal one of the biggest cuts in State personal income tax in the nation? Senate Ways and Means Chairman Brian Taniguchi explained that the proposed repeal of the tax cuts was to assure there would be enough money to pay for the raises demanded by HSTA and UHPA.

I was stunned. The Senate was about to repeal one of the biggest tax cuts in State personal income tax in the *nation*—just to appease the unions!

"I can't imagine Calvin [Say, the Speaker] will let the House pass this bill, but if he does, I'll have no choice but to veto it," I said to my chief of staff, Sam Callejo (Charlie Toguchi had retired in 1999).

"I'll go downstairs and talk to the Speaker," he replied.

Say was no novice; he knew that if the House repealed the tax cuts ($750 million over four years) the Republicans would use it like a sledgehammer against the Democrats in the 2002 election.

Taniguchi and the Senate leadership must have known the House would not pass the bill, but they were so worried about angering the two unions that they put on a show for them even though they knew they couldn't deliver.

But Taniguchi and the Senate leadership were not finished pandering to the unions. On April 4, the day before the unions went on strike, Taniguchi set aside $250 million in the Senate version of the State budget—$200 million for the teachers and $50 million for the University faculty—for the pay raises HSTA and UHPA had demanded. It was no coincidence that the $200 million set aside for the HSTA was exactly the amount the union had proposed as a compromise.

On April 5, the HSTA and UHPA went on strike, shutting down the State's entire public education system. The strike made national headlines. Taniguchi denied that his committee was trying to undermine the State's contract negotiations, saying his intent was rather to show support for the teachers and faculty. I was flabbergasted—he actually seemed to believe what he said.

When asked by reporters where the $250 million would come from, Taniguchi said $80 million would come from "raiding" special funds; the rest would come from tapping into the State's "rainy day" fund and program cuts to the proposed State budget. As part of the cuts, Taniguchi eliminated $8.8 million for drug treatment programs. Other programs he cut out or reduced included appropriations for school computers and textbooks.

If Taniguchi and the senators thought giving the teachers and faculty the pay raises they demanded was more important than drug addiction treatment programs, computers and textbooks, that was their right. The legislative process, after all, was about setting priorities.

But Taniguchi either ignored or dismissed that the added cost of pay raises does not end with the termination of the contract; it carries over through subsequent years. Taniguchi had patched the $250 million together by raiding special funds, eliminating social programs, reducing funding for needed school equipment and supplies and dipping into the State's emergency funds. But these were one-time funding sources. Where would the funding come from after the two-year contract expired? He never answered that question.

Not surprisingly, for the duration of the strike, HSTA leaders and teachers would repeatedly refer to the $250 million set aside as proof that the State could afford their pay raises, and that I was stubborn. It was definitely a factor in prolonging the strike.

The House leadership had stood firm against repealing the tax cuts. But it had been a struggle for the Speaker to persuade his worried members to reject the Senate's $250 million. Under pressure from his younger leaders, Say felt that the House could not remain silent. Led by Vice Speaker Sylvia Luke and House Majority Whip Brian Schatz, a group of about two dozen House Democrats gathered at the State Capitol and held a press conference declaring their support for the strikers. It was quite a performance.

In an obvious reference to me, Luke scolded, "We must put aside the pettiness and egos."

Not to be outdone, Schatz declared, "Every day teachers get a little more demoralized, and if the intention of the governor is to … break the spirits of our educators, then we can't support it."

Luke and Schatz were part of the new generation of politicians: well-educated, bright and young (both were in their early 30s), lacking in life experience and highly political. As Luke would tell me later, the House Democrats were going to override my veto of the age of consent bill because they were concerned about the Republicans attacking them for being "soft on crime"—a tactic the GOP had used to defeat six House Democrats in the 2000 election. Off to an early start in the parade of panderers was conservative Republican State Sen. Fred Hemmings. At a February 27 meeting with constituents, Hemmings quipped, "The money's there. Even though there's a need to pay teachers, Ben wants to finance a huge fish tank in Kakaʻako."

Hemmings seemed to live for opportunities to deliver one-liners, which he apparently believed were a sufficient substitute for doing his homework. Given to uttering Newt Gingrich-sounding slogans, at times Hemmings sounded as if he were speaking in tongues.

Never one to concern himself with details, Hemmings was wrong about the proposed Kaka'ako "fish tank," which, in fact, would have been financed by revenue bonds and a $20 million contribution from the private sector—unlike the proposed "fish tank" in Ko Olina, for which Hemmings would vote to give smooth-talking Ko Olina resort developer Jeff Stone a $75 million tax credit against the general fund in 2002—the same general fund from which public education and social programs for the needy schools are funded. There were a few legislators in both the House and Senate who were embarrassed by the Senate's ploy. But they were not in leadership positions, and most were inclined to remain silent. One House Democrat, Ed Case, who would eventually go on to Congress, did not take part in the House news conference or walk the picket line. Case was the only one who spoke out publicly against the Senate's largesse for the strikers:

"I believe the Senate is passing out an irresponsible budget which is short-term-related and does not provide for long-term sustainability, at least without cutting deep into government programs. I don't think that's feasible. In my own mind, what is probably feasible is somewhere in the range of 15 percent or so, give or take."

It must be disconcerting for the other House members to listen to this guy make sense day after day, I said to myself. The man had guts.

On March 29, I was shocked when Lt. Gov. Mazie Hirono, speaking at a Democratic Party issues forum, told the audience that she wasn't there "to represent the governor" but to support the teachers. Sitting in the audience were Karen Ginoza and Alex Mallahoff, presidents of HSTA and UHPA, respectively. They must have been delighted by what they heard.

That hurt. Hirono and I had won two tough elections together, coming from behind each time to overtake our opponents. We were close friends and political allies, but she had never expressed misgivings about my handling of the negotiations. Still, I said nothing about it to her. Nor did she say anything to me.

The day the strike began, Hirono was seen walking the picket lines, encouraging the strikers. Apparently, she had done it because Jeremy Harris, her likely opponent in the 2000 Democratic primary, and Linda Lingle, the presumptive Republican gubernatorial candidate, had already walked the picket lines. A story about the strike in the *New York Times* ran the headline: "Lieutenant Governor Breaks with Her Boss."

Later, when the news reporters finally caught up with me, one of them asked what I thought about Hirono walking the picket line. "She wanted to go out and express her support for the teachers and demonstrate some empathy and compassion; I think that is fine and I feel the same way, too," I replied.

It wasn't fine, of course. Under Hawai'i law, if I were to drop dead or become incapacitated for any reason, Hirono would succeed me as governor. Put in simplistic terms, her walking the picket line was about as appropriate as a backup quarterback cheering for the opposing team. There are many defining moments in every politician's career—her decision to walk the picket line was one of them.

"This won't help her; the old folks won't like it," former Gov. Ariyoshi would later tell me. By "old folks" Ariyoshi was referring to the older AJAs, for whom loyalty is a very important virtue.

Later during the strike, Hirono's office issued a press release that restated her support for the strikers and strongly suggested that I was treating the strikers unfairly. The suggestion that I was unfair bothered me. When the reporters asked what I thought about the press release, I let out my frustrations.

"If she wants to be governor, she should act like one and get all of the facts before she says anything!" The news media, of course, played it up.

Hirono and I had been close for too long for this one incident to change my feelings about our friendship. It did, however, affect my opinion on whether she would be the Democrats' best hope for governor in 2002.

For the duration of the strike, the only ones supporting me were the members of my Cabinet, U.S. Congressman Neil Abercrombie and Charles Toguchi, both of whom I had asked to help with the negotiations. No two politicians understood the public education system and the unions better than Abercrombie and Toguchi. Toguchi, himself a former teacher, had served as State superintendent of education from 1986 to 1994, when he resigned to become my chief of staff, and he had been an HSTA strike captain in the 1973 teachers' strike. Abercrombie was a former UH professor and had served as chairman of the State Senate Education Committee from 1979 to 1983. Both were favorites of the unions.

Predictably, public sentiment ran heavily in support of the strikers. To spare me bad news, my staff advised me against reading the emails and letters my office was receiving. I did read them, of course, usually at the end of the day. No other technology gave the public greater instant access to their political leaders than email. I received hundreds of them. Most of the messages were reasonable, earnest pleas to settle the strike; some showed the ugly side of people; and a few were downright racist.

One email read, "Who do you think you are, Ferdinand Marcos?" The reference to the former Philippine dictator brought a few chuckles from the male members of my staff. The women who read it didn't see any humor in it. In keeping with my practice of never turning the other cheek on racist insults, I emailed back: "And who do you think you are—Tojo?"

Humor can be a great stress reliever.

Some teachers turned the strike into class projects, encouraging their students to write to me. Not surprisingly, I didn't receive one letter that agreed with me on the strike. But most of the letters I received from the students were pretty well written. The best letters came from elementary students in the so-called "good" public schools. One day, I received a packet filled with a couple of dozen letters written by students from a high school class (I shall not name the school). Nearly all the letters were filled with grammatical, spelling and syntax errors. In my layman's opinion, most of them were writing at a fifth- or sixth-grade level.

One morning, Michael Fisch, who was then the publisher of the *Honolulu Advertiser*, came to my office for a meeting. We were supposed to meet on some other issue (I don't remember what it was), but I decided to show Fisch the letters because I wanted him to get a dose of the reality of public education. Perhaps it would help him understand better why I had made teacher accountability a big issue in the strike negotiations.

"Mike, I want to show you something in confidence. Take a look at these letters I received from _____ High School," I said, handing him the letters.

"My goodness, this is terrible," he said, grimacing, after he reviewed them.

"And these are juniors," I said.

"It's sad—our democracy requires a well-educated population...." he lamented, his voice trailing off as he looked at the letters again.

"You know, unless these kids get some help, they won't have much of a chance to get ahead in the real world," I said.

Fisch had been in Hawai'i for less than five years and had immersed himself in community affairs. We had had a few dinners together with our wives, and I had gotten to know him well enough to believe he was a very thoughtful and compassionate man. The letters seemed to have made a real impact on him. *Good*, I thought; *maybe the next editorial the* Advertiser *runs will show more understanding of why I've taken such a strong position in the contract negotiations.*

By the end of the first week of the strike, I decided that the State should not continue to pay its share of the strike health benefits. "That's the way it is when workers in the private sector go on strike; they don't get paid and the employer stops paying for their benefits," I said tersely to my negotiator and staff, whose faces showed doubt about the political wisdom of my decision.

I knew that ordering the State to stop paying for the strikers' health benefits would cause an uproar among the strikers, but I thought it was important for them to understand the hardship experienced by private-sector workers, who have no benefits when they go on strike.

A few days later, Davis Yogi, my chief negotiator, said wryly, "Gov, I think they got the message, but it's disrupted the negotiations and it may lead to the unions filing a lawsuit."

"Okay, let's announce publicly that I'm deferring my decision to stop the payments for now and leave it at that. But if this strike goes on and it screws up graduation, I'll stop payments for as long as the strike goes on. Let them sue us—

they don't have a case. The truth is when they go on strike the State's obligation to pay benefits stops."

On April 12, the *Star-Bulletin* reported that 13 percent of the UH professors on strike had returned to their classrooms. Each day, I got reports that more faculty members were returning to work. A UH professor who is a close friend had assured me earlier that the majority of the faculty would not abandon their students. Apparently, many were worried about their students being able to get the required 15 weeks of instruction to earn credit for their semester courses and, of course, their looming graduation. By April 18, the day UHPA and the State settled, an estimated 30 percent of the faculty had returned to their classes.

Under the new contract the faculty would receive a 10-percent pay raise—4 percent in the first year, 6 percent in the second year. Included was a 2-percent merit raise through a system to be developed jointly between UHPA and the UH president. It was a fair compromise: The faculty got a pay raise the State could afford and, for the first time, merit pay became part of the contract.

After the strike ended, a member of the UHPA bargaining team was quoted as saying, "We never dreamed it would last so long ... the State just had no intention of settling." That was an incredible admission of how little thought UHPA had put into the decision to strike. It was naïve for UHPA to think the State would just roll over and agree to its demands. Apparently, there were some professors who were upset that they had to strike to get the pay raise they ultimately got under the new contract. Jim Mak, a professor of economics who was well known in the community, sent an email message to faculty members raising the question of whether UHPA should be decertified.

I could not agree more. I've been a strong supporter of unionism, but I don't think that university professors and school principals should be unionized. Once I asked Alex Mallahoff, then the president of UHPA, what the existence of a union did to promote excellence at the University. Mallahoff, a distinguished professor of oceanography, smiled and said bluntly, "Nothing." He was being honest.

The great research universities that excel in our country thrive on competition and accountability. Few of them are unionized. Their faculty members can gain job security by earning tenure. At the University of Hawai'i, however, the faculty has double protection: tenure and the union. It's no secret that UH deans and department heads complain frequently about how difficult it is for them to weed out incompetent or underperforming faculty. While higher salaries are critical in attracting outstanding faculty, boosting the pay of underperforming and incompetent faculty will not give UH the faculty it needs to become the great university it should be.

However, in 2001, UHPA was a fact of life with which I had to deal. Our proposal for merit pay was a small step toward creating an environment in which UH professors were rewarded for excellence in teaching rather than just for research or published writings. Generally, unions frown on merit pay because they see it as a form of discrimination that is subject to abuse. As far as I was concerned, it was a deal-breaker. No merit pay, no new contract. The State was not going to come out of the negotiations empty-handed. In the end, a compromise was reached and the parties agreed on the new contract.

The settlement with UHPA allowed us to concentrate on our negotiations with HSTA. On Thursday, April 19, our chief negotiator, Davis Yogi, walked into my office with a wry smile on his face.

"Gov, I just found out that HSTA rented the Stan Sheriff Center for this coming Monday."

"That means they're ready to settle."

"Right, they need the lead time to notify their 13,000 teachers to meet and vote to ratify the new contract," Yogi said. "Do you want me to push them on the negotiations?"

"Actually, Davis, I've been thinking about keeping them out for another week, to teach them never again to leverage our kids' education for pay raises. Frankly, another week or two and I think we'll break this strike!" I said grimly.

Yogi, who had done a yeoman's job as our chief negotiator, looked at me wanly and in disbelief.

"Uh, Gov … you're not serious, are you?"

"Oh, it was just a passing thought," I chuckled, though actually I had given the idea some serious consideration. "No, don't change anything; our settlement offer was given in good faith, just hold firm. If they get over their hang-up on the retroactive pay raises, they'll settle over the weekend and then we can wrap up this damned strike and go home. Remind Karen [Ginoza] and Joan [Husted] that our new contracts with HGEA, UHPA and UPW do not include retroactive pay."

"I think we'll settle over the weekend," Yogi replied.

"I'll be surprised if we don't," I said.

The next day, Friday, April 20, Joan Husted told newspaper reporters she was not optimistic that a settlement would be reached. The big obstacle, Husted suggested, was retroactive pay. She knew that the new contracts between the State and the three other public-worker unions did not include retroactive pay raises, and that there was no way I would agree to them for the HSTA. As far as I was concerned, like Taniguchi, she was grandstanding for the rank and file. This was the kind of shibai that made me consider holding off settling for another week.

As expected, a settlement was reached over the weekend. On Monday, April 24, the majority of the 13,000 voted to ratify the new contract. HSTA agreed to a $113 million contract: $111 million were recurring or carry-over costs and, the remaining $2 million paid for one-time bonuses. The new contract was a good one for the teachers and for the State. Among its provisions were a number of incentive-driven ways for ambitious teachers to boost their salaries through professional-development programs and earning advanced degrees.

The public-relations campaign of HSTA President Ginoza and chief negotiator Husted had generated high expectations among the rank and file. As *Star-Bulletin* reporter Richard Borreca wrote in 2002: "Teachers and University faculty quickly personalized the strike and flooded Cayetano with bitter emails, attacking him and the State's refusal to give larger pay raises." From the union's perspective, having a common enemy or scapegoat was an ideal way to unify the members. I had no doubt the teachers resented hearing my blunt remarks about having to cut social programs for the poor and needy in order to pay for their raises. Moreover, the perception that I was "hardnosed … a pit bull … stubborn" made it easy for the unions to goad teachers and University faculty into disliking and, in some cases, hating me.

Did it bother me? Of course. Every politician would prefer to be liked. Today most politicians work incessantly at it. It's easier to duck responsibility as one of 76 legislators. But governors don't have that luxury. The one thing that helped shore up my resolve was the realization that, in this modern political era, when politicians are beset to do the bidding of powerful special-interest groups such as unions, big business and single-issue religious fanatics, the only thing the poor, the needy and the public have going for them are the good consciences of their political leaders. That may sound corny and overly idealistic, but it was at the core of every major decision I made in my 28 years in politics.

Anger can be an effective motivator; it can inspire unity, but it can also obfuscate the hard facts.

The stark reality of the $113 million settlement was a far cry from the $260 million pay-raise package HSTA had demanded and the $200 million Taniguchi had set aside for the raises. For a paltry $17 million more (the State's last offer was $96 million), 13,000 teachers went on strike, disrupting the lives of thousands of parents, depriving 185,000 schoolchildren of 21 days of schooling and costing each teacher about $1,500 in salary that they were unlikely to ever recover.

The danger of setting high expectations is that, repeated often enough, such expectations evolve into promises, and the failure to deliver them causes frustration, disappointment and anger. I thought the new contract was good and fair. Apparently, however, a growing number of teachers became upset that walking the picket line for nearly three weeks had not produced the raises to which their leadership had said they were entitled. Ultimately, the rank and file took their frustrations out on their leader. In 2003, Ginoza was defeated in her bid for reelection. The new president, Roger Takabayashi, had pledged a more collaborative approach to future collective bargaining with the State.

On May 23, 2001, journalist Bob Rees wrote in his *Honolulu Weekly* column that the State had "taken the unions to school." To be honest, that was pretty much how I felt about it. ❖

CHAPTER TWENTY-TWO

Veto Power

The State Health Plan

Historic" was how the *Star-Bulletin* described the 2001 legislative session. Indeed, in terms of government reform, it was the most productive of my two terms as governor.

Since 1995, our efforts to reform State government and its civil service system had made little progress. Economic revival, balancing the State budget and Hawaiian affairs overshadowed all other issues. Our attempts to bring about reform through legislation—strongly opposed by the public-employee unions—were rejected by the Legislature. Legislative leaders made it clear that they wanted me to reform government through the collective-bargaining process. In other words, I would have to find ways to buy reforms. *Fine*, I thought, *but with what?*

The unions had done a great job for their members. It was unreasonable to expect them to give up their benefits for nothing. Reform rarely comes without cost. Finding ways to reduce the cost of State government by "buying back" some of the worker benefits and restoring more work days was a huge challenge.

Hawai'i's State employees enjoy one of the best—if not the best—fringe-benefit packages in the nation. State employees earn 21 vacation days, 21 days of sick leave and 13 days of paid vacation per year. Theoretically, a State employee could be off work for a total of 55 days in a 260-day work year, compared to an average total of 36 days for most Mainland State employees. No matter how hard or efficiently Hawai'i State employees worked they could not match the productivity of other states in delivering services.

But our biggest concern was the State employees' health fund. The costs of the health-fund plan, which provided medical, vision, dental and drug benefits—and lifetime free coverage for employees' spouses—were skyrocketing.

While the public, State employees and union leaders were preoccupied with the ongoing HSTA-UHPA strike, HGEA Executive Secretary Russell Okata and UPW Director Gary Rodrigues were meeting with me privately to resolve our differences on their unions' respective contracts.

More often than not, interpersonal relationships are critical to getting things done in politics. I had good, close relationships with both Okata and Rodrigues. Negotiations were best conducted privately, allowing the parties to speak freely and in confidence. I was very comfortable meeting and discussing matters candidly with them.

As a matter of course, we opened the State's books to all four public-employee unions to show that the State could not afford the pay raises they demanded. The reaction of the different union leaders to the information was a barometer to how the negotiations would progress.

Okata and Rodrigues, with years of experience negotiating with the State, understood the details of the State budget better than the other labor union leaders. Furthermore, they both realized that if I had to lay off State workers—which I would likely do if I agreed to union demands—those cut would come mainly from the ranks of their respective members, not from HSTA's teachers (there was a teacher shortage) or UHPA's professors (the University was quasi-autonomous).

We settled our differences with HGEA on its arbitration award and agreed to a new contract with UPW. In return, the two unions agreed to revise the way employee fringe benefits were awarded. Sick leave and vacation benefits for starting employees were reduced from the current 21 days to 15 days for the first five years of their employment; thereafter they would increase to 21 days and, for 25-year employees, 25 days. It was a modest concession from the unions, but it was a start.

Meanwhile, as Taniguchi and others were pandering to the striking teachers and professors, a freshman senator was quietly gathering support to pass Senate Bill 1044, which would establish a single health plan for all State employees. It would be the biggest reform of State government in decades.

A 1999 State auditor's report had concluded that, unless reforms were made, the cost for the State employee health fund, which covered approximately 47,000 full-time State workers and 31,000 retirees, would escalate to $1 billion by 2013. The cause was that State employees had the option of joining either their respective union health plans or the State's health plan. If the employee opted for the union health plan, the State would transfer or port its share of the cost of the employee premiums to the union. The union health plans were customized to attract workers who were least likely to use health benefits, leaving mostly retired State employees, who were more likely to use health benefits, enrolled in the State plan.

This process of "cherry-picking," as it was often called, resulted in huge savings for the more efficient union plans, while the cost of the State's less efficient plan—filled with retirees—was rising rapidly. The savings was a cash boon to the unions, making it possible for them to enhance their health plans and provide better coverage for their members, or use the money for other purposes, for which there was literally no connection to health benefits for the employees.

Senate Bill 1044 was designed to reduce costs by placing all State employees in a single State health plan, thus eliminating cherry-picking. Our administration had been introducing a similar bill since 1996, but the unions managed to kill it every year. The first big break came in 2000, when Senate President Norman Mizuguchi retired. Mizuguchi, who had close ties to HGEA, had been instrumental in killing our reform bills.

Both Senate President Robert Bunda and Speaker Calvin Say had been in the Legislature long enough to understand the reasons for the looming crisis. Not surprisingly, Say would not push his Democratic House members to pass SB 1044 unless the Senate was willing to go along. Otherwise, he would be exposing them unnecessarily to the wrath of the unions. With Mizuguchi gone it was a new ball-game. Bunda was supportive of SB 1044 but was reluctant to take the lead.

Few legislators understood the health-fund system. It was complicated, and actuarial experts who briefed legislators were usually talking over their heads. But every legislator understood the experts' conclusion: The State's health-fund system was headed for big trouble—a billion dollars' worth by 2013.

One senator who understood the problem better than anyone in the Legislature and was willing to take the lead in doing something about it was Democrat Colleen Hanabusa. A first-term senator and the leader of a faction of four or five strongly supportive freshmen senators, Hanabusa was the major force behind moving SB 1044. While HSTA and UHPA were preoccupied with the strike, she began working quietly to help senators understand the health-fund system and the ramifications of doing nothing.

Hanabusa was born and raised in Wai'anae—a blue-collar, impoverished area where the overwhelming majority of the residents are Hawaiian and where families suffer from the highest incidence of social ills such as drug use, spouse and child abuse, other crimes and teen pregnancy in Hawai'i. As one of the state's top labor lawyers, she could have easily afforded to move to a more affluent neighborhood; that she continued to live in the area impressed me.

Hanabusa had been instrumental in orchestrating the Senate's rejection of the confirmations of Margery Bronster and Earl Anzai. The incident left me wary, but it also stamped her as a leader in the Senate.

Despite strong but belated opposition from the unions, SB 1044 somehow emerged out of the Senate and House conference committees. On May 1, SB 1044 and other reform bills had made it to the floors of the Senate and House for votes.

After six years of failing to pass the bill, I was delighted when I was told that the conference committees had reported the bill to both houses for vote. I had less than two years left in my second term. The opportunity would not come again. I cancelled appointments and spent much time personally lobbying senators to vote for SB 1044. Ultimately, I was convinced that every senator (I wasn't worried about the House) agreed that the State health fund should be reformed and that SB 1044 was the vehicle to do it. But I had been in politics long enough to know that didn't assure they would vote for it.

The unions, apparently lulled by the highly publicized strikes and the fact that they had killed the bill for six consecutive years, had been initially caught off guard, but in the week before the May 1 vote they put on a fierce, full-court press, buttonholing legislators and urging them to kill the bill.

Only 12 of the 22 Democrats in the Senate were willing to vote for SB 1044. Among the 10 who were against it was a faction of six Democrats who were so vehemently opposed to Bunda as president that they refused to accept committee chairmanships. Two of the 10, Matt Matsunaga and Ron Menor, had already decided to run for lieutenant governor and apparently saw no point in angering the unions.

Questioning the reliability of the projections on how much SB 1044 would save the State, Democratic Sen. Cal Kawamoto, a former fighter pilot who had flown numerous combat missions in Vietnam, left the impression he worried more about his life in politics than he had in the war. "What figures do we believe? Do we sacrifice our political careers for that? We want to come back," he pleaded shamelessly.

Thirteen votes were needed to pass the bill. One Democratic senator, Avery Chumbley, had assured Hanabusa that he would change his vote if a 13th vote was needed. I had heard similar promises many times before and took no comfort in it. *Surely,* I thought, *the three Republican senators—all critics of big government—will provide the margin needed to pass the bill.*

I was in for a surprise.

The affable and likeable Bob Hogue, a first-time senator who was contemplating a run for Congress, had already caved in to HSTA lobbyists, promising them that he would vote against the bill.

Fred Hemmings also capitulated. He declared that he would vote against not only SB 1044 but also SB 1096, a reform bill that authorized privatization and repealed the State's one-sided mandatory arbitration law. These were only Band-Aid solutions, he said without offering alternatives. As for SB 1044, Hemmings revealed why, in his two decades in politics, he had accomplished virtually nothing. "We're doing this [SB 1044] because of cherry-picking by unions," he blurted out. "I'd like to ask, who's handing out the cherries?"

It remained for Sam Slom to prove there was at least one true conservative Republican in the Senate. I had my differences with Slom. Indeed, the political dirty trick he and a Republican hit group had pulled on Vicky and me regarding our Waiʻalae Iki parcel during the 1998 election had told me much about his character. After the 1998 election, I never thought I'd ever set foot in Slom's office, but SB 1044 was the most important government reform in decades, and Slom could provide the elusive 13th vote.

I made an appointment to meet with Slom at his Senate office. We had what I would describe as a "cordial" conversation about the bill. Slom promised he was open to supporting the bill. I left his office confident he would be the 13th vote. SB 1044 was big, the kind of reform a conservative like Slom could not turn down.

On May 1, the Senate passed SB 1044 by a 13 to 12 vote.

The House followed suit, approving the bill by a 38-13 vote, with nine Republicans and four Democrats voting no.

Caught literally flat-footed, union leaders were furious.

UPW's Rodrigues had warned angrily the week before the vote that the bill would "cost the workers all the pay raises that we negotiated for because it is not true ... that it'll save the State health-fund plan." But Rodrigues, described as the "26th senator" by some creative news reporters, was under indictment by the federal government for fraud relating to his union's health insurance plan, and his political influence had been greatly damaged.

HSTA President Ginoza, revealing her inexperience, threatened retribution: "Our teachers are very much interested in the electoral process, and we will start looking at the issues of support for education and labor. They have long memories."

HGEA's Okata decried the "major shift" in public policy, complaining, "The public employees have become scapegoats." Although HGEA was the biggest public-employee union and probably the most effective in political campaigns, Okata was not one to issue threats. Unlike David Trask, his fiery and outspoken predecessor, Okata tended towards understatement, which belied his toughness, and he was patient, a great virtue in politics.

Unlike Ginoza, Okata had been taught by experience that politics is a long-term game. Win some, lose some. Okata understood fully that he would need legislative support on other issues important to his union down the road. (Shortly after I retired in 2002, Okata led the unions in successfully lobbying the Legislature to reinstate mandatory arbitration.)

At the outset of the 2001 legislative session, union demands for pay raises totaled more than $500 million. The new collective-bargaining agreements totaled approximately $300 million—$200 million less than the unions had demanded. The State got some modest concessions in return. The $200 million difference made it possible for our administration to continue some important social and educational programs. Given the antics of the Senate and political grandstanding by the House, the collective-bargaining negotiations had become a personal test of character for me. I was very satisfied with the final outcome.

On May 3 I held a public bill-signing ceremony of SB 1044 and SB 1096. All the legislators were invited. Usually, legislators eagerly attend bill-signing ceremonies as a chance for photo ops and publicity. But this time, no legislators showed up. After waiting for about 10 minutes, I signed the bills into law, with only the news media for an audience. Later, when asked by reporters about the absence of legislators at the bill signing, Senate President Bunda explained that Democrats had to be sensitive to the unions. "Why rub salt into their wounds?" he asked.

The Age of Consent

When the distinguished Republican U.S. Sen. Warren Rudman, described by *TIME* magazine as one of the "most effective, influential" senators, was interviewed by *TIME* after his retirement from the Senate in 1992, he lamented the lack of political courage among his former colleagues. When he was a Marine captain serving in Korea, Rudman said, he commanded young Marines who were ready to risk their lives for their country, and many did lose their lives. But he was disappointed with his colleagues in the Senate, he said, because too many of them were not even willing to risk their political lives for their country.

Rudman put his finger on what had become the current state of politics throughout the nation. There was no better example of it than the 2001 Legislature's actions on the Age of Consent bill.

The Age of Consent bill was introduced to protect minors from participating in consensual sex by raising the permissible age from 14 to 16. To address the potential problems that might arise in the case of consensual sex between high school friends or sweethearts, the bill included a sliding scale defining the age gaps at which a minor could engage in consensual sex. For example, under the sliding scale, if a 19-year-old had consensual sex with his 14-year-old girlfriend he would face a 20-year prison sentence. But if his girlfriend was 15 at the time, it would not be a crime.

I had no objection to raising the age from 14 to 16, but I felt that the sliding scale defied reality and common sense. Furthermore, the 20-year felony prison sentence was too harsh. It was the same prison sentence a criminal would receive for forcible rape or even murder.

I wasn't the only one opposed to the bill. Honolulu's tough law-and-order prosecutor, Peter Carlisle; the Commission on the Status of Women and the *Honolulu Advertiser* were among others opposed to it. Nevertheless, the bill unanimously passed the House; only one senator, Democrat Les Ihara, who thought the penalty was too harsh, voted against it.

The bill had languished in the Legislature for four consecutive years, but the Republican success in incessantly attacking Democrats for being soft on crime had apparently cost six House Democrats their seats in the 2000 elections. In 2001, the Democratic majority, many of them wary of the soft-on-crime label being used against them again in 2002, voted to approve the bill. Republicans who had been milking this issue at the expense of the Democrats were delighted. "This bill," Republican Minority Leader Galen Fox said, "will protect 14- and 15-year-olds."

That all but one legislator had voted for the bill meant there were more than enough votes to override my veto. I had hoped the Legislature could amend the bill to meet with my objections, but the House Democrats rejected the idea. My staff cautioned me that public sentiment favored the bill. It didn't surprise me. Protecting

14- and 15-year-olds was like motherhood. But I wondered how many really understood the specifics of the bill.

"One day," I remarked to my staff, "a 19-year-old honor student, who comes from a good home, who never committed a crime in his life, is going to face a 20-year prison term because he had sex with a 14-year-old girl he thought was older." I vetoed the bill.

My veto provoked wails of criticism from the Republicans. Minority leader Fox called my veto a "misstep" and invited Democrats to join Republicans in overriding it. Initially, Say and Bunda said publicly that an override was unlikely. But neither could ignore the growing concern among their members about the political ramifications they would face in the 2002 elections if the bill did not become law.

In the Senate, freshman Sen. Jonathan Chun of Kaua'i began lobbying his colleagues, urging them to override my veto.

"Chun's in big trouble on Kaua'i," Lloyd Nekoba, who was now my political liaison to the Neighbor Islands, told me. "First, he pissed off people on Kaua'i—especially the haoles—with his big talk and vote against Margery Bronster. And then he really pissed off the unions when he voted for the new health fund [SB 1044]. Our guys, Turk Tokita and his group, don't like him, and Turk told me they're going to support Gary Hooser against him in 2002."

"Hooser, the haole councilman?" I asked.

"Yeah, Turk said they all like him. He's a straight shooter, gets along great with local people."

"Good, Chun doesn't give a damn about 14- and 15-year-olds; he wants the override to show he's not soft on crime."

On July 9, 2001, House Vice Speaker Sylvia Luke and a few other House leaders met with me in my office to tell me they were going to override my veto. I wasn't surprised. I had sensed that the mood of the Legislature had changed over the past week. Our meeting was brief.

"Governor, we're here to tell you that the House and Senate Democrats have decided to override your veto on the Age of Consent bill," she said.

"Don't you think it's a bad bill?" I asked.

"Governor, we agree with you that it's a bad bill, but in the last election we lost six Democrats who the Republicans had targeted for being soft on crime," she replied.

"Let me get this straight: You think it's a bad bill but you're worried that the Republicans are going to use it against you if it doesn't become law?" I asked, barely able to hide my disgust.

"Governor, I'm going to close my eyes on this one—we have to override your veto, otherwise the Republicans will use it against us in the election."

Realizing it was futile to discuss the merits of the bill, I cut the meeting short. "Okay, you guys, do what you gotta do, but I'm going to hold you people accountable publicly."

On July 10, the Legislature overrode my veto by a nearly unanimous margin. The news media played up the override as "historic" and a personal defeat for me. Indeed, they were right that it was historic. It was the first time a Democratic governor's veto had been overridden by Democratic legislators. I was disappointed, of course, but when I found out the real reason the Democrats had overridden my veto, I felt contempt more than anything else. We had scored big on collective bargaining and civil service but lost the fight on the Age of Consent bill.

When reporters asked me to comment, I disclosed my conversation with Luke and the other House leaders. "It's not about protecting 14- and 15-year-olds," I told one television news reporter, "it's all about politics."

Luke, claiming that I had quoted her "out of context," retorted, "What he needs to understand is that this Legislature is not like the old-time Legislature."

Well, at least she's got that right, I thought.

On November 1, 2005, Fox resigned from the House of Representatives. Unknown to the public and news media, on December 18, 2004, he had been convicted of sexual battery against a female passenger on a flight from Honolulu to Los Angeles. Fox denied to local reporters that he had done anything wrong. "In my heart," he told news reporters, "I know I didn't do it."

In federal court, however, Fox admitted to U.S. District Court Judge Margery Nagle that he had unbuttoned and unzipped the jeans of an Asian female passenger sitting next to him, whom he had overheard telling her parents sitting across the aisle that she had taken Dramamine and was going to sleep. Fox also admitted to the judge that he was rubbing the woman's crotch when she suddenly awoke and confronted him. He was arrested by FBI agents when the plane landed in Los Angeles.

Shortly after his conviction, Fox disclosed it to Republican Gov. Linda Lingle, who kept the incident under wraps for a year, leaving it to Fox to break the news.

Fox could have been charged with a felony. I wondered why he was not. Lucky for him—if he had been convicted of a felony he would have been another face on Hawai'i's registry of sex offenders.

On July 25, 2006, the news media reported a double suicide on the little island of Lāna'i. The bodies of 24-year-old John Etrata and 15-year-old Ariel Aki were found in a field about a half-mile from the Lāna'i Police Station. Etrata and Aki were lovers and had been living together for about three months.

Most people would disapprove of a relationship between a 24-year-old and a 15-year-old. But as it happens, Lāna'i is the state's least-populated island, except for Ni'ihau, with only 2,400 or so residents. It is the kind of community where everyone literally knows everyone else. It is a place where such a liaison was more likely to happen than in urban Honolulu.

Etrata was no lecherous older man, no pimp preying on young girls. Friends described him as a "good boy," a construction worker and a good fisherman. The only time he got in trouble with the law was when he let Aki, who did not have a driver's license, drive his car and was cited for it by the Lāna'i police. Ultimately, the police began to investigate Etrata's relationship with Aki and, in mid-July, arrested him for sexual assault involving a minor.

Apparently, the age gap did not bother Aki's mother or the Etrata family. Aki's mother later told the news media that Etrata should never have been charged with a sex offense. Etrata's sister spoke highly of her brother's relationship with Aki, noting that "they really seemed happy together."

The pair had killed themselves with Etrata's hunting rifle. Each left farewell letters. The contents of Aki's letter were not mentioned by the news media, but Etrata's sister was quoted as saying her brother mentioned how his time with Aki had been the happiest in his life.

No one knows for sure why they killed themselves. But I wondered how shocked Etrata must have been when he found out—as he must have—that he faced a 20-year prison term for being intimate with Aki. Ironically, had Aki been a year older, they—with her parents' consent—could have been married. ❖

CHAPTER TWENTY-THREE

Nine-Eleven

A State of Emergency

Governor, it's Kim [Murakawa, my press secretary]. Turn on your television; there's something going on in New York."

It was about 3:50 a.m., September 11, 2001. I switched on my television set just in time to see a rerun of an airplane crashing into the North Tower of New York's world-renowned World Trade Center. I wasn't really sure what was happening until moments later when I saw a second airplane crash into the South Tower.

I asked Murakawa to immediately put in calls to Edward Correa, the adjutant general of the Hawai'i National Guard; Sam Callejo, my chief of staff; and Brian Minaai, the director of the Department of Transportation.

As I awaited their calls and hurriedly dressed, I continued to watch, transfixed by the images on the screen. The sheer audacity of the attacks, the apparent sophistication and precision of their planning, seemed surreal.

Vicky and I had visited New York in July 2000. One evening we had dinner at the internationally acclaimed Windows on the World restaurant on the 107th floor of the World Trade Center's North Tower. Among its many features, the elegant restaurant, with its thick, wraparound glass windows, offered a spectacular panoramic view of the city. However, the night we were there the clouds (perhaps it was fog) were so low and thick we could see nothing. But on September 11, the morning sky was clear. I was heartsick as I imagined the shock and terror the doomed patrons and restaurant workers must have felt when from out of the panoramic view they saw the huge airliner coming at them.

"Governor, this is Mert Agena [Brigadier General Clarence Agena]. Ed Texeira from Civil Defense notified me about the attacks this morning."

"Is General Correa out of town?"

"Yes, sir, he's attending a U.S. Army seminar with General [Eric] Shinseki in Malaysia. I'm acting TAG [The Adjutant General]."

"Any more news on the attacks?"

"No, we only know what we've seen and heard on the television news and radio. According to the latest report a third hijacked airliner was used in a suicide attack on the Pentagon; apparently many people were killed." Later, the news media reported that a fourth hijacked airliner had crashed in a field in Pennsylvania.

Incredible—the United States is the world's richest, most technologically advanced super power, with the most powerful military on the planet, but on September 11 everyone—President Bush, Vice President Cheney, Congress, governors, mayors, legislators, the military—were getting their information about the terrorist attacks from the same sources as the public: the television and radio news media.

The State had a contingency plan that I would be discussing later that morning with the generals and my Cabinet. I didn't need a plan, however, to know that taking steps to assure the public they were safe was foremost.

"General, I want you to deploy our guardsmen to secure every airport and harbor we have in this state."

"Sir, I've already notified our Quick Response Team—as soon as they're ready I'll deploy them immediately."

"How will they be dressed and equipped?"

"For this kind of crisis they'll be wearing combat gear and Kevlar vests and helmets, and they'll be carrying M16s."

"General, no loaded weapons—have them use empty clips and keep the loaded clips in their belts. The last thing we need is a nervous guardsman accidentally firing a shot."

"In emergencies like this, we take that precaution as a matter of course. They are a well-trained unit, sir."

"Yes, I know." But the thought of 50 or so guardsmen at the airport, dressed in combat gear, armed with automatic weapons, reminded me of my 1989 visit to Israel, where the ubiquitous presence of Israeli soldiers armed with submachine guns at Tel Aviv's Ben Gurion Airport unsettled me rather than making me feel more secure.

A few minutes later, Agena called again.

"Sir, the president has activated our Air Guard, and Admiral Blair has ordered the Air Force to take command."

By law, the governor is the commander in chief of the National Guard unless it is activated by the president. Under the circumstances, I wasn't surprised. "How many F-15s do we have in the air?" I replied.

"Our normal practice is to have at least two armed and ready to go around the clock. But right now we have four ready to go, and we've put the entire unit on alert."

"Good," I replied, confident that our Air Guard, which had been consistently ranked as one of the best in the nation, was more than up to the task. "Who's in command?"

"Lieutenant General Lanny Trapp is acting commander of the Pacific Air Force Command [the commander, General William Begert, was in Alaska]. Brigadier General Albert Richards, [commander of the Hawai'i Air National Guard] is assisting. They're in the process of ordering all international civilian flights from Asia to the Mainland to either turn back or divert to land in Hawai'i."

"How many planes are we talking about?"

"Between 27 and 30; we don't have a firm count right now."

"Damn, most of those planes are probably the big 747s; only HIA [Honolulu International Airport] and Kona have runways long enough for 747s," I replied, worried that some of the big planes could be ordered to land on Maui or Kaua'i.

"Sir, the planes will not be permitted to land at HIA; they'll be diverted to the Neighbor Islands. The 747s will either have to turn back or land at Kona. HIA is only a few miles away from Pearl Harbor and downtown Honolulu—it's too much of a risk to allow them near HIA."

"And if the pilots don't comply?"

"An F-15 will be escorting each civilian plane; if the pilots don't follow orders and veer away, our F-15s may be ordered to shoot them down."

"Shoot them down?" I asked incredulously. "My God, each of those planes must be carrying hundreds of passengers—who will give the order to do it?"

"Well, sir, the 'command kill' [that's what Agena called it] was authorized by the president down to the Secretary of Defense and then to the commander in chief of the Pacific Command, Admiral [Dennis] Blair."

I was horrified by the thought of our Air Guard pilots shooting down a commercial airliner carrying hundreds of innocent civilians. I asked my staff to contact Blair immediately. As the commander in chief of the U.S. Pacific Command, Blair commanded all American military forces in the Pacific and Asia. He was one of four commanders in chief I had worked with during my two terms. Like the others he was part of the impressive new breed of post-Vietnam War military officers. Vicky and I had become friends with Blair and his wife, Diane, and I was particularly impressed with how easily he interacted with State officials and local community leaders.

"Hi, Ben. I hope you didn't mind my borrowing a few of your F-15s," Blair said with a chuckle.

"No problem," I replied, trying to sound cool myself. "Denny, I've been told that our Air Guard pilots could be ordered to shoot down any commercial airliner that does not comply...."

"Well, I don't think that will happen, but, if it did, it would be the last resort," he interrupted me, sounding more serious. "The Secretary of Defense has ordered me not to allow any civilian plane or commercial airliner from Asia to land on the Mainland. And so we're informing them to either turn back or land at designated airports in Hawai'i."

"Well, I'm a little worried. I assume many of the pilots of those planes are foreigners who probably don't know what's happening and may be reluctant to comply. Who is handling this?" I asked.

"Well, Lanny Trapp is the acting commander of the Pacific Air Force Command but Tom Wascow is the director of operations, Pacific Air Forces. He's been designated the area air defense commander for the Hawai'i Air Defense Region and he's on top of it. I'll have him call you to explain what's going on." A few minutes later, the general called.

"Governor, Tom Wascow here. Admiral Blair asked me to call you."

"Yes, General, thanks for calling. [Wascow was a lieutenant general.] I'm very concerned about the fact that our Air Guard may be ordered to shoot down commercial airliners—can you explain the procedures on this?"

"Yes, the order came down the chain of command—from the president to the secretary of defense to Admiral Blair and finally to me. The big problem right now is we are still trying to verify the identities of the pilots. Until we do, if they don't obey our orders—then we have to take steps to protect our civilian and military people here and on the Mainland from a possible attack. There are maneuvers that the F-15s can try to force the planes to land. But if they veer off we may have no choice but to shoot them down."

"Who has the final say on this?"

"Well, if there is time, I'll clear it with Admiral Blair and he'll clear with the secretary of defense, who will clear it with the president. Once cleared, I'll have the responsibility to give the order. If there is no time—it will be my call."

"How are you keeping track of all of this?"

"I have a lieutenant colonel at the Military Intelligence Center at Schofield closely monitoring all of the incoming aircraft."

"A lieutenant colonel?"

"He's a combat veteran, a very experienced and highly competent pilot. He's one of my best."

The general was cool, very professional and assuring. But the thought of our Air Guard shooting down a commercial plane carrying hundreds of innocent civilians filled me with anxiety.

Around noon, Trapp and Richards briefed me and selected Cabinet members and legislative leaders at my office. They repeated what Wascow had told me and informed us that they were still verifying the identities of the pilots of the planes; those who were confirmed would be allowed to land their planes at HIA. Later that afternoon, I learned that six Japan Airlines planes had returned to Japan, while 21 other international airliners had landed safely at various airports in Hawai'i. Before this, at 9 a.m., I held a live, televised press conference at the State Capitol.

Jackie Kido, my director of communications, and Kim Murakawa had put together a memorandum of talking points. When I read it, I told Kido to take out words like "horrified," which, of course, was exactly how I felt when I first watched the television news, but I was concerned that such words would suggest weakness to the statewide audience and news media. I may have overreacted on my choice of words, but perception is reality in politics, and it was important for me to show resolve and confidence.

The press conference went well enough. I gave a short statement explaining the security measures we had taken, what we were doing to follow up and how much we knew about the attacks, and then I fielded questions from the news media. Although most of the media was aware that civilian airplanes were being ordered to turn back or land in Hawai'i, I did not disclose, nor did our incurious reporters ask, about the possibility that a plane could be shot down.

The order grounding all civilian aircraft had been issued by Secretary of Transportation Norman Mineta. Mineta, a Democrat, had been a trailblazer and role model for young Asian-American politicians. He was the first Asian American to serve as mayor of San Jose and was later elected to the U.S. House of Representatives, where he served with distinction for 20 years before resigning in 1995 to go into the private sector. In 2000, he was appointed Secretary of Commerce by President Bill Clinton. In 2001, President Bush appointed him to serve as Secretary of Transportation. Mineta was the only Democrat in the Bush administration—a measure of the respect he had earned on both sides of the aisle.

Later that day, Mineta made personal calls to inform the states' governors about his decision to shut down all civilian flights. I was one of those Mineta called. I appreciated the phone call, hoping to be briefed in greater detail about the grounding of all civilian aircraft. It turned out to be more of a courtesy call than anything else.

"Ben, we're asking all of the governors to shut down their airports."

"Norm, why should I agree to shut down our airports?" I asked, realizing immediately that I could have phrased the question less bluntly.

He seemed to struggle for an answer. "For patriotism!" he finally blurted out, apparently annoyed and sounding as if I had asked the dumbest question he had ever heard.

For patriotism? I had a high regard for Mineta and had expected a more illuminating response than that. The federal government had the authority to ground commercial civilian aircraft and take control of the runways, but the airport facilities belonged to the State, and State cooperation was needed to shut down the facilities. The State airports included restaurants, gift shops and car-rental companies, and were filled with hundreds of workers and stranded passengers who had already checked out of their hotels. I was not inclined to do something just because the federal government ordered it. All I wanted was some specifics as to why the airport should be shut down, and for how long, so we could figure out what to do and what was needed. If information was available and it was appropriate to release it, the public was entitled to know. Uncertainty fuels fear, and there was a great deal of uncertainty among the public.

Mineta's sharp retort suggested that even the federal government didn't know much more than the general public. He wanted the airports closed. Period. I wasn't satisfied with his answer, but, under the circumstances, I conceded. The September 11 attacks had caught our federal government flatfooted—a lapse that would later be exposed as America's biggest intelligence failure since Pearl Harbor.

In the following days we were briefed on the potential of bioterrorism, the use of chemical toxins or deadly infectious viruses. Along with other elected officials, I had been briefed on this subject previously, but the probability of such an attack in Hawai'i had seemed so remote that I'd never paid much attention to it until September 11.

Hawai'i was as well prepared as any other state for a potential biological or chemical attack by terrorists. In 1997, funded by federal grants, the State, counties and federal government had started working jointly to develop contingency plans for acts of terrorism. But the preparation was a work in progress. What had been developed so far was a plan that called for a coordinated response, with State, counties, federal agencies, private hospitals and pharmacies working together. That could be done relatively easily, but our isolation left us with limited health resources and hospital capacity. Having the plan on paper was one thing; carrying it out successfully was problematic.

Various scenarios ran through my mind. One frightening thought was the 1995 sarin gas attack in Toyko, when, in five coordinated attacks, members of a Japanese radical group released sarin gas on several lines of the Tokyo Metro, killing 12 people, severely injuring 50 and causing temporary vision problems to nearly a thousand others. (Sarin was one of the gases used by the Nazis to execute Jews during the Holocaust.)

During the 1991 Persian Gulf War, our military intelligence suspected that the Iraqi dictator Saddam Hussein had developed enough anthrax, along with a new, vaccine-resistant smallpox virus, to kill every person in the world. Consequently, vaccinations against anthrax and smallpox were produced and given to approximately 500,000 U.S. troops. Perhaps because the threat had been viewed mainly as a military one, little was done to assure the vaccines would be available to the U.S. civilian population. The day after September 11, I was told that the available supply of anthrax vaccine for civilians was enough to cover only a fraction of the population; the availability of a vaccine for smallpox—a disease that had been considered eradicated in U.S. since the 1970s—was virtually nil.

Both anthrax and smallpox viruses posed threats of death or serious injury to those who were infected. If inhaled, anthrax was almost certain to cause death. Skin contact could cause either death or injury.

There is no known cure for smallpox; vaccination is the only prevention. By 1900 widespread vaccinations had eradicated smallpox in the United States. By the late 1970s, smallpox had been eradicated throughout the world. In 1972 mandatory smallpox vaccination for American schoolchildren was discontinued. Thus, on September 11, 2001, there were at least three generations of American citizens who had not been vaccinated against either anthrax or smallpox.

During the first week of October, a number of cases of anthrax were reported in Florida, New York, Nevada and Washington, D.C. In most of the cases, the suspected anthrax was discovered in the mail. Not surprisingly, many of the anthrax reports turned out to be false alarms. But in the months that followed, news reports revealed that anthrax had caused the deaths of five people; 17 victims survived but had been physically injured or impaired.

Within two weeks, Hawai'i began getting its share of anthrax scares. One day, Mo Bright, one of our front office receptionists, opened a letter and found it filled with a white powder. Bright, clearly worried, quickly notified Jackie Kido, who called 911 for the Honolulu Fire Department's hazardous materials (HAZMAT) unit. While the HAZMAT team, who in their protective suits resembled astronauts, combed the entire floor for traces of anthrax, Bright, a retired State worker and grandmother who had come out of retirement to work in my office, was kept isolated in the office for several hours (Jackie Kido stayed to comfort her, putting herself at risk). At the same time, the third, fourth and fifth floors of the State Capitol were evacuated and sealed off as the HAZMAT team did its work. Tests by the Navy's laboratory at Pearl Harbor indicated that the white powder was not anthrax but a harmless look-alike sent by some prankster. In addition to the emotional toll it took on Bright and the other office workers, the false alarm had shut down the State Capitol for nearly four hours.

Starting in mid-October, there was a flood of anthrax reports that kept the city's HAZMAT team, police, State health department and postal authorities stretched to the limit.

"It's gotten ridiculous," Felice Broglio, a U.S. Postal Service spokeswoman, told the news media. "People need to think about why they might be a target. No one is out to get the people of Hawai'i."

"The situation is getting out of hand, and we need to apply some common sense," said Bruce Anderson, State health director.

The worst anthrax scare came on October 23, when the city's HAZMAT team responded to a call from an architect's office claiming that an employee had received a letter in an envelope that had an "unusual texture." HAZMAT, using newly purchased test devices, reported that the suspected substance on the envelope tested positive for anthrax.

Mayor Jeremy Harris immediately sent an email to City employees instructing them not to open any mail. Word of Harris' email spread quickly, and City employees not only stopped opening the mail, many stopped working, effectively shutting down the City government. A shutdown and evacuation of the architect's office and nearby buildings was ordered. Hundreds of office workers could be seen milling about in the streets. Several thoroughfares running through the city were closed.

Inevitably, the news media quickly learned about the HAZMAT test findings and covered the incident on live television. As I watched the live televised news from my office, I saw hundreds of people gathered in the streets and Harris, holding a cell phone to his ear, standing near the HAZMAT team. "There's Harris making like he's Rudy Giuliani," Nekoba chuckled.

"Yeah, he could use some good publicity," I replied. A few days earlier, the newspapers had run stories about the State Campaign Spending Commission's investigation of Harris' campaign fundraising.

The incident turned out to be a false alarm. The only reliable, certified laboratory to test for anthrax in Hawai'i was the Navy's facility at Pearl Harbor—a fact of which Harris and the other mayors were well aware. Tests by the Navy laboratory of the suspicious-looking substance were negative—contradicting the two positive findings for anthrax by the city's uncertified test equipment.

In his eagerness to be out front, Harris had ignored the protocol set up by the joint terrorism committee: Suspected anthrax findings were to be sent to the Navy laboratory for testing. Instead, Harris had approved HAZMAT's use of newly purchased but uncertified, unreliable test devices from a private vendor. For more than four hours, the anthrax false alarm disrupted workers, caused a massive traffic jam and virtually shut down Honolulu's financial district.

Harris' actions left me exasperated. There were more than a dozen reports of anthrax in Hawai'i, all of them false alarms. People were edgy, and it was up to State and county leaders to keep them calm.

"Every time there is an anthrax report, every time there is a false alarm—everything comes to a screeching halt. We cannot continue to live like this," I said, venting my frustrations as I thought about what lay ahead for us.

"And you're going to support the guy for governor?" Nekoba teased.

"Let's not get into that," I replied. "It's a long story."

Clearly, terrorists did not need to hijack a 747 to poison a city's air quality or water supply with chemical toxins or deadly viruses. But the reality was that neither the states nor the counties had the resources to deal effectively with the myriad of complicated problems involved in fighting terrorism. The federal government would have to provide the resources and take the lead.

With the American people aroused, angry and determined to fight back, President Bush was handed an opportunity most political leaders dream of but rarely get—the chance to unify the people under a common cause.

I had first met Bush while he was serving his final term as governor of Texas. Once, when I was attending a Western Governors Association conference hosted by Bush in San Antonio, I was the only governor who had not brought his or her spouse (Lorraine and I were separated at the time). On the way to a tour of the Alamo, Bush noticed I was sitting alone in the back of the bus. He left his seat in the front next to his wife, Laura, and came over and sat next to me, keeping me company for the remainder of the trip. With an impish look, he started talking to me in Spanish. He knew, of course, that I was not a Hispanic ("Chicano" was the term of choice back then), but he wanted to show off a bit. He spoke Spanish, I couldn't. We had a big laugh about it. His coming over to keep me company was a nice gesture.

In the aftermath of September 11, I looked to him for leadership. He was our president, and I wanted him to succeed in leading our country out of the crisis. His address to a joint session of Congress will probably be seen as the highlight of his otherwise troubled presidency. He was firm, clear and inspirational; his speech appealed strongly to the people's sense of patriotism and rallied the nation. I was proud of him. (I felt empathy for Bush as he struggled with the post-invasion consequences of the 2003 Iraq War but, by 2004, I concluded that he was in over his head.)

Leadership was on my mind at the time. The 2001 legislative session had been a good one for our administration, but the struggle over hot issues such as civil service reform, OHA and the ceded lands, Bishop Estate and the statewide teacher-University faculty strike had taken a toll on me. Emotionally and physically, I felt drained. I was getting only three to four hours of sleep a night. I was frustrated and tired of dealing with Democratic legislators who seemed to stand for little except their reelections. The year 2002 was my 28th and final year in politics—I felt a real temptation to coast, to take a trip, some goodwill tour to a foreign country (I did—to Vietnam). Vicky mentioned that I was grumpy. One thing for sure, I needed a vacation.

But everything changed on September 11. Knowing that people looked to me for answers, I felt a sense of urgency to respond, to lead. My adrenalin was running high again; the fire inside me that had kept me going in politics for 27 years was burning stronger than ever.

We had our work cut out for us.

Tourism Hits the Skids

The three-day air travel shutdown had brought the airline industry to its knees. Experts estimated that 4,500 civilian planes were grounded. Throughout the nation, millions of passengers were either stranded or had had their flights cancelled. Thousands of airline employees were laid off. The shutdown had a similar ripple effect on workers in related industries. After the three-day ban was lifted, it would take nearly a year before the volume of air travel reached pre-September 11 levels and, under the new, stringent security measures imposed by the federal government, air travel would never be the same.

The nation's economy—which had already shown signs of a downturn before the September 11 attacks—was slipping into the throes of an economic recession. Not surprisingly, the states in which tourism was a big part of the economy were hit hardest. For Hawai'i, which relies on airlines for about 99 percent of its tourist and resident travel, the shutdown was devastating.

Within several weeks of the attacks, the streets of Waikīkī looked deserted as thousands of potential tourists cancelled hotel reservations and the number of visitors dropped sharply. Consequently, thousands of workers in the hotels, airlines and other tourism-related businesses were either laid off or had their work hours reduced. On tiny Lāna'i, for example, 400 of the island's 1,100 tourism workers were laid off. By the end of September applications for unemployment benefits had doubled, and the State employment office was swamped with applications from people looking for jobs. With commercial air travel at an all-time low, the state's airport vendors were hit particularly hard; their business volumes had dropped precipitously.

Hawai'i's economy was tanking. I was back at square one—it was 1994 all over again.

A crisis often brings out the best and worst in people. In the days following September 11, there would be ample proof of this truism.

On September 18, I called for a meeting of leaders from business, labor unions, community organizations and legislators of both parties. The response was heartwarming. Everyone pledged to work together to develop an economic stimulus plan and find ways to help the unemployed and comfort those who needed spiritual help. Democratic legislative leaders pledged their support, and Minority Leader Galen Fox, speaking for House Republicans, was earnest about setting aside partisan politics to work with my administration and the private sector.

The response of Hawai'i's people, fueled by an upsurge of patriotism and compassion, inspired me. By the afternoon of September 11, people were already standing in long lines outside blood banks waiting patiently to donate their blood. Stores ran out of American flags as the public bought them up, and in the following weeks, community groups, churches, charitable organizations as well as individual citizens volunteered their services to help. *This must have been the way it was when Pearl Harbor was attacked in 1941*, I thought.

I am not a religious person. Born and baptized a Catholic, I left the Church long ago. But I realized that many looked to their churches for comfort and solace. I called on Dan Chun, the reverend from First Presbyterian Church, which Vicky attended regularly, and asked if he would meet with other religious leaders to coordinate their efforts with the State to help those who had lost their jobs or were otherwise in need of spiritual support. Within a week, they had organized an ad hoc group and developed a plan to hold a statewide interdenominational memorial service for the victims and provide counseling services and spiritual replenishment to people in need of help and comfort.

Non-profits stepped forward. I called on Susan Doyle, head of the YWCA, to organize the non-profits as Dan Chun had done with the churches to provide volunteer services to people with emotional or mental problems and those suffering from post-September 11 depression. The Hawai'i Food Bank, a statewide non-profit organization, was typical. Inundated with donations of food from the public, businesses, unions and schools, the food bank coordinated its efforts with the State, the county and churches to help unemployed workers and their families on every island.

The business community came up with innovative ideas to help the victims and promote Hawai'i tourism simultaneously. The most unique came from the tourist industry: Hawaiian Airlines pledged to reserve two airliners to transport 1,200 New York firefighters, police and rescue personnel or their surviving families to Hawai'i free of charge for a week's vacation with gifts, a lū'au and free hotel rooms provided by various hotels in Waikīkī. The plan was bold and generous and reflected the compassion and empathy felt by Hawai'i's people for their fellow Americans in New York—and the effort was given considerable coverage by the national television networks and by major newspapers such as the *New York Times*.

It was a good time to be governor.

In November, I traveled to New York to attend a travel conference and present New York City Mayor Rudy Giuliani with gifts from the people of Hawai'i. Among the gifts were a check for $125,000 from the Hawai'i Visitors and Convention Bureau and paper lei with messages and prayers strung by schoolchildren—including one strung with 1,000 one-dollar bills. (As I presented Giuliani with the lei, he turned to an aide and joked, "I don't know if I should be photographed accepting this much cash.") A hula hālau (dance troupe) traveled with us and performed for students at several elementary schools. Americans from every state were sending help to New York, but the response of Hawai'i's people was very special.

Several weeks later, Vicky and I greeted the first contingent of New Yorkers—600 of them—widows, mothers and fathers whose sons had been killed at the towers; firefighters; rescue personnel and police officers who had survived the attacks. Selected by Mayor Giuliani, they were flown to Hawai'i on the two specially designated Hawaiian Air planes and feted by the hotels and businesses at the lū'au given in their honor at the Ko Olina resort. I met a mother and her pregnant daughter-in-law who had both been widowed when their firefighter husbands perished in one of the towers. "My husband was a fire captain and our son had just joined his unit," the older woman, tears welling in her eyes, told me. Many New Yorkers came up to me to express their appreciation. We were deeply moved by their emotional expressions of thanks. A lighter moment came when a Bermuda shorts-clad NYPD officer happily told me, "Governor, if one of our guys ever gives you a ticket in New York—you just tell him you're from Hawai'i, he'll take care of it." It was an experience, I thought, that our fellow Americans from New York would never forget. And neither would we.

Focus on the Economy

"In Chinese, the word 'crisis' is composed of two characters. One represents danger and the other represents opportunity," President John F. Kennedy once said. Indeed, I thought the September 11 crisis had presented us with an opportunity to make life better, to do good things for which, in ordinary times, the necessary political environment would be lacking.

"Nothing big ever got done by people who think small," I would say to legislative leaders, and I repeated the line in my 2002 State of the State Address. With that thought in mind, in mid-October I submitted our economic stimulus plan to a special session of the State Legislature.

The plan's objectives revealed the limitations of a tourism-dominated economy: Our main options were to boost tourism and encourage construction. The plan included a request for a $1 billion CIP (capital improvement program) appropriation, tax breaks totaling $76 million and a $10 million emergency appropriation to market tourism. Among the capital projects were allocations for the public schools and the University of Hawai'i, a new prison, a new campus in Kapolei for the UH-West O'ahu campus, the new John A. Burns School of Medicine (JABSOM) complex and the aquarium in Kaka'ako.

Given the Senate's earlier proposal to repeal tax cuts to pay for State employee pay raises, I knew that legislative approval of our proposed tax breaks was problematic (I would later withdraw the proposal). But I had high hopes that our request for the CIP appropriation would be approved. I knew that the legislators would struggle over approving our bigger projects, but I informed them that I was open to their substituting projects of their own or negotiating a compromise. The interest rates on bonds were favorable and the new construction would create jobs and improve the state's aging infrastructure.

In 1997, the Legislature reluctantly approved our request for the billion-dollar CIP appropriation (roughly twice the amount of the annual request). By 2002, we had already built a record number of new schools (eventually 16 would be built), as well as nearly 1,000 new classrooms and new facilities on every campus of the UH system.

But still, it wasn't enough to bring the public schools and the University up to speed. Decades of under-funding had resulted in a crisis of repair and maintenance and a failure to build new facilities or renovate old ones to keep up with the growth in demand for services. In 2001, the University of Hawai'i had a repair and maintenance backlog of more than $200 million. Combined with the DOE repair and maintenance backlog of about $640 million, it should have been clear to everyone that trying to reduce it without significantly increasing the CIP budget was like walking on a treadmill. Not surprisingly, as Hawai'i's population grew, overcrowding became a major problem in our public schools. Unlike an individual family, whose costs for repair and maintenance get smaller as children become adults, and which spends less as mortgages are paid off, the State government gets bigger and more costly as the population increases.

The irony was that this situation had accrued during times when the economy was growing and there were surpluses, when constitutionally required tax rebates were paid to taxpayers. These things happen because long-term thinking is not politically rewarding. "The future doesn't vote," UH professor and futurist Jim Dator once wrote. Indeed, politicians are more apt to address problems that catch the public's eye or are currently hot; simply put, long-term thinking is not a good vote getter because most voters are not long-term thinkers.

It would take the equivalent of a Marshall Plan to make a significant improvement in the state's aging infrastructure. (Sadly, most younger legislators apparently did not know about the Marshall Plan's historical role in rebuilding post-World War II Europe.)

In my September 18 meeting with legislative leaders, I briefed them on our ideas for our economic stimulus plan and asked them to work with us or develop their own ideas to shore up the economy. Speaker Calvin Say joined me, telling the news media, "We have to do something out of the box." Senate Leader Colleen Hanabusa pledged, "We have a commitment that something be done."

Their remarks buoyed my spirits, but when we announced the details of our economic stimulus plan, the legislators were skeptical.

The Legislature, of course, is a separate and equal branch of government. Its duty is to check the executive branch. The problem was that it offered much criticism but no viable alternatives. What really irked me was that the same legislative leaders who shamelessly pandered to the public-worker unions' demands for pay raises—and didn't bat an eyelash when it came to disbursing pork-barrel money to private interests—were now getting religious about State spending.

"A billion dollars in bonds comes up to about $50 million a year in debt service," Say said. He had a point, but his attitude said much about why the State government's capital infrastructure had been so neglected; inaction only meant the problem would get worse. As a former finance committee chairman, Say knew that a dollar in debt service is paid off over 20 years, whereas a dollar in pay raises carries over literally indefinitely and has a greater impact on State finances. Of course, he also knew that it was politically incorrect to publicly mention such differences.

Senate President Bunda complained to news reporters: "Is this really diversifying the economy? It is a billion dollars over and above what is already allocated. The question is, Did he go overboard?"

Bunda missed the point. We were trying to create jobs. The fastest way to do it was to increase spending for construction to improve the sorry state of our public schools and University campuses. Our billion-dollar CIP proposal was not a new idea. In fact, Hawai'i's four mayors were trying to expand their CIP spending for the same reasons—as was the Bush administration and every state in the union.

As for the tourist industry, Bunda told reporters if the State was to aid the tourist industry, it would be better off if we could negotiate with the airlines on their fares and the hotels about their room rates. In fact, he suggested that "perhaps the State could buy a large amount of airline tickets to give to travel agents so they can bring in tourists."

I had a tough time swallowing that one. I wondered whether Bunda was just being facetious or had gotten his ticket-buying idea from Rod Tam, his inept, incompetent political ally, whom he had rewarded with the chairmanship of the important Senate Economic Development Committee. "That idea must have come right off the top of Tam's head," I told a staff member. (Bunda never publicly mentioned the ticket-buying scheme again.)

Bunda and Say weren't the only ones who got religion about State spending. According to the *Star-Bulletin*, Brian Taniguchi, chairman of the Senate Ways and Means Committee, said that I should spend the $500 million of CIP appropriations still on the books before asking for an extra $1 billion. Taniguchi's point was that the State bureaucracy could not process a billion-dollar CIP appropriation in a timely fashion.

His remarks revealed a misunderstanding of the process. Actually, I had released a good part of the 1997 $1 billion CIP appropriation for projects that the DOE and the University had deemed important. The results spoke for themselves: The record number of new schools, the new classrooms and facilities built on every UH campus, and the thousands of jobs this construction had created had helped bring about the economic recovery in late 1998.

Moreover, as a matter of sound fiscal practice, governors release the funding in increments; first for planning and design and then, when timely, for construction—much the way an ordinary citizen who is building a new home pays his contractor.

Timing is important. The Legislature is a part-time body and is in session for about four months. The governor cannot spend funds for any capital facility unless there is a specific appropriation approved by the Legislature. Because an appropriation cannot be approved until the State Budget Bill is passed in the final days of the session, nearly a year could pass before the governor is authorized to release funds for the planning and design of a specific project.

I wondered how many of the young legislators really understood the CIP process. But it did not matter. Taniguchi was being a bit disingenuous. He wanted the $500 million released because it included millions in legislative pork-barrel capital-improvement appropriations. As a former legislator I understood why many legislators placed a great deal of importance on their pet pork-barrel projects for their reelection campaigns (I was among a minority of legislators who did not). I was told that some of the Democratic legislators had complained about my restricting or vetoing their pork.

"These guys never quit," I replied tersely. "The damned economy is tanking, people are losing their jobs and they worry about their pork."

Actually, I had no problem releasing pork-barrel appropriations if the sponsoring legislator could show me that the State benefited in some way. In fact, some legislators would meet with me privately and offer good reasons why I should release their pork, which, more often than not, I did. Others did not bother because their pork was intended to benefit private special interests or ranked low in priority by the State departments.

Taniguchi's selective parsimony did not apply to his pet projects. For example, he had included an $8 million appropriation in the State budget to bail out the Japanese Cultural Center of Hawai'i (JCCH), which had suffered an operating loss in that amount. Several Japanese-American businessmen called me to say that they were embarrassed by Taniguchi's action, that the JCCH had not asked for the appropriation, and that the JCCH members would straighten out things themselves. They urged me to veto the $8 million, which I did. Subsequently, a group of young AJA businessmen, led by Island Insurance CEO Colbert Matsumoto, reorganized the JCCH and paid off the debt without State or county assistance.

Another example was former Speaker Joe Souki's $3 million pork for a new bridge across the Ala Wai Canal. If built, the bridge would mainly benefit Outrigger Hotels & Resorts' new shopping-mall development in Waikīkī. It was no secret that Souki was very close to Outrigger executives. If Souki wanted to help Outrigger, that was his business—but he would have to persuade me that it was in the public's interest also for the State to spend millions (the $3 million was only for planning and design) to build a bridge that would benefit mainly a private development. He didn't bother, and I vetoed the appropriation. (One thing I liked about Souki: He never used affordability as an excuse to oppose any CIP appropriation.)

The hidden message in Taniguchi's remarks was that the chances my request for a $1 billion CIP funding would improve if I released pork-barrel funding. I was open to considering each pork-barrel appropriation on its merits, but I was not willing to horse-trade just to get the $1 billion appropriation. At any given time, there are hundreds of millions of pork-barrel and low-priority appropriations on the books; if a governor released every appropriation passed by the Legislature it would bankrupt the State government.

Marketing Muscle

Meanwhile, I had appointed three businessmen—Walter Dods, chairman and CEO of BancWest; Peter Schall, Hilton Hawaiian Village vice president; and Tony Vericella, Hawai'i Visitors and Convention Bureau chief executive—to

~~develop an emergency tourism-promotion strategy.~~

After working literally around the clock for days, the weary trio briefed me on their proposed marketing plan. The plan would be financed by a $20 million package. Visitor attractions would put up $5 million, with another $5 million coming from hotels and other tourism-related businesses and a $10 million matching grant for advertising being provided by the State.

"For example," Dods explained, "we are working on things the visitors can do for free. We're asking the hotels to come up with package discounts, discounted hotel rates, free tickets to attractions such as the Bishop Museum and Contemporary Arts Center, and we are also looking at the idea of 'Hawaiian dollars' that tourists can spend in participating hotels and restaurants. So far, we've had tremendous cooperation from the industry—many remember and don't want a repeat of how the industry was devastated by the 1991 Gulf War."

Dods continued: "We've put together an entire marketing plan which includes an intense outreach effort. We want you and Governors Ariyoshi and Waihee to head a Hawai'i delegation to Japan, where we will use our connections for all of you to meet with Prime Minister Koizumi and other Japanese political leaders. We also want you to head a Hawai'i delegation to New York to meet with Mayor Giuliani and address the international conference of travel companies that will be held there."

"What about our advertising campaign?" I asked. "It seems to me that Hawai'i has a real edge—we're isolated and safer than the Mainland states. Look at the WTO [World Trade Organization] disaster in Seattle in 1999. Compare that to the ADB [Asian Development Bank] conference we had here in May [2001]. The WTO conference was a fiasco. It attracted more than 50,000 people from all over the world who opposed the WTO policies—and they brought Seattle virtually to its knees as demonstrations erupted into riots and violence. The ADB is just as controversial, and every one of its past conferences has been disrupted by demonstrators—except the one here in May. ADB President Tadao Chino told me that their Hawai'i conference was the "most peaceful and successful in the ADB's history."

(Hawai'i, by the way, was the first choice of the selection committee for the 1999 WTO meeting. San Diego was ranked second, but Seattle was chosen, for understandable political reasons. According to one source, Washington's U.S. Sen. Slade Gordon was one of 10 Republicans who voted "not guilty" in President Clinton's impeachment trial before the U.S. Senate, which acquitted him by a 55-45 vote. The WTO was understood to be Clinton's way of saying "thanks.")

"Yes, Hawai'i is a pretty safe place," Dods replied. "But we don't think our advertising should specifically use words like "safe" or "secure" because we may be inviting trouble—terrorists or some nut may want to prove otherwise. And just one act of terrorism will hurt our tourist industry—possibly for years."

"Governor," Vericella interjected, "we don't ignore the safety issue in our advertising—instead we send that message subtly." He began placing storyboards on an easel, pointing to one or another as he spoke.

"There are several themes running through our plan. For example, we use the title "Hawai'i Now More Than Ever." Keywords like 'serenity' and phrases such as 'replenish the spirit' all speak to Hawai'i's strengths as a tourist destination. Our beautiful environment, the warmth of our people, the aloha spirit. And these themes, the words and phrases we use in our ads, also suggest strongly that Hawai'i is a safe place for tourists to visit. We know from past experience that these themes work for us.

"Now, advertising itself will not do the job. To help us market Hawai'i we intend to fly in at our expense the leaders of the major travel companies, American and foreign. We'll host them, show them what we've planned and work out agreements with them to market Hawai'i. These people know the industry very well, and they understand how to sell Hawai'i as a safe destination to their clients."

I was impressed. I accepted the plan with only a few minor changes. On September 28, we presented the plan at a public hearing before the Senate Tourism Committee, which was chaired by Donna Kim, a State senator representing the Kalihi area.

Kim had grown up in Kalihi and graduated from Farrington six or seven years after I did. She was a cheerleader—a testament to her Filipino-Korean good looks. She was bright, graduating magna cum laude from Washington State University. A veteran of the City Council and the Legislature, she had developed a reputation for being tough—and vindictive.

Kim did not like what she saw. "We saw four themes, and I don't see anyone jumping up and down," she said flippantly after listening to Dods and Vericella present our tourism marketing plan. "We have to solve the issue of safety and fear. Advertising is not going to take away the fear factor."

Watching the hearing on the State Capitol television channel, I thought, *Good enough, Dragon Lady* (my moniker for her), *but what's your proposal?*

"The State should subsidize air marshals for all flights to and from Hawai'i and hire more security personnel to speed up checking in and out at the airports," she said, lecturing Dods and Vericella. "And why aren't we using 'patriotism' as a theme?"

Dods and Vericella kept their cool, and during the intense discussion it became pretty clear that Kim hadn't done her homework. No specifics, no cost estimates, no discussion of the fact that air marshals were exclusively under the jurisdiction of the federal government and that at that very moment Congress was struggling in its debate over the feasibility of deploying air marshals on the thousands of commercial aircrafts that carry millions of passengers every day.

As for a patriotism theme, Vericella pointed out that theme was being used by nearly every state on the Mainland and it would be a mistake for Hawai'i to use its limited dollars to follow suit. Apparently, Vericella had rubbed her the wrong way and, as I would learn later, she did not forget it.

Disagreeing with the plan was one thing, but Kim showed no respect, no appreciation for the hard work the three business leaders had put into developing the State's economic stimulus plan. Why would any sane citizens volunteer their services if they were disrespected like that?

"Nearly three weeks have passed since 9-11, and they don't have a clue on what to do about the economy," I said to my staff, "just criticism, sniping. Talk is cheap. If they don't like our proposals then what are their alternatives?"

On October 11, Bush ordered air strikes against terrorists in Afghanistan, fueling speculation about the impact increasing hostilities would have on Hawai'i's tourism industry. The grim memory of Waikīkī's nearly deserted streets during the Gulf War came to mind. After consulting with Bunda, Say and other legislative leaders, we agreed that a Special Session of the Legislature should be held. I issued a proclamation scheduling the opening of a five-day session on October 22.

On October 22, the Democrats submitted a package of 17 bills, which included some of our proposals and a bill that would expand the governor's emergency powers to suspend or waive State leases, rents and fees to help airport concessions and vendors who were struggling to stay in business.

The Republicans also submitted bills. One of their bills proposed repealing the 4-percent general excise tax on food. Politically, the bill played well with the public, but every legislator knew that it wasn't realistic; the tax brought in more than $100 million annually—between 25 percent and 30 percent of it from non-residents. When Say announced that the House would not hear the bill, Galen Fox complained that Say's decision was eroding the post-9-11 spirit of bipartisanship. Fox was right, but the Republicans were partly to blame for introducing a bill that had no chance of passing and with which they had played politics in every year of my governorship. Say had made the right call. The post-9-11 spirit of bipartisanship was falling apart.

Excluded from the Democrats' package were my requests for a $1 billion CIP appropriation and funding for the proposed aquarium in Kaka'ako. Say and Bunda argued the State could not afford it and reduced the request to $100 million. Instead they hoped to spur construction by giving 4-percent tax credits for residential renovations or purchases up to $250,000 and new hotel construction. Instead of the $100 million for which I had asked to build the new campus for UH-West O'ahu, they put in $8 million for planning and design. Token funding for the new John A. Burns School of Medicine (JABSOM) complex in Kaka'ako was also included.

Overall, the Democrats' package had been agreed to by the Republicans except for one bill. "The emergency powers bill is essentially a blank check, and we won't sign off on that," said Fox, House Minority GOP leader.

By the third or fourth day, I extended the five-day special session on a day-to-day basis to fix bills that had fatal drafting errors or had not been very well thought out. For example, one bill provided for a 10-percent tax credit to developers whether or not they paid any taxes. That would have been a windfall to developers. I informed the legislative leaders that I would be forced to veto the bill unless it was changed to a non-refundable tax credit, which meant that developers would be entitled to refunds based on what they actually paid in annual taxes. The bill was amended and passed, and I signed it into law.

Ultimately, the special session boiled down to a raging controversy over the bill that would expand the governor's emergency powers. The bill had been authored by Colleen Hanabusa, apparently one of the few legislators who realized the urgency of fast-tracking job creation to replace the thousands of jobs that were lost after the 9-11 attacks.

The emergency powers bill was intended to authorize the governor to adjust State lease rents to provide financial relief to lessees whose businesses were failing and to waive procurement procedures for small contracts to create jobs. By State law, any construction contract over $25,000 could only be awarded by bid or under the request-for-proposal (RFP) procedure. Each method was time consuming. The law required that a call for bids or RFPs be advertised in a major newspaper for three consecutive weeks. Under post-9-11 circumstances, the law was an obstruction to fast-tracking job creation.

The Republicans had already announced their opposition to the bill. It didn't take long for Fred Hemmings to come up with another of his one-liners, mockingly calling the bill the "King Ben" bill. Hemmings had a propensity for using inflammatory words in place of reason. He had made a career out of accusing me, Ariyoshi, Waihee and other Democrats of everything from nepotism and cronyism to corruption. He called the proposed aquarium in Kaka'ako "a big fish tank" and dismissed a long-term-care proposal by an ad hoc committee comprised of respected citizens headed by Vicky as a "fraud" and "vickycare." Hemmings was not just any senator—he was the Republican Minority Leader. He wasn't interested in bipartisan cooperation—he was fishing for newspaper headlines.

It got to the point that whenever Hemmings mouthed off I thought about the day he came to see me for help with his proposed surfing restaurant idea in Waikīkī. "This guy will kiss your ass one day to get what he wants and try to kick it the next day for newspaper headlines—remember that," I told my staff.

The criticism, however, was not limited to the Republicans. Anthony Gill, a UHPA attorney and the son of long-time Democrat and former congressman and Lt. Gov. Tom Gill, issued a scathing letter.

"It [the bill] is astounding in hubris, insulting in its ignorance of American tradition, disproportionate in its remedy, and dumb in its conflation of the themes of natural disaster and the economy," Gill wrote, revealing his own hubris.

Gill's brother, Gary, was a member of my Cabinet. The Gills were unabashed liberal Democrats. In 1974, I had supported Tom Gill in his losing effort against

Ariyoshi in the Democratic gubernatorial primary. I was drawn to him in large part by his idealism. But over the years I concluded that one reason the acerbic Tom Gill was never elected governor was, in fact, the unyielding nature of his idealism.

I wondered whether I would have reacted as the younger Gill did had I not been the governor. The big difference, of course, was that I was more familiar than Gill or any other politicians with how badly people were hurting. Small businesses were struggling to stay alive, and I saw the desperation and fear in the eyes of those who ran the social programs that served the poor and the needy.

For crying out loud, I said to myself, *the bill doesn't waive the right to due process, the right to a jury trial—we're trying to provide relief to the vendors holding State leases who are on the verge of bankruptcy and trying to create construction jobs quickly by waiving an obsolete law that requires bids for any job over $25,000. When the revenue runs out people suffer—it's as simple as that. The guy doesn't have a clue,* I concluded. *He's had his head in the clouds too long with those elitists at UH.*

I was being unkind, and unnecessarily so. But Gill's letter revealed a major flaw in American liberalism: Too many are stuck in their fixation with rights and procedures at the cost of efficiency and common sense.

Gill wasn't the only critic from the public. Hanabusa told news reporters that she had been receiving angry letters, some again comparing me to Philippine dictator Ferdinand Marcos. I had the feeling that the residue of anger fomented against me during the strike in April was still festering among certain groups of people. I didn't mind the racist remarks during the strike, but after 9-11 they began to annoy me. I told my secretaries that if we received any racist calls or letters to let me know. I intended to respond personally.

As noted, Hanabusa was one of the few legislators who really understood how difficult it was to fast-track job creation under existing State law. She proposed some amendments that allowed for greater transparency and oversight and shepherded the bill through the Senate. The House accepted the amendments and I signed the bill into law.

In her first term as a senator, Hanabusa had emerged as a leader in the otherwise leaderless Senate. I disagreed, of course, with her role in organizing the opposition against the confirmation of Margery Bronster, but I had to respect that she had pulled it off. She was also instrumental in the passage of the new State health fund—the biggest civil-service reform in years. It was a remarkable show of leadership for a freshmen senator.

On November 2, the Legislature adjourned the special session. In a revealing admission of the Legislature's failure to "think outside of the box," as Say had pledged to do in mid-September, Rep. Joe Souki (D, Wailuku), Transportation Committee chairman and former House speaker, told the news media:

"It would have been better if the governor didn't call us back ... it raises the hopes of the public, but what do they expect 76 legislators to do in a week—solve all the problems of the economy?" he said. "I hope we don't become the scapegoat."

Harry Truman once denounced his Congress as "a do-nothing Congress." I couldn't say that about the Special Session of the Legislature because there were a few useful bills that were passed. But as I told news reporters, I was disappointed because "I had lobbed them an air ball that they could've hit out of the park—but they chose to bunt instead."

By law, the opening of the Regular Legislative Session is held on the third Wednesday of January—approximately three months away. We would have another crack at the Legislature then.

A few days before my final State of the State Address, a reporter queried several legislators on what I should cover. "As a statesman going out of office, he has certainly accumulated wisdom. He should say what we should be doing," Bunda replied, causing me to wonder where he had been for the seven years I was governor. Say quipped, "He should just say, 'Thank you for the opportunity of letting me be your governor for the past eight years.'

"You can propose all these new programs, but when the new administration comes in, everything is going to be scrapped," he added.

Curious remarks for someone who had preached a week after 9-11 that "we have to do something out of the box." Apparently, in the three months that had elapsed since Say made those remarks, he had been persuaded to hunker down and stay inside it. ❖

CHAPTER TWENTY-FOUR

A Year to Remember

Special Interests

O n January 22, 2002, I gave my eighth and last State of the State Address. I implored the legislators to think "big" in addressing the economic crisis brought on by the 9-11 attacks if they disagreed with our economic stimulus plan. I called on them to come up with alternatives. I cited the heroic examples of the New York firefighters, police officers and rescue personnel who had lost their lives in doing their jobs—"Do your job even if costs you your job...." I poured my heart and soul into that speech. It was well received, and several news reporters wrote that it was the best I had ever given. But I had been in politics long enough to know that any impact it had on the legislative leaders, particularly *this* group, would be temporary at best.

In December, a month before my State of the State, the Council on Revenues had revised its revenue projections downward. The State government faced a $350 million shortfall in general-fund revenues over the next two years. To balance the State budget, House and Senate leaders proposed an 8-percent across-the-board budget cut which, after seven years of budget cutting, I found unacceptable.

If it came down to it, I was inclined to veto the State Budget Bill. The Legislature would be left with a choice: override my veto (which would make the Legislature accountable for the consequences of an 8-percent cut) or redo the budget and restore funding for critical State social programs. The more I thought about the idea the better I liked it. I wasn't about to leave the governorship the way I came in 1994, having to cut State services for the most vulnerable of our state's citizens.

After seven years of legislative sessions, it was difficult to figure out where the Democrat leadership was coming from. Occasionally, when their backs were against the wall, they could muster the political will to pass important legislation such as our Health Fund bill, perhaps the most important reform bill passed during my two terms. But more often than not they were more likely to descend into pure politics to serve their personal interests such as their overriding my veto on the Age of Consent bill—an act Vice Speaker Sylvia Luke had admitted shamelessly to me was based on political self-preservation. Time had sapped the idealism out of veteran leaders like Say and Bunda—all of which was reflected in their opening-day speeches, the paucity of floor debates on important issues and the ease with which special interest legislation was passed. And what I found particularly disturbing was that this was happening to some of the younger legislators as well.

To be clear, dealing with special interests has been part of the legislative process ever since legislatures were established. Furthermore, it would be wrong to dismiss legislation simply because it benefits a private party. For me—and I believe for most of the legislators with whom I served—the key question is whether the special-interest legislation benefits the public to an extent that justifies the cost. This is a subjective weighing process that a legislator makes on a case-by-case basis, in which the legislator should always err on the side of the public's best interests.

Never, however, during all of my years in public office had I witnessed special-interest legislation approved with so little debate and discussion and with such ease as was the case with the 1998-2002 Legislatures.

In 2001, for example, I vetoed a bill that would have mandated the three Neighbor Island counties to provide a "food recycling" service. The mayors of all three counties asked me to veto the bill, arguing that it did little to protect the public health and would require the counties to purchase new equipment and contract with private vendors they could not afford. My budget analysts found out there was only one company that could provide this service to the counties and that it was a big supporter of and contributor of campaign funds to the senator who had introduced the bill. With a stroke of my pen, I could create a new business in the three counties for a certain company, but neither the senator nor any of the bill's supporters was willing to come forward and vouch for the bill. I vetoed it.

But there was no more egregious an example than when the Legislature passed a bill that provided for both an increase in the minimum wage and a 20-percent tax credit for hotel renovations and new construction. I had been given a Hobson's choice: accept both the increase in the minimum wage and the 20-percent tax credit by approving the bill or kill both by vetoing it. I believed that an increase in the minimum wage was long overdue, but the 20-percent tax credit was outrageous, an unwarranted gift to the hotel industry and landowners. If I approved the bill, more of the same would follow. Increasing the minimum wage would have to wait. I had little choice but to veto the bill.

The ploy disgusted me and told me much about the main characters involved. I wasn't surprised that Big Island Democrat Bob Herkes was behind it. Herkes, a Democrat of convenience, a full-time employee of the Bishop Estate and a strong ally of Speaker Say, didn't blink an eye when it came to doing favors for business interests. I had known Say for more than 20 years, serving with him briefly in the State House. Say had a tough time saying "no" to his friends.

"The Speaker knew you would probably veto the bill, and he let it go to accommodate Herkes," a House member told me later.

"This is typical of the kind of games they play down there," I replied tersely. "Cal must know I have no choice but to veto the bill—it just pisses me off that he would play games with the minimum wage."

What, I wondered, *was the Senate Democrats' excuse for passing Herkes' bill?*

After the 2001 Special Session in October, I literally gave up trying to reason with some of the Democratic legislative leaders. There is little to discuss when the other party is consumed with self-preservation and politics. To be sure, there were many good people in the Legislature, but none of them were in the leadership. Moreover, although they were well educated, many of the young legislators lacked real-life experience and too often behaved as if they were students who were reluctant to speak out publicly or question their mentors—"boy-sans," as Gov. John A. Burns would have described them.

Seven years of dealing with the Democratic leadership revealed that they reacted to public opinion more than anything else. Faced with the proposed 8-percent cut, I decided I would just lay out in public what I would do if I had to slash the State budget. "Let's see how they react when the public finds out we can no longer spare the Department of Education as we did during my first term. And this time I'll lay off State workers *first* before I cut social programs," I told my staff.

To avoid cutting the State budget we proposed using the State's Hurricane Relief Fund (HRF) and Rainy Day Fund and doubling the tax on alcohol. The HRF had $213 million in reserves. The Rainy Day Fund, approximately $40 million. The tax on alcohol would raise another $40 million. The HRF and the tax on alcohol were two politically charged proposals that would test the legislators' resolve or compel them to come up with alternatives.

The HRF was created in 1993 to provide coverage to homeowners after private hurricane insurers began leaving the Hawai'i market in the aftermath of Hurricane 'Iniki in 1992. By 1999, the State had stopped writing hurricane policies, because private insurance had returned to the market. By 2001, there were no outstanding policies. The law that established the HRF provided that once the fund was terminated, its reserves had to be deposited to the general fund. As far as I was concerned, the Legislature was well justified in repealing the HRF law to use the funds to balance the State's general fund operating budget.

The Republicans, however, had politicized the issue, arguing that the HRF funds should be returned to the policyholders. *Nonsense,* I thought. An HRF policy was an insurance policy, and its holders had no more right to be reimbursed with the HRF funds than they had to the earnings of their private auto insurance or homeowner's insurance companies.

What should have been an easy argument to refute was made politically difficult by the hapless Democratic leadership who insisted on holding public hearings throughout the State to get "feedback" (a favorite, overused phrase) on the issue. Not surprisingly, the Republicans flooded the hearings with testimony from their party faithful demanding that the former policyholders be reimbursed from the HRF reserves. This argument soon took on a life of its own. Republicans like

Hemmings argued that the public testimony was proof that the public supported the idea of giving the money back to the policyholders. Politically, the skittish Democrats had mousetrapped themselves.

The other, more rational argument against using the HRF reserves was that the fund should be kept intact in case there was another hurricane. But the HRF had been a stopgap measure intended to fill in the homeowners' needs for hurricane insurance *after* a hurricane hit and the private sector got out of the market; it was not intended to compete with private insurers once they reentered the market. If there were another hurricane, there would be a considerable gap between the time private insurers exited the market and the time existing insurance policies were not renewed; the State would have ample time to reestablish the HRF.

Actually, the most important reason for the HRF was that with private insurance no longer available, the HRF policies fulfilled the mandatory requirement of all home mortgages for wind or hurricane insurance coverage. Without it the banks and financial institutions holding the mortgages could be forced to foreclose.

But by 2001 the situation had changed. The private sector was back in the market, and all HRF policies had expired. There was no need for the HRF's continued existence. To allow the HRF's $213 million to sit collecting interest while the State was struggling with the aftermath of an "economic hurricane" was a waste.

I knew our proposal to double the State liquor tax would face strong opposition from lobbyists, restaurants and other businesses, but I hoped that the legislators would see wine, liquor and beer as luxury items, as I did—luxuries not essential to the health and welfare of the public. As expected, the Republicans opposed any tax increase, as did some Democrats. Raising taxes—even on alcohol—is a tough sell in an election year.

When the news media queried me on the legislators' grumbling about our proposals, I replied: "What are the Legislature's alternatives?"

Dinner in D.C.

In late February, Vicky and I traveled to Washington, D.C., for my final National Governor's Association (NGA) winter conference. The trip was a welcome respite from our legislative problems.

The NGA conference is held semiannually, but the Washington, D.C., winter conference is considered the most important because it gives the nation's governors the opportunity to meet and discuss State issues with the president behind closed doors. Because of the 9-11 crisis, this NGA winter conference was particularly important.

The NGA conference includes a series of events. Among them on this occasion was an opportunity to hear from important guest speakers ranging from best-selling authors (Tom Friedman, author of *The Lexus and the Olive Tree*) to corporate CEOs (Carly Fiorina of Hewlett Packard) to renowned scholars, scientists and the president's Cabinet members.

Traditionally, the president hosted the governors and their spouses to a formal black tie dinner at the White House. I don't like wearing a tuxedo, but having dinner with the president was special. I had attended six of these dinners hosted by the Clintons; this would be my first with the Bushes (I had not attended the 2001 NGA conference.) Not surprisingly, there is a certain protocol to every White House function. For this dinner, each governor and his or her spouse would be announced by a Marine officer in full dress uniform. Another Marine officer would then escort the governor and spouse up a red-carpeted ramp to meet the president and the first lady, who stood approximately 25 to 30 feet away at the doorway to the White House.

I hadn't seen George Bush since he'd hosted the 1997 Western Governors Association conference in San Antonio. I was curious to see how he was holding up as president. As Vicky and I waited our turn to be announced, I was thinking hurriedly of something profound to say to him.

As we neared the president and first lady, he grinned impishly, stepped forward on the red carpet and, swinging his arms as if he was teeing off on the golf course, said, "Ben, when I go to Hawai'i, I'm going to get you on the golf course and kick your ass!" Vicky was a bit taken aback (later she asked me if Bush always spoke like that), but I just laughed. "My game sucks, Mr. President, but I'd be happy to take you on." *First*, I thought, *he showed off by speaking Spanish to me in San Antonio and now he threatens to kick my butt on the golf course. Well, so much for profound remarks; he hasn't changed.*

At our dinner table, I was seated between U.S. Attorney General John Ashcroft and Secretary of Defense Donald Rumsfeld. These guys were conservative Republicans (Ashcroft more so), so I made it a point not to discuss political issues. *Keep it social*, I thought. Ashcroft, a former governor of Missouri, was pleasant, and we exchanged small talk. I learned that he loved to sing and apparently was good at it. Rumsfeld was silent, acknowledging only those who greeted him. The slight frown on his brow suggested he would have preferred to be somewhere else. I empathized with him; the war in Afghanistan had already begun (at the time, I was clueless about the *other* war he was planning), and he no doubt had better things to do than dine with governors.

In an attempt to stimulate conversation with Rumsfeld, I thought I'd be positive and tell him how much I appreciated the Navy's handling of the *Ehime Maru* tragedy. On February 9, 2001, the *Ehime Maru*, a small Japanese fishing training ship carrying a crew of 35, had been sunk in Hawai'i waters after a collision with the *U.S.S. Greeneville*, a U.S. Navy nuclear submarine. The accident occurred when, in a demonstration for some civilian visitors, the *Greeneville* performed an emergency surfacing maneuver. As the submarine quickly surfaced, it struck the

Ehime Maru, which sank within a few minutes. Nine of the smaller ship's crewmembers were lost, including four high school students.

The tragedy became a national cause célèbre in Japan as the news media ran stories suggesting that the *Greeneville*'s captain had allowed a civilian to control the submarine and that the *Greeneville*'s crew had not gone to the aid of the *Ehime Maru*'s crew. Unfortunately, the latter was true, but only because Navy regulations required that under emergency circumstances the submarine must be sailed to safe waters immediately. Whatever the justification for the Navy regulation, there was no doubt in my mind that the image of the big submarine leaving the surviving *Ehime Maru* crewmembers behind treading water in its wake would enrage the already angry Japanese public.

Upon learning about the tragedy, President Bush had quickly offered his condolences to Prime Minister Mori. I thought the Navy was handling the incident about as well as could be. Our government leaders had made all the right moves and said the right things. At the dinner, I leaned over to express my thanks to Rumsfeld.

"Mr. Secretary, I want to thank you for the Navy's efforts in trying to raise the *Ehime Maru* and recover the bodies. The Navy has done a fine job," I said. I wasn't prepared for his reply.

"Ahhh—we all know those people are dead and yet we're spending millions of dollars to raise the ship and recover the bodies. All that … it's a waste of time and money!" he replied tersely without even looking at me.

Son of a bitch! I said to myself, *the man has no compassion for the victims' families.* Yes, yes, we all knew they were dead, but at least the U.S. Navy top command understood the importance in the Japanese culture of recovering the remains of the nine crewmembers for proper interment, even though Rumsfeld didn't.

Years earlier, I had been part of a group of 20 lieutenant governors who met with then-President Reagan, Vice President Bush and Secretary of Defense Caspar Weinberger. After hearing Weinberger express his hardnosed views on communism and national defense, I had left the meeting thinking that the guy was dangerous. I was beginning to have similar thoughts about Rumsfeld.

I didn't say another word to Rumsfeld during the rest of the dinner. He must have sensed I was bothered by his remarks. At the end of the dinner, he stood up, looked at me, placed a hand on my shoulder, smiled wearily and said somewhat contritely, "Governor, we'll keep looking." I thanked him.

In October, the Navy managed to raise the *Ehime Maru* from a depth of 1,500 feet, tow it to shallow water, recover the remains of eight of the nine lost crew, tow the ship back to deep water and sink it. It had taken nearly a year and an estimated $40 million to complete the operation. Undoubtedly, the Navy higher-ups were mindful that the *Ehime Maru* tragedy was turning into a major public-relations disaster for Japanese-American relations. There were 120 million Japanese citizens scrutinizing the Navy's response to the tragedy. In my eyes, the Navy responded sensitively and superbly by compensating the victims' families and the survivors for their loss and conducting an inquiry that was objective and fair to the beleaguered, guilt-ridden captain of the *U.S.S. Greeneville.*

At about 9 p.m., the dinner was over and the Marine Band played while some governors and spouses took to the dance floor or engaged in conversation over cocktails. Fifteen minutes later, Bush grabbed the microphone.

"Well, folks, Laura and I are packing it in for the night. I'm an early riser, but you can stay and enjoy yourselves," he said, abruptly interrupting the dancing and conversation as he and the first lady started walking up the stairway to the second floor.

I stifled a laugh. Bush had just done what every governor in the room wished they had the nerve to do at one time or another at one of their own social functions—end it.

Bush and Clinton were so different. Clinton loved to entertain, whereas Bush merely seemed to tolerate it. I remembered once when Vicky and I (along with two other governors and their spouses) stayed overnight at the White House, Clinton gave Vicky and the others a tour of the different rooms. I had stayed alone overnight once before (in the Lincoln bedroom), so I had been through the tour. While Vicky and the others were being shown around by Clinton, I stayed in my room watching the fights on HBO. By the time I joined Clinton and the group, it was nearly 1 a.m. and the president was still going strong, showing us things like the saxophone he played on *The Arsenio Hall Show* after his disastrous speech at the 1988 Democratic Convention.

The next morning, we met with Bush. At the outset, the president and the chairman of the NGA both gave introductory and perfunctory remarks. The press was then ushered out of the room, and except for the Secret Service and a few of the president's Cabinet members, no one besides the governors was allowed in the room.

There was a bit of irony about this meeting. When Bush was still governor he let it be known that he thought the NGA conference was a waste of time and, in fact, as far as I recall, he attended only several. I wondered whether he thought these meetings were a waste of time—or just the meetings with Clinton.

In any event, we were briefed on Bush's post-9-11 plans for homeland security, the economic stimulus package, the impact on air travel and the airline industry and other related matters. The question-and-answer discussion was somber as some of the governors raised security issues peculiar to their respective states and others asked questions about the availability of federal funding.

As the discussion went from 9-11 to other, more mundane (comparatively speaking) issues, Bush showed his propensity to inject humor at the most unlikely times when Gov. William Janklow of South Dakota stood up to ask a question.

Janklow, a four-term, outspoken, feisty conservative Republican who would be great cast in a movie as a redneck Southerner, had arrived late at the president's dinner the previous night. He had gone straight from the airport to the White House. Dressed in a shiny baby blue suit, a dark blue shirt and a bright yellow tie, Janklow stood out among the rest of the formally dressed crowd.

Before Janklow could ask his question, Bush interrupted him.

"Bill, I notice you're wearing the same blue suit you wore last night."

Caught off guard, Janklow mumbled something I could not hear. Some of the other governors, including me, started smiling.

"And I see you got on the same yellow tie and blue shirt you wore last night," Bush deadpanned.

This time there was some outright laughter as the normally garrulous Janklow seemed at a complete loss for words. After a pause, a subdued governor finally asked his question—something about a federal regulation and prairie dogs.

Well, the president hasn't lost his sense of humor, I thought—*he must be fun on the golf course.*

(In 2003 Janklow, who had been elected to Congress, was convicted of negligent homicide after his car ran a stop sign at high speed—he had been cited for speeding on several occasions—and killed a motorcyclist. He resigned and was sentenced to 100 days in jail, a tap on the wrist compared to what he would have gotten under Hawai'i law. His law license was also revoked, ending his political career.)

A Red-Hot Issue

Meanwhile, the Hurricane Relief Fund had become something of a political football. With Republicans turning up the political heat by demanding that the HRF funds be paid to former policyholders or remain intact, some Democrats, mainly in the supposedly more mature Senate, were desperately trying to find ways to avoid using HRF funds. I made my feelings known to the news media:

"All of this debate over the Hurricane Relief Fund and the confusion that now reigns among the people is so unnecessary. It's a result of the politics that have been played with the Hurricane Relief Fund. It's unfortunate because now the Legislature, the Democratic majority, is so concerned about the public reaction that they're beginning to turn over every rock and hiding place looking for money."

My remarks were directed to the Senate. The House, led by House Finance Committee Chairman Dwight Takamine, had approved a bill authorizing the use of $100 million in HRF funds. In the Senate, Ways and Means Chairman Brian Taniguchi agreed, stating publicly that he had reluctantly come to the conclusion that it was the only way to avoid drastic budget cuts. He was supported by Senate Vice President Colleen Hanabusa.

Senate President Bunda, however, was opposed to the House plan. So adamant was he that when his staff thought they had found $45 million in "unencumbered contracts" he immediately announced it to support his opposition against using the HRF. Senate Vice President Hanabusa was skeptical and asked publicly that if the $45 million in unencumbered contracts existed, why was it that Ways and Means had not known about it?

The term "unencumbered contracts" was something of an oxymoron, as no contract exists between two parties unless it is encumbered or, in legal terms, consideration was given by each side. Even the State cannot legally cancel a contract on a whim. The $45 million in "unencumbered contracts" did not exist. Bunda's staff had made a colossal error—a product of their apparently hurried but surely shoddy research. Anxious to avoid the political repercussions of using the HRF monies, Bunda had compounded his staff's error by announcing it publicly. Once the gaffe was exposed, he never mentioned it again.

Meanwhile, the Republicans must have been delighted at the mischief they were causing. Their relentless criticism had made the HRF a red-hot political issue. I was amazed at the number of former policyholders who believed that if the HRF was terminated they were entitled to be reimbursed for the premiums they had paid for their HRF policies.

Undaunted by his earlier blunder, Bunda then managed to persuade 16 senators—who undoubtedly wanted to the issue to disappear—to sign a petition opposing the use of the HRF. A petition to Taniguchi? This was like the president of the United States petitioning the secretary of the Treasury. In the normal political world, such differences were worked out privately or in closed caucuses. Once again Bunda had failed to support his Ways and Means chairman. Bunda, like Say, had acquired his post as a compromise between opposing factions, and the petition incident revealed the fragility of his presidency.

With Bunda and a majority of the senators opposed to using HRF funds, leaders in both houses scrambled to develop a financial plan for the State budget. In late April, the House and Senate approved a new financing plan: Only the $29 million interest on the earnings of the HRF would be used; another $140 million would come from raiding special funds, $10 million from the Rainy Day Fund and $10 million from a 50-percent increase in the tax on alcohol.

The infusion of these funds meant that instead of making an 8-percent across-the-board budget cut, we would have to cut only 2.5 percent. My Cabinet members indicated to me that they could manage a 2.5-percent reduction without a significant reduction in services. I wasn't happy about using special funds, most of which were for services far more important the HRF, but it was something I could live with. I agreed to approve the plan.

Bunda, an insurance agent by profession, went to great lengths to tout the fact that only the interest earned on HRF funds was being used and the "base," as he called it, was left untouched. It was obvious that Bunda and other Senate

Democrats were driven more by the goal of depriving the Republicans of a campaign issue rather than concern as to how the budget cuts would affect social programs.

Left out of the State budget bill were funds for the new campus for UH-West O'ahu, the Kaka'ako aquarium and my request for a $1 billion CIP appropriation to improve the aging infrastructure of State facilities—particularly those of the public schools and the University system. Instead of the $1 billion I had requested, only $100 million was appropriated. (As of 2001, the repair and maintenance backlog for DOE, UH and other State departments was nearly a billion dollars.) Although the Legislature approved the use of part of the tobacco settlement funds for the new John A. Burns School of Medicine, I was disappointed by their timidity in not coming up with big ideas of their own.

Not surprisingly, the Republicans blasted the Democrats for a lackluster session. As Minority Floor Leader Charles Djou put it, "The only thing they [the Democrats] can brag about is they didn't use the Hurricane Relief Fund."

Not quite.

While the Democratic leadership was struggling over the HRF, other Democrats were moving forward with some important legislation. Our bills for mandatory drug treatment before incarceration for first-time offenders, bulk prescription drug rates for residents, health insurance oversight and a cap on gasoline prices were all passed.

Unfortunately, our Death with Dignity bill, which had passed the House, was defeated by a 14-11 vote in the Senate. After three hours of emotional debate, three senators changed their votes at the last minute. Had the bill passed, Hawai'i would have joined Oregon as the only other state to authorize and offer the option of euthanasia to the terminally ill.

I was buoyed, however, by the passage of the so-called "Gas Cap" bill. In January 2002, the State's 1997 lawsuit against the oil companies for price-fixing had been settled for $20 million (two companies had settled earlier in 2002 for $15 million). The $35 million settlement was disappointing, but the litigation revealed facts that would not otherwise have been available to the State. Hawai'i's gasoline consumers paid the highest gasoline prices in the nation, mainly because of the lack of competition. Hawai'i's oil companies comprised an oligopoly: Two oil refineries controlled the price of gasoline and did as they pleased. Chevron, for example, made 22 percent of its profits in gasoline in Hawai'i—and yet Hawai'i comprised only 3 percent of Chevron's market nationally.

Contrary to popular belief, transportation costs were minimal, only 3 to 5 cents a gallon, and surprisingly, because crude oil from Alaska and Indonesia came directly to Hawai'i, gasoline could be produced in Hawai'i at or below the cost of gasoline in California. Those kinds of facts justified the regulation of gasoline prices in Hawai'i. The Legislature passed the bill but extended its implementation date by two years to allow the State to set up the logistics to administer the gas cap law—the first of its kind in the nation.

Through most of the legislative session I had been critical of the Democratic leadership, but some good things had been done, and I felt strongly that I should acknowledge those responsible for it. When the news media asked me—as they always did—how I would rate this Legislature's performance, I responded with praise:

"There was a point in the session when I felt that they weren't going to do anything bold, and they proved me wrong. And I'm really very, very pleased and proud of those young chairs, in particular, because I think they bode very well for the future of the Legislature."

My congratulatory remarks were not intended for the leadership. The bills were the product of the committee chairs rather than the leadership, but they did little to produce jobs and help struggling businesses. In this context, the Republican criticism was not far off the mark. Only seven months after the September 11 attacks, the Democrat leadership had allowed the Hurricane Relief Fund to become a bigger issue than was warranted, overshadowing any kind of meaningful discussion on the real economic issues: creating new jobs for the thousands of jobless workers and relief for the State's struggling businesses.

In my eyes, the cries of fiscal responsibility cited by the Democratic leaders as a reason for not increasing funding for new construction and attacking the nearly $1 billion backlog in repair and maintenance—for the public schools, the University, State hospitals, prisons and other aging State facilities—were arguments of convenience. When it was to their political advantage, they could be big spenders.

There may have been another other reason for their reluctance: "They don't want to give you another $1 billion because you're not going to be here next year [a polite way of saying I was a 'lame duck'], and if Lingle is elected she'll control how it's spent," a legislator confided to me. The thought had never occurred to me. When it came to playing politics these guys had no peers.

Conflict at Ko Olina

To stimulate private construction, the Legislature relied mainly on giving tax credits as incentives to developers and landowners. Theoretically, tax credits didn't cost the State anything. If a tax credit helped create new construction projects, thus creating new jobs, the State could afford to give up the new taxes which it otherwise would not have collected anyway. I supported tax credits, and there were a few useful ones relating to new home construction or renovation that had been passed, but there were also several tax credit bills that were not in the public's interest.

For example, during the 2001 Special Session, the bill to give developers a 10-percent "refundable" tax credit for new construction or renovation had been introduced, which would have been a bonanza to developers if it hadn't been corrected—at my instigation—to provide a non-refundable credit. The bill, I learned later, had been introduced to help Jeff Stone's Ko Olina Resort development.

In the 2002 legislative session, a tax credit bill intended to encourage new private construction projects was written in a way that would allow all construction projects—new and current—to qualify for the tax credit. Tax credits are designed to encourage *new* construction, which in turn creates jobs and more tax revenues. Giving tax credits for ongoing construction projects that were already paying taxes didn't make sense. Either the author of the bill had erred in drafting it, or the bill was worded to give developers of ongoing projects a tax break. The error was so blatant that I was inclined to believe the latter. *How*, I thought, *could 76 legislators miss the error?* I vetoed the bill.

The most controversial bill of the legislative session was the $75 million tax credit for Ko Olina. During my 28 years in politics, the Ko Olina bill was the first I had seen that was intended to benefit a specifically named private developer.

In drumming up support for the bill, Jeff Stone put on quite a show for the legislators. Letters of support from representatives of the Hilton Hotels chain, Intrawest Resort Corp, a $2 billion asset Vancouver corporation, and the Ritz-Carlton Hotels suggested strongly they were seriously considering investing in Ko Olina. Vendors who did business for Stone were called to testify in support of the bill—all singing the same song: The aquarium would be a catalyst for the development of the Ko Olina Resort.

Stone stated that the project would create as many as 23,000 construction jobs and 10,000 permanent jobs while also generating $60 million in annual tax revenue. He did not believe the facility would lose any money. "Look at the model for any other state," he claimed. "[Aquariums] do generate one million to three million people a year."

I wondered which aquariums Stone had visited. The reality, I learned after touring some of the better-known aquariums on the Mainland, was that few aquariums turn a profit, and stand-alone aquariums like the one planned for Ko Olina almost never do. They usually require subsidies or private grants to survive. Aquariums—like convention centers—are rarely self sustaining and are often looked upon as loss leaders to attract tourists and local visitors to the area, which in turn benefits business overall.

Incredibly, Stone's patronage studies claimed the Ko Olina aquarium could attract approximately the same number of patrons (750,000 paying customers annually) that our studies showed an aquarium in Kaka'ako Makai would attract. How was this possible? Kaka'ako Makai was only a mile or two away from Waikīkī's 34,000 hotel rooms and was located in the heart of urban Honolulu, while Ko Olina was nearly 25 miles away and virtually isolated on the Leeward Coast.

"Ko Olina will create hundreds of jobs for the residents of the Leeward Coast," an exuberant Hanabusa claimed. *Fair enough*, I thought, *but only time will tell whether her ebullience is justified.* But if Hanabusa wanted to provide jobs and opportunities for her constituents on the Leeward Coast, I noticed she had done little to support the building of the proposed new campus for the University's West Oʻahu campus in Kapolei, the designated Second City located a few miles from Ko Olina. Surely, the new college would have provided construction and a variety of jobs and, perhaps more important, provided educational opportunities for her constituents and spurred development of the area.

More troubling were the serious questions of fairness. Tax credits are usually written to apply generically to a specific industry and apply across the board. "Unlike other tax credits that are targeted at a specific industry, this credit will largely benefit a handful of taxpayers who have already secured a position in this particular development site," State Tax Director Marie Okamura testified in opposition to the bill at the hearing.

As I watched all of this, I wondered if there were any legislators who had the guts to ask the hard questions. There was not a peep from the Democrats—or from conservative Republicans like Slom and Hemmings who had made careers in opposing social programs for the needy, or from the young legislators who were learning quickly the politics of "going along to get along." The only legislators who raised questions about the credibility of Stone's claims were Republicans Charles Djou of Oʻahu and Jim Rath of Kona, Hawaiʻi. The legislators I served with in the 1970s and 1980s would have given Stone's study a much-deserved thrashing.

There was, however, at least one voice of refreshing candor that came from the resort industry. A week before I vetoed Hanabusa's bill, Stan Brown, who was then vice president of Japan, Hawaiʻi and South Pacific Marriott Hotels, wrote me a letter (paraphrased in part):

"Dear Governor Cayetano," Brown wrote," I want to inform you that whether or not you veto the Ko Olina $75 million tax credit bill makes no difference to Marriott's investment strategy in Hawaiʻi. The first phase of our time-share project in Ko Olina has been a great success and Marriot is committed to building the second phase regardless of what happens to the bill."

Brown's letter was unsolicited but welcomed. It confirmed my belief that market forces would drive the development of Ko Olina. And although he did not come out and say it, I sensed Brown wanted to divorce himself and Marriot from the exaggeration and hype being tossed around by some of his industry colleagues in support of the bill.

The late journalist Bob Rees once wrote that Hanabusa possessed "one of the brightest minds" in the Legislature. I agreed. As a freshman senator, the Stanford Law School graduate had emerged as a leader in the Legislature. She had carved out a reputation as one of the state's top labor lawyers and counted the AFL-CIO among her clients. Nevertheless, despite strong union opposition, Hanabusa had taken the lead in passing bills that established the new State Health Employees Fund and repealed the mandatory arbitration law which as written was stacked against the State. For a first-term senator it was a remarkable show of intellect and leadership.

I respected her for her leadership ability, and I sensed that she was destined to run for higher office one day—which made her unprecedented actions following my veto of her 2002 Ko Olina bill inexplicable to me. She had sued to overturn my veto. It was a first in Hawai'i's history. Not surprisingly, the State Circuit Court ruled against her. She appealed—only to have the Hawai'i Supreme Court rule against her.

Hanabusa was too good a lawyer to believe her lawsuit to overturn my veto had a scintilla of a chance of succeeding. And she was too smart to swallow the exaggerated claims of Jeff Stone and his supporters. *Why*, I wondered, *did she go to such extremes? Did she do it to show the people in her district that she was fighting to create jobs?*

Experience teaches that there are many intangibles that may affect a politician's decisions—things not taught in high school Civics 101. Interpersonal relationships—friendships, family, loved ones—rank high on the list.

In March 2004 the *Honolulu Advertiser* ran a story by investigative reporter Jim Dooley that revealed new facts exposing an undisclosed possible conflict of interest that Hanabusa had as a result of her relationship with Stone, who had also been one of the main figures in the State's 1997-98 investigation of the Bishop Estate.

> State Sen. Colleen Hanabusa, backer of the controversial $75 million tax-credit program benefiting Ko Olina resort developer Jeffrey Stone, lives in a luxury Ko Olina townhouse purchased by her fiancé from Stone, and works in a downtown law office subleased from Stone, according to real estate and business records.
>
> Hanabusa, Stone and State Sheriff John F. Souza III, who is engaged to Hanabusa, said their business relations have been aboveboard, conducted at market prices and unrelated to the Ko Olina tax-credit legislation signed into law by Gov. Linda Lingle in May. The measure, which provides massive State tax breaks to companies that build a "world-class aquarium" at Ko Olina, has helped spur a rapid rise of property values in the Leeward resort community.
>
> Souza bought the townhouse in the recently completed Kai Lani development in June, less than a month after Lingle signed the tax-credit package into law. Hanabusa introduced the bill in early 2002, and it was passed by the Legislature but vetoed by then-Gov. Ben Cayetano. Hanabusa, an attorney, sued Cayetano over the veto and reintroduced the bill in January 2003. The Legislature approved it in May.

Having failed to overturn my veto through the courts, Hanabusa reintroduced the $75 million tax credit bill in the 2003 legislative session. Once again, with little debate the bill was passed by the Legislature and signed into law by the new governor. The bill was passed with such overwhelming approval that I began to question whether my conclusions about it were wrong.

A year or so later, I ran into Hilton Hawaiian Village managing director Peter Schall, who had testified in 2002 that Hilton was committed to building a new hotel at Stone's resort. "Peter," I asked, "does Hilton still plan to build another hotel at Ko Olina?"

"No," he replied curtly and walked away.

I wasn't surprised by Schall's answer. Three or four years before the Ko Olina bill was introduced in 2002, Schall told me that Hilton was investing more than $100 million to build a timeshare project next to its flagship hotel in Waikīkī. By 2002, that project had been completed and, given that investment, I doubted that Hilton would invest another $100 million or so to build another hotel at Ko Olina. They did not, and I doubt they will anytime soon.

In 2007, I ran into Jeff Stone at the opening-day ceremonies of the State Legislature. He was sitting in front of me in the section reserved for guests of the new Senate president, Colleen Hanabusa. At the close of the ceremony, he saw me and said, "Governor, you were right, the market will determine how Ko Olina develops; I'm going to give back the tax credit." A few days later, Stone was quoted in the newspapers as saying that he had decided "to give back the $75 million tax credit."

"Give back the tax credit"? How big of him, I thought. But it wasn't his to give back. He either applied for the tax credit or chose not to. Instead, he acted as if he owned it. Who could blame him? Stone had literally smooth-talked the compliant, incurious, self-interested Legislature into passing the biggest State tax credit in history exclusively for his company—and with virtually no questions asked. Handsome, charismatic, charming, articulate and smart, the crafty and personable Stone could sell, as they say, a refrigerator to an Eskimo.

(In January 2008, the Disney Corporation announced that it would build an 800-room hotel/timeshare in Ko Olina. I assumed that Disney's decision was market driven, spurred by the success of Marriott's two timeshare projects at the resort. In April 2008, Stone reneged on his promise to "give back" the $75 million tax credit, at least all of it. Instead, he applied for a tax credit of $3.5 million for a seawater well his company built to determine, he said, if there was enough water for the never-to-be-built aquarium. Not surprisingly, the $3.5 million tax credit was approved by the governor. Interestingly, no one questioned why it was necessary to construct a sea well for information that engineers could have obtained through test bores and other methods. The sea well, however, will not be wasted—it came as no surprise when Stone announced that it would be used for his resort.)

The Ivory Tower

While most politicians were busy trying to find ways to boost Hawai'i's ailing economy in 2002, some, like Speaker Calvin Say and Senate Tourism Committee Chairperson Donna Kim, were busy trying to find ways to help their special-interest friends and expand their political clout.

Say became Speaker when a majority of House Democrats found then-Speaker Joe Souki's dealings with special interests such as the Bishop Estate an embarrassing political liability. Say was the compromise choice to succeed Souki and restore the House's tarnished image. Souki's antics had concerned me as well. After I was reelected in 1998, I offered Souki an appointment to a seat on the Public Utilities Commission—not because he was particularly qualified for the job but because I shared the concerns about his ties to special interests and wanted a new Speaker. He declined.

After Souki was ousted as Speaker, the House Democrats gave him a new title to assuage his hurt feelings. "Speaker Emeritus" they crowned him—about as unflattering as the term "lame duck." To paraphrase Bill Clinton—I felt Souki's pain.

It didn't take long for Say to realize what a good thing Souki had had going for him. Shortly after he became Speaker, Say was offered and accepted a directorship on the Board of Directors of City Bank. Many legislators hold full-time jobs with private employers, but the propriety of a legislator sitting as a director was questionable. Unlike employees, a director owes a fiduciary duty to his company and its stockholders. This can pose a potential conflict with the fiduciary duty the legislator owes to the public. It didn't matter what I thought, of course; Henry Peters had set the precedent when he served as a Bishop Estate trustee and Speaker simultaneously—killing all bills he deemed detrimental to the Bishop Estate's interests—before he too became an embarrassing political liability for Democrats and was ousted.

One morning, I got a call from Evan Dobelle, the recently appointed president of the University of Hawai'i, which provided some insight to Say's role with City Bank.

"Governor, do you know a Richard Lim from City Bank?"

"Not well, but I know who he is. Why do you ask?"

"Well, Lim asked for a meeting, and he brought along Calvin Say and Brian Taniguchi. Pres [Prescott Stewart, a Dobelle staff person] was with me. I discussed ideas that the faculty and students have for University Avenue, past the Varsity Theatre down to King Street. Then Lim started talking—and he did all of the talking while Calvin and Brian looked on. The tone of Lim's words bothered me. In essence he seemed to be suggesting that if I wanted to get anything done at the University I should call him."

"What did Calvin and Brian do?" I asked Dobelle.

"Well, afterward I turned to Calvin and Brian and said, 'What was that all about?'" he replied.

"Did they say anything?"

"No. They just sat there looking down at their shoes—and that bothered me more than what Lim was saying. Calvin has been helpful to me and the University. I couldn't understand his behavior."

"Looking down at their shoes?"

Years later, I got a slightly different version of the Lim-Dobelle meeting from a former UH regent who had arranged the meeting and was also in attendance.

"I was asked to arrange a meeting with Dobelle and I did," the regent told me. "I had no idea what Lim wanted to meet about, so I asked Calvin and Brian if they knew. They both said they didn't."

"How did Lim come across?"

"Well, he did all of the talking, and after a few minutes I felt Dobelle didn't like what he was hearing. And I think everyone was kind of caught off guard by what was being said."

"Including Calvin and Brian?"

"Probably—I think they were surprised too."

Dobelle thought Lim was trying to intimidate him. If he was, then having the Speaker of the House and the chairman of the Senate Ways and Means Committee in tow only added to that impression. If Say and Taniguchi were surprised by Lim's words, the right thing for them to do would have been to contact Dobelle later and clear up any misunderstanding. They didn't.

The Hawai'i Tourism Authority

In 2004 Calvin Say lost his directorship when City Bank was bought out by Central Pacific Bank. Central Pacific paid a premium $91.83 price per share, up from its original offer of $21.83 less than a year earlier. So Say didn't walk away empty-handed. His director's stock options provided a handsome return.

Like his predecessor Joseph Souki, Say had also developed a close friendship with Outrigger Hotels & Resorts executives, in particular Max Sword, Outrigger's popular liaison to the Legislature. When Say served as chairman of the House Finance Committee he worked out an agreement to borrow Outrigger employees on "loan" from the hotel to serve on his staff—a practice which has become increasingly common at the Legislature. After he became Speaker, Say appointed Sword to the Judicial Selection Commission.

In 1998, at the urging of Souki, I appointed Outrigger CEO David Carey to the fledgling Hawai'i Tourism Authority (HTA). There was no question about Carey's qualifications for the post. Moreover, Souki had been a member of the 1997 Economic Revitalization Task Force that created the idea for the HTA.

Politically, I felt he was entitled to Carey's appointment.

In 2002, Carey's four-year term was coming to an end. Say, who also had a close relationship to Outrigger, wanted to ensure that Outrigger, if not Carey, would continue to control Carey's soon-to-be-vacant HTA seat. As events will demonstrate, Say was not subtle in his efforts to please Outrigger. First, though, some history on the HTA:

The Hawai'i Tourism Authority, the creation of which was a proposal of my 1997 Economic Revitalization Task Force, was established by the Legislature in 1998. One of the HTA's primary objectives was to develop a statewide strategic plan for the development of tourism. Funded with a percentage of the transient accommodation tax, HTA received $60 million in 1998 to carry out its mission. By 2002 it was receiving $65 million. A major part of HTA's strategic tourism plan was to develop a marketing plan to better promote Hawai'i as a tourist destination.

Under the State constitution, the governor is authorized to make appointments to boards and commissions subject to the advice and consent of the Senate. For four of the nine appointments to the HTA, the governor is required to select from a list of three names submitted by the Speaker or the Senate president for each appointment. The other five appointments are made by the governor, subject to the advice and consent of the Senate.

In 2002, Say forwarded a list of three names to fill Carey's HTA seat. The list included the names of Carey and two Outrigger employees. In other words, no matter which of the three I appointed, Outrigger would still control the seat. I was disappointed by Say's ploy. "Tell him if he wants to make the appointments to HTA, he should run for governor," I grumbled to a staff member.

When the news media asked Say about his ploy to ensure that Outrigger would continue to have a seat, he replied dismissively, "What's wrong with Outrigger?"

There was nothing *wrong* with Outrigger. Clearly Carey, an experienced hotel executive, was well qualified. What was wrong was Say's manipulation of the system to keep Carey or Outrigger in control of the HTA seat. I wasn't going to reappoint Carey, because reports I had gotten about his HTA board performance indicated that virtually every move he made was designed to help the hotels. But the HTA was not intended to serve as a clearinghouse for the hotel industry—there was much more to Hawai'i tourism than the hotels. I was also looking for non-tourism people who could provide more balance on the HTA board.

The intent of authorizing the Speaker and Senate president to submit a list of three names for the HTA was to assure more objectivity in the governor's appointments. Say had made a mockery of the law's intent. I refused to make the appointment.

Say's antics proved a larger point: The process is only as good and objective as the people who control it. The HTA nomination process had empowered the Speaker and the Senate president to influence the governor's appointments to the

HTA Board. And Say had perverted that power. But Say had one thing going for him: No one cared about a dispute between the governor and the Speaker.

By 2002, the HTA had $65 million to dole out to public relations firms, consultants and other vendors. This fact was not lost upon other tourism executives, some who were groping for ways to get their people on the HTA board. For example, shortly after I appointed two HTA members, they were offered and accepted jobs by businesses in the tourist industry. The two were good people; nevertheless, I asked one to resign, which she did, and told the other that I would not reappoint her after her term expired.

But Say was not the only one playing games with the HTA appointments. According to former Honolulu Councilman Gary Gill, who served in my Cabinet, Donna Kim once told him that an astute politician should seize every opportunity to enhance his or her political power. This trait would become apparent in Kim's actions relating to Larry Johnson and later Tony Vericella.

Kim had a much-deserved reputation for taking slights very personally. When she served on the City Council her numerous quarrels with Mayor Jeremy Harris had filled her with enmity for the man. One of Harris' many sins against her came when Harris wondered aloud publicly why Kim's name was on the deed to one of the City's affordable housing units, which had been sold to Kim's parents. She could hardly hide her anger when she explained to me that her name was on the deed because she had had to co-sign for her parents, who would not have been able to afford to buy the unit by themselves. Inasmuch as I didn't have a high regard for Harris, I empathized with Kim.

UH President Evan Dobelle got an insight into Kim's feelings about Harris when she called him to her office one day and asked why he had participated in Harris' Visions program. Puzzled, Dobelle explained that as the UH's new president he thought it was important for him and the University that he accept the mayor's invitation to participate. According to Dobelle, Kim told him, "Well, I think you should know that Harris is my enemy." (Dobelle would later join Harris on Kim's list.)

I knew that Kim was not happy with the way Tony Vericella, chairman of the Hawai'i Convention and Visitors Bureau (HVCB) at the time, had responded to her criticism of the post-September 11 emergency tourism marketing strategy that he, along with First Hawaiian Bank's Walter Dods and Hilton's Peter Schall, had developed. Vericella's big mistake had been exposing Kim's shallow, poorly thought-out ideas for marketing at the public hearings.

The day I received Senate President Bunda's list of candidates for appointment to the HTA Board, I noticed that Lori Stone, wife of Jeff Stone, was one of the three. Bunda had no special tie to Jeff Stone, so I figured Lori Stone was on the list because of Kim, who at the time was a close confidant of Bunda. Initially, I did not intend to appoint Stone, because I thought Jeff Stone had too much influence over

Hanabusa and Kim in the Senate.

But I noticed that Bunda—at the time an ally of Kim's—had "stacked" the list in favor of Stone. Stone's qualifications were so obviously better than those of the other two nominees (imagine a coach having to choose a quarterback from a list that included NFL All-Pro quarterback Brett Favre and two high school quarterbacks)—that I chuckled when I realized it.

A staff member, however, suggested that I appoint Stone to the HTA as a courtesy to Donna Kim, who as chairperson of the tourism committee had significant clout over our tourism bills. As a sop to Kim, and hoping to assuage the ill feelings she had developed against Vericella and to maintain good relations for the sake of our tourism programs, I appointed Stone. I would learn soon enough that it wouldn't make a difference.

Shortly after I appointed Stone, I told Kim that I was going to appoint Larry Johnson as one of the five governor's appointees to the HTA board. Johnson was well qualified to sit on the board: Over a 40-year period, he had risen from management trainee to chairman of the Bank of Hawai'i. Born and raised in the Islands, Johnson understood how local people tended to view the tourism industry. He was well liked and popular among community and business leaders. The next day, I got a telephone call from First Hawaiian Bank. It was Walter Dods.

"Governor, Donna Kim just called me and told me that Larry [Johnson] was not going to be confirmed and that I should suggest to you that you withdraw Larry's appointment so you won't be embarrassed," Dods said, obviously irritated over Kim's antics with Johnson.

"What? I find that hard to believe," I replied

"I don't know what her problem with Larry is all about, but I think you should call her and clear it up."

I called Kim immediately.

"Donna, Walter Dods told me you have a problem with Larry Johnson's appointment."

"Yes, Larry's going to have problems being confirmed," she replied.

"What's the problem?"

"Well, I'm having trouble with some senators who don't like him; I don't think he has the votes to be confirmed," she said.

"I find that hard to believe," I said tersely.

"Well, like I told Walter you may want to withdraw his name and save yourself from being embarrassed," she said calmly.

"Who are these people [senators]? Give me their names so I can meet with them personally to clear up their hang-ups with Larry," I replied.

"Uh ... I'll get back to you," Kim said, after a long pause.

I had a good relationship with Kim and trusted her—but that pregnant pause in her reply created some doubt in my mind. Johnson was popular with the Democratic majority. The only senator I thought did not like Johnson was Republican Sam Slom, who had once worked for Johnson at Bank of Hawai'i. Slom's hostile feelings about Johnson would emerge at the public hearing on Johnson's confirmation.

I started making personal calls to Democrat senators. The response I got from Senator Cal Kawamoto was typical:

"Cal, Donna told me that Larry Johnson might have a hard time being confirmed. How do you feel about him?"

"I don't have a problem with Larry. He's been very good to my community in Waipahu."

"Do you know of any senator who has a problem with Larry?"

"Not among the Democrats. I'll vote to confirm him. He's a straight shooter. He's well qualified."

I called on a few more Democrats, and each one responded with surprise. "What's Donna's problem with Larry?" one asked.

Sam Callejo, my chief of staff, and Lloyd Nekoba, one of my liaisons to the Legislature, had polled other Democratic senators; all said they would vote to confirm Johnson. I decided to discuss the matter with Johnson himself. I told Johnson about Kim's antics and asked him how his meeting with Kim had gone. He was surprised Kim had suggested I withdraw his appointment.

"I thought my meeting with her had gone over very well," Johnson told me. "She never gave me any reason to suspect that my confirmation might be in trouble."

"What kind of questions did she ask you?"

"Nothing unusual—except she asked me whether I knew Tony Vericella and if so, how well I knew him."

"She asked about Tony?"

"Yes, I told her that I knew Tony very well."

"Anything else?"

"She asked me whether I golfed with Tony. And I told her that Tony often plays with our golf group on Sunday at Waialae [Country Club]."

"Sounds like she knew that you and Tony were friends," I said. "She say anything else?"

"No, that's about all I remember. Frankly, I'm surprised—I thought our meeting went over pretty well."

I wasn't sure about Kim's motives, but I concluded that although she had nothing personal against Larry Johnson, the thought of Tony Vericella having a good friend like Johnson on the HTA board was not to her liking. As chairperson of the Senate Tourism Committee, Kim had the authority to hold Johnson's appointment in committee. Despite the assurances of the senators I spoke with, I wasn't going to take any chances. I called Walter Dods and told him what was happening.

Although their banks were competitors, Dods and Johnson were good friends and often worked on community projects together. I asked Dods if he would organize business leaders to testify in support of Johnson's confirmation at the public hearing held by Kim's tourism committee. He outdid himself. At the hearing, business and community leaders appeared in droves to testify in support of Johnson's confirmation. Aside from Slom's hostile questioning, not one person spoke against him. Kim had no choice but to recommend Johnson's confirmation.

Having mousetrapped herself into an embarrassing position, Kim lashed out at me, accusing me publicly in a floor speech of threatening the senators if they did not vote for Johnson. It was false, and every senator knew it. But her accusations were more to salvage her public image as a crusader for truth than in service of truth itself.

Much of Kim's enmity to Vericella was because he wouldn't do her bidding. Kim went ballistic when she learned that in 2002 the HVCB had approved a three-year, $3.9 million franchise agreement in the Disney movie *Lilo and Stitch*. Kim thought it was a waste of money.

The unique agreement was an example of Vericella's outside-the-box philosophy during his tenure as chairman of the HVCB. The animated movie was about a Hawaiian girl who adopts an unusual pet who is actually a notorious fugitive from the law. Under the agreement with Disney, the HVCB acted as a consultant in the production of the movie, mainly to assure that the script accurately portrayed Hawai'i and that Hawaiian landmarks and historical sites were clearly mentioned in the film. The agreement was the first of its kind for Disney and the HVCB.

The movie became a bona fide hit. It was nominated for an Oscar, and in less than a year after its release in 2002, the film had earned more than $250 million in worldwide box-office revenues. Disney would later produce a sequel, *Lilo & Stitch II*, and a television series of the same name on the Disney channel.

Five million DVDs and videos were released in December 2002. Each DVD contained a 15-minute chapter called "Disneypedia: Hawai'i," a narrated travelogue of the Hawaiian Islands. It was the first time Disney had included such marketing on a DVD or video.

And the HVCB was given the right to participate in the launch of every phase of Disney's strategic marketing of *Lilo and Stitch*—the introduction of the animated characters at Disney's theme parks, the television series, the sale of retail items and Disney's online programs.

This was innovative marketing. Unlike a 30-second television commercial, which the viewer can turn off or ignore, "Disneypedia: Hawai'i" was much more likely to capture the attention of people who went to see *Lilo and Stitch*. Moreover, Vericella told me, HVCB studies revealed that family travel had increased dramatically after September 11. *Lilo and Stitch* was designed to penetrate that market.

"We'll be selling the film in video and DVD for another 50 years," a Disney executive was quoted by the *Star-Bulletin*.

None of this mattered to Kim. She wasn't interested in learning how the marketing of movies and DVDs had changed. She was angry because Vericella had not cleared the project with the HTA board, though under HVCB's contract with HTA he was not required to do so. That the movie was a huge success only fueled her resentment.

At a cost of $1.6 million, the HVCB had gotten more advertising mileage from its agreement with Disney than it had from traditional advertising. But under pressure from Kim, the HTA board terminated the three-year agreement with Disney.

In 2002, Kim turned to her favorite weapon: the legislative audit. At her request, the legislative auditor audited both the HTA and the HVCB. The audit was fraught with errors and misstatements, but it gave Kim what she needed to harass Vericella. In 2003, among its findings the audit reported that Vericella had used State funds to pay for $137 in parking and speeding tickets, $174 for family travel and $359 for in-room movies rented at hotels—or roughly $700 in total.

As one exasperated HVCB director told me, "Parking tickets? Rented movies? Give me a fucking break!" *My feelings exactly*, I thought. I knew how hard Vericella worked. He was a dynamo when it came to marketing Hawai'i. Once he told me, "Governor, the world knows the word 'Aloha'—our marketing strategy will teach people the meaning of the word "Ohana.'"

After the audit, the HVCB board of directors met in executive session and emerged with a vote of confidence for Vericella, urging him to stay on with the HVCB.

But a week later, Vericella decided to resign. I was impressed by what he had done at the HVCB and urged him to stick it out. But he said, "She tries to micromanage everything we do. She calls vendors to tell them what to do and leaves them with the impression that she'll make life miserable for them if they don't go along. She even got the HTA to include in its contract with the Bureau a provision that forbids the HVCB from criticizing the HTA.

"She's out to dismantle the HVCB and the network the Bureau has established over more than 50 years in different countries. If she gets her way, the HVCB's presence in those places will disappear. I don't need this, the Bureau doesn't need it—it's best that I leave."

With his departure, Vericella took with him years of experience and contacts throughout the U.S., Asia and Europe. And the HVCB brand name, which had taken more than 50 years to establish in foreign countries such as Japan and Australia, would be wiped out shortly thereafter.

Kim enjoyed playing the "gotcha" game. Her good looks belied her pernicious nature. ❖

CHAPTER TWENTY-FIVE

The Election of 2002

The Changing Face of Island Voters

I n describing the 1998 gubernatorial election, *Star-Bulletin* editor David Shapiro wrote:

"After all the hope and hype, Republicans found a way to blow the big one—just as they did in the 1990 U.S. Senate race and the 1994 governor's race. No governorship for the GOP, no gains in the Legislature or Congress.

"It was the same old story. Republicans started with a big lead based on voter discontent with 44 years of Democratic rule. Instead of pressing the lead, GOP strategists dodged tough issues so as not to antagonize prospective Democratic supporters. Democratic leaders countered with loyalty appeals that worked because, in the end, timid Republicans hadn't given Democratic voters compelling reason to leave home."

Hubris, overconfidence and mismanagement of the campaign cost Linda Lingle the 1998 election. It was the fourth of eight elections in which I had come from behind to win. And it was the sweetest. Lingle and the Republicans had played fast and loose with the facts; instead of telling the voters what they stood for, they opted to do foolish things like stooping to attack my wife, and they were brimming with so much overconfidence that they were virtually measuring the drapes in my office. They had a good time of it until the final votes were counted or, as the saying goes, the fat lady sang. On Election Day, Joe Napolitan had advised me, "No matter what happens, be gracious." It was a struggle, but I managed to defer to Napolitan's advice.

But I could see there were storm clouds in the future for the Democratic Party. We had won Oʻahu and Kauaʻi, but for the first time since 1954, the Republican gubernatorial candidate had won the Big Island and Maui. The lopsided haole vote in Kona had cut our early Statewide lead from 12,000 to the final margin of 5,253 votes. The haole vote had finally emerged as a potent voting bloc. Inspired by Lingle's candidacy, haoles took 1998 as a turning point. They had turned out in record numbers to vote heavily for her and the Republican ticket.

To be clear, I believe there is nothing wrong when an ethnic or racial group that has never had political power before turns out in a big way for one of their own who is breaking long-standing barriers. Thus, in 1960 Irish Americans voted proudly in record numbers to elect John F. Kennedy as the first Irish-Catholic president. Similarly, in 1974 Japanese Americans did the same to elect George Ariyoshi as the first Japanese-American governor of an American state, as did Hawaiians for John Waihee in 1986. This is the history of immigrants in America. And it is a sign of the positive growth of the diversity and multiculturalism of our country. That kind of voting is different from when an individual or racial group votes because it believes it is racially superior to another or to preserve its hegemony over others.

Despite Hawai'i's worldwide reputation for racial harmony, race has always been a factor in its elections. And judging from some of the angry, racist emails (one persistent emailer from the Big Island kept writing, "When Lingle is elected, she will show you what white people can do"); letters; telephone calls; and organized, in-your-face heckling I was getting, I'd had no doubt that race would be a bigger factor in 1998 than in previous elections.

Elections are usually highly charged contests for power, and it is not unusual for supporters to sometimes become overzealous in supporting their candidates. But I had never experienced a campaign as nasty as the 1998 campaign. For example, at one of our rallies in Waipahu two young, blond women tried to navigate their way through the sea of my mostly brown-skinned supporters to flash me the Lingle T-shirts they were wearing under their jackets; during a walk-through at Aloha Stadium prior to a UH football game, a short barrel-chested haole male walked right up to me and opened his vest to flash a T-shirt showing a picture of my face crossed diagonally by a red line. This kind of heckling was not only widespread and organized; it seemed designed to provoke a reaction from me.

We were getting clobbered so badly in haole enclaves like Kona and Lahaina that Joe Napolitan and Jack Seigle recommended I make only token appearances there, leaving the serious campaigning in those areas mainly to my wife, Vicky, whose smile and bubbly personality—Napolitan predicted—would warm even the coldest and most hostile Republican heart.

The resurgence of the haole voter was no surprise. Republicans like Andy Anderson had long and openly predicted it (although it came too late for his campaigns for governor). Veterans of the 1954 Democratic Revolution such as Mike Tokunaga also saw it coming. Tokunaga was from a generation that had experienced racial discrimination and almost total domination by haoles firsthand. Even by 1994, that bitter history was still too fresh for many of his generation to feel at ease with haoles.

A member of the famed 100th Battalion and a close confidant of Gov. John A. Burns, Tokunaga was a thoughtful and reflective person. Once, after the 1994 election, we talked about the emerging haole vote:

"Ben, all we local people wanted was a piece of the pie—that's what 1954 was all about and that's why a lot of us went off to war. The difference is that many haoles want to control everything—it's their culture—that's the way they've been brought up. Over time, things between local people and the haoles will get better. But now that you are governor you should do what you can to find ways to bring them into the Party—otherwise the Republicans may be running things again."

Ironically, the only racial discrimination I experienced personally was in Hawai'i. During my nearly nine years of living in Los Angeles, amidst the racial turmoil, the riots and the police shootings, the whites I met treated me as an equal; a few touched my life and played important roles in shaping my values. And I developed cherished and enduring friendships with them.

I wasn't blind to the racial turmoil between whites and the growing Chicano and black communities in Los Angeles. Indeed, there is much written in our nation's history about the mistreatment of the American Indians, blacks, Asians and Chicanos—shameful episodes in our nation's history. Yet the fact that in 2008 an American who is hapa (half- or mixed-race—in Barack Obama's case, part black and part white) was able to capture the presidency speaks volumes about the growth of multiculturalism in America and its impact on the evolution of our nation's democracy. Racism is a product of culture, not genetics, and just as it is taught and learned, so tolerance and respect for others can be taught and learned.

Many of the Mainland haoles who moved to Hawai'i during the early post-statehood years were hippies, or else well-heeled types who seemed to know or care little about Hawai'i's history or the local culture. In fact, for a variety of reasons, many of them tended to be uninvolved with or indifferent to local politics, turning out to vote mainly in presidential elections.

Things began to change in the 1970s and '80s. The introduction of 747s and other wide-bodied aircraft made it possible for greater numbers of passengers to travel to Hawai'i faster and at reasonable cost. And during times when the Mainland economy was in a deep recession, Hawai'i's economy had continued to grow, literally without pause for nearly three decades, attracting a growing number of middle- and working-class haoles.

By the mid-1980s haoles had become the largest racial minority group in Hawai'i (there is no majority group), making up roughly 33 percent of the population, surpassing Japanese Americans, the base of the Democratic Party. AJAs, who once comprised as much as 40 percent of Hawai'i's population, had declined to approximately 23 percent. A consequence of this demographic shift was its impact on jobs that were usually held by local people.

One morning during my 1986 campaign for lieutenant governor, I was having breakfast with some Maui supporters at a hotel in Lahaina when I noticed that four of the five waitresses on duty were haoles, while the busboys were all locals.

"I feel as if I'm in Newport Beach," I chuckled, nodding toward the pretty haole waitress who had just waited on us. "I guess times are really changing—when my father was working as a waiter at the Outrigger Canoe club, no haole would be caught dead working as a waitress."

"Oh, there are a couple of restaurants in Lahaina with nearly all haole workers. Maui's changing. Give or take another five to 10 years, the haoles will be the majority on Maui," my friend replied.

"Do you get a lot of haole transients here?"

"Not as many as people think. As usual, you have some who are well off, but most are working people who are willing to wait tables or take other jobs that the old kama'āina haoles wouldn't even dream of touching."

"Yes, back then the haole bosses wouldn't hire haoles who were willing to work as waitresses, clerks, those kinds of jobs—they'd give them some supervisory job or tell them to go back to the Mainland," I said recalling what Richard Dumancus had told me.

"Yeah, the bluebloods felt it was bad for their race."

"So how do locals and haoles get along here?" I asked.

"The kids get along fine. With adults, it's mixed. Some get along very well and others don't. Too often they don't understand us and we don't understand them. And when they complain about racial discrimination against them, some locals take a "Well, now they know how it feels" attitude, which doesn't help any."

"Do they turn out to vote?"

"More and more, and they tend to vote Republican. Here on Maui, fanatics like Rick Reed are very popular because they thumb their noses at the local Democrats. What's sad is that too many haoles who were Democrats on the Mainland become Republicans once they get here."

"What's the Party doing to bring them in?"

"Here the haole Democrats are usually teachers, university professor types, union members or gays and lesbians. The big problem is that the Party has become too insular; many of the older Democrats are reluctant to share power even with younger local Democrats."

"But that's how the old guard is. At the 1984 convention Milton Holt and his gang tried to kick us out of the party because we organized a coalition with the Republicans."

"Well, here most of the local guys have no time for haoles who they think don't respect local people or our local traditions. Their attitude is "Well, if that's the way they feel, fuck 'em."

On the surface the divide between the local and haole communities was generally not overt, but in politics it manifested itself starkly in different ways. For instance, during the 1978 Constitutional Convention, a clandestine political screed called "Palaka Power" was published. ("Palaka" is the Hawaiian word for the plaid blue-and-white checkered material once widely used for shirts worn by plantation workers.)

The title demonstrated the power of words. The paper touted "localism" as a means of preserving local values. By itself there is nothing wrong with touting "localism" or "local values" in Hawai'i any more than in states on the Mainland. But the words "Palaka Power" sounded too much like "Black Power," the provocative slogan of the black extremists of the 1960s that had struck anxiety in the hearts of not only white people but people of color as well.

When it was reported that "Palaka Power" had been distributed only to Con Con delegates who were local, and that it was being used to depict initiative and referendum as a political tool that Mainland haoles would use to wrest political power from locals (both proposals were defeated), it only widened the divide between the two groups.

Preserving local values was important, but "Palaka Power" seemed written to exclude political outsiders, haole and local. I felt excluded. And I think most of the independent Democrats I was allied with felt the same way.

At times, the news media's treatment of incidents between locals and haoles could not but aggravate matters. "Kill Haole Day"—a news story headline about an incident between haole and local students—is an example. No one can pinpoint the origin of this provocative utterance, but when I first heard it I took it as the kind of wild hyperbole one hears when juveniles fight. But the way the newspapers played it up annoyed me.

It seemed that for several years at least—and even today—whenever there was a fight or an incident between haole and local students, the news media, particularly the newspapers with their haole-dominated editorial boards, repeatedly reprised "Kill Haole Day" in their news stories—as if it were a Hawaiian tradition. Those who wonder about the power of the press need only search for "Kill Haole Day" on the Internet, where the phrase is now forever memorialized for the entire world. Little wonder that haole parents feared having their children attend local public schools.

For many Mainland haoles, living in an American state run by non-white governors, with the State Legislature, county councils and a congressional delegation dominated by non-white locals, was a rude cultural shock. It required adjustments some had difficulty making. At times, their dissatisfaction reached extremes. During the George Ariyoshi years (1974-1986), for example, disgruntled haoles living in Kona and Kailua organized movements to establish separate county governments for their respective areas. The idea had no chance of succeeding (the county councils were dominated by locals), but it was another example of the haoles' frustration with their lack of political power.

Shortly after my election in 1994, I made a courtesy call to then-Maui Mayor Linda Lingle. Prior to our meeting, some of my key local Maui Democrats could hardly utter a complimentary word about her. "We called her first administration the "white house" because it was nearly all haole," one of them chuckled.

Lingle had greeted me warmly. She is an athletic-looking, handsome woman, at least 6 feet tall, with a pleasant and disarming smile. We had a good discussion of state and Maui issues and engaged in some small talk. I was impressed with her. I thought we connected well. Before I left I asked her the obvious question.

"I'm surprised you're not a Democrat. You strike me as a liberal and a natural Democrat. Why are you a Republican?"

"Well, I didn't feel welcomed by the Democrats—besides, I couldn't get elected here on Maui as a Democrat," she replied, smiling wryly.

Too bad, I thought. Lingle was clearly a rising star in Hawai'i politics. But her answer said much about the state of the Democratic Party. Just as the Republican Party was stereotyped as the party of the haoles, so too had the Democratic Party become the party of locals and organized labor.

The challenge of attracting more haoles to the Democratic Party was not lost on Democratic Party members. In 1986 Democrats elected local haole businessman Jack Richardson (1986-92) as party chairman. Richardson was followed by former State Senator Dennis O'Connor (1992-94), retired educator Richard Port (1994-96) and former City Councilwoman Marilyn Bornhorst (1996-98). Like Richardson, O'Connor was a local haole; Port and Bornhorst were Mainland haoles who were longtime Hawai'i residents.

As governors, Ariyoshi, Waihee and I appointed haoles to top positions in our respective Cabinets. Eileen Anderson became Ariyoshi's director of budget and finance, Warren Price and Jack Lewin were Waihee's attorney general and director of health, respectively, and Margery Bronster became attorney general in my administration.

I didn't appoint Bronster because she was a haole—the only other finalist for the position was also Caucasian. When it came to Cabinet appointments, my policy was simple: If all things are equal among applicants, then I will consider their race or ethnicity. As much as possible, I wanted my Cabinet to look like the face of Hawai'i.

The problem, of course, was far deeper than could be cured by symbolic changes in the infrastructure of the Democratic Party or Cabinet appointments. The divide was most prominent at ground level—where the respective cultures and attitudes clashed daily and in many different ways. Many haoles were unaccustomed to not being in control, and I sensed that too many reacted as if they resented it.

My narrow win over Lingle in 1998 left no doubt in my mind that the Democrats' best chance of retaining the governorship was to field a haole candidate against her in 2002. Like it or not, Lingle had become the Republican White Hope. To win, the Democrats had to find their own. Honolulu Mayor Jeremy Harris came to mind.

In many ways, Harris and Lingle were like peas in a pod. Both were Mainland haoles who had become successful politicians in Hawai'i. Harris was in his second term as Honolulu's mayor, Lingle had served several terms as mayor of Maui; both were given high favorable ratings in political polls.

But there were some big differences that favored Harris. As mayor of the City and County of Honolulu, Harris governed some 80 percent (approximately 900,000) of the state's population. Lingle's experience as mayor of Maui County, with approximately 12 percent (about 100,000) residents, paled by comparison. Furthermore, Harris was sharper. His grasp of the details of City issues was impressive. Lingle, on the other hand, seemed more scripted than knowledgeable—an impression I had gotten from our debates in the 1998 election.

In a head-to-head race, I believed that Harris and Lingle would probably split the haole and Hawaiian vote—but Harris would beat Lingle decisively among the majority of AJA and Filipino voters who remained loyal to the Democratic Party.

For me, supporting Harris for governor in 2002 came only after prolonged soul-searching. My personal experiences with him, his betrayal of Frank Fasi and his never-ending self-serving political antics—all of this left me with little reason to trust or like him. In the political arena, he seemed willing to do anything, or hurt anyone, just to win. Harris' redeeming quality was his liberal philosophy. Unless it interfered with his ambitious personal plans he would support programs for the needy, implement policies to protect the environment and appoint good judges.

Be that as it may, I had never supported a candidate for governor in whom I did not believe. I didn't believe in Harris—but I would support him because I believed he could win.

The Mazie Factor

There was another contender.

Mazie Hirono was born in Fukushima, Japan on Nov. 3, 1947. When Hirono was about eight years old, her mother fled an abusive marriage and moved with Hirono and her two brothers to Hawai'i. Naturalized as a U.S. citizen in 1959, Hirono was graduated with honors from Kaimukī High School and as a Phi Beta Kappa from the University of Hawai'i at Mānoa. She earned her law degree from Georgetown University Law Center in Washington, D.C., where she focused on public interest law. In 1981, she was elected to the State House, where she served until her election as lieutenant governor in 1994 and reelection in 1998. Hers was an inspiring personal story—the kind political consultants dream about for campaigns.

Hirono had set her sights on running for governor in 2002. Since her reelection as lieutenant governor in 1998 and after eight long frustrating years in that office, the time had come. Earlier that year (or perhaps in late 2001), she met with Jack Seigle. Hirono wanted to hire Seigle, who had been my political consultant since 1986, for her 2002 gubernatorial campaign, but he declined.

Later, Seigle told me, "I told her I didn't think she could win. She asked me why not, and I told her frankly that I didn't think she had the 'passion' it would take to beat someone like Lingle. I liked Mazie and didn't want to see her hurt, so I didn't want to get involved."

Once, I think it was in late 2000, UPW leader Gary Rodrigues—a strong Hirono supporter—asked me whether I would appoint Hirono to either the Intermediate Court of Appeals or the Hawai'i Supreme Court. Rodrigues, who was a member of the Judicial Selection Commission at the time, said that if Hirono applied for the positions, he was sure she would make the list of finalists. Then it would be up to me to appoint her. I told Rodrigues that I believed Hirono would make an excellent judge or Supreme Court justice and I would appoint her if her name was submitted to me.

(In March, 2001 Rodrigues and his daughter were indicted by a federal grand jury for taking kickbacks on union contracts and money laundering relating to his union's health insurance fund. On November 19, 2002, they were convicted, a sad end to an otherwise outstanding career as a labor leader. Nevertheless, I was confident if Hirono applied for a judgeship she would be a finalist.)

When I broached the idea to Hirono, not only did she adamantly reject it, she lectured me for implying that she would not make a good governor because she was a woman. Frankly, I was tired of hearing that kind of talk. I had appointed the first woman to serve as State attorney general and more women to Cabinet and State boards and commissions than any other governor. Rodrigues had made the proposal because he thought Hirono would do well in one of those positions and didn't think she could win as governor. It was that simple.

By 2001 Jeremy Harris had moved far ahead of Hirono. He had been campaigning for governor in one way or another ever since he was reelected mayor in 1996. By early 2002, Harris already had a substantial campaign war chest and was raising even more money. In addition to his well-oiled O'ahu campaign organization, Harris had already set up campaign organizations on the Neighbor Islands.

Hirono, meanwhile, seemed as unprepared and underfinanced in 2002 as she had been when we ran for reelection in 1998. During that campaign, I had been shocked to learn that after four years she still hadn't raised enough money to afford headquarters on the Neighbor Islands. Nor did she have much of a campaign organization.

Vice President John Nance Garner IV once described the office of the vice presidency as "not worth a bucket of warm piss," a description which could also apply to the office of the lieutenant governor. Having served eight frustrating years in that post myself, I knew the limitations of the position. The harsh reality is that a lieutenant governor's success rests on his or her ability to make something out of nothing. The lieutenant governor cannot be successful without some help from the governor.

Thus, Gov. George Ariyoshi, himself a former lieutenant governor, had assigned then-Lt. Gov. John Waihee to help negotiate a settlement of the United Airlines strike, a task in which Waihee seemingly enjoyed some success. Likewise, Gov. Waihee had given me the opportunity to create the A-Plus After-School Program, which proved highly popular. I had tried to do the same for Hirono by asking her to take the lead on cutting bureaucratic red tape (a program which she named SWAT) and later to establish preschools (Pre-Plus) in the public schools. Sadly, by late 2002 little had been accomplished.

There was a growing perception that Hirono had just been biding her time. In a 2002 story, *Honolulu Advertiser* reporter Kevin Dayton wrote:

"While in eight years she has had her hand in a number of modest initiatives, her critics say Hirono did little to expand the political heft of the lieutenant governor's largely ceremonial position. Even some who like Hirono's politics complain that she acted like someone simply putting in her time, like a confident executive assuming the big promotion is just around the corner, as it was for George Ariyoshi, John Waihee and Ben Cayetano."

Dayton may not have meant it literally, but the notion that lieutenant governors are routinely "promoted" is a myth—a reflection of the low esteem with which that office is perceived. If it had been left to the Democratic establishment, neither Waihee nor I would have been elected lieutenant governor or governor. As for Hirono, who was somewhat of a feminist, she seemed to assume that it was time—her time—for the election of Hawai'i's first woman governor.

The governorship of Hawai'i is bigger than any individual. I did not think Hirono was the best candidate for the job. For me, a defining moment came during the 2001 teacher and University faculty strikes. I was not surprised when Harris and Lingle walked the picket lines, as I considered both of them the foremost practitioners of the politics of self-promotion. Still, when Hirono also walked the picket line and made remarks suggesting that I was treating the strikers unfairly, I was shocked.

Frankly, I didn't think by walking the line Hirono had gained any political mileage. But the incident convinced me that she was better suited to serve in the legislative or judicial branches of government rather than the governorship. Being governor can be a lonely job and one which at times requires taking strong positions against one's political allies.

The widespread perception that Harris was the only Democrat who could beat Lingle made it difficult for Hirono to raise campaign funds. Contrary to popular belief, loyalty in politics is not automatically transferable from one politician to another. Potential donors who had supported me in many elections told me repeatedly that they would gladly support Hirono if she ran for mayor but not for governor. "She can't beat Lingle," many would say. By the end of 2001, the relentless Harris had all but wrapped up the Democratic primary election for governor.

In March, Hirono, perhaps finally realizing the huge odds against her, announced that she was dropping out of the governor's race and would run for mayor instead. This was good news; it meant a potentially hotly contested Democratic primary between Harris and Hirono would be avoided and she would be running for an office for which she had an excellent chance to win.

Meanwhile, certain factions were encouraging two Democratic State senators, Matt Matsunaga and Ron Menor, to run for lieutenant governor. Both had strong Democratic roots. Their fathers were part of the 1954 revolution. Matsunaga, the son of the late U.S. Senator Spark Matsunaga, was expected to draw heavy support from the AJA community, where his father was a revered figure. Menor, the son of the late Benjamin Menor, who was the nation's first Filipino-American State senator and first Hawai'i Supreme Court justice, would keep Filipino voters in the Democratic column. Both were in their early 40s, graduates of respected law schools (Menor was the class valedictorian for his graduating class at UCLA) and experienced legislators. A Harris-Matsunaga or a Harris-Menor ticket would be hard for Lingle to beat. I felt encouraged by the prospects of a Democratic victory.

But on May 30, Jeremy Harris made a shocking announcement: He was dropping out of the race for governor!

"I couldn't believe it," former mayor Frank Fasi was quoted in the *Star-Bulletin*. "Then again, I thought to myself that the fact that he is not running is the best thing that's happened to the people of Hawai'i."

"I don't hate him anymore," Fasi added, his Sicilian blood filled with schadenfreude at Harris' humiliation and self-inflicted fall from grace. "He tried. He had some good ideas … but I'll say this: Jeremy Harris' worst enemy is Jeremy Harris," Fasi said grimly about the "son" who had betrayed him.

Harris made his announcement on the day before the start of the 2002 State Democratic Convention. A few days earlier, Harris' campaign manager Rick Tsujimura had told the news media that Harris would formally announce his candidacy for governor at the convention. As usual, Harris had played it close to his vest, not even having the courtesy to tell the stunned and embarrassed Tsujimura beforehand about his decision not to run.

Only three weeks earlier, the Hawai'i Supreme Court had reversed a circuit ruling holding that Harris' campaign activities amounted to a formal announcement for governor, which by law required Harris to resign as mayor. The then-ebullient Harris had all but danced a jig, announcing happily that he would resume his campaign for governor.

In anticipation of Harris' resignation to run for governor, a number of politicians, including Hirono, City Councilman Duke Bainum, former Councilman Mufi Hannemann and former City Prosecutor Keith Kaneshiro, had already began campaigning to succeed him as mayor.

Hannemann's reaction to Harris' announcement sized up the feelings of most of the stunned candidates: "I am extremely disappointed … we raised a lot of money.

We had a first-class campaign and we were getting endorsements ... we were so focused there was going to be a mayor's race in 2002 that there was no plan B."

At his press conference Harris said his polls showed him trailing Lingle by 22 percent. "I can't in good conscience ask all of my supporters to go out and give their hearts and souls for a campaign that I don't believe that I can now win," he said.

Harris attributed the drop in his polls to a "year of bad publicity." And when pressed further by the news media, he replied dismissively: "Folks, politics is a rough and tumble sport, and the Democratic primaries have traditionally been very rough and tumble, so I don't have any recriminations or blame on why our numbers have fallen and why we're no longer able to beat Linda Lingle in the general. The fact of the matter is, that's just the way it turned out, and I think my responsibility is to do what's right."

"I don't know of a single soul telling him to do this.... He hasn't even campaigned yet," a stunned John Waihee said.

Perhaps it was God. To assure everyone that he had consulted the Almighty before he made his fateful decision, Harris had asked the Rev. Dan Chun of First Presbyterian Church to stand by his side at a press conference on the steps of City Hall where he announced his decision not to run. Harris gazed serenely at the Reverend and announced piously, "Dan and I prayed a lot on this, including just before we came out here. My dropping out of the race is the right thing to do."

"I felt like throwing up," one of my Cabinet officers told me later.

It was shibai—all of it. The last poll I saw showed Harris and Lingle in a statistical dead heat in mid-April. Based on my 28 years of experience, I knew it would have taken a scandal of gargantuan proportions for Harris to drop 22 percent behind Lingle in a month. Furthermore, even if Harris had been behind, he could still have won; he had seen firsthand how in 1998 a united Democratic Party had helped us overcome Lingle's (coincidentally) 22-point lead in June and beat her in the November general election. Similarly, in 1994 we overcame Pat Saiki's 32-point lead to win. Harris knew very well how formidable a united Democratic Party could be at the polls.

In 2008, at my request, Pat Loui of the highly respected Hawai'i polling company Omnitrak showed me the results of polls Omnitrak conducted in January 2001 (Lingle 43 percent, Harris 39 percent) and February 2002 (Lingle 42 percent, Harris 37 percent). Given the 4-percent margin of error, these results indicated a statistical tie. Loui could not show me the April and May polls it had taken, because those were paid for by a client, but she did tell me that the results for those months were "consistent." The Omnitrak polls confirmed my belief that Harris' own "poll" was a figment of his imagination.

Harris was entitled to do whatever was in his best personal interests. The fact that the majority of Democrats were relying on him to run for governor did not diminish that right. But he owed his supporters the truth—particularly those who, as Harris himself put it, "gave their hearts and souls" to his campaign. Had he said that he was dropping out for "personal reasons" and left it at that, no one could have argued about it. But to concoct an elaborate lie was an act which itself betrayed those very same supporters.

So why did he drop out? I suspected that Harris was worried about the investigation into his campaign fundraising by the Honolulu City prosecutor's office.

To be clear, the State Campaign Spending Commission had been investigating the campaign contributions made to me, Harris, Hirono, Waihee and Lingle. Among the issues being investigated was the practice of "bundling" contributions to get around the legal limit on a donor's campaign contributions to an individual candidate. At the conclusion of its investigation, the commission asked the City prosecutor to investigate Harris' campaign fundraising.

Any candidate for a major public office who handles his own campaign fundraising is asking for trouble. During my 28 years in public office, I received campaign contributions from thousands of donors (10,000 is a modest estimate), the overwhelming majority of whom I either did not know or had no personal or professional relationship with. The chances for misunderstanding, error, fraud or bribery either by those who solicit contributions for the candidate or those who are solicited increases dramatically in the bigger races. My policy, like Waihee's and Lingle's, was to insulate myself from potential abuses by assigning the responsibility to a committee comprised of trusted supporters. It was also my policy, whenever it appeared we had received "bundled" contributions, to turn the matter over to the commission, which we did on several occasions.

Harris was different; it was his nature to micromanage and control everything in which he was involved. The editor of one of our major daily newspapers once offered this observation about Harris: "If the topic of discussion was sewers, Harris would try to convince you that he knew more about sewers than anyone else." I had no doubt that there was little about his campaign fundraising that Harris did not know.

In 2008 Jackie Kido, my former Director of Communications, told me how she had accompanied Harris and several others to campaign for me on Kaua'i during the 1998 election. At a dinner Kido attended with Harris, Peter Char (Harris' political confidant), Turk Tokita (my Kaua'i campaign chairman) and several others, the topic of then-Republican Kaua'i Mayor Maryanne Kusaka's strong support for Lingle came up. Upon hearing this, Harris turned to Peter Char and told him to call "our people," including engineering firms and others, and "tell them they need to cut Kusaka off." Kido said she was surprised at how open Harris was in talking about his control over those with City contracts.

The prosecutor's investigation took a terrible toll on Char, who was Harris' closest ally and who had once served as deputy treasurer of his 2000 mayoral campaign. Char was a highly respected attorney, had been selected by *Honolulu* magazine as one of Hawai'i's Best Lawyers and had been widely acclaimed for his community work. Among his legal peers and friends, Char was considered a man of high integrity and ability, but when he got too deeply involved in politics he was like a duck out of water.

Apparently, the ensuing rampant speculation that Harris and perhaps even Char would be indicted for unlawful campaign spending offenses proved too much for Char. Shortly after the investigation was started, his health deteriorated and he suffered a stroke. Given the close relationship of the two men, prosecutors apparently felt that if Harris had violated the State's campaign spending laws, Char was likely to know something about it. There was little doubt that at the very least, Char would be called to testify before a grand jury.

As a former criminal defense attorney, I had seen dozens of my clients wilt emotionally under the pressure of a looming grand jury indictment. But most of my clients were tough, hardcore types. Char was a sophisticated gentleman admired and respected by all who knew him. In mid-January 2003, less than three months after the November 2002 general election, Char suffered a final and fatal stroke. He was 60.

(Subsequently, a half-dozen companies and individuals pled guilty to campaign-spending violations. A few were fined, other violators served short jail sentences—but no indictments were ever filed against Harris himself. The CEO of one of the State's largest engineering firms pled no contest to laundering $139,000 to the Harris campaign, and Harris' confidante Mike Amii was convicted for ordering a city staffer to work on Harris' political campaign. In 2008 a Honolulu jury returned a $3 million verdict in favor of a woman whose contract had not been renewed by Amii, after she questioned why the Harris administration was awarding millions of dollars in job-training and employment services contracts without putting them out for competitive bid.)

During his May 30 press conference, Harris said he had "no recriminations" about his withdrawal. Notwithstanding my obligatory public statements about Democrats having to "move on" and so forth, I felt literally consumed by self-recrimination. I didn't trust Harris; when it came to politics I believed him to be a person who would say or do anything to get his way—but I had supported him simply because I thought he could win.

Cynical pragmatism had overcome my idealism. It was time for me to get out of politics.

Harris' withdrawal did little to change minds about Hirono's slim chances of beating Lingle. Consequently, there was a mad scramble among Democratic leaders to find a candidate who could win. Two names promptly popped up: banker Walter Dods and Hawai'i County Mayor Harry Kim.

Dods, whose mother was a coffee shop cashier and whose father was a Honolulu cop, had gone directly to work for a bank after graduating from St. Louis High

School, working his way through the University of Hawai'i. Eventually he worked his way up from bank clerk to become CEO and chairman of Hawai'i's largest bank, First Hawaiian, ultimately becoming the first Hawai'i banker to serve as president of the prestigious American Banking Association before his retirement in 2002.

Dods had long been active behind the scenes supporting Democratic politicians, including me. He was respected among the predominantly haole business community leadership and was popular with local labor and community leaders.

The prospect of Dods' candidacy excited me. He would draw support from the business community and would beat Lingle handily among Democrats and the labor unions. Dods himself seemed eager to run. But he would run only if his wife, Diane, and their adult children, agreed. Diane, who had been a longtime aide to U.S. Senator Daniel K. Inouye, probably understood the burdens that political life imposed on families better than Dods himself. She and their children unanimously opposed Dods' running for governor. Honoring his family's wishes, he dropped out of the running.

I was disappointed, but then who could blame him? The state of politics, not only in Hawai'i but throughout the nation, had sunk to such a low, and holding public office had become such an intrusion in one's private life, that it scared away many talented people like Walter Dods.

Harry Kim was the other possibility. In 2000, he had been elected as the nation's first Korean-American mayor. In my eyes, his rise in local politics was nothing short of phenomenal. In his first try at public office, his opponent in the Republican primary was Lingle's hand-picked candidate, Hilo businessman and former Democratic State Representative-turned-Republican Harvey Tajiri. In picking Tajiri, Lingle, who had become the Republican Party chairman after her loss in 1998, had shunned the chairman's customary practice of staying neutral in the primary election. She had anointed Tajiri to carry the Republican banner into the general election. In the primary election, the unflappable Kim trounced Tajiri by a 2-to-1 margin and then went on to easily defeat Democrat Fred Holschuh in the general. Later, a humbled Holschuh summed up his loss to Kim, explaining that he felt as if he was running against "a mystique."

Kim had run on a pledge not to accept more than $10 in contribution from any person. He didn't need money or advertising. His 16 years of service as the Big Island's civil defense coordinator for a county that has been hit with more tsunami and volcano eruptions than any other in the state had established him as a leader and molded into a folk hero of sorts among locals and haoles alike.

"I'm a little Democrat, a little Republican, a little Green, a little independent, and a little disappointed in government," he said during the campaign. In fact, his Cabinet appointments revealed he was more of a Green Democrat than anything else. For his managing director he picked liberal Democratic State Senator Andy

Levin and environmentalist (and Democrat) attorney Christopher Yuen to head the county's planning department.

Later, Kim told me that Lingle had not even given him the courtesy of a phone call prior to the primary election or during the general election. "She called me after I won the general election and offered to set up a blue ribbon committee to help select my Cabinet," Kim told me with a chuckle. His amusement betrayed his response to Lingle's offer. (Kim has since disavowed his connection to the Republicans.)

Kim is a unique persona in local politics. The more I learned about him, the more I liked him. His speeches reflected a deep love for Hawai'i's multicultural people and its beautiful environment that manifested itself in his county policies. He is humble, idealistic and honest. He is respected by haoles and locals, Democrats as well as Republicans. He would have made a great Democratic candidate for governor. Unfortunately, Kim was undergoing some health problems at the time—he had reportedly suffered a mild heart attack—and after much soul-searching decided not to run.

And so the Democratic Primary boiled down to a contest between former State Representative Ed Case and Lt. Gov. Mazie Hirono. I felt that Case had a better chance against Lingle than Hirono did.

A Democrat who came from a family of longtime moderate Republicans—including his famous first cousin, America Online founder Steve Case—Ed Case was born and raised on the Big Island. After graduating from Hawai'i Preparatory Academy and later Williams College, he worked for several years as an aide to U.S. Senator Spark Matsunaga in Washington, D.C., before leaving to earn his law degree from Hastings School of Law. His first marriage produced two sons but ended in divorce. Later he married his high school classmate, Audrey Nakamura, on whom Case admitted to reporters he had had a big-time crush since their school days.

Narrowly defeated in his first two tries at running for the State House of Representatives, Case was finally elected in 1994. He stood out as a State representative, often speaking on hot issues avoided by his colleagues. He had been assigned by then-Speaker Joseph Souki to chair the Hawaiian Affairs Committee. The assignment was a no-win hot seat shunned by other legislators. Reportedly, Souki had assigned Case to the chairmanship as a form of punishment. (Case got even by later leading a group of dissidents that deposed Souki and replaced him with Calvin Say.) Case took the assignment seriously and proposed a bill that offered a reasonable and thoughtful settlement of some big Hawaiian issues. He was rewarded for his temerity by being hung in effigy by angry Hawaiian activists who seemed more angered by the color of his skin (Case is local but looks very haole) than the substance of his proposal. It took courage for Case to step up like that, and I respected him for it.

To the public, Case was a fresh face not tied into the so-called old-boy politics (actually, he was an eight-year veteran of the State House and had served as its majority leader). The 40ish Case was telegenic, smart and articulate. He had that youthful "John F. Kennedy" look—an asset that was beginning to attract local and haole voters alike.

With Matt Matsunaga as the front-runner in the lieutenant governor's race (Ron Menor had decided not to run after Harris dropped out), the possibility of a Case-Matsunaga ticket with a united Democratic Party behind it was beginning to look like a dream team. Case didn't have Harris' experience, campaign organization or war chest—but he had established a solid reputation as an independent and honest legislator.

As governor, I was obliged to stay neutral in the Democratic primary. It was no secret, however, that I was pulling for Case to win.

At one point Case, who was relatively unknown statewide, trailed Hirono by 26 points. Although his campaign was underfinanced, Case wisely threw most of his resources into television ads and began to cut into Mazie's lead. Hirono had heavy union support, but Case had the momentum. As he became better known, he quickly closed the gap. Unfortunately for Case, time ran out. On Primary Election Day, Hirono edged Case 75,186 to 72,753—a margin of only 2,433 votes. It was a remarkable showing. Had the primary election been a week later Case probably would have won. Post-election analysis indicated that he had been beaten mainly in the absentee balloting where many voters had cast their ballots early, often without knowing much about him.

With Case's defeat in the primary, the Democratic Party was left with a troubling scenario: two Japanese Americans, Hirono and Matsunaga, against Lingle, a Mainland haole, and James "Duke" Aiona, a native Hawaiian. To be sure, all-AJA governor-lieutenant governor teams had won in 1974 (Ariyoshi/Jean King) and in 1978 (Ariyoshi/Nelson Doi). But Hawai'i's demographics had changed substantially since then. And Case's narrow loss to Hirono in the primary was a sign that the emerging haole vote would prove to be a big factor in the 2002 and future elections.

Meanwhile, Lingle, who had attacked me as a "big money" candidate for spending $5 million in the 1998 election, had raised some big bucks herself—more than $5 million, as compared to Hirono's $1.5 million—giving her a nearly three-to-one advantage. Moreover, the Republicans had fine-tuned their campaign organization and were far better organized and more efficient than the Democrats.

Harris' abrupt withdrawal from the governor's race had hurt Hirono. And by dropping out of and then dropping back into the governor's race, she could not avoid creating the impression that she was indecisive. Furthermore, her inability to raise campaign funds was compounded by the Campaign Spending Commission's investigation, which made potential contributors wary of getting involved in politics at all. Finally, her highly competitive race with Ed Case in the Democratic primary had drained her campaign war chest of funds desperately needed for television and radio spots and newspaper ads against Lingle in the General Election.

Hirono faced huge odds. Still, if Hirono and Matsunaga could find some way to galvanize and unite the various Democratic factions as she and I had done in 1998, they had a chance—a slim one to be sure—of winning.

My role in Hirono's campaign was limited as it became obvious that Hirono wanted to keep some distance between us. After eight years of playing backup to me, Hirono, who had been an active legislator, apparently wanted to show the public that she was, as they say, "her own person." I understood. There is a subtly demeaning aspect to the office of lieutenant governor which at some point often compels its occupants to either quit or try to prove that they are competent and capable.

Furthermore, my decisions on civil service reform, budget cuts and Hawaiian issues such as the ceded-lands dispute and our investigation of the Bishop Estate, compounded by the 2001 teacher and UH faculty strikes, made me persona non grata among certain groups—a fact not lost on Hirono and her campaign supporters.

Once when I suggested to Hirono that she run on "our" record (for example, the big tax cut, the record number of new schools we built), she abruptly cut me off, stating that she was "not the boy from Kalihi" and would run on her "own record." Her big problem, I thought, was that as lieutenant governor she *had* no record of accomplishment to speak of. Still, I wanted to help, of course, and I told her to let me know how they wanted me to help and I would do it. Other than that, I never offered advice again.

As if the odds against her were not big enough, aside from Bob Toyofuku, Hirono's longtime political confidant, the day-to-day responsibility of running the campaign was in the hands of a group of young women whose political inexperience soon emerged. About two weeks into the general election, Charlie Toguchi, my former campaign manager who had volunteered (he wasn't asked) to help Hirono, expressed surprise that many of the old-time Democrats were not involved in her campaign. Toguchi quickly began contacting them to help out. "No one asked them," Toguchi said, surprised that such a basic step had not been taken.

Despite Lingle's nearly three-to-one advantage in campaign funds, the Democrats were slowly uniting behind Hirono. A *Star-Bulletin* poll published on October 27, nine days before the election, showed Hirono and Lingle in a dead heat at 40 percent each with a 4-percent margin of error.

On November 1, Hirono and Lingle had their final televised debate. The two candidates were asked a question posed by OHA on restoring $10.3 million in disputed revenues from ceded lands that were owed to OHA. Lingle said that if elected, she would immediately move to transfer the funds, while Hirono said the money would have to be appropriated by the Legislature, but that she would introduce such a bill when the Legislature convened in January.

"I support the resolution of the ceded-lands claims," Hirono said, "but I don't believe the law would allow the governor to simply pass the money over without legislative approval."

Lingle—once again demonstrating her propensity to say whatever worked at the moment regardless of its truth—had one-upped Hirono by saying the money "should be taken straight out of the State's account."

"It can't wait to go to the governor," Lingle said.

Hirono was right. Basic textbook civics teaches that the governor cannot spend money unless it is authorized by the Legislature. The law under which the $10.3 million was supposed to be paid had been ruled null and void when the Hawai'i Supreme Court reversed the *Heely* decision. In other words, there was no legal authority to justify paying OHA the $10.3 million. Naturally, though, Lingle's answer resonated better with OHA, which was more interested in getting the money than heeding the niceties of law.

News of the *Star-Bulletin* poll showing the two candidates tied must have gotten to the Bush administration. And Lingle, who had predicted that George W. Bush would go down in history as a "great president," got help from the White House. On November 1, the Center for Disease Control (CDC) issued a press release rating Hawai'i and Wisconsin as the two states least prepared to deal with bioterrorism. Later, it was learned that the CDC must have used outdated information to evaluate Hawai'i's readiness and had not used the progress reports from the states for which the deadline for filing still had not passed.

Fortunately, Bill Raub, deputy assistant secretary for public health emergency preparedness in the U.S. Department of Health and Human Services, who reviews state bioterrorism plans for his department, said about Hawai'i's bioterrorism plan: "We're encouraged by progress in Hawai'i and every other state."

Four days before the general election, Michael Liu, assistant secretary of the U.S. Department of Housing and Urban Development (HUD), had demanded that the five-member board of the State Housing and Community Development Corp. of Hawaii (HCDCH) resign by Nov. 15. Liu had sent the news media a copy of his letter even before we received it.

"It's very interesting that Mike Liu, former Republican State representative and Republican candidate for lieutenant governor, should issue something like this four days before the election—and immediately forward it to the press," I told reporters.

Liu, who had in previous years given the HCDCH good evaluations, released a "review report" of the Housing and Community Development Corp. indicating that the agency's managers were incapable of successfully managing and overseeing agency funds. The report cited a $771,000 sole-source contract awarded by Sharyn Miyashiro, the agency's former executive director, to a construction company in which her ex-husband had a financial interest. According to Mike Liu, her failure to disclose her ex-husband's interest violated HUD rules.

"Sharyn divorced her husband more than 25 years ago," I replied angrily to the news media. "Divorces terminate relationships, not start them. Tell me where does it say in the federal law that Sharyn Miyashiro had to disclose that non-relationship to the (HCDCH) board? Mike Liu should be ashamed of himself.

"As to the particular contract Mr. Liu refers to, when questions first arose, I asked my attorney general to investigate and urged Mr. Liu to contact the U.S. attorney if he suspected any criminal activity in the issuance of the contract."

A subsequent analysis of the contract in question concluded that the price was about 10 percent less than it would ordinarily have cost. It was all political—cheap shots. I was so angry at Liu and the Bush administration that I told the news media, "If HUD is not satisfied with the State's performance, the State would be ready to begin negotiations to turn over all of its public-housing units back to the federal government."

The 2002 election returns told a fateful story for Democrats. Surprisingly, the voter turnout was low—58.1 percent compared to 68.6 percent in 1998. Lingle beat Hirono 197,009 (51.6 percent) to 179,647 (47.1 percent)—a margin of 17,362 votes. The race between the two was reasonably competitive in all ethnic groups except for the haole group, where Hirono got less than 13 percent of the vote.

Lingle received about 2,000 fewer votes than she had in the 1998 general election. But Hirono's vote total was a shocking 24,557 fewer votes in 2002 than it had been in 1998. Against Hirono, Lingle won in new growth areas and did better in areas Hirono and I had won in 1998. In the Mānoa House District, for example, a strong Democratic district dominated by mostly AJA residents where we beat Lingle soundly in 1998, Hirono beat Lingle in 2002 by only 13 votes.

Given the controversies in the final days of the election, my sense was that many of those 24,557 voters who did not show up at the polls for Hirono were unhappy with the Democrats but could not bring themselves to vote Republican.

In any event, the election was over. After 40 years, the voters had finally elected a Republican governor. Like Ariyoshi, Waihee and me, Lingle was a first—Hawai'i's first woman governor.

A New Beginning?

I had nearly a month left in my final term before Lingle's inauguration on December 2, 2002. Besides working with her people in making the transition from my administration to hers, we had the responsibility of preparing and submitting the State budget to the Legislature. That seemed to go smoothly enough.

However, while we were still negotiating an agreement with a private company to build a new prison, Lingle demanded that we stop the negotiations, suggesting publicly that there was some kind of sweetheart deal in the works. She had been saying such things ever since she had decided to run for governor in 1997. To put it mildly, I was pissed. Nevertheless, I publicly invited her to sit in on the negotiations. She never responded. Finally, I called Sam Callejo, my chief of staff.

"Sam, we don't need to take this shit from her. The hell with it, let's leave it to her. Cancel the negotiations. Let her learn the hard way." (As of August 2008, Lingle still had not built a new prison. She has stated that she will not build a prison in any area where the residents are opposed to it. Translation: There will be no new prison built.)

Her desire to establish a "New Beginning" even extended to firing the four maids at Washington Place. All immigrants—two Chinese, two Filipinos—the maids were never involved in any kind of political activity. They worked hard and were respectful to the governors and first families they served. And they would have given Lingle no less. Fortunately, the Legislature had given me the authority to create a half-dozen new positions by executive order. I issued an order creating four custodial positions for the four maids from which they could eventually earn civil service status and benefits.

On December 2, 2002 Lingle's inaugural ceremony was held at 'Iolani Palace. The weather was perfect, a sunny, bright day tempered by a cool breeze. Lingle's family was sitting on the stage at the Capitol rotunda. Jerry Cutter, Lingle's uncle, whom I had gotten to know during my association with David Schutter's law firm, waved at me. Cutter is a gentlemen and a class act, someone I had liked and respected ever since we met. It was a proud moment for him to watch his niece Linda Cutter Lingle make history. I waved back. I was happy for him.

An Inaugural Address gives the new governor the opportunity to express his or her hopes for the future and objectives for the present and to call on all to unify and work for the common good. Lingle's address sounded as if she was still on the campaign trail:

"Too often in Hawai'i, the first order of business for the newly elected has been to sort people into two categories: political supporters and everyone else. People in the first category often received favorable treatment. People in the second category received what they perceived to be retribution for supporting the 'wrong' candidate. This kind of 'help your friends, hurt your enemies' thinking has damaged our state's reputation and ability to thrive. It must stop. It will stop. A New Beginning means zero tolerance for political rewards and retribution. Sorting people into political friends and enemies, or insiders and outsiders, has created a culture of mediocrity by discouraging public debate and excluding people who might otherwise contribute. Who you know became more important than what you know."

Later, an editor at the *Honolulu Advertiser* told me he thought that part of the speech was "ungracious." In my opinion she was offering a handshake with one hand and a slap in the face with the other. I sensed from the body language of some of the Democratic leaders sitting on either side of me—Inouye, Akaka, Ariyoshi, Waihee—that their reactions were similar.

She still hasn't got over it, I thought. In 1998 she had "snatched defeat from the jaws of victory," and her bitterness showed over the four years that followed. And now when she had the chance to put all of that behind her and issue a call for bipartisanship to the Democrats she blew it.

As we walked to our car, a reporter came over and asked what I thought of Lingle's speech.

"Off the record," I replied.

"Okay."

"Listen, Lingle is the only governor in this state's history who was convicted of a crime, who had the Hawai'i Supreme Court rule that as mayor she had hired her ex-husband illegally and still hasn't reimbursed the county the $100,000 she paid him; she is the only governor who had federal and State tax liens against her because she didn't pay her taxes like everyone else. Not Bill Quinn, John Burns, George Ariyoshi, John Waihee or yours truly. So what did I think of her speech? It was fine until she started talking about restoring integrity to government. I find it a bit annoying that someone with her background should preach to the rest of us," I said.

"Off the record?" the reporter asked, obviously hoping I'd change my mind.

"Yeah. Off the record. After all, this is supposed to be a day of hope when everyone agrees to work for the common good. I wouldn't want to spoil that, now would I?"

In the weeks that followed, I naturally found myself reflecting more and more on my 28 years in politics. There had been times in my life when earning a college degree was just a remote thought, when making it through law school and becoming a lawyer seemed an impossible dream—and a career in politics had never even entered my consciousness. Luck, helping hands from others and family had made it possible.

And at each step in my political career—from the State Legislature to lieutenant governor and finally governor—I never ceased to be amazed at my good fortune, and I never forgot what a great privilege I had been given by the good people of our state to serve. I was far from perfect in my actions; in hindsight there are things I should have done differently, but I gave it everything I had, trying to make life better for our people.

A friend once lamented that it was too bad that I became governor during the worst economic downturn in Hawai'i's history. "Just think about the things you could have done if you'd had the money," he said. To be honest, yes, I thought about it, but ultimately I was just glad that I was called upon to lead the state during such tough times. Frankly, I believed I was the right man for the job. And it became a rite of passage for me—like the ones I experienced growing up as a kid in Kalihi—to do it right, using my intellect and the wise counsel of my Cabinet and friends, to make sound decisions in the public's interest without fear of the political consequences.

When I began my political career in 1974 I was a 34-year-old lawyer full of idealism, ready to change the world. A veteran legislator who took a liking to me took me aside and offered the following: "Ben," he said, "you remind me of myself when I first got into politics. I was a reformer; I wanted to change the world. You're no different. But after being in this business for 20 years now, I think the best any politician can hope for before he leaves is that he helped make life a *little* better for our people."

He was right. ❖

Acknowledgments

It would have been very difficult to write this book without the support of a number of people.

I want to begin by thanking my wife, Vicky, and my children, Brandon, Janeen, Samantha, Marissa and William, for their love and support. I wrote most of this book at home, and Vicky's patience and understanding were critical. My thanks also to my Aunt Rachel for her stories that revealed a side of my mother I had not known before and to my brother, Ken, for his courage and love.

I was fortunate to have had a first-rate Cabinet during my eight years as governor—truly dedicated and outstanding public servants who were underpaid and overworked. When I called on a number of them for assistance, they responded unhesitatingly in helping me resurrect some of the stories in this book. And so I extend my warmest thanks to Earl Anzai, Mert Agena, Sam Callejo, Susan Chandler, Evan Dobelle, Gary Gill, Ray Kamikawa, Janet Kawelo, Wayne Kimura, Neal Miyahira, Kim Murakawa, Seiji Naya, Lloyd Nekoba, Edward Richardson, Charles Toguchi, Mike Wilson and Davis Yogi. I want to especially thank Jackie Kido, who served in my administration as Director of Communications. After I retired in December 2002, Jackie decided to become a lawyer, earned her law degree from UCLA and is now a practicing attorney in Honolulu. Through it all, she took the time to read and scrutinize every chapter of this book. As a former writer, her insights and criticisms were invaluable, and I adopted many of her suggestions in the book.

Also, my thanks to attorney Colbert Matsumoto and University of Hawai'i Professor Randy Roth for reviewing my chapters on the Bishop Estate controversy, and to Neil Abercrombie, Jeff Agader, Jim Bickerton, Ed Case, Walter Dods, Randy Hack, Clayton Hee, Randy Iwase, Duke Kawasaki, Bert Kobayashi, Pat Loui, Oliver Lunasco, Joe Napolitan, Dennis O'Connor, Robert Richards, Jack Seigle, Buddy Soares, Jane Sugimura, Fred Trotter and Tony Vericella for their important input on other issues. Thanks also to former *Honolulu Advertiser* editor Saundra Keyes and to the *Advertiser*'s former publisher Michael Fisch, who gave me unlimited access to their newspaper's invaluable archives. There are others who helped but I know prefer to remain unnamed; I take this means to thank them also.

And my warmest appreciation to my publisher at Watermark Publishing, George Engebretson, for having the patience of Job. Writing this book took much longer than I expected, and I made many mistakes in doing it. But through it all, George showed an understanding and patience that says much about him as a person. Thanks also to Frederika Bain, Kathy Reimers and Aimee Harris at Watermark for their assistance in editing and fact-checking.

Finally, my heartfelt thanks to the owner of Watermark Publishing, Duane Kurisu. Duane is a very successful businessman and philanthropist, and Watermark is just one of his many business ventures. When he approached me about writing this book, I joked that I thought he'd lose money on it. But like many who've gotten to know him, I've come to understand that with Duane it's not about money. He wanted someone to write a book that would give future generations an insight into what life was like for local people who grew up in post-World War II Hawai'i, particularly the social and political events from 1974 to 2002. I hope this book meets his expectations.

Index

About the Author

Benjamin J. Cayetano served as governor of Hawai'i from 1994 to 2002 and was the first Filipino American elected as a United States governor. He currently lives in Honolulu with his wife, Vicky.